TOSCANINI

TOSCANINI

Harvey Sachs

PERENNIAL LIBRARY

Harper & Row, Publishers, New York
Cambridge, Philadelphia, San Francisco, Washington
London, Mexico City, São Paulo, Singapore, Sydney

First PERENNIAL LIBRARY edition published 1988.

Library of Congress Cataloging-in-Publication Data

Sachs, Harvey, birth date.
   Toscanini.

   "Perennial Library."
   Includes index.
   Bibliography: p.
   1. Toscanini, Arturo, 1867–1957. 2. Conductors (Music)—Biography.
ML422.T67S34   785'.092'4 [B]   78-17245
ISBN 0-06-091473-4 (pbk.)

88 89 90 91 92 MPC 10 9 8 7 6 5 4 3 2 1

To my mother and father

Contents

Illustrations

Frontispiece Toscanini, at about the age of 25, when he conducted the world premiere of *Pagliacci*.

Notes and Acknowledgements

The following chapters constitute a biography and not a work of musical criticism. Some of the problems of Toscanini criticism are touched upon in the concluding section; but I am much more concerned here with establishing a credible and substantial outline of the subject's extraordinary life and with describing his character, surroundings and working methods than with discussing his performances or recordings.

The research has been very extensive, and I want to mention some of the people who have assisted me. Their number is so great that I am necessarily forced simply to list most of them. I am particularly sorry about that since working or talking with these people has in almost all cases been a great source of pleasure, as well as having been highly useful.

Two people, above all, deserve my gratitude: my wife, Barbara, whose patience, advice and support have been immeasurable, and music critic B.H. Haggin, without whose recommendation this book would not have been written. Mr Haggin has given unstintingly of his time, knowledge and experience at every step. Seven other people have been of especially great assistance to me during various phases in my work: Dr Peter Aistleitner of Hamburg; Mr Thomas S. Hathaway of Toronto; Miss Linda Osband, editor, and Miss Gill Hudson, editorial assistant at Weidenfeld and Nicolson; Mr Robert Hupka of New York; Dr Jonothan Logan of Cambridge, Massachusetts; and Miss Friedelind Wagner.

Warmest thanks also go to the following institutions and individuals:

Italy. Maestro Giampiero Tintori and his assistants Adriana Corbella and Lorenzo Siliotto of the Museo Teatrale alla Scala, Milan; Dottoressa Agostina Zecca Laterza and assistants at the library of the Conservatorio di Musica 'G. Verdi', Milan; Signor Mainardi of the Casa Toscanini, Parma; Signor Gaspare Nello Vetro of the Conservatorio di Musica 'A. Boito', Parma; Maestro Mario Medici of the Istituto di Studi Verdiani, Parma; Maestro Fausto Broussard and Signora Luciana Pestalozza of the Ricordi Co., Milan. Individuals: Michelangelo Abbado, Franco Abbiati, Guglielmo Barblan, Sandro Cicogna, Beniamino Dal Fabbro, Mario Delli Ponti, Gianni Eminente, Natale Gallini, Gianandrea Gavazzeni, Anna Gerardi, Antonio Ghiringhelli, Carlo Maria Giulini, Mariantonietta Maestri, Maria Majno, Giuseppe Marchioro, Luciano Martini, Maria Cecchini Montarsolo, Giulio Riccardi, Ada Rossi, Lily Seppilli, Wally Toscanini, Antonino Votto.

USA. Mary Ellis Peltz and Heloise Pressey of the Metropolitan Opera Archives; Mary Decamp, archivist of the New York Philharmonic; Marilyn Dean of the Central Records Dept. at NBC; James Dolan of the Los Angeles Philharmonic;

NOTES AND ACKNOWLEDGEMENTS

Mary Dupré of the Philadelphia Orchestra; William Bernell of the San Francisco Symphony; Meredith Armstrong of the Cincinnati Symphony; and the YIVO Institute of New York. Individuals: Ruth Bloch, Robert Bloom, Hugo Burghauser, Arthur Feher, Arthur Fierro, Frances Holden, Clyde J. Key, Alexander Kipnis, Erich Leinsdorf, Stephen Matyi, Milton Sachs, Leonard Sharrow, Dario Soria, Jerome Toobin, Walfredo Toscanini, Daniel Whitman.

Great Britain. Miss R. Campbell of St Antony's College library, Oxford; G.M. Jones of the BBC Written Archives Centre; Evelyn Barbirolli, Ray Burford, Prof. Dennis Mack Smith.

Argentina. Maestro Juan Emilio Martini of the Teatro Colón, Buenos Aires; F.M. Beatty of the British Council, Buenos Aires; Diana Talkowsky.

Austria. Prof. Otto Strasser of the Vienna Philharmonic; Frau Neunteufel of the Salzburg Festival archives.

Belgium. M. Daniel Depauw of the Opéra National, Brussels.

Brazil. W.E. Moss and Bruno Furlanetto of the British Council; Da. Mercedes Reis Pequeño of the National Library, Rio de Janeiro.

Canada. Enrique Tabak, Philip Wults.

Germany. Mr Herbert Barth; Dr Manfred Eger of the Richard Wagner Gedenkstätte, Bayreuth.

Israel. Mr Heinz Berger of the Israel Philharmonic; Mr Yaacov Snir of the Central Library of Music and Dance, Tel-Aviv.

Netherlands. Bruno LaRooij.

Sweden. Mr Åke Pihlblad and Mr Anders Ramsay of the Stockholm Philharmonic; Mrs Iwa Aulin Voghera.

Switzerland. Mme Danielle Deyer of the Bibliothèque Cantonale, Lausanne; M.L. Kaufmann of the Lucerne Festival; Mme Juliette Ansermet; Frau Elisabeth Furtwängler.

A great deal of translating was necessary for the documentation which this book contains. The author assumes responsibility for most of the translations from Italian, French, German, Portuguese, Spanish and Swedish; his wife translated from Hebrew.

The following list of rates of exchange should help to make fees and other figures more easily comprehensible to English-speaking readers:

Year: 1900 £1 = $4·87 = 25·2 lire
    1910   1 = 4·86 = 25·2
    1920   1 = 4·86 1 lira = $9\frac{1}{2}$ old pence = $0·19
    1935   1 = 4·86
    1950   1 = 2·80 = 1,750 lire

I have given opera titles according to current English usage. Thus: *The Magic Flute*, not *Die Zauberflöte*; but *Die Meistersinger*, not *The Master Singers*.

All operas conducted by Toscanini in Italy and South America were performed in Italian, regardless of their original languages, excepting the 1925 *Pelléas* done in French at La Scala. In the United States and Austria, all operas conducted by him were done in their original languages, excepting the 1913 *Boris Godunov* performed in Italian at the Metropolitan Opera.

Foreword

Biographies of performing musicians are generally of limited value except as entertainment. If the biographer attempts to give non-technical analyses of musical performances—which are in themselves analyses, in part—he may find himself drowning in descriptive explanations of non-verbal phenomena; while if he simply decides to describe a career, the result is often little better than a combination travelogue/who's who.

But Arturo Toscanini's important rôle in the history of operatic and orchestral performance, as well as his uncompromising character, have made him the subject of numerous works—biographical, descriptive-analytical and anecdotal—varying greatly in quality. He himself apparently was never tempted to write either memoirs or musico-philosophical reflections, nor did he grant interviews; but several people who knew him produced valuable books which reveal aspects of his working methods and personality. Among these are *This Was Toscanini*, by Samuel Antek, who played in the NBC Symphony for the full seventeen years of its existence; *The Toscanini Musicians Knew*, a compilation of testimony by singers and instrumentalists who worked with the conductor at various times during his career, by music critic B.H. Haggin; and Haggin's earlier *Conversations with Toscanini*. There have also been books like the meretricious *Toscanini: An Intimate Portrait*, by Samuel Chotzinoff (numerous descriptions of the Maestro at dinner parties—and what could be less intimate than a dinner party? —plus a great amount of sheer invention, much of it malicious) and a number of biographies, which Walter Toscanini, the conductor's son, characterized as being 'of little value due to the fact that they contain a lot of misinformation and mistakes'.[1]

Over thirty books have, in fact, been published about Toscanini, not even taking into account revised editions and translations, pamphlets, lengthy articles, discographies, etc. Seven of these books are full-length biographical works, and should be mentioned briefly. (See Bibliography for their exact titles and other data.)

The first, by Tobia Nicotra, was written in Italian but published only in English (1929). It is superficial, full of errors and invented conversations, and was written when Toscanini still had twenty-five active years before him. Nicotra was later arrested for forging valuable manuscripts (one of which, incidentally, was bought by Toscanini) and was then released by the Fascists who needed his help in forging their enemies' signatures on incriminating documents.

Paul Stefan, the Austrian critic, published his Toscanini biography in 1936, and it was quickly translated into English. While it is a great improvement upon Nicotra's, it also presents a very restricted view of the subject: it is hard to write a thorough biography of a very strong-willed person who is indifferent or hostile to the project.

A breakthrough came in 1947 when Alfredo Segre's long article, 'Toscanini, the First Forty Years', appeared in *The Musical Quarterly*. Not only was Segre able to talk with members of the Toscanini family and even with Toscanini himself, who had opened up a bit in his old age, he was also willing to begin examining the records of the past in order to give the story of Toscanini's youth a less mythological tone than his predecessors had done.

Two lengthy biographies were published in 1951 by journalists, Howard Taubman in America and Filippo Sacchi in Italy. Taubman's version of the first half of Toscanini's life is based very closely on Segre's. Considering the scarcity of documents then available, it is a useful work, although one senses the author's reluctance to touch certain issues, such as the treatment Toscanini received at the hands of his 'friends' at the National Broadcasting Company, or important aspects of the conductor's personal life. Sacchi's book, in its original form (the American translation is abridged), gives a charming and informative picture of the Italian musical environment of Toscanini's youth; but it is still very inadequate regarding purely factual material, especially where the enormous American portion of Toscanini's career is concerned.

Andrea Della Corte, critic and musicologist, produced the most thorough of these biographies in 1958, the year after Toscanini's death. Della Corte was the first not to be daunted by the incredibly copious but totally scattered and disorganized documentary material extant in countless Italian libraries, archives and private collections. There were still serious gaps and errors, but it was an important and admirable work which, however, was never issued in English.

Seventeen years separated the Della Corte book from its successor, written by George R. Marek. During that period a vast amount of source material came to light, and much of it was published in several non- or partially-biographical Italian works. Unfortunately, Marek, a former RCA vice-president, did not take full advantage of these items, nor did he follow the rewarding paths they hinted at. His book offers a devout layman's approach, couched in nebulous terms, to Toscanini's work, while not providing the compensation of setting straight the bare facts of his life. There are literally dozens of major and minor inaccuracies, mistranslations, chronological and metaphorical mix-ups, and page after page of digressions. Marek says that Walter Toscanini had asked him to write a biography of his father and that he had refused. He changed his mind, however, when Walter was dead and when the family archives which Walter had assembled and had presumably intended to make available to him were no longer available to Marek or to anyone else.

The only biography to follow Marek's until now has been that of Giuseppe Tarozzi, a Milanese journalist (1977; available only in Italian at this time). It is largely a poorly written re-hashing of the now out-of-print Sacchi book.

Part of the confusion regarding simple factual information can be ascribed to Toscanini's utter lack of interest in keeping records of the events of his career. When, in 1886, at the age of nineteen, he made his extraordinary conducting début in Rio de Janeiro, he did not bother to save any programmes or reviews, or even to write to his parents about the unusual event. And as late as 1964, seven years after Toscanini's death, his son was gathering together such basic materials as dates and programmes from the Scala Orchestra's famous North American tour, which Toscanini had led in 1920–1. When one considers that he was active as a conductor for sixty-eight years and that his repertoire must have been one of the most enormous in the history of his profession, it becomes obvious that a great deal more than anecdotage and speculation is required if one wishes to attempt a serious, complete and well-documented chronicle of the man's life.

The present biography is the first to be published by someone too young to have met Toscanini or to have attended one of his concerts. It is also the first to be written by someone with a certain experience as a performing musician, and by someone who has, for twenty years, watched all varieties of conductors *rehearsing* orchestras. Obviously, it is a great disadvantage not to have heard Toscanini conduct: although his recordings give a reasonably accurate picture of his musical ideas *when those recordings were made*, they very inadequately represent his 'sound', which by all accounts was remarkable and unique. ('I went to his rehearsals,' said Otto Klemperer, who was not given to adulation, 'and I remember I went to different places in the empty hall—how he could make this sound! I felt this is a miracle—perhaps from any movement—and I could not find it.'[2]) Not having known his subject personally also makes a biographer's task much more difficult; but there is at least a chance that the subject's character will emerge somewhat better balanced and less polemicized as a result.

Some years ago a book about famous conductors was published in Britain by a nearly unknown conductor. It served to demonstrate that little musicians writing about big musicians can be a dangerous affair, fraught with temptations to make the subject—or victim, as the case may be—conform not only to the author's preconceptions of him (twist or change data as you please), but also to his preconceptions of the subject's art. The resultant vitriol stew can then be delicately seasoned with the author's own frustrations. I sincerely hope that that situation has been avoided here, and that whatever technical familiarity I have with the profession has merely served to avoid some of the witchcraft terminology so often adopted by those writing about 'hypnotic' conductors and their 'entranced' orchestras.

Material used in this book has been collected over a seventeen-year period, most concentratedly during the past two years, spent mainly in Italy. If and when the Toscanini family archives are made available for research, unknown data will undoubtedly come to light. Nevertheless, this book is based on very extensive documentation; verbal statements and other forms of second-hand testimony have been checked to the greatest degree possible, and speculative remarks by the author are clearly recognizable as such. I shall hazard—perhaps immodestly—the guess that the possible eventual release of the family's material would augment but not greatly alter the contents of the book.

If the subject of this book were a literary figure, or someone who had written great quantities of letters whereby one could follow his day-to-day life with some sort of regularity, a good biographer would first publish the prime source material in a separate volume and would then write an interpretative biography. But that is not the case here. Toscanini's letters—at least those which have so far come to light—are relatively few and often uninformative. Therefore, where useful and interesting letters do exist, I have chosen to incorporate them into the text.

Antonino Votto, who was Toscanini's assistant at La Scala during the 1920s, once made the following statement: 'For everything concerning the figure of Toscanini, I am like St Thomas: I relate only what I myself saw and heard.'[3] Although I, unfortunately, cannot make that claim, I have tried to keep that admirable thought in mind throughout the writing of this book, and I hope that the result is not completely unworthy of the subject.

TOSCANINI

I
Parma and Rio de Janeiro

'Royal Prefecture of Parma—Cabinet
Political report No. 2383
To the Ministry of the Interior—Florence
Confidential
Parma, 7 November 1866
   ... Yesterday evening five or six citizens belonging to the radical party met at the home of Gardelli, the pharmacist, in Via Santa Croce, in order to discuss badly-needed assistance for the periodical, *l'Unità italiana*. The barristers Magradi and Spinazzi were noted among them. A new assessment was made, and a certain Toscanini, Claudio, son of Angelo, 30 [sic] years old, tailor, and Ceresini, Augusto ... both resident in Parma and both already compromised in the Aspromonte affair, were charged with collecting donations to that end. Their footsteps will be followed. The Prefect'[1]

Italy was on the verge of becoming a nation by the time Claudio Toscanini's generation reached adulthood. The *carbonari* and *federati* of the 1820s had given way to Mazzini's *Giovine Italia* in the '30s, which had been followed in turn by the stop-gap reforms of the '40s, the revolutions of '48, Cavour's manoeuvrings throughout the '50s, and finally the climactic battles, diplomatic deals and plebiscites of 1859–61. A movement which had begun as an expression of discontent with unenlightened foreign rule on the part of middle- and upper-class radicals had eventually spread to large numbers of people at all levels of society.

Claudio himself came from a lower-class but relatively well-off family in Cortemaggiore, a beautiful village lying in the Po plain, very close to Cremona and Piacenza, and a mere eight or nine miles from the even tinier village of Roncole, Verdi's birthplace. We do not know how many generations of Toscaninis had lived in the Emilia region; but the name Toscanini means 'little Tuscans', so at some time the family had emigrated from Tuscany. Claudio's father, Angelo, was the owner of a spinning mill which had outlet shops in both Cortemaggiore and Piacenza. Legend has it that Angelo and his first wife produced three children in quick succession, after which the poor woman committed suicide by throwing herself down a well. His second wife, Eligia Bombardi, is said to have given birth to twenty-five children, of whom Claudio was the youngest. The infant mortality rate was high in those days, and by 1833, the year of Claudio's birth, the Corte-maggiore census book listed only ten Toscanini children.

At the age of twelve, Claudio lost his temper during an argument with his father and hit him in the face with a handkerchief. Overcome with fear and remorse, he ran away from home, travelling on foot to Parma, some thirty miles to the south-east, where he stayed at the home of a step-sister and worked as a tailor. In 1859 he decided to join Giuseppe Garibaldi's republican army. The previous year Count Cavour, who was the prime minister of King Victor Emanuel II of Piedmont, had plotted with Napoleon III to create a kingdom of northern Italy, which would include Piedmont, Lombardy, Venice and the central Italian duchies. A war with Austria was provoked, and Garibaldi and his followers, subordinating republicanism to nationalism, rushed to the aid of Piedmont and France. Having won the battles of Magenta and Solferino, the allies triumphantly entered Milan; but at that point Napoleon III decided to pull out. An armistice was signed with Austria, leaving Piedmont and Lombardy weakly confederated, and leaving Claudio and his fellow redshirts free to return to their homes.

It would be useless to speculate whether Claudio had imbibed republican ideals which had then led him to enlist in Garibaldi's forces, or whether it was the very potent romantic legend of the general and his wild band—appealing, in any case, to someone of Claudio's adventurous temperament—which had led first to his participation with them and only afterwards to his familiarity with the ideology, at least in its rough outlines. In any case, when Garibaldi and his 'Thousand Men' rid Sicily of the Bourbons in 1860 Claudio was again among the *garibaldini*. Afterwards he was conscripted into the regular army, probably in Sicily, but when Garibaldi decided two years later that Rome should be annexed immediately to the new Italian state and that the temporal power of the papacy should be ended, Claudio deserted the regular forces to join his hero. The consequences of all this were unfortunate: the redshirts were surrounded and beaten by the regulars at Aspromonte in Calabria, en route to Rome; and although Garibaldi and his 'irregulars' were granted an amnesty a few weeks later, Claudio and other deserters were imprisoned and sentenced to death. Many of them did, in fact, face the firing squad. Claudio was spared that fate but re-sentenced to three years in prison—a sentence which he served, fully, under horrifying conditions. He contracted scurvy and lost all his teeth, but managed somehow to survive.

Not long after his return to Parma he fell in love with a twenty-six-year-old woman named Paola (Paolina) Montani, a native of the city, daughter of Pietro and Carolina (née Notari) Montani. They were married on 7 June 1866 at the church of Santo Spirito. Within a few days Claudio received a secret message that the general was gathering his troops to help in the imminent war to take Venice and the Trentino from Austria. Three years of prison had not altered Claudio's principles a bit: he bade his wife goodbye and went off to fight at Condino and Bezzecca. The Italians were defeated, but Austria ceded Venice to France in gratitude for Napoleon III's intermediary efforts, and the French allowed the city to hold a plebiscite, whose issue favoured union with Italy. (The Trentino remained Austrian until 1918.)

When, after four months, Claudio came home from this last campaign, he found his wife pregnant with their first child; but this did not deter him from becoming involved in the business referred to in the Prefect's letter. The so-called 'radical party' to which he adhered was the *Associazione unitaria democratica*, an anti-royalist party led by Mazzini, then in exile. Apparently Claudio's actions were not subversive enough to have caused him real difficulties. He is mentioned again in official correspondence as someone who should be kept under surveillance, but nothing more serious seems to have developed.

The child, a boy, was born at 3 a.m. on 25 March 1867 in the Toscanini flat at No. 13, Borgo San Giacomo (now Borgo Rodolfo Tanzi). Claudio, despite his anti-clericalism, carried the infant that same day to Parma's thirteenth-century Baptistery, one of the most beautiful buildings in Italy. *Infantulo imposui nomina Arturus Primus Alexander Secundus*, reads the baptismal record. The 'Arturo' remained but the 'Alessandro' was not used again.

Although the house on Borgo Tanzi is now a museum filled with relics from its most famous resident's career, the fact is that within a few months of Arturo's birth the family had moved to Genoa, where Claudio hoped to open a new and more promising tailor's shop. Unfortunately, the baby's health was poor. He was thin, delicate, and suffered constantly from various illnesses. Paolina, for one reason or another, decided to take him back to Parma and leave him with her parents. According to the family story, the child was so sickly that he was kept on a strict diet of broth and mush. One day he saw a plate of beans in olive oil on the table and pointed at it wilfully: 'That's all he needs!' said one of his aunts; but the grandmother replied, 'If he wants beans, give them to him. He's going to die anyway, so it's better to make him happy.' And whether because of or in spite of the beans, his health began to improve almost immediately.[2]

In Genoa, Paolina gave birth to a second child, a girl who was given the name Narcisa; and soon afterwards Claudio, whose hopes for quick success in the Ligurian capital had not been realized, decided to return to Parma to make another new start. The economic situation of the Toscanini family was neither bright nor promising. Claudio's seven years as a *garibaldino* had been the high point of his existence, and the excitement had ended when he was only thirty-three. He was a good-natured fellow who found it difficult to work steadily at his trade; it was much more interesting to walk around town taking part in clandestine political discussions which were in fact known to everyone, or to tell stories of battles won and lost, of what the general had had to say on any given subject, of prison life. (His granddaughter, Wally Toscanini Castelbarco, who was only six when Claudio died in 1906, still remembers, seven decades later, seeing him in his red shirt—his most prized possession—which he had last worn in combat some forty years earlier.) An unfortunate tendency to drink developed and he disappeared from home for days at a time. Added to this lack of diligence was the fact that his participation in the Aspromonte affair had disqualified him from even the most meagre military pension.

Paolina was the opposite of her husband. Hard-working, proud, harsh and undemonstrative, she raised her four children (two more daughters, Ada and Zina, followed Narcisa), took care of the household and ran the tailor shop. She was determined, according to her granddaughter, not to let people know how poor the family was. Arturo and his sisters received little maternal affection.

The working-class families of Parma, which was a city of 45,000 in 1870, lived mainly in the district called Oltretorrente—'the other side of the stream'—and that is where Arturo Toscanini was born; but Claudio, on his return from Genoa, decided to set up his new shop and home on the opposite side, in the heart of town, perhaps hoping that business would be better there. Nonetheless, Arturo's maternal grandparents, aunts, uncles and cousins still lived in Oltretorrente, and it was there that he spent much of his early childhood. He found more warmth among the Montanis than in his own home. Still, the Toscanini household was not entirely devoid of interest for the boy. Culture, for Claudio's family and many like it, was not something carefully nurtured or regarded with wonder from a polite distance: it was an important and natural part of life. Quite apart from the fact that Parma's residents were and still are surrounded by architectural masterpieces of nearly every period from the Romanesque to the Neo-classical, and that painting and sculpture are richly represented in the city, there was widespread enthusiasm at all levels of society for the other arts as well—particularly literature and music. Literature, to the general public of that time, meant above all the high romantic poets and novelists of the early nineteenth century. Workers at the Toscanini shop would often take turns reading aloud to each other—and the repertoire included not only works of Italian masters: Toscanini, in his extreme old age, still remembered making his first contact with Scott's *Ivanhoe* (in translation, of course) and other foreign works in this way as a small child. The importance of these early impressions cannot be overvalued. All his life, his affinities remained very closely connected to the romantic movement and its immediate offshoots. His tastes not only in music but also in literature and painting were firmly rooted there, and it is natural that that is where he felt most at home.

The Parmesans have long had a reputation among fellow Italians for their fine cooking, their leftist political leanings and above all their passion for opera. This madness for *la lirica* is not as strong today as it was a hundred years ago, when the beautiful Teatro Regio (1829) was to a great extent the focal point of the city's existence. Every season's operatic productions received numerous performances to accommodate the avid audience, many of whom came night after night to hear the same opera, to find out whether this or that singer would sing this or that aria (or note) as well or as poorly as the night before, to see friends, and perhaps to go to a café afterwards, where opinions on the proceedings were delivered and where the latest theatre gossip was joyfully discussed in minute detail.

Claudio sometimes sang in the chorus at the Regio, and his shop assistants went to the theatre each evening to help dress the cast. The Montanis were also amateur singers and impassioned opera enthusiasts, and it was probably Grand-father Montani or one of his sons who first took Arturo, age four, to hear one of Verdi's more recent operas, *Un ballo in maschera*, from the Regio's *loggione*—that famous gallery which terrified singers for so many decades. The child had already heard various arias from *Ballo* sung repeatedly around the shop and it seems that at some point during the performance he joined one of the artists, singing the not very accurate version he had learned at home and provoking laughter among the public.

This premature début was not hailed in the press, and in fact there are few indications of very early manifestations of musical talent on Arturo's part. A young girl named Medea Massari, who spent much time in the Toscanini house-hold learning tailoring skills, recalled many years later that Arturo was 'like an old man' and not at all a noisy child. He was very serious and stubborn and did not enjoy playing with other children; but he was fascinated by any musical sounds. Medea added that Arturo did not like to sing and that he had a raspy voice (this persisted throughout his life). He did, however, love to play with a little two-stringed 'instrument' which the girl had fashioned from a hollowed-out corncob.

His memory of kindergarten, looking back on it some eighty years later, was mainly that of falling in love with a girl in his class, whom he disliked being away from even during the afternoon nap, when the girls and boys were separated. 'The little thing, whom I loved very much, died a few years later,' he remem-bered, 'and even when I was already at the Conservatory, I would often look towards the cypress trees growing near her grave.'[3] Arturo was sent to the elementary school in Via Caprazucca, where he did well in the first two grades. One of his teachers, a Signora Vernoni, exercised what turned out to be an enor-mous influence upon his future. She had been very surprised to observe that he could memorize poems after a single reading, and was even more surprised when the boy asked if he could visit her home to try her piano. Permission was granted, and Arturo immediately began to find the notes of some of the arias and songs he had heard people singing. Signora Vernoni paid a visit to Claudio and Paolina and suggested that they try to enrol Arturo at the Conservatory.

The idea did not displease the elder Toscaninis: Parma's Royal School of Music was a very reputable institution; moreover, if a child were gifted enough, lucky enough, or had parents who knew the right people, he might even be accepted as a resident scholarship student, whose tuition and living expenses would be absorbed by the state. Thus, after Arturo had been given a ninety per cent mark in his final examinations at the end of second grade, Claudio saw to it that his son received some basic piano lessons from a local tuba player named Bonini, and then made an application, in comically stiff and ungrammatical style, to the Conservatory's director, Giusto Dacci:

'Parma, 9 September 1876
Most Illustrious Director,
    Toscanini, Claudio, of Parma resident at Strada dei Genovesi 65 by profession tailor.
    Having a son named Arturo approximately $9\frac{1}{2}$ years old who seems very inclined towards Instrumental music, who knows how to read, and write, and instructed with music lessons.
    It is for this that he presents to Your Most Illustrious Lordship his most fervid supplications in order to receive the favour that his son were admitted as a resident student at this Royal and Most Honoured Musical Institute, the influence of which upon the son having the necessary requisites will certainly one day be able to call himself very fortunate together with his poor family ...'[4]

Admission examinations were held early in November, with eighteen boys trying for the one available 'resident' post. (There were twenty-three residents in 1876–7.) Arturo did not obtain that place, but was the second of three boys accepted as external students with the agreement that they would be taken as internal students when positions were open. He spent a year living at home while taking lessons at the Conservatory and then, in February 1878, after another letter from Claudio to the director and another examination, he was admitted as a scholarship student.

Parma's Conservatory was founded by Marie Louise in 1821 in what had formerly been a Carmelite convent, and it is still located there today, although students no longer live in it. The building itself—parts of which date from medieval times—has been cleaned up and inoffensively modernized in recent years; but old photographs demonstrate that it cannot have been a pleasant place in which to live in Toscanini's day. He was not, however, used to a comfortable way of life; certainly the school did not represent a lowering of his standard of living. He slept in a large, barren dormitory room with eleven other boys, ate poor meals (often fish on the verge of going bad and wine of lowest quality), said his compulsory daily prayers, and wore the school's military cadet-like uniform. There was a single water closet, which did not include a bathtub: baths were provided once a year at the Civic Hospital. Straw for the mattresses was not replaced often enough and bed linen was changed so infrequently that the dormitory rooms often stank. Nevertheless, all students had to have certificates of vaccination prior to admittance and cholera vaccinations whenever outbreaks occurred in the country.

During his first two years Arturo studied *solfeggio* (sight-singing), rudiments of theory, keyboard harmony, piano, chorus, music history and non-musical subjects. From his second year onwards, his principal instrument, by assignment, was the cello—although he would have preferred the piano—which he studied under Leandro Carini; and his more advanced work in harmony and composition was done with Dacci himself. Dacci's Christian names were Giusto Severo Pertinace (Just Severe Pertinacious); not surprisingly, he was a moralistic and pedantic man, but very highly respected throughout Italy as a pedagogue.

'I was a hard-working student because I liked music and did not have to force myself to study it,' Toscanini would later recall; 'but I wasn't what you would call exemplary in regard to personal appearance. My uniform was often in disorder and I often didn't have as many buttons as I needed for the buttonholes in my shoes.' As punishment for this, he once had to pass a whole morning locked in a small room with his cello. After a while he called a custodian to ask permission to go to the toilet, but was told to control himself. Time passed and finally, in desperation, he decided to use his cello for a non-musical purpose. Next day, forgetting what had happened, he took the cello to his lesson. While Arturo was still playing his scales Prof. Carini exclaimed, 'Student Toscanini, what's the matter with that sweaty cello?'[5]

In those days the teachers were present at the school every day except Sunday, which meant that students were able to work under direct and steady supervision. Carini did not, in fact, allow his youngest students to practise by themselves: he worked with them daily. Instruction was conservative but thorough and discipline was strict to the point of absurdity. From Dacci's diary:

'18 January 1877. A love letter sent by the cleaning lady, Bianchi, to Student Copelli was found. Copelli was put in solitary confinement on bread and water for 24 hours. The woman was fired immediately.[6]

14 March 1877. I have ordered that the Students' hair be cut immediately, but not too short, the weather being too cold.[7]

[1885]. . . . With the intention of providing himself with fresh water, Internal Student Enrico Preti poured, from the window of his room, a glass of water which accidentally landed on the cat belonging to the wife of the aforementioned Signor Ferrari, said cat having been in the school courtyard. The lady, believing the liquid poured to have been urine, took offence and, addressing the students, also called her husband who, complaining about the deed in very harsh terms, provoked not very polite replies on the part of the students.'[8]

Preti was punished for this last crime, with the result that some days later the cat disappeared. Arturo and several of the other older students participated in the murder, skinning, cooking, serving and eventual eating of the animal—a nefarious *vendetta* not made public until 1930.

There was definitely a touch of prison atmosphere at the school. Classes were held from 8 a.m. until noon and again from 2 until 6 p.m., six days a week. The building itself has two cloisters where the boys were able to get some fresh air and probably some exercise as well; however, internal students were only allowed to leave the premises once or twice a week, when they were led through the city streets by an adult guard. Students who had reached a certain level of instrumental proficiency were required to play in the orchestra at the Teatro Regio, but even those trips—a distance of about a thousand feet—were accompanied. It seems, though, that the older students managed somehow to pay visits to the local brothels, and that the school authorities remained determinedly ignorant of this fact.

Families of the young musicians were permitted to visit once a week in the Conservatory's receiving room, but Paolina did not feel that her family was well enough dressed for these events; so she contented herself with seeing her son on Sunday mornings at the Church of the Five Wounds, where the students were led for compulsory services.

This was the institution which Arturo attended for nine years, seven and a half of them as a resident; and it was an experience which he did better than merely survive. From early on it was apparent that he was not only musically gifted, but also in possession of an amazingly strong internal discipline and a mind which demanded to know everything about whatever fascinated it. His name rarely appears on Dacci's 'bad boy' lists, and not once is he mentioned as having complained about the meagre quantity and poor quality of the food—the most common cause of dissatisfaction. He more than once sold part of his food ration in order to buy music. Fortunately, his health was excellent: Dacci records only once that the boy was in bed, suffering from chilblains—not surprising considering that the building was poorly heated during the winter.

By the time he reached adolescence Arturo Toscanini was completely possessed by his love of music and by his desire to get inside it, and the other aspects of his life were of secondary importance. One could call this a distorted point of view; and the distortion was so pronounced in this case that it was eventually to make life difficult for many people who came in direct contact with it, and sometimes insufferable for the man who was its direct victim. But the mental discipline which that distortion demanded also brought its own form of healthiness. It is no exaggeration to say that this book is the story of that distortion and its consequences.

We do not know many details of the boy's studies at the Conservatory, but we do know that he made a deep impression on his teachers and fellow students. His exceptional memory and extraordinary powers of concentration must have made him rather a terror at times, although he was modest and quiet by nature and not apt to boast of his talents or to use them to put others in a bad light. He wanted to make music all the time, and would beg and cajole other students to get together during free hours to play, under his supervision, arrangements he had made of symphonic and operatic compositions. School regulations did not permit these gatherings, and this was probably one of the reasons why it was possible to entice people into participating. His obvious abilities and unhesitating criticisms earned him two well-meant nicknames, which he hated nonetheless: *Genio* (Genius) and *Forbsòn* (a Parmesan dialect word meaning 'shears'). His cello technique developed well; and he taught himself to play orchestral scores and everything else at the piano. At about the age of fifteen he began to compose in earnest and by twenty-one he had produced over two dozen short works. Of these, more later.

Practical performing experience of a varied nature was not neglected at the Conservatory. We know, for instance, that Arturo sang in the chorus in a performance of the Cherubini *Requiem* in memory of Victor Emanuel II, shortly after the king's death in 1878; that he acted as accompanist for instrumentalists at Conservatory recitals; and that he played cello in various small ensembles and orchestras both in and outside the school. But these were of little importance compared with the experience of playing in the orchestra at the Regio. Between 1881 and 1885 he sat in the theatre's famous string section, which Verdi had called the best in Italy just a few years earlier; and one can be sure that he not only played but also watched and listened greedily to all that went on around him.

Nowadays established opera companies seem to avoid, if possible, playing works written within the past fifty years; but during Toscanini's time at the Regio all of the twenty operas performed had been written since 1835, which meant no Gluck, Mozart, Beethoven or Weber, no Rossini or Bellini. The general public considered most of those composers—even if their works were known only by name—to be worthy but somewhat boring representatives of styles not suited to modern tastes. Verdi, who was born and spent most of his life in or near Busseto—'practically at the gates of Parma', as any *parmigiano* will tell you—was the great champion of the local repertoire, with five of his operas, from the early *Ernani* to the most recent *Aida*, having been produced during Toscanini's five seasons. Donizetti, Meyerbeer, Bizet and Ponchielli were represented by two works each, and single operas by Gounod, Thomas, Gomes, Pacini, Auteri-Manzocchi, Palminteri and even Wagner were produced.

Wagner was not at all popular in Italy, and very little of his music managed to reach Parma, as Toscanini himself wrote many years later:

'The first impression I received of Wagner's music goes back to 1878–79, when I heard the *Tannhäuser* Overture at a concert of Parma's Quartet Society—and I was bewildered. I remember a detail: my teacher brought a cello part of this overture to school for me and made me study various passages, which were very difficult for me at that time. In 1884 Parma was the first Italian city to perform *Lohengrin* after its success in Bologna and its failure in Milan. I was in the orchestra. It was then that I first acquired a great, marvellous awareness of Wagner's genius. From the first rehearsal, or rather from the first bars of the Prelude, I was overwhelmed by magical, supernatural feelings; the celestial harmonies revealed a new world to me, a world of whose existence no one had even the slightest intuition until Wagner's transcendent spirit discovered it.'[9]

Since Dacci believed that Mendelssohn had reached the limits of the harmonic universe, the young Toscanini studied secretly whatever Wagnerian music he was able to find.

In the spring of 1884 Toscanini, then seventeen, appeared as cellist, composer and conductor on a programme given by Conservatory students in the foyer of the Regio. He played the Introduction and Polonaise for cello by E. Dunkler and then conducted his own Andante and Scherzo for orchestra. This concert was reviewed in no fewer than ten newspapers—four from Parma, three from Milan and one each from Rome, Piacenza and Ravenna—all praising his as the best of the student compositions, lauding his cello playing and making no reference to his or anyone else's conducting! (There was no formal study of conducting in those days; but all composition students at the Parma Conservatory were instructed in instrumental coaching.)

Dacci made Toscanini assistant instructor of harmony for the 1884–5 school year—the boy's last at the Conservatory—despite some clashes that almost caused his expulsion. The troubles had begun the previous spring when a dozen students, including Toscanini, had angered Dacci by refusing to attend confession or to take communion. Then, in August 1884, during his summer holidays, Toscanini went to the nearby town of Carpi to play first-desk cello in an opera-ballet by Guglielmo Branca, without obtaining the required permission from Dacci. The director's amazingly efficient 'secret police' found out about this crime, and although Toscanini probably suffered nothing worse than a reprimand, the ridiculous strictness of the rules must have been irksome to an independent seventeen-year-old. Things went along well enough that autumn, and in September and October he played in an orchestra directed by a young fellow Parmesan named Cleofonte Campanini, a talented musician whose successful career would later be overshadowed by Toscanini's. Performances were given at the National Exposition in Turin and also in Milan; these were the young cellist's first visits to two of the cities which were to play an important part in his life.

We read in Dacci's diary that on Sunday, 11 January 1885, fifteen students —Toscanini among them—refused to get up early to go to mass. When they finally did leave their beds Dacci informed them that they would have to go to a later mass during the time reserved for the weekly family visits, and then ordered them to go immediately to their respective study rooms. They refused. Dacci was dumbfounded and told an assistant to take the names of the disobedient boys.

'Toscanini, in the presence of his companions, declared that he wanted his name to be first on the list. . . . I had his father sent for at once and told him that if his son did not write a letter asking to be pardoned, he would certainly be expelled from the School. . . . The young Toscanini, who was also in the Office, walked out of the room—another scornful act. The same day I informed the Royal Commissioner of the occurrence . . .'[10]

The letter was not forthcoming and Dacci, who was probably worried about losing his best student only a few months before graduation, convinced some of the professors to write the letter and to persuade Toscanini to copy and sign it, which he did.

In July he took his last examinations. He received the maximum number of points and highest honours in cello and composition, as well as the Barbacini Prize of 137.50 lire, presented annually to the outstanding graduate.

He must have played in Carpi again that summer, which would hardly be worth mentioning except that Carpi was the home town of an impresario named Claudio Rossi, who was then putting together an opera company to take to Brazil the following spring. Toscanini was noticed either by Rossi himself or by his brother Lelio,[11] and was engaged as principal cellist and assistant chorus-master—exceptional responsibilities for such a young man. After playing another winter season at the Regio he packed his few belongings and left his native city, where he was never to reside again. In Genoa he said goodbye to his parents and sisters, who had recently moved back there, and embarked with the rest of the company.

The crossing took about twenty-five days. Toscanini spent much of his time practising and studying. Since there was a piano on board, some of the singers asked him to coach them in their rôles, which he happily agreed to do. There were some well-known artists among the singers, including soprano Nadina Boulicioff; mezzo-soprano Medea Mei; her husband, tenor Nicolai Figner; baritone Paul Lhérie, who had begun his career as a tenor and had sung Don José at the world première of Carmen in 1875; and bass Gaetano Roveri. They appreciated the young man's gifts and his seriousness. Also on board was Ferruccio Catellani, an ex-classmate from the Conservatory who had been engaged as concertmaster.

Toscanini passed his nineteenth birthday at Cádiz, one of the ship's ports of call; and the troupe arrived at São Paulo in mid April. (Years later he told his grandson that the musicians used to return to the boat each night to sleep, although this did not continue throughout the whole tour.) It was not until their arrival that the company met their conductor, a thirty-five-year-old Brazilian named Leopoldo Miguez, and it did not take long for them to realize that he was incompetent—or to make him realize that they knew it. There was tension as well between Miguez and Carlo Superti, the assistant conductor and co-administrator of the company. Superti was probably not much better equipped as a conductor than Miguez (a few years later he made such a mess of a performance of *Don Carlo*, which he had stepped in to conduct as a substitute at La Scala, that the public shouted him out of the theatre); but he was Italian, as were most of the artists, and he was not as overbearing as Miguez. Much later Toscanini referred to Superti as 'a good violinist and ballet conductor'.

The São Paulo season began with *La favorita* on 17 April. 'The company cannot be perfectly judged by the first performance,' wrote the critic of *O Pais*. 'I would say, however, that the public, judging by its behaviour and by the conversations in the corridors, had hoped for somewhat more.' Critical opinion varied somewhat from performance to performance, but did not reach extremes of enthusiasm or opprobrium. This began to change towards the end of the two-month stay in São Paulo. The same critic wrote:

'The last performances were tempestuous and a great revolution was expected at the last one. As always happens when a row or disturbance is anticipated, nothing can stop it. There was a furious stamping on Thursday, which set off a battle between the stampers—university boys—and other spectators who applauded.'[12]

By the time the company transferred to Rio de Janeiro, where they were to open at the Imperial Teatro Dom Pedro II on 25 June, internal dissensions had become unendurable. The singers called for Miguez to resign, while the latter blamed all the difficulties on the singers. At the first performance (*Aida*) the chorus was judged too small and not good, the ballet 'couldn't be worse', and the orchestra 'did not seem balanced or obedient'. Miguez, although 'an inspired composer', as a conductor had a beat that was 'too much the same . . . bland'. At the next night's performance of *Faust*, 'the prelude, the peasants' chorus, the fair and the march—not to mention smaller details—were badly played, partly due to the orchestra, partly to the poor preparation of the chorus'. Toscanini always remembered that 'the band on the stage was at war with the orchestra in the pit'.

During the next few days mutual recriminations flew back and forth, with the end result that on the day of the next performance—another *Aida*—Rossi received a letter of resignation from Miguez, for reasons of health. Since the whole theatre-going community in Rio was aware of the divisions within the company, and since feelings of national pride for Miguez were bound to come into play, it was apparent that there would be trouble that night, and that the whole tour might be facing disaster. Superti was designated to conduct, and everyone hoped for the best.

Towards the end of his life Toscanini recalled that he had spent the early part of that evening—Wednesday, 30 June 1886—at his *pensione* with a young contralto named Eugenia Mantelli, 'going over Schubert *Lieder*'.[13] (But some people who knew him well say that he had another version of the story, in which Schumann's music had nothing to do with his own and Signorina Mantelli's activities that evening.) 'Then I took the tram and arrived at the theatre. There was a hell of an uproar!'

At 8 p.m. the ballet master went before the public to announce Miguez's 'indisposition' and the substitution of Superti; but jeers, anti-Italian slogans and rude catcalls greeted poor Superti as he made his way to the podium. Well-dressed gentlemen in the loges banged their canes on the floor, and the police stood by in case the situation should get out of hand. Superti could not begin because of the noise and withdrew. Rossi appeared on stage, accompanied by an interpreter, and again began to explain that Miguez had withdrawn for reasons of health. The rest of the explanation could not be heard over the fresh outburst of noise.

What was to be done? Were the company forced to end the tour after only two performances in Rio, there would not even be enough money for the return voyage. Another attempt had to be made, and several singers put forward Toscanini's name. He recalled:

'Everyone knew that I knew the operas by heart: I used to coach them at the piano without looking at the score. I didn't want to go out; but a woman in the chorus—a Signora Leoni from Parma—ugly as the devil—begged me to go. They wanted me to put a frock coat on, but I said no, no.... I wore my orchestra uniform.'

He took the baton, walked to the podium and sat down. (Yes, sat down! Toscanini did not always stand at rehearsals and performances, as many people believe: in his early years he followed the tradition that opera conductors sit, even at performances; and there is a photograph from as late as 1910 that shows him sitting while rehearsing the Metropolitan Opera orchestra.) It was now 9.15; the audience had shouted and waited for an hour and a quarter. They had paid their money to hear an opera and had had the satisfaction of chasing Miguez's rival from the auditorium. And here, furthermore, was a young boy who had calmly walked to the podium and seemed ready to begin. The noise abated to the point where the orchestra could probably be heard. There was no orchestral score on the podium—only a piano score from which Superti had been ready to direct. Without referring to it, Toscanini raised his baton and began to conduct.[14]

In later years he said that he had no memory of the public's reaction as he walked out, of starting to conduct, or of what happened during the first scenes. He conducted as if in a dream, 'as if I were drunk'; and it was not until he came to the chorus's entrance, 'Su! del Nilo al sacro lido', well into the first act, that he became aware of what he was doing. 'As soon as the chorus came in, I *conducted*. I didn't have the technique, but I conducted.' All his life he would remember two errors he made that evening—one wrong downbeat and one short memory lapse. By the time the performance had ended a disaster had turned into a triumph. It is easy to understand the feelings of astonishment, admiration and gratitude on the part of his fellow performers—not to mention poor Rossi, who must have been on the verge of hysteria. During the next few days reports of the début appeared in the local papers.

'*Gazeta de Noticias*, 1 July. Toscanini is a youth of nineteen who is said to be a musical prodigy. He knows sixty operas by heart—or perhaps 120. It is he who coaches the artists at home, accompanying them at the piano without looking at the score, which he knows even in his sleep. Lively, alert, enthusiastic and courageous, Mr. Toscanini turned out at the last moment to be a sure-handed and secure conductor. It would seem, from the applause and salutations he received, that yesterday's was the well-known situation: *le roi est mort, vive le roi*. It must be admitted that this young maestro is worthy of holding the baton.'

'*Diario de Noticias*, 2 July. This boy, barely nineteen years old but already an excellent musician, succeeded admirably, revealing directorial qualities of a superior level.'

'*A Evolução*, 3 July. In the end . . . a young boy, a modest cellist, Mr. Toscanini, was designated to conduct. Bravo! to the inspired youth. This beardless maestro is a prodigy who communicated the sacred artistic fire to his baton and the energy and passion of a genuine artist to the orchestra. . . . After he took over the conductor's podium, the stamping dwindled away by itself and the stampers only spoke of the extraordinary turn of events.'

Letters from Miguez and Rossi explaining the former's resignation also appeared in the press; but all this had become past history, as an article in *O Pais* (4 July) demonstrates:

'Mr. Arthur Toscanini is definitely remaining at his post as conductor, and we are convinced that he will carry it out worthily, since he gave more than enough proof in *Aida* of competence, *sang-froid*, enthusiasm and vigour. He brought off *Traviata* in the same way the day before yesterday; and according to report, although these are his first conducting experiences, he has been preparing himself for the task for some time, only wishing that it would happen later, in order to learn by heart the entire operatic repertoire and to acquire practical orchestral experience.'

Rossi had in fact asked Toscanini to continue as conductor of the company. There were twelve operas in the repertoire at Rio (*Rigoletto* and *Trovatore* in addition to *Aida* by Verdi, *Marion Delorme* and *La gioconda* of Ponchielli, Donizetti's *La favorita*, Thomas's *Hamlet*, Meyerbeer's *Les Huguenots*, Gounod's *Faust*, Gomes's *Salvator Rosa* and a new Portuguese work called *Laurianna* by

Machado); and Toscanini conducted all of them from memory. Of course he had
studied, helped to coach and played cello in these operas for many weeks, so it is
not surprising or miraculous that he knew them well. (All but two of these works
had been performed at the Regio in Parma during Toscanini's five seasons as a
cellist there.) His memory, nevertheless, was something extraordinary. Stravinsky
wrote fifty years later:

> 'Conducting an orchestra without the score has become the fashion, and is
> often a matter of mere display. There is, however, nothing marvellous about
> this apparent *tour de force* . . .; one risks little and with a modicum of assurance
> and coolness a conductor can easily get away with it. It does not really prove
> that he knows the orchestration of the score. But there can be no doubt in the
> case of Toscanini. His memory is proverbial; there is not a detail that escapes
> him, as attendance at one of his rehearsals is enough to demonstrate.'[15]

Many people have said that Toscanini conducted without a score because he
was extremely myopic and refused to wear glasses. While it is true that in later
years his eyes were very weak and that he wore glasses only when absolutely
necessary, there is no evidence of any eye problem in his youth. He conducted by
memory in the first place because it was easy for him, and secondly because, as he
gained experience, he realized that not having to refer constantly to the score
increased his ability to communicate with his musicians and left him free to
concentrate on what he was hearing.

The experience he gained in Rio was invaluable; and towards the end of his life
he spoke with particular gratitude of the help he had received from baritone Paul
Lhérie:

> 'He was a great artist; Verdi had chosen him for his second *Don Carlo*. I
> learned things from him there that I later tried to teach to other baritones. But
> he was a great talent—greater even than Maurel. He didn't have Maurel's
> voice, but he was more refined. His Rigoletto made you cry. . . . Once, he said
> to me, "Look, Toscanini, I sing a bit slowly here, but you move ahead and I'll
> follow you." Ehhh, what I learned from him! Then there was a certain
> Collione—a beautiful tenor voice, but an imbecile . . .'

Between 30 June and 16 August Toscanini conducted twenty-six performances. He was an incompetent businessman whose finances, until he married,
were always in a state of havoc; so he did not think of requesting a higher salary
as the company's conductor—and Rossi, naturally, did not think of offering him
one. He did, however, have his *serata d'onore* at a performance of *Faust* on
5 August. These traditional 'honour evenings' were given for some of the principal artists during the course of an opera season. The designated performer, in
addition to receiving his fee, would be given a certain percentage of the night's
net profits from ticket sales, plus a laurel wreath or some similar token of esteem.

'They gave me a *serata* without telling me,' Toscanini recalled. 'I looked at the playbill posted on the theatre when I arrived that evening and I was surprised to see my name in large print.' *O Pais* reported the next day:

'The opera *Faust* was sung yesterday at the Teatro Imperial in a benefit performance for Maestro Toscanini. In the interval between Acts II and III, the orchestra, under the direction of the beneficiary, played the grandiose *Guarany* Overture [by Gomes] quite perfectly. The public applauded him at length and called him to the stage; then the company's artists appeared, bringing him various gifts and, after the presentations, they applauded him enthusiastically, joining in the acclamations of the whole theatre. Following this ovation he led Bolzoni's Minuet, written as a quintet and played by the orchestra's strings. It could not have been played with greater polish. The enthusiasm shown for this magnificent composition is indescribable. It was repeated, and so was the applause. His Majesty the Emperor sent to ask the name of the piece performed and Mr. Toscanini went to the imperial loge in order to show him Bolzoni's score.'

And from *O Rio de Janeiro* (7 August) we learn that after the repetition of the Minuet,

'. . . the clapping was repeated, Toscanini was called to the stage, and the timid Maestro came on stage only to flee, frightened by his glory, which is already great and which will be immense.'

Among the gifts Toscanini received were a cup, saucer and silver spoon, a silver-framed blotter, a jewelled ring, a gold pencil case, and so on; and Emperor Dom Pedro presented him with a diamond ring. 'He spoke Italian,' recalled Toscanini, 'and so did his daughter. I put everything I had been given in a drawer at the hotel and it was all stolen from me. It's not that I was stupid, but you know, I was still a kid, I had always lived at the Conservatory . . .'

The Rio season ended with a performance of *Huguenots*, and the next day, at the city's Beethoven Club, Toscanini accompanied Catellani in pieces by Vieuxtemps and Wieniawski. Rossi tried to organize a season in Buenos Aires; but when the project did not materialize he dissolved the company and left, still owing several thousand francs to each of the principals and smaller sums to everyone else. Since this left many of them without enough money to pay their return fare, they collectively organized a special concert for 23 August. At the piano, Toscanini was to have accompanied a duet from *I puritani*; this had to be replaced at the last minute by a song by Denza, which he sight-read, transposing up a semitone. He also accompanied other singers in short works and repeated the Vieuxtemps piece with Catellani, then conducted the orchestra in short pieces by Gounod, Celega, Taubert, Bolzoni (the popular Minuet again), Haydn and Rossini (*William Tell* Overture). Three days later Toscanini and most of the rest of the company boarded the French vessel *Savoie* for the return trip to Europe.

Music historian Guglielmo Barblan has aptly said that if someone were to do today what Toscanini did in Rio in 1886, the fuss and international publicity would be endless. But Toscanini disembarked at Genoa late in September, greeted his family, gave his mother what remained of his earnings and returned to anonymity. 'Yes,' he said nearly seventy years later, 'I had conducted many operas; but I got back to Genoa and put myself to work playing the cello.'

2

Journeyman

'I took up the cello and didn't seriously think of myself as a conductor,' Toscanini recalled in extreme old age; and he added typically: 'And was I supposed to go around telling people I was a conductor? I was nineteen years old and looked even younger . . . And anyway, who would I have told?'[1]

He began immediately to hunt for a job in the cello section of an opera orchestra; but the search had hardly begun when he received a letter from Nicolai Figner in Milan. Figner, who had been the Rossi company's lead tenor, was a Russian, a friend of Tchaikovsky, very popular in St Petersburg, and married to Medea Ivanovna Mei, the mezzo-soprano who had also taken part in the Brazilian tour. (Four years later, the couple sang lead rôles in the world première of Tchaikovsky's *Pique Dame* in St Petersburg.) The letter expressed surprise that Toscanini had not gone immediately to Milan to seek work as a conductor. (Milan was and still is the centre of musical activity in Italy; in those days impresarios and agents from other towns, big and small, generally went there to engage performers.) When Toscanini replied indecisively Figner sent him money for his train fare and paid for his lodging at a small hotel in the centre of the city. 'I owe him my career,' Toscanini said of Figner years later. Mei was at that time trying to change from mezzo-soprano to soprano. Toscanini coached her in the new rôles she was learning; and Figner even had the young man teach him the part of Lenski in Tchaikovsky's *Eugene Onegin*—an opera then unknown in Italy. (Toscanini led its first performance there in 1900.) He found himself on the stage of La Scala for the first time when the Figners had him accompany their auditions for a committee which included conductor Franco Faccio, publisher Giulio Ricordi and impresario and critic Carlo D'Ormeville.

Shortly afterwards the Figners introduced Toscanini to Giovannina Lucca, then one of the foremost music publishers in the country. They all went to lunch at her villa on Lake Como one day, and Toscanini impressed her with his familiarity with Wagner's music—of which she was the Italian publisher—when he played parts of *Tannhäuser* and *Lohengrin* from memory. Figner was to sing in November in a Turin production of a recent opera by a young composer named Alfredo Catalani; and at a certain moment the tenor said to Signora Lucca, who had published the work: 'Why not have Toscanini conduct the opera?' She was understandably hesitant. The opera, *Edmea*, had already been produced twice —in Trento and at La Scala—under the direction, respectively, of Alessandro Pomé and Faccio, two of the best-known conductors of the day, and the Turin production would be an important one. Pomé had already promised to conduct the performances, although he wasn't so sure about being able to participate in the rehearsals.

It must be understood that in those days there were still conductors who believed in the early nineteenth-century division of labour between the *maestro concertatore*, or 'rehearser', and the *direttore d'orchestra*, or conductor. The former was often a barely competent time-beater who was, illogically, entrusted with the enormous task of preparing the production; while the latter was a more established 'personality' who would—with luck—arrive for the last rehearsals and lend the attraction of his name and presence to the performances. Signora Lucca didn't quite know whether a *concertatore* would be needed or not and, if so, whether someone as young as Toscanini, gifted though he obviously was, would be acceptable to Giovanni Depanis, the impresario of Turin's Teatro Carignano, where the opera was to be staged; but she would make some inquiries.

The first performance was scheduled for early November. Since Toscanini had not returned from Brazil until the end of September and since these discussions could hardly have taken place less than two weeks later, one cannot help being struck by the fact that a new production of a nearly unknown opera was being organized not more than three weeks before it was to go on stage.

This was not at all unusual at that time, partly because the physical aspect of staging was in no way as complicated as it is today and partly because the musical preparation was rarely as thorough as we would like to believe it is—and as it occasionally is—today. Scenery and costumes were often used interchangeably from one opera to another and acting as we know it did not exist. Filippo Sacchi, writing in 1967 about provincial operatic performances he had seen at the turn of the century, reported that certain emotions were represented by a 'pre-determined set of facial contortions and gestures: high notes were pre-announced by bringing a foot forward in a certain way; amorous tenderness was indicated by languidly inclining the head to a certain degree.'[2] The choruses knew how to stay out of the way. As for musical preparation, the singers generally informed the *concertatore* how they wanted their arias done; and the orchestra was rehearsed enough to make sure that the players were kept more or less together and in the right key, since transpositions were frequent. Despite the battles of Verdi and other musicians to make Italian opera a convincing combination of music, poetry and action, it remained, for the public at large, almost entirely an arena for the display of vocal technique.

As soon as Figner received the piano-vocal score of *Edmea* he set up an ambush. Calling on Toscanini, he led him to the piano in the hotel lobby to read through

the opera. 'I was sight-reading well,' the conductor would recall, 'and sweating.'
At the end of the second act a gentleman who had been sitting in the lobby un-
noticed by Toscanini stepped forward. 'Did you already know this opera?' 'No,
I'm reading it for the first time.'

The gentleman nodded to someone behind him, who also came up to the
piano. Figner introduced them: Depanis and Catalani. It was now fairly certain
that Pomé would not be able to go to Turin even for the performances of *Edmea*.
Toscanini told Carlo Gatti years later:

'Catalani wanted me and Depanis consented. Imagine choosing me, unknown to all, young—too young—to conduct a nearly new opera, to take it
before the public that most appreciated and liked the composer . . .

Signora Lucca was not opposed to my engagement. I went to Turin;
Depanis had last-minute doubts, because of my youth. I had barely begun
the rehearsals. Maestro Bolzoni, a Parmesan like me [whose Minuet had
been so successful in Rio] . . . was conductor of the "Popular Symphonic
Concerts" and was also about to begin his rehearsals . . . Bolzoni's orchestra
was basically my Teatro Carignano orchestra. He felt that his cellos needed
reinforcement. He asked me to enter the section; I accepted and sat at the
rear. Depanis thought that I would lose my authority over the Carignano
musicians . . .

He was quickly reassured. The first cellist of Bolzoni's orchestra and also of
mine was Casella, professor at the music academy, well-known soloist and
chamber music player, and father of Alfredo, the pianist and composer . . . At
one rehearsal of *Edmea* Casella didn't play a solo passage correctly. I asked him
to do it again. It didn't go well. We did it again, two or three times. Casella got
tired and shouted, "Is this going to go on much longer?" I replied calmly,
"Until the passage goes well." He said, "Perhaps I ought to leave?" I shut up:
let him decide as he pleases. Casella got up and left with his cello. Didn't come
back again, either.'[3]

Despite little disturbances of this nature, not unknown even today in Italian
orchestral life—nor in that of other countries, for that matter—the rehearsals
proceeded well, and the orchestra and cast were more than satisfied with their
conductor's work. Toscanini frequently consulted Catalani on various details,
and the thirty-two-year-old composer was very impressed by the quality and
conscientiousness of his younger colleague's work.

On 4 November 1886 Toscanini made his Italian professional conducting
début, with great success. There were twenty curtain calls for the artists and for
Catalani, and nine more performances followed the first one. (Operas were not
generally presented for a pre-determined number of nights: they were given as
long as they attracted a sufficiently large public. Ten performances was a very

substantial number for a new work by a young and not very famous composer.)
The critic for the *Gazzetta musicale di Milano* wrote:

> 'The chorus was irreproachable, the orchestra exceptionally attentive and
> correct. Toscanini's début was a triumph. It is a splendid dawn on the artistic
> horizon ... He conducted from memory with the sureness and energy of a
> proven maestro ... A thoughtful, studious, intelligent youth has built a solid
> base for enduring fame ...'

Ernesto Ferrettini, in the *Gazzetta piemontese*, referred to Toscanini's 'secure
rhythm, communicativeness, *sang-froid*, diligence, unyielding memory', while
lamenting the fact that inadequate rehearsal time had left some problems of
balance. Other journalists were similarly enthusiastic, and Catalani himself wrote
to a friend: 'One would think that this weren't the first time he had climbed on to
the conductor's stool, but that he had been doing so for twenty years. He is a
real phenomenon; his career is assured.'[4]

Toscanini's friendship with Catalani was to be of enduring importance for both
of them. The composer, who was born in 1854 in the ancient Tuscan town of
Lucca, just two blocks from the house in which his rival Puccini was born four
years later, had studied music with his father and uncle and later at the Milan
Conservatory. *Edmea* was his fourth opera, having been preceded by *La falce*
(1875), *Elda* (1880) and *Dejanice* (1883)—the last much admired by Mahler in his
youth. Catalani was a tall, thin man with a handsome face and a long, bushy
moustache. When Toscanini met him he was already suffering from the tuber-
culosis that would kill him before he reached forty. He was nervous, pessimistic
and easily discouraged—not the sort of person who was a natural winner or even
survivor in the extremely competitive world of Italian opera. Toscanini's
thorough musicianship and good instincts were an aid to Catalani in his last years,
and his admiration was a comfort for him. In turn, Toscanini matured as an artist
and as a human being through the friendship, and Catalani's unhesitant trust in
him helped his career and morale.

Following the *Edmea* success Toscanini was asked to stay on at the Carignano
to rehearse Wagner's *Flying Dutchman* for the still absent Pomé, and he continued to play in Bolzoni's orchestra. He also went to the nearby town of Asti
to give a cello recital and received, shortly afterwards, a note from a Parmesan
friend and ex-classmate, violinist Enrico Polo. 'All our school companions have
asked me to tell you that they, too, have had the greatest happiness in learning of
your successes,' wrote Polo. 'I saw Catellani, who told me about all your
American triumphs. Bravo! You knew how to seize fortune; hold it tight, so that
it will be ever more favourable towards you.'[5]

By the end of that eventful 1886 Toscanini was back in Milan, where he had
decided to make his home. Since he did not want and could not afford to live in
hotels and eat in restaurants, he arranged for his parents and sisters to transfer

there as well. Claudio was again unemployed in Genoa; in Milan he was soon able to find work in an already extant tailoring establishment, instead of having to start another business of his own.

On 5 February 1887 Verdi's *Otello* was premièred at La Scala. Toscanini had been anxious to be involved with the preparations which were supervised by the seventy-three-year-old composer himself, although conducted by Faccio. Italian opera orchestras were formed anew each season at that time, and Toscanini was hired as second cellist for the December–April period which included *Aida* (with the same principal singers who were to appear in *Otello*: tenor Francesco Tamagno, baritone Victor Maurel and soprano Romilda Pantaleoni), Donizetti's *Lucrezia Borgia*, Bizet's *Pearlfishers* and *Flora mirabilis* by Greek composer Spyros Samaras (with soprano Emma Calvé). The *Otello* première was the occasion for a great public outpouring of love and admiration for Verdi; but the production itself was not all it might have been. A general problem was that the orchestra at La Scala, as in most other houses at that time, did not play from a lowered pit, but right at ground-floor level. This not only disturbed the view, but also created serious balance problems between voices and instruments in a work like *Otello*, with its massive orchestral textures. Nor was the cast entirely satisfactory. There seems to have been near unanimity on Maurel's excellence as Iago, but Tamagno did not satisfy Verdi or a large segment of the public. Pantaleoni's coarse tone and poor intonation caused Toscanini to wince and grimace during the rehearsals. When Faccio noticed this he had the young cellist fined. (Pantaleoni was Faccio's mistress.)

Toscanini was also fined for his part in a minor orchestral insurrection. At that time opera performances at La Scala were always followed by ballets. Scenes from a ballet, *Rolla*, had been appended to *Otello*, and Toscanini and a group of other youngsters in the orchestra, indignant at the affront to Verdi's new masterpiece and at the inhuman physical effort they were required to make by having to play ballet music after this particularly exhausting opera, protested by purposely playing *Rolla* badly. Their protest failed and all guilty parties were fined. The orchestra also baulked at the difficulties of the opera, and Verdi sighed and accepted compromise solutions, such as having the famous passage for double basses *soli* in Act IV played by one bass only, to avoid excruciating intonation problems.

During a rehearsal of the love duet in Act I, which begins with a passage for four cellos alone, Verdi came off the stage, where he was directing the action, and down to the orchestra. 'Second cello!' he said. Toscanini, surprised, stood up. 'You're playing too softly; play louder next time.' The parts are marked *piano* and *pianissimo* at that point, but Verdi wanted a singing, sustained tone quality. It was a small, unremarkable incident, but it made a considerable impression on Toscanini, who later referred to it hundreds of times. He also recalled that after the hysterical ovations and pandemonium at the first performance he went running home, woke his mother and shouted: 'Mamma, Verdi is a genius! Down on your knees to Verdi, down on your knees to Verdi!'

Following the Scala season Toscanini, now twenty, was engaged to conduct Meyerbeer's *L'Africaine* in the Piedmontese town of Casale Monferrato in June, and he returned there in October and November 1887 to direct *La gioconda* and *I lombardi*. This marked the beginning of a decade of wandering, fighting and learning—a period which, on the whole, cannot have been very enjoyable for him, but during which he mastered his profession. Engagements were irregular and ill-paid; he worked with third-class casts and orchestras, travelled on third-class trains and stayed in third-class hotels; and he began to acquire the resilience necessary for survival in the rough Italian theatrical environment.

Many people who have written about him seem to believe that from the very outset of his career, he had a clear and coherent picture in his mind of all the reforms he wished to accomplish, of all the bad customs to be swept away, of how to deal swiftly and categorically with theatrical agents, impresarios, prima donnas and recalcitrant players, and that he would accept nothing less than compliance and perfection from all who worked with him. This is a totally absurd notion. In the first place—as mentioned earlier—conductors at that time were by no means the authoritative figures they became a generation or so later. They had to cede, to a great degree, to the wishes of the singers, to the traditional 'adjustments' and interpolations made in the score; and Toscanini, in his earliest years, went along with this, too—not out of laziness, but because he had not yet formulated other ideas. He could not demand flawless and beautiful playing from the orchestras he worked with because they were simply incapable of it. (For that matter, he had never heard a fine orchestra.) Nor could he demand efficient organization in towns where three or four operas were given in a year, where sets, costumes and singers were imported from Milan—take them or leave them—and where orchestra musicians were gathered from the highways and hedges and contracted for very short periods. What immediately set him apart and attracted attention were his striking gifts and his rigorous self-discipline. His score was closed during rehearsals; he not only *knew* every note and dynamic mark but could also *hear* when something was missing or incorrect or out of tune; and he was terribly serious in his approach to what he was doing. All this obviated many of the problems that normally face a very young and inexperienced conductor working with a group of professional musicians.

After Toscanini's first performance at Casale the local critic made the following observations:

'He revealed himself to be an artist of rare genius, with an extraordinary memory, versed in the musical disciplines, diligent, careful . . . He knows how to draw every minute detail from the orchestra. Modest and therefore un-affected, he conducted the performance of the grandiose score [*L'Africaine*] with admirable ease and not less energy. . . . All the most intelligent people, first and foremost the members of the orchestra, are enthusiastic about his ability.'[6]

At his *serata d'onore*—probably the last performance of *L'Africaine* in mid-June—he played a few cello pieces between two of the acts.

His friend Polo received a card from him at about this time:

'Since I'm going back to conduct at Casalmonferrato this October, I'll need, besides several first violins for the section, a concertmaster; and I naturally thought immediately of you, because after *Gioconda* we're doing *Lombardi*, and you know what there is in that opera. [Note: Toscanini is referring to the difficult violin solo in the Trio from Act III.] I think the pay will be seven lire per day.'[7]

Found among Polo's papers at his death was a manuscript of virtuosistic variations which Toscanini had composed for his friend to interpolate, in the mistaken but traditional way, into the famous solo.

At one of the *Gioconda* performances the audience shouted for a *bis*—a repetition of an enthusiastically received aria or other segment—and Toscanini refused to grant it. This was an unheard-of affront, and it was the first skirmish in a war which Toscanini was to wage over a twenty-year period. The public complained loudly, and a military man in uniform shouted at him, 'You are an arrogant young conductor!' Toscanini turned around: 'You are wrong, you dog!'[8] More shouting and disruption. He waited until the theatre grew quiet, then continued the performance—without the *bis*. Afterwards the soldier sent an intermediary to the conductor's dressing room and challenged him to a duel. Toscanini had never handled arms. He did not accept and eventually the incident was forgotten. But what is interesting is that already at this early moment in his career he felt that interrupting a drama to repeat some highlight was wrong from an artistic point of view, although he was inconsistent for years in applying his no-*bis* rule.

At another *Gioconda* performance the lead soprano, Lola Peydro, who was having her *serata d'onore*, sang the song 'Son gelosa', composed by Toscanini and probably accompanied by him. His career as a composer was short-lived. It began when he was about fifteen with some songs with piano accompaniment, written as class assignments. One of the earliest of these, although of little artistic interest, is quite remarkable harmonically. It is called *Pagina d'album*, is only forty-six bars long, was improvised in the presence of his teacher and later written down. Its bold—not to say excessive—use of lowered triads very much anticipates Puccini, who was then a student at the Milan Conservatory.

Toscanini began to compose in earnest, and seven of his compositions were published between 1887 and 1889. Six of these are songs; the seventh is a

Berceuse for piano. A total of twenty-six compositions are known to exist today; eighteen of these are songs with piano accompaniment, three are for orchestra, one is for piano solo, one for violin and piano (later arranged for violin solo and string quartet), and three I have not seen. The texts which Toscanini chose for his songs are largely ultra-romantic poems by famous poets of the day, while the song *V'amo* is a setting of a translation of a Heine poem. *Nevrosi* and *Autunno*, both dedicated to one Emma Gorin, were published by Giovannina Lucca, Milan, probably late in 1887. The other printed works were published by Giudici e Strada, Turin; neither company exists today.

Autunno, a short, sad piece in F minor, is undoubtedly the only work by Arturo Toscanini which suggests that some day its composer might have produced something of artistic merit. But this was not to be. On 2 June 1888 he went to Bologna to hear the first Italian performance of *Tristan und Isolde*, and by the time the second act had ended, he had made up his mind to compose no more. Not long afterwards he decided to oppose all further performances and publication of his extant works. In 1965 Walter Toscanini told me that he remembered hearing his father play and sing *Son gelosa*—but only once, 'maybe forty years ago'; and he also said that towards the end of his life his father had been challenged to write out some of his youthful compositions from memory, at a distance of sixty to seventy years. This he did—texts included—and with few discrepancies. In fact, he became so intrigued that he even tried writing rhythmic English translations of some of them. George Marek (author of *Toscanini*) came across the sketches of two of these translations, *Autunno* and *Mignon*, and guessed—without telling anyone he was guessing—that they were poems written by Toscanini 'in his old age . . . poems of longing, longing for youth. Even he knew he had to die.'[9]

Toscanini was not going to be a composer, nor was he going to continue to play the cello much longer; he was going to be a conductor. It was in his nature to want to do one thing with his life and to want to do it excellently. Filippo Sacchi, a longtime friend, said: 'He instinctively respected those who knew how to do their jobs well: if someone's job was just nailing nails, and if he nailed them well, Toscanini respected him.'[10] This anti-dilettantism was an essential part of his nature, even during his youth; so when someone asked him years later why he had given up composition, he answered: 'I knew that whatever I composed would have fallen below the standard I set for myself.' And to another inquirer: 'So very many masterpieces are necessary to a man's spiritual life; there is no need and no place for mediocrity.'

A month after the Casale engagement had ended he was in Verona to conduct a short season which opened with *Carmen* on 26 December 1887, continued with Donizetti's *Lucrezia Borgia*, and ended early in February 1888 with Thomas's *Mignon*. The Donizetti production had its trying moments, gleefully reported by Verona's newspaper, *L'Arena*, 13 January:

'The latest adventures of Signora Borgia ... took place last evening at that theatre which the profane call the Filarmonico, but which the knowledgeable refer to as the Fiascomonico. ... The public [in effect] told the impresario: "Listen, we're highly indulgent and of good will, as you can tell by the crowd; but we aren't dunces, and although we regret it, we cannot allow Signora Wiziack [the Lucrezia] to undergo the agonies of seeing her poisoned son die. Since she was already moved to the point of ... making us fear that she would faint before getting to the end of Act I, we beg her to withdraw so that such dolorous scenes will not recur." '

Wiziack was a once-decent singer who no longer had enough voice or stage presence to be convincing, and the performance had ended half-way through the first act. A replacement was sought and a second and more successful opening took place five nights later. On 19 January 1888 Signora Ravogli—the Carmen—had her *serata*, at which she was accompanied by Toscanini on the cello and a Maestro Fiorinotto at the piano in a *Serenata* by Braga, during the interval after Act III. 'Maestro Toscanini, the valorous conductor, ... showed himself to be a very great player and an incomparable artist,' reported the *Arena*. It is amazing that those qualities could be recognized through the execution of Braga's piece which, however, the audience insisted on hearing a second time.

It was a long wait to the next engagement—a production of *Aida* at Macerata in August. The previous June, as already mentioned, Toscanini had gone to Bologna to hear *Tristan*, conducted by Giuseppe Martucci. Composer and pianist as well as conductor, Martucci was among the first musicians to help familiarize Italian audiences with the music of the German symphonists and Wagner. Toscanini, all his life, held Martucci in the highest regard as man and artist.

In October, two months after the Macerata performances, Toscanini was engaged by Milan's famous Teatro Dal Verme to conduct Verdi's *La forza del destino*, Ponchielli's *I promessi sposi* and Antonio Cagnoni's *Francesca da Rimini*. This was his first conducting appearance in Milan and it was a big step for a twenty-one-year-old. In those years La Scala was not the only Milanese theatre with an opera season. The Milanese still have a justifiable reputation as theatre-goers and opera enthusiasts; but it is astonishing to think that around 1850, when the city had a population of 200,000, one-tenth its present size, there were ten theatres that put on regular opera series. The three principal houses (La Scala, Teatro della Canobbiana—now Teatro Lirico—and Teatro Carcano), in them-selves had a combined seating capacity of over 7,000. The Dal Verme was built in 1864 and was quickly ranked above the Canobbiana and the Carcano. Toscanini's entrance there was well received by public and critics, and the members of the cast, orchestra and chorus presented him with a specially bound, gold-embossed volume of the Beethoven overtures (Breitkopf edition), signed by all of them, as a token of their esteem. It was a gift which he kept much longer than the traditional laurel wreath given him by Cagnoni at the last performance, and it can still be seen at the Parma Conservatory, filled with the young conductor's pencilled-in dynamic markings and other annotations.

The Dal Verme season provoked the first criticism of Toscanini's basic idea of a piece of music: Amintore Galli, writing in *Il secolo*, referred to Toscanini's abandonment of the traditions in his performance of *La forza del destino*. As is customary among critics, Galli did not state what those traditions were, what they were based upon, and in what ways they had been abandoned. The young conductor was beginning to develop and implement ideas of his own and, in so doing, to make supporters and critics.

Two or three weeks after the Milan series, which ended late in November, he was in Novara to conduct a two-month season which included *Aida*, *Huguenots* and *Forza del destino*. These were the inaugural productions of the new Teatro Coccia. Toscanini had a special problem in the Meyerbeer work because the tenor was having an affair with the lead soprano and, as a result of excessive love-making, was exhausted and voiceless by the second performance. There is no record of the soprano's having suffered any ill effects.

Returning to Turin for the first time since his début more than two years earlier, Toscanini conducted *Carmen* at the Teatro Vittorio Emanuele (March and April 1889) with Adele Borghi in the title rôle. (She also sang *Son gelosa* at her *serata* on 14 April.) Many elements in the company were not equal to the task and public disapproval was so strong that several singers were replaced. In May —still in Turin—the Teatro Carignano engaged him to lead a revival of *Edmea* and a remounting of another production of *Carmen*—the same one which, under the direction of Leopoldo Mugnone a year earlier, had been attended repeatedly and enthusiastically by Nietzsche. From Turin it was on to Genoa for another encounter with Cagnoni's *Francesca* at the Politeama Genovese, beginning 8 July. Audiences were tough in those days:

'Excepting Boronat, Sottolana and Pagnoni ... the artists left much to be desired. Therefore, the public remained unsatisfied and the opera ended in absolute silence. Maestro Arturo Toscanini, who conducted the orchestra—a haphazardly gathered troupe—knew, however, how to wring very fine effects and to lead with mastery ... He received warm applause after the overture. Succeeding performances went much better, achieving a most brilliant result. ... There were sixteen performances.'[11]

Giulio Gatti-Casazza, a student of nautical mathematics from Ferrara who also happened to be a budding impresario, heard this Genoese production of his friend Cagnoni's opera and afterwards met its conductor:

'Toscanini was really a handsome young fellow, very elegant and affable indeed, a thing that surprised me, since I had heard that he was an extremely severe person with an inexpansive personality ...

In spite of the fact that the Politeama orchestra was rather mediocre, Toscanini had succeeded in obtaining a thoroughly fused and coherent performance, full of colour and warmth. Everyone spoke of him as the most important factor in the entire performance . . .'[12]

Gatti-Casazza was only twenty at the time—even younger than Toscanini. Nine years later they would be running one of the world's major opera houses together.

After a two-month rest (probably unwanted) Toscanini went to Voghera, a small Lombard town, for a short season which was originally to have comprised *Aida* and *Norma*. Extensive documentation of this season has been preserved, so it is possible to observe closely the sort of circumstances in which Toscanini was working at this point in his life.[13]

Late in July members of the town council and various influential citizens who made up the theatre's directorate agreed to hire a Milanese impresario named La Via to put together the autumn season at the Teatro Sociale. La Via was given 9,500 lire to cover expenses. Among other things, he was charged with engaging a '*maestro concertatore* who will also have to act as conductor' and who must direct the scores 'exactly as they are written, excepting the customary changes and deletions, and [supervise] the staging as indicated in the respective texts'. There were to be forty-six orchestra musicians (apart from the stage band), including fifteen out-of-town players, 'and these will have to play the parts assigned them by the conductor at the first rehearsal'. There would also be a chorus of twenty-four male and eighteen female voices, eight ballerinas and, of course, the eight solo artists. Having engaged Toscanini, La Via wrote to the directorate: 'He is a very young conductor, but he already has good experience with orchestra and stage.' When the soprano who was to have sung Norma had to withdraw, a replacement was found and Donizetti's *La favorita* was substituted for the Bellini opera. Rehearsals for *Aida* began on 10 October. They did not always go smoothly, which is hardly surprising considering that forces at least twice as numerous and probably several times as good were needed for a decent job. There was an unsuccessful barrister in Voghera who used to augment his meagre income by playing double bass in dance orchestras and during the opera season. At one rehearsal Toscanini turned to him in exasperation and said in Parmesan dialect: '*Vucat, c'al brusa qul cason le.*' ('Mr Barrister, go out and burn that big box.')

Aida opened on 20 October and the local critic wrote that Toscanini had shown himself to be a 'very intelligent, passionate and faithful interpreter of Verdi's music'.

'Rarely have we in our theatre heard the orchestra perform its duty with such precision, energy and shading as under Toscanini's direction; and the public, after the second act finale, gave him a clamorous demonstration . . .'

Olga Dettloff, the Aida, sang yet another *Son gelosa* at her *serata* on 7 November, and we read that 'the piece was a great success ... The public would very much like to hear this *romanza* again.' *La favorita* opened two nights later, but was less successful because the prima donna didn't please the audiences. On 17 November, the fiftieth anniversary of the première of Verdi's first opera, *Oberto*, Toscanini sent a congratulatory telegram (paid for by the management) to the composer on behalf of all the members of the Voghera company. On the 22nd he took up the cello to perform in a musical *soirée* for invited guests at the palace of a local nobleman, Sartirana. In addition to conducting Bolzoni's Minuet and Theme and Variations for String Quartet, and a Gavotte by clarinettist Guido Rocchi, a classmate from Parma, Toscanini played Dunkler's *A Tear* and Mariani's *The Abandonment*, both for solo cello. 'We need not waste a single word to describe the performance these pieces received or the success they achieved as a result,' wrote the same critic. 'It is enough that it be known that Toscanini is a cello soloist so distinguished as to need fear no rival.' Two nights later, at the last performance of the season (*Aida*), which was also Toscanini's *serata d'onore*, the young man played two cello pieces by Dunkler, in what was probably his last public appearance as an instrumentalist, and conducted Rocchi's Gavotte and Lully's Minuet for string quartet.

'Maestro Toscanini was singled out for continuous demonstrations of esteem and affection, and at certain moments the ovations intended for him reached the point of rapture. After the second act he was given a beautiful laurel wreath, an artistic scroll, several jewels of no little value, flowers, etc., etc., as well as a large gold medal presented by the honourable Directorate of the theatre. Maestro Toscanini was so moved ... that although accustomed to triumphs, he will not soon forget that beautiful Sunday evening, we are sure, just as we shall never forget having had him as the leader of our theatre's orchestra.'

The next stop was Brescia, where he arrived in mid-December—with his mother to keep house for him—to prepare and conduct a production of *La gioconda* at the Teatro Grande. There he remained to direct *Le Villi*, the little-known first opera of the then little-known composer Giacomo Puccini. By the end of February Toscanini was again in Genoa, this time at the Politeama Regina Margherita, where he conducted *Mignon* and *Carmen*. Alfredo Segre says that upon arriving in the city Toscanini went directly to the theatre.

'In the lobby he met a man who was busily sweeping the floor. He asked him where the impresario could be found. "I am the impresario," answered the man, who was in fact Signor Chiarella. "And you, what do you want?" "My name is Toscanini. I'm the conductor. You have assigned me only 24 chor-isters. I want 48." A heated argument ensued, up and down the hall, while the impresario continued to sweep the floor. "I'll give you thirty, is that all right?" he finally proposed. "Then I'll return to Milan," said Toscanini, walking away abruptly. He got the 48 choristers.'[14]

That was fine; but a somewhat more bitter situation developed over Toscanini's subsequent demand that a substantial number of replacements be made in the orchestra. This, of course, caused great outcries among those who were replaced and necessitated further expenditures on the impresario's part.

It is clear that Toscanini, at twenty-three, was entering a crucial period. His career was still in its infancy, he was still working at third-rate theatres, and still struggling for economic survival; yet he had already decided that it was time to start establishing some basic conditions, in the absence of which he would not work. Since his return from South America he had conducted about two dozen operatic productions and had developed a clear idea of what was possible and what was not. Many musicians who worked with him years later, when he was at the peak of his fame, have said that one of his most amazing abilities was that of being absolutely uncompromising within an absolutely realistic framework. And the same was true in Genoa in 1890. He did not try to convert a third-rate company into a first-rate one during a one-month engagement; he tried, rather, to make that particular company achieve the maximum of which it was capable. As regards the replacement of musicians, several things must be made clear. First of all—and as has already been stated—the opera houses of the day did not have permanent orchestras working under long-term contracts. There were players, however, many of them untrained and of very low calibre, who were accustomed to being re-hired each season at certain theatres without having to re-audition, and who looked upon these engagements as signs of God's mercy made manifest through the impecuniousness of impresarios (who did not want to pay higher fees to more competent musicians) and through the ardent desire of average *maestri* not to rock the boat, at any cost. Toscanini was not afraid of boat-rocking. In fact, he began to see it as the only way of rousing dormant colleagues. So he insisted on the rules, and that meant auditions.

The internal logical process which led him to decide that the established order of things had to be upset brought with it personal difficulties. Clear-headedness, diligence and obstinacy were qualities he was born with; but the ferociousness needed to back up these other characteristics, to demonstrate just how serious he was and to try to alter the firmly entrenched system within which he was con-demned to operate—this was something not at all native to his personality. According to all reports of people who knew him in his youth, he was shy and quiet by nature, and many who knew him in later years felt the same was true then. No matter: the music was of such overriding importance to him that he would do whatever had to be done to upset the lethargy of routine. It is at this point that one begins to hear not only about his purposefulness, his adamant refusal to bend to points of view which he believed wrong, but also about the unleashing of a terrible temper in confronting fellow musicians and the organizers of his musical world. He personally felt like a whole human being, like one who was making use of all his vital energies, only when he was putting body and spirit into what he considered his very great task; he was incapable of understanding how others who called themselves musicians could behave otherwise, could wish to relax, to say 'I'll work on that later.' He was not a religious man, but his view of art was a moral one: it was wrong to let anyone who did not want to commit himself totally to pursuing 'the maximum' even approach such greatness. And so the twist in his personality developed, a twist he himself resented and perhaps often regretted, but did not renounce. He could rehearse patiently for hours when he felt everyone was working at highest capacity; but when he suspected less than one hundred per cent cooperation he became a monster. Something in him would snap; he would break batons, scream obscenities (of which he had a rich repertoire from his childhood days in Parma's working-class neighbourhoods), tear up scores, throw music stands into the empty auditorium, and hurl insults at principal offenders. Singers often left his coaching sessions in tears and orchestra players left rehearsals wrung out from tension and exhaustion. There were many, especially in those early years, who detested him; but there were others, even then, who decided that the tension and exhaustion of a serious struggle to achieve something were better than the anaesthetizing boredom of mediocrity.

His enemies could not convincingly accuse him of carrying on as he did out of vanity—this young man who did not make the *bel gesto* for the public but who conducted so simply and directly, and who always seemed to want to run away from applause. He worked incredibly hard, staying up nights to study and spending his days running from coaching sessions to staging rehearsals to choral rehearsals; he learned his scores with penetrating thoroughness, drove himself to the limit during rehearsals, always concentrating, and perspiring like an athlete. He was not happy. While still in his twenties he wrote to a friend: 'Believe me, I am a miserable wretch! . . . Nobody's life is embittered as much as mine by this accursed theatre! . . . The worst of it is that I thus, in turn, embitter others' lives, unconsciously, unintentionally.'[15]

But the results began to tell. Reviewing the *Mignon* production, the critic for Genoa's *Il secolo XIX* wrote that 'having achieved a complete overhauling of the orchestra, Toscanini finally avenged all the crimes that have been committed in the name of Art'.

Carmen and *Mignon* in Genoa, *Mignon* and *Carmen* in Turin—with a *Faust* thrown in as well. The latter engagement took place in April and May 1890; and afterwards Toscanini returned to his family in Milan, where he found himself unemployed for four months. The Toscaninis had taken in lodgers at that time, including Polo, Rocchi and other young Parmesan musicians. Maestro Toscanini was still Arturén (dialect form) among all these people; he enjoyed participating in the endless discussions, musical and otherwise, and he loved to tease mercilessly his sisters Ada, now fifteen, and Zina, thirteen. Even dour Paolina would be dragged into some of the merriment when her son—in order to show his friends how strong his mother was—would climb on to the table and insist that she lift him down and carry him to his room. Of course he spent most of his time studying, and one of his friends always kept as a souvenir Toscanini's piano-vocal score of *Parsifal* which, since he could not obtain the orchestral score, he had filled with detailed annotations, such as: 'The triplet pattern is begun by the 2nd and 3rd flutes and bass clarinet—on the 2nd quarter the 1st bassoon enters—on the 3rd the 2nd bassoon.' He played the piano for hours each day and also read as much as possible, Carducci and Leopardi having been his great favourites then.

Of his love life at that now remote time we have very few details. Several people who knew him well in later years have said that Toscanini was more abundantly successful in his sexual relationships with women than any other man they had ever known or heard of; and everything indicates that the situation was no different in his youth. He was good-looking—short and slender with well-proportioned features, very deep-set eyes and a bristly moustache which he had grown while still in his teens—and he always dressed fashionably, formally and immaculately. His energetic character, his growing reputation as a brilliant musician and his natural charm (when not studying or rehearsing) added to his attractiveness.

In October 1890 he left Italy for the first time since his return from South America, having accepted an offer to be assistant to conductor Edoardo Mascheroni for a season at the Teatro Liceo in Barcelona. It is hard to understand precisely why he took this post. Mascheroni, who was only eight years his senior, had conducted the first Italian production of *Fidelio* in 1886 and would later direct the première of Verdi's *Falstaff* at La Scala (1893). Perhaps Toscanini thought he would enjoy working with Mascheroni or perhaps he simply wanted a holiday from the internecine strife of the Italian theatrical world. Not surprisingly, Mascheroni was less than ecstatic about having someone as gifted as Toscanini as his assistant. Segre reports:

'Mascheroni, at the very last moment, assigned to Toscanini *Capuleti e Montecchi*, an opera by Bellini, written especially for virtuoso singers and for this reason rarely revived. Mascheroni hoped that the opera would turn into a fiasco. But to his great disappointment, under Toscanini's direction it became one of the greatest successes of the season. To stem the rising tide, Mascheroni somehow persuaded the impresario to withdraw the opera after the third performance.'[16]

When the season ended Toscanini returned to Italy. He went to Senigallia during the summer (1891) to conduct a production of Pietro Mascagni's *Cavalleria rusticana*—his first encounter with this work which had been premièred in Rome a year earlier. Mascagni was one of a group of young composers which included Leoncavallo, Giordano, Cilea and, at least to an extent, Puccini, all of whose first real successes date from the 1890s. They were by no means a formal group, far less a school, although the term *verismo* (realism) was soon applied to their output in an overgeneralized way by those with a mania for pigeonholing. These were artists who faced very similar creative difficulties at the outset of their careers and who found divergent but related solutions to their problems. Their greatest difficulty was Giuseppe Verdi, who had by then dominated the Italian operatic world for nearly half a century, who had recently pulled the rug out from under the feet of his younger contemporaries with *Otello*, and who was soon to do the same thing in an even more astonishing and decisive way with *Falstaff*. A whole generation of composers had been trying desperately either to be like Verdi or to be unlike Verdi, and had simply been forgotten. Another huge problem was the gradual internationalization of the repertoire. Wagner, Bizet, Massenet had found their ways into Italy, and young composers could not avoid feeling their influence, in regard to both aesthetic theory and compositional practice.

One of the ways of 'getting around' Verdi, and Wagner as well, was the adoption of 'realistic' plots and texts, as opposed to the worn-out, idealized concoctions of their Italian predecessors or the mythological-philosophical inventions of Wagner. The public, it was felt, was ready for up-to-date stories of everyday life, such as Zola and Verga were presenting in their books; and the new operas would be composed in a way that would be a synthesis of the best elements of Italian national traditions and of new foreign influences. In the prologue to *I pagliacci*, which was soon to be premièred under Toscanini's direction, Leoncavallo—who wrote his own libretto—made Tonio say: 'The author has sought to depict a slice of life for you. His only maxim is that the artist is a man and that he must write for men. —And he was inspired by the truth.' Fatuous but sincere. Unfortunately, the *veristi* did not have Verdi's genius for delineation of character, Wagner's overwhelming originality or Bizet's freshness. Their art was a hybrid one; their works enjoyed great popularity for a time and then began to disappear from the world's stages, to the point where—Puccini excepted—each of these composers is represented in today's active international repertoire by one opera, at most.

Toscanini's attitude towards the *veristi* was ambivalent. His interest in new musical currents, national and international, was enormous until he reached middle age, and there is no question that he wanted to do his best for these compatriots who were also his contemporaries; but he did not really find their music to his taste—again excepting (though not always excepting) Puccini. In fact, he found it in many ways rather crude; and that is precisely why his admiration of and hopes for Catalani were so strong. Catalani's style was altogether more refined and Toscanini undoubtedly dreamed that his friend would eventually find a better solution than Mascagni, Leoncavallo and even Puccini had found to the problems touched upon above. Catalani died before reaching artistic maturity, and Toscanini regarded this not only as a personal loss but as a tragedy for Italian music. Perhaps this was an exaggerated estimate of Catalani's potential; but Toscanini could never quite forgive the *veristi* their success, accompanying as it did the near oblivion of his friend's work. What neither Toscanini nor others could easily have realized in the 1890s was that opera, as a form that met—without even trying—the criteria of being contemporary, popular in the broadest sense and artistically satisfying, was gradually dying, after a century of glory.

He conducted another production of *Cavalleria* as well as Verdi's *Luisa Miller* at the Teatro Carignano in Turin in November and December, with a fine cast in both works. While there he was contracted by impresario Luigi Piontelli for his most important engagement to date: a two-month season—five operas—at Genoa's principal theatre, the Carlo Felice. Arriving there late in December, Toscanini found an orchestral situation similar to the one he had found at the same city's Politeama Regina Margherita two years earlier. His solution was no different: auditions. This time his action set off a wave of factionalism, recriminations and counter-recriminations. The first opera was Meyerbeer's *Le Prophète*, and the critics were divided into two camps—those who felt that Toscanini had distorted the work and those who felt that, although the cast was not very good, the young conductor had done what he could and had, in any case, obtained exceptional results from the orchestra. G.B. Vallebona, in his history, *Il Teatro Carlo Felice (1828–1928)*, said:

'Despite the care taken by Maestro Arturo Toscanini, this opera was a fiasco at its opening night, and the performances were therefore suspended. After a few days it was taken up again, lightened by some cuts and with the performance improved. It was presented for a further thirteen evenings, but without enthusiasm.'[17]

The second opera was Verdi's *Simon Boccanegra*, with baritone Ramòn Blanchard and soprano Cesira Ferrani. 'The result was very attractive,' writes Vallebona, 'because of the fine balance between orchestra and stage; but the public was sparse throughout the nine performances.'[18] Mascagni's recent *L'amico Fritz*, which followed *Boccanegra*, was a tremendous success, and Toscanini permitted four *bis* on the first night. At all ten performances, according to our chronicler, 'the attendance was extraordinary, with great applause for all the artists and the orchestra'.[19]

Catalani arrived for the rehearsals of his *Loreley*, which Toscanini was to bring before the Genoese public on 18 February 1892. In a letter to a cousin the composer wrote: 'I heard *Amico Fritz*. I had been told so many bad things about it that I found it better than I had expected.' But he confided to Giuseppe Depanis, son of the Turin impresario: 'I am a bit apprehensive because *Amico Fritz* always fills the theatre and has many partisans.'

Poor Catalani! In this case, he needn't have worried. Toscanini rehearsed and conducted *Loreley* with the fervour of a disciple. Before rehearsals had begun the two men had been in correspondence over various details. Catalani's messages demonstrate his faith in Toscanini, who was not yet twenty-five:

'In regard to deletions I put myself entirely in your hands. Do anything you wish. With your artistic taste, you can't do it any way but well . . .

I think that in the second act the waltzes or the epithalamium must be cut. You'll do whatever you think best. I know I am in good hands and therefore I remain absolutely confident . . .

. . . I believe that no one else can divine and interpret me as you do . . . I trust you for everything . . .'[20]

Loreley was enthusiastically received at all four of its performances. After the opening night the normally reserved and pessimistic composer wrote to publisher Giulio Ricordi:

'Yesterday evening's success was really splendid. I could not have wished for a greater one; and it was all the sweeter to me as I did not expect it, not knowing this public. After the first and second acts I received extremely warm ovations. Then, the last act was . . . but it is useless for me to continue flattering myself! . . . Toscanini is a great and true artist; that is all there is to be said.'[21]

And to Depanis:

'Toscanini has proved himself a first-rate conductor as well as a true artist . . . I received six curtain calls, which never happened to me before.'[22]

The last opera of this series was *Vindice* by one Umberto Masetti (a pupil of Martucci), now as forgotten as his opera which, according to Vallebona, 'barely survived four performances, always with a small audience'.[23]

Toscanini had hoped to return to Milan as soon as *Vindice* had ended—around 1 March; but he could not move. It seems that at that time his family was again living in Genoa. *Wanderlust* and a new desire to make a fresh start had apparently again taken hold of Claudio, who was nearly sixty. One can easily deduce, in the absence of concrete evidence, that Papà Toscanini had involved his unwitting son—or at least his son's name—in one of his mad business ventures, and had promptly found himself in debt. Toscanini's reaction, on being told of the situation, is not hard to imagine. Nevertheless, he now considered it his responsibility. He gritted his teeth and wrote to Piontelli on 7 March:

'I must ask a great favour of you . . . Because of various family obligations (not trifling ones), I find myself in very great need. I will need 300 lire and I don't know where to turn; I beg you to be kind—to get me out of this mess. I hope that the time to return it to you will not be very far off; for now I can do nothing but be grateful to you . . .'[24]

Ten days later:

'After two beseeching letters and a telegram I received notification from you yesterday, saying that a telegraphic money order would be sent me during the morning..... The morning passed, the evening passed, another morning and... nothing, nothing, nothing..... Dear Piontelli, I cannot believe that you are laughing at my present very critical position: —I believe that you have forgotten..... So for the last time, I beg you, I pray you to send me 300 lire . . . I cannot leave Genoa if I do not have this sum; and believe me, I find myself thus out of kindness, too much kindness, towards a family that is very ungrateful towards me . . . You, who told me that in the fall, at Carnival and at Lent I would be engaged by your theatres, would be able to trust me, that if I cannot pay my debt today, it will be tomorrow . . .'[25]

And the next day:

'I have received your money order . . . An immeasurable proof of your generous heart..... [Note: Piontelli had sent him 200 lire as a gift "for services rendered last season".] You have been so kind and so tactful as to make it seem that I deserve that which I absolutely do not feel I deserve, since I have not rendered you any service at all, but have merely done my duty weakly . . . I hope that I shall soon be able to reciprocate such kindness, at least in part . . .'[26]

With this situation resolved Toscanini was able to return to Milan, where another very important assignment awaited him in May. He had again been engaged by the Teatro Dal Verme, this time to conduct a revival of Thomas's *Hamlet* and the world première of Leoncavallo's *I pagliacci*. According to Taubman, Verdi himself had been hearing good things about the young conductor and had recommended him to the famous baritone Victor Maurel, who was to sing in both operas; Maurel had then recommended Toscanini to Leoncavallo's publisher, Edoardo Sonzogno, and to the Dal Verme's impresario. *Pagliacci* was written in a new style and was difficult to prepare. After the very successful first performance Toscanini returned home so exhausted that he threw himself down on his bed, still wearing his shoes, tails and starched shirt, and fell asleep.

Most of the summer was free for study and relaxation, following which he plunged into eight months of relentless activity. The first engagement was a labour of love for him: Catalani had asked him to conduct a production of his latest opera—and his last one, as it turned out—*La Wally*, at the Teatro del Giglio in Lucca, his home town. The composer's usual trepidation about such a venture was exacerbated in this case because it was the first time one of his operas was being presented in Lucca, and he feared that the Puccini family—his fellow townsmen—had been plotting against him. (Paranoia is not at all uncommon among musicians.) 'I am not sure that my townspeople will like my music,' he wrote to Depanis, 'accustomed as they are to inflated operas with bombastic finales.'[27] (That meant Puccini's *Edgar*.) But once again, he needn't have worried, as a telegram to Depanis the day after the opening reveals:

> '*5 September. Wally* success enthusiastic, indescribable. Audience deeply impressed. Six *bis* . . . Toscanini's conducting admirable—After opera a torchlight procession, serenade, impressive demonstration, whole population attended . . .'[28]

The opera was performed fourteen times.

From Lucca Toscanini went to Genoa, where Alberto Franchetti's opera *Cristoforo Colombo* was to be premièred at the Carlo Felice. It had been commissioned by the administration of the explorer's native city for the 400th anniversary of the discovery of America. A charming story which appears in nearly every biographical book or article on Toscanini describes how Luigi Mancinelli, who had been engaged to conduct the opera, quarrelled with the composer or the impresario and left after only three performances; whereupon Toscanini was searched out, handed a score which he studied overnight, and sent out to the podium the next evening to lead the performance from memory. (One article even stated that Mancinelli had committed suicide; but in fact he lived until 1921.) The true story is quite different, as this letter from Catalani to Depanis proves:

> 'Milan, 23 September. . . . I arrived yesterday from Genoa and will return there Tuesday to start rehearsals. When you announce that *Colombo* will open on 1 October, please also announce that *Wally* will begin on the 12th; the conductor will be Toscanini, who will also take over the direction of *Colombo*, since Gigi [Mancinelli] has to leave for Madrid after three performances . . .'[29]

All arranged in advance. Actually, *Colombo* did not begin until 5 October and Mancinelli was able to lead only two performances. Toscanini was offered a new dress rehearsal but said that he didn't need one. He had attended Mancinelli's performances to learn the tempi, etc.—which in any case could not have been greatly altered at a dress rehearsal—and Giovanni Monleone remembered seeing him in one of the loges, 'all absorbed, with his head in his hands'. Verdi was present and applauded enthusiastically at the last performance on 23 October; this was the only time he heard Toscanini conduct.

Wally began on the 17th and received seven performances. 'I am really happy with the success,' wrote Catalani to Depanis.[30]

Toscanini had to dash to Rome as soon as his Genoa duties ended. His first engagement in the capital was to take place at the Teatro Costanzi, and he could not have had more than three or four days of rehearsals for the first production, *Carmen*, which opened on 30 October. This was followed by the world première of the now forgotten *Gualtiero Swarten* by Andrea Gnaga, which starred Tamagno—who also sang in the next opera, *La forza del destino*. Toscanini was also to have conducted a production of Mascagni's new opera, *I Rantzau*; the production took place, but without Toscanini. After the work's wildly successful première in Florence on 10 November the Costanzi orchestra had sent a congratulatory telegram to Mascagni, who had interpreted it in his own way and had wired back: 'Will be happy to bring you my thanks, proud to captain, myself, famous Roman orchestra, first restaging my new opera.'

Toscanini took this badly. What Mascagni wanted was to have him lead the rehearsals, then to direct the first performances himself, and finally to give the baton back to Toscanini for the remaining performances. This was not an uncommon tribute to composers in those days, but it was not normally done when the regular conductor was someone with Toscanini's reputation. For reasons of pride Toscanini objected; and when an article appeared in a Rome paper, the *Fanfulla*, stating that it was he who had proposed this idea to Mascagni, he sent an open letter to the *Tribuna*—probably the only time in his career when he replied publicly in such a matter.

'The *Fanfulla* would like to have it believed that it was I who spontaneously offered Mascagni the honour of conducting *I Rantzau*. This is not true. Far from giving up this honour, I would have liked to have retained it, and I would have felt myself equal to the task—and with no strain—*even given the limited amount of time*; but Mascagni wanted to keep for himself the honour of the first three performances... I, on my part, beg him to take the remaining ones as well.'

Rantzau opened on 26 November—with Mascagni, of course; but a chronicler says that when Toscanini returned to conduct a performance of *Forza del destino* a day or two later, 'the whole audience rose to its feet in a warm and impressive demonstration, and he was presented with a laurel wreath, a gift from Tamagno'.[31]

Looking back on this episode not many weeks later, Toscanini must have regarded it as trifling compared with what he was by then undergoing. From Rome he had gone to Sicily, where he was under contract to direct a four-month season at Palermo's Politeama Garibaldi. The opening production was *Pagliacci* (24 December). The impresario evidently had not been aware that Palermitans traditionally went out to play *tombola*—something like bingo—on Christmas eve, before going to mass. Few people attended the performance, and those who did created a disturbance during most of it. The opera was received enthusiastically after that and Leoncavallo was in attendance on the third night.

The next opera was *Cavalleria*, which had already been performed in Palermo two years earlier, with great success. The singing in this new production did not please the public, or at least a powerful and vociferous segment thereof, despite the fact that some well-known voices were participating (Garulli, Ferni-Germano *et al.*). There was such pandemonium on the second night that the performance had to be suspended; and the hostile demonstration continued outside the theatre afterwards. The critic for *L'amico del popolo* wrote:

'Old and new grudges and jealousies and more or less dishonest interests joined together. Yesterday evening's scandalous exhibition arose from this strange coalition, which had attempted to set the stage through the press and through gossip. By this we do not wish to state that the performance of *Cavalleria rusticana* at the Politeama is perfect, nor that the public may not show its dissatisfaction in a correct and dignified way; but we do not think that yesterday evening's scandal can legitimately be justified.'

The 'dishonest interests' alluded to were those of the mafia, who resented Toscanini's refusal to follow their orders as to which arias were to be encored—presumably because one or another mafia boss was interested in one or another of the female singers. The company went to the mayor to declare the season suspended; but after a day or two the situation was at least superficially cleared up and the next opera, *Loreley*, was staged on 28 January 1893 in the presence of its composer. Catalani was now seriously ill but had made the cold and turbulent winter voyage by boat. Fortunately, the production was successful and he received a tumultuous ovation.

The season continued with Toscanini's first *Norma* (12 February) and his first Wagner, *The Flying Dutchman* (2 March)—although he had rehearsed the latter for Pomé in Turin in 1886. *Barber of Seville* was next, and according to Segre, at the second performance,

'. . . at the beginning of the overture, the audience began to clamour for something that, at the time, Toscanini could not make out, so great was the turmoil. He continued to direct, then he became so upset that he threw his baton at the audience and walked out of the theatre. Only forty years later, speaking by chance with an old man from Palermo, did he get the explanation: the audience wanted him to play the "Hymn of Garibaldi" inasmuch as it was March 19, Saint Giuseppe's day, and Giuseppe was also the name of the hero of Italian independence [after whom the theatre was named].'[32]

The last two productions were *Rigoletto* and *Gioconda* (4 and 15 April). One local critic summarized the season as 'unfortunate and wretched' and said of Toscanini:

'Excepting *Loreley* and *Gioconda* [he] did nothing well . . . did not know how to get the desired effects from the orchestra . . . did not rigorously observe the metronomic indications . . . Above all, he was absolutely incompatible with the public which, irritated more than once by his obstinacy, demonstrated its feelings by whistling. Did Toscanini believe he could veil his defects as a conductor by keeping the score closed on the music stand?'[33]

It will come as no surprise that Toscanini never again conducted in Palermo.

Strangely enough, the next ten months were spent without an engagement. He had been offered a rather lucrative contract, but the names of the theatre and city were not revealed to him. Suspecting that he was being involved in foul play against a colleague, he refused to sign. It may be that he was offered other jobs in the autumn; but in August he had suffered a blow which temporarily took away his desire to work: the death of Catalani.

From 1890 onwards Catalani had been professor of composition at the Milan Conservatory. Whenever he and Toscanini had found themselves in Milan at the same time, they had met as often as possible. Carlo Gatti, who was one of Catalani's pupils, wrote later:

> 'Catalani sought him out continually, went to his home to visit him . . . I remember, because I sometimes went along; and if Toscanini wasn't there he would stay and wait for him, asking his mother to let him sit there, and he would remain silent for a long time . . . Toscanini's mother would look at him with pity . . . Catalani often asked Toscanini to sit at the piano and play him his music . . .'[34]

Around 1 August 1893 Toscanini and some other friends saw Catalani off on a holiday in the high Alps. A violinist named Landucci happened to sit down in the composer's train compartment and noticed that he was having trouble talking and breathing. By the time they reached Chiasso, just across the Swiss border, Catalani was hemorrhaging seriously. He returned to Milan with help and was put to bed. Toscanini was informed and rushed to his friend's flat. For days he, Luigi Illica (the librettist and playwright) and Catalani's cousins took turns watching over the ailing man, whose suffering was so great that Toscanini once had to restrain him from throwing himself out the window. Teresa Junck, his benefactress and lover, arrived; but he did not even want to see her. Late at night on 6 August Toscanini left Catalani's bedside and went home to sleep. Returning early the next morning, he found him dead.

Toscanini was distraught; it took him a long time to recover from his grief. Long afterwards he said: 'I always think of him. The place he left will never be filled for me. And yet he who so yearned for joy was doomed never to know it.'[35]

In November Leoncavallo wanted Toscanini to conduct the première of his *I Medici* at the Dal Verme; but Sonzogno, the publisher, objected—and the publishers were omnipotent in those days. The reason for his attitude was the scandal Toscanini had provoked in Rome a year earlier over *I Rantzau*, another Sonzogno

opera. In his unpublished autobiography—of which only fragments remain—
Leoncavallo said that Sonzogno told him: 'If you are so fond of Toscanini, then
go ahead; but I will not go to the theatre that evening.'[36] Rodolfo Ferrari was
chosen to conduct.

Finally, in March 1894 Toscanini began conducting again. The first engagement he accepted was in Pisa, where he directed his first productions of *Otello* and
of Puccini's recent *Manon Lescaut*. He wrote to Puccini, inviting him to attend a
performance of his opera, and reported: 'The tenor, Rosati, *is an idiot,* but he
makes up for this misfortune by having a beautiful voice, warm and expressive.'
During a performance of *Otello* a small bomb went off backstage, injuring no one
but breaking glass and making a lot of noise. Toscanini immediately had the
orchestra play the Garibaldi Hymn and the Royal March to restore calm in the
theatre; the performance then proceeded. The name of the terrorist was never
discovered, but the general opinion was that the incident was related to some of
the replacements Toscanini had made in the orchestra.

In May Toscanini conducted Massenet's *Le Roi de Lahore* in Ravenna and in
August and September he did a series of three productions in Brescia: Massenet's
Manon, *I puritani* and *La traviata,* with fine singers such as Cesira Ferrani,
Roberto Stagno and Gemma Bellincioni. Along with a production of *Cristoforo
Colombo* under his direction in October, Treviso heard his very first performances
of *Falstaff,* which had been premièred at La Scala the previous year, and which
was to be performed in a greater number of productions or seasons (twenty-
seven) than any other opera in Toscanini's repertoire. While in Treviso he
attempted to learn to ride a bicycle—the old-fashioned high-wheeled type—took
a bad fall, and resumed studying scores.

The next stop was Bologna (November–December 1894), where he opened
with *Falstaff,* using the same cast he had trained in Treviso. Gatti-Casazza had
attended the Rome production of *Falstaff* with the same cast that had appeared in
the première at La Scala; 'then I heard it again at Bologna . . . directed by Arturo
Toscanini in a distinctly superior manner'.[37] Other productions during Toscanini's one-month Bolognese stay were the world première of *Savitri* by Natale
Canti and *Colombo*. The same three operas were included in his two-month
season in Genoa, which began on 26 December. In addition, he directed
Cavalleria and *L'amico Fritz* as a double bill, his first production of *Tannhäuser,*
and *La forza del destino*.

During the *Falstaff* rehearsals in Genoa Toscanini had argued with Pini-Corsi,
the baritone who was taking the rôle of Ford (as he had done in the original Scala
production), over the tempo of the phrase '*Quella crudel beltà*' in the second act.
Toscanini wanted it done at the speed indicated by Verdi in the score, Pini-Corsi
insisted that the composer himself had had him sing it more slowly. Verdi was
spending the winter in Genoa, as he often did, and Toscanini's friend Piontelli,
the impresario, had arranged to take the entire cast over to give the old man their

Christmas greetings. Toscanini, whose natural timidity was intensified in the composer's presence, eventually summoned up all his nerve and asked Verdi's opinion on the point in question. Pini-Corsi, of course, presented his side, too. Verdi declared Toscanini in the right; and when Pini-Corsi maintained that he had been singing as Verdi had instructed, the composer related that in 1867 he had patiently rehearsed his *Don Carlo* in Paris for months and that the result had been satisfactory. He had left Paris for a month and upon his return had found that not one tempo remained as he had wanted it.

Unfortunately, *Falstaff* was not a popular success. Verdi did not attend the production but kept himself informed of the situation. On 30 December 1894 he wrote to Giulio Ricordi:

'*Falstaff* is a fiasco! But really a first-rate fiasco. Nobody goes to the theatre! The beautiful part is that they say that an opera so perfectly performed and so well-blended has never been heard before! In that case it must be that the music is accursed!'[38]

And on 11 January:

'Last evening at the Carlo Felice there was a reduced *Falstaff*—not paunch-wise but price-wise!! I daren't say it! 1·50 lire. Result? The same.

If I were Piontelli I would make another attempt. I would remove all the seats from the theatre. I would set up a great bar near the orchestra, with six or more barmaids, and four newsboys outside the theatre shouting, "Ladies and gentlemen, come right in, come into the theatre gratis. Performance gratis, chorus and orchestra gratis, everything gratis!! You only have to pay for your beer at five *centesimi* a mug!!! Step right up, step right up, ladies and gentlemen!! A real stroke of luck!!"

With this system perhaps Piontelli would find a few pennies in his cash box...'[39]

Having conducted an incredible fifty-nine performances in under sixty-five days, Toscanini moved on immediately to Pisa, where he again led *Falstaff* and *Colombo*. Piontelli was the impresario; and he was probably asking himself soon afterwards why he didn't find a more tranquil occupation. The following paragraphs appeared in an article by Garibaldo Bagnolesi in the *Corriere dell'Arno* in 1945:

'[Toscanini] had barely read through a third of the first act [of *Falstaff*] when he stopped and told Piontelli that it was not possible to be ready by the set date because many players were inadequate. The impresario asked the Maestro to choose the best and to release the others. Toscanini chose 26 players who, however, declared their solidarity with those fired; and this led to a strike. There was a furor which almost came to blows, but Piontelli, undaunted, declared that if those chosen by Toscanini continued the strike, he would be forced to bring a whole orchestra from Milan!

The uproar was so great, in and out of the theatre, against Piontelli and against Toscanini, that the prefect had to intervene in person to reconcile the parties. Since Toscanini was immovable about the choice that had been made, Piontelli—to please the prefect—said he would pay a fixed sum to those who had been fired; but only those players chosen by the Maestro could remain in the orchestra. That settled, Toscanini began to wire Parma, Modena, Bologna, Milan . . . and by that evening he could count on forming a seventy-piece orchestra of highest quality.

Piontelli had aroused so much unjustified antipathy that some ugly prank was anticipated which would jeopardize the season; the authorities therefore took serious measures to insure that the production was not disrupted. The first night arrived; the crowd overflowed the theatre. All of Tuscany was amply represented. The production was judged superb . . . Toscanini received ovations throughout the performance.'

During this conflict Toscanini had received an anonymous letter which he kept all his life. I quote the translation given by Segre:

'You are too proud and you have hurt us; and therefore for us your orchestra does not exist. If another conductor who enjoys our favour were in your place, you would hear tremendous applause. . . . To tell the truth, you are a nice young man, full of intelligence, and you will become great; but all intelligence disappears in one who is impolite towards the audience. You are a misanthrope, you don't want to be introduced to students or important men. . . . We have rendered great honours to conductors such as Mugnone, Mancinelli, Catalanotti, Mascagni and Mascheroni, because they are kind and polite, and you would have enjoyed our favours had you not such a horrible character. . . . We warn you that the audience will ask for several encores and you had better execute them without being begged to. . . .'[40]

From Pisa Toscanini went to Venice (April–May 1895) where he worked simultaneously at two theatres—the Malibran and the Fenice—both under the auspices of Piontelli. The popular priced series at the Malibran opened with *Falstaff*. 'The performances came off well,' said the *Gazzetta di Venezia*, 'mainly because of the outstanding orchestral playing, always perfectly balanced, under the guidance of Arturo Toscanini.' This production was transferred to the Fenice and then back to the Malibran, receiving twenty-four performances in all. Next came *La forza del destino*, again at the Malibran:

'Several *bis* were requested and obtained by the less demanding spectators; but—and above all—there was a repetition requested by all without exception:

the overture, which was played with fire, with fusion, with colour, under the valiant direction of Arturo Toscanini. The orchestra was truly the absolutely superior part, consistently admirable.'[41]

At the Fenice he conducted *Colombo*, *Le Villi* and the world première of an unfortunate work, *Emma Liona* by Antonio Lozzi. Segre says that he also gave a concert which was attended by the royal family, and which included, among other works, the overtures to *I vespri siciliani*, *William Tell* and *Tannhäuser*; but I have not been able to find any confirmation of this in the Venetian papers of the time, although it is true that members of the royal family were in Venice at the time.

Toscanini conducted *Colombo* in Trento in June and *Tannhäuser* and *Loreley* in Treviso in October.

It was now over nine years since the episode in Rio; his reputation as an exceptional musician and as a difficult and uncompromising person was established. At that precise moment a far-sighted and dedicated man conceived a plan which was to put Toscanini in the conductor's chair at one of the most important theatres in the country. At twenty-eight, his years of apprenticeship were about to end.

That man was Giuseppe Depanis, the already-mentioned lawyer and music critic from Turin, whose father, Giovanni, was the impresario who had engaged Toscanini to conduct *Edmea* in 1886. The younger Depanis had been one of Catalani's closest friends and had observed Toscanini's artistic growth from the outset. Piontelli had stood by Toscanini—and continued to do so—because he had faith in his abilities and instincts. Depanis had the same, but he also understood and shared many of the conductor's aspirations. He and Toscanini were in agreement about the reforms which ought to be undertaken in the theatre regarding repertoire, performance practices and audience comportment. Far from balking at or fearing Toscanini's extreme intransigence, Depanis welcomed it; and he felt that the time had come to provide a situation in which his friend could operate without having to create an entirely new working environment virtually every time he rehearsed a new production. In addition, Depanis was a city councillor. He was concerned with the reorganization of Turin's musical life and was in a position to do something about it. Writing thirty years later, he recalled:

'After a fierce campaign waged by the local newspapers, the Turin City Council approved the foundation of a municipal orchestra and called upon Arturo Toscanini to form and conduct it. It was necessary to cut to the quick, to make painful choices [Note: obviously, the orchestra had to be composed of the best elements of Turin's other 'occasional' orchestras], to break with deep-rooted customs, to collide with personal interests; and nothing less than Toscanini's unyielding temperament was required. . . . There were lively protests and formidable arguments: these are inevitable in a radical reform, as are partial and involuntary injustices. But on the whole, the new orchestra turned out to be a solid, compact and marvellous instrument, and Toscanini a great conductor.'[42]

Links were also developed between the new orchestra and the already extant municipal music academy, so that the latter fed the former. The entire plan was revolutionary in its day.

Toscanini's previous appearances in Turin had been at the city's secondary theatres. Now it was time to make his entrance at the famed Teatro Regio, at the head of the new orchestra, and in an enormously demanding production: *Die Götterdämmerung*. Wagner's entire *Ring* tetralogy had been performed in Italy twelve years earlier by a touring German company under the direction of Anton Seidl; but the Regio *Götterdämmerung* was the first performance of the work by an Italian company—and in Italian, of course.

It was no coincidence that Toscanini's first season as what would today be called musical director of a major opera house began with Wagner. The Turin situation was the partial realization of an idea, or series of ideas, which had been developing in his mind for some time, and which would culminate twenty-five years later at La Scala; and the great first force behind his plans was Wagner. We have seen how his love of the German composer's works took root during his Parma years, when the newness, forbiddenness and unique beauty of the music had attracted him powerfully. His study of all of Wagner's scores and his experience conducting two of the earlier operas during the intervening years had greatly increased his admiration. Verdi he had imbibed with his mother's milk; but there is no doubt that Wagner was the great love of his youth. His re-evaluation and full recognition of the Italian master came after his whole-hearted embracing of Wagner, surprisingly enough.

Tied in closely with this was his admiration of Wagner's writings—not the racial and chauvinistic ones, but the ideas on conducting and on the reorganization of theatrical practices. Wagner insisted that the conductor must seek not only technical excellence in working with the orchestra but must also use his imagination and intellect to try to grasp the outpouring of nervous energy, the difficult struggle towards expression, that lie behind the notes on the printed page. Toscanini's sentiments on this point were very strong indeed. He also believed, with Wagner, that the only way to reach a higher level of performance in the theatre was to develop a system wherein each element of production was conceived and executed with maximum dedication and competence, in perfect relation to all the other elements and with greatest respect for the intentions of the composer. Like his contemporary Mahler in Vienna, Toscanini felt that the conductor was the person who logically should assume the burden of responsibility in the battle to actuate such a system; and he was determined to do anything towards that end. Although possessing a completely different personality, he believed, like Wagner and Mahler, that it was not his job to make life easier or more pleasant for himself or his colleagues, but to produce the best possible results in his work. Depanis, who was already a second generation Wagnerite (his father had laboured on behalf of Wagner's music in Italy and had even attended the first Bayreuth festival in 1876), again supported Toscanini fully in every way, as did Piontelli, who had been given a four-year contract by the city as the Regio's impresario.

Among the singers who auditioned for the *Götterdämmerung* production was a young woman named Ida De Martini, whom Toscanini chose as Woglinde, one of the Rhine Maidens. Ida was accompanied to the audition by her mother—the widow of a Milanese stockbroker—and sister Carla. Toscanini found the De Martini sisters charming and was soon in love with Carla, who was only eighteen but intelligent, lively and beautiful. By chance, his friend Enrico Polo, who had been in Germany studying with Joachim, was now in Turin to head the violin faculty at the music academy and to be concertmaster of the new orchestra. When Toscanini introduced him to the De Martinis Polo promptly fell in love with Ida; and eventually the two friends married the two sisters.

When *Götterdämmerung* was produced on 22 December 1895 the Turin audience actually heard only about three-fourths of it: Toscanini had decided that a public which was almost entirely unfamiliar with the mature Wagner's musical idiom could not reasonably be expected to digest the enormous work at a first attempt; so he eliminated the Waltraute episode and made several other cuts as well. The singers had been coached meticulously and only ten days of orchestral and ensemble rehearsals were required.

The production was more than successful. Carlo Bersezio, in the *Gazzetta piemontese*, wrote that there was 'a fusion and blend of the elements, care in the interpretation and playing, refinements of colouring and expression' thanks to Toscanini's 'high dedication and rare intelligence'. After 'Siegfried's Funeral Music', the audience 'broke into a real ovation and called in one great voice for a *bis*, which was not given'. Incredibly, *Die Götterdämmerung* received twenty-one performances that season.

The next opera was *Falstaff*; and it was probably at the first ensemble rehearsal in costume for this production that Toscanini stopped the orchestra at one point, ran up on to the stage, walked quickly towards the frightened chorus and said, 'Let me see your shoes.' Surprised, they stuck out their feet to let him look. Toscanini said calmly to the stage coordinator, 'You must have different shoes made for them,' described how the shoes should be, then returned to the orchestra and continued the rehearsal. This is the earliest recorded incident pertaining to Toscanini's attention to non-musical details of operatic production.[43]

Arrigo Boito, the composer and poet, had been enthusiastic about the

Götterdämmerung production and had returned for *Falstaff*. He congratulated Toscanini afterwards, and this was the beginning of a friendship which lasted until Boito's death—and, in a very real sense, even beyond.

After another staging of the unfortunate *Savitri* the attention of the Italian musical world was again focused on the Piedmontese capital for the world première of Puccini's *La bohème* on 1 February 1896. The composer, who had originally wanted Leopoldo Mugnone to conduct the first production, arrived early in January for rehearsals and found Toscanini 'highly intelligent and a very sweet, kind man'.[44] But he was not happy with the choice of Turin for the first production: he would have preferred Rome or Naples, where he felt the lighting and acoustics would have been better. Besides, he had doubts about some of the singers. 'This Marcello [Wilmant] is absolutely no good,' he wrote to Illica, one of his librettists. 'He doesn't understand anything at all, and he wouldn't make it even if we rehearsed as much as at Bayreuth.'[45] And in another letter: 'I fear that the opening will have to be postponed because of some inadequate artists! And this is a disaster for me.'[46] He was completely satisfied with Cesira Ferrani as the first Mimì (she had also been the first *Manon Lescaut*) and he was in love with her, too; she, however, was in love with Toscanini.[47]

Bohème was a great and ever-growing success with the Turin public—twenty-three performances were given—but was received rather sourly and with predictions of a short life by the critics, who nevertheless praised Toscanini's direction as 'excellent, perfect . . . with that valour, that artistic conscience that make him one of today's best . . . an elect spirit . . . aristocratic temperament . . .'

After a production of an older work, Paer's *Il maestro di cappella* (1821), Toscanini's first Regio season ended with *Emma Liona*. All in all, there had been fifty-nine performances of six operas in just over two months, and Toscanini and the new orchestra had clearly been appreciated.

The spring of 1896 marked Toscanini's début as a symphonic conductor. His first full-length concert took place at the Regio on 20 March, again under Piontelli's auspices, and the programme consisted entirely of works barely known in Italy at that time: Schubert's 'Great C Major' Symphony, Tchaikovsky's 'Nutcracker' Suite, the Italian première of the 'Tragic' Overture by Brahms, who was still alive, and the 'Entrance of the Gods into Valhalla' from *Das Rheingold*. (And if Toscanini could say, right from the start, Wagner *and* Verdi—not Wagner *or* Verdi—he could do the same for Wagner *and* Brahms.) The concert was actually to have taken place a few days earlier, but a problem had arisen: since the Regio stage was still cluttered with scenery, Toscanini had rehearsed the orchestra from its 'opera position' on the ground floor. (There was no pit.) He had warned Piontelli that he would need a rehearsal on the stage to test the acoustics, but Piontelli had told him that it was not necessary. 'I say I will not conduct concert,' Toscanini told B.H. Haggin more than sixty years later. 'This man was like father to me; but when is time for concert I am in bed. Manager

[Piontelli] come to hotel; but I stay in bed.' The audience was sent home and the concert postponed until Toscanini got his rehearsal.[48]

A month later he gave four concerts at La Scala—his first conducting appearances there. In addition to the Schubert, Tchaikovsky and Brahms works that had been on his Turin concert, his programmes included Haydn's 'Clock' Symphony, Beethoven's First, short pieces by Grieg, Verdi, Saint-Saëns and others, and excerpts from the *Götterdämmerung* Prologue, with some of the same singers who had performed the opera in Turin, but with famed tenor Giuseppe Borgatti replacing Raffaele Grani in the rôle of Siegfried.

'A theatre such as we have never seen before: completely sold out. A success such as we have never seen before: great applause for all the pieces and a *bis* for Wagner's *Götterdämmerung*. A conductor such as we did not have, unfortunately, during the past season: Maestro Toscanini, a youth who knows how to command . . . on a level with the most glorious veterans of the conductor's stool.' [Romeo Carugati, *Lombardia*, 27 April.]

The reviews of these concerts are unanimous in their praise of Toscanini. Even the difficult Amintore Galli of *Il secolo* (see p. 31) wrote after the first concert that 'last night Toscanini achieved a great success which has an artistic significance of high importance'. It was obvious that Toscanini and La Scala were destined to establish a closer relationship.

In June Toscanini was in Trento to conduct *Un ballo in maschera* and *La bohème*. When his future sister-in-law wrote to scold him for not writing to her sister, he replied:

'25 June 1896. . . . I tell you that I don't like Trento at all. The air doesn't do anything at all for me—everything that surrounds me is unpleasant—even the customs are intolerable . . . After all this, you can easily imagine what kind of mood this very irritable creature is in these days, the victim, moreover, of terrible rheumatic pains which have taken hold of my back and right arm and have even made breathing painful! As many times as I have set out to write to Carla or to your mother, I have had to give up because I felt incapable of formulating a single thought . . .'[49]

And from Milan on 3 July he wrote to Depanis:

'I learned from Count Torazzo that you are persisting in your idea of no longer wanting to concern yourself with the Orchestra. If you knew how much displeasure this news gave me, you would not hesitate an instant to retract this bad proposal, and you would return—as I hope—to continue to give me your most valuable cooperation. I still trust in your goodness, in the sweetness of your character and in the affection which you have shown me under a thousand guises; and once the ugly impression made by my rude behaviour has melted away you will again be the affectionate friend of before, without rancour, without any sort of bad impression. Nothing could be more important to me than to receive a letter from you; I needn't tell you with what trepidation I await it.'⁵⁰

The rude behaviour most likely refers to the incident of the postponed concert in March. Depanis returned to his voluntary duties.

Toscanini conducted *Bohème* in Brescia late in August, and led the same opera plus *Le Villi* in Bologna in November and December. He wrote to Polo, who was in Turin:

'3 December. I think you've become a real sluggard! Ida is very displeased that you don't write to her and don't even answer her letters. Are you so busy that you can't give her two minutes? Tell me if the orchestra is better this year and if Maestro Martucci was satisfied.

I'm angry that I won't be able to have the second part of Berlioz's Dramatic Symphony *Romeo and Juliet* played on the first concert I conduct [later that month].—The society doesn't want to pay for the music, so I shall have to do Buzzi-Peccia's symphonic poem *Re Harfagar* instead. . . .'⁵¹

Toscanini's interest in Berlioz at the very outset of his symphonic conducting career, and at a time when the Frenchman's music was infrequently played, especially in Italy, is remarkable. Composers who did appear on his two programmes in Turin were Haydn, Beethoven, Weber, Mendelssohn, Wagner, Chabrier, Grieg, Catalani, the above-mentioned Buzzi-Peccia and, most surprisingly, the recently-deceased Bruckner (Adagio from the Seventh Symphony), whose music Toscanini would conduct on only four other occasions in his entire career.

By the end of December his second Regio season had begun with Giordano's *Andrea Chénier*, followed by Saint-Saëns's *Samson and Delilah*, Boito's *Mefistofele*, *Tristan und Isolde*, and Buzzi-Peccia's *La forza d'amore*. It was neither as interesting nor as successful as the previous season. The production which aroused the greatest anticipatory interest was *Tristan*, and some idea of the time and energy that went into the preparations is given in this letter to Carla De Martini, whom Toscanini was to marry four months later.

'[February 1897, 1 a.m.] Dearest, I am just getting home this minute after 4¼ hours of rehearsal. I am completely exhausted. I began at 10:30 this morning by teaching the English horn player his little solo in the third act. At 11:30 I ate two eggs in great haste and at 12 I rehearsed the orchestra alone—then I continued with the artists until 6. Eleven hours of rehearsal in all for your poor Arturo. I can truly say that I earn my pay by the sweat of my brow! This evening, though, even my mind is tired. This blessed *Tristan* is very, very difficult—then to get it into the blood of the stupid mass which (with some exceptions) makes up the totality of the production—that is, the orchestra, soloists, etc., etc.—I guarantee you that patience superior to mine is needed. God make me find it. The bass clarinet riled me so this morning that I wound up chasing him out of the orchestra. Apart from that outburst the thermometer of my poor nerves is low enough. Tomorrow I shall rehearse with all the artists and soloists—In the evening another rehearsal of the whole opera with every-one—Piontelli has purposely not scheduled a performance [that evening] in order to hasten our opening. Two more rehearsals Wednesday—Thursday, rehearsal in the morning and dress rehearsal in the evening—Saturday, rest for the soloists and perhaps also for the orchestra, and Sunday, the big première. Will it go well? Let's hope so. If my Carlottina were there that evening I would be sure of victory, but since I can't hope for that, I can only sigh! I'll have a calm heart and I'll be able to say that I did what my understanding indicated.

I know that many people are coming from Milan; also Bologna and Florence. There is an atmosphere of anticipation. I won't hide from you the fact that this opening gives me a certain feeling of apprehension, especially after the fiascos of *Götterdämmerung* and *Don Carlo* at La Scala. My dear Little Round Ball, why haven't you written me any nice little notes these days? I need a sweet and affectionate word to make this undefined sadness that has been tormenting my heart for several days disappear. Who can do this for me better than my Carlottina? Instead, she has been silent for two days. Are you also rehearsing a Tristan?

I am still thinking about your suggestion that we live at your house, without ever being able to persuade myself that this is really a good idea. Polo is also of my opinion, as is Piontelli. On the other hand, I would like to have your mother together with us. All this puts me in an embarrassing situation. . . .'[52]

Unfortunately *Tristan* was disturbed by a battle between Toscanini and the audience over whether or not the theatre should be kept dark during the perform-ance. It was Toscanini's belief that a total theatrical illusion could only be created in a darkened house, and this was his first attempt at imposing this idea on a public accustomed to walking, talking, eating, looking at each other, flirting, playing cards and following libretti while 'listening' to an opera. The majority of the audience did not appreciate being plunged into darkness, and they voiced their protest—while the counterprotests of the Wagnerites in the theatre did not diminish the confusion. (Sacchi called this a situation in which the Illuminists were actually the Obscurantists and vice-versa.) Toscanini had to stop conduct-ing, and when the management turned the lights on, he lost his temper and smashed the light on his stand. A compromise decision was made and the remainder of the performance took place in half-light; but Toscanini was so intensely aggravated and disgusted that he directed the rest of the opera sitting in his chair with his right hand resting on his knee, barely moving his baton. Poor Polo virtually had to lead the orchestra while the prompter tried to assist the singers. It was an incident which left bitter feelings on all sides, and only six performances were given in all.

Toscanini was anxious to conduct more symphonic music, so Depanis and Piontelli asked him to lead five concerts at the Regio in March, in the course of which he gave his first readings of the Beethoven Sixth Symphony and Violin Concerto (with Eugène Ysaye), Schumann's Second and Tchaikovsky's Sixth symphonies, and shorter works by Weber, Corelli, Berlioz, Bach, Haydn, Cherubini, Wagner and Verdi as well as contemporaries Grieg, Raff, Smetana, Saint-Saëns, Dvořák, Goldmark and Bolzoni.

Having passed his thirtieth birthday, he went to Venice in April to conduct *Bohème* at the Teatro Rossini. There was fierce competition at the time between Puccini's opera and a Leoncavallo work by the same name, and Toscanini's firm support for Puccini won the conductor—accidentally and temporarily—the gratitude and support of the powerful publisher Giulio Ricordi.

On 21 June Toscanini married Carla De Martini, who was not yet twenty years old; their wedding day may have given the girl an idea of what the rest of her life was to be like. Their daughter, Wally, related the story seventy-five years later:

'Papà hated publicity, so he kept the date a secret. To avoid surprises, he decided to have the wedding far from Milan. [Piontelli] had a villa at Conegliano Veneto. Papà chose that town for his wedding.

'Our father had an instinctive aversion for celebrations, for official receptions, for everything that wasn't spontaneous and sincere. So he decided that there would be no ceremony, no traditional invitations, no formal luncheon afterwards. Only a few intimates were invited. He left Milan secretly by train with his fiancée. Mamma remembered that it was a beautiful trip. Papà was cheerful, calm and very affectionate. But at the Conegliano station came the tragedy. [Piontelli] had not been able to keep the secret and news of the wedding had spread through the town. There was a great crowd at the station, headed by a band, waiting to greet the Maestro. When our father looked out the window and saw those people, he became livid with rage. . . . He got off the train without saying a word, paying no attention to his fiancée, who was trying vainly to hold on to his arm. He went into the church and went through the ceremony with a clouded face. At the meal afterwards he didn't touch the food nor even a drop of wine. He refused the toasts of the few relations and friends and didn't say a word to anyone. There was a funereal atmosphere. After the meal, Mamma and Papà left in a carriage for their honeymoon [in the Dolomites]. Papà didn't say a word all day. Mamma always said: "That was the worst trip of my life." Towards evening Mamma started to cry. Then the gruff

Toscanini tried to overcome his bad humour and with an effort started to break the silence he had kept up to that moment.'[53]

Toscanini's own family had not been invited to the wedding.

Neither the disturbance at the Turin *Tristan* nor that of the wedding day was the most upsetting occurrence of 1897. That honour belonged to Toscanini's engagement at Bergamo in August and September, where he had been invited to direct performances of Donizetti's *La favorita* and *Lucia di Lammermoor*. The composer is Bergamo's most famous native son, and these productions were scheduled in honour of the centenary of his birth. The exact background of the story is unclear; but it appears that the cast of *Favorita*, which opened on 21 August, left quite a bit to be desired. The critic of *L'eco di Bergamo* praised the orchestra—'balanced and well directed'—but complained about the cast, whom he refused even to name, excepting the 'fine' baritone Caruson. According to Della Corte and Segre, Toscanini went on preparing *Lucia*, but at the last moment refused to conduct it. This was supposedly because two singers were taken ill and Toscanini was dissatisfied with the impresario's suggestions for replacements, favouring instead a postponement which the impresario rejected. But Giuseppe Valdengo claims that Toscanini told him the following story many years later:

'The second opera was supposed to have been *Lucia*, with the soprano Gemma Bellincioni and her husband, the tenor Roberto Stagno. At the time fixed for the [first] rehearsal I was in the hall waiting for the cast; the two famous artists arrived a good half hour late. Stagno sat down slowly and comfortably and, leaning on his ebony cane with its silver handle, said to me: "Do you want *Lucia* sung the old way or the new way?" I only knew one *Lucia*—the one written by Donizetti. I took it badly and thought to myself: this tenor is so famous that he knows two *Lucias* while I only know one. I replied: "Signor Stagno, excuse me a moment." I went out the door and quickly downstairs, ran to find the impresario and told him: "Listen, find another conductor because I'm not conducting *Lucia* with that guy; he knows two *Lucias* and I only know Donizetti's." And I ran out. The chorus master Eraclio Gerbella conducted in my place, and I don't know which of the two *Lucias* was performed.'[54]

Whatever the truth may be, this was the result:

'*L'eco di Bergamo*, 7 September. . . . Saturday evening there was a public pandemonium such as we believe the old theatre has never seen before. There was a real revolt against the company, accused of excessive abuse of the Bergamo public. . . . Saturday's violent scene, more than just the effect of momentary disappointment, was the result of discontent which goes back to the first performances of the current season. . . . Who is to blame? For the record it must be reported that the public was a little surprised, upon entering the theatre, to see a printed notice in the foyer which announced that Maestro

Toscanini, taken ill at the last moment, had had to leave the direction of the performance to Maestro Gerbella, the chorus director. [Note: Gerbella had been one of Toscanini's teachers at the Parma Conservatory.] These notices always leave many sceptics, of course . . .'

After the second act the audience became so unruly that benches were thrown from the gallery. The police had to be sent for to suspend the performance and clear the theatre. Despite this, Toscanini decided to fulfil his contract to direct several symphonic concerts before leaving the town. During the first one, which was poorly attended, a clique of his detractors began screaming, 'Out with Toscanini! Out of the theatre!' He turned to the audience, shouted 'Absurd!' and left the stage. Having calmed down, he was persuaded to return and finish the concert; but once on the podium his rage boiled over again and he conducted—as at the *Tristan*—perfunctorily and rigidly. He refused to honour the rest of his contract and returned to Milan.

At the Teatro Dal Verme from October to early December he directed *Bohème*, *Lucia* and *Manon Lescaut*, and underwent what was probably the last *serata d'onore* of his life—at which he conducted 'Siegfried's Rhine Journey' and Smetana's *Bartered Bride* Overture in addition to the evening's opera.

His third Turin season opened on 1 January 1898 with the Italian première of Mancinelli's *Ero e Leandro* and continued with revivals of *Mefistofele* and *Bohème*, after which Puccini wrote to thank Toscanini, 'sublime and incomparable *condottiere*'. There was a rare production of *Die Walküre* and the world première of *La Camargo* by one Enrico De Leva; and the season ended with *Norma*. *Camargo* was a failure; but one piece—a minuet which served as an intermezzo between the first and second acts—pleased enough of the public that a *bis* was requested. Toscanini felt sorry for the poor composer and told the orchestra to replay the minuet. No sooner had they begun than another segment of the audience began to protest against the repetition. Toscanini stopped, signalled for the curtain to go up for the second act, as if to go on without the *bis*, but then had the orchestra play the minuet again. The disrupters were caught by surprise and remained silent to the end.

Following the opera season Toscanini directed four light symphonic concerts, on one of which Spanish violinist Pablo de Sarasate was soloist in Bruch's *Scottish Fantasy*. At the second concert Toscanini was invited to the loge of Princess Elena, who decorated him with the cross of *cavaliere*; and two days after the last concert (19 March) Carla gave birth to the Toscaninis' first child, who was named Walter after the hero of Catalani's *Loreley*. Commenting once years later to B.H. Haggin about Walter's tendency to be late, Toscanini said: 'Is good, but not punctual. Only once was punctual: I was married June 21; he was born March 21.'[55]

In May Toscanini began an enormously demanding series of concerts in conjunction with an international exposition which was being held in Turin. In fact, there were forty-four concerts in all between 1 May and 31 October, with a break from mid-July to the end of August. For the record, there were 213 performances of 133 works by 54 composers; 48 of the works were being heard in Turin for the first time, including Brahms's Second and Fourth symphonies, Dvořák's Symphonic Variations, Grieg's *Peer Gynt* Suite, Schubert's 'Unfinished', Schumann's Fourth and Saint-Saëns's Third symphonies. The great event of the series was the Italian première on 26 May of three of Verdi's Four Sacred Pieces—the composer's last major work—which had first been heard in Paris a month earlier.

In studying the *Te Deum* Toscanini had had some doubts about slight tempo modifications, particularly let-ups in the overall velocity, which he felt were implicit in the music at certain points but which Verdi had not indicated in the score. He made Depanis write to the composer, who was in Genoa, to request a meeting. Verdi replied on 18 April:

'. . . Maestro Toscanini and Maestro Venturi [the chorus master] may come when they wish. I am always at home after midday.

A chorus of 200 voices is too large, in my opinion. These great masses always have a fat and swollen colour, and their pronunciation is too *unholy* (so to speak). . . . 120 voices would suffice. . . .'[56]

In Genoa the visitors from Turin were kindly received by the old man. The conversation turned to the Sacred Pieces and Toscanini hoped that the composer would play the *Te Deum* at the piano. But instead Verdi said, 'No, no, you play it.' Toscanini began to play; and at one point he made a slight *rallentando* (relaxation of the tempo) that was not printed in the score. 'Bravo,' said Verdi. Toscanini stopped playing and said, 'Maestro, if you knew how much this has been bothering me . . . Why didn't you write the *rallentando*?' And Verdi replied: 'If I had written it, a bad musician would have exaggerated it; but if one is a good musician, one feels it and plays it, just as you've done, without the necessity of having it written down.'

Ten days before the performance of the Sacred Pieces Toscanini received a letter from Boito:

'I have a mad craving to hear a good rehearsal of the Maestro's Three Pieces; please tell me on what day and at what time I could satisfy this desire.'[57]

And a few days later:

'You are too "intuitive" not to have guessed that my request to attend one of your rehearsals hid my intention to drag the Maestro along to Turin with me, to take him there without anyone's knowing a thing (thus avoiding any demonstration), to procure for him the intellectual joy of your interpretation, for you his great praise, and for myself this double satisfaction. But all my strategy ended in nothing. The Maestro is not to be moved, resists Giulio Ricordi's insistent prayers and my own, and doesn't give in. Perhaps he is afraid of exposing himself to a strong emotional reaction. His will be done. . . . I plan to join a group of friends to attend the performance and to admire you as I always do.'[58]

These extremely kind letters were meant in all seriousness by Boito, who was then, at the age of fifty-six, one of the most important figures in the Italian artistic world. But he did not tell Toscanini the main reason for his invitation to Verdi. Boito had recently been named vice-president of La Scala's governing board, and he had wanted Verdi's moral support in his major project: to make Arturo Toscanini, thirty-one years old, musical director of La Scala.

3
La Scala

In February 1776 Milan's principal opera house, the Regio Ducale Teatro, was destroyed in a fire. Within twelve days a committee of ninety noblemen had sent initial plans to Vienna for the building of a new theatre. (Austria ruled Lombardy at that time.) With the combined financial support of the Austrian royalty and the Milanese nobility and the incessant efforts of 300 workmen, the new edifice was completed in just over two years, on the site of the former church of Santa Maria della Scala. It soon developed an excellent reputation. 'I arrive [in Milan] at 7 in the evening, dead tired, and run to La Scala,' wrote Stendhal in 1817. 'I run to the leading theatre in the world.' All four of Italy's great nineteenth-century *operisti*—Rossini, Donizetti, Bellini and Verdi—had works premièred there, and the most famous singers performed there.

Until 1815 La Scala was run entirely by the *palchettisti*—the noble families who subsidized the theatre and who hereditarily owned the loges or boxes (*palchi*) which they occupied. They licensed impresarios to organize the operas and ballets and also to run a gambling casino in the foyer, which helped pay for the productions. From 1815 onwards the Austrian government provided a generous subsidy and the casino was eliminated. After the birth of the Italian state the new government continued to give an annual grant. In 1897, however, during a period of austerity, the Crown ceded its 'property'—a euphemism in this case for 'responsibility'—to the city of Milan, which shortly afterwards decided that the money would be better spent elsewhere and abolished the subsidies. Thus, in June of that year La Scala was closed. On 26 December, which would have marked the opening of the new season, someone posted a sign on the main door of the theatre: 'Closed because of the death of artistic feeling, civic responsibility and common sense.'

Soon afterwards a committee was established to work out a solution to the problem, and a radical change in the operation of the theatre was eventually prescribed. The *palchettisti* increased their contribution, the city reduced its own from the pre-shutdown level, and a society of shareholders was formed to provide an operating capital of 300,000 lire. An administrative council was set up under the presidency of Duke Guido Visconti di Modrone, one of the city's best-known aristocrats, with Boito as vice-president; the rest of the board of governors was comprised largely of well-known figures in Milan's musical world, noblemen and legal consultants. Instead of accepting bids from impresarios each season, the council decided to hire a professional general manager on an experimental three-year basis; and this manager, together with the conductor, would be responsible for the season's productions. Consultations and negotiations were initiated, and after a time the council's nominees for these positions were presented to the board for approval.

In an obscure theatrical yearbook published in 1899, an article entitled '*Storia della questione della Scala*' contains the following interesting item:

'The nomination of Arturo Toscanini as Conductor raised a hurricane of suspicions, not because of his artistic ability, which is undoubtedly great and beyond discussion, but because of his personality which, according to some, is not adapted to maintaining that tranquillity and that dignified severity which are necessary if the productions are to proceed in the interests of the Administration. The choice of [Giulio] Gatti-Casazza as general manager was also fought doggedly by some who felt the young administrator was not sufficiently experienced for a Theatre of such great importance . . . But it must be admitted that these little battles, fought on the sidelines and provoked more by personal ambition than by artistic or managerial considerations, did not make a breach in the spirits of those who—not mistakenly—based the most fervent hopes for and the surest guarantees of La Scala's good fortunes on the two young directors.'[1]

Boito and his supporters on the board had their way, and news of the reorganization and of the new directorate was made public late in June 1898. It is true that Gatti-Casazza's only previous post had been at Ferrara's Teatro Municipale, but it had been a most useful apprenticeship. Besides, some hoped that his imperturbability and box office sense would help to balance Toscanini's fiery temperament and idealism. For his part, Toscanini brought with him an already vast experience: in the twelve years since his début he had conducted 113 productions and countless performances of 58 operas—staggering statistics—not to mention the repertoire of 150 symphonic compositions which he had acquired in only two and a half years.

In addition to studying for and rehearsing the vast series of concerts he was still directing in Turin, Toscanini now had the additional task of organizing the Scala season. During the month's break between the two parts of the series he went with Carla, Walter, and Ida and Enrico Polo to Ceresole Reale in the mountains near the French border, to study, to clear his head—and to do some mountain climbing! Some details of this first Alpinistic adventure were recounted many years later by Swiss musicologist Aloys Mooser:

'In the company of a Scottish mountaineer, I had reached Col du Géant [Mont Blanc *massif*] during an awful blizzard which had overtaken us two hours earlier and which now made the tiny cabin-refuge *Torino* tremble . . . Having lit a fire [we were joined in the cabin by] a half-dozen Italians, who had come via Courmayeur and Entrèves. All of a sudden one of them exclaimed: "Eh, Toscanini!" That name made me perk up my ears. As a professional musician I had already had many occasions to read articles from Italian newspapers which had spoken of a young conductor by that name who showed exceptional talent, and for whom it was agreed there would be a most brilliant future. "Which Toscanini?" I asked. "That one there! The little one! The Maestro!" . . . I hastened to meet this artist whom fortune had so providentially put in my path. . . . Once the hot soup had been distributed Toscanini and I stretched out on the camp bed where, curled up side by side under a wretched cover, the better to fight the cold, we began a spirited conversation which continued for the two-and-a-half days during which the storm kept us prisoners in the *Torino*, while our companions in misfortune played cards badtemperedly to kill time. Having revealed . . . that I was then living in St. Petersburg, where I was attached to the Imperial Theatres, I was surprised to hear him ask me point-blank: "So you have seen *Boris Godunov*?" I fell from the clouds. If at that time there weren't twenty people in the west who knew the great composer's opera, the situation was hardly more encouraging in Russia, where the official milieu, the court, the public, many professional musicians and the majority of the press considered Moussorgsky a sort of failure nearly bereft of talent to whom one could attach no importance. At that time none of his works was admitted on the imperial stages, and to get to know *Boris Godunov*—of which my teacher Mily Balakirev had spoken with delirious enthusiasm—I had had to read the full score at the piano . . . And it was nearly 3000 kilometres from there, in an ice-covered hut perched at an altitude of 3350 metres, that a young Italian musician was talking to me about this work. I do not know how, but he had come to know it, he had studied it in great detail, and he had immediately perceived its moving grandeur and burned with a desire to see and hear it on the stage. "Some day I shall conduct it," he declared to me in a determined tone of voice. . . .'[2]

At Ceresole Toscanini continued to send and receive letters regarding planning for the Scala season. The following excerpts from two of his letters demonstrate not only his careful attention to the composition of his orchestra, but also his human concern for the various players—which may not have manifested itself during rehearsals, but was obvious at other times.

'28 July 1898. Dear and distinguished Prof. Romeo Orsi [principal clarinet of the Scala orchestra and head of the orchestral society], As I have to deliver a complete list of the orchestra members to . . . Gatti-Casazza as soon as possible, I turn to you in the hope that you will help me with this difficult task. . . . If you would send me a complete list of the members . . . I would be very grateful. At the same time I shall ask you another favour! If by chance you should meet Prof. Zamperoni [principal flute], advise him not to leave his position at La Scala. I firmly believe that his reasons for wanting to withdraw from that job, however eloquent and persuasive, are not entirely acceptable to those who know Prof. Zamperoni at all well. It may be that he suffers from nervousness, but this is nothing new, and still he has always played well. He says he is old; but I would like to have an orchestra completely made up of old-timers like himself but who can play as he does—and I would accept them with great enthusiasm! . . .

I don't know where to find a really good bass clarinettist! Is there no clarinettist in Milan who would agree to play bass clarinet? Also, I hope Sonzogno will agree to play first horn. Can you give me his address?

Distinguished Professor, please excuse all the annoyances . . . have pity on me and remember that I should be happy to serve you in any way I can. Accept my heartfelt thanks and a cordial handshake. . . .'[3]

And to Zamperoni on 17 August:

'Your letter has made me very unhappy . . . It would be a shame if you were to leave the post which you have filled with honour for twenty years, especially today when we are all cooperating to restore Italy's greatest theatre to its glorious old traditions. Dearest Professor, I tell you plainly that I cannot begin to think of replacing you—Who knows whether your health, which is delicate today, won't be flourishing again tomorrow! Accept my best wishes with an affectionate handshake and write me later when you have completely changed your mind, which will be most gratifying for me. . . .'[4]

To no avail: Zamperoni had to be replaced. Meanwhile, final plans were still being made for the remaining Turin concerts. Toscanini wrote to Depanis in July:

'. . . I have so little desire to go to Milan that I'll also include in my contract the article which your letter suggests. If it isn't accepted, so much the better for me.

Joachim wrote to Polo that he can't come to Italy in the fall, having already made tentative arrangements for concerts in Germany; and his daughter's wedding is taking place at that time. This news displeases me very much and I predict that our negotiations with the other soloists will also go badly. You'll see that Saint-Saëns will also be busy for that period! We should have thought about it earlier.

. . . Please tell Blanchi to send me the Strauss and Franck scores as soon as they arrive. . . . Sonzogno has not yet replied. Fontana will be better able to inform you about [?]; for my part you can send him to hell with a kick in the tail, that scoundrel! . . .'[5]

The terms Toscanini had insisted upon in his Scala contract were the right to choose the operas, the singers, the orchestral players and the scenographers, to determine the number of rehearsals, and to set the date of each production according to the progress of the preparations. In short, he was to be artistic director.

Another letter to Depanis (14 August) deals at length with the hiring of orchestra musicians and with mountaineering conquests, and then continues:

'I'm really leaving Ceresole unwillingly! If I had at least been able to reach the top of the Paradiso! I had to give up the Levanna because my wife wouldn't hear of letting me go, since it is a more difficult ascent... Enough. The day after tomorrow I'll take up the baton again instead of the alpenstok [sic], to climb the less dangerous mountains of eighth-notes and sixteenth-notes. . . . I've gained weight. I always have a musician's appetite. . . .'[6]

Back in Turin Toscanini received frequent visits and letters from his new Scala colleagues. Gatti-Casazza wrote in his memoirs:

'With Toscanini, Boito and I discussed matters along general lines. . . . We decided to favour as much as possible the youthful element. At any rate, this was more in keeping with the youthfulness of Toscanini and myself. . . . In little more than a month, the personnel of the various departments—administrative, scenic, costuming, orchestra, chorus, ballet school—all these were chosen and reorganized. During the same period we mustered our company of singers.'[7]

Along with Bolzoni, Martucci and others, Toscanini judged a composition competition in Turin early in October, and on the last day of that month he conducted the last concert (attended by the Queen) in the enormous series. Very soon afterwards, he and his young family left for Milan. 'Other cities envied our having Toscanini,' wrote Depanis years later, 'and Milan was able to attract him into the Scala orbit. It was predestined that that happen: La Scala was worthy of Toscanini and Toscanini was worthy of La Scala. But it was a grave loss for Turin . . .'[8]

After a month of rehearsals the Scala season opened on 26 December with Wagner's *Die Meistersinger*. The work had been presented before in Italy with substantial cuts; this was the first time it was being heard nearly in its entirety. The cast included Antonio Scotti (Sachs), Emilio De Marchi (Walter) and Angelica Pandolfini (Eva). Chorus master was Aristide Venturi—the same man who had been chorus master of the Rossi company in Rio. The critics generally complained of the opera's length but were satisfied with the production:

'Toscanini was victorious . . . Rarely have I had the fortune of hearing a mass of instruments so together and so in tune. . . . The interpretation was truly outstanding: apart from his memory, which is simply marvellous, he attended to every detail with maximum precision, and he knew how to obtain the desired effect in the climactic moments without ever exaggerating. . . . He showed himself to be an extremely fine artist. [Annibale Ponchielli, *Sera*, 27 December.]'

'It was a performance of the highest order, such as we have not been able to enjoy in Vienna, Berlin or Paris, and not even at Bayreuth, the Wagnerian temple. The orchestra was stupendous, well balanced, directed with admirable sureness by Maestro Toscanini . . . [Giulio Ricordi, *Gazzetta musicale di Milano*, 29 December.]'

'The outcome of *Meistersinger* was very good and the performance—especially by the orchestra—very praiseworthy. [At the end] there was a great shout for Maestro Toscanini, enlightened, serious, calm and energetic conductor. Yesterday evening's main triumph was his. [Romeo Carugati, *Lombardia*, 26–7 December.]'

Among the innovations which Toscanini had insisted upon were a new curtain which opened laterally, like the one at Bayreuth, instead of vertically, so that the audience did not first see the singers' feet, then their knees, then their waists, etc. He also ruled that women sitting on the ground floor should not be allowed to wear hats, and that there should be darkness in the house during performances.

If *Meistersinger* was a triumph, the next production—*Norma*—was a nightmare. Toscanini had searched long and hard for a soprano who he believed would be capable of bringing off the taxing lead rôle successfully. He finally hired Ines De Frate and the rehearsals went forward. That he anticipated no major disasters can be discerned from the tone of this letter to Piontelli—undated, but obviously from the first days of January 1899:

'. . . Cosentino [a singer represented by Piontelli] has arrived and has already rehearsed with piano. This evening he will rehearse with the orchestra. I didn't know that Brogi [another singer] gets 1500 per performance—you who knew it did badly by not asking more for Cosentino. You must realize that I was forced by Gatti-Cassaccio's* pressures to send my first telegram! Yesterday evening, however, after I received your wire informing me of Brogi's fee, I let him hear a few words with pepper added and told him that *Piontelli had done badly by not asking 2000 per performance* and that it bothered me to have allowed him to wire you in my name!

Enough. Norma opens Wednesday—Thursday we'll know the result—The public is so stupid that I don't know whether I should hope or despair.

* A comical and not exactly kind play on Gatti-Casazza's name. *Cassa* means case or chest or even cash register—which may well be the sense intended here. The suffix *accio* gives a word a derogatory and diminutive quality.

Goodbye, dear friend; come to Milan soon to hear Meistersinger—you'll see that you'll like it, except for its length . . .'[9]

At the *Norma* dress rehearsal, those in attendance seemed to feel that all was going well; but at the end of the first act Toscanini remained standing silently on the podium. Old Duke Guido came up to him and asked if there was something wrong. Toscanini replied that the whole production was wrong. He was very sorry, but it would have to be cancelled.

Cancelling a production at the dress rehearsal, after vast expenditures of time and other resources on the part of hundreds of people, is something one does not often read about in operatic annals. Toscanini had decided, however, that De Frate was good in the lyrical parts but simply inadequate in the more dramatic passages. Could he not have determined that during the earlier stages of preparation? Could he not have found another Norma? There is no answer to the first question because we do not know what went on at the rehearsals or how mentally at odds with himself Toscanini was from the outset, how hard he may have tried to compromise with himself in order not to bring grief and embarrassment to a singer who was not an ungifted artist. The answer to the second question is that one is not likely, a few days before the first performance, to find a soprano capable of singing Norma decently.

Toscanini knew very well that he had done something highly questionable that would put his competence in doubt and his position in jeopardy, since it would play directly into the hands of those who had opposed his appointment. But he refused to back down, despite the pleas and protests of Boito, Gatti-Casazza, the Duke and Giulio Ricordi. It was finally suggested that an assistant conductor replace Toscanini; but he replied that the quality of every aspect of the production was his responsibility, according to the terms of his contract, and he could not allow a production to go before the public if he deemed it unworthy. No *Norma*.

The extent to which Toscanini was vilified for this decision can be seen in an article which appeared on 17 January 1899 in a libellous but popular (in theatrical circles) one-man newspaper called *Il corno* (*The Horn*), of no fixed address, written by a certain Pompeo Ferrari:

Bluebeard's Gallantries

'. . . Who could not have foreseen that La Scala would be made the laughing-stock of Art under the sceptre of that little king who answers to the name of Maestro Toscanini?—a man who has built his fame upon the absolute ignor-ance of every form of politeness, upon the dominance that an unconscientious, overbearing person can have over an artistic organization which, by its own responsibility, has been made childishly fearful and submissive? We said it repeatedly: if La Scala is really to be saved, full powers must not be given to this abortion of Luciferian arrogance who was incautiously chosen to direct its artistic destiny. Toscanini, like any other conductor, has to be under contract; and as such, if he ruins things by his extravagant demands, he must still be subject to dismissal by the company. . . . Toscanini is the absolute financial and artistic ruin of La Scala . . .

As the first edict of his reign as czar, Toscanini gets rid of seven *comprimari* [singers of secondary rôles] who had already drawn their quarterly pay. No little financial damage, and inexplicable artistic nastiness. Seven artists who have to fight for a living—ruined; a slap at the union of theatrical agents, thus declared incapable even of finding a *comprimario*. [Note: These scandal-mongering journals were, of course, financed by singers and agents who used them for publicity purposes.]

. . . Toscanini, the famous Bluebeard, only knows how to conduct operas which are unknown to others—such as *Die Meistersinger*—to prove his superiority—and to cause repertory operas like *Norma* to fail—so as not to reveal his own lack of knowledge . . .' [Note: Toscanini had conducted *Norma* in Palermo in 1893 and in Turin only a few months before the Scala misfortune.]

Many years later Paul Stefan heard Toscanini say, in response to someone who had praised *Norma*: 'Have you ever heard this opera? I have never heard it the way it must really be given. I tried to perform it but I didn't succeed. And so I had to give up...'[10]

He found himself embroiled in fresh difficulties over the season's next opera, Mascagni's new *Iris*. Some weeks earlier he had gone to Rome to hear the première, which had been a near disaster. The composer himself had conducted, and had allowed the singers to persuade him to make all sorts of transpositions, rhythmic changes, and the like, to 'facilitate' the production. Afterwards, of course, Mascagni blamed the failure on the singers and, meeting Toscanini in a café the next day, told him that at La Scala he must forbid them 'to tear the music to shreds, and make them perform it as we ["we" composers] have written it'. Toscanini replied: 'My dear Maestro, how can you expect me to be firm with these artists? The same ones whom you are now condemning will also be singing at La Scala and will be able to argue that they have performed the opera in this way and with this freedom under your direction.'[11] Mascagni had no valid excuse; but eventually the two musicians hit on the idea of having the composer send a letter to the conductor wherein Toscanini would be 'constrained' to make the singers perform the music as written. Ricordi found out and asked that the letter be addressed to him so that it could be used for other productions as well. This was done, and the rehearsals began. But Toscanini and Ricordi, aware of Mascagni's unpredictable temperament, had decided upon another ruling as well. On 16 January Mascagni wrote to Toscanini:

'. . . The "absolute ban" imposed upon me by Signor Commendatore Ricordi, forbidding my coming to Milan for the rehearsals and first perform-

ances, has justifiably made me a bit suspicious. If you, my dear Toscanini, still
have the same feelings which you so kindly expressed to me in Rome, you
ought to show me the courtesy of informing me on this matter, and perhaps of
letting me know in time to take a little trip to Milan and attend (absolutely
incognito) the dress rehearsal.

From third persons (since the Ricordi Company tell me nothing), I learn
that you are putting your whole soul into the preparations and conducting of
Iris. This is a great comfort to me. I thank you with all my heart . . .'[12]

Iris opened three days later; but while the performance was judged 'ideal',
'superb', 'marvellous' and 'greatly superior to the composer's own version'—thus
helping to mitigate the effects of the *Norma* scandal—the opera itself was
received rather coldly. This, of course, was a double affront to Mascagni: not
only was his work unsuccessful, but his conducting was also described as inferior
to Toscanini's. 'Concerning the outcome of *Iris* in Milan,' the furious composer
wrote to Ricordi on 26 January, 'I am very satisfied, since, truly, everything was
done to cause a shipwreck. . . . I alone knew how *Iris* should be done; but by
some absurd quirk nobody thought that the author's ideas should and must be
preferred. Patience!' The final crazy turnaround in the episode came only five
days later, when Mascagni finally attended a performance of the Scala *Iris*. By
then the public and critics had warmed somewhat to the opera, and the *Gazzetta
musicale* reported that Mascagni, 'as a result of the audience's insistent applause
and the wishes of his valiant interpreters, presented himself, albeit reluctantly,
before the curtain . . . and thus, together with the artists and Maestro Toscanini,
was called out twice after the first act, three times after the second, and twice
after the third.'

Meyerbeer's *Huguenots*, the next opera, did not provide any new cataclysms
within La Scala; but it was not well received by the critics, who almost unani-
mously claimed that the traditional cuts should have been made, that the singers,
chorus and orchestra all seemed somewhat insecure in places, and that certain
tempi were too fast. This time Toscanini decided that the critics were at least
partly right; and he decided to perform the opera without the fifth act, as was
commonly done.

Unfortunately, another difficult situation was rapidly materializing which was
to torment Toscanini for years to come. His innovations regarding repertoire
and production procedures were leading him to a direct confrontation with
Giulio Ricordi, who was no mean adversary. The Ricordi Company had been
founded nearly a century earlier and was one of the largest and wealthiest music
publishing firms in the world. Signor Giulio had inherited power from his father
and grandfather; he was accustomed to being listened to and obeyed by composers, impresarios, performers and everyone else in the operatic world. Toscanini was a terrible irritant to him not only because they disagreed about many

things, but because the conductor did not know how to pretend to agree, how to smile and smooth things over. It seemed to Signor Giulio that Toscanini, who was younger than the publisher's own son, Tito, was determined to show all and sundry how operas should be performed; and if the Ricordis and others didn't approve, he just shrugged and continued fixedly along his path. Signor Giulio also considered Toscanini an unregenerate Wagnerite; and although Ricordi had purchased the Italian rights to Wagner's works from Giovannina Lucca, he still looked upon the German composer as a latter-day Attila, to be kept at bay at any cost.

There was another aspect to the problem as well. Signor Giulio was an amateur composer who wrote pieces with titles like *The Stolen Bucket* and *Pulcinella in Love* under the pseudonym of J. Burgmein. Amateurs generally have a hard time getting their music played, but this obviously was not the case with Burgmein/Ricordi. He had written to Toscanini the previous autumn, suggesting that the conductor include *Pulcinella* on one of his Turin concerts. Had Toscanini replied negatively, the situation would have been difficult enough; but he did not reply at all. Eventually the alarmed Depanis had answered for him; but Ricordi knew what had happened, and it did not predispose him in Toscanini's favour.

Before long, the powerful *Gazzetta musicale di Milano*, which was published and partly written by Signor Giulio, began to open fire on Toscanini. This did not help the young man's reputation but it strengthened his determination. Much sadder is the fact that Ricordi, one of the few people who had direct and constant access to Verdi, partly poisoned the composer's opinion of Toscanini by sending him very one-sided opinions of the reforms being carried out at La Scala. This part of Verdi's correspondence was not published in Toscanini's lifetime. Had he seen it, it would have wounded him deeply to learn of the old man's disappointment in him.

'Genoa, 11 February 1899. . . . I heard news of the *Huguenots* at La Scala. It is a result which allows one to foresee a considerable crescendo. I was surprised, however, by the comments made about the chorus, and even more by those regarding the orchestra! The devil! You can't believe in anything anymore; but it's good to see clearly how things stand.[13]

27 February. . . . About La Scala, I can only repeat my old ideas to you, simple ideas, but perhaps useful and, I believe, possible, given the current circumstances. If Toscanini is not capable, the others are even less so. Soon comes the *Falstaff* revival. Everything is against it. Falstaff [Scotti] will be good (maybe!) but not Alice [Pandolfini] . . . And notice that the protagonist of *Falstaff* is not Falstaff but Alice. What am I going around saying? Waste of time! Forget that I said it and *addio* . . .[14]

Toscanini was in the process of achieving some of the things Verdi had struggled much of his life to achieve and had then given up. Years earlier the composer had written to the very same Giulio Ricordi:

'. . . I want one single creator, and I shall be happy if [musicians] perform simply and exactly what is written. I often read in the papers about *effects unimagined by the composer*; but I, for my part, have never found such things . . .'[15]

And two years after the première of *Otello* Verdi wrote thus to Ricordi:

'Regarding the music, it should not be necessary to make concessions, either in the instrumentation or in the tempi . . . There is *only one* interpretation of a work of art and there must be *only one* . . . The performance [at the première] was never good, or at least the interpretation was not according to my ideas. Afterwards I regretted, and I still regret, not having been more severe and exacting in principle.'[16]

This concept of 'only one' interpretation does not mean that a performer will or even ought to play a piece the same way every time. On the contrary, it means that a serious musician will constantly be seeking to come closer to a full understanding and to a totally effective execution of any given work.

After Toscanini's first *Falstaff* at La Scala (11 March 1899) Boito wired an enthusiastic report to Verdi. The old man wrote back (12 March): 'Thank you for the telegram and I congratulate the valiant performers.' And to Toscanini he wired, 'Thanks, thanks, thanks.' But Ricordi soon sent Verdi a copy of his own review which contained remarks like:

'It is undeniable that last Saturday's interpretation was characterized by rigidity, thus cancelling a large part of the effects admired before in the same theatre in the same opera . . . We see a serious danger for Italian art . . .'[17]

Verdi responded (18 March):

'I read your vigorous and very nice article (*Falstaff*). If things are as you say, it is better to return to the modest conductors of earlier times (and anyway there were Rolla, Festa, De Giovanni, etc.). When I began scandalizing the musical world with my sins, there was the calamity of the "rondos" of the *prima donnas*; today there is the tyranny of the conductors! Bad, bad! But the first is less bad!!'[18]

Of course, Verdi did not see an article by Enrico Carozzi in the *Gazzetta teatrale italiana* which appeared after the *Falstaff* and which stated that 'one could almost say, reading between the lines of certain reviews, that a crusade is under way against Toscanini, who is under contract for three years at La Scala'. One critic who agreed with Ricordi (Colombani in the *Corriere della sera*) did mention, in fairness, that the performance 'was approved by the one who could express the composer's intentions better than anyone else [Boito]'.

Massenet's *Le Roi de Lahore* and Rossini's *William Tell* ended the Scala season —the former received apathetically and the latter enthusiastically, even by Ricordi. In all, there had been fifty-three performances of six operas. The overall attitude towards the new conductor was one of perplexity: his talents were astonishing but his ideas were often shocking.

A series of five concerts followed the opera season; on the first of these Milan heard three of Verdi's Sacred Pieces for the first time. Verdi had been opposed to Boito's idea of having the works given at La Scala,

'... first of all because I don't believe they will have any effect there ...; secondly because my name is too old and boring! Even I'm bored when I have to name myself. Add to this the critics' observations! It's true that I don't have to read them ...'[19]

After the performance of *William Tell* he had written Boito:

'From you, from others, and even from the papers I have learned of Tamagno's great success in *William Tell*. I am happy for the dignity of the theatre. And now?—There is only one reasonable thing remaining to be done: *Close the Theatre immediately!*'[20]

But eventually he gave in and Boito wrote him:

'The performance in the hands of Toscanini and Venturi, who learned the interpretation from you and who made such a striking impression in Turin, could only be outstanding, *and was outstanding* ...'[21]

An oratorio, *The Resurrection of Lazarus*, by a then popular composer-priest named Lorenzo Perosi, was also played on the series as were works by Schumann, Schubert, Brahms, Berlioz, Franck, Wagner *et al*. The last concert took place on 11 May.

Toscanini had put himself in the hands of a Viennese concert agent at that time in the hopes of getting a guest engagement with the Vienna Philharmonic. (I have not come across any other example of his having arranged or sought to arrange engagements through an agent during his entire career!) The agent, a certain M. Täncer, described 'Signor Artur Toscanini' as 'unusually brilliant, not only in the direction of operas, but also ... in symphonic works'. In short, he is described just as every client is described by every agent. The Philharmonic administration made this notation on the letter: 'Brought to our attention 20 May 99.'[22] Toscanini first conducted the Vienna Philharmonic thirty-four years later.

Accompanied by Gatti-Casazza, Toscanini made his first trip to Germany in July, in order to attend the Bayreuth festival. He heard the entire *Ring* conducted by Siegfried Wagner, *Meistersinger* with Hans Richter and *Parsifal* with Franz von Fischer. *Parsifal* at that time was played only in Bayreuth and nowhere else; Toscanini found the work overwhelming, the performance less so. He sent Polo a postcard (28 July) which shows Wagner's grave; next to it Toscanini wrote: 'Here is the tomb of the greatest composer of the century!'[23]

The 1899–1900 Scala season was somewhat calmer but certainly no less demanding than its predecessor. Toscanini had decided that there should be in effect two opening productions, and he chose a pair of frighteningly difficult works. On 26 December he directed the first Italian production of *Siegfried*, which was very warmly received, with Giuseppe Borgatti in the title rôle; and the next night he led a revival of *Otello* which included the opera's original protagonist, Tamagno, and Emma Carelli as Desdemona. Segre reports:

> During the rehearsals of *Otello* an argument broke out between Tamagno and Toscanini, reminiscent of the one Toscanini had had with Pini-Corsi five years before. Tamagno insisted that he was singing a certain passage in the last act the way Verdi had taught him when directing the rehearsals for the world première . . . Toscanini pointed out that he was also present at those rehearsals as second cellist and that he was certain that *his* tempi were the ones Verdi had requested and that they were written in the score. Faced with Tamagno's stubbornness, Toscanini . . . invited the singer to come and ask Verdi personally to decide the dispute. They went to the composer's residence and Verdi congratulated Toscanini for the remarkable accuracy of his memory. To this, Tamagno grumbled that composers and conductors were always changing their minds.'[24]

Several critics complained that Tamagno was still greatly exaggerating the rôle during the performance. Enrico Carozzi wrote: 'I was assured last night that at the rehearsals Maestro Toscanini pointed out to the great singer the uselessness of these outbursts: why, then, did he persist with them?' Apart from that, the success was 'triumphal' (Carlo D'Ormeville in the *Gazzetta dei teatri*). 'After the fourth act, an extraordinary ovation. And it was only just.'

Lohengrin next—lauded, as usual, by the Wagnerites and barely tolerated by the unconverted, like D'Ormeville:

> 'Chorus and orchestra manoeuvred like German regiments on the field at Potsdam. A defile formed to perfection! Duke Visconti, who attended the review accompanied by Maestro Boito, his chief of staff, was highly satisfied. The burgrave-critics added the satisfaction of His Majesty to the order of the day.'[25]

During a rehearsal of *Lohengrin* on 16 January someone rushed in to tell Toscanini that Carla had just given birth to a girl. The orchestra congratulated him; he tried to continue rehearsing, but couldn't keep his mind on what he was doing. Finally he dismissed the orchestra and ran off to see his wife and daughter, who was given the name Wally, again in tribute to Catalani's memory.

Following the world première of Cesare Galeotti's *Anton* came the Milanese première of Puccini's *Tosca* (17 March), which had first been presented in Rome two months earlier. The composer and conductor had already agreed on the cast in October (Darclée—Tosca, Borgatti—Cavaradossi, Giraldoni—Scarpia). In a letter to his friend Primo Levi three days before the opening, Puccini wrote:

> 'All's well at La Scala. The performance will be *superb*. Toscanini, the sets, the chorus, the atmosphere—outstanding; and the singers come off better in this blessed theatre than in other theatres. Giraldoni, for instance, is much more effective vocally here—much more!'[26]

And to the same friend on 3 April:

> 'I leave for Torre del Lago tomorrow. *Tosca* has conquered the general affections here, filling the theatre every evening ... The performance has been excellent because of Toscanini and a few others, especially Giraldoni ...'[27]

The season ended with the first Italian production of Tchaikovsky's *Eugene Onegin*, which was listened to with mild interest and was given only three performances. 'The orchestra was excellent, directed conscientiously and with love by Toscanini who, after the first and third acts, was called on to the stage with the singers' (*Lombardia*, 8 April). In all, there were fifty-eight performances of six operas that season.

There was a series of four concerts in the spring; and during the same period Toscanini took the orchestra on a tour which included Parma (the first of his very few professional appearances in his home town) and seven other northern Italian cities.

Among La Scala's board members was Giuseppe Gallignani, director of the Milan Conservatory, a musician held in high esteem by Verdi himself. Gallignani, like his friend Boito, was a great admirer of Toscanini. At the end of the conductor's first Scala season Gallignani had persuaded him to sit on the examining committee for composition students at the Conservatory. The next year Toscanini went further and volunteered to participate in two concerts at the end of the school year. Thus, on 21 and 28 June he conducted a student orchestra, enlarged by a few professionals (mainly graduates of the Conservatory), in compositions by students Arrigo Pedrollo and Italo Montemezzi, as well as smaller pieces by other composers.

While planning and studying for his third Scala season Toscanini agreed to direct the world première of Leoncavallo's now forgotten *Zazà* at Milan's Teatro Lirico on 10 November 1900. This temporarily restored him to the good graces of Leoncavallo and his publisher Sonzogno, after the treasonous position he had

taken in the 'Battle of the Two *Bohèmes*'. The production was a success; but for
Toscanini the engagement was important in another way.

The opera's protagonist was soprano Rosina Storchio. Born in Mantua, she
studied at the Milan Conservatory, which she left in 1890, and débuted as
Micaela in *Carmen* two years later; at the time of *Zazà* she was twenty-eight and
singing at the most important Italian opera houses. Contemporary photographs
show her as slender and beautiful, and it is said that she was an extraordinarily
sensitive and intelligent musician. During a rehearsal of the third act of *Zazà*
Toscanini exclaimed: '*This* is an artist!'—a rare compliment from him. They fell
in love; and although the details of their relationship are still unclear today and
may always remain so, it is known that they had a child, a boy named Giovannino,
who was born in March 1903. He was palsied and died at the age of sixteen.
Storchio and Toscanini remained lovers for several years; professionally, they
appeared together until 1915. She ended her career in 1923 and eventually died
in obscurity after a lengthy and paralysing illness. Their relationship had a
disastrous effect on Storchio's life, and it would not leave Toscanini unscarred.

Despite his heavy work schedule and his affair with Storchio, he spent much
time with his young family. Wally recalled:

'He very much enjoyed playing with us. Mamma said that when he was home
he took care of the babies himself. He bathed us, swaddled us and gave us our
pabulum. He passed hour after hour reading pediatric and child care books. I
remember him as a very affectionate father. When he came home he was
greeted with shouts of joy. . . . When we were small he never shouted at us. We
knew what he expected of us. There was a law which had to be observed by
everyone in our house. Papà told Mamma what he wanted of us and she passed
it on. We always obeyed because we adored him. This . . . lasted until he left
for America [i.e. for New York in 1908]. From that time on nearly his entire
life was absorbed by his artistic activity and he no longer had much time for us.
From then on we were raised by a nursemaid, Nena Rama, who became our
second mother. She always lived with our family and she is entombed next to
Papà and Mamma.'[28]

Toscanini had planned to open his third season, like the first two, with
Wagner—*Tristan*, this time; but Borgatti, the tenor, was taken ill and *Tristan* was
replaced by *Bohème*, which was to have been the second production. In the rôle
of Rodolfo was a twenty-seven-year-old Neapolitan tenor named Enrico Caruso,
who was making his Scala début. He was also suffering from fever, exhaustion
and acute nervousness, and had fought with Toscanini over whether to sing half-
voice or full-voice during the dress rehearsal. (Toscanini insisted that singers sing
full-voice at all rehearsals; in those days, when they could not travel fast enough
to take on the excessive number of engagements they often do today, this require-
ment was not deleterious to their vocal apparatus.) The performance failed and

Emma Carelli, the Mimì, wrote that 'the curtain fell in deathly silence after each act'. Most of the critics were understanding and lauded the excellent orchestral playing, but Giulio Ricordi took the opportunity to ride roughshod over Toscanini. The day after the opening Puccini sent a note to the conductor:

'This evening I'm going to breathe better air; I'm going into the country for two or three days. Last night, at the beginning of the last act, I left and didn't greet you as I would have wished. Excuse me, I was too saddened . . . For the second performance, please remember especially Carelli, her costume and make-up. Tell her to try to act the character a little . . . and not to slow down her part so "tiredly". I can only thank you for all the care you've taken with my opera . . .'[29]

Successive performances went much better.

With Borgatti recovered, *Tristan* opened on 29 December and was an extraordinary success. (Amelia Pinto sang Isolde.) The composer's son, Siegfried, attended the performance of 12 January 1901 and was astounded by the level of excellence. He did not hesitate to express his admiration to Toscanini, who must have been very gratified. At Bayreuth in 1899 Toscanini had not wanted to meet Cosima Wagner 'because she was like a queen';[30] nevertheless, when Siegfried told his mother about the Scala *Tristan*, she sent a grateful letter (18 January) to the conductor:

'My son has given me an account of the performance of *Tristan* which he attended in Milan, and he has told me so many good things about it that I take upon myself the duty of expressing to you the contentment I feel in knowing that a work of such great difficulty has been performed with care on a foreign stage.

My son stressed the meticulous zeal which you brought to the orchestral preparations and the excellent result obtained by this zeal, along with your ability as conductor. He also told me that the singers knew their rôles perfectly and delivered them with passion and enthusiasm.

Lastly, he told me with great satisfaction about the sets owing to the talent of Mr. Fortuny [Italo-Spanish scenographer]. And—to crown it all—he praised the attention of those gathered, the intelligent liveliness of the audience.

All these indications of your respect towards and instinct for the incomparable work to which you have dedicated yourself with so much ardour made my son very happy to have been a witness, and at a distance I join in his satisfaction.'[31]

News of the production reached America as well. On 10 February the *New York Times* reported:

'At La Scala, Toscanini has arranged a plan for lighting by which all the light can be thrown from one side of the stage, and yet with sufficient brilliancy given to prevent too heavy shadows. When this plan was put into operation at the ... production of *Tristan und Isolde* ... the German managers all sent representatives to observe its workings. It must have been very successful. Siegfried Wagner, who was present, ... told Toscanini that the production excelled even those of Munich and Berlin.'

Besides the new lighting system, another innovation Toscanini realized around this time was the removal of the traditional post-opera ballet on nights when works of Wagner or other long operas were performed—a tradition which had bothered him since his days as an orchestra member. He did not have to conduct the ballets; but he felt that it was cruel to make the orchestra work to the point of exhaustion and detrimental to the effectiveness of both the opera and the ballet. Eventually ballet performances were given on separate evenings.

Mascagni's latest effort, *Le maschere*, was premièred in seven Italian cities simultaneously on 17 January—a typically circus-like publicity venture on the part of this composer whom one critic called 'the travelling salesman of his art'. Six of the seven productions were disasters, including Milan's. In fact, there was a repetition of the *Iris* situation, except worse: Toscanini and the cast were praised and Mascagni and his opera were damned. This time Mascagni could not say that Toscanini had ruined everything, because he had himself attended some of the rehearsals and had stated immediately afterwards: 'I found in Toscanini an unsurpassable conductor and interpreter, and the singers [Caruso, Carelli, *et al.*] were worthy of this champion.'[32] D'Ormeville, in the *Gazzetta dei teatri*, lauded Toscanini and added: 'He was unable to save *Le maschere*; but not even the Lord in his infinite power could have done so ...'

Two or three days after the première Toscanini called on Verdi, who was spending part of the winter at the Hotel Milan, up the street from La Scala. The composer, now eighty-seven, had heard about *Le maschere* and asked how Mascagni had treated the rôle of Tartaglia, a stutterer. 'He has him sing stuttering, like this,' replied Toscanini, singing a phrase or two. Verdi observed that most stutterers do not stutter when they sing. When Toscanini told him that the best-liked part had been the pavane in the second act, Verdi asked feebly, 'What is a pavane?' Then, getting a grip on himself, he said, 'Oh yes, now I understand.' Toscanini left, saddened at seeing the tough old man beginning to decline. That visit took place on 19 or 20 January. On the 22nd Verdi suffered a cerebral hemorrhage and died five days later.

La Scala closed its doors as a sign of mourning, and on 1 February Toscanini conducted a memorial programme of excerpts from seven Verdi operas, with ten soloists including tenors Caruso, Borgatti and Tamagno. The composer had left instructions forbidding any public funeral, and these wishes were respected; but a month later, when the bodies of Verdi and his wife were transferred from Milan's Cimitero Monumentale to a special tomb in the rest home for aged musicians which he had had built at Piazza Buonarroti, there was an enormous show of love and grief by a large portion of the city's population plus visitors from all over Italy and abroad who followed the procession. From a platform in front of the cemetery Toscanini conducted an orchestra and 800-voice chorus in *Va pensiero sull'ali dorate* from *Nabucco*; and this was repeated after the evening's performance at La Scala.

The fourth opera of the season was Goldmark's *The Queen of Sheba*, a curiosity which was followed by Donizetti's *L'elisir d'amore*.

'Toscanini prepared and conducted this love elixir with the same conscientiousness with which he had revealed that other one. [*Tristan*, of course.] In the orchestra, everything was neat, clear, clean; there was never any lack of spirit, nor of honest and clear-headed moderation in the effects. [Gustavo Macchi, *Tempo*, 18 February.]'

Elisir was Caruso's first great triumph at La Scala. Gatti-Casazza says that before going out for a curtain call with the cast, Toscanini embraced the tenor and said to Gatti: 'By God, if this tenor continues to sing like this, he'll have the whole world talking about him!'[33] Years later Toscanini told Haggin:

'I write to Boito: "You must come to La Scala to hear *Elisir d'amore* with young tenor who sing like angel." But in 1901 is already change; and in New York—! I tell him: "Yes, you make much money—but no! *no! NO!!*"'[34]

Singing alongside Caruso in the next production—Boito's *Mefistofele*—was the young Russian basso, Feodor Chaliapin, making his Scala début. He left an interesting account of his first meeting with Toscanini in his autobiography (co-written by Maxim Gorky):

'The conductor looked quite ferocious to me. A man of few words, unsmiling, he corrected the singers harshly, and spared nobody. Here was a man who really knew his job, and one who would brook no contradiction. I remember his turning to me in the middle of [a piano] rehearsal, and asking in rasping tones if I intended to sing the opera as I was singing it then [half-voice]. "No. Certainly not," I said, embarrassed. "Well," he replied, "I have not had the honour of going to Russia and hearing you there. Thus I don't know your voice. Please be good enough to sing as you intend to do at the performance."

I saw that he was right, and I sang in full voice. Often he would interrupt the other singers, offering advice, but he never said a word to me. I didn't know how to take this, and it left me with a feeling of uncertainty.

Again the next day there was a rehearsal . . . [which] began with the Prologue. I gave it full voice, and when I had finished Toscanini paused for a moment, his hands lying on the piano keys, inclined his head a little, and uttered one single word in a very hoarse voice, "Bravo." It was quite

unexpected ... Elated by this success, I sang with tremendous enthusiasm,
but Toscanini never uttered another word. ...

At the staging rehearsals ... Toscanini would come and watch me, order me
to stand this way, that way, the other, sit like this, like that, walk that way, not
this way. He would wind one of my legs round the other corkscrew-fashion, or
make me fold my arms à la Napoleon. In fact what I was being instructed in was
the technique of provincial tragedians, something with which I was already too
well acquainted. If I asked him why he found this or that pose necessary, he
replied with the utmost confidence: "Perchè questa è una vera posa diabolica"
(because this is a truly diabolic pose). ...'[35]

Chaliapin says that he was able to convince Toscanini to let him try acting the
part as he saw it, and that Toscanini was convinced by his conception of it.

The production was another great success—something which could not be said
of the season's next and last opera, *Messalina* by Isidore De Lara. This work had
been performed in Monte Carlo two years earlier. Tamagno was in the cast; and
Toscanini later told Haggin:

'To get Tamagno ... we must take Calvé ... When she sing this opera for
me composer play piano; and I ask him: "You are satisfied?" He say: "Yes,
I am satisfied." Calvé tell me when I may come to hotel for rehearsal; and
I tell her we make rehearsal in theatre. She leave the same day'; and he
chuckled.[36]

The public reacted violently to *Messalina* and the opera received only one
performance. The critic for the journal *Trovatore* wrote:

'The orchestra was conducted by Toscanini in the usual way, that is, stupen-
dously. Too bad that so much ability and so much intelligence were in large
part wasted.'

Toscanini had decided not to conduct a concert series following the opera
season in 1901. Instead, he had accepted an invitation to spend his summer conducting Buenos Aires' winter season at the Teatro de la Ópera. It is true that
Toscanini was a work maniac by nature; but it must also be pointed out that his
Scala salary was rather modest—about 12,000 lire per season (five months)—
whereas many singers earned that much in two weeks. He was the head of a
growing family—Carla was expecting a third child (another son, Giorgio, was
born in September)—and the Argentinians were offering him the equivalent of
10,000 lire per month for three months.

Some of the best singers from La Scala—Caruso, Darclée, Borgatti and
others—had been contracted along with him, and they all embarked together in
mid-April. It was Toscanini's first ocean voyage since the Brazilian adventure
fifteen years earlier, and he enjoyed it very much. The season opened on 19 May

with *Tosca* and continued with *Tannhäuser*, *Samson and Delilah*, *The Queen of Sheba*, *Aida*, *Rigoletto*, Franchetti's *Asrael*,* *L'elisir d'amore*, *Otello*, *Lohengrin* (with Caruso!), *Iris*, *Traviata*, *Tristan*,* *Colombo* and *Medio Evo latino** by Ettore Panizza, a young Italo-Argentinian musician who would later be Toscanini's devoted collaborator at La Scala.

Toscanini returned to Milan in mid-September and immediately began preparing for his fourth Scala season. (Both he and Gatti-Casazza had had their contracts renewed.) As has always been the case with opera companies everywhere, there were 'new' financial difficulties. This time La Scala's solution was to supplant a few insolvent noblemen on the board of governors with some wealthy industrialists.

In November Toscanini conducted the première of Perosi's oratorio *Mosè* at the church of Santa Maria della Pace; a month later the opera season opened with *Die Walküre*, which the critics praised while again lamenting the conductor's stubbornness in not making big cuts. This was followed in January by Donizetti's *Linda di Chamounix*, Humperdinck's *Hänsel and Gretel* and, on the first anniversary of the composer's death (27 January), the Verdi *Requiem*. Toscanini was confronting this score for the first time. The critics were ecstatic and the public beside itself. At the end of the *Dies irae*, the audience rose to its feet shouting 'Toscanini!' and applauding and cheering madly. All this excitement was only a foretaste, however, of what would happen two weeks later.

It was mentioned earlier that while Toscanini was born to the music of Verdi, the real love of his youth was Wagner. We not only have his words on the subject (the card he sent Polo from Bayreuth); we also have the record of his first three-year term as musical director of Italy's greatest lyric theatre. He had decided to begin each of those seasons with Wagner and had led a fourth Wagner opera as well. During the same period he had conducted only two Verdi operas—and which ones? *Otello* and *Falstaff*—precisely those works which do not belong to the mainstream, to the 'popular' Verdian repertoire, separated as they are from their older sisters by a large time-gap and by the radically different compositional procedures which had matured in their creator during that period. Of course Toscanini had conducted eight of the pre-*Otello* operas during his years of apprenticeship; but not one of them had so far appeared in his Scala repertoire —nor, for that matter, had he touched any of them during his three seasons at Turin's Regio.

His love of Wagner was certainly not the only factor contributing to this attitude. I think that more than anything else, Toscanini was undecided in his approach to these works. He had grown up hearing them performed in the 'traditional' way—with interpolated notes and cadential passages, illogical transpositions, and tempo fluctuations which went far beyond the bounds of inflection

* Argentine première.

or *rubato* into the realm of gross distortion. The victims hardest hit by these practices were the three operas which had come to form the core of the Italian operatic repertoire: *Rigoletto*, *Il trovatore* and *La traviata*. Every little provincial theatre in the country performed these works according to the local requirements —with or without certain instruments, with or without certain arias or ensembles, and so on. Expediency had become habit, habit custom and custom tradition— and not only in the provincial theatres. It took years for Toscanini to decide that the investigative method he applied to other music, the method of trying to find and play what was in the score instead of trying to adapt the score to his own or others' needs and preferences, was an equally just and logical process when applied to the more thickly encrusted Verdi works. That decision made, a huge amount of courage—not to mention determination and severity—was required to put these ideas into practice. By the time he planned his fourth Scala season he must have felt that he had enough support and good feeling behind him to be able to risk an experiment; and his choice fell upon what was then the most down-trodden and battle-weary work in the repertoire, *Il trovatore*.

When Giulio Ricordi heard of Toscanini's plan he made up his mind to prevent the production's taking place. While the attitude of most Milanese musicians and critics towards Toscanini had shifted from one of mistrust to admiration to enthusiasm, Ricordi's had hardened into one of implacable opposition. The idea that this insolent conductor, this importer of Ostrogoth culture, was now going to Wagnerize and 'metronomize' *Trovatore* was more than he could face. He informed the Scala directorate that the Ricordi Company would not permit them to schedule *Trovatore*.

It was not unusual for publishers temporarily to refuse performance rights for a new opera to a particular theatre, if they wished to have the work done first in a different theatre or city; but to refuse performing rights to *any* theatre, let alone La Scala, for *Trovatore*—which was about to celebrate its fiftieth birthday—was an unheard-of action and a terrible affront to Toscanini. A great furore ensued, and one can easily believe that Toscanini's way of trying to deal with the problem did not help matters. Sacchi says that Tito Ricordi was present one day during a heated argument between his father and Toscanini. At one point he interrupted and said: 'You're both impossible characters'; to which Toscanini replied: 'Yes, but I keep to my own affairs, while your father insists on sticking his nose into everyone's business!' Signor Giulio's action seems particularly ungenerous in view of the incalculable service Toscanini had done his company through his successful performances of works by many of Ricordi's younger composers. Toscanini refused to back down. Eventually, some well-timed diplomatic action on the part of Boito and others convinced Ricordi to relent, if ungraciously.

It is hard to imagine how Toscanini must have felt as he walked into the auditorium to begin the first performance. A good many people in the audience knew something of what had taken place. There were people twice his age present who had heard *Trovatore* done *à la mode* for decades; and there was a younger element made up of people who believed that the opera was simply not worth the effort, that it was hopelessly crude and bereft of musical value. Carlo D'Orme-ville, who had by no means been a convinced Toscaninian three years earlier, described the event in the *Gazzetta dei teatri*:

> 'When the curtain fell on the last scene of the last act, I saw Maestro Toscanini radiant, as I believe Napoleon III must have been after Solferino, when he sent that laconic and eloquent telegram to Paris: "Great battle, great victory." . . . And Maestro Toscanini was right to be proud of the triumphal success, because a large part of that success was due to him, personally.

> When one is able to imagine such a brilliant reconstruction of an opera used and abused in the most infamous circus tents that call themselves theatres; when one has the talent to create—permit me the word—that first scene in such a way as to give it tone and colour of absolute and surprising newness; when one arrives at bringing into relief every smallest detail, at animating every scene, at bringing life into every particular; when one obtains such an admir-able orchestral ensemble and such exquisite refinements from the chorus; when one suggests to the scenographers a real artistic revolution, indicating everything to them, explaining and almost guiding their pencils and brushes with a firm hand; when one understands that only an artist like Pogliaghi must be entrusted with the difficult task of banishing the customary old plumed helmets and dragging capes to construct a completely new and harmonic ensemble . . . —it must be said that if Fortune smiles on audacity, she has shown, perhaps for the first time, that she is not blind.

> Maestro Toscanini knew how to will and knew how to obtain all this; and I think—may the intransigent Wagnerites not curse me!—that much greater talent and much greater authority is needed to will and to obtain all this than to prepare and conduct a *Tristan* or a *Walküre*. I have had my say and I have let off steam. Who can say that I am wrong?'

Gustavo Macchi wrote in *Tempo*:

> 'Nor can one say that the success was owing to the tenor's high C or the bravura of individual artists. They were all excellent . . . , fused into a won-derful ensemble under the baton of Toscanini, the real soul of the whole success, faithful and simple before Verdi as he was before Wagner and Donizetti. Faced with this interpretation of *Trovatore*, no one will again dare to doubt Toscanini's worth, impartiality or artistic honesty.'

There was someone who continued to doubt: Giulio Ricordi, who wrote in the *Gazzetta musicale*:

> 'For many, Toscanini is now as infallible as the Pope! He is actually superior to Verdi himself, the author of *Trovatore*—who, however, never prepared and

conducted it like this! [Note: It is unlikely that Giulio Ricordi ever heard Verdi conduct *Trovatore*.] My goodness gracious! One mustn't criticize the King!'

Many Italian music historians consider that production to have initiated the 'Verdi Renaissance'—which might better be termed the 'Verdi Restoration'—in a double sense: the reconditioning-restoration of a work of art, and the restoration of Verdi to his rightful position.

The highly successful world première of Franchetti's *Germania* (11 March, with Caruso) followed *Trovatore*, and was succeeded in turn by a rarity, Weber's *Euryanthe* (with Storchio). This work, written in 1823, had never been heard in Italy. Toscanini prepared it lovingly; but while the overture was received well—too well, in fact—the rest of the performance was interrupted by vociferous members of the audience who did not feel that Weber was worthy of La Scala. All in all, the opening night was a turbulent affair:

'. . . After the overture the audience gave Toscanini an ovation and scream-ingly requested a *bis*. Perhaps it was too much to demand; but the custom of the *bis* is prevalent these days and the master in the theatre is the audience. Maestro Toscanini did not want to concede the repetition of the piece and went on. But the public in turn increased their shouts for the *bis*, so that the curtain, which had already been raised, had to be lowered again. The con-ductor wanted to win the struggle and again began the measures which announce the first chorus. New and louder shouts of *bis*. Then Toscanini, out of spite, put his baton down, jumped down from the podium and went out quickly, leaving the orchestra high and dry.

The inexplicable occurrence, the discourteous action towards the audience which had paid homage to the young conductor, aroused a great clamour . . . Was it possible that a serious person in such a high position . . . would throw down the gauntlet before an audience from which he had received nothing but signs of honour? Had Toscanini perhaps become an old-fashioned *prima donna*, overcome by hysteria, who, because of the "vapours", denied her talent to the public?

Mr. Barilli, in the name of the Scala administration, came out to announce that the conductor suddenly felt indisposed. This was received with a certain disbelief; but when it was learned that Toscanini is exhausted by the work of rehearsing and conducting the operas and is in a grievous state since his wife and children are ill, the nervous outburst was readily forgiven and as soon as he reappeared in the orchestra the audience welcomed him kindly. However—he had to repeat the overture, and it was the only *bis* of the evening.

This incident unfortunately upset those on stage and the interpretation as a whole suffered.'[37]

Euryanthe was performed only three times.

In April Toscanini conducted four concerts with the Scala Orchestra. *Till Eulenspiegel* figured on the opening programme and was such a success that it was repeated in its entirety and apparently willingly on Toscanini's part. (One wonders how the horn players felt about it.) The remaining programme centred around Beethoven's Ninth Symphony, which Toscanini was conducting for the first time, although he had directed the second and third movements during the marathon Turin series four years earlier. Amazingly, this was only the fourth performance of the work ever heard in Milan, and it was greeted with great enthusiasm. Nappi, critic for *Perseveranza*, gives us the distressing information that Toscanini eliminated the bass drum and cymbals (and triangle?) from the *Alla marcia* section of the last movement—something he never did again, so far as is known.

He went to Hamburg that spring to see Raoul Gunsbourg's staging and sets for Berlioz's *Damnation of Faust*, which he wanted to make use of for a Scala production the following season. After Hamburg Toscanini stopped in Berlin and in Eisenach, where he visited Bach's birthplace, and then returned to Italy to join his family at Tai di Cadore in the Dolomites. He wrote to Polo (26 June) requesting a copy of a guidebook for mountaineers, but dashed off to Germany again soon afterwards to attend the Bayreuth festival. He was particularly anxious to hear *Parsifal* again—in addition to the *Ring*—because he hoped to conduct part of it at La Scala during the coming season. From Bayreuth he returned to Tai for some climbing; but by the end of August he was in the town of Lugo in the Romagna region to prepare and conduct *Aida*. Then, after spending two weeks at Montecatini spa—I believe to try to alleviate the muscular pains, particularly in his right shoulder, which were to plague him intermittently all his life—he rejoined his family at Salò on Lake Garda. With them he returned to Milan to complete plans for the coming season, which opened on 22 December with *The Damnation of Faust* (with Giovanni Zenatello).

This work received the incredible number of twenty-four performances; but the next opera, Verdi's *Luisa Miller*, had a very mixed reception. Romeo Carugati wrote in *Lombardia*: 'The performance . . . was mediocre, because concord and conviction were lacking.' *Mondo artistico* said that the performers, 'first and foremost Toscanini, made every effort to save the opera' but that 'the work, which is certainly not one of Verdi's best, bored people . . .' *Lega lombarda* reported that Toscanini 'infused the action with all [Verdi's] passion, without ever giving way to excess or cheap, mannered effects . . .'.

Oceana by Antonio Smareglia was given its world première on 22 January 1903. It was an immediate success but a long-term failure; and Franchetti's *Asrael*, the next opera, was fortunate and unfortunate in the same way. This was followed by *Un ballo in maschera*, which had been analysed, purified and galvanized in the same way as *Trovatore*—and with similar results. The only

Wagner that year was the Prelude and third act of *Parsifal*, done in concert form, and greeted with tolerant boredom by most of those present, including the majority of the critics.

There had been considerable tension between Toscanini and the Scala administration during the 1902–3 season. Part of this was caused by the death of Duke Guido Visconti di Modrone in November 1902. The old Duke was an extremely well-liked and civic-minded man who was mourned even in the left-wing press. He had always donated great amounts of time and money to La Scala and his charm and personal honesty had won Toscanini's confidence. At his death the presidency of the Scala board was assumed jointly by his five sons, headed by the eldest, Duke Uberto. Uberto was also willing to do his best for La Scala; but he was a socialite who saw the theatre as an extension of the salon. To say that he and Toscanini did not understand each other is to put the case mildly indeed.

At the end of the 1901–2 season Toscanini had finally decided to ask for a raise in his salary—something he could easily have done at least two years earlier. His wife had probably made him look realistically at the situation. He went to Gatti-Casazza, reminded him that after four years he was still earning only 12,000 lire per season, and pointed out that the previous season Emma Carelli's salary had jumped from 12,000 to 36,000, while the soprano's work at La Scala amounted to only a fraction of his own. Would it be outlandish on his part to ask for 20,000? Gatti replied that it certainly would not be, and that he would talk to the Duke in the autumn. Meanwhile, the old Duke died and the matter was passed on to Uberto. Seeing Toscanini in the corridor one evening, Uberto's brother Giuseppe told him that it had been decided to increase his salary to 18,000. That was the wrong kind of answer to give Toscanini. He turned his back on Giuseppe and walked away.

The season, as we have seen, went ahead anyway (whether at 12, 18, or 20,000 I cannot say, since the records no longer exist), and so did Toscanini's war of nerves with the public. The only scheduled repertoire opera with pre-assured audience appeal was *Ballo*; and when Toscanini was called to come out for a bow on the opening night of that production, he refused, 'as usual' (*Lombardia*, 12 March). The audience regarded this as a most discourteous act.

At the same time, his personal life was a nightmare, with Storchio in the last stages of her pregnancy; and less than three weeks after the birth of their poor child came the *Parsifal* opening. Toscanini was furious at the blasé reception accorded the excerpts, and at the second (and last) performance, when a tiny handful of listeners asked for a *bis* after the prelude, he conceded the encore—as if to fling the music in the face of the majority of the audience. That was on 13 April.

The last performance of the season—a repetition of *Ballo in maschera*—was scheduled for the next night. Toscanini had agreed to return to Buenos Aires that spring and his boat was to depart from Genoa on the 15th. He had asked to be excused from the last Scala performance—to have one of his competent assistants, Pietro Sormani or Tullio Serafin, conduct. The request had been denied.

Toscanini conducted the performance, and all went well until the aria *E' scherzo od è follia* in the second part of the first act. The *Corriere della sera* gave this account in the next day's paper:

'. . . A part of the audience wanted a *bis* of the aria . . .; but since the tenor, Zenatello, did not appear disposed to concede it, Maestro Toscanini signalled to proceed. The refusal was interpreted badly by part of the audience and the requests for the *bis* became more heated and insistent, while the other part shouted for the performance to go on. The clamour for and against the *bis* went on thus for a long time. Finally the performance continued. After the act, however, a stage boy came out to inform the public that Maestro Toscanini had suddenly begun bleeding and that Maestro Sormani would have to substitute for him.

Not everyone was persuaded by this. The same people who had attributed the refusal of the *bis* to Maestro Toscanini, accusing him of permitting a *bis* only in those operas which he liked best, now believed that he had had himself replaced . . . as an act of spite. Thus, when Maestro Sormani stepped on to the podium, there was an applause of protest, so to speak.'

Toscanini arrived home, still in full dress. His surprised wife asked him, 'What's wrong? Is it finished already?' 'Yes. For me it's finished.'[38]

According to some sources, the story that Toscanini was bleeding was true: in a fury, he had put his hand through a window or some other glass object, causing a minor injury. In any case, he had made up his mind not to return to La Scala. Five years had been enough—too much, rather. What he would do instead he did not know; but anything or even nothing would be better than returning to those idiots. The next morning at six he left for Genoa, where he boarded the *Sicilia* for the voyage to Argentina—after having sent a telegram to La Scala stating that he would not set foot in that theatre again.

In Buenos Aires Toscanini worked with a group of singers that included Caruso, Giuseppe De Luca, Darclée and Zenatello. The season opened on 19 May with *Tosca*† and continued with *Germania, Gioconda, Damnation of Faust,**† *Elisir,*† *Hänsel and Gretel,*† *Iris,*† *Rigoletto, Mefistofele,*† *Adriana Lecouvreur,**† *Aida,*† Massenet's *Griselda,**† *Manon Lescaut,*† *Traviata* and *Meistersinger.*† De Luca sang Beckmesser in *Meistersinger.* Earlier in the year the baritone had sent the following letter to his agent:

* Argentine première.

† Also performed on tour at Teatro Solís in Montevideo, Uruguay.

'Although unwillingly, I shall study the rôle of Bekmesser [sic] anyway. I say unwillingly because these are parts which ruin the voice; but to please Maestro Toscanini, what wouldn't I do?'[39]

During the nine months following the Buenos Aires season the only conducting Toscanini did was a pair of concerts at Bologna's Teatro Comunale on 29 March and 4 April 1904. The programmes included his first performances of three short works that he was to conduct regularly in the future: Sibelius's *Swan of Tuonela*, Dukas's *Sorcerer's Apprentice* and Smetana's *Moldau*.

Some weeks earlier the première of *Madama Butterfly* had taken place at La Scala with Campanini conducting and Storchio in the lead rôle. Shortly before the opening Puccini had told Toscanini that he wanted his opinion of the score. They met at Storchio's and the composer played a few carefully chosen excerpts at the piano. Toscanini then asked to look at the score. He felt immediately that the two-act format was a grave error: both acts were too long, particularly the second. 'I thought at once, this length is impossible,' he said years later; 'For Wagner, yes! For Puccini, no!'[40] Knowing what effect his negative judgment could have on morale at that late stage, he simply complimented what he felt were the strong points of the score and gave Puccini his best wishes. As much as he might have wanted to attend the première, he refused to enter La Scala. He may have expected a lukewarm reception for the opera; but he could not have anticipated the catastrophic fiasco that in fact took place. One can only imagine his feelings on learning that at one point, when a breeze on stage had made Storchio's kimono billow out, someone in the audience had shouted: '*E' incinta!* [She's pregnant!] *Il bambino di Toscanini!*' By the time the performance had ended to the accompaniment of catcalls and whistles from the gallery, Puccini was crushed and Storchio hysterical. The opera was thoroughly overhauled by the composer and was presented with great success in its three-act form at Brescia in May—not with Storchio, however.

She was in Buenos Aires by then, where Toscanini was conducting another winter season. This year his singers included Garbin, Amato, Borgatti, Didur, De Luca *et al.*; and the repertoire consisted of *Lohengrin*,† *Faust*,† *Linda di Chamounix*,† Giordano's *Siberia*,* *Butterfly*,*† *Bohème*, *Falstaff*, *Wally*,*† *Freischütz* (the only time Toscanini ever conducted this work) and Massenet's *Manon*,† in addition to five of the operas done the previous season.

Storchio was at least partially compensated for the Scala disaster when she and the revised *Butterfly* were warmly received by the Argentinian public.

In October and November Toscanini directed *Meistersinger* and Meyerbeer's *Dinorah* at Bologna's Teatro Comunale. Marco Enrico Bossi, the organist and composer, recalled that at the opening night of *Meistersinger*, as Toscanini raised

* Argentine première.

† Also performed on tour at Teatro Solís in Montevideo, Uruguay.

his baton to begin the prelude, a terrified voice called out from the gallery: 'Maestro, Maestro, you've forgotten your music!'

'I remember [continued Bossi] the laughs that would follow the funny stories which he would tell wittily and picturesquely in one or another Bolognese café, after the rehearsals and performances ... The hilarity would spread through the company, the circle of friends would grow, and this would be surrounded in turn by the waiters who ... had become deaf to the calls of the other customers scattered here and there in the café ...'[41]

Toscanini and family transferred to Rome for the winter of 1904-5. He had wanted to be able to familiarize himself with the archaeological and artistic wealth of the capital while preparing for concert engagements during the coming months, and he had thought it would be a pleasant change for Carla and the children as well. In January they all went to Sicily, where they visited Agrigento and its temples, Siracusa and Taormina, among other places. Back in Rome he wrote to a friend:

'This sweet and peaceful rest has not, however, completely distracted me from all musical occupation. I have made the acquaintance of some very interesting works. Strauss's "Domestic" Symphony—his last-born—is a formidable composition from a technical point of view, with flashes of genius, but very debatable as an artistic direction; or at least the artistic dogma launched by this highly capable secessionist is not to be accepted wholly and blindly.'[42]

Toscanini introduced several of Strauss's works in Italy; but he never conducted the 'Domestic' Symphony.

He directed two concerts in February at the Accademia di Santa Cecilia—his first Roman appearances in nearly thirteen years. Count Enrico di San Martino Valperga, who was then president of the academy, wrote in his memoirs:

'Toscanini ... was preceded by his reputation, not only as having the most distinguished qualities, but also as having a terribly difficult character. But justice requires recognition of the fact that the first part is true but that the accusation is unfounded. We always found Toscanini to be not only a most valuable artistic collaborator but also a wise and affectionate advisor on every problem, in the theatre as well as the concert hall.'[43]

The programmes of those two concerts (for which he was paid 2,000 lire) were highly varied: Wagner, Berlioz, Catalani, Strauss, Beethoven, Martucci and Sibelius. The performance of Martucci's recent Second Symphony was the occasion for a letter (15 February) from Toscanini to his admired friend:

'Yesterday I began rehearsing the Symphony and after two hours of assiduous study I was not able to get through the first movement. What a horrid orchestra! How badly they read! And they play worse! I haven't conducted their like in years. I have to think back to a rather remote period in order to remind myself of impressions similar to the ones revived in me by this Roman orchestra. These people have lost the feeling for playing—I won't say well, but at least correctly. I nearly slaughtered myself trying to put together the first Concert which the public and *magna critica* judged highly successful. And here it is really the case that he who is satisfied enjoys himself. I was disgusted by it.

Today I was able to read through the first movement better and to run through the Scherzo which turned out to be less difficult than the first movement. Tomorrow I shall give over to the Scherzo again and I shall read through the Adagio. I can already hear those cellos and those infamous double basses wreaking havoc on those poor notes. Enough, I've armed myself with patience. I hope it will serve to get everything that these not good, but good-hearted players (since that is how they have been with me) can give. And to think that you read through the whole Symphony in two rehearsals at Bologna!

I told Count di San Martino that eight rehearsals will be necessary for this concert; I am sure that he will be able to satisfy me somehow or other. . . .'[44]

During the first days of April Toscanini conducted four concerts in Bologna. Among the works new to his repertoire were Sibelius's *En Saga*, Strauss's *Death and Transfiguration*, Elgar's 'Enigma' Variations and the *Prelude to the Afternoon of a Faun* by Debussy, a composer who was to become particularly close to his heart. His two concerts at the Teatro Vittorio Emanuele in Turin a month later also included some of these pieces.

He had of course put much time and effort into the choice of repertoire for these series, as can be seen from an unusual letter he sent Polo on New Year's day, 1905. Polo had studied with Joachim in Berlin and had maintained an interest in German musical developments. It was he, for instance, who had first brought Toscanini's attention to Brahms. Recently he had read of the première of Mahler's Fifth Symphony in Cologne the previous October, had procured the score and had sent it to his brother-in-law in Rome. This is Toscanini's reaction to what was probably his first contact with Mahler's work:

'. . . You'll easily be able to imagine how much joy and how much curiosity its unexpected arrival gave me. I read it immediately, or rather devoured it— but unfortunately, during this ferocious musical meal, the initial joy and curiosity gradually waned, changing in the end into a sad, very sad hilarity.

No, dear Enrico, believe me, Mahler is not a genuine artist. His music has neither personality nor genius. It is a mixture of an Italianate style à la Petrella [popular nineteenth-century opera composer] or Leoncavallo, coupled with Tchaikovsky's musical and instrumental bombast and a seeking after Straussian peculiarities (although boasting an opposing system) without having the originality of the last two. At every step you fall, not into a commonplace, but into some triviality. Just look at this: [here Toscanini has written out eight bars of the recurring theme of the opening funeral march]. Petrella and Leoncavallo would look disdainfully at this nice little march motif . . . Mahler is shameless enough to introduce it into the first movement of a symphony . . . Can you imagine a more awful hatchet job than this other one that I'm copying for you: [here he has transcribed the first thirteen bars of the brass—No. 7 in the score]. And this is coloured by lamenting violins and wailing woodwinds. . . .

. . . Add to this technical difficulty and exaggerated proportions.—So, the idea of a possible performance in Turin has thus faded. Where can I turn next? Tchaikovsky's Fifth Symphony and one in D minor by Dvořák will arrive in a few days. Let's hope for better luck. I'm also awaiting the Elgar Variations.'[45]

Neither the Tchaikovsky nor the Dvořák appealed to him. The Elgar piece became a staple of his repertoire; but not a single work of Mahler ever appeared on one of his programmes. He directed Sinigaglia's 'Piedmontese Dances' during the Turin series; but a segment of the audience objected to the use of traditional local tunes. 'The battle disturbed the solemn correctness of the Hall for several minutes,' reported one critic.

In June Toscanini took the Turin orchestra to Milan for two concerts at La Scala—his first appearances there in over two years. Things had not been going so well since his departure: discipline had broken down in the orchestra and the backstage area was often overrun with gallant gentlemen—Duke Uberto and his friends, for the most part—arranging dressing-room suppers with their favourite singers and ballerinas. Campanini, Toscanini's successor, was a competent conductor; but Toscanini was a very hard act to follow, as dozens upon dozens of conductors were to discover during the next fifty years. He finally gave up and was succeeded by Mugnone for the 1905–6 season. Toscanini's reappearance in Milan, even at the head of an out-of-town orchestra, was greeted with excitement by that very large segment of the public that had been sorry to see him leave in 1903. When he walked on stage to begin the first concert, 'the whole audience broke into a warm, spontaneous, affectionate and prolonged ovation' (D'Ormeville). And the *Corriere della sera* said:

'Toscanini is already to be counted among the greatest of living conductors. But a scrupulous sense of the highest artistic demands, an unyielding intransigence respecting certain production compromises . . . has prevented any diminution of his fame . . . And perhaps also because of this his glory seems more dazzling and pure: it is certain that also because of this his art grows ever greater and more beautiful.'

The Bohemian composer Johann Bohuslav Förster attended Toscanini's rehearsals for these concerts and made the following comments in his memoirs, *Der Pilger*:

'Toscanini speaks little and is cautious; but every phrase, be it harsh or subtly ironic, demonstrates that a precise goal motivates his thoughts: the most complete of interpretations. He could be defined as the eternally dissatisfied. Although he aims for the greatest precision, he does not weary the orchestra ... He occupies himself with the sense of the work ... It is surprising that he preserves a physical calm, even in the most excited passages.'[46]

The Toscanini family spent the summer of 1905 at Pré St-Didier in the Valle d'Aosta, from which point Papà made several ascensions, along with a guide, a porter and Gino Mella, a relation of Carla's from Milan. The first expedition lasted about three weeks and took him through Courmayeur to the summit of Mont Blanc. ('We have reached the top of Mont Blanc,' he wrote on a postcard to Polo; 'Dante, Beethoven, Wagner!!! Quivering with rapture.'[47] They then descended to Chamonix, across the Argentière glacier, Col Chardonnet, *fenêtre* St-Solenar, Lac Champey, Ferret valley and back to Pré St-Didier. After a rest he made another lengthy excursion from Degioz in Valsavaranche and attempted to climb the 'arduous and beautiful' Grivola. He wrote to Polo on 25 August from the 'very charming village' of Cogne: 'Gave up the Grivola because of blizzard; I'll try again today. Sunday I'll do the Herbetet and will end my climbs for this year, seeing as the Matterhorn is impossible because of bad weather.'[48]

From October to early December Toscanini conducted a series of operas in Bologna: *Butterfly* with Salomea Krusceniski, *Siegfried* with Borgatti, *Hänsel and Gretel*, and the world première of Vittorio Gnecchi's *Cassandra*. Musicologist and composer Francesco Vatielli, who was connected with the Teatro Comunale at that time, wrote:

'At the first Bolognese performance of *Siegfried* one of the singers (an excellent one), who was treading the boards of the Comunale for the first time, showed signs of great fear and worry. A few moments before the curtain was to go up Maestro Toscanini passed next to him, serious and morose as usual. "Good evening, Maestro," said the singer, greeting him. "How will the opera go?" "Eh!" answered Toscanini, "I really don't know. There are too many beasts in this opera. There are birds, there's the dragon, there's the bear, and there's —you!" And he went quickly down to the orchestra.'[49]

A few days after finishing the Bologna season Toscanini was in Turin to conduct opera at the newly restored and reopened Regio for the first time in nearly eight years. The series again included *Siegfried* and *Butterfly* as well as *Damnation of Faust*, *Loreley* and *Siberia*. Aside from the Berlioz work, his original plan had been entirely different: he had wanted to do Strauss's new *Salome* (for which arrangements could not be made in time: the world première was given in Dresden only on 9 December), *Wally*, Mascagni's *Amica* and a new opera called *Chopin* by Giacomo Orefice—in addition to Wagner's entire *Ring*! This last project proved to be too big to consider seriously. In fact, Toscanini never conducted an entire *Ring* (nor did he ever perform *Das Rheingold*, excepting a few excerpts in concert form).

The Turin opera season was followed by three concerts (15, 18 and 19 March) at the Regio. New to Toscanini's repertoire were *Nuages* from Debussy's *Nocturnes*, Strauss's *Don Juan*, Borodin's *In the Steppes of Central Asia*, and Elgar's Introduction and Allegro for strings. He then took the orchestra on a ten-day tour: two concerts in Milan, three in Venice, and one each in Parma, Bologna, Trieste, Brescia and Como.

On 28 March 1906 Claudio Toscanini died at the age of seventy-three; he was buried in his red shirt.

The Toscanini family spent the summer of 1906 in Buenos Aires. This time De Luca, Anselmi, Krusceniski, Garbin, Storchio, Didur and others sang with him; and the repertoire included *Rigoletto*,† *Wally*,† *Don Pasquale*,† *Gioconda*, *Butterfly*,† *Walküre*, *Manon*,† *Mefistofele*, *Traviata*,† *Colombo*, *Tosca*, *Barber of Seville*,† *Tristan*,† *Don Giovanni*, *Loreley*† and Franchetti's *Figlia di Iorio*.* This was the only time Toscanini ever performed *Don Giovanni*. He had De Luca as the protagonist, Tolexis as Anna, Anselmi as Ottavio, Storchio as Zerlina and Didur as Leporello. The reviews of the time—like most reviews of all times—give us little idea of what the production was like. *La Nación* (30 July) wrote that De Luca was not right for his rôle, and that Toscanini had disregarded the public by choosing Didur instead of Ercolani. Everyone else was fine and the orchestra very clear. 'In a word, a mediocre *Don Giovanni*, which constitutes an unpardonable act of disrespect.' *La Prensa* found De Luca 'an intelligent interpreter'; but the production as a whole was 'not completely satisfactory. We found it uneven, unhomogeneous, and defective in many ways.... The *mise-en-scène* was very beautiful and the orchestral part delicately coloured.'

Shortly after the Buenos Aires season had begun four and a half year old Giorgio Toscanini contracted diphtheria; he died on 10 June. Toscanini had loved his youngest child very much; he was crushed not only by grief but by guilt as well. Although he was not religious in any formal sense and heartily detested the clergy and the Church, he believed in God, considered himself a Christian, and had also imbibed many peasant superstitions in his childhood. And since that childhood had been darkened by the irresponsibility of a vagabond father, he was all the more convinced of the necessity of a stable family life. He was categorically and narrow-mindedly opposed to divorce and to anything else that might, in his opinion, imperil the family. (Not surprisingly, several of his descendants have led peculiar and even disastrous lives.) Yet his relationship with Storchio was still going on, and there were others, too. According to some, he was with Storchio at the moment of Giorgio's death. Given his provincial nineteenth-century point of

* Argentine première.

† Also performed on tour at Teatro Solís in Montevideo, Uruguay.

view, his actions were morally reprehensible. He could not forgive himself but
neither could he control himself in the sexual–amorous aspect of his life. He ate
and drank extremely sparingly, slept little, worked like a beast of burden,
shunned high society, and demanded the utmost of himself at all times; but he
could not resist women and they could not resist him. As far as Giorgio was concerned, there can be little doubt that Toscanini regarded his death as in some way
a retributive act.

Poor Carla was beside herself: it was an even worse blow for her than for her
husband. He had his work; she had only her family. Besides, she could not have
been unaware of his escapades, particularly his affair with Storchio and their child
out of wedlock; and when she learned of the incident at the *Butterfly* première
—that is, when she learned that *everyone* knew—she must have been terribly
wounded and humiliated. After all, she was still in her twenties and still beautiful;
she worshipped her husband and did everything to make his life easier for him.
What more did he want? It is said that she wanted to leave him after the child's
death; but the marriage was patched up, and eighteen months after the despair of
Buenos Aires Carla gave birth to a girl who was named Wanda Giorgina.

Toscanini, of course, drowned his grief and his guilt in the theatre. Wally has
related that 'the day after Giorgio died Papà went out and conducted. He had a
sense of duty to the point of exasperation, and he was ashamed of his feelings.'[50]

The Toscanini family had been *en route* to their wretched South American
summer when an item appeared in the *Gazzetta teatrale italiana* (30 April)
stating that after long negotiations, Toscanini would be returning to La Scala for
the coming season, 1906–7.

Among the conditions he had set were an official ban on the *bis*—finally
implementing a rule which had existed at La Scala since 1793; prohibition of
access to the stage by anyone who was not involved in the production; and the
construction of an orchestra pit. A commission which included Toscanini, Boito
and Puccini was appointed to examine this last matter; and they designated a city
engineer, Cesare Albertini, to study the designs of the best orchestra pits in
Europe. Eventually the task was carried out satisfactorily, although opposed by
Boito and Giulio Ricordi. The latter categorized the action as part of the 'fad for
aping Bayreuth', despite the fact that Verdi himself had spoken in favour of a
lowered pit as early as 1871.

It was unfortunate that the operation was not completed in time for the new
season because, after a successful opening production of *Carmen* (19 December),
the operatic series proceeded with one of the most orchestrally massive operas
ever written—Richard Strauss's *Salome*.

A year earlier, when Toscanini was preparing the 1905–6 season at the Regio,
he had asked the Turin directorate to enter into negotiations with Strauss's
representatives about obtaining rights to the first Italian performance, and had

then begun exchanging letters with Strauss himself concerning the barely completed work. Their correspondence was in schoolboy French. Toscanini's first letter to Strauss is dated 27 July 1905:

> '. . . I hope that your beautiful score has been completed by now, and I also hope that there will be no difficulty in satisfying my ardent desire to perform *Salome* in Turin. . . . I have another reason for wanting so strongly the fulfilment of this wish: I would consider myself infinitely happy to be able to meet you personally on that occasion.
> . . . I found the *Salome* poem in French, as Oscar Wilde wrote it: it could serve for the Italian translation. Please accept . . . my hearty compliments on your very nice choice of such a beautiful and musical subject. . . .'[51]

Strauss replied on 2 August:

> '. . . I greatly rejoice in your great interest in my works . . . The piano score will be finished around 15 September, the orchestra score at the end of October. At the moment I am busy putting Wilde's original French version into harmony with my music, and after this French transcription a friend of Mons. Cesare Pollini [pianist, composer and musicologist] in Padua will do the Italian translation. I hope that all this can be done by the end of October.
> The study of the vocal parts with the singers will require at least two months. When do you expect to give the first performance in Turin? In my opinion this will not be possible before the middle of January. The orchestra is very big and very difficult; but there is no chorus. . . .'[52]

It soon became clear to Toscanini and the Regio directorate that they could not be certain that *Salome* would be ready for inclusion during the 1905–6 season; they therefore postponed the project until the following year. Not many months afterwards, however, Toscanini was re-engaged by La Scala and a difficult situation developed: Strauss and Fürstner, his publisher, had promised, if unofficially, the Italian première to the Regio, while Toscanini felt that since the idea and initial efforts had been his, the première was rightfully his. He was determined to take the responsibility and the honour for this important endeavour; and he therefore wanted the première transferred from the Regio to La Scala.

Upon returning from Argentina he had learned that Strauss himself had been engaged to lead the first production at the Regio. Toscanini and Carla, with Polo to act as interpreter, took a train to Berlin to talk with Strauss about possibly altering his plans. Arriving at the composer's house in Potsdam, Toscanini suddenly turned and ran away—whether out of shyness or because he anticipated an unpleasant situation is hard to guess. Carla and Polo caught him and convinced him to come back, and Strauss welcomed him warmly. Toscanini asked whether the première could be changed to Milan; but Strauss replied that he and Fürstner had already given their word to Turin. The conductor then proposed giving the opera simultaneously in both cities, to which Strauss responded that if Milan were willing to pay a fee equal to that being paid by Turin.... At that point Toscanini stood up, said that Strauss's respect for his word of honour was evidently just a question of money, and walked out. That same day (9 October 1906) he received a letter from the composer:

'I am very sad that you are angry with me; but this series of mistakes is truly not my fault. Just think: last year you, D'Ormeville and I corresponded about the performance of *Salome* in Turin and I promised you the Italian première. This whole summer D'Ormeville, Fürstner and I have corresponded about the performances in Turin and Milan. D'Ormeville knew that I had promised you the première. You yourself spoke with Gatti-Casazza about this première; he must have known that you wanted the première. After having waited the whole summer I finally met with D'Ormeville and Gatti-Casazza. They both knew that I was going to conduct in Turin on 26 December, and despite that, at the moment we came to discuss the conditions, royalties, etc., Mr Gatti-Casazza told me that he did not intend to give *Salome* before February.

After that date had been voluntarily set by Mr Gatti-Casazza, and thinking that it would not be possible to give more than twelve or thirteen performances in Milan from mid-February to April, I said that I found a percentage of 3,000 francs too small and I asked for 10,000 francs—more if Milan should give more than ten performances. Is it not true that these conditions were set with the understanding that Mr Gatti-Casazza had voluntarily renounced the first Italian performance and that *Salome* would be given in Milan only during a two-month period (the end of the season)?

Is it not true that it is now a totally different thing when Mr Gatti-Casazza asks for four months, when he asks for the première on the same day as Turin, which is paying 15,000 francs? It is therefore clear that the conditions change as the proposals change. I do not like to cause confusion—I, who am accustomed to keeping my promises to everyone, all the more so to you, dear Maestro. But really, I repeat, the fault lies with Mr D'Ormeville, who did not keep you informed of our correspondence regarding Turin—the fault lies with Mr Gatti-Casazza, who knew the Turin dates (26 December) and assured me, despite that, that he wished to give *Salome* in February. Is it not true that I had to believe that you were in absolute agreement with Mr Gatti-Casazza when he mentioned February for the Milanese première, that that was your wish and that you had renounced the right to the first Italian performance?

I hope that this explanation is clear enough and that you are persuaded that I have done the correct thing. You have the right to my promise ... allowing you to give *Salome* on 26 December, the same day as Turin. But Mr Gatti-Casazza cannot ask that the contract which was sent, which was based upon completely different proposals, can now be fulfilled by me, when he requests the première instead of the second production for Milan, and when he requests the right to perform *Salome* for four months instead of two.

... Tomorrow morning at eleven I shall meet you at Fürstner's, and I hope that you will no longer be angry with your very devoted [etc.].'[53]

Toscanini responded:

'I want to tell you right away that I am not at all angry with you: I am only very astonished that, having expressed to you a simple and more than natural personal wish to give *Salome* on the 26th in Milan, you do not want to interpret this wish in its true significance, bringing the matter into altogether commercial territory. I repeat to you that it is not the Scala directorate that is asking your permission to move the Milan opening forward, because in that case or in any other the directorate could never give more than fifteen performances of your opera; but it is I [who ask it] for entirely personal and artistic satisfaction. However, if you plan on insisting upon your decision to change the terms of the contract for the favour I have asked of you, then I am obliged to ask you to leave things as they are: we shall give *Salome* in Milan at the previously decided time, because I cannot permit the directorate of La Scala to make a sacrifice to please me.

In any case, I shall be at Mr Fürstner's at 11 o'clock. Please accept my best wishes [etc.].'[54]

Strauss saw things in terms of his legal right to earn a much larger sum of money, while Toscanini was asking a personal favour for which—according to his way of thinking—the question of money could not enter in. (Toscanini also refused to see that Turin should not have been expected to pay much more than La Scala if they were to have a co-première.) The meeting at Fürstner's must simply have confirmed Toscanini's decision, as stated in his letter, to let the matter drop and to accept the second production for La Scala. A month later (12 November) he wrote to Strauss from Milan (original in Italian):

'... The episode is now turning to your advantage. I began piano rehearsals of *Salome* some days ago, and you cannot imagine what a titanic, superhuman effort the singers must make to try to overcome the colossal difficulties, made even more serious by a bad translation. This has convinced me how brilliantly stupid I was to have fixed a date for the performance of an opera without having taken into consideration its difficulties, an opera in which there are— to the ears of our Italian singers—extraordinary harmonic irregularities and great difficulties to overcome.

I considered it my duty to inform the Scala directorate of all this; consequently *Salome* can be performed in the first days of January at the earliest— all the more so, as I must prepare *Carmen* at the same time.

As you see ... the matter has taken a turn for the better, not by my merit but by your good fortune, according to your wishes and those of the Turin company. I hope that it will not be necessary to add to all that has already been said and debated on this subject. Please believe always in my admiration for your art [etc.].'[55]

'My admiration for your art'—but not for *you*. As the weeks went by, what Toscanini considered to be Strauss's betrayal rankled increasingly. When he saw the rehearsals were not going badly, he formed a plan: La Scala announced the *Salome* opening for 26 December—the same night as the Regio première; the directorate had probably decided to let Strauss make an issue of it if he cared to. The Turin production was then moved forward to the 23rd (eventually the 22nd)—and here one must surmise that the Regio directorate and Strauss did this in order to avoid a confrontation. At that point the Milanese decided on another tactic. D'Ormeville discussed the situation in retrospect in the *Gazzetta dei teatri* (27 December):

'. . . I can well understand the Scala-ites' desire to return victorious, and I understand even better Maestro Toscanini's noble ambition to leave his personal mark upon an artistic event of such high importance. But it seems to me that one must not forget that the direction of the Turin *Salome* was put in the hands of Maestro Strauss himself.

. . . The Scala-ites . . . had a meeting and hit on an expedient which was craftier than it was brilliant and more spiteful than courteous: they decided to have a dress rehearsal on the evening of the 21st . . . which was attended by subscribers, journalists, benefactors, friends—anyone. What was the aim?— That of letting the Milanese hear *Salome* first?—I think that at bottom the real aim was not that, but rather to avoid having the Turin fiasco damage the Milan performance in advance.

The Turin fiasco?—Yes. The Scala-ites are convinced, in their arrogant egoism, that nothing good can be done outside La Scala, just as the Pope is persuaded that *nulla salus* is possible outside the bosom of the Holy Mother Church. But if no one believes any longer in the infallibility of God's Vicar, why ought one believe in that of my dear friends Toscanini and Gatti-Casazza? . . .'

In the end Turin's production was officially called the première, and nearly all the critics lauded both equally highly—although the Regio's Gemma Bellincioni was generally preferred in the lead rôle to La Scala's Salomea Krusceniski. (Toscanini told a friend, decades later, that Krusceniski was the only woman with whom he had ever been madly in love who had refused him.) Strauss was furious with Toscanini. He did not attend the Milan production and allowed himself to be convinced by third parties of its great inferiority. He wrote to his wife on 26 December:

'You say: "I didn't pack you off to Turin." That's right. But how necessary it was that I look after the thing is attested by the Milanese *Salome* production, where Toscanini, with a pitilessly raging orchestra, is said to have simply slaughtered the singers and the drama (à la Mottl). It's a wonder that the work was successful there anyway. Had I not been here early, however, and shown people how the work looks, *Salome* could have been lost to Italy for many years. Eyewitnesses who have heard the Milan production testify that it is an entirely different piece here. In Milan the *Kapellmeister* [Toscanini] performed a symphony without singers; here, on the contrary, the orchestra accompanies and one understands the singers' every word.'[56]

It seems that Strauss changed his mind about Toscanini when he eventually heard him conduct. George Szell, who was Strauss's assistant for some time, said that someone reported to him that Strauss had said: 'When you see that man conduct, you feel that there is only one thing for you to do: take your baton, break it in pieces, and never conduct again.' Toscanini never again conducted *Salome* nor did he ever conduct any other Strauss opera.

The Scala season proceeded with *Gioconda*, *Tristan*, *Aida* and *Wally*. On 17 March Toscanini led a revival of Gluck's *Orfeo*. (It had, however, been given at La Scala nine years earlier.) He demonstrated great interest in this work throughout his life, and it remained the oldest opera in his repertoire. Before the opening, the newspaper *Sera* announced:

'Toscanini, adhering to Gevaert's precedent and Saint-Saëns's opinion, will not play the overture; and at the end of the first act he has inserted an aria from Gluck's *Alceste*—an opera written five years after *Orfeo*—in place of the aria in the score, the attribution of which is uncertain . . .'

Reviews ranged from enthusiastic to bored; and Maria Gay, Zenatello's wife, who had been warmly received as Carmen, was generally criticized as Orfeo. Carugati's article in *Lombardia* (18 March) was entitled 'Morpheus at La Scala':

'Last night an elegant and classical musical dormitory was inaugurated at La Scala under the direction of Maestro Toscanini, who did everything in his power to bring sleep to the visitors. . . . I had the impression that instead of classical serenity, there was a predominance of Olympian boredom . . .'

The last operas of the season were Cilea's *Gloria*, in its world première, and *Cavalleria rusticana*; neither production was successful. Cilea had wanted his work withdrawn before it was produced because he had had second thoughts about its quality; but Toscanini had insisted on proceeding with it. Actress Eleonora Duse, who was performing at the Teatro Lirico on the evening of the première, helped to draw the audience away from La Scala. The performance was highly praised, but the opera was apathetically received and was withdrawn after a second hearing. Toscanini had little sympathy for Cilea's music and never again directed a note by him. Many years later, when both men were past eighty, Cilea still loathed Toscanini. He wrote to a friend: 'For now, I do not hope to return to La Scala. As long as Toscanini is mixing in there, it is better for me to stay far away and—wait.' (Toscanini was still mixing in when Cilea died in 1950.)

In April and May Toscanini directed two pairs of concerts with the Scala orchestra. Once preliminary plans had been made for the 1907–8 season he and his family went on holiday to Giomein, where he became acquainted with the writer Edmondo De Amicis.

The opera season began on 21 December with *Götterdämmerung*, again minus Waltraute, as in Turin in 1895. Toscanini conducted from the newly completed orchestra pit, and the critics were extremely laudatory. D'Ormeville: 'Maestro Toscanini surpassed himself. I have admired him many times in other Wagner operas, but perhaps never as in this one.' Nappi (*Perseveranza*): 'On the whole it may be the most complete Wagnerian performance yet offered us by Arturo Toscanini . . . Under his baton the orchestra is a great organism animated by a powerful life impulse.'

Successful productions of *Tosca* ('a strong and incisive interpretation by Toscanini and a very effective ensemble on stage,' wrote Puccini to his friend Clausetti) and *Colombo* came next, followed by Gustave Charpentier's *Louise*, which was a critical success but did not please the general public. The New Zealand–born soprano Frances Alda made her Scala début in this work, and wrote of her first meeting with Toscanini in her memoirs, *Men, Women and Tenors*:

'In the rehearsal room at La Scala, Gatti sat off in one corner. . . . Toscanini sat beside the pianist. He kept his eyes closed as he listened, only lifting a finger now and then to mark the time. . . . I sang the rôle straight through . . . The pianist struck the final chord . . . No one spoke. Then Toscanini leaned across the pianist's shoulder and closed the music book on the rack. Only then did he open his eyes and look at me. Blandly, in Italian, he asked: "In what language were you singing?"

. . . I glared at Toscanini, at the cowed and silent pianist, at Gatti-Casazza brooding in his corner. Without deigning to reply I marched out of the rehearsal room, out of the theatre, and back to the Hotel Milan. . . .

Now, recalling that childish fit of temper and hurt pride on my part, I think too of the innumerable times later on that Toscanini taught me the rôles I was to sing; his infinite patience and inspiring enthusiasm, and all that I owe him. And I feel like humbling myself before the forbearance of a very great artist.'[57]

Reviews of the next opera—a re-mounting (16 February) of the previous season's *Gioconda*—contained shocking news for the Italian musical world: Toscanini and Gatti-Casazza would be leaving La Scala at the end of the season. Gatti would become general manager of New York's Metropolitan Opera Company and Toscanini would share duties as principal conductor there with Gustav Mahler.

There had been a fruitless contact between Toscanini and the Metropolitan as early as 1903; then, in 1906, Toscanini had been approached by the Metropolitan's then general manager, Heinrich Conried, who had used the services of Otto H. Kahn, millionaire chairman of the executive committee—who in turn had worked through Count di San Martino. The conductor had not yet returned to La Scala and was not entirely happy with the prospect of doing so; but he did not know enough about the situation at the Metropolitan or about Conried, and he preferred, for the moment, to face known difficulties in Milan to unknown ones in New York. By the spring of 1907 Kahn had begun looking for a replacement for the ailing Conried, and had again turned to San Martino for advice. The Count had discreetly contacted Gatti-Casazza through a mutual friend. When Gatti told Toscanini about this inquiry Toscanini advised him to find out more, and added that if Gatti accepted, he would be willing to go as well. He was not happy with Duke Uberto and the Scala board of governors and would gladly try to work elsewhere. He was encouraged to hear that Mahler had already been hired at the Metropolitan for 1907–8: although he was not an admirer of Mahler's music, he knew his reputation as an extraordinary conductor and operatic reformist. 'I hold Mahler in great esteem,' he told Gatti, 'and would infinitely prefer such a colleague to any mediocrity.'[58] (There were, of course, plenty of mediocre staff conductors to contend with, too, at the Metropolitan.) Gatti eventually entered into secret negotiations with Kahn and others and the final decision was made by the beginning of 1908.

In May Toscanini received a formal contract from the Metropolitan engaging him for the three seasons beginning 1908–9, 'but either party to the contract will have the right to dissolve the present contract after the first . . . or second season . . .' (This cancellation clause was dropped in a revised contract signed by Toscanini in New York in December.) The document further stipulated that Toscanini had 'right of use of all that concerns the performing of the art'; that he was to arrive in New York between 15 October and 1 November and to remain at the disposal of the Metropolitan until 30 April; that he would receive 25,000 lire per month; that he would 'have the right to all his travels free of expense both ways, either by steamer or by rail, in the first class for himself and the members of his family'; that 'all expenses . . . on his travels for lodging, etc., on account of preparing performances of the Metropolitan' would be reimbursed; and that he would 'come to an understanding with the Manager . . . as to the distribution of the repertoire.'[59]

News of the imminent departure of the two men was greeted with great dismay in Milan—and not without accusations of unpatriotic behaviour and 'dollaritis'. Most commentators refused to consider the possibility that Toscanini might have had valid reasons for being dissatisfied with La Scala or that he might have had a legitimate desire to meet a new challenge under different circumstances.

In this atmosphere of bitterness and bad feelings, the next production, *La forza del destino*, turned into a disaster and was withdrawn after only one performance. The orchestra and chorus were praised, but the cast did not please. Toscanini was soundly thrashed for his choice of singers and for his decision to revive the work itself, which the critics referred to as 'overcome with age', 'a mish-mash' and 'no longer an opera that can please the Scala public'. Leonora was sung by Ester Mazzoleni, who recalled the events of that production:

'. . . Burzio, who was supposed to have been Leonora, had sung *Tosca* and *Gioconda* at La Scala between December 1907 and the following February; but she quarrelled with Toscanini. I was asked to study the part and I put everything into it. I had done the piano rehearsals and was ready to rehearse with the orchestra; but right at that moment it seemed that Burzio was going to give in, and I was asked to wait. Imagine how I felt! However, before half an hour had passed someone came to tell me that Toscanini wanted me. I flew on to the stage and, greeted very affably by the Maestro, I made a good showing. It was the first in a series of replacements: the tenor, Dygas, took sick and the rôle of Alvaro was given to Calleya, who had to learn it in a very few days; finally, the baritone, a Frenchman, was replaced at the last moment by Amato.

Calleya was Burzio's lover at the time. At the opening . . . (which was also the closing), trying to help him, she began beating time for him from a box she had taken over the stage, which only resulted in making him more nervous, to the point where poor Calleya began "*O tu che in seno agli angeli*" at the wrong time and Toscanini stopped him and made him begin again. That was enough to irritate the audience and to seal the fate of the production. In the nervous tension which spread onstage, even Amato ended by losing his calm: in the duet with the tenor, he held a long note longer than necessary and the annoyed public sentenced him to death. As for me, God helped me and I was successful [not according to the critics], as was Nazzareno De Angelis as Padre Guardiano. But the opera was not performed again because Toscanini feared the public's reaction after that decisive evening. I saw him in a corner of the stage as I was about to leave the theatre. He was scowling and enraged, with his arms folded and the air of a defeated Napoleon. He saw me, too, and greeted me with a "brava" repeated three times—accompanying it with a healthy admonition (which was a deeply-felt allusion to Burzio): "See that you, too, don't become a goddess!" '[60]

Two weeks after this fiasco Toscanini presented the Scala public with what he would always consider one of the most important products of his labours there: the first performance in Italy of Debussy's *Pelléas et Mélisande*. The project had begun nearly four years earlier in Bologna. At the time he was directing a production of *Meistersinger*, and was sitting in his dressing room before a performance one evening when his attention was drawn to the new score. 'I was struck by the sobriety of those pages, in which everything is essential,' he said later. Writing to a friend shortly afterwards, Toscanini said:

'I hardly even knew the name of [a] composer who has won all my sympathy: the Frenchman Debussy, with his *Pelléas et Mélisande* . . . His art overturns everything that has been done until now. He doesn't have Strauss's technique, but he is a greater genius, more elegant and undoubtedly more daring. On first venturing upon him, you are completely disorientated; but once you have begun to converse a little more familiarly in his language—and that of his inspirer Maeterlinck—you end by being fascinated. Thinking of the theatre, of Maeterlinck's characters, I can confirm my opinion that Debussy's music is the fulfilment of that art. However, our public today, in all countries, is not yet mature to sense this, let alone to accept it.'[61]

It has already been noted that Debussy's orchestral music began to appear on Toscanini's concert programmes almost immediately (April 1905); but *Pelléas* was his great dream. He had originally scheduled Mancinelli's opera *Francesca da Rimini* for the 1907-8 season, but replaced it with *Pelléas*. This predisposed the nationalistic element of the public and critics against the French opera. Toscanini supervised every aspect of the production with extraordinary care, even by his rigorous standards. He went so far as to have the stage hands wrap cloth around their shoes to help prevent extraneous noises. Fiorello Giraud and Cesira Ferrani sang the lead rôles, with Amato as Golaud. 'To each of them,' wrote Gatti-Casazza, 'Toscanini had transfused his entire being.'

Debussy had been invited to attend the preparations and the opening, but was unable to do so. He wrote to Toscanini: 'I put *Pelléas*' fate in your hands, sure as I am that I could not wish for more loyal or more capable ones. For this reason as well, I would have liked to have worked on it with you; it is a joy which one does not often find along the path of our art.'[62]

D'Ormeville attended the public dress rehearsal and published a report on the day of the première (2 April):

'. . . When the last note of Debussy's music evaporated . . . a spontaneous and impulsive shout escaped my lips: Viva Toscanini!—And the thousand voices of the attentive and alert listeners who filled the hall . . . echoed that shout.

Yes. Viva Toscanini—because if we had the chance to hear a work which merits the esteem, attention and respect of those who do not allow themselves to be misled by . . . misconceived chauvinism, we owe it to the high level of his ideals, to the firmness of his character, and to his apostolic faith. . . . La Scala must be open to every artistic manifestation, wherever it may come from. He alone fought against everything and everyone, and so he was the real victor. . . .'

The première itself was disturbed by some loud protests from members of the audience who were angered by the lack of 'melodies' and 'excitement'. Most of this commotion took place during the second scene of Act III (*les souterrains du château*); but the *Corriere della sera* related the next day that 'Maestro Toscanini calmly continued to conduct, so there was no break in the performance, nor even a moment's hesitation on stage.' He had, in fact, warned the singers to watch his baton no matter what happened in the hall. By the end of the act—the scene between Golaud and Yniold—there were enthusiastic outbursts in the audience. When the opera ended, 'the roaring, general applause sealed the success and the victory', wrote S.P. in *Sera*. 'First the singers were called before the curtain twice, then three more times with Toscanini, whose appearance was greeted by resounding ovations. Toscanini, too, was clapping his hands, . . . to show that the audience had lived up to itself . . .'

Debussy sent Toscanini a photograph of himself which he had inscribed: 'To Maestro Toscanini, whom I shall never be able to thank enough'; on the back he had written the first bar of Act III Scene 2 (*Lourd et sombre*), with the comment: '. . . at which point Toscanini came out victorious all the same'.[63] In retrospect Toscanini regretted having done the work in the Italian translation, although that was then a rigid rule at La Scala, and one to which he was not generally opposed. He felt that the sound of the words in *Pelléas* was so closely united to the music that it could not be sacrificed. During the 1920s he conducted *Pelléas* at La Scala in French, although he continued to do all other foreign works in translation.

The opera season ended with a highly successful production of *Mefistofele*, again with Chaliapin. This was followed by what should have been a normal series of symphonic concerts, the first two (each given twice) to be led by Martucci, and two more by Toscanini. A few weeks earlier, a Milanese composer and teacher, Gaetano Coronaro—Catalani's successor at the Conservatory—had died; Toscanini was asked by Count Guido Visconti di Modrone, head of the Concert Society and Uberto's younger brother, to include a work by Coronaro on one of his programmes. Toscanini replied that the intention was fine, but the music itself was not good enough (or he did not like it well enough) to be included on one of his programmes. The Society's response to this was to take the second concert away from Toscanini and to give it to young Ettore Panizza; and Toscanini counter-attacked by suing the Society. He lost the suit and conducted two performances of his one concert, which included his first presentation of Strauss's *Ein Heldenleben*—judged 'crazy and bizarre' and 'madhouse music' by the local critics. He spent part of the summer with his family at Champez in the Alps; and late in September or early in October he set sail for New York.

4
The Metropolitan

New York first heard of Toscanini's appointment in a report cabled from Milan on 4 February 1908; and although he was quoted a day later as having said that no contract had yet been signed, an official announcement was made on the 12th. Two days earlier the *Tribune* had stated:

> 'Signor Toscanini, who was much desired because of his conceded eminence as a conductor, made [the appointment of Gatti-Casazza] a condition precedent to his acceptance of the offer to him; and the men concerned with the revolution in the affairs of the Metropolitan were impressed with the idea that the coming of the manager of La Scala would bring prestige to the new administration. Signor Toscanini is an admirable conductor and an artist of strong and aggressive methods.'

Considering that Toscanini and Gatti-Casazza had not always been in agreement at La Scala, and considering that they distrusted each other's point of view and that they had never developed a warm personal relationship (they always used the formal *lei* or *voi* form in addressing each other, never the informal *tu* which Toscanini and most of the associates of his younger years—including Puccini—used) it might seem strange that Toscanini set this particular pre-condition; but there were two very good reasons for his stand. He knew that Gatti was capable and hard-working and he also knew that he could maltreat and torment him as much as necessary in order to have his way. After more than twenty years in the theatre Toscanini was certainly aware of what demands he might reasonably make on his associates. If on occasion (actually on very few occasions) his demands were unreasonable, the cause was not a lack of practical judgement, but rather a decision to override practicalities in an attempt to reach what he considered to be a more important goal. Toscanini's image of a general manager was that of someone responsible for handling finances, for maintaining relatively peaceful and happy relations among the members of the company, and for doing his part in implementing the artistic decisions which he, Toscanini, made. The tactics he employed were straightforward and—when he felt it necessary—violent. Gatti's phlegmatic temperament was legendary, and it enabled him to survive fourteen years of collaboration with Toscanini—a situation which Sacchi described as the cohabitation of a tortoise and a cat.

Many of the Metropolitan's star singers and other members of the company were not delighted with the news of Toscanini's imminent arrival. Shortly after his appointment was announced the *New York Times* reported that Caruso was considering dissolving his contract: he was not—according to a friend—very happy about Toscanini's accession. Five years had passed since they had last worked together, and it may be that the tenor, who had meanwhile become the favourite of the New York public, was not anticipating with pleasure the inevitable battles and crises of nerves that the conductor brought with him. That at least was an honest reason. In some other cases, the reasons were chauvinistic more than anything else. The German element at the Metropolitan had dominated for the full quarter-century of the company's existence, and the sudden enthroning of two Italians was opposed in advance by many. Most upset of all seems to have been American-born soprano Emma Eames, who referred to Toscanini and Gatti-Casazza in her memoirs as 'these Italians'. She tried unsuccessfully to prevent their accession to the Metropolitan's directorship, and claimed that this was due to her 'perfect understanding of Italian operatic ideals'.[1] She does not clarify what she thought those ideals were; but in any case, if she was expecting Toscanini's operating methods to conform to some perconceived notion, she was in for a great surprise. Certainly no one in Italian operatic circles considered Toscanini's ways to be typical of the system as a whole. Eames had long been considering retiring, although she was only forty-three at the time. When the Toscanini–Gatti nominations were confirmed she announced that their first season would be her last—this before she had even met the two men, let alone worked with them.

Mahler's reaction to the Toscanini appointment was a far more reasonable one. He had begun conducting at the Metropolitan in the 1907–8 season; he was kept apprised of the negotiations with Gatti and Toscanini and on 20 January 1908 wrote to Alfred Roller that the board planned 'to make the current manager of La Scala manager of the Metropolitan, to call the highly praised conductor Toscanini for the Italian operas and to give me, so to speak, the German operas. —But this is all Music of the Future. I for my part must first see how all this affects me.'[2]

Toscanini, however, was not interested in conducting only Italian operas: he wanted to maintain the same sort of international repertoire to which he had been accustomed in Italy. In planning his first New York season, he let the Metropolitan board know that he wanted to conduct *Tristan*. Mahler had directed the opera the previous year; when he heard about Toscanini's request he wrote the Metropolitan from Europe:

'If, recently, I have allowed the new conductor to arrange things as he likes— out of consideration for my colleague's wishes—I have, nonetheless, explicitly reserved *Tristan* for myself. I took special pains with *Tristan* last season, and I can say that the form in which the work currently appears on the New York stage is my spiritual property. If Toscanini, for whom, although I do not know him, I have the greatest respect and whom I shall be honoured to greet as a colleague, were now to take over *Tristan* before my return, an entirely new stamp would be given to the work, and I would no longer be able to resume its direction in the course of the season. I must, therefore, strongly request that you reserve the direction of this work for me, and that you therefore programme it after 17 December.'[3]

Contrary to Alma Mahler's elaborately fabricated story that her husband wearily relinquished *Tristan* to Toscanini, which the latter had made 'his supreme object and an indispensable condition',[4] we find that in fact Toscanini acceded to Mahler's request and only conducted *Tristan* in the following season, when Mahler had all but ceased to conduct at the Metropolitan in order to devote more time to the New York Philharmonic; and contradicting her statement that when she and her husband eventually heard Toscanini's performance of *Tristan* they found the nuances 'distressing',[5] we have Bruno Walter's statement that Mahler had told him, 'he conducts it in a manner entirely different from ours but magnificently in his way'.[6]

Of course Mahler and Toscanini were two very unusual and very different personalities, and there cannot have been much warm feeling between them. Forty years later Toscanini told Taubman that Mahler's *Tristan* had ' "no passion in it; but the poor man was tired and sick" '.[7] To Haggin he said that Mahler was a ' "crazy man" ';[8] and it would not be surprising to discover that Mahler had felt the same way about his younger colleague.

Upon arriving in New York, one of Toscanini's first tasks—and one which he had undertaken on his own initiative—was to supervise the selection of the chorus for the French–Italian repertoire, in cooperation with chorus master Giulio Setti. Shortly afterwards he began orchestral rehearsals. The mother tongue of most of the company's orchestra members in those days was either English or German. Toscanini knew by heart the texts of all the German operas he conducted, but he was never at home in the language; and while his English eventually became fluent if imperfect, it was very primitive in 1908. He had never faced similar circumstances before (Argentinian musicians had easily been able to understand his Italian) and this increased his normal nervousness. He told Bruno Walter many years later that he had been 'extremely nervous' before his first rehearsal; and he even took pains to prepare and write out a short message in English which he read to the orchestra before that rehearsal, expressing his hopes for a productive and happy association. Although he was to begin the season with *Aida*, he chose to start his rehearsals with the more complicated *Götterdämmerung*, which was to open a few weeks later. No doubt the orchestra had heard in advance about his memory, but there was general shock when he appeared in the pit to rehearse this vast work without a score. The impression was strengthened when the new conductor began to hear and correct errors in the printed parts which had gone undetected by well-known German conductors for many years; and the way in which he immersed himself and his co-workers in the very substance of the music aroused immediate respect, admiration and enthusiasm. At the end of the rehearsal the orchestra broke into applause and bravos.

Aida (16 November) was an enormous success. The cast included Emmy Destinn, who was making her Metropolitan début in the title rôle, Caruso, Scotti and Louise Homer. 'The spirit that pervaded it was clearly instilled by the new conductor,' wrote Richard Aldrich in the *Times*. 'He is . . . a dominating power, a man of potent authority, a musician of infinite resource.' And Henry E. Krehbiel of the *Tribune* said that 'in the best sense he is an artist, an interpreter, a re creator. Without such men music is as lifeless to the ear as it is on the printed page.'

Three days later he conducted *Butterfly* with Farrar and Caruso. (At the Metropolitan many operas ran simultaneously, as opposed to La Scala's system of having only one or two running at any one time.) On the 23rd he substituted for an ailing staff conductor, Spetrino, at a performance of *Rigoletto* in Brooklyn —his only performance of that work during his Metropolitan tenure; and he did the same that week for *Tosca*, given at home. Only two weeks after Toscanini's début mezzo-soprano Maria Gay wrote to her Milanese agent: 'The Gatti–Toscanini directorate is going admirably well here; more and more the Italian operas are magnificently successful and the others are falling apart.'[9]

The bad fortune of the non-Italian operas was soon reversed by Mahler's return and by Toscanini's entry into the French and German repertoires. On 3 December he directed *Carmen*—probably his first performance of a work in a language other than Italian—with Gay and Caruso in the lead rôles; and a week later New York heard his performance of *Götterdämmerung*, with Fremstad and Schmedes. In addition to restoring the Prologue and Norn scene, which had been omitted in Metropolitan performances since 1900, Toscanini also included the Waltraute episode (with Homer), which he had cut in his two previous productions of the work. (This according to Seltsam's *Metropolitan Opera Annals* and Homer's daughter; but Kolodin and Aldrich claim that Waltraute was cut.) Aldrich wrote that Toscanini 'presented a performance of remarkable energy and dramatic power, as well as one of great musical beauty.'

On 17 December Toscanini conducted a double bill of *Le Villi* (American première) and *Cavalleria rusticana*, which was followed in January by another American première: *La Wally*. This was a tribute to the dear friend of his youth; but it was also the last production he ever conducted of a Catalani opera. Two nights later he participated in a concert at the Metropolitan for the benefit of the victims of a recent Italian earthquake by conducting the quartet from *Rigoletto* with Alda, Gay, Bonci and Amato; and on 21 February he led the Verdi *Requiem* with Destinn, Homer, Martin and Hinckley. The impression was so great that three more performances were scheduled that season and two the following year.

Falstaff had already been a basic element of the Toscanini repertoire for nearly fifteen years when New York first heard him conduct it on the afternoon of 20 March, with Scotti. That evening he led the second scene of Act II of *Aida* as part of a Metropolitan Pension and Endowment fund benefit gala (Mahler directed Act I of *The Bartered Bride* on the same programme); and a few days later he conducted the Prologue to *Mefistofele* with Didur and the quartet from *Rigoletto* (same soloists as 10 January) on another special concert. In total he directed forty-five performances of ten operas, four concerts, and parts of three benefit programmes during his first Metropolitan season. He also led eighteen tour performances, scattered throughout the season, in Brooklyn, Philadelphia, Baltimore, Chicago and Pittsburgh.

He can only have been delighted with the extremely high calibre of the singers with whom he worked in New York; nevertheless, he did not modify his principle that all artistic decisions must in the end be made by him—and this did not appeal to many of the famous artists in the company. Erich Leinsdorf, who worked as Toscanini's *répétiteur* at Salzburg in the 1930s, has pointed out that when Toscanini was working with singers

'... who had many years' experience in the parts they were singing with him, he would very willingly let them be and not try to mould them in a new way. The same was true of solo wind players in the orchestra. He was a generous man. He was only impatient with the wrong mentality. If he felt that people were not serious or that they were stupid, that was something he could not stand.'[10]

Of course, it was also possible for an artist to be serious, intelligent and capable and to have a view of a rôle or of part of a rôle that clashed with Toscanini's. In such a case, Toscanini's opinion was that that artist must be persuaded or forced to conform to his overall vision of the opera—otherwise the work could not be presented as a unity. Since he was not patient, diplomatic or compliant, this standpoint sometimes led to open conflict.

It is interesting to examine the accusations made against him by his implacable enemy, Emma Eames:

'As an operatic conductor he left much to be desired by comparison with such great ones as Seidl and Mancinelli. He was charming and amiable, and rehearsed at the piano with me, taking all my shades and intentions. Once before the public, however, the opera was his and his alone. He had such a marvellous and exact memory that he could reproduce always what he had heard one do at any one particular rehearsal, and only that.'[11]

(This estimate was based upon the three performances of *Aida* and possibly one of *Tosca* which she sang with him—nothing else.) In other words Eames was not complaining that Toscanini made her alter her way of singing a rôle: he was simply requiring her to *have a way* of singing it, to reproduce in performance essentially what she had done at rehearsal. Today this is a basic and unarguable tenet of operatic performance and falls more into the realm of professional behaviour than artistry. It is one of the countless examples of what Carlo Maria Giulini meant when he told me that 'Toscanini fought terrible battles in order to achieve things which everyone today takes for granted. Even musicians who disagree with him are the direct beneficiaries of his work, of his struggle.'[12]

Toscanini felt very strongly that without an enormous amount of discipline, a serious artistic achievement was not possible. Therefore, he prepared every detail of a work with great care, tried to leave nothing to chance, and considered the conductor's task to be that of putting together a thoroughly integrated and unified production of an opera—not to accompany each singer in the most convenient way possible.

Many singers understood and agreed with Toscanini's objectives and were ready to cooperate with him. Louise Homer's daughter and biographer, Anne Homer, has written that although Toscanini's discipline required 'a devastating concentration, a tension, a sometimes violent, slashing, relentless rehearsal session that was often, for the singers, a nightmare . . . under his guidance they might awake from the nightmare astonished, invigorated, inspired, with an altogether new vision of this rôle.'[13] Frieda Hempel, who sang with Toscanini during his last three Metropolitan seasons, said in her memoirs: 'I considered him to be one of the greatest conductors of all time . . . We were good friends and often worked together. Unfortunately, I never sang an Italian opera with him [she did actually sing in *Un ballo in maschera* with him] . . . but his understanding of the German spirit and feeling was excellent.'[14] The admiration and devotion of other artists who worked with him have already been reported in this book, and there will be other instances.

On 27 February 1909 the Metropolitan released the news that Toscanini's and Gatti's contracts had been extended for a further two seasons—which had already been decided three months earlier. It was probably at this time that a group of singers signed a petition requesting that Andreas Dippel, who had been retained from the previous administration to help in the transition and to serve as Gatti's co-manager, have his contract renewed as well. This was a thinly veiled protest against the new directorate, and it had been signed by Farrar, Sembrich, Eames, Scotti and Caruso. Dippel remained another season and was then dismissed.

Having conducted his last performance on 10 April, Toscanini returned to Milan, where he led three 'Popular Orchestral Concerts of Professors and Students' at the Conservatory on 2, 4 and 17 June. The ticket sales for these concerts went towards furnishing the Conservatory's new concert hall. New to

Toscanini's programmes were *La Mer*, the recently deceased Rimsky-Korsakov's 'Antar' Symphony and young Maurice Ravel's *Rhapsodie espagnole*. A seventeen-year-old student named Victor De Sabata, who was to become one of Italy's best-known conductors, played cymbals in Mendelssohn's *Midsummer Night's Dream* Wedding March. In his enthusiasm, the young man fell over backwards after his first entrance during the first rehearsal, knocking over the timpani. Toscanini and the orchestra laughed heartily.

On 1 June Giuseppe Martucci had died in Naples, and a month later Toscanini made one of his rare appearances in that city, where he led a memorial concert of Martucci's music, with Krusceniski as soloist. Part of the summer was spent in the Alps with his family, and he later went to Munich to attend a Brahms festival conducted by Fritz Steinbach. 'I have enjoyed myself beyond words,' he wrote to Polo on 12 September. 'Brahms is great—Steinbach marvellous.'[15]

Toscanini's second New York season opened on 15 November with *La gioconda* (Destinn, Homer, Caruso, Amato). Two nights later he conducted *Otello*, with Leo Slezak making his Metropolitan début in the title rôle. *Butterfly* soon reappeared under his direction, and on the 27th he led his first North American *Tristan*. 'New York music lovers had an opportunity to enjoy the reading which when it was originally published stirred Milan and attracted general attention throughout Europe,' wrote W.J. Henderson in the *Sun*.

'Its presentation here fully justified the enthusiasm in Italy and the warm praise awarded by the German critics. Mr. Toscanini's interpretation of the first act was unexpectedly subdued, and while musically finished, seemed to promise a want of vital emotion in the remainder of the performance. But it became evident that the distinguished conductor conceived the first act in a mood of restrained intensity and reserved the outpouring of thrilling passion for the second. Here, indeed, the waves of turbulent orchestration surged in inspired grandeur. From the summons to Tristan to the end of the act the music was filled with emotional fervour, and the majestic climaxes were brought out with a superb power, yet with never a step beyond the limits of musical beauty. Mr. Toscanini . . . assumed his rightful position among the most interesting Wagner conductors known to this public.'

Aida was revived on 3 December; three weeks later Toscanini presented his version of Gluck's *Orfeo* to the public, a year and a half after the unsuccessful Scala production. The previous March, he had invited Louise Homer, whose voice appealed to him, to sing the part of Orfeo, which she had long wanted to do. She studied it with him in great detail, and her copy of the score contains his blue-pencilled instructions—*agitato, con passione* and so on. He interpolated the aria *Divinités du Styx* from *Alceste*, as well as a trio from *Paride ed Elena* and a chorus from *Echo et Narcisse*; and he eliminated the overture. Sets designed by Jacques Pacquereau and painted by Paul Chauvanne were imported from

Paris. Gadski sang Euridice and young Alma Gluck made her Metropolitan début as the Happy Shade. Krehbiel called the production 'the most interesting event of the operatic season thus far . . . Mr. Toscanini's treatment of the music was reverential—more than reverential—it was loving, and his spirit had its counterpart in that of Mme. Homer.'

A month later Toscanini conducted the American première of Franchetti's *Germania*, and *Falstaff* was revived on 16 February. He led the third act of *Gioconda* at a pension fund benefit performance on 1 March; and the New York public was able to hear his *Meistersinger* at the end of that month. Aldrich wrote:

'That Wagner's comedy did not reach a performance at the Metropolitan Opera House till the last days of the season has been a matter for surprise and disappointment. But this season it was transferred [from Alfred Hertz] to the care of Mr. Toscanini; and the delay in the production has been due to his exigencies in the matter of rehearsals. Although many of the principal singers are the same and the scenic arrangements have not been changed, the work was necessarily entirely restudied under Mr. Toscanini. And how thoroughly this was done yesterday's performance bore eloquent testimony. It was indeed worth waiting for. . . . New York has heard representations of *Die Meistersinger* . . . that have been memorable in many ways; but yesterday's was one of the most remarkable of them all . . . Nothing Mr. Toscanini has done, not even his reading of *Tristan*, has equalled his performance of *Die Meistersinger*.'

Toscanini later said that this was one of the productions that had given him greatest satisfaction.

At the end of the season, during which he had conducted thirty-nine performances of nine operas, plus twenty-two tour performances in five cities, he and Gatti took the company—excluding the orchestra—to Paris for a brief season of Italian opera at the Théâtre du Châtelet. Between 19 May and 25 June 1910 they presented *Aida, Cavalleria rusticana, Otello, Falstaff* and *Manon Lescaut* in a total of eighteen performances, with singers such as Caruso, Amato, Destinn, Homer, Rappold, Fremstad, Slezak, Alda, Scotti, Bori and Farrar. The opening night —and the rest of the tour as well—almost turned into a disaster when the Metropolitan administration was accused of discriminating against French singers. This seems to have come about through the machinations of Marie Delna, a French contralto who had sung two performances of *Orfeo* with Toscanini during the previous season and who had had a serious argument with him, following which her contract had not been renewed. A segment of the Parisian press began a malicious campaign against Toscanini and Gatti; and at the first performance—*Aida*—the conductor was greeted with calculated hostility by a portion of the public at the beginning of the second act. However, he continued to conduct, Homer continued to sing Amneris's solo, and the disrupters were subdued. The performance proceeded normally and the rest of the season was highly successful, even from a financial point of view: an average of $10,500 per night was taken in—a huge sum for those days.

The orchestra at Toscanini's disposal was that of the Concerts Colonne. He had considerable trouble in rousing the players from their lethargy and unloosed more than one cataclysmic storm during the rehearsals; but Gabriel Pierné, who was then conductor of the Colonne Orchestra, recalled years later that he as an observer and his musicians as participants were all convinced that Toscanini was the greatest living conductor.

The biggest surprise of the Parisian adventure was the overwhelming success of *Manon Lescaut*. The opera was already seventeen years old, but had never been heard in Paris because of national pride in Massenet's somewhat older *Manon*. Most surprised of all was Puccini, who wrote to Giulio Ricordi: 'A real and total triumph. Performance unique. I don't think I've ever had such an organic and perfect ensemble for *Manon*.'[16] Toscanini had made some modifications in the orchestral score of the opera, with Puccini's permission, although the score he used in Paris actually shows very few annotations in his hand: some accent marks, some changes in the use of mutes, a few remarks like *leggerissimo* and *en dehors*, and a few bowing changes.[17] Further alterations may have been decided upon during rehearsals. In any case, after returning to Milan the composer wrote to Toscanini, who was still in Paris:

'The Ricordi Company have finally decided to print [a new edition of] the *Manon* score. You will be sent a copy which you will want to edit. Believe me, you couldn't do me a bigger favour. Thus, with your corrections of colourings and effective bowings, etc., etc., I'll finally be able to have a definitive *Manon*, and to free her from the anarchy that binds her. My soul is full of your performance and of the goodness of your spirit; I hope to see you soon.'[18]

While in Paris Puccini and Gatti reached an agreement on presenting the world première of the composer's nearly completed opera, *La fanciulla del West*, at the Metropolitan during the following season.

On 19 June the visiting company gave a benefit performance at the Opéra, and managed to raise 200,000 francs for the survivors of a recently sunk submarine. The programme included the second act of *Tristan* (the first time since the Franco-Prussian war that German had been sung at the Opéra), the third act of *Bohème*, an act of *Otello* and the final scene of *Faust*. Debussy attended several of the Metropolitan's Parisian performances, and he and Toscanini met.

Having returned to Italy, Toscanini spent some time at the Montecatini spa. Puccini wrote him there on 28 July to inform him that he was about to finish *Fanciulla* and to invite him to come and examine it with him. That visit took place some time in August. By mid-October Toscanini was back in New York preparing for a crushingly difficult season. Mahler had now completely severed his ties with the Metropolitan, having conducted only three performances the previous year; and although the conducting staff now numbered nine, as opposed to four during Toscanini's first season, his workload had become heavier than ever.

His choice for the opening night (14 November) was Gluck's *Armide*, given for the first time at the Metropolitan, with Fremstad, Caruso, Amato and Homer. 'If the public fails to receive the opera with enthusiasm it will at least recognize the stupendous conception of genius . . .', wrote Henderson. 'The production as a whole . . . was a new laurel in the crown worn jointly by Messrs. Gatti-Casazza and Toscanini.'

In addition to *Armide*, within the first ten days of the season he conducted *Aida*, *Butterfly*, his first Metropolitan *Bohème* and *Gioconda*. On 10 December came the anxiously awaited première of *Fanciulla*, with Destinn, Caruso and Amato. Rehearsals had begun six weeks earlier and Toscanini had wired Puccini, assuring him that all was well. 'You can't imagine how much pleasure your telegram gave me,' the composer wrote back on 28 October. '. . . I had been awaiting it for three or four days, and there was a bit of anguish in that wait. Now I am calm and happy . . .'[19]

Accompanied by his son Tonio and Tito Ricordi, Puccini arrived in New York to oversee the last three weeks of rehearsals, and David Belasco, whose play *The Girl of the Golden West* had served as the basis for the new opera, supervised the staging. Posterity has relegated *Fanciulla* to a rather low position among Puccini's works; but it was received with near ecstasy by the capacity audience who had paid double the normal ticket prices to attend the first night—much the same as people who today pay £70 to attend a performance at one of the famous European music festivals are easily convinced that they have heard something extraordinary. This great-grandfather of the 'spaghetti western' was kindly, if not rhapsodically, received in the press as well, and Aldrich commented that 'the presentation of the opera was one of Mr. Toscanini's masterpieces.' Puccini was given royal treatment in New York; and from aboard the *Lusitania* which carried him back to Europe at the end of December, he wrote melancholically to Carla Toscanini:

'You have been so good and kind to me, so gently attentive; Toscanini so patient and so affectionately friendly! My thoughts are full of you both, and I envy you. I, too, would like to be like you, with your family all together, with your children who love you so much, with friends who surround you and believe in you. Unfortunately, I feel alone in the world and so I am always unhappy. And yet I have always tried to love and have never been understood —that is, I've always been misinterpreted. Now it is late, I'm too far along. Keep your friendship for me, so that I can at least have good and intelligent people who tolerate and understand me.'[20]

1 and *2* Toscanini and his
wife, Carla De Martini, *circa*
1900

3 Battle over the Italian première of *Salomé* (1906): a contemporary Milanese cartoonist shows Toscanini whacking Richard Strauss over the head with his baton (*Museo Teatrale alla Scala, Milan*)

4 Letter from Toscanini to Puccini, from Pisa, 1 March 1894, concerning the preparation for Toscanini's first production of *Manon Lescaut* (*collection of Robert Hupka*)

5 Toscanini, *circa* 1915, when
he resigned from the
Metropolitan Opera

6 Toscanini at Verdi's
birthplace, Roncole (Busseto),
at the time of the Scala
company's performances of
Falstaff at Busseto, 1926

7, 8 and 9 Three of Toscanini's singers: tenor Francesco Tamagno as Arnoldo in *William Tell*, baritone Mariano Stabile as Falstaff, and tenor Aureliano Pertile as Des Grieux in *Manon Lescaut*

Opposite 10, 11, 12 and *13* Four of Toscanini's sopranos: Cesira Ferrani as Mimì in *Bohème*, Rosina Storchio as Zazà, Salomea Krusceniski as Salomé, and Gilda Dalla Rizza

14 After a performance of *Falstaff* at Salzburg during the 1930s. To Toscanini's left: Maria Caniglia (Alice) and Mariano Stabile (Falstaff).

15 Toscanini with his son, Walter, in the basement of their home in Riverdale, New York, where Toscanini's recordings were stored (*from the collection of Walter Toscanini*)

16 Toscanini at the Dead Sea, Palestine, 1936 or '38 (*courtesy RCA Records*)

17 Concert at Lucerne with
Vladimir Horowitz as soloist in
Brahms' Piano Concerto No. 2,
29 August 1939. (The last
concert given by Toscanini in
Europe until after World War
II.)

18 4 July 1946 – Toscanini
arrives at Lucerne station for
concerts with the Scala
orchestra. *Left* (looking
backwards) Dr Walter Strebi,
head of the festival; *right* (with
cane) Dr Aloys Mooser,
musicologist, whom Toscanini
had first met on Mont Blanc,
1898. (*Lucerne Festival
archives*)

In a less depressed mood, he informed Clausetti: 'Musical performance magnificent and *mise-en-scène* surprising. Caruso great, Destinn very fine, Amato excellent; Toscanini immeasurable and good, a real angel.'[21]

Toscanini's season proceeded with a remounting of *Orfeo* in December, *Tristan* and *Meistersinger* in January, *Germania*, *Tosca* and *Otello* in February, *Cavalleria* in March and, on the 29th of that month, the American première of Dukas's *Ariane et Barbe-bleue*, with Farrar and Rothier. He also led the first act of *Armide* at a benefit afternoon on 6 April. Sixty-six performances of fourteen operas in five months, not to mention tour performances in seven cities.

In February Toscanini had met one of his most famous compatriots, pianist and composer Ferruccio Busoni, who was in the midst of an American tour. On the 21st he had heard Mahler conduct Busoni's *Berceuse* with the New York Philharmonic. (It was one of Mahler's last appearances: he returned to Europe shortly afterwards and died in May.) Four days later Busoni wrote to his wife: 'This evening I shall probably be with Toscanini who, it seems, was charmed with the *Berceuse*. That may help the opera [*Die Brautwahl*]—when once it is finished.' And a few days later:

'Last Sunday (the 26th) I was at Toscanini's. He lives in a private suite in a big hotel [the Ansonia] and keeps his own Italian cook.

It was the most pleasant evening I have spent since you left. The food was excellent and the conversation animated and interesting, right up to midnight.

Consolo [pianist and teacher] was there. I played them the Sonatina, the Mephisto Waltz, the St. Francis legends. I was brought still more into the right atmosphere by a Steinway which thunders and *sustains the tone* (it is so long since I had this pleasure!). Toscanini is the most intelligent musician I have met up till now (with perhaps the exception of Strauss). Tremendously lively, quick, far-sighted, and artistic.

He repeated whole pages out of my aesthetic. I mean, he spoke my thoughts and did not say one word which I could not corroborate with my whole heart. He seemed to have a particular sympathy for me, for (according to Consolo) it is seldom he is so communicative.

He looks scarcely thirty years of age, but he is 44. His blindness is a legend. He does not even use glasses. His memory is a phenomenon in the annals of physiology; but this does not impede his other faculties as is often the case with such abnormalities. He had just studied the very difficult score of Dukas's *Ariane et Barbe-bleue* and the next morning he was going to take the first rehearsal—from memory! But such achievements must wear him out; he is a bundle of nerves . . . I hope with all my heart that life will bring me still more closely in touch with him.'[22]

Not long afterwards Busoni wrote to a friend that Toscanini was interested in his opera; but in fact it was never performed under his direction. Their friendship never developed—partly, no doubt, because they were rarely in the same place at the same time. In a letter to Egon Petri in 1912, the pianist criticized Toscanini for working in America instead of Italy—an odd remark coming from someone who spent the greater part of his life outside his native country. But he added: 'If he did his damned duty and stayed home, people would put every difficulty in his way.'[23] According to Toscanini's daughter Wanda, her father once attended a Busoni recital in New York. The pianist's interpretation of Beethoven's 'Waldstein' Sonata was so distasteful to him that he walked out before the concert had ended. This act was noted by many and provoked a scandal; but Busoni himself was not offended and sent a note to Toscanini stating that he would be happy to see him the following Sunday at his next recital, and promising to play 'well' this time. 'Papà was amused to see that "well" in quotation marks,' said Wanda, 'and he went to the concert that Sunday. He took a seat in the front row, remained to the end, and applauded enthusiastically.'[24]

In 1917 Busoni wrote to Toscanini:

'Right now I am finishing a short and bizarre opera, *Turandot* (on the Venetian Gozzi's original text);—and for the admiration and affection I bear you, as well as for whatever value I attribute to my new work, I should like to ask your permission to put your name on the dedicatory page.

I would ask you further—although I know and understand your aversion to writing—to confirm this great favour with a short note; otherwise I should not take the liberty of putting your name on the work . . .

I greet you with affection and respect.'[25]

The opera was published with a dedication to Toscanini who, however, never conducted it. He did, on the other hand, play two of Busoni's orchestral pieces, the *Berceuse* and *Rondò arlecchinesco*, fairly frequently in later years; and when he learned that the pianist's widow was in difficult economic straits he made her a gift and sent out the following message:

'This is an appeal to all lovers of music, to help in an hour of need, Madame Gerda Busoni—the widow of one of the greatest musicians of our time, Ferruccio Busoni. I shall be personally grateful for your contribution.' [Original in English.][26]

On his return to Italy in the spring of 1911 Toscanini stopped briefly in Milan and then went to Rome to direct *Falstaff* and the Italian première of *Fanciulla* at the Teatro Costanzi; these productions coincided with the fiftieth anniversary celebrations of the Kingdom of Italy. Tenor Giovanni Martinelli, who was twenty-six at the time, related the following story about his participation in the production:

'I had received word in Milan to go to Casa Ricordi for an audition. I entered a beautiful hall, someone sat down at the piano and said, "Sing something." . . . At the end, I saw an old man come in through a door curtain. It was Giulio Ricordi, followed by two other people—Puccini and Maestro Toscanini, no less. They had heard me sing and were now muttering among themselves about my vocal possibilities. Turning to me they said, "You must come to Rome, because we're beginning rehearsals of *Fanciulla del West*." "But I don't know a note of *Fanciulla del West*!" "No matter: we'll teach it to you."

In Rome they had me follow all the rehearsals of *Fanciulla* with tenor Amedeo Bassi, until one day Toscanini said to me: "Bassi will have to go to London [after the first performances] and we'll have to continue here with a substitute." Then he sat down at the piano and had me sing. Out of nervousness, I was unable to hear the entrances, so I didn't follow the Maestro at all. All at once he rudely interrupted me, closing the score. (Toscanini was a great, good man, because when he took a liking to someone he supported him; but he also had moments of terrible outbursts.) He turned to his assistant and said in Parmesan dialect, "This guy is too green for me."

You can imagine how I felt at that moment; but I think that a good star was protecting me and told me to reply, "Look, Maestro, I'm so happy to have been with you for half an hour and to have seen Rome that I'll gladly leave." Toscanini smiled at me and said to his assistant, "You take him for awhile, continue to study and rehearse, and we'll pull the thing together". . . .'[27]

In July Toscanini gave three performances of the Verdi *Requiem* in Rome—two at the Augusteum and one at the Costanzi. It was probably after his return to Milan that month that he bought the home on Via Durini which would be his favourite residence for the rest of his life. It is a three-storey building which dates from the seventeenth century, with a beautiful courtyard and a wrought iron balcony.

August found Toscanini at Moncenisio in the Alps, where he relaxed among friends and relatives and took long walks, prior to a series of concerts he was to give under Depanis's aegis at Turin's International Exposition. His eyes were bothering him and his myopia seemed to be worsening; and he wrote Depanis from Moncenisio:

'I have followed my oculist here; he tortures me daily with rather painful eye injections. . . . I can go to Turin around 10 September and stay there until the 28th. I'm including four programmes. They don't sparkle with novelty, but novelties (and I've looked through many of them) are not all interesting. . . . Suggest some changes if you like, and I'll be happy to satisfy you.'[28]

An exchange on the programming ensued, and Toscanini wrote again to his friend:

'Concerning Sinigaglia's *Piedmont Suite*—yes, it's new, but we're still dealing with those rhapsodies fabricated out of popular Piedmontese themes; and if this time there is no "The Sun is Shining" or "Ciao, ciao, ciao", we find instead "The Violet" and similar folk tunes. The *Suite* is dedicated to me—help! . . . I have no desire to look at new scores . . . Dr. Precerutti has begged and prayed me to let my eyes rest. They will still be subjected to other injections and various sorts of maltreatment even during the period of the Turin concerts.'[29]

Between 16 and 29 September Toscanini conducted five concerts on the series. Among the other conductors were Debussy, D'Indy, Elgar, Kajanus, Mengelberg, Serafin and Steinbach.

In New York Toscanini opened his fourth Metropolitan season on 13 November with *Aida*; and by the end of the month he had conducted *Fanciulla, Tristan, Butterfly* and *Gioconda*. *Tosca, Armide* and *Orfeo* were added in December. On 3 January 1912 he led the American première of Wolf-Ferrari's *Le donne curiose*. *Ariane* returned to the repertoire that month, *Otello* in February; and in March, besides *Meistersinger*, he led his first American production of Massenet's *Manon*, with Farrar and Caruso. On 28 March the *Corriere della sera* reported that Toscanini and Gatti-Casazza had had their contracts renewed for a further three-year term. The statistics for this season are fifty-eight performances of thirteen operas with—this time—only five tour performances. This murderous schedule (for example: evening of 3 February—*Tristan*; afternoon of the 4th—*Fanciulla*; same evening—*Butterfly*) apparently did not exhaust his energies, because instead of returning to Italy at season's end, he went to Buenos Aires where, between mid-May and early September, he conducted *Tristan, Aida, Mefistofele, Manon, Don Pasquale, Manon Lescaut, Bohème, Germania, Tosca, Ariane et Barbe-bleue, Butterfly, Rigoletto, Falstaff, Götterdämmerung* and Humperdinck's *Königskinder*. (Some sources also list Massenet's *Werther* and Gounod's *Roméo et Juliette*; but those were in fact directed by Bernardino Molinari.) The Dukas and Humperdinck productions were Argentinian premières. These were Toscanini's first appearances at the Teatro Colón, which had opened since his previous visit to the city in 1906. They were also his last appearances as an opera conductor in South America.

The *Manon* production was the cause of a confrontation between Toscanini and tenor Giuseppe Anselmi. Conductor Lorenzo Molajoli sent this gossip from Buenos Aires to another conductor:

'31 May. . . . A terrible argument arose between Toscanini and Anselmi at the first piano rehearsal, since Toscanini insisted that Anselmi sing everything as written in *Manon*; but you well know that in order for a singer to create an effect in these operas, the conductor has to be a bit elastic, as long as one isn't talking about Wagnerian operas. [!?] So Anselmi rebelled, and besides calling him a despot, he told him that he had sung the opera with conductors like him and *better*, and that he wouldn't tolerate his despotism. He did not want to sing anymore with him; and in the end he said goodbye to everyone, adding, "Excuse what has happened, and best wishes to everyone except you"— addressing Toscanini. Now it turns out that Toscanini refuses to conduct *Manon* and the other operas in which Anselmi is to sing.

It seems impossible, but although some have censured Anselmi's act, *everyone is happy about it*. And this is due to Toscanini's *popula>.ty* in the theatre.

News! Molinari took the orchestra rehearsal but it fell apart; and peace has been declared between Toscanini and Anselmi, with Bori [who was singing the title rôle] as intermediary. . . . But what a bad figure Molinari cut! And to think that it was Toscanini who had him hired and that he gets 6,000 lire per month. Lucky people who find protectors even when they are not qualified!'[30]

And unlucky people who find themselves the subjects of gossip: Molinari was certainly far from being an unqualified conductor.

Returning to Milan around the end of September, Toscanini began a series of consultations concerning several musical projects. The first of these involved preliminary planning for producing Boito's long-anticipated second opera, *Nerone*, which the composer had been contemplating and working on for forty-five years! He had now finished the massive vocal score and was torturing himself with the orchestration; and he hoped to present the work at La Scala in the autumn of 1913, with Toscanini and Caruso—both of whom accepted his invitations. Toscanini and Boito met several times during the former's Milanese sojourn. Shortly before the conductor's departure for America the old man wrote him:

'You are again going to carry the divine light of Art to distant peoples. May heaven grant your quick return among us with that light! You are the last ray that remains; all the rest is darkness. Safe journey. Safe return. An embrace.'[31]

Another dozen years were to pass before Toscanini would conduct the première of his friend's opera.

The second project involved negotiations with La Scala concerning the Verdi centenary, which was to take place the following year. Of this, more later. But the final and most immediately fruitful consultations led to Toscanini's agreeing to conduct two concerts at Milan's Teatro del Popolo on 10 and 11 November. This theatre had close ties with the Italian Socialist Party and its newspaper, *Avanti*. Admittance to the first performance of the Beethoven-Wagner programme cost forty *centesimi*—next to nothing even in those days—and was very strictly limited to workers and their families. The second performance (same programme) was open to everyone at prices several times higher, with the receipts going towards the workers and staff of the theatre itself. Toscanini was honoured at a reception afterwards. He must have gone to Rome the very next day to begin rehearsing a concert of music by Cherubini, Brahms, Beethoven, Debussy and Wagner, presented on 17 and 20 November, following which he returned to Milan for a week and then left for New York.

This was the first time since his arrival at the Metropolitan that he had not conducted an opening night. He began with *Orfeo* on 19 December and continued through mid-March with eight other operas from past seasons. Then, on 19 March 1913, he fulfilled the dream which he had expressed to Aloys Mooser in a blizzard-bound hut on the Mont Blanc *massif* fifteen years earlier: he conducted his and America's first performance of Moussorgsky's *Boris Godunov*. He had begun rehearsing the opera in January and the preparations were extraordinarily thorough. Sets and costumes were again imported from Paris (designers Golovine and Benois), and Rimsky-Korsakov's heavily altered version of the score was used. Haggin questioned Toscanini about this in 1949:

'He conceded that Rimsky's correction of the consecutive fifths in the Simpleton's song had spoiled the passage, but insisted that the editing as a whole had made the work a success. I cited Rimsky's own statement in *My Musical Life* that the Musorgsky original had been a success when it had first been produced. "Yes," said Toscanini, "but only in Russia." '[32]

The opera was performed in Italian with Didur as Boris, Homer as Marina, Rothier as Pimen, and Paul Althouse, in his Metropolitan début, as Dmitri. Henderson commented:

'That the production of last evening impressed itself upon the audience as a remarkable disclosure of novelty in subject, method, and style was unquestionable ... Over all the guiding genius of Mr. Toscanini was felt to hold its masterful grip ... The orchestra has a place ... quite equal to that of the voices. One follows the opera with unceasing admiration for the use of musical resource ... The orchestra played well indeed and the whole interpretation of the work was made vital and beautiful by the sympathetic guidance and fine intelligence of Arturo Toscanini ...'

At the time of the *Boris* opening an American magazine called *The Century* had carried a lengthy article by Max Smith, a journalist who spoke Italian well and had become friendly with the conductor. Because he was able to question Toscanini and his wife on Toscanini's study methods and because he was privileged to attend rehearsals, parts of the article are of considerable value.

'... Toscanini's method of study is as follows: first, he sits down at the piano and plays the score carefully, with his extremely short-sighted eyes held close to the page. In this way he supplements and sharpens his photographic vision through his keenly retentive ear. Subsequently he studies the score apart from the piano, only now and then calling upon the instrument for assistance. Stretched at ease in bed or relaxing comfortably in a chair, he pores over his volumes for hours at a time, spending occasionally a whole night at work. . . .

. . . Toscanini gives personal attention to each of the principals, sometimes going to their homes and playing their accompaniments himself, before he meets them for a combined rehearsal. It is interesting to watch him at that stage, sitting at some distance from the piano, which is manipulated by an assistant conductor, clapping his hands in rhythmical command, often singing in unison with his pupils, shouting his directions, giving this order or that, criticizing, encouraging, blaming, approving, and all without referring to the score.

The next step . . . is the rehearsal on the stage to the accompaniment of a piano. On such an occasion you will see stage-managers and assistant conductors scurrying about among the singers, hinting, helping, suggesting. You will see the prompter sitting in a chair . . . following the vocal score and reading aloud the first words of every line in the text. The conductor, you will observe, is also on hand, not only to keep his artists within the rhythmical limitations defined by him, but to cooperate with those whose immediate duty is to map out the dramatic scheme of the play, to tell the actors . . . how they must move about, with what gestures they must express their feelings. . . . At times, indeed, he will act a whole scene to convey his intentions graphically. . . . Even more enlightening is his verbal comment and criticism, inspired by a penetrating knowledge of the interlocking artistic values, dramatic, poetic, and musical.

. . . With most musical directors . . . the first general rehearsal has many interruptions. Singers stand inactive while the orchestra practices a part of the score which did not go quite as it should. Musicians grow fidgety waiting for some stage tangle to be settled. The strain upon all of pauses, discussions, and repetitions is at times intolerable. When Toscanini marshals his forces this is not the case. The previous preparations . . . have been carried out with so elaborate a care . . . that when the parts are finally assembled every piece of the complicated operatic machinery fits perfectly into its particular place. Even under Toscanini, to be sure, there may be occasional halts and repetitions, and woe to him who has to shoulder the responsibility! But these are the exceptions not the rule.

. . . Toscanini's abhorrence of applause, manifested frequently in the Metropolitan Opera House, is not an affectation, as some observers have suspected. "I cannot give the exact reasons," he explained; "but noisy demonstrations of approval always have given me an acute sensation of pain. It is not timidity, I know. It is an instinct. I had the feeling as a boy when I played the cello for the first time in public. As soon as the hand-clapping began I could not resist the impulse to rush into hiding." . . .[33]

Toscanini conducted his first Metropolitan *Don Pasquale* on 5 April, and eight days later led his first concert in New York since the Verdi *Requiem* performances several seasons earlier: Wagner's *Faust* Overture, Strauss's *Till Eulenspiegel* and Beethoven's Ninth Symphony, with soloists Hempel, Homer, Jörn and Griswold. The *Herald* carried an interesting report of the event.

' "Since when does Caruso sing on Sunday night?" asked a man who arrived early at the Metropolitan Opera House last night, for the line of ticket buyers completely encircled the building. Mr. Caruso was not to sing, but Mr. Arturo Toscanini . . . was to appear for the first time [sic] in America as a symphonic conductor. Every seat had been sold days ago, and when the limit of tickets of admittance had been disposed of last night there were still hundreds of persons in line.

"The ticket rack was emptied in two hours last Tuesday," said Mr. Earle R. Lewis, treasurer, "and since then we must have disappointed fully 5000 persons."

It was a distinctly musical gathering, including conductors, composers, pianists and almost everyone prominently concerned with or interested in music. Many were eager to criticize the Italian for his conducting of Beethoven. . . . The answer of the critics and all was that they applauded each number, and after the final movement of Beethoven's Ninth Symphony, which ended the concert, they remained to cheer and cheer. The auditorium emptied so slowly that finally the lights were turned down, as the conductor would not appear again. . . . Mr. Toscanini's reading was not that of an Italian, but of a master of all schools, upholding his foreign reputation as a remarkable symphonic conductor. . . .'

Richard Aldrich wrote in the *Times*:

'He revealed in the fullest measure the qualities of the great symphonic conductor. . . . In all the nuances of the performance the melodic line was not interrupted; nor in all the plastic shaping of the phrase was the symmetry of the larger proportion of the organic unit of the whole lost sight of. It was rhythmically of extraordinary vitality. . . . There were subtle and significant modulations of tempo, but never of a disturbing sort.'

Toscanini told Haggin that the soloists in that performance of the Ninth (which was repeated on the 18th) were

' ". . . best I ever have; and was good orchestra." This reminded him of the rehearsal at which the Metropolitan orchestra "play like pig" and he swore at it in Italian. When, subsequently, the Italian was translated, the orchestra was offended and said it wouldn't play for him until he apologized. To the mediator who came to see him Toscanini explained that he couldn't apologize because "orchestra play like pig." But he proposed the solution that worked: "I go to rehearsal and smile and say "*Good* morning." '[34]

Besides arriving a month later than usual, Toscanini had been ill during part of the season, so the records show only thirty-six performances of eleven operas, along with six out-of-town appearances. He had, however, conducted approximately 175 performances—almost entirely operatic—during the previous year and a half, on three continents, at a time when travel was slow. A rest was badly needed, especially for his eyes, and he did no conducting for the next four months, which were spent in Italy.

Then, in September and October, in honour of Verdi's 100th birthday (10 October 1913), he conducted new productions of *Traviata* and *Falstaff* at the tiny and beautiful theatre in the composer's home town of Busseto. He personally and lovingly supervised every detail of the project: he brought his friend Albertini from Milan to see to the lowering of the orchestra pit; asked the impresario Borioli from Turin to organize the 'season'; saw to it that the best singers were obtained—Bori, Garbin and Amato, among others; carefully selected most of the players for the reduced orchestra; and put the remaining choices in trusted hands. I had the fortune of speaking personally with one of the members of that orchestra, some sixty-four years *post factum*. Prof. Giulio Riccardi was then eighteen years old and a recent graduate of the Parma Conservatory, where he had studied violin with Toscanini's ex-classmate Eurialo Allodi. Riccardi still recalls that before the first orchestral rehearsal, Toscanini came up to him at the last stand of the second violins, greeted him warmly, and told him of the letter of recommendation Allodi had sent him on the young man's behalf. It was a simple and natural gesture, and very effective in calming the nerves of an inexperienced musician.

Riccardi says—and written testimony left by others corroborates this—that Toscanini was very happy at Busseto. 'Rehearsals went very smoothly; no details were overlooked, but the Maestro was in excellent humour. I remember that at the first ensemble rehearsal of *Falstaff*, he stopped once during the second part of Act 1 and went on to the stage to correct something in the "*Bocca baciata*" passage; then he returned to the pit, began the scene again, and went straight through without stopping. It was incredible! Everything had been so well prepared in advance.'[35]

The Busseto performances were an act of homage on Toscanini's part, and it had certainly entered his mind that a regular Verdi festival ought to be organized in the area, just as Germany had its Wagner festival in Bayreuth. This idea is still resuscitated from time to time in Italy, but nothing has happened so far.

Following the enthusiastically received Busseto series Toscanini returned to La Scala for the first time in five years to continue the Verdi celebrations with three performances of the *Requiem* (12, 14 and 18 October, with an orchestra of

120 and chorus of 360) and six of *Falstaff* (starting 21 October with basically the same company as that of Busseto but with Scotti instead of Amato in the title rôle and with, of course, normal-sized orchestra and chorus). Public and critical acclaim for these performances was boundless.

Many years later playwright Renato Simoni remembered seeing Boito in tears at one of the *Falstaff* rehearsals. Two days after the opening, Toscanini received a beautifully bound copy of Verdi's newly published correspondence (*I copia-lettere*), with this inscription in it: 'To my very dear Arturo Toscanini, in remembrance of the immense intellectual joy he gave me with the *Falstaff* at Busseto and at La Scala—Arrigo Boito.' Toscanini immersed himself in the volume; and it is interesting to examine some of the annotations he made in it.

He has written 'to be observed' next to this statement in Verdi's letter of 11 April 1871 to Giulio Ricordi:

'On the divining powers of conductors . . . and *on creating at every performance* . . . This is a principle which leads to bad taste and falsity . . .'

Toscanini has underlined the sentence beginning 'I want only one creator', cited earlier, as well as most of this statement:

'You previously referred praisefully to an effect which Mariani drew out of the *Forza del destino* Overture by bringing in the brass in G with a *fortissimo*. Well, I do not approve of that effect. Those brass—*mezza voce*, according to my idea—had to express the Friar's religious chant, and could only do that. Mariani's *fortissimo* completely alters the character, and that fragment becomes a warlike fanfare, which has nothing to do with the subject of the drama.'[36]

In another letter to Ricordi (10 July 1871) Toscanini has underlined this entire paragraph:

'. . . *the invisible orchestra*. This is not my idea, it is Wagner's; and it is a very good one.—It seems impossible that in this day and age one still tolerates see-ing our wretched frock-coats and white bow-ties, mixed together with an Egyptian, Assyrian or Druid costume, etc., etc...; and furthermore, to see the orchestra, *which is part of the fictitious world*, almost in the middle of the ground floor, in the world of the hissers or applauders. Add to all this the obscenity of seeing the harpists' heads, the double bass players' cuffs, and the conductor's windmill.'[37]

Beneath this statement Toscanini has written, 'Not at all Wagner's [idea], but that of the first Italian melodramatists.' Following Verdi's letters to Faccio and Boito (27 March and 26 April 1884) in which the composer offers to renounce his rights to the *Otello* libretto, Toscanini has commented: '. . . always a marvellous man, and at what a distance he keeps *everyone*.'

After a grovellingly ingratiating letter written by Bossi to Verdi (9 June 1895) with requests for a recommendation, judgements on his compositions, and an autographed photograph, Toscanini notes: 'Like the doorkeeper in a monastery' and 'Wasn't he ashamed to write letters like this to Giuseppe Verdi...?' And next to Verdi's dignified but critical response Toscanini writes: 'After this answer Bossi continued to understand nothing and to annoy Verdi—a real sandalled friar.'

Immediately after the *Falstaff* performances Toscanini left for New York, where he opened the season with *Gioconda* on 17 November. Five nights later he brought the Verdi centennial celebrations to America with a new production of *Un ballo in maschera*, with a cast that included Caruso, Amato, Destinn, Matzenauer and Hempel. 'The mounting of the old opera was artistic and brilliant,' wrote Henderson. 'Mr. Toscanini conducted, and to him was due the intelligent treatment of the choruses and ensembles and the effective performance of the score.' Before the end of 1913 he had also conducted *Butterfly*, *Boris*, *Tosca*, *Aida*, *Tristan* and *Manon*; and on 2 January he led the American première of *L'amore dei tre re* by Montemezzi, who, as a student, had had one of his compositions performed by Toscanini at the Milan Conservatory in 1900.

Toscanini's share of the season continued with *Meistersinger*, *Don Pasquale* and *Orfeo*. A hand injury incapacitated him for a few days in March; but on the 25th he directed the first American performance of Wolf-Ferrari's *L'amore medico*. On 14 April he participated in a benefit gala by leading the second act of *Butterfly*. This season's totals were fifty-three performances of thirteen operas and seven presentations in other cities.

A letter which Toscanini sent to his sister-in-law Ida Polo on 26 January 1914 contains, after the personal news, an eye-catching sentence:

'A few lines in a great hurry . . . Carla has just now cabled me that the voyage has been fine and that Wally hasn't suffered at all. So much the better. So tomorrow morning I'll go to meet them. I can't tell you how happy I am and how strange it seems to me to be seeing Wally here in New York.—Since I left Milan my health has improved markedly. My digestive system . . . has never been better in 46 years. I don't know what's happened nor to whom I owe this marvellous change. . . . Everything is going well, or at least normally, here. *L'amore dei tre re* has been dazzlingly successful with the public and press . . . Like no other opera by any other modern composer. I am still incredulous over it.

Kahn has offered me a blank contract for another three or five years; but I shall not make any decision of the sort. . . . If you see Walter and Wanda, tell them not to study but hug them warmly for me.'[38]

It is clear that well over a year before his departure from the Metropolitan Toscanini was already contemplating resigning. Kahn's invitation to name his own fee and other terms was not sufficient to overcome either the questions of artistic conscientiousness or the personal problems that were beginning to weigh upon him.

Looked at superficially, it would seem that his situation at the Metropolitan was ideal. The orchestra and chorus were excellent and the company of singers was certainly the best available to any conductor in the world; he was admired by the overwhelming majority of the public and press; he received a very large salary; and his duties in New York left him free to go where he pleased and to do as he pleased for half of every year. On the other hand, he regretted the lack of a sense of direction within the company. 'Is no discipline,' he later told Haggin. 'With me, yes; but with other conductors, no.'[39] And it was typical of his seriousness to be disturbed because decent conductors among his colleagues who happened not to have his startling gifts and his quick temper did not obtain the best results of which they were capable. The Metropolitan's 'star system' also had its disadvantages: for every artist like Homer or Hempel who showed some understanding of and sympathy for what he was trying to achieve, there was an Eames or a Delna who really could not see the significance of making an opera into an artistic whole, since the public came to hear displays of vocal technique. Then there were the Metropolitan's well-meaning but often unthinking guarantors, Kahn himself among them, who were perfectly willing to pay their top stars $2,500 an evening—a considerably higher sum than the average American's annual income in those days—but were unwilling to pay a relative pittance to hire a few extra musicians for the stage band in *Ballo*. (Toscanini was told to take players from the pit orchestra for that purpose.)

Private difficulties were also straining his nerves. He was in the midst of another serious love affair, this time with Geraldine Farrar. The American-born soprano, daughter of a popular baseball player, had studied in the United States and Europe—with Lilli Lehmann, among others—had débuted in *Faust* under Karl Muck's direction in Berlin in 1901, and had joined the Metropolitan five years later. Her voice, according to many who heard her in the theatre, was very intense and beautiful and she was a conscientious artist, a dynamic presence on stage, and exceptionally beautiful. At the apex of her fame in New York, during the years around the First World War, her popularity was second only to that of Caruso. She even appeared as a silent film actress, and one music critic referred to the hordes of adolescent girls who worshipped her as 'Gerry-flappers'.

When Toscanini arrived in New York in 1908 he was forty-one years old, Farrar twenty-six. She was a very stubborn person and they did not get along well at all. The story has often been told—and may even be true—that Farrar stopped him during one of his outbursts and reminded him that she was a star. 'I recognize only the stars in the sky, which are perfect,' he is said to have replied. It will be remembered that Farrar was also one of the artists who, in 1909, had signed the petition to retain Dippel and curb the powers of Toscanini and Gatti-Casazza. But at some point the bad relations had begun to change and had metamorphosed into something quite different. Toscanini again found himself in the exasperating position of being torn between his belief in the family and his extreme susceptibility to beautiful and fascinating women. This particular situation would soon influence the course of his career.

In Italy once again for the summer, he made arrangements to conduct in Russia in the autumn; but the outbreak of the war ended that project. He and his family spent much of the summer at Viareggio, by the sea, with the Puccini family. 'Papà and Puccini would discuss music and politics,' recalled Wally.

'Puccini was pro-German, while Papà hated the Germans. I remember that on the eve of the first world war their arguments became very animated. One day Puccini complained that everything was going badly in Italy, there was no order, everyone cheated, the authorities acted in their own interests and the poor always got the worst of it. He ended his speech by saying, "Let's hope the Germans come to put things in order." Papà turned into a wild beast. He jumped to his feet and shut himself in the house. He said that he wouldn't go out anymore because if he were to see Puccini he would hit him. Some friends came to our house to try to make peace between the two, but Papà chased them out brusquely.... Friends came to the window and said, "Puccini has repented, he asks you to forgive him. Come out, go visit him." Papà shouted, "If I meet him, I'll box his ears!" After a week, however, they were reconciled.[40]

While in Viareggio Toscanini had been approached by some city officials from Lucca about conducting Catalani's *Loreley* in the composer's home town in the autumn; but that plan, like the Russian one, came to nothing. On 19 October Toscanini, Caruso, Bori and De Luca participated in a special performance of *Pagliacci* and Act II of *Butterfly* at Rome's Teatro Costanzi, for the benefit of Italian emigrants who had had to return home at the outbreak of war.

By coincidence, a few weeks earlier Leoncavallo had seen Gatti-Casazza and Caruso at Montecatini and had read them the libretto of his projected but never completed opera, *Avemaria*. 'Please note', wrote the composer to Illica shortly afterwards, 'that I preceded the reading ... by stating that I was reading [to them] and not to the conductor of the Metropolitan because I well knew that where Toscanini reigns my works will never be given.... I took the occasion to tell them some hard truths.'[41] The fact that Toscanini had performed *Pagliacci* many times and would continue to do so, although it was far from being one of his favourite works, meant nothing to Leoncavallo. Years later Toscanini spoke bitterly of composers who 'complain that their names remain tied to only one or two operas, and who implore one to go through all their works again, to dust them off ...' And in fact, when Toscanini and Caruso again scheduled *Pagliacci* for another benefit in Milan the following summer, 'there was Leoncavallo', said Toscanini, 'to urge me to conduct *Zazà* instead, adding that it made him unhappy to be eternally and solely the composer of *Pagliacci*. And what could I do? Believe me: no matter how good the conducting or interpretation, it cannot galvanize an uneven opera.'[42]

Toscanini's seventh season at the Metropolitan turned out to be one of his most demanding and varied ones—and also his last. It opened on 16 November with *Ballo*. Three nights later he conducted his first *Carmen* in nearly six years, with Farrar singing the lead rôle for the first time. (Toscanini generally insisted on having Carmen sung by a mezzo-soprano, as indicated in the text; but for Farrar ...) *Aida*, *Boris*, *Butterfly*, *Tristan* and *Tosca* followed—French, Italian, Russian and German operas, and all within the first three weeks of the season! On 19 December he presented the first New York performance in twenty-seven years of *Euryanthe* (with Hempel). Krehbiel wrote:

'Last year when the first intimations were whispered that Signor Toscanini contemplated a revival of the opera it was explained that his reason, outside his own admiration for the score, was that he wished to supply the missing link between operas of the old type and Wagner's lyric dramas and knew that *Euryanthe* was that link. He must have been gratified at the popular reception of the opera yesterday. ... All the singers found themselves buoyed up by Signor Toscanini's marvellous orchestra. The Italian master revealed what is meant by the studious preparation of an opera—the kind of preparation of which all the German operas in the Metropolitan's list stand in great need.'

Manon was added to the repertoire a few days later, and on 25 January 1915 Toscanini directed the world première of Giordano's *Madame Sans-Gêne*, with Farrar, Martinelli and Amato. Martinelli later recalled:

'At one rehearsal ... everything went wrong. Toscanini said to me: "YOU! You sing like a police dog!!" I said to myself, "Maybe he's right." Toscanini shouted at everyone—Farrar, Amato ... Finally he shouted, "*Basta* [enough], *riposo* [rest]!" We sat around, silent, looking at each other, not knowing what to do. At one moment, he looks around at everyone, then picks up his hat. He goes up to De Segurola and says, "Put a few pennies in the hat." The same with Amato and Farrar. Finally he comes to me and says, "Listen, there's not much, I think just seventeen cents—go and have your hair cut." Everyone laughed and from that moment we all had the courage to joke with him, and the rehearsal went beautifully.'[43]

In February Toscanini conducted *L'amore dei tre re* and *Il trovatore*. Again, Martinelli has left interesting recollections of the Verdi production.

'[Toscanini] was determined to present *Trovatore* as Verdi would have wanted it. The result was a veritable revolution in thought on the opera. The first rehearsals for *Trovatore* were called in October of 1914. We had a minimum of fifty rehearsals of two hours and more. Think of it! . . . Our cast included Emmy Destinn, Margarete Ober, Pasquale Amato and Léon Rothier as well as myself.

Toscanini pointed out that the score of *Trovatore* was in eight scenes, each an entity in itself. He staged the opera himself, since he wanted to be certain that at every point the stage action would not interfere with his direction and that his baton would be visible to the singers at all times. I remember that the first of these rehearsals was to set the chorus and the bass, Ferrando, sung by Rothier, for the "*Abbietta zingara*" in Act I. This scene takes about five minutes to sing. Toscanini took more than two hours to arrange the singer and chorus, placing and moving them as he wanted.

Certain cuts were restored, such as Leonora's "*Tu vedrai che amore in terra*", . . . and other arias deleted. Toscanini allowed me the interpolated B-flat at the end of "*Deserto sulla terra*" and also in "*Ah! sì ben mio*". Toscanini pointed out that the two verses of "*Ah! sì ben mio*" were identical, and for this reason the B-flat was allowed even by Verdi. [He also permitted the two high Cs in "*Di quella pira*".]

Toscanini stressed the importance of the words in emphasizing the story of *Trovatore*. The recitative before the long lyric line for the tenor in the duet "*Mal reggendo*" . . . is a good case in point; and the final part of this duet, taken at a pace reminiscent of the galloping of a horse (but never must that horse slow down!), makes a tremendous effect because of the persistently quick and rhythmical tempos which continue to the very end."[44]

Meistersinger and Mascagni's *Iris* completed his season's repertoire. (He also began rehearsing Borodin's *Prince Igor* for the following season.) At an afternoon performance of *Carmen* on 18 March Martinelli, who was replacing Caruso as Don José and singing the rôle for the first time in French instead of Italian, became nervous and jumped several pages. Toscanini and the orchestra followed; but the conductor was furious afterwards—not so much with Martinelli as with the Metropolitan management, who had not allotted sufficient rehearsal time to allow the tenor to feel more secure with the rest of the ensemble. Worse was to come on 13 April at another afternoon performance of *Carmen*, again with Martinelli, and this time with Tegani substituting for Amato, who was ill, as Escamillo. Tullio Serafin, who was then in New York on his way to Havana, attended the performance in the company of Titta Ruffo, Maria Gay and Giovanni Zenatello. Toscanini had hoped to show them the Metropolitan at its best; instead, Farrar did not sing well, Tegani left a great deal to be desired, Martinelli was still somewhat insecure (there had been no further *Carmen* performances during the intervening four weeks), the orchestra was not alert and the stage band began playing ten bars early.

This pushed the enraged Toscanini to make a decision. There had been rumours throughout the season that he would be leaving the company, and the Metropolitan's new economic austerity programme—which, according to Kolodin, applied not only to singers' often exorbitant fees, but also to production details which could lower the overall level of performance—had brought him closer to making a resolution. Now, after the *Carmen* disaster, he informed Gatti that he would conduct the next evening's performance of *Iris*, for which it was too late to find a replacement, but that he was cancelling the remaining six performances on his schedule for that season. He was also cancelling the huge symphonic concert scheduled for the 18th (Brahms's Second, Beethoven's Sixth, *The Sorcerer's Apprentice*, *En Saga*, *La Mer*, Roger-Ducasse's *Sarabande* and the *Tannhäuser* Overture) to which he had been happily looking forward, as well as tentative plans for a concert tour with the Metropolitan orchestra and a quartet of soloists; and he added that he would not be coming back the following season.

Months later, after his return to Italy, he wrote to Max Smith:

'. . . Please, dear friend, make this explicit declaration on my behalf concerning my spontaneous withdrawal from the Metropolitan, and even make it public if necessary: "I have given up my position at that theatre because my aspirations and artistic ideals were unable to find the fulfilment I had dreamt of reaching when I entered it in 1908. Routine is the ideal and the basis of that theatre. This can suffice *for the artisan not for the artist*." [Note: Italicized words in English in the original.]

"Renew yourself or die." Voilà tout. This is the *only* reason which made me leave the Metropolitan. All the others that have circulated in the papers are false and unfounded. . . .'[45]

Beyond a doubt, Toscanini would not have left the Metropolitan had he not had reasons for grave artistic dissatisfaction. And yet, these were not his only reasons, although he himself may have wished to believe so. Documentation from the summer of 1915 demonstrates not only that the Metropolitan directorate was willing to make every single concession demanded by Toscanini, but also that he considered accepting their proposals.

All the problems which had bothered him at the Metropolitan in past years had been exacerbated during the 1914–15 season. In addition he had had an unpleasant confrontation with Giorgio Polacco, with whom he had been sharing the Italian repertoire since November 1912. Polacco had been telling people that Toscanini was making sure that he got less interesting operas to conduct. 'It was not true,' Toscanini later told Taubman.

'I told him so plainly, and I told him I wanted no more to do with him. [Note: the facts support Toscanini: during the 1914–15 season Polacco conducted *Bohème*, *Gioconda*, *Traviata*, *Cavalleria*, *Pagliacci*, *Aida*, *Huguenots*,

Manon Lescaut, Tosca, Butterfly, and a new work—hardly an uninteresting list for someone who specialized in Italian repertoire.] After that he kept trying to telephone me to explain himself. After I left the Metropolitan, he would phone me in Milan when he was in Italy and I would not talk to him. One day, during the first war, Carla and I went to a hospital for wounded soldiers, and on the street we met Polacco. I wouldn't talk to him. Carla scolded me. "You're impossible," she said. So I told Polacco to come and call on us the next day at 3. I meant to be polite. But when he came in, I got angry again, and I talked to him in the worst way. I told him everything. I was brutal . . . Later, I was ashamed. . . . But I told the truth.'[46]

Toscanini's great New York crisis, however, came in the form of an ultimatum from Farrar, who told him that if he loved her, he must leave his family for her. But the family, for him, was something that went beyond his most intense—and intensely egoistic—desires. He broke with her, whether verbally or simply by leaving New York is impossible to say at this time. Obviously, he could not face the prospect of having to see her again, day after day, in a working relationship, with everything else changed; and this as much as anything was responsible for his finding the idea of a return to New York unbearable.

Not many months later, the beautiful Geraldine married Lou Telegen, an actor, partly to spite Toscanini. The marriage did not last long. She and Toscanini continued to correspond, and Carla would suffer when she found Farrar's letters, left absent-mindedly in books or dressing-gown pockets. They resumed their friendship, on a different basis, many years later

On 16 July 1915 Gatti-Casazza, then in Milan, sent Kahn a long letter which bears partial quoting here. (I am translating from the original Italian version of the letter; I have not seen the translation which Kahn read.)

'. . . Apropos the war in Europe, I can tell you that the Toscanini case can be compared with the Balkan affair. And just as no diplomat would be able to find a convenient solution in the Balkans, so with the Toscanini case it will not be my diplomacy nor anyone else's which will succeed; only pure luck or, better, certain fortuitous circumstances, will permit a favourable outcome. I am now taking advantage of a mutual friend [D'Ormeville?] who in analogous circumstances was able, with great tact, to provoke in him a spiritual condition which led him to do, for the sake of contradiction, precisely that which he had intended not to do. . . .

A few hours ago I had lunch with Toscanini, who has now undertaken to lead an enormous popular benefit concert at the Milan arena, as well as a popular benefit [opera] season in September and October at the Teatro Dal Verme. He told me that he is tired and worn out and that he does not know how he will be able to fulfil the duties he has undertaken . . . Naturally, I no longer had the nerve to talk about the Metropolitan even in distant terms, and

I put off the discussion until the end of this month when the concert, at least, will be done. Anyway, our friend hopes to have had more time to prepare the way.

If circumstances permit you and Mme Kahn to speak with Toscanini and to argue with him, and to give him the occasion for one of his great eruptions, this might be useful; but a letter or mere telegram would have no practical result at this time. It might give him a chance to answer definitely in the negative, and that would complicate things rather than facilitating them. But whenever this case ... seems to be ready for a move on your part, you may rest assured that I shall let you know ...

Toscanini is tired and not in good health ... He is a rabid nationalist and he does not wish to abandon his country under present conditions in order to work in surroundings where the German element is numerous. Furthermore, I am sure, as are his friends, that in this entire affair there is some great point of honour, for intimate reasons, which constitutes the principal reason for Toscanini's present behaviour. He does not say this, however, and, not wanting to say it, he rehashes all the old accusations against the Metropolitan to justify his conduct. To these accusations I responded thus: Excuse me, Maestro, what can you complain about, considering that everyone at the Metropolitan, from Mr. Kahn down to the lowest staff member, is ready to do whatever you wish? Is it a question of financial conditions? We can always reach an understanding on that. Is it a question of a title? In that case, why have you refused that of General Music Director? Is it a question of repertoire, artists, rehearsals, performances, etc.? But I wish for nothing more than to go along with you, whom I consider an associate, not an employee, and whom I try to satisfy in everything possible. If I cannot always comply with your ideas, it is because you often do not state them. ... For that matter, in the last two seasons we have always been in perfect agreement and have not had even the smallest argument. As concerns the coming season, you are aware of everything: we have decided on reconfirmations and non-confirmations of artists together; the same for the choice of operas, etc. ...

Toscanini was unable to respond seriously to these arguments; however, he ended with the usual refrain that we do not value him as he deserves and that I only think about saving pennies for a Board of Millionaires.

I ask you, Mr. Kahn, how can one argue and make decisions under these conditions, while trying not to vex such an opponent? Not even Job in the Bible was put to such a test of patience.

... Here is how I intend to proceed: When the terrain has been conveniently prepared and an opportune moment has presented itself—this might happen in the first half of August—I shall propose to Toscanini that he come to New York at least for the last three months of the coming season, 1916, in order that the season not be deprived of one of its most important artistic assets, and also to discuss with you and with me a definite arrangement for future seasons.

If you are in agreement, this arrangement could consist of a sort of dual management in which I would be the General Manager and Toscanini the General Music Director. The two directors would have to choose by agreement (and allowing for the prerogative of the Executive Committee) the repertoire, the artists and artistic staff, and to establish the yearly schedules—performances, rehearsals, etc. All of Toscanini's complaints ought thus to be eliminated . . .

If you and he will accept it I am sure that we could march along in perfect harmony. If, however, Toscanini will not even be happy with this . . . what more can I do? It would really mean that what we guess to be the case is absolutely true, and that is, that there exist special motives in Toscanini's soul for leaving the Metropolitan, which have nothing to do with art, and which we do not have the means to eliminate.'[47]

The benefit concert took place at the end of July and Kahn sent a cheque for $1,000. Toscanini did not respond. But early in August, as Gatti had predicted, negotiations made some headway, and it is clear that Toscanini was seriously thinking of going back to New York. Kahn wrote him:

'I am happy to learn that you are considering Gatti-Casazza's proposal, which has my full approval, not only because it contains a public expression of our admiration and gratitude for that which the Metropolitan owes to your unique genius, but also because it will give your great personality greater scope and effective power in the Metropolitan's artistic development. I convey the feelings of the Board, the New York public and myself in expressing the sincere hope that we shall be able to continue to enjoy the inspiration of your splendid art. I assure you that I shall do, with pleasure, everything possible to render your work here pleasant and satisfying.' [Author's translation of the Italian translation sent to Toscanini.][48]

But in the end Toscanini decided not to accept the Metropolitan's proposals. He had left the company forever.

The last season, in which he had conducted fifty-nine performances of fourteen operas, and seven tour performances, had brought his seven-season total, including tours, to 446 performances of thirty-one operas in New York, nine other American cities and Paris. Obviously, his loss was grave for the Metropolitan in ways far more important than the sudden absence of a tireless workhorse. An article by H.T. Parker in the *Boston Evening Transcript* of 30 September 1915 sounds more like an obituary notice than a simple farewell: '[. . . In] the whole range of music of the theatre from Gluck to Dukas—he penetrated substance, style and spirit and transmitted them eloquently to his audience. . . .

The nervous force within him he infused into music and play, singers, band and audience until, when he was at his highest and fullest . . . it made the atmosphere of the opera house electric.'[49] And Martinelli said: 'He was the heart and soul of the Metropolitan.'

Toscanini's earlier than scheduled departure from New York was unarguably fortunate for him in at least one way: he was able to book passage on an earlier ship than originally planned. The ship on which he had first been booked was the *Lusitania*, and the voyage was to be the vessel's last.

The years 1915–20 constitute the most puzzling period in Toscanini's life—puzzling because of his enthusiasm for the most senseless and awful of all senseless and awful wars, puzzling because of his apparent lack of interest in resuming his work at war's end, and puzzling because of his short-lived venture into politics.

It is quite true that Toscanini was a rabid nationalist, as Gatti said, and that he hated the German militarists, as Wally Toscanini said; but it must be remembered that his ideas on these subjects had been imbibed principally from his father and other direct participants in the *Risorgimento*. He actually knew very little about politics; but he was absolutely certain that the Trentino, Alto Adige, Istrian peninsula and so on rightfully belonged to Italy. Claudio Toscanini had told his son many times how he had faced death to help get the Austrians out of Lombardy at the battles of Magenta and Solferino, and how he had left his pregnant wife in order to help in the attempt to wrest the Trentino from Franz Josef. Claudio and his red shirt had long since been laid to rest, but old Franz Josef was still occupying the Trentino half a century later. The time had come to carry the *Risorgimento* to its conclusion; and Toscanini, like so many others who should have known better, became first an interventionist and then an ardent supporter of the war whose triumphal issue made Europe ripe for the glorious events which followed.

With Italy's official entry into the war, Signora Carla enrolled in the Red Cross. She and Wally, now fifteen, did sewing at home and also helped in the hospitals. (When asked nearly sixty years later what worthwhile instruction her mother had given her, Wally replied: 'She sent me into hospitals instead of churches.') Wanda was only eight; but to Walter, seventeen, the war was an adventure. He joined the Red Cross as a volunteer at the front, and on turning eighteen enlisted in the army.

Toscanini began to plan war benefit performances, the first of which was the mammoth concert on 26 July 1915 at Milan's outdoor arena, already referred to in Gatti-Casazza's letter. A chorus of 1,500 and a proportionately large orchestra participated in this event. The *Corriere* reported that great applause greeted Toscanini on his entering the stadium. Next, the first batch of the city's seriously wounded were carried in, and all 150 of them were heartily applauded. The

programme, all Verdi, began with the *Forza del destino* Overture and contained
short excerpts from five other operas. It ended with the *Hymn of the Nations*
and the singing of patriotic anthems by the audience of 40,000. The performance
raised 70,000 lire.

As soon as the concert was out of the way Toscanini personally undertook the
organization of a special opera season at the Teatro Dal Verme. He wrote to some
of the best-known singers of the day to enlist their support for this venture, whose
beneficiaries were to be the numerous Milanese musicians who were unemployed
because of the war and the subsequent closing of most of the theatres. In con-
nection with the production of *Pagliacci* scheduled for this series, Toscanini
received a letter from Leoncavallo early in September; and it must have reminded
him of a similarly absurd request made by Mascagni years earlier.

'I read in the papers that the baritone Montesanto will sing in the big
performance of *Pagliacci* . . . I am sure that you will see to the perfect execution
of my work, as you usually do . . . Montesanto sang under my direction in
California, and I know his great merits and his defects. If I allowed certain
things there . . . this must not happen under your direction.

He has the habit (imitating Battistini, the "god") of singing the Prologue
in tails and then taking the part of Silvio!!! I absolutely cannot allow that the
Prologue be sung in a frock coat, but rather in Tonio's clothes; and much less
that whoever sings the Prologue then sing the other part. There is a philo-
sophical and moral reason why Tonio and not Silvio must sing the Prologue,
but it is useless to explain this to singers. . . .

I embrace you with unaltered affection and great admiration.'[50]

Just how unaltered Leoncavallo's affection was we have already seen. And why
do so many composers wish to abdicate responsibility for achieving decent
performances of their works when those works are being performed under their
direction? It is both disgusting and pathetic to think of the elephantine Leoncavallo, already in his late fifties, insulting Toscanini behind his back and then
commanding him not to permit the liberties which he had permitted in his own
work!

The Dal Verme season opened on 18 September with the Italian première of
Madame Sans-Gêne and continued with a double bill of *Pagliacci* (with Caruso,
Muzio and Montesanto) and Wolf-Ferrari's *Il segreto di Susanna*. There were
productions of *Traviata* (Toscanini's last appearances with Storchio), *Tosca*
(with Muzio), *Ballo* (with Bonci and Mazzoleni) and *Falstaff* (with Giacomo
Rimini and Tito Schipa)—forty-three performances in two months, with an
intake of 369,000 lire.

Bernardino Molinari came from Rome to hear some of the Dal Verme performances and invited Toscanini to direct some concerts in the capital with the
same charitable purpose as that of the operatic series in Milan. Toscanini agreed

to direct three performances of the Beethoven Ninth in January and, at about the same time, tentatively accepted the direction of a short opera season in Turin in January and February. However, he found himself so overwhelmed with the distribution of the Dal Verme profits—which he had agreed to administer personally—that the Turin project had to be cancelled. Nor could he conduct the Ninth in Rome: Molinari wrote to inform him that military conscription had decimated the ranks of all the decent choruses in the city, and that the programmes would therefore have to be altered. On 18 December Toscanini wired Molinari, asking him to postpone the concerts by two weeks. Finally, three concerts were arranged for the Augusteum on 30 January and 6 and 9 February. New to Toscanini's repertoire were excerpts from *Petrouchka*, Rachmaninoff's *Isle of the Dead* and Busoni's *Berceuse élégiaque*. He returned to Rome in March to conduct another concert and in May directed three concerts in Turin. There was so little musical activity that for five months he did no conducting; then he made another trip to Rome for more concerts at the Augusteum. The first programme, 19 November, began with Corelli's 'Christmas' Concerto and Martucci's First Symphony. After the interval another Italian work—Tommasini's *Chiari di luna*—was given its first performance, and was followed by the 'Forest Murmurs' from *Siegfried*. Violinist Augusto Rossi, who was in the orchestra, recalled that during the latter piece, a segment of the public which opposed the playing of German music during the war began to raise a furore.

'. . . At one point Maestro Luigi Mancinelli, who was much beloved by the Roman public and particularly so by Toscanini, came down from his box . . . jumped on to the stage . . . and embraced the conductor in fraternal friendship, demonstrating his solidarity. This had the effect of calming the storm . . . and the concert began again.

After the "Forest Murmurs" we began the "Funeral Music" from *Götterdämmerung*. The Maestro began it with the timpani entrance. A voice was heard from the hall: "For the dead in Padua!" ' [Note: Padua had recently suffered civilian casualties during an aerial bombardment.][51]

The result of this shout was an even greater uproar than before. Toscanini folded his arms on his chest and waited for the noise to abate. When it did not, he left the hall, ending that concert and cancelling the remaining ones. A few days later an order was issued banning German music in Rome until war's end. Toscanini did not conduct again in the capital until 1920.

The following months were musically barren ones for him. We learn from a letter Puccini wrote to Alfredo Vandini (18 January 1917) that there was a plan to produce the composer's latest opera, *Il tabarro*, in Turin under Toscanini's direction, 'but I fear it will come to nothing. For now, nothing is sure, either in Rome or in Turin. Quite the contrary! The singers are lacking—they are at the front.'⁵² Toscanini went to Naples to contribute his services in conducting *Madame Sans-Gêne*, but a strike for higher pay was called by the orchestra and chorus at the dress rehearsal. He left, and the opera was eventually directed by someone else. His fiftieth birthday was passed in forced withdrawal from his profession and in sorrow over the prolongation of the horrible and seemingly interminable war.

He had given so freely of his energies and other resources that he found himself in serious financial difficulty. The house on Via Durini had to be sold; but the people who bought it allowed the Toscanini family to rent it, and eventually sold it back to them when Toscanini had begun earning money again. During all the war years and for some months thereafter he did not earn a penny.

He followed the events of the war in great detail, mainly through the reports of the *Corriere della sera*, and used to mark daily troop movements at the front by shifting pins with little flags attached from one point to another on a large map. Several of Italy's leading generals had been presented to him at his various benefit appearances; and although he found most of them unpleasant (he said they reminded him too much of singers), he took a liking to General Antonio Cascino, who invited him in the summer of 1917 to form a military band and play for the soldiers who were engaged along the Isonzo front. Toscanini was enthusiastic about the idea and immediately began engaging musicians and selecting music.

One day, Walter Toscanini—who was then nineteen and an artillery officer on the same front—heard the sounds of a band playing marches and anthems, and playing them well. He said jokingly to a friend that the band sounded so much better than the usual military ensembles that he could almost believe that his father had trained it. Some days later he received a call from General Cascino's headquarters with an invitation to come for lunch. Knowing how difficult a trek it was over mountainous terrain, he replied that he had already eaten. He was then *ordered* to come for lunch. Arriving tired and angry, he was incredulous to see his father and Cascino himself come out to meet him, and even more surprised to learn that it had indeed been Papà who had led the band. Later in the afternoon, as the elder and younger Toscaninis walked together along a mountain path, they came to a shell hole, filled with water. They separated to walk around it, and at that instant a stray shell whizzed along the path. The pressure knocked them both to the ground; and although the shell itself was a dud, they would both have been decapitated, in all likelihood, had they not had to walk around the hole.

At the end of August Toscanini led his band during the Italian assault on Monte Santo. Pietro Toschi, who later taught composition at the Santa Cecilia academy, was in the brigade. He remembered that after each piece Toscanini shouted, 'Viva l'Italia!' The bass drum was ripped by shrapnel, but none of the players was hurt. On 3 September the *New York Times* reported:

'Arturo Toscanini, the noted Italian conductor, has been decorated by the Italian government for great bravery under fire. Signor Toscanini kept his military band playing during the battle of Monte Santo in the present offensive on the Italian front. The soldiers stormed the enemy's position to the strains of martial music.

In the midst of the fighting and at a time when the Austrian barrage fire was at its height, Signor Toscanini led his band to one of the advanced positions where, sheltered only by a huge rock, he conducted a concert which did not stop until word had been brought to him that the Italian soldiers had stormed and taken the trenches of the Austrians to the music of his band.'

Toscanini remained at the front until the defeat at Caporetto, late in October. When the retreat began the general command forgot about the band, which was then at Cormons, and Toscanini calmly continued to lead his musicians in the prelude to Act III of *Traviata* and Martucci's *Novelletta*. With the Austrian troops already nearing the town, he finally decided to dismiss the band. Then he ran about procuring wagons and train cars to evacuate the players, went to the hospital to pick up Walter, who was convalescing from a wound, accompanied him to the army hospital at Udine, and took a slow train back to Milan. 'I still remember when he came into the house,' said Wally in 1972.

'He opened the service door; his face was ashen and dirty and his eyes swollen from crying. Mamma, thinking that something terrible had happened to Waltèr, jumped to her feet and screamed, "Walter, Walter!" My father said, "No. It's Italy. Italy is finished." He embraced my mother and began to weep.'[53]

Within a few weeks his old friend Gallignani had managed to draw him out of his despair, to some extent, by convincing him that he must participate in a new project to aid Milanese musicians, whom the war had now reduced to penury. They sent out joint letters of appeal to government ministries, banks, newspapers and private individuals for initial financial support. Toscanini himself contributed 1,000 lire—as much as some of the banks gave.

Twelve concerts at the Conservatory were organized for successive Sunday afternoons from 6 January to 24 March 1918, and three extra popular concerts were added at the end. Public support was great and 100,000 lire was raised. Some members of the public made donations beyond the price of admission; and two English girls, both artists and both named Nora, sent a combined contribution directly to Toscanini's address along with a note of thanks 'for Beethoven's "Third", performed so perfectly.' Gallignani and Toscanini also received letters of protest—anonymous ones as well as civil and signed ones— over the inclusion of compositions by German and Austrian composers. The programmes were not altered, however, and no untoward incidents occurred.

(No music by Wagner or contemporary Germans had been scheduled.) Several works new to Toscanini's repertoire and almost entirely 'Allied' appeared: *Ibéria* and *La Demoiselle élue* by Debussy (who died while the series was in progress), Franck's Symphony and excerpts from his *Psyché*, Respighi's *Fountains of Rome*, Glinka's *Kamarinskaya*, D'Indy's 'Istar' variations, Mozart's 'Prague' Symphony, Vivaldi's Concerto Grosso in E minor and Violin Concerto in A minor, Rimsky-Korsakov's 'Russian Easter' Overture, Malipiero's *Pause del silenzio*, Stravinsky's *Fireworks*, and pieces by seven other composers.

In June Boito died. He had been in poor health for some time, but his greatest suffering came from the still unfinished *Nerone*. Eleonora Duse, Boito's former lover and constant friend, had written to another friend on 6 February 1918:

'It seems that no one mentions the war to him, or the battles, or the Piave, or the Neva, or Toscanini, or the holy *manuscript* of *his opera*, which is the most *interior* part of his soul . . . I cannot forget that . . . when he became aware that he was not yet ready *for the departure*, mere mention of *Toscanini's* name caused bitter weeping . . . because it reminded him of the Work and the long wait, and the promise of years and years, and the discomfort that Toscanini wouldn't believe and wouldn't think well of it! *Nobody, nobody can help me—* he said, sobbing . . . —but perhaps Toscanini could, and if *he were allowed to see him and talk to him, what balm it would be for him!*'[54]

When Toscanini heard that Boito was dying he went to visit him at the clinic: but a friend of Boito's turned him away because a rumour had been spread that Toscanini had spoken badly about *Nerone*. A few days later he went back to the clinic and this time was permitted to spend some time with the old man, who was so weak that he spoke only with difficulty. Toscanini returned home and shut himself in his study. He and a few others spent the entire night before Boito's funeral sitting beside the bier. Precisely twenty years ago that month Boito had persuaded the new directorate of La Scala to engage Toscanini as conductor.

La Scala housed a special opera season for the benefit of operatic artists, war invalids and war orphans, and Toscanini participated by conducting *Mefistofele*, with Gigli and De Angelis. During rehearsals for this production word came that the war had ended.

Obviously he was glad about this; nonetheless, he found himself in a generally depressed state. 'He was discouraged,' said Wally, 'and it seemed as if he had even lost his enthusiasm for music.' Most probably, he wondered what the next few years could possibly hold for a musician. Much of Europe lay in ruins and the economic condition of the formerly belligerent nations was disastrous. He could have returned to America, but he did not want to abandon his country at such a difficult moment. There are times when every intelligent person is overwhelmed by the utter futility of his own existence, and Toscanini was in any case not a cheerful character by nature. He flourished only when working insanely hard, and at a pitch of tension which would have destroyed any normal human being. Between the spring of 1915 and that of 1920 he did less work in total than he had formerly been accustomed to doing in a single year. The less he did, the more withered and useless he felt.

There was some discussion of his going to London in the spring of 1919 to conduct the European première of Puccini's *Trittico*; but the composer had heard through mutual 'friends' that Toscanini had made unfavourable remarks about the three one-act operas, and he was furious. He wrote to his friend Sybil Seligman in London:

> 'I've heard about Covent Garden—I protested to Ricordi's because I don't want that *pig* of a Toscanini; he has said all sorts of nasty things about my operas and has tried to inspire certain journalists to run them down too. He didn't succeed in every case, but one of his friends (of the *Secolo*) wrote a beastly article under his inspiration—and I won't have this *God*. He's no use to me—and I say, as I have already said, that when a conductor thinks poorly of the operas he has to conduct, he can't interpret them properly . . .'[55]

The Puccini–Toscanini relationship was to be mended, broken again and re-mended during the remaining five years of the composer's life. It is certainly possible that Toscanini had spoken ill of these operas—he did so in later years, and never conducted them—but it is extremely unlikely that he would have been so malicious or so stupid as to have influenced critics to write against them. (Vincent Seligman, Sybil's son, felt the same way.) He did not go to London, but it cannot now be determined whether this was because of his dislike of the operas, Puccini's opposition, or simply non-agreement on a contract.

Turin heard his first post-war concerts in May and June. He led two performances of a programme which included, among other works, Mozart's Symphony No. 39 in E-flat—new to his repertoire. These were followed by three performances of the Beethoven Ninth. Canadian tenor Edoardo Di Giovanni, who was later general manager of the Metropolitan Opera Company under his real name, Edward Johnson, sang in these concerts and recalled that the contralto soloist, Ida Bergamasco, was so nervous at the first piano rehearsal that she made a bad entrance. Toscanini began the passage again, but the same thing happened. *Da capo* again, but this time she couldn't produce a sound. She began to cry; Toscanini said nothing. Finally, she regained control of herself. '*Ancora*,' said the Maestro, and then muttered: 'And they say that I am impatient.'[56]

It was true, however, that he was impatient, and a far more serious incident occurred during one of the orchestra rehearsals for the Ninth. It so happened that Annibale Pastore, professor of theoretical philosophy at Turin University, had obtained permission to attend the rehearsals in order to help document a book called *L'entusiasmo* which he was preparing. He witnessed the occurrence and reported on it.

'During the *finale*, when the tremendous outcry of the chorus must rise to maximum power . . . there were three dry taps of the baton . . . The Maestro turned to one of the second violins, seated at the second stand, and shouted: "What kind of scratching is that? Two centimetres of bow!" And he threw his crumpled handkerchief, which he had been using to fan himself, at him. The violinist answered: "I'm playing, not scratching. And you? Why did you throw your handkerchief at me?" Toscanini, still trembling, responded: "I throw everything I have into it; and you—nothing. You ought to throw your bow into it." So saying, . . . he stepped involuntarily off the podium and approached the second stand of second violins.

The violinist persisted: "I've always done what's possible, and you are impolite." Toscanini: "Ah, what's possible? And this?" And with a nervous motion of his baton he struck the bow sidewise. It broke, and on the rebound hit the violinist on the forehead. The violinist was about to react; then players and soloists threw themselves in between and held them back. . . . The violinist was led away by a colleague. On leaving the stage he turned and shouted at Toscanini: "You aren't a maestro, you're a scoundrel."

The rehearsal was interrupted . . . After half an hour it began again with the orchestra only. The Maestro conducted with a muffled voice, very pale, seated. The next day . . . Toscanini came on to the stage as if in a dream, without looking at anyone. He stepped on to the podium, ordered the orchestra to begin . . . Then, after the usual glance around at the whole orchestra, he noticed the presence of the second violinist, stepped down eagerly and went over to shake his hand. . . .'[57]

Despite the handshake and the purchase, by Signora Toscanini, of a good bow for the man, the head injury was the cause of a lawsuit. Toscanini was absolved on the basis of Pastore's ridiculous theories of 'holy furore', 'the artist prey to the tyranny of the tragic (not individual) will' and the like. Fortunately, this is the only recorded case of physical violence in the history of Toscanini's turbulent rehearsals.

On 14 June, four days after the last Turin performance of the Ninth, he conducted the first of four Milan performances of the work, with the same soloists but a different chorus and orchestra. The Prelude and 'Good Friday Spell' from *Parsifal* were also included in the Milan programmes.

Seven months passed before he next conducted, and during that period Toscanini went through the most peculiar episode in his life—one which he would come to regret.

There are various versions of Toscanini's first encounter with journalist Benito Mussolini, who was sixteen years his junior. According to some, this took place when Toscanini went personally to protest against the stand of Mussolini's newspaper, *Il popolo d'Italia*, against the playing of German music during the war; others say that it happened at a political meeting which Toscanini attended at a school on Via Santo Spirito; and there are still other versions. Mussolini made a positive impression on Toscanini, and that impression was strengthened by the admiration which some of the conductor's artist and intellectual acquaintances—notably the Futurist writer F.T. Marinetti—demonstrated towards the journalist.

The new movement, later transformed into Fascism, began with a meeting of some 200 people in a hall at Piazza San Sepolcro in March 1919; and Toscanini soon found himself supporting a political party for the first time in his life. 'Proto-Fascism' was a purely Milanese movement, not a national one, and its original adherents advocated a socialistic policy which had nothing in common with Mussolini's later actions. The *Sansepolcristi*, as these men were called, put forward a programme which included the formation of a constituent assembly which was to be the Italian section of an international constituent assembly; the proclamation of an Italian republic; women's suffrage; the abolition of the upper house of parliament, of all titles of nobility and of compulsory military service; international disarmament; election of judges; dissolution of limited liability companies; abolition of the banks and closing of the stock exchange; limitation of private capital; confiscation of unproductive capital; land for the peasants; union participation in the management of industry, transport and public services; eighty per cent tax on war profits; death duties; and confiscation of unused houses and ecclesiastical property.

Obviously, this was anything but a right-wing programme. In view of the terrible economic deprivations and general post-war upheaval in the country, Toscanini, like many others, felt that there was a real need for these drastic changes. (It should also be mentioned that there was no racism attached to proto- or early Fascism, and in fact there were many Jews among its early supporters. The Italians did not become Aryans until 1938.) When, at the last moment, Mussolini decided to put forward a list of candidates for the parliamentary elections of 16 November 1919 the conductor's name appeared on that list. According to Wally Toscanini, this happened when Marinetti and other important members came to talk with her father and convinced him that, although there was no chance of victory, the party needed a name as well-known as his in order to gain credence. He did no active campaigning.

The Milanese Socialists received 170,000 votes in the election, while Mussolini's group received under 5,000. None of its candidates was elected—not even Mussolini. His political career was believed finished, whereas he had merely lost his taste for elections. But Toscanini's official political career was indeed finished. He, like the other candidates, had pledged 30,000 lire towards the party's expenses and, according to Cesare Rossi, he paid up without complaining. Before long, his relationship with the transformed *fascisti* would change radically.

In January 1920 Toscanini conducted five concerts in Rome, incorporating into his programmes several of the new works he had done in Milan two years earlier. He was then to have gone to Prague for concerts and opera performances, but contracted influenza and had to give up the project. After having returned to Rome for four more concerts in May, he went to Padua to conduct six concerts the following month at an international fair, and then repeated the same programmes in Ferrara, at the invitation of Gatti-Casazza, who was a native of the city and spent his summers there. Gatti wrote to Edward Ziegler of the Metropolitan staff:

'I had the occasion to meet him . . . after four years that I had not seen him nor come in contact with him. My impression is that his character has remained the same as we knew it. Further, I have noticed in him a pessimism and a discouragement more accentuated than in the past. I attended his concerts and it is only justice to say that as an artist he is superior to any comparison.' [Translation from the Metropolitan archives.][58]

The previous autumn Emilio Caldara, Milan's socialist mayor, and Luigi Albertini, editor of the *Corriere della sera*, had begun to think seriously about reopening La Scala which, like all of the country's artistic institutions, had fallen on hard times during the war. La Scala's situation was particularly difficult since Duke Uberto Visconti di Modrone had given up the presidency of the theatre in 1917 and no likely successor had presented himself. Caldara and Albertini approached Toscanini. Would he be interested in returning to La Scala? He was hesitant. A theatre run as La Scala had previously been run, or as the Metropolitan was run, did not appeal to him at all. A whole new system was required—a new artistic organization and a new way of financing the theatre. Such a project would be time-consuming and arduous. The idea was put forward to begin by forming a new orchestra and to take it on an extended tour, perhaps even to America. Toscanini was willing. Inquiries were made by cable to Otto Kahn late in October for a tour of a 100-member Toscanini orchestra, unlimited number of concerts beginning January 1920, at a total weekly cost of $11,500 plus $30,000 for the voyage. The answer was that it was too late for that season: try next year. The suggestion was followed.

On 14 July 1920 La Scala's administrative council met and nominated Toscanini 'plenipotentiary director'. Plans for the forming of the orchestra were finalized and others for the establishment of the new operatic organization were begun. The culminating decade of Toscanini's life in the theatre had been initiated.

5
Milan and New York

Throughout the first half of 1920 Toscanini, Caldara and Albertini had struggled with the immensely complicated task of creating an entirely new organization for La Scala. The problems were technical, financial and artistic.

Toscanini's old friend and associate, the engineer Cesare Albertini (not to be confused with Luigi Albertini), was again brought in to supervise the modernization of the technical apparatus. He made a tour of Europe's most advanced theatres and began performing surgery on La Scala early in August. The forestage area was shortened, the pit was enlarged and put on a lift, the roof over the stage was raised twenty-three feet, and a new dome was installed to house an up-to-date lighting system.

The economic question was harder to resolve. It will be remembered that when Toscanini first took over the musical direction of La Scala in 1898 the theatre had just undergone a reorganization which divided financial responsibility among the hereditary boxholders, the city government and a society of shareholders. The presidency was filled by a nobleman-boxholder, and the general manager and musical director were responsible to him. Now, in 1920, Toscanini insisted that that system be scrapped. His new plan, formulated in close collaboration with Caldara and Luigi Albertini, was a revolutionary one: La Scala was to be reconstituted as an *ente autonomc*—an 'autonomous society'. The old societies of boxholders and shareholders were to be dissolved, and the theatre's four tiers of boxes were to be made available to the general public by annual subscription or by individual admission, just like seats on the ground floor or in the two galleries. (As a gesture of goodwill, for nine years the former boxholders were given first option on retaining their boxes—at the established rate, however; and during the same period they received nominal interest payments on their expropriated holdings.) The city would relinquish its titular ownership of the theatre and bestow it on the theatre itself, although the mayor would automatically assume its presidency. Furthermore, the city would make an annual contribution of 350,000 lire; and the financing would be completed through public subscription, private donation and the levying of a two per cent surtax on the admission prices of all the other theatres, cinemas and places of public entertainment in Milan and its *provincia*. The reasoning was that since La Scala was being democratized, since its doors were being opened—at least ideally—to everyone, everyone had to pay for it.

If Toscanini's ideas on renovating La Scala's technical structures and re-systematizing its fiscal foundations were clear and functional, his conception of its artistic administration, of the methods to be adopted in order to bring worth-while productions before the public, was of a lucidity and a practicability extra-ordinarily rare in the history of the modern lyric theatre. In so far as the consistently high level of results is concerned, it is safe to say that the Toscanini system at La Scala was without a doubt a uniquely successful and unrepeatable achievement.

In essence the system was this: everyone who had anything to do with any aspect of artistic production was personally responsible to Arturo Toscanini. His jurisdiction extended to everything, and all decisions devolved ultimately upon him. It is true that Angelo Scandiani—a former engineer for the Italian Edison Company and a very fine amateur *basso* who had sung Gurnemanz in Toscanini's 1903 performances of the *Parsifal* excerpts at La Scala—had been named *direttore generale*; but his function was in no way to be compared to that of an old-time impresario nor even to that of a manager like Gatti-Casazza, who had been mauled by Toscanini in many an encounter. Scandiani was, in fact, just what Toscanini had always wanted Gatti-Casazza to be: an efficient administrator who did what he was told. Anita Colombo, an intelligent and indefatigable young woman, was hired as a sort of administrative assistant. She was extremely capable and Toscanini seems to have relied more on her than on Scandiani.

He wanted a new, hand-picked orchestra, which would be made up of Italy's finest players; he chose the experienced Vittore Veneziani—a former Martucci pupil—to select and train the chorus; he hired a group of highly gifted musical assistants; he selected the heads of the scenographic and technical departments; and he attacked the most difficult question of all—that of developing a resident company of outstanding singers who would allow themselves to be formed by him in their rôles. In effect, he was establishing a repertoire company. The reasons for doing so, and the exceptional results, will be dealt with further on.

The new orchestra—initially called the Orchestra Arturo Toscanini and fin-anced by a society nominally headed by Carla Toscanini—had been formed by late August 1920. Rehearsals probably began not long afterwards; and since La Scala was undergoing restoration, the sessions were held at the Conservatory. A substantial repertoire was prepared—thirty-one pieces by twenty composers—and on 23 October the new orchestra began what must still hold the record as the longest and roughest tour ever undertaken by a major orchestra. They opened in Milan and by 29 November had given thirty-three concerts in twenty-one Italian cities. Everywhere, they met with great popular and critical enthusiasm.

An 'illegal' concert was given with the tacit consent of the government in the contested city of Fiume (Rijeka). After the war, nationalistic elements within Italy had strongly favoured the annexation of the city; but Yugoslavia and the United States were entirely opposed to the idea, and the Italian government did not take a very decisive stand. In September 1919 author Gabriele D'Annunzio—in his rôle of 'Man of Action'—had led a troop of soldiers into the city and had occupied it. Even the horrors of the world war had left Toscanini's nationalism intact, and he considered it a duty and an honour to play for D'Annunzio and his men. The soldiers put on a limited display of military exercises, complete with battle cries, for the Maestro and his orchestra, who also received various medals for their moral support of the Fiume adventure. In tribute to what D'Annunzio called the 'Symphoniac' and his 'Orphic Legion', the poet made a speech filled with phrases like, 'His sceptre is a light wand . . . and it raises up the orchestra's huge billows, releases the great torrents of harmony . . . Who is he, then? He is a Leader, as I am a Leader, O my people.'[1] The city's Teatro Verdi was jammed beyond normal capacity for the evening's concert, which was, of course, greeted with hysterical ovations.

On 30 November Toscanini and the orchestra embarked at Naples for the second part of their tour, which took them to the United States and Canada, with Kahn and the Metropolitan acting as financial backers. Originally planned to last ten weeks and to cost about $180,000, in the end it lasted sixteen weeks and probably cost proportionally more. 'If everything goes along as per schedule,' Ziegler had written to Kahn the previous June, 'there should be no loss in this tour; but then such affairs seldom do, especially when dealing with as uncertain a quantity as Toscanini.'[2] That the Metropolitan directorate looked upon the tour as a way of creating a *rapprochement* between Toscanini and their opera company is clear from a letter Gatti had sent Kahn from Italy in July:

'. . . I quite agree with you that during his stay in America we must show him the greatest sympathy and the best cordiality. . . . We shall study the most convenient way to make a demonstration that may put in everyone the persuasion of the sincerity of our sentiments . . . He told me that he would prefer that his concerts took place at Carnegie Hall instead of the Metropolitan and this for considerations of acoustics; moreover, that he now hates the theatre, the singers and scenic performances, etc., etc., and that if he accepts to go for some time to the Scala, it will simply be for the fact to render a service to a great national institution, etc., etc., considered all these expressions, it is to be thought that he would probably not accept a proposal that would come from you or from me, to conduct a performance at the Metropolitan.

Perhaps the best way to obtain his consent would be to organize at the Metropolitan, a special performance, at a matinee or Saturday evening, which would be in favour of some Italian institution . . .' [Translation from Metropolitan Opera archives.]

No such special performance ever took place. It has been reported elsewhere that while Toscanini had assumed that Kahn was backing the orchestra as a goodwill gesture, the orchestra was in fact being 'resold' at a much higher price than what they had asked as a guarantee, bringing Kahn (and presumably the Metropolitan) a nice profit. Toscanini is said to have been furious when he discovered this. I have found no way of confirming or denying this story.

The orchestra was given two free days after arriving in New York on 13 December. On the second evening all the players were guests of the Metropolitan at a performance of Halévy's *La Juive* with Caruso. The tenor was already very ill then and died eight months later.

On the 16th Toscanini and company journeyed to Philadelphia to begin making a series of records for the Victor Talking Machine Company, across the river in Camden, New Jersey. Toscanini was fifty-three years old and had been a conductor for thirty-four years when these records were cut. He was to be professionally active for another thirty-four years. Nuccio Fiorda, who was on the Scala coaching staff and also assisted in the orchestra's percussion section, has left this account of the sessions:

'The orchestra—reduced to its bare essentials—was stuffed and squashed into an enormous wooden niche . . . The double basses were partially reinforced by the tuba. The agreement with the Victor Company stated that no record could be marketed without the Maestro's approval. The "wax recording" technique did not allow for direct playback from the wax of a recorded piece of music; this would cause it to be destroyed irremediably. Consequently, once listened to, it was necessary to re-do the whole thing! But unfortunately this "re-doing" happened rather frequently, given the Maestro's dissatisfaction. One day the establishment's director said, "If Toscanini comes back again, the company will go bankrupt!" '3

Enrico Minetti, who was later concertmaster of the Scala Orchestra but was then playing in the section, said that Toscanini had 'indescribable outbursts of anger!'

' "No, no," he said, "not like this, it's no good! All our work destroyed and useless: tempi changed, wrong sonorities, no dynamics, no shadings—a real pile of rubbish!" . . . After this disastrous trial, the Maestro swore never to make another record. Fortunately, this was not to be the case.'4

Seven days in December and eight in March were spent in the studio; the total yield in marketable recordings was approximately fifty minutes of music, eventually released on single and double-faced discs. Listening to them today, one can easily sympathize with Toscanini's intense displeasure. Like other recordings of the period, they do not give any idea of what the orchestra itself sounded like, and the dry, compressed acoustics of the studio may even have caused Toscanini to alter his tempi considerably. The records' interest is therefore principally historical and not musical.

While staying in Philadelphia Toscanini and many of the orchestra members enjoyed listening to a black jazz band which played in their hotel in the evenings; and Fiorda reports that the Maestro was particularly delighted by the percussionist's way of throwing his sticks into the air and catching them behind his back.

The orchestra moved back to New York on Christmas day and opened its tour with a concert at the Metropolitan (a Vivaldi Concerto Grosso, Beethoven's Fifth Symphony, Respighi's *Fountains of Rome* and Debussy's *Ibéria*). Performances were also given at the Hippodrome Theatre and Carnegie Hall. Travelling aboard a special train, to which they returned each night, they then visited Baltimore, Philadelphia, Boston, Washington, Montreal, Toronto, Cleveland, Detroit, Chicago, Des Moines, Tulsa and twenty-nine other cities. Many famous musicians heard Toscanini for the first time during this tour, and some of them made their reactions public. Pierre Monteux wrote three years later:

'All my friends and colleagues had told me so many good things about him that I wanted very much to hear one of his concerts . . . My impression was that everything I had heard on the subject was very pale next to the reality! I had before me, very simply, a man of genius, a conductor such as I had never seen in my life, a real revelation in the art of conducting and in the art of interpretation. . . . This great Master is, in my opinion, not only "your" [Italy's] greatest Maestro but "the greatest of all".'[5]

The composer Ernest Bloch commented:

'I was astonished when I saw this little, sad-looking man come forward; he seemed ill-at-ease before the crowd and had none of that repugnant obsequiousness of virtuosi who seek to flatter the public... I liked that attitude immediately. It revealed a whole side of Toscanini's character which I later found again in his conducting. I shall never forget the Prelude and *Liebestod* from *Tristan*, which he conducted that evening. It was really *all the music* contained within that amazing work.'[6]

Violinist Fritz Kreisler, some of whose German colleagues had told him that Toscanini did not know how to play Beethoven's Fifth Symphony correctly, remarked: 'I don't believe Toscanini is wrong: but even if he were, I should rather hear it wrongly played by Toscanini than correctly by anyone else.'[7] Conductor Arthur Bodanzky said: 'He is simply the conductor's conductor'; and Leopold Stokowski, who was offered a free ticket, insisted on paying, commenting, 'Everyone must pay to learn something.' It may also have been at this time that Paderewski first heard Toscanini. He later wrote in his memoirs: 'When all is said and done, there is nobody—nobody to be compared with Toscanini, for he is a transcendent genius—a genius of the first order. One cannot speak in any ordinary terms of Toscanini.'[8]

The orchestra returned to New York for additional concerts several times during the tour. It happened once that at the very last moment before a performance, someone informed Toscanini that the third trombone was not to be found; it was too late to hire a replacement and Toscanini angrily led the concert with only two trombones. Afterwards, it was learned that the man had been arrested for trying to molest a woman in Central Park. 'It's always the same thing with these Italians!' Toscanini shouted; and the intervention of Gatti-Casazza and the Italian consul general was required to pay the $90 fine and to have the man liberated.

The day after a concert in Buffalo, Toscanini and a few of the musicians went to see Niagara Falls. One of these companions was Ermanno Marchesi, who had shown a certain fearfulness during the ocean voyage to America.

'When there were storms, the Maestro would stay on the deck to enjoy the spectacle with greatest enthusiasm. He always wanted to try all the fastest and most modern means of transportation. The trouble was that he invited others, less courageous than himself, to come along. . . . To cure my timidity he went with me in a shaking airplane over Niagara Falls.'[9]

Following the March recording sessions there were two more weeks of concerts—the last on 2 April—and then the orchestra boarded ship for Italy. They had given sixty-eight concerts in America; but the ordeal was by no means over. On arriving in Naples the orchestra began another Italian tour which would take them to nineteen cities (thirty-six concerts) between 20 April and 16 June—with a two-week break in May.

That Toscanini was generally satisfied with the results of the American adventure is clear from the fact that he talked to journalists upon his return to Italy. The following quotations are drawn from a dispatch dated 18 April to the *Corriere della sera*, and from Raffaelle De Rensis's book *Musica vista*:

'. . . Excepting some organizational and travel inconveniences, nothing disturbed the breakneck race—the only way to put it—across the States. Confidence, stamina and ardour helped us from the first concert to the last. The first one took place at the Metropolitan and the audience's welcome was enormous . . . It must be said above all that this artistic trip had moral results which really moved us. In the USA and Canada . . . we were truly welcomed as ambassadors of Italian art. . . . We were greeted everywhere with demonstrations in honour of Italy.

Of course in smaller and less-developed cities, I made up less demanding programmes; but I did not eliminate . . . Beethoven, Wagner, Brahms . . .

What was extremely comforting for me was the welcome given the newest Italian music. In general, it was judged very favourably . . .

"The Scala orchestra!..." Toscanini is radiant when he talks about it. . . . "You know that the Americans admire it for its really perfect discipline, among its other virtues!" And he adds: "It is an orchestra which I hope always to have." '

By the time the marathon tour ended in Milan, the orchestra had given 133 concerts in just under eight months and had been heard by over a quarter of a million people.

In that same spring of 1921 Alfredo Frassati, Italy's ambassador to Germany, had been asked to inquire about the possibility of securing Toscanini to lead the Berlin Staatsoper. This attempt was made through Toscanini's good friend, the sculptor Leonardo Bistolfi, who was also an intimate friend of Frassati; but the project never came to anything. Toscanini had pledged himself to La Scala.

The first season of the new *ente autonomo* was to include ten operas, all in entirely new productions. Toscanini would conduct five of the works, and the remaining five would be led by Ettore Panizza—although Toscanini had a controlling hand in everything.

He had little time for rest after the tour: his attention was required in matters regarding the completion of the theatre's technical modernization, in the selection of singers and assistants, and even in overseeing the scenography. Giuseppe Marchioro, son of one of La Scala's famed scenographers, Edoardo Marchioro, said that each spring Toscanini would examine the preliminary sketches for the painted backdrops and the *maquettes* for the next season's new productions. In the autumn he would sit in the auditorium and look at the finished sets as they were placed on the stage with an approximation of the correct lighting. At both times he maintained the prerogative to accept, suggest modifications to, or reject the scenographers' work.[10]

Panizza had proposed Antonino Votto, barely twenty-five years old, as one of the principal coaches and musical assistants, and Toscanini had tentatively agreed. One afternoon in the summer of 1921 Votto had come to La Scala, as was his habit, to study scores on the piano in the upstairs foyer, which was then used as the main rehearsal room. Panizza entered at one point, with Toscanini—whom Votto had not met before—and a violinist. Toscanini greeted Votto warmly, then asked if he would please play through the Franck Sonata with the violinist, who was auditioning for the orchestra. 'Fortunately,' Votto recalled, 'I had played the piece before. When we got to the end, Toscanini smiled, clapped me on the shoulder and said, "The violinist plays well, but the audition was actually for you!" '[11]

Cesare Albertini, the engineer, wrote about Toscanini's organizational abilities in an article in June 1924:

'. . . This is another of the external manifestations of a very well-balanced and harmonious intellect . . . A deep penetrator of people's hearts, Arturo Toscanini chooses his colleagues with shrewd prudence. He does not love those who adulate him, nor those who present themselves to him prostrate or dully submissive . . . He wants colleagues who are intelligent, who know how to argue with him; he listens to their objections, and he trusts those who show that they really know something; he greatly appreciates those who spiritedly try new paths, even if those paths are full of difficulties . . .

There is no one who does not feel flattered and honoured by the faith Arturo Toscanini puts in him, in his strong and serene way . . . Those who see this tireless artist at work from morning till late at night, those who see him instruct the principals, chorus, secondary singers, take care of the stage production, co-ordinate the work of musical assistants, scenographers and stage directors, deal with administrative problems and relations with the public and press . . . those who see him always ready to do his duty, cannot avoid feeling his fascination and cannot avoid being attracted to such a formidable example. Thus . . . he has been able to achieve organizational miracles. . . .'[12]

When Toscanini had first taken charge at La Scala in 1898 he had worked under the sign of Wagner; but during the 1920s the house god was Verdi, without question. Not surprisingly, the conductor wished to reinaugurate the theatre with his favourite opera, *Falstaff*. Baritone Mariano Stabile made his Scala début in the title rôle—a part he was to sing nearly 1,200 times during his long career. He recounted the story of his engagement nearly half a century after the event:

'. . . They had begun to review the names of those who could possibly have taken the part of the protagonist. . . . Toscanini canned all those who had already done Falstaff. . . . "If only there were a young man who could do this part, maybe I would teach it to him myself." Then Calusio [a member of the coaching staff] turned to the Maestro and said, "I think that there is a young man who could do it." . . . So Maestro Toscanini said to Calusio, "Listen, without mentioning La Scala or myself, have him study the first part and the monologue from the last act. When you think he's ready, let me hear him."

I began to go to Calusio every morning at ten to study the part which Toscanini had indicated . . . Finally, after nearly two months . . . he said to me, "Look, Friday at 5 p.m., there will be the person who has to hear you." "And where do I meet you?" "At Piazza della Scala." . . .

La Scala was upside down, the stage apparatus was missing, the seats were missing, everything was missing. In the rear I saw a group of people; Maestro Toscanini was among them . . . I began to sing the first act." . . . Afterwards Maestro Toscanini said, "Sing me the monologue from the last act . . . When I finished singing . . . I went to where the little group of people, including

Toscanini, was standing. There was one of those pauses that used to kill people; he would twirl his moustache with two fingers ... Then, finally, he said to me, "You sing too metronomically." "Maestro," I said, "I didn't come here to have you hear how I sing *Falstaff*. I came to have you hear whether I have the potential to be able one day to sing *Falstaff* with you, if you tell me what to do, how to do it." This, naturally, impressed him. Another terrible silence... "Okay, show up here tomorrow at six and I'll be able to tell you something."

Of course I didn't sleep that night ... I went there the next afternoon and found the Maestro ... "Are you free?" "Yes, Maestro." "Do you know where Via Durini is?" "Yes." "Come to my house tomorrow morning at ten." ... At precisely ten o'clock we began to go over the monologue from the third act, "*Mondo ladro, mondo rubaldo*"; and until one or 1:30 I repeated those words, because he wanted me to bring forth a sort of regurgitation, that *oahhh* of the fat man, the drunkard, the glutton ... So we finished ... and he said, "Goodbye, see you tomorrow at ten." Naturally, another night passed with visions and—anyway, after two or three days of going to him, I had calmed down, he used *tu* with me, began to tell me stories ...

... One day two o'clock struck. Maestro Toscanini never got up from the piano, because he didn't smoke, didn't drink cocktails, didn't eat, was never hungry; so at one point Signora Carla came in and said, "But Arturo, don't you understand that Stabile has to go eat? Won't you let up and let him go home?" So then I went out, joking and laughing.

Finally, after seven days of this Calvary, he accompanied me to the door of his apartment and said, "Go to La Scala, go to Scandiani, whom I'll call now and who will give you a contract for La Scala." Imagine my joy! ... Then I went to study with Maestro Calusio. Sometimes, however—once, twice or three times a week—we both went to the Maestro's on Via Durini to have him listen to what we had studied.'[13]

La Scala re-opened its doors on 26 December 1921. The first night was nearly a disaster. It was a period of great political turmoil in the country, and some months earlier a bomb had gone off during a performance at Milan's Teatro Diana, causing deaths and serious injuries. Now a rumour had spread that there would be a bomb at La Scala as well. The public were searched on entering the theatre, which slowed down the process of getting to their seats. Nevertheless, Toscanini began the performance precisely on schedule; and some of the blameless latecomers, on entering the hall and finding that the opera was already under way, complained vociferously. Toscanini continued to conduct and the situation eventually became more tranquil. Successive performances were received with great enthusiasm. Verdi's ironic suggestion of free admission and cheap beer to attract an audience to *Falstaff* was no longer applicable.

Toscanini's second opera of the season was also by Verdi; but this time the choice fell on one of the great popular works of the composer's middle period—*Rigoletto*—which opened on 14 January 1922. And if Stabile was to become a fixture in the great Toscanini–Scala company of the 'twenties, so were two of the protagonists of this production—soprano Toti Dal Monte and baritone Carlo Galeffi.

Carla had heard Dal Monte as Gilda in Naples some months earlier and had recommended her to her husband—who already knew her voice from the performances of the Ninth Symphony they had done together in 1919. She later recalled her *Rigoletto* rehearsals with Toscanini:

'I shall always remember "my" rehearsal in La Scala's red room. For the whole first part of the second act—duets with the tenor and baritone—Toscanini stopped me very few times ... He urged me in particular to connect more smoothly the phrase "*Quanto affetto e quali cure*". He had me repeat it, and was satisfied after the second time. But then I came to the famous "*Caro nome*". I was very worried, and tried to do my best. Toscanini stopped me and said, "Listen, dear, you sing this *romanza* technically perfectly, but holy God!—you need more than that. First of all, I'll tell you that all of Verdi's women love in the same way ... They all have the same sort of heart-beat. And yet there are differences. Why do you think Verdi wrote this "*Caro nome*" in such a *staccato* style? For laughs? No, no, no. Verdi used this technique of short pauses to make the girl's anxiety more real. She's experiencing love for the first time and she feels almost breathless at the thought of the man she loves, who has inebriated her with so many pretty words.'[14]

Dal Monte said that when she sang Gilda's death scene, '*Lassù in cielo vicina alla madre*', Toscanini told her that at this point the girl is 'more there (in heaven) than here', and that the voice must have a truly delicate and angelic quality. The soprano also reported that the staging rehearsals were 'very laborious':

'Toscanini taught Galeffi his whole scene in the third act, transforming himself into Rigoletto, showing him every gesture, every expression, every 'spoken' recitative, every anguished outburst of wrath. How infinite were the sensations that man knew how to present, and how he knew how to get to the bottom of Verdi's creation, through music and words!'[15]

Tenor Giacomo Lauri-Volpi, who sang the Duke of Mantua in this production, has stated, apropos of Dal Monte, that at one rehearsal Toscanini asked her to sing 'Caro nome' in a fuller and rounder voice. She replied, 'Maestro, if I sing it as you would like it, I won't make it to the end.' Toscanini said nothing and let her do it her way. He also restored a passage often cut—the '*Oh quanto affetto*' referred to earlier. The tenor said:

'Toti Dal Monte did not reveal herself through the "*Caro nome*", but actually through that phrase, through that verse which the public had not known before . . .'[16]

Lauri-Volpi himself fared less well in his relations with Toscanini. The tenor wanted to insert a 'traditional' cadenza into the famous '*La donna è mobile*' but Toscanini wouldn't hear of it. Votto was playing piano at the rehearsal and recounted many years later:

'When Lauri-Volpi told him that even Caruso had done it the Maestro replied that Caruso had done it, but with a different voice and in a different style. Then the dissension arose, because after the four subscription performances of *Rigoletto* the Duke's part was taken over by *utilité* tenor Alessio De Paolis, who did another three performances.'[17]

Lauri-Volpi did not perform again with Toscanini for seven years.

On 16 February Toscanini led his first Italian production of *Boris Godunov*, with Zygmunt Zalewski in the title rôle. This was followed on 22 March by *Mefistofele*, in which Aureliano Pertile, who was to be his favourite tenor throughout the decade, sang *Faust*. Like Dal Monte, Pertile had been recommended to Toscanini by Signora Carla, who had heard him in the same rôle at Verona's Arena. Toscanini had originally scheduled another tenor for the part but had not been satisfied with him. Pertile had been called in at the last moment, a day before the first orchestral rehearsal. At the end of that rehearsal Toscanini is said to have exclaimed: 'At last I've heard someone sing my way! That's the way to sing!'

Pertile was a lyric tenor with a naturally beautiful if unextraordinary voice. His approach to singing was intelligent and he was dedicated in his work. Although lacking originality, he was malleable, quick to respond, and of a phlegmatic temperament. This combination of talent, adaptability, eagerness to learn and work, and absence of 'star' mentality was, of course, a perfect formula, as far as Toscanini was concerned. Not only did he assign the tenor many important rôles: he also frequently turned over to him, on short notice, parts initially assigned to other tenors who had left him dissatisfied. During Toscanini's eight Scala seasons Pertile sang lead rôles with him in no fewer than twenty-seven mountings of fourteen operas—rôles as diverse as Edgardo, Alfredo, Radames and Walther von Stolzing. He happily admitted that he owed very much to Toscanini:

'Imagine what help a good singer can receive from such a teacher. There is always the possibility of being told to go to the devil; but if one is capable of doing well and of overcoming the awe one feels before such a remarkable personality, one obtains everything—stimulus, sureness, self-confidence, in addition to an artistic formation. To such a Maestro go my devoted thoughts, my gratitude and my admiration.'[18]

The last production of the season was *Die Meistersinger*, with Marcel Journet as Sachs. Making his Scala début as Pogner was young bass Ezio Pinza.

'. . . Instead of a routine audition, I was to take part in a rehearsal with the other singers, who had already worked with the Maestro for about a month. Along with everyone else, I reported ten minutes ahead of time, and was awed by the hush in the vast room, as though Toscanini were already there. He appeared exactly on time, looking much smaller than I had expected, but instantly filling the hall with his presence. Everyone rose with military precision, like soldiers greeting a general. Without a nod, a smile or a word of salutation, Toscanini announced, "We will begin with the entrance of the Meistersingers."

That meant he was starting with me. In fact, the major part of that rehearsal revolved around my rôle. I concentrated on what I was doing with such single-mindedness that I could form no idea of Toscanini's reaction, and impatiently waited for the rehearsal to end; then the Maestro would surely pronounce his verdict. He did nothing of the kind. Without as much as a glance in my direction, he said, "Rehearsal tomorrow at the same time." And he left the room.

One of the baritones patted me on the shoulder. "Congratulations, Pinza, you're in!"

"But the Maestro said nothing!" I remonstrated.

"You can always tell by his face. Didn't you see it?" '[19]

Journalist Giulio Ciampelli has described Toscanini during a staging rehearsal of the third act of that *Meistersinger* production—literally running and jumping all over the stage, first to this group, then to that one, demonstrating positioning, gestures, clapping his hands to keep the piano and the massive forces together, shouting and singing.

Having conducted fifty-five opera performances between December and May, Toscanini led the orchestra in three concerts at La Scala and three more at the Teatro del Popolo in June and July. Beethoven's Ninth was the main work on the Scala programmes. Renato Simoni was present at the rehearsals of the Ninth and noted some of Toscanini's remarks:

'I don't want to hear the notes any more, there must be no more notes. Only spirit here!' . . . 'Abandon yourselves to your hearts; it's not enough to interpret the signs you have on the paper in front of your eyes. Look, I'm shuddering here. You must shudder, too.' . . . 'What you're expressing is serenity, contentedness, but it's not joy yet. You have to look for it in yourselves, not in the music . . .'[20]

Ciampelli reports that Toscanini planned a series of open-air concerts for great numbers of people in the Public Gardens; but the project was never realized. The conductor took a very brief holiday and then returned to Milan to work on the coming season.

We learn from other sources that Toscanini had drawn a very modest salary for his work at La Scala. At the end of the first season, which had so great an artistic and popular success, the governing board sent him a cheque for 100,000 lire—a gift above and beyond his salary. He returned it, saying that he had been paid quite adequately. In consternation, the directors sent the cheque back to him, saying that it was but a small token of their appreciation for his work. This time Toscanini graciously accepted the gift, but immediately made an anonymous donation of 100,000 lire to the theatre. He also wished to set an example in other fiscal matters; and so, for instance, he insisted on paying full price for a box for his family at La Scala, when, in fact, he was entitled, at least by tradition, to the use of one gratis.

A reporter for the American magazine *Musical Courier* managed to talk to Toscanini at La Scala in July, when the conductor was auditioning and rehearsing for the new season. The journalist asked him whether it was true that the Chicago Opera Association had invited him to conduct there and that he had asked a fee of $50,000 per season, which had been considered too high. Toscanini replied that Giorgio Polacco had written him the previous year, to ask whether he would like to become co-principal conductor with him in Chicago. The letter had been co-signed by Mary Garden, the soprano, who was then the company's manager. Not only had he not asked for $50,000: he had never even answered the letter. He explained to the reporter that he did not want to share the directorship of an opera company with Polacco or with anyone else, and that in any case he had no intention of ever working again in a traditionally run theatre like that of Chicago or the Metropolitan.

The second season, which Toscanini shared with Panizza, Antonio Guarnieri and Franco Ghione, opened on 2 December, again with *Falstaff*. Just a few weeks earlier, the Fascists had marched on Rome and the King had docilely put the government in Mussolini's hands. The events leading up to the march and the march itself had upset Toscanini, and he was disgusted by Mussolini's failure to make good his anti-monarchical statements of 1919. On the eve of the march he had told a friend, 'If I were capable of killing a man, I would kill Mussolini.' At one of the *Falstaff* performances a group of Fascists in the theatre began crying out to have the party hymn, *Giovinezza*, played, just as the third act was about to begin. Toscanini refused and began the act, but the disrupters would not be silent. He broke his baton, left the pit and went backstage, shouting and cursing. One of the administrative directors finally announced to the public that the hymn would be played at the end of the performance. Toscanini returned to the pit and the opera was played to its conclusion. Maria Labia, who sang Alice in the production, related:

> 'When the opera ended the manager told us: "Stay where you are, everybody, and sing the hymn accompanied by the piano." Toscanini intervened: "They're not going to sing a damned thing; the Scala artists aren't vaudeville singers. Go to your dressing rooms, all of you." And we went. The hymn was played at the piano because the orchestra, according to Toscanini, did not know it....'[21]

Many of Toscanini's intellectual and artist friends were shocked or at least puzzled by his behaviour in this matter. There were many intelligent people who were convinced that Mussolini was indeed the man of destiny, that he had arrived on the scene at precisely the right time, in order to solve the country's problems. Now, at the very moment of Mussolini's accession to power, one of Italy's best-known artists seemed to be turning against him. Toscanini's act was rationalized by many as a purely artistic matter—that is, that he did not want political songs performed alongside serious works. This, of course, is nonsense. He had always followed the protocol of playing national anthems under circumstances which he felt required such a gesture. Obviously, Toscanini was neither a profound political thinker nor a prophet: he could not have foreseen the disastrous course of the following two decades. But he simply did not like Mussolini's tactics, even at this very early time; and Wally Toscanini said that when Mussolini retained the militia as a paramilitary force (February 1923) her father said, 'He is not interested in the country—he is interested in himself.' The conductor's relations with the new régime were to worsen.

Toscanini's second production of the season was the world première of *Dèbora e Jaéle* by Ildebrando Pizzetti. Born and trained in Parma, like Toscanini, Pizzetti was one of Italy's most important composers of the period between the two world wars. He worshipped Toscanini and accepted his musical suggestions as if they had been made by a divine being.

A revival of *Manon Lescaut* (26 December; with Juanita Caracciolo and Pertile) was the occasion for a reconciliation between Toscanini and Puccini. Their rift in 1919 over the composer's *Trittico* had not been healed during the intervening time; in fact, Puccini's comments on Toscanini in letters from that period could almost be called schizophrenic. On 15 February 1921 he wrote to Carlo Paladini:

> '*Bis* are no longer permitted—Toscanini has settled it thus. I read bewildering things about him in today's *Corriere*. He who was so uninterested at first glance, with his eye fixed on Art, has had himself recorded along with his

orchestra! This great animator of foreign things, so little sensitive to our music, [is the subject of] articles and exaltations, as if he, a new Guido D'Arezzo, had discovered the notes of St. Joseph's hymn! As fas as I'm concerned, he has a great, prodigious memory; but music has to make the soul vibrate. In his hands its physiognomy changes ... Toscanini is fine for concerts, especially if he is conducting Debussy's embroideries and cold and colourful things. For the rest, where the soul vibrates humanly—*nihil*—or little more.'[22]

When, that summer, La Scala was planning the Milanese première of the *Trittico* for the coming season, under Panizza's direction, Puccini's opinion of Toscanini seemed to have changed. He wrote to Carlo Clausetti of the Ricordi Company on 4 July:

'. . . As for the direction of the opera, I firmly maintain that if the opera is not conducted by Toscanini I shall be damaged by it—not only materially (that is, in the performance), but morally. I know Milan (remember *Butterfly*) . . . Without Toscanini, the opera would be presented in an inferior light.

I would rather you think up a way of making "peace" between him and me. I have no deep rancour—it is not in my nature. If you yourself want to try, very well; and if you don't feel up to it, look for someone who has either the authority or the power of friendship to convince him to accept the direction of the *Trittico*. . . .'[23]

The tactic did not work, and Puccini refused to believe that Toscanini simply and truly did not like this particular work. A few weeks later the composer wrote to his friend, Count Riccardo Schnabl-Rossi:

'*Trittico* at La Scala but Panizza will conduct. Toscanini will only conduct *Falstaff* and works he already knows—so they tell me—and I think it is in order not to have to conduct me. He is really a bad man—perfidious—and I deny that he has the soul of an artist—because those who really do are not so full of wickedness and also, I think, envy! At bottom, I couldn't care less—but it bothers me for the Milanese, because with another conductor my opera won't be seen in the best light by the more or less intelligent public.'[24]

And to Renato Simoni, in August:

'There's a thorn in my side: that Toscanini, who persists in his enmity to me! And why? Who knows! I certainly would like peace, but he continues in his hostility.'[25]

The following January Puccini heard *Rigoletto* at La Scala and wrote to Schnabl:

'*Rigoletto* is really well played, without *fermate* or corrections of Verdi['s work]. Toti is excellent, Galeffi and Lauri-Volpi good. Toscanini's tempi are serene and right, third act excellent, even dramatically. The quartet nothing great, but there are few voices around. . . . Intimate, excellent staging. Fourth act not extraordinary; however, it's a production that takes hold.'[26]

It may well have been at the time of the *Rigoletto* that Toscanini and Puccini mended their friendship and began to think about reviving *Manon* for the following season. They met at Viareggio in August to discuss further modifications to the score, which Toscanini had already helped the composer to doctor twelve years earlier. 'Toscanini is here, two steps away from me,' he wrote to Schnabl on the 13th. 'He'll conduct my *Manon* at La Scala. I've done some substantial retouching on the score.'[27]

Puccini attended rehearsals for the production and wrote to Schnabl on the day of the opening:

'This evening *Manon*, a great *Manon*; and if the public isn't moved it will mean that we're living on Saturn instead of Earth. I assure you that Toscanini is a real miracle of feeling, of refinement, of sensitivity, of balance. What a pleasure the rehearsals were for me. Never, never have I so enjoyed hearing my music.'[28]

The public was indeed moved and *Manon* had to be performed seventeen times that season—more than any other opera. The day after the opening Puccini sent a lengthy letter to the *Corriere della sera*, which I translate here in part:

'Your music critic states that I have retouched the instrumentation of *Manon*. "Especially in the second and fourth acts, there are several retouchings, and others are evident even in the first act." He is referring to some trifling modifications of colouring; but the score printed by Ricordi can testify to the fact that I have not done over the instrumentation of the opera. My *Manon* is exactly that of thirty years ago, only it has been directed by Arturo Toscanini, which means directed in a way that brings its composer the great and rare joy of seeing his music illuminated with the same brightness that he saw and dreamt at the moment of composing it and never saw thereafter. For too long it has been the custom in Italy to present the so-called repertoire operas—that is, those which have resisted time and unfaithful performances—in an indecent style: one orchestra rehearsal, none for staging, and off goes the worthless thing, deformed by the abuses with which it has become encrusted, little by little, due to the bad habits of conductors and singers.

When Arturo Toscanini, with that conviction and love which are enflamed by his marvellous art, takes the scalpel in his hand and clears away the filth, and brings the opera back to its natural state, revealing the true intentions of the composer to the public, the old opera seems new to the public and they say it's something different. No, it is simply itself, enlivened by the greatest animator the art of music can boast of.

At La Scala these miracles are happening frequently nowadays; and last night, when the emotion of the public . . . took hold of me as well, and when I felt impelled to embrace our Toscanini, that embrace was not only a gesture of selfish gratitude for the performance of my *Manon*. No, it was the gratitude of one artist towards another artist, who had succeeded in making La Scala into a real temple for artistic consecrations and re-consecrations. What he has accomplished at La Scala is wonderful. I visit all the world's theatres, and I see and study what they do. This seems to me the moment to say that what is being done at La Scala today is not being done in any other theatre. Toscanini has achieved here not only the work of organization: he has created an institution which is the pride of Italian art . . . This nucleus of energy, guided and animated by Toscanini, gives results which, as happened last night, make *Manon* appear to be a new opera—to the extent that even to me it seemed to be thirty years younger. . . .'[29]

Before leaving Milan Puccini wrote Toscanini (2 February 1923):

'Dear Arturo, You have given me the greatest satisfaction of my life. *Manon*, in your interpretation, is beyond what I thought it to be in those distant days. You have done this music of mine with unapproachable poetry, *souplesse* and passion. Last evening I really felt your whole great spirit and the love you bear your old friend and companion of early days. I am happy because you, more than anyone else, knew how to understand my youthful and passionate spirit of thirty years ago. Thanks, from the bottom of my heart!'[30]

Re-mountings of *Meistersinger* and *Rigoletto* in January and February were followed by Charpentier's *Louise* on 25 February, with Fanny Heldy and Pertile. Journet and then Pinza took the rôle of the father. *Boris* succeeded *Louise* and was followed in turn by a completely fresh version of one of the most hackneyed repertoire operas, *Lucia di Lammermoor*, with Toti Dal Monte, Pertile and Pinza. Toscanini had performed the work only once before.

The previous autumn 'la Toti' had sung in a production of *Rigoletto* in Bergamo under the direction of Antonio Guarnieri, who had told her to sing 'Caro nome' down a semitone, and to put back all the traditional pauses on high notes, cadenzas, etc., which Toscanini had made her remove. Toscanini was angry when he found out about this. The soprano knew that he had been told and arrived for her first piano rehearsal of *Lucia* in a nervous state.

'. . . He sat down at the piano. My heart was in my mouth, for fear of an outburst. He banged out a few chords, then exclaimed furiously: "How could you have permitted yourself to sing *Rigoletto* in a different way from the one I taught you? And to think that I raised you up among the elect! You're a circus artist, that's what you are! You're not going to sing with me any more!" He slammed down the keyboard lid, got up and left without even giving me a chance to defend myself.

. . . I threw myself into an armchair and cried my heart out. Then Scandiani came to console me. He urged me to be patient and calmed me by assuring me that the tempest would pass as it had come. . . . Little by little, I recovered my tranquillity; thus, when the Maestro returned [after half an hour], still very out of sorts but less hostile, I was able to meet the test. The Maestro probably noticed that my eyes were red. In any case, seated at the piano, he began the rehearsal.

I didn't fail to notice that as I sang with increasing courage, he became calmer. Thank you, Donizetti! When we came to "*Verranno a te sull'aure*," Toscanini stopped me. "You sing this phrase well," he said; "but there isn't enough air in your voice. There must be more colour, more sweetness, more expression."

. . . When we came to the "mad scene", I sang my cadenza with a certain trepidation. The Maestro asked me, "Who taught you this cadenza?" "Paolantonio" [her coach], I answered, "as he did all the other ornaments in the score." "Yes, it's all right, it's all quite good . . .; but it's too short. You must add a couple of bars. Tell him."

At the end of the rehearsal the Maestro got up from the piano and said to me very affectionately: "You're still good, despite everything, and you have a beautiful voice."

. . . The *Lucia* rehearsals were detailed and enervating. . . . There were thirteen staging rehearsals for the "curse scene" alone. At one of the last ones . . . I plucked up my courage and said, "Maestro, we haven't rehearsed the 'mad scene' yet—how shall we be able to do it?" He looked me up and down, then said jokingly, "Come on now! You've acted crazy all your life; don't you think you'll be able to do it on the stage?" I insisted. "All right," he said; "we'll rehearse with the piano tomorrow at three."

The next afternoon . . . I made my entrance from the top of the stairs. . . . Toscanini stopped me immediately. "Remember that madmen stare straight ahead of themselves first, and then speak," he admonished. . . . At one point Toscanini rested his hand lightly on my shoulder, and in a thin voice, without looking at me, said: "That's enough... the rest is a concert piece... with the flute . . ." '31

Elsewhere the soprano reported that while rehearsing the '*Verranno a te*' Toscanini told her, 'You know, this is a woman who meets her lover at night secretly. *You're* worried about singing *piano* and that's all. Forget the *piano*, it's not *piano*; the heart must be in this phrase!'32

Pertile was asked to sing Edgardo in *Lucia* when another tenor had not pleased Toscanini.

'I did not know the opera. I learned it with Toscanini in five days; however, I had only one ensemble rehearsal ... I went calmly enough to the opening, but hesitant for fear of being inadequately prepared. I got lost for a moment during the famous ensemble ... After the performance ... I said to Maestro Toscanini: "I'm sorry about the mistake, Maestro. Please let me have a rehearsal with the orchestra." ... He said: "Calm down, get some rest, and come to the next performance." I did so and everything went well.'[33]

A month after the first *Lucia* performance Toscanini led a new production of *Madame Sans-Gêne*. The following production, however, was welcomed with surprising apathy. Mozart's *Magic Flute* had not been heard at La Scala for 107 years. The Scala public were not accustomed to hearing spoken dialogue at their theatre, and many regarded this masterpiece as a sort of operetta, beneath their dignity and of little musical interest. It received only three performances. Toscanini was so enraged that instead of withdrawing it from the repertoire, as others had suggested, he chose it for the opening of the following season.

His last opera that year was *Mefistofele*, and he also directed two performances of the Verdi *Requiem* in May. Some months earlier, during a visit Mussolini had made to Milan, the new prime minister had had himself photographed at La Scala together with Toscanini, the company's principal singers, and the heads of the administrative and technical staffs. He had also extracted a promise from Toscanini to bring to Rome the artists who had sung *Falstaff* at La Scala and to prepare a special performance of the opera for 10 May at the Teatro Costanzi, in honour of the visit of King George v. But the *Corriere* of 23 April reported that owing to health problems, Toscanini was 'greatly disappointed' to have to cancel the project.

He was suffering from visual disturbances and gastric problems at the time; but the fact that he managed to prepare and conduct two new productions and one old one, as well as the *Requiem*, at La Scala between mid-April and mid-May leads one to make other conjectures about his reasons for not going to Rome.

Mussolini's visit to La Scala was to be his only one during Toscanini's tenure there. The two men met two or three times during the 1920s: Toscanini feared that if he did not talk to—or rather listen to—Mussolini when asked to do so, the consequences would have been grave for La Scala, since it was a federal law which permitted the *ente autonomo* to exist. However, he paid no attention to the orders given him, and the Fascists did not have the courage to attack him—at that time.

Puccini's letters also indicate that Toscanini was not well during this period. Furthermore, diplomatic relations between Puccini and Toscanini had again deteriorated, simply because Ghione and not Toscanini had directed the new

Bohème production at La Scala (2 June). The composer was totally unreasonable and childish on this point. Toscanini had conducted about seventy-five perform-ances of eleven operas that season; the only composer who had had more than one work led by him was Verdi (two). His production of *Manon* had given Puccini 'the greatest satisfaction of my life' just a few months earlier; and Puccini was completely aware of his friend's poor health. Nevertheless, when Toscanini requested his presence at Ghione's last *Bohème* rehearsals, Puccini wired irritatedly (28 May): 'If you don't conduct, I don't feel interested in being present'.[34] Then, when Toscanini behaved with restraint and refrained from responding to this and similar messages, Puccini complained to Schnabl (3 June):

'*Bohème* last night at La Scala—I received a telegram reporting an excellent outcome: sixteen curtain calls. The God didn't conduct! Maestro Ghione con-ducted. I'm angry about this. He's a strange guy—after all the good he did for *Manon* and the celebrations in my honour—then he never responded to the telegrams I sent him from Vienna asking the date of the première [Note: and yet Toscanini had requested his presence at the last rehearsals; certainly by then Puccini must have been aware of the opening date] or to another long telegram in which I begged him to conduct. . . . I know that he's ill; but a little friendship, a little thoughtfulness and even good manners... Enough. I couldn't care less.'[35]

Still more fluctuations were to occur in this difficult friendship.

German conductor Wilhelm Furtwängler made his first appearances at La Scala in June, leading the Scala Orchestra in two concerts of music by Stravinsky, Wagner, Beethoven, Schumann, Reger and others. Berta Geissmar, his secretary, later wrote that during one of Furtwängler's rehearsals,

'Toscanini, who had been sitting unnoticed at the back, suddenly rushed forward and shook him warmly by the hand; he and his family were extremely friendly to him during this whole visit. The year after, Furtwängler visited La Scala to attend some of Toscanini's own operatic productions.'[36]

Three days after opening the 1923–4 Scala season with *The Magic Flute* (17 November) Toscanini directed a revival of *Aida,* which was followed by an important new production of *La traviata* (28 November). This was also the Scala début of the gifted and beautiful Gilda Dalla Rizza. Interestingly, Dalla Rizza was a lyric soprano who had made her name mainly in the forceful rôles of the *verismo* school and who was in no way accustomed to singing rôles like Violetta, which demand an extreme vocal agility. During most of this century, such parts have generally been assigned to the so-called *soprani leggeri*; but Toscanini wanted a weightier voice which was also capable of great lightness—a voice, in fact, like that of Storchio, who had by then retired from the stage. Dalla Rizza talked about this in an interview published some years ago:

'I met with the Maestro before 1923, because he was looking for a voice, a temperament adapted to *La traviata* . . . He listened to many voices, also better ones than mine, I believe; but since they were all "light", they could not, according to him, adapt to the character of Violetta. . . . "Try a bit of Violetta's part for me" [said Toscanini]; "let me hear a bit of your *agilità*." "Maestro," I answered, "I've never sung *agilità*. What do you want to hear from me?" I sang and he said: "Right now you sound like a double bass, but try studying it anyway."

Flattered by this, I began to work on the first act [the one with the greatest technical difficulties] of *Traviata* for four months, twice a day, with Maestro Calusio, who patiently tried to convince me that I would succeed. . . . One morning he said, "Gilda, La Scala can't wait any longer. We must decide— otherwise they'll take Muzio." Muzio was then the queen of sopranos. Finally, I decided, and I wired La Scala that I accepted. . . .

I remember that I wanted to do the first orchestra rehearsal alone, without the other soloists and without the chorus, for fear of becoming nervous and of not giving what I had given at the piano rehearsals; Toscanini was very under-standing and agreed to this. The character of Violetta had been taught me by Forzano [Note: Giovacchino Forzano, the playwright and jack-of-all-theatrical-trades whom Toscanini had engaged the previous year as principal stage director]; but there was not a single staging rehearsal in which the Maestro did not participate as well. I remember that during an ensemble rehearsal for the second act, he persisted in telling me that I wasn't putting everything possible into the famous "*Dite alla giovine*". I tried and tried again but I wasn't able to express all the emotion that Toscanini demanded. At one point—who knows why?—I put myself into it with all my will, all my soul, all my heart, and I burst into real tears. "That's it, that's it!" he shouted at me from the podium. "*Traviata* needs emotion!" "Yes, Maestro," I replied; "but if this happens to me on stage I don't know how the thing will end!" Toscanini gave everything of himself when he conducted; and when I sang, he would sing with me to make me feel the expression. . . .

The blessed first night finally arrived, and I don't know which saint helped me, because my success actually came in the first act. . . .'[37]

Manon Lescaut returned to La Scala under Toscanini's direction on 16 December, this time with Dalla Rizza in the lead rôle. It is hard to imagine Toscanini's state of mind during that performance, given the events of the previous two days.

His old friend Giuseppe Gallignani, who had directed Milan's Conservatory since 1897, had, without knowing it, been the object of a campaign against him within the powerful Ministry of Public Education in Rome which had been taken over by the ever-stronger Fascists. Gallignani had shown no particular sympathy towards the new administration; and since he was seventy-two years old, it was easy for his power-hungry enemies within the Fascist block at the Conservatory to convince the authorities to have him replaced. This was done, with no prior warning or even hint, in the form of a cruel telegram from Rome, telling him that he had been retired. The poor man was so shocked and distraught that he went home and the very same day, 15 December, threw himself out the window. Toscanini was one of the first to hear about this, and his grief was only equalled by his anger. He immediately sent a telegram to the Ministry in Rome:

'Maestro Gallignani, who did what no Minister or Director-General knew how to do for our Conservatory, has committed suicide. Gentlemen of the Ministry of Public Education, Ministers and Directors-General: I tell you that this suicide will weigh upon your consciences forever.'[38]

The next day Toscanini attended the funeral, as did the mayor and other city officials, faculty and students of the Conservatory and a wide representation of the city's artistic and intellectual community. Sacchi reports that outside the church, as the coffin was being placed on a carriage to take it to the cemetery, a huge wreath bearing the words 'The Minister of Public Education' was placed next to it. Suddenly, Toscanini rushed forward and said hoarsely, 'We'll get rid of that immediately.' He grabbed the wreath and threw it as far as he could. No one dared oppose him. At the Cimitero Monumentale, a city representative made a commemorative speech, and then one of the Conservatory professors prepared to make an address. The would-be speaker was a man whom informed sources referred to as one of the leaders of the effort to have Gallignani removed. Again, Toscanini stepped forward in agitation. He grabbed the professor's notes from his hand, threw them to the ground, stepped on them, and shouted: 'No! You will not speak!' Again, no one dared breathe. 'Avenged at last,' says Sacchi, 'the poor dead man was lowered into the grave. . . . Even many years later the workers at the Monumentale remembered it as the most exciting funeral they had ever seen.'[39]

Four days later Toscanini presented his new production of *Tristan* to the Milanese public, with Stefano Bielina and Nanny Larsén-Todsen in the principal rôles. The most unusual aspect of the event was that Toscanini, instead of having Forzano stage the opera, with his own intervention, had hired the Swiss theatrical theorist Adolphe Appia. Appia's mystical and symbolic approach to the staging of Wagner's operas was at that time considered by many to be the limit in avant-garde folly; but it is now recognized as the forerunner of modern Wagnerian interpretation. Toscanini was most interested in Appia's ideas, and he and his family were very kind and helpful to Appia during his Milanese sojourn; but the general public were puzzled by and cool towards the production. However, conductor Gianandrea Gavazzeni, who was then a student, recalled that 'we

young people were very taken with this new attempt and enthusiastic about it'.
Luciano Alberti, a specialist in the history of operatic staging, has said:

'Appia was a theorist; his practical experience was limited and of minor importance next to his theoretical work. . . . Appia's experience at La Scala . . . would seem to have met with resistance from the general situation—the presence of a permanent director like Forzano, among other things. It would appear, therefore, that even at La Scala, Appia was unable to do the *Tristan* he wanted. . . . Nevertheless, it must have been a spectacular production, eliminating as it did all the bric-à-brac. It was the triumph of darkness, in the second act: a circle of torchlight around the two lovers was the only scenic element. . . .'[40]

The Appia experiment may have been an isolated one at La Scala; but it reflected a serious desire on Toscanini's part to make Wagnerian staging more palatable. He once said:

'Listen to *Siegfried*: you can imagine the leaves rustling in the trees. Then look at the stage: a tree painted on paper. It's ridiculous! You can't present these operas without murdering them! In the music there's genius; on the stage you have fat and clumsy singers. It's a travesty!'[41]

Toscanini's staff conductors that season were Vittorio Gui and Arturo Lucon, and young Antonio Votto was given his first opportunity to direct a few performances. Toscanini watched over all the productions carefully, and no doubt made life miserable for his junior colleagues. He attended others' rehearsals and did not refrain from making brutally honest comments when he felt his intervention was warranted. Toti Dal Monte relates that after a rehearsal of the second act of *Barber of Seville* under Lucon, in which she had included much traditional ornamentation in her aria, 'Una voce poco fa', and in the duet with Figaro,

'Toscanini hurtled himself into my dressing room like a comet. He swore and insulted me: "superficial", "ham", "circus-tent singer" were the most gracious epithets. When the outburst had ended, he slammed the door and left; and I, stupefied, was left to cry.'[42]

A few days later she began rehearsals for Bellini's *La sonnambula*, with Gui conducting.

'Toscanini was always there, prodigal of advice for Borgioli, Pinza and all the others. He didn't interest himself at all in me, or at least so I thought. . . . At one of the last rehearsals I was about to cross the ramp [set up during rehearsals to enable people to walk from the auditorium over the orchestra pit and on to the stage], so high and narrow that it made one feel dizzy. . . . I felt a robust hand take me by the arm; I turned, and it was Toscanini himself. Joking, he crossed the ramp with me. When the scene had ended . . . I said to him: "Dear Maestro, you haven't said anything to me so far. Please listen to me: I'm waiting for your comments." He looked at me smilingly and replied: "For the last act, I have nothing to tell you. I would only like you to move the tempi. We all know that you sing well; but for pity's sake, don't just stand there listening to yourself. Move, move more—especially in the recitatives."

The next morning, at the dress rehearsal, I had only one thought: move, speed up, and lighten the interpretation. While I was dressing for the first performance, Toscanini shouted through the door: "I heard you last night. Sing as you did before, because yesterday you weren't yourself anymore." '[43]

A more horrifying Toscanini 'intervention' occurred the following season when Gui was preparing the première of *Il diavolo nel campanile* by Adriano Lualdi. There is a place in the score where the orchestra musicians are instructed to play whatever they please—free improvisation. Some of the comedians in the orchestra made rude oral noises as well as instrumental ones during the first rehearsals, and Gui let them have fun; but when the same thing happened at the dress rehearsal he literally put his foot down. The cloud of dust that went up from the podium after he had angrily stamped his feet caused further noises— of protest, this time—from the orchestra. 'Gui, beside himself, left the podium and ran up to tell Toscanini,' recalled Minetti, 'and the orchestra left the "mystic gulf" commenting excitedly on what had happened.' Minetti continued:

'. . . The Maestro suddenly came down the steps leading into our waiting room . . . like an avalanche, screaming as I had never heard him scream. There was a very heavy, thick table in the middle of the room. Toscanini grabbed it by one side and started to shake it and to make it dance, while continuing to scream and inviting us to fight with him. He looked like one of the Furies.
. . . My colleagues, pressed against the walls all around the room, their faces livid, sought to disappear. One, creeping along next to the wall, tried to get to the w.c.; others tried to flee to the next room. . . . The principal double bass, poor fellow, had the nerve to defend himself since, . . . justifiably, he did not want to be considered guilty. Toscanini, in his anger, said everything in his vocabulary to him, too; then still challenging us to fight, raving and threatening, he departed, having injured his wrist during the gymnastic exercise with the table. He left us pale with fear.'

The orchestra decided to demand an apology from Toscanini.

'The next morning . . . he came down into our room to make peace. The lights weren't working in the basement room. Somehow, one chap managed to find a candle and to light it; others lit matches. Toscanini gave a shadow of a greeting in a low tone of voice. Everyone present was a bit embarrassed. It

was at that point that our old, half-crazy bass clarinet player—the one who
lived in an attic with a chicken ... —spoke the famous phrase about the "sun
and the candles", in a clear allusion, after which the Maestro muttered,
"Imbecile!" in a half-gruff tone, and left. Peace had been made!'[44]

In January 1924 Toscanini presented Gluck's *Orfeo*, with the same cuts and
interpolations he had used at the Metropolitan. Fanny Anitùa sang the lead, and
Ernst Lert, whom Toscanini had brought in to assist Appia in the *Tristan*
production, was responsible for the staging. (He remained to do most of the
German operas during the next few years.) During the rest of the season Toscanini led operas already in the repertoire from previous years; however, the season
ended with a world première which was an international musical event: Boito's
long-awaited and today all but forgotten *Nerone*.

The poet and composer had died leaving what was to have been his masterpiece in an unfinished state, after fifty years of work and planning and self-
torture. 'Long before his death, poor Boito had announced to me many times the
completion of *Nerone* and his wish to have it performed at La Scala under my
direction,' Toscanini told Raffaelle De Rensis in 1929.

> 'Every time, because of his now legendary self-dissatisfaction, he would
> postpone his proposal, tearing up paper, changing or redoing entirely whole
> scenes and acts. When he died, the opera was found to be complete in the
> piano-vocal version, but incomplete in the instrumentation. However, the
> abundant and precise annotations were such that it was sufficient to follow
> and interpret them to finish the instrumentation. This was done scrupulously
> by Maestro [Vincenzo] Tommasini and myself.... [Boito's] annotations
> concerning the harmonization and orchestration were correct, since his
> intuition for sound hardly ever failed him; but as soon as he had to make them
> concrete, to realize them, he wandered away from his intuition and did not
> achieve the effects he had planned and wanted. At that point there would be
> second thoughts, discouragement, piles of paper in the waste basket, and
> indefinite postponements.'[45]

Boito died leaving no family and had made his friend Luigi Albertini his heir
and executor. Albertini had put the *Nerone* task in Toscanini's hands, and at first
the conductor had worked with Antonio Smareglia in attempting to complete the
opera. It may be that Toscanini was not satisfied with Smareglia's work, or that
he ran out of patience at having to play every scrap of Boito's sketches over and
over again at the piano for the poor blind man, or that they simply had a dis-
agreement at some point. In any case, Toscanini eventually chose Tommasini
as his collaborator. They worked on the score during whatever spare time was
available to Toscanini during his Scala seasons and especially during the summers. By the spring of 1923 they had progressed far enough for Toscanini

to make plans for a production the following season, and news of the forth-coming première was made public. That summer he and Tommasini completed the opera.

The première took place on 1 May 1924; it was the most massive undertaking of Toscanini's Scala tenure and probably of his entire career. Pertile took the part of Nero, and his colleagues included Rosa Raisa, Journet, Galeffi and Pinza; Lodovico Pogliaghi designed the sets and costumes; Edoardo Marchioro and Alessandro Magnoni painted the sets; Forzano and Toscanini supervised the staging; and Cia Fornaroli—who later married Walter Toscanini—was the *prima ballerina* (as she was in most of the Scala productions during the 1920s). Rehear-sals ran day and night for two months. Excitement over the event was feverish: composers, critics and admirers of Boito came from all over Europe and from North and South America. Seats had to be set up in the foyer for members of the public who would not be turned away: nothing could be seen, but at least some-thing could be heard. Mussolini telephoned Scandiani from Rome after the first act to inquire about the success up to that point. The public's reception of the work and the production was overwhelming.

Camille Bellaigue, the French music critic who had been a friend of Verdi and Boito, wrote: 'With Boito gone, only Toscanini could be the all-powerful soul of this great body.'[46] This statement proved to be true in a sense unintended by Bellaigue: when Toscanini ceased to conduct the work, when his personal involvement was withdrawn as a result of his withdrawal from regular operatic conducting, *Nerone* rapidly fell altogether from the repertoire, where it had never really managed to establish itself. It is resurrected extremely rarely, as a sort of monstrous curiosity piece. Boito's masterpieces remain the libretti of *Otello* and *Falstaff*.

Having conducted eighty-one performances of fourteen operas that season, Toscanini gave a concert in nearby Varese with the Scala Orchestra on 13 June; they then departed for a two-week tour in Switzerland, where they gave three concerts in Zürich, two each in Berne, Lausanne and Geneva, and one in Basel—all welcomed with enthusiasm.

Paolina Toscanini died in July at the age of eighty-four; she had been tough, bitter, pessimistic and hard-to-get-along-with to the end. Her remains were placed in the family tomb which her son had had Bistolfi build in the Cimitero Monumentale in 1911, and which already housed the bodies of Giorgio and Claudio Toscanini.

Shortly afterwards Toscanini and Scandiani went to Paris, where they dis-cussed the possibility of a series of guest performances at the Opéra by the entire Scala company. This proposal had been made by Jacques Rouché, the Opéra's general director, who had gone to Milan and had been astounded by what he had seen and heard at La Scala. At the meetings in Paris Rouché suggested bringing six Italian operas plus *Meistersinger* to the Opéra between mid-May and mid-

June of the following year; but there were both financial and physical problems
involved in the proposed visit, and in the end it never took place.

Meanwhile, the temperature of the Toscanini–Puccini relationship had again
dropped drastically, and this time the childish behaviour was Toscanini's.
Long before the *Nerone* première Puccini had had serious doubts regarding the
quality of the work; and although he had not been so foolhardy as to have
expressed them to Toscanini, he had made disparaging remarks to others about
the futility of Toscanini's dedication to the task. ('I have learned that Toscanini
and Tommasini are going to withdraw to some villa on Lake Como to manipulate
Nerone,' he had written to Riccardo Schnabl in June 1923.)[47] Word of this
blasphemous attitude had reached Toscanini who, in a fit of pique, had left
orders that Puccini be banned from the dress rehearsal of the opera. This turned
out to be the last time the already ill composer was to visit Milan; he had come
especially for the event and had left terribly upset and offended. After several
months he decided to tell Toscanini what was on his mind. He wrote him that
the exclusion from the rehearsal had hurt him badly, that he had departed the
city 'full of bitterness, an ungreeted guest'.

> 'You can understand me—it's rather painful for a man who, like myself, has
> worked his whole life, not ingloriously, for a man whose name keeps itself
> alive and unvanquished in the world, and who, for his age, ought to have the
> right to some respect—to see himself treated this way in his own country, and
> by the best! Yes, it is really discomforting and unjust, and I can't tell you how
> sad at heart I am because of it. You would do me a great favour if, appreciating
> as they deserve to be appreciated the feelings of loyal friendship which have
> moved me to write you, you would answer me (4 August).'[48]

Two weeks later he wrote Schnabl:

> 'I'm not well, I have a persistent sore throat, chronic laryngitis—four speci-
> alists have seen me and have advised four different cures! [Note: Puccini died
> of throat cancer several weeks later.] . . . War of the deaf with Toscanini . . . It
> is said that I spoke badly of *Nerone*, God superdamn it! *Turandot* lies un-
> finished; I haven't touched the piano or written a line in months.'[49]

What was bothering the composer above all was that he wanted Toscanini to
conduct the première of the nearly finished *Turandot* at La Scala, but dared not
ask under the circumstances. Finally, early in September, Toscanini went to
Viareggio to visit Puccini. On the 7th the composer wrote to Schnabl:

> 'Toscanini has just left and all the clouds have dispersed, which makes me
> very, very happy. I'm sure that in his hands *Turandot* will have the ideal
> performance. And this will be in April, so I have all the time in the world to

finish the bit that I still have to do. I showed him and played him some parts and I think he was very satisfied. And so the whole disagreeable situation has ended.'[50]

Wanda Toscanini had accompanied her father on that visit to Puccini and said many years later that he was very embarrassed on leaving because he liked *Turandot* but could not really show any great enthusiasm for it.

During much of September and October Toscanini was in Bologna to prepare and conduct the second production of *Nerone*. Puccini's condition had worsened and other specialists had diagnosed cancer. Toscanini was one of the few friends to have been told about the situation, and he went back to Viareggio from Bologna twice in October and again on 3 November, on the eve of Puccini's departure for the radiological clinic in Brussels from which he would not return.

Toscanini suffered a shock while in Bologna. Seven years earlier Wally, then seventeen, had fallen in love with Count Emanuele Castelbarco, who was already married and had two children. Knowing that her father would be unlikely to show sympathy and understanding in the matter, she kept it hidden from him. But when, in 1924, foreign divorce proceedings were finally initiated, Castelbarco's wife went to Toscanini in Bologna and informed him that Wally was destroying her marriage and family. He took this news very badly, and on returning to Milan he let his daughter know exactly how he felt. 'Glasses, dishes and everything else he could put his hands on went flying,' she recalled many years later. 'He said terrible things to me and he hit me. It was the first time he had ever lifted a hand against one of his children. He did it with great sorrow, and he later asked me to forgive him.' At first he told her to leave home; but when she actually began to pack he changed his mind.

Another six years passed. Castelbarco obtained a divorce in Hungary, and Wally—after swallowing a glass of cognac—went to tell her father that she wanted to marry Castelbarco, 'but I don't want to lose you'. He told her that since she had loved Castelbarco for so long, he, as her father, had no right to ask her to give him up. But he added that he never wanted to meet him. The marriage took place at Zoltán Kodály's home in Hungary. Toscanini did not attend but sent a telegram to Wally saying, 'May God bless you as I bless you.' For yet another three years the situation remained difficult. Wally could not be received by her father or his friends unless she left her husband behind; and even when Toscanini's granddaughter, Emanuela, was born, he insisted on seeing her and her mother without her father. Then, in 1933, a chance encounter changed everything. Toscanini was in Vienna to conduct some concerts; Carla was with him, as were Wanda and her fiancé, Vladimir Horowitz. Wally was also there with her husband and daughter—in a different hotel. When Toscanini was busy with concert preparations the rest of them would go sight-seeing together. One day

they happened to see Toscanini walking towards them. Castelbarco started to
leave the group, but Wanda told her brother-in-law to stay. 'It's time Papà
stopped this.' Wally later related: 'When we were in front of him I said, "Look,
Papà, Emanuele is here, too." He turned towards my husband, smiled at him,
shook his hand and said, "Pleased to meet you." It was as if nothing had happened between them. From that moment on my husband was welcomed into the
family.'[51]

It was an all-too-common and pathetic case of a would-be family man tyran-
nizing over his loved ones and trying to force them to conform to a moral
system in which he believed but to which he himself was incapable of adhering
in practice. In 1924, when Toscanini learned of his daughter's affair, he himself
was as involved as ever in numerous passing 'diversions'. His fame was now
world-wide and his good looks seemed, if anything, to increase with age. He
continued to be very careful about his appearance. 'He went to the best tailor,
always wore highly polished shoes, and used eau de Cologne d'Orsay—even on
his moustache,' said Wally.[52] In the theatre his philandering was notorious,
although in all fairness, I have yet to hear a story of a singer who was not given
a rôle because she had not gone to bed with him, or of one who was given a rôle
only because she had. In addition to singers and ballerinas, there were many
society ladies who threw themselves at him, not to mention women who were in
some way associated with artistic and intellectual circles. 'He had many lovers
and was unfaithful to all of them,' Wally said. 'He would even have affairs with
two or three of them at a time. . . . If he became aware that they were taking
things seriously, he abandoned them. He was cruel. . . . It didn't bother us
[children] at all. On the contrary, we found Mamma tiresome about this. "You
would have to turn all your lady friends out of the house," we used to tell her.
She wouldn't confront him; she would become rude and bad-humoured.'[53]

Toscanini's fourth Scala season opened on 15 November with *Nerone* and
continued with *Boris* four nights later. On the afternoon of 29 November he was
in the midst of an orchestra rehearsal when Puccini's friend and librettist
Giuseppe Adami came down to the pit and walked over to him. 'He turned to
me, and understood in a moment,' said Adami. ' "Dead?" "Dead." He dropped
his baton, ran to his dressing room, threw himself face down on the sofa . . . and
broke into tears.'[54]

Toscanini had sent Carla to Brussels to be among the close friends who would
look after Puccini in his last days. Now, he and another friend took upon themselves the unpleasant task of breaking the news to the composer's ailing widow,
Elvira, who had never been told of the seriousness of her husband's condition.
They remained with her until nighttime. On 3 December Toscanini conducted
the Scala Orchestra in the Funeral Elegy from *Edgar*, Puccini's second opera, at
the funeral in Milan's cathedral. The composer's body was put temporarily into

the Toscanini family vault at the Monumentale, while a tomb was prepared for him in Tuscany.

Having led Mascagni's *Iris* on 6 December, Toscanini prepared and conducted the world première of Giordano's *La cena delle beffe* (20 December). On the afternoon of 29 December he directed a concert in memory of Puccini at the Milan Conservatory, where the composer had been a student. The programme was played and sung by a student orchestra and chorus, and included the Prelude to Act II of *Le Villi*, the third act Intermezzo from *Manon* and an unpublished *Requiem* which Puccini had written when Verdi died. That evening, at La Scala, he led the *Villi* piece, the *Edgar* Prelude and Funeral music and a special performance of *Bohème*.

Afterwards, journalist Ugo Ojetti, a well-known correspondent for the *Corriere della sera* who was acquainted with Toscanini, had dinner with him at his home. He noticed and remarked on a bust of the conductor near the piano. Toscanini said it was by his friend Wildt, and that he had paid 30,000 lire for it. But he couldn't stand it: every time he sat down at the piano it looked 'twice as big and twice as ugly' to him. Ojetti promised to help him think of some delicate way of getting rid of it—by giving it to a gallery, perhaps—without hurting Wildt's feelings. Ojetti had close connections with the Fascists, and he noted in his diary after returning home that while her husband was out of the room, Carla had told him of her fear that Toscanini would be offered a senatorship by the régime. (There were rumours to that effect at the time.) She said that at one time he would have welcomed the honour, but that now he would certainly reject it, 'and who knows what words he would use?'[55]

The previous June the Italian Socialist Party secretary, Giacomo Matteotti, who had been involved in a series of parliamentary reports which unmasked the totalitarian objectives of the government, had been murdered. Toscanini, like millions of other Italians, had been outraged. A farcical trial had been held for the material suspects—whereas Fascist bosses including Mussolini himself had almost certainly approved the murder. By then, however, Mussolini's position with the military and the monarchy was firmly established, and he was able to suspend many of the country's democratic institutions early in 1925. When orders reached La Scala that pictures of the Duce and the King must appear in every public place, including theatres, Toscanini refused to comply. And in fact, as long as he was at La Scala the pictures were not shown.

From January through April 1925 he conducted *Traviata*, *Louise*, the world première of Riccardo Zandonai's *I cavalieri di Ekebù*, *Manon Lescaut*, *Orfeo*, *Rigoletto* and *Falstaff*. For the first time in twenty-three years Milan heard him conduct *Il trovatore* on 30 April, with Pertile, Raisa, Anitùa and Benvenuto Franci, and the reaction was, if anything, even greater than it had been at the startling 1902 production. Franci has told of his audition for the rôle of the Conte di Luna:

'Toscanini said: "You're a bit of a screamer . . . , a bit of a shrieker! When we do *Trovatore* at La Scala, I'll teach you; because I heard, for instance, that when you sang '*Leonora mia!*' you threw in a G. What are you going to do with that G? This is a count talking, not a rag-picker, not a screamer. So you must sing it as Verdi wrote it—without the G!" And in playing the composer's version for me, he said to me: "Hear how beautiful it is?" And he was right.'[56]

Turin saw Toscanini direct an opera for the last time in March, when he led a third production of *Nerone*. The previous year he had visited the city to inspect the operation of lowering the Regio's pit, which he had made one of the conditions of his leading the opera there.

His last production of the Scala season was a revival of *Pelléas* (May), this time in French, with Fanny Heldy, Alfred Legrand and Journet. Panizza, Gui and Votto had shared the conducting duties with him during the season; he had directed seventy-four performances of fourteen operas.

In June he began another Swiss tour with the Scala Orchestra: two concerts each in Lausanne and Geneva, one each in Basel and Zürich. Unfortunately, the tour's Swiss sponsor, Ernst Stamm, involved himself in some dishonest dealings. There were to have been more concerts, but the orchestra had to return to Milan after its first Zürich performance and Stamm was arrested for circulating bad cheques. Conductor Fritz Busch had hoped to go to the second Zürich concert, which was then cancelled.

'My Zürich colleague, Volkmar Andreae, knew that [Toscanini] had gone with friends and musicians to a small Italian tavern, and we followed him there. In a few minutes Toscanini and I were absorbed in the most animated conversation on musical questions, although to this day I cannot understand how. We both suffered from the results of the Tower of Babel. Our exchange of ideas was the product of Toscanini's Wagner German and my smattering of broken Italian, helped out on both sides by loud singing and violent gesticulation. The contact we made here lasted for twenty years, with an improved linguistic foundation. [Note: Busch learned Italian; Toscanini did not learn German.] I may say it was friendship, until Toscanini, with increasing age, silently withdrew, except for a specially intimate circle, from those who did not force themselves upon him.'[57]

Following the Swiss misadventure two concerts were quickly arranged in Milan to make up the loss to the orchestra. Toscanini insisted that the entire proceeds of these two special performances be turned over to the players.

A festival sponsored by the International Contemporary Music Society was held at the Teatro la Fenice in Venice in September, and Toscanini attended, after having spent part of his summer at Alpino, a tiny village high over Stresa on Lago Maggiore. The man who had introduced to Italy many works of

Wagner, Brahms, Strauss, Debussy and dozens of his compatriots was now nearing sixty and, not surprisingly, his opinion of much of what he heard was negative. At the end of the series he was heard to exclaim: 'Now they should disinfect the theatre.'

More concerts were given at La Scala under Toscanini's direction in October —three different programmes on the 12th, 14th and 16th. The opera season opened on 14 November with a new production of *Un ballo in maschera*. Pertile, Galeffi and Maria Carena sang the principal rôles. By the end of December Toscanini had also conducted new productions of *Faust* and *Butterfly* as well as bringing back five works from the repertoire—eight operas in six weeks! He was able to do this because he had perfected a repertoire system in which everything was prepared so meticulously that productions could be reassembled from previous seasons with an absolute minimum of rehearsal time. Thinking back on that system half a century later, Gianandrea Gavazzeni said:

'It was an altogether new way of working for the Italian operatic tradition, because he instituted a custom, a method—a tyranny, one could say . . . Before Toscanini, yes, there were good performances, there were great conductors, there were great singers, but not yet a method for a complete realization from the aesthetic and even moral points of view. La Scala was completely reorganized for Toscanini, in respect to its rehearsal habits, to the way of conceiving its programme, to the method of making singers study, and also in respect to educating the public. The public with Toscanini, during that era, was educated to consider the theatre not as something for amusement, but as something with a moral and aesthetic function, which enters into the life of a society, into the life of a culture.'[58]

Of course things did not always work perfectly: Votto remembered that at a performance of *Meistersinger* one year, there were some serious mistakes in one of the big ensemble scenes. He saw Toscanini in the wings after the act had ended, crying from shame and anger, and murmuring, '*Non ci posso credere*' ('I can't believe it') over and over again. And when *Dèbora e Jaéle* was brought back one season Toscanini himself made a serious error at the dress rehearsal— which was to have been the only rehearsal. Votto reported that Toscanini was so shocked and upset that he dismissed everyone and rescheduled the rehearsal. However, Votto made it very clear that these were very rare exceptions.

Discipline within the company was rigid, and nerves were strained when Toscanini was conducting. When overworked or under emotional tension for one reason or another he was more prone to angry outbursts which were sometimes unreasonable or disproportionate to the crime. There is the story of a violinist in the orchestra, a certain Licari, who would always go through a series of extravagant preparatory motions before picking up his instrument to begin a passage; and he so exaggerated this process that often he would not have the violin and bow in place until the very last instant—and sometimes entered altogether late. Toscanini was annoyed by this—as anyone would have been; but one day he could stand it no longer. According to Sacchi, Toscanini turned to Licari and said:

' "You always prepare at the last moment. I want to see the violins in position two bars before the attack. I don't want to see any sluggards. You are a sluggard." ... Licari, uncertain at first, turned to his stand partner: "Who is he talking to?" ... "I'm talking precisely to you. You're a sluggard, you don't know how to play the violin, and next year you won't be back in this orchestra." "No matter," replied Licari jokingly. This really infuriated Toscanini: "You don't know how to play the violin; as a teacher, you're a cripple, and you can only produce cripples." At that, Licari got up and left the hall; and Toscanini shouted ... "Finally that creep is gone. I've had him on my nerves for five years!" '59

Toscanini received a court summons over this affair, but the case never proceeded any further. The judge gave his opinion, *in camera,* that Toscanini had the right to unrestricted 'artistic censure'. Toscanini stated that he had not intended any personal offence to Licari (!) and the latter signed a declaration withdrawing the charges. At the moment Licari was about to sign Toscanini exclaimed: 'What an imbecile!' His lawyers pounced on him and begged him not to ruin everything, to which he replied, 'I said it because if I were he, I never would have signed!'

The *Corriere della sera* reported that on the morning of 28 December Toscanini went to the Milan Prefecture at the request of Mussolini, who was visiting the city. It must have been this meeting which Toscanini later told friends had been a long harangue on the Duce's part. Toscanini, who was kept standing, stared at a spot on the wall over Mussolini's head while being reprimanded for his bad behaviour and warned of the possible consequences for La Scala. When the lecture had ended, Toscanini left. The *Corriere*—which had by then been taken out of Albertini's hands and muzzled—said that 'the Prime Minister . . . showed great interest in the proceedings at La Scala and in [Toscanini's] imminent trip to America.'

In fact Toscanini, along with Carla and Wally, was to leave that same afternoon for Cherbourg; two days later they embarked on the *Berengaria,* bound for New York. He had arranged for a seven-week leave of absence from La Scala in order to accept an engagement as guest conductor with the New York Philharmonic.

Attempts had been made in the summer of 1922 to secure Toscanini's services for the Philharmonic's 1923–4 season. The first approach was carried out through Loudon Charlton, who had managed the Scala Orchestra's American tour; but according to a letter in the Philharmonic's files, Toscanini 'could not consider conducting so many concerts as the Philharmonic schedule seemed to call for' and 'must have at least two weeks before the season in which to prepare the orchestra'; and he made 'other conditions financially and otherwise quite beyond the power of the Society'.[60] New efforts were made through the orchestra's regular conductor, Willem Mengelberg, and his manager, S. Bottenheim, but to no avail.

Nearly three years passed before Clarence H. Mackay, the millionaire chairman of the orchestra's board of directors, who was to the Philharmonic what Kahn was to the Metropolitan, arrived at the right solution to the problem. He dispatched Max Smith, the conductor's Italian-speaking New York journalist friend, on what turned out to be a successful mission to engage Toscanini. On 5 April 1925 Smith was able to wire Mackay:

'Maestro coming for period beginning January 14th. Decision just communicated cost him tremendous struggle because unanticipated troubles and difficulties here placed him in cruel dilemma. Strain on me also great. Inasmuch as till now remuneration has not been mentioned or even touched upon directly or indirectly, may I ask without being misconstrued whether offer by you to assume cost of American tax and ocean expense would not be noble gesture by you towards this man of incomparable genius. Hope I am justified in having offered six preparatory rehearsals including day of first concert and further rehearsals on every other open day of engagement, but realized importance of avoiding all obstacles to acceptance. Moreover wife advised me six preparatory were essential to success.'[61]

One can only guess that the 'troubles and difficulties' mainly involved the reaction of the Scala directorate; and in fact, after Mackay had wired Smith his delight and thanks, Smith replied on 12 April:

'You may now count absolutely on Maestro's promise but direction of Scala greatly upset because of his decision. Has asked me to request as special favour one month's respite for him wherein to decide whether to come at time now set or at an earlier date.'[62]

The original date was eventually maintained and Toscanini began planning his programmes. Smith sent a tentative list to New York on 2 August and added:

'Now that Toscanini is actually coming to America he seems to be much interested in his coming work with the Philharmonic. He asks about the various musicians in the orchestra. He is curious about this and that thing. He is now looking extraordinarily well. In fact, I don't believe I have ever seen him in such good health.'[63]

Later that month a contract was signed by Toscanini and sent to New York. He would receive $20,000 for conducting eleven performances with the orchestra; his income tax would be paid by the Philharmonic; and he would be given an

additional $1,500 for travel expenses. By October the series had been expanded
to fifteen concerts, with an additional $2,000 for two of the extra performances.
(The other two, given for student audiences, he directed gratis.)

The Toscaninis arrived in New York on 5 January 1926 and the first Phil-
harmonic concert took place at Carnegie Hall on the 14th. The programme
included Haydn's Symphony No. 101 ('The Clock'), Respighi's *Pines of Rome*
(American première), Sibelius's *Swan of Tuonela*, 'Siegfried's Death and Funeral
Music' from *Götterdämmerung* and Weber's *Euryanthe* Overture. As anticipated,
the concert was a very great success. Later programmes in the series contained
Beethoven's *Leonore* Overture No. 3 and First, Third and Fifth Symphonies;
Brahms's 'Haydn' Variations; a Prelude, Chorale and Fugue by Bach, arranged
by Abert; the Nocturne and Scherzo from Mendelssohn's *Midsummer Night's
Dream*; Schubert's 'Unfinished' Symphony; *La Mer*; Scenes I and IV from
Petrouchka; Mozart's 'Prague' Symphony; the Prelude and *Liebestod* from
Tristan; Vivaldi's Concerto grosso in D minor, Op. 3 No. 11; and works by De
Sabata, Martucci, Tommasini and Roger-Ducasse. A benefit performance for the
Italian Welfare League, two performances for students and one performance each
in Philadelphia and Brooklyn were included among the fifteen concerts. The
Brunswick Company recorded the *Midsummer Night's Dream* excerpts in the
fifth-floor 'Chapter Room' of Carnegie Hall. The last concert took place on the
afternoon of 7 February and the Toscaninis departed for Italy that same evening.

During his stay Toscanini had gone as Respighi's guest to a concert of the
International Composers' Guild, where he had immediately involved himself in
an argument with Edgar Varèse. The composer's widow, Louise, gave an account
of the clash in her *Varèse: A Looking-Glass Diary*:

'Like Varèse, Toscanini was notorious for his uncontrollable temper, and when
he shouted at Varèse that it was a disgrace to make people listen to the kind of
music he not only sponsored but wrote, Varèse met him temper to temper,
insult for insult. It was quite a spectacle. From then on, the slightest mention
of Toscanini was like the *muleta* to a bull; Varèse charged. . . . Varèse insisted
that Toscanini was incapable of conducting anything better than Italian opera
and that he had the mentality of a coiffeur and looked like one. Salzedo [the
harpist], who was an admirer and friend of Toscanini, argued with Varèse in
vain.'[64]

Furtwängler, who had been very successful in his guest appearances with the
Philharmonic, began to lose support with the orchestra's management soon after
Toscanini's arrival. Varèse and Furtwängler were quite friendly—although the
German conductor had no more to do with Varèse's music than did Toscanini—
and Louise Varèse reports that 'Furtwängler was very bitter and Varèse had the
pleasure of joining him in flaying Toscanini alive, blood dripping from every
word'.[65]

Edward Ervin, the Philharmonic's assistant manager, accompanied the Toscaninis to the ship on which they were to return to Europe and talked with the conductor about details of his visit during the next season, which he had apparently agreed upon during his stay. The visit would take place during the same period (mid-January to early February).

On his return to Milan Toscanini plunged at once into a terrible schedule which bound him to putting seven works—including one Italian première and one world première—on the stage during the remaining two months of the season. Gluck's *Orfeo* (27 February) was followed five nights later by the first Italian performance of Debussy's 'mystery', *Le Martyre de Saint-Sébastien,* on a text by D'Annunzio.

As early as 1910, when the two men were still labouring on the piece, they had wired Toscanini: 'We believe that you alone will be able to give perfect life to our work',[66] but the première had taken place without him. A plan to stage *Le Martyre* at an earlier Scala season had gone unrealized. The 1926 production took place with Ida Rubinstein speaking and dancing the rôle of the saint. The critic for *Unità* wrote:

'Several times, Bakst's marvellous sets seemed barely noteworthy, since the orchestral sounds aroused much richer images. . . . It was, therefore, an extraordinarily interesting artistic event, but the Scala public did not seem to appreciate it as it deserved.'

At the performance of 13 March D'Annunzio, who was in the theatre, made an improvised speech in tribute to Debussy and Toscanini.

Saint-Sébastien was succeeded by a revival of Montemezzi's *L'amore dei tre re,* which was followed in turn by *Nerone, Pelléas* and *Traviata*; but the great event of the season, for the general public and the press, was the world première of Puccini's last opera, *Turandot,* on 25 April. It is also the last episode in the strange story of the Puccini–Toscanini friendship.

At the time of his death Puccini had not quite completed the last act of the opera. It seems that the Ricordi Company had asked Toscanini to suggest someone to finish the work, and Toscanini had recommended Riccardo Zandonai. Puccini's son Tonio opposed this on the grounds that Zandonai was too well-known a composer in his own right. Franco Alfano's name was then put forward and Toscanini gave his approval; but Votto says that 'Toscanini was very angry when Alfano brought him the finished product'.[67] However, according to a letter Alfano sent to Gaetano Cesari, critic of the *Corriere della sera,* Toscanini had insisted that Alfano expand the finale beyond the version he had originally presented; and it was precisely this expanded version which was most severely criticized and eventually reduced. In any case, it is said that after the dress rehearsal Alfano approached Toscanini and asked him, 'What do you have to say,

Maestro?' Toscanini replied: 'I say that I saw Puccini approaching from the rear of the stage to clout me.'[68]

Another problem was the selection of singers for the three principal parts. Lauri-Volpi, Gigli and Martinelli claimed that Puccini had told each of them he was thinking of *his* voice for the rôle of Calaf; but Toscanini chose Miguel Fleta, whom the composer could not stand. Likewise, Dalla Rizza and Dal Monte claimed similar pledges for the part of Liù; but Toscanini chose Maria Zamboni. Finally, Rosa Raisa and Maria Jeritza were both said to have been considered as possible Turandots; and in this case Toscanini chose Raisa.

First, Calaf: Lauri-Volpi had had, as we know, a serious falling-out with Toscanini in 1922 which had not yet been forgiven by the conductor. Gigli felt that the rôle was unsuited to his voice. Martinelli was told by Gatti-Casazza that he would not be rehired by the Metropolitan if he sang in *Turandot* at La Scala. (Lauri-Volpi and Gigli were also under contract in New York and may have received similar warnings.) Gavazzeni, who was present at the dress rehearsal of the opera, recalled that although Fleta had trouble with Alfano's final duet, the rest was superb. 'With all due respect for all the other Calafs in *Turandot*'s history, I've never again heard anyone sing the beginning of *"Non piangere Liù"* as he sang it. And even the problem of *"Nessun dorma"*—leaving aside the B-natural which some other tenors might have done more brilliantly—but all the preceding phrases were extraordinary.'[69]

Liù: Gavazzeni also felt that Puccini's ideas about Dalla Rizza and Dal Monte for this rôle were misjudgements. 'I maintain that Toscanini's choice of Zamboni was correct, because Zamboni, for the quality of her sound, was highly suited to the part.'[70] This, of course, is his opinion against Puccini's.

Turandot: Basso Tancredi Pasero, who was in the Scala company from 1926 onwards, said that Raisa was better suited to the rôle than Jeritza. 'A fine artist, Jeritza, a little bizarre in her stage mannerisms—she would throw herself to the ground; but when she went up a bit in the high register, she forced. You don't fool around with Turandot: that's a great part, and it has had few great interpreters.'[71] Jeritza was also singing at the Metropolitan then, so she may have been told what Martinelli was told. Furthermore, Raisa also claimed to have been promised the part by Puccini, and Gavazzeni said that the choice was 'absolutely ideal'.

Giorgio Gualerzi, an important historian of the Italian lyric theatre, feels that part of the reason for Toscanini's choice of singers was a deliberate desire to countermand Puccini's wishes, caused by some contention they had had over a woman. He is not specific, however; and although such a situation may well have existed, I think that the facts reported above and the success of the production prove that Toscanini's choices were made according to the dictates of his tastes and conscience, and not out of vindictiveness towards a friend who had already been dead over a year.

The rehearsals were many, long and difficult. Not long before the opening Toscanini informed the company that the very first performance would be given without Alfano's ending. And in fact, after the death of Liù in the third act Toscanini dropped his baton, turned partially towards the audience and said: 'The opera ends, left incomplete by the death of the Maestro.'[72] With tears in his eyes, he left the podium and made his way out of the pit. No one dared applaud until finally someone shouted 'Viva Puccini!' which touched off an enormous ovation. There was an interesting report in the next day's *Corriere*:

> 'During the interval the audience awaited the previously announced arrival of Mussolini. But the Prime Minister did not want his presence to distract the public in any way: their attention had to be entirely devoted to Puccini.'

What had actually happened was rather more complicated. Mussolini had turned 21 April into a national holiday he called the Birth of Rome, and he ordered all places of public entertainment to play *Giovinezza* at their performances on that day. In 1925 Toscanini had made sure that a rehearsal, not a performance, was scheduled at La Scala that evening. Now, in 1926, he received word from highly-placed persons that he was not to use the same trick again. He ignored the order and again scheduled a rehearsal. Mussolini, who arrived in Milan a day or two later, was furious, and sent for the theatre's directors. They were told that if they could not control Toscanini, they would either have to get rid of him or never expect to see Mussolini in the theatre. He wished to attend the *Turandot* première, but *Giovinezza* would have to be played.

The Scala directors found themselves in an unenviable position, caught between the wrath of Mussolini and the wrath of Toscanini. They told the conductor of the prime minister's order; Toscanini retorted that they could have *Giovinezza* played if they would get someone else to conduct both it and *Turandot*. At that point, of course, Toscanini was more essential than Mussolini to La Scala's well-being, so *Turandot* was performed with the Maestro and without the Duce. When, after the third performance, Toscanini—who was on the verge of total nervous exhaustion at the end of this particularly demanding season—left the remaining performances to Panizza and went to the Ligurian coast for a rest, the Fascist press circulated rumours that he had left La Scala for good because he objected to a new law which formed a national corporation of opera house managers. In effect, the Fascists were giving La Scala a chance to dump Toscanini and Toscanini a chance to withdraw without hurting his pride. Toscanini remained.

A consequence of his state of exhaustion was that he was unable to conduct either *Tristan* or the first Scala production of Stravinsky's *Le Rossignol*, which he had been preparing. Stravinsky had attended some of the rehearsals of his work and reported in his autobiography:

'Toscanini received me in the most charming fashion. He called the choruses and asked me to accompany them on the piano in order to give them such instructions as I might think necessary. I was struck by the deep knowledge he had of the score in its smallest details, and by his meticulous study of every work which he undertook to conduct. This quality of his is universally recognized, but this was the first time that I had a chance of seeing it applied to one of my own compositions. . . . I have never encountered in a conductor of such world repute such a degree of self-effacement, conscientiousness, and artistic honesty. What a pity it is that his inexhaustible energy and his marvellous talents should almost always be wasted on such eternally repeated works that no general idea can be discerned in the composition of his programmes, and that he should be so unexacting in the selection of his modern repertory!'[73]

Stravinsky's criticisms are justifiable. It is hard to imagine what Toscanini could have had in mind when he followed performances of Schubert's 'Great C Major' Symphony with Busoni's *Berceuse élégiaque*, Tommasini's Prelude, Fanfare and Fugue, and Rossini's *William Tell* Overture, or when he preceded the Beethoven Ninth with *Till Eulenspiegel* or Franck's *Rédemption*. Then, too, he certainly led huge quantities of third-rate music, as a glance at the repertoire list in the back of this book will indicate. He also did things in questionable taste with certain pieces of first-rate music—such as performing isolated movements from Beethoven's string quartets with an entire orchestral string section. (In the case of the C Major Quartet, Op. 59, No. 3, he once used the first movement introduction as a lead-in to the last movement!)

But what is bad music depends upon whom you ask. Toscanini tended to lead inconsequential Italian music, while others led inconsequential music from other countries. Furthermore, conductors face a problem not encountered by other musicians. A solo pianist, for example, may choose to exclude most or all of Mozart's music—or Schubert's or Brahms's or even Chopin's—from his repertoire if he wishes: he plays in a different city each night and may play the same programme twenty times in a row if he likes. A conductor, however, generally gives a series of concerts in the same place with the same orchestra, and the orchestra has as great a cultural function in a city as a museum or a library. The conductor's responsibility is civic and social as well as artistic. Toscanini was keenly aware of this; but as he grew older, and as his tastes ceased progressing with the times, his attempts to vary his programmes centred more on the exhumation of obscure items which he found interesting for one reason or another than on the investigation of current musical developments. After all, he entered the Parma Conservatory in the year in which Brahms's First Symphony was premièred, the year of the first Bayreuth festival—six years before Stravinsky was born; and although he was still active in the year in which Boulez's *Le Marteau sans maître* was premièred, his musical tastes can hardly have been expected to encompass all or even most of the myriad musical developments of the whole intervening period. Besides, if a musician performs *any* piece of music—contemporary or otherwise—purely out of a sense of duty, the results are often more harmful than helpful to that piece and its composer.

To return to Stravinsky and La Scala: the composer eventually was called to return to Milan to replace Toscanini in conducting his music, and was 'astounded by the high standards and rigorous discipline of the Scala orchestra'.[74]

Eric Walter White, in his book on Stravinsky, gives evidence that Toscanini was not as impressed with Stravinsky as Stravinsky was with him. He says that according to Ernest Ansermet, who was very friendly with Stravinsky in early years and with Toscanini in later years, Toscanini ' "lost all confidence in his [Stravinsky's] musicality when he heard him count the time out loud as he played through part of [*Le Rossignol*] on the piano." '[75] Whatever the truth of the matter, it is certain that close relations never developed between the two musicians.

In total, Toscanini had led fifty-one performances of fifteen operas during the 1925–6 season; other conductors had been Panizza, Votto, Gabriele Santini and, of course, Stravinsky. How much Toscanini was able to rest that spring and summer is open to question: he was preparing an opera season in which he would conduct six new productions and several old ones, studying for his Milan and New York concert series and organizing another tribute to Verdi at Busseto.

Meanwhile the Philharmonic directors were extremely interested in Toscanini's rift with the Fascists: they saw in it a means of obtaining his services for a more extended length of time, and possibly of making him musical director. As early as 7 May—immediately after reports of Toscanini's Milanese problems had been circulated in the press—Arthur Judson, the orchestra's manager, had written to Mackay:

'This puts us in the position of being compelled to make an immediate decision for the season 1927–28. . . . I think it would be wise if you were to cable Mr. Smith and ask him to keep Toscanini from committing himself to anything abroad or the Metropolitan here until I have a chance to talk with him the first part of June. I have reason to suspect that Mr. Kahn may seize this opportunity to get him for the Metropolitan, which would, of course, be disastrous for the Philharmonic. . . . My suggestion is that we engage him for a term of years as *the* conductor of the Philharmonic and that we either bring over one or two guest conductors in the middle of the season in order to give him a rest, or that we engage an assistant conductor of his choice, such as Molinari, to relieve him from time to time.'[76]

Judson, together with Maurice Van Praag, who played in the orchestra and was its personnel manager, and with whom Toscanini seemed to get on well, visited him in Milan in June; and Van Praag sent this memorandum to Mackay on returning to New York:

'Mr. and Mrs. Max Smith met us at the station. . . . We drove over to Maestro;
he was happy to see us and though he looked sad and worried it was not long
before I had him in good humour. Gave him your love, and he then told me
how kind you were to him last winter, and how happy he was with the Philharmonic; but when he came back to La Scala he could not stand to hear their
terrible playing. I then asked him why it was he bothered with them at all,
when you Mr. Mackay were willing to give him the best Orchestra in the world
to conduct without any friction or discontent on the part of the musicians, as he
has in Italy. I told him it was impossible for him to think of retiring as he is the
only great conductor living today. This touched him and his answer was, "My
dear Van Praag, Mr. Mackay, you and all my friends in America are very kind,
but I am nearly sixty years of age, why should I keep on? Here in Milano, I
have much trouble and cannot leave them." Judson then spoke to him about
taking the Philharmonic for a tour in Europe, maybe in 1928. This interested
him very much, and Judson pressed on by saying you would like to have him
next season as your regular conductor. He did not answer, so we left him,
promising to have dinner with him at his home the following day. On the way
to the Hotel, Max Smith told Judson if he would offer Maestro $100,000 for a
season he might accept; but Judson said $75,000 was the highest he could pay.
Next day he [Toscanini] spoke to me alone saying he was interested but an
entire season was too much. Then we spoke of our plan for him to conduct ten
weeks, then have an associate conductor conduct the Orchestra for six weeks,
while he went to Palm Beach for a vacation, then to come back to us and
conduct eight weeks. This pleased him I could see, so said no more about it till
later. We then spoke of you and he is in hopes of meeting you soon. Next
evening heard the Scala Orchestra in concert, Molinari conducting. The
Orchestra played poorly. No wonder Maestro is unhappy.'[77]

The real issue was that Toscanini still had several big projects which he wished
to bring to fruition before leaving the theatre. It was precisely forty years that
month since he had conducted *Aida* in Rio de Janeiro. Although the Scala
Orchestra could not live up to the standards of a wealthy and internationally
renowned symphonic ensemble like the Philharmonic, it was, by all reports, an
outstanding operatic orchestra. Beyond that, Toscanini had, as we have seen,
developed and set into motion the operatic organization which had been his
dream and his goal for so many years, *and* in his own country—which was a very
important factor from his point of view. In short, he could not yet make the
decision to leave, despite the Fascists, the orchestra, the much lower salary, and
the constant state of total war that was needed in order to get the results he wanted
in the theatre.

Shortly after Judson's and Van Praag's departure, Bruno Walter arrived in
Milan for a concert with the Scala Orchestra, and he and Toscanini met for the

first time. 'The meeting, casual though it was, made a deep and lasting impression on me,' wrote Walter in his *Theme and Variations*. '. . . I wished I could come to know the man better and fathom the secret of so exceptional a being. My wish was to be fulfilled later. Our paths crossed, and I owe to the activity of the eminent musician and powerful man a wealth of valuable musical experiences.'[78]

In September Toscanini returned to Busseto after an absence of thirteen years to lead *Falstaff* in commemoration of the twenty-fifth anniversary of Verdi's death. Although he took his Scala ensemble, which had performed the opera with him dozens of times, it was necessary to re-rehearse because of the completely different acoustical conditions in the tiny theatre. The orchestra was reduced to fifty; and Orio Vergani, who covered the event for the *Corriere*, heard Toscanini tell the musicians at one rehearsal: 'Here you must play better than anywhere else... I would give anything if Verdi could hear *Falstaff* performed here!'

Rehearsals for a complete cycle of the Beethoven symphonies at La Scala—to mark the approaching 100th anniversary of the composer's death—occupied him on his return to Milan. These performances took place on 7, 8, 9 and 12 October and were repeated in Turin on the 13th, 14th, 16th and 17th. The First and Ninth symphonies were given again in Milan at a special reduced-price concert on the 20th. Walter Toscanini had brought a recording apparatus into La Scala and had tried to record some of his father's rehearsals for this cycle; but the results were a failure.

An interesting detail of one of those rehearsals was recounted to me by French conductor Louis Fourestier, who had obtained permission to attend the sessions. While working on the Seventh Symphony Toscanini had spent a great deal of effort on balancing the oboes, clarinets, bassoons and horns in the sustained opening chord of the second movement. 'His ear for balance was astounding and exquisite,' Fourestier said; 'but after all, that is a physiological phenomenon more than anything else. After he had reached his goal and had achieved the *diminuendo* in the same gradation from each player, he said to the first oboe: "Your note—your E—make it sing! It's a melody!" *One* note, a melody... *That* was genius!'[79]

According to Taubman, the Beethoven cycle in Turin was so successful that the management there sent Toscanini an extra cheque, above and beyond his pre-arranged fee. He returned it with thanks, saying that he had been paid well enough. While Toscanini asked for and received astronomical fees when working for organizations which could afford to pay them, he did not do so elsewhere. Returning to La Scala from his visits to New York, he would make complicated calculations to determine how much of his salary should be returned to the theatre; and when the management would insist that as artistic director he was entitled to the full salary, he would protest and insist even more until (as usual) he got his way. In general, he had a Robin Hood attitude towards musical organizations: rob the rich and give to the poor. Many of his most important engagements were done for small fees or none at all. He usually asked his wife to collect and sign for his fee, and knew nothing of what happened to the money from that point onwards. 'He had no practical sense and never had a *lira* in his pocket,' said Wally.

The sixth season of the *ente autonomo* opened on 14 November with Toscanini's only production of *Don Carlo*. The so-called 'third edition'—i.e. in five acts, without the ballet—was given for the first time at La Scala. This was followed by *Dèbora e Jaéle* on the 28th; but Toscanini was suffering terrible pain in his right arm, and so conducted no other operas before his departure for New York at the end of December or early in January.

In New York the inflammation continued to torment him, and he was also suffering from bronchitis and nervous depression. His doctor ordered total rest. He cancelled most of his scheduled concerts, but decided to disobey the doctor and lead four performances (two different programmes) before leaving.

Some accusations have been made against Toscanini in regard to the repertoire he chose for that season. Daniel Gillis, in his book *Furtwängler and America*, says that in February, 'Toscanini, now quite recovered, though his physician had reportedly advised a long rest, agreed to conduct two Beethoven programmes. . . . The second was to feature the Ninth, with singers "already prepared by the Schola Cantorum". The singers had indeed been prepared for the Ninth—but it was to have been Furtwängler's Ninth.' Gillis continues:

> 'Furtwängler . . . was shocked at the arbitrary decision by the Philharmonic Board to transfer this program to Toscanini. He told a friend in New York, Albrecht Pagenstecher—as Pagenstecher recalled the incident many years later—that he had learned that Toscanini's illness had been feigned and that Toscanini had threatened to cancel all his commitments and return to Italy unless he was allowed to conduct the Ninth in place of Furtwängler.'[80]

The case was not quite as Gillis states it. On 3 March 1926—nearly a year earlier—Toscanini had wired the Philharmonic (and the wire is still in the orchestra's files) indicating that he wished his first performance of the Ninth the following season to take place at Carnegie Hall and not at the Metropolitan, as originally planned, because the first performance should take place in the same hall in which it had been rehearsed. Furthermore, the same Van Praag memorandum to Mackay which was cited earlier shows that as of mid-June Furtwängler had not yet submitted even a partial programme list for his Philharmonic concerts.

In October the Philharmonic management had received a letter from Anita Colombo stating that Toscanini would like to do a complete Beethoven cycle as part of his New York series that winter. They replied that that was impossible because other all-Beethoven programmes had already been promised to other conductors, but that of course the Ninth was still reserved for Toscanini. It seems that he made another attempt to have his way on that point; but after another No, Smith cabled Mackay from Milan (20 November): 'Our friend now satisfied not to conduct Beethoven cycle. Is preparing programs and will send them soon.'[81]

The two programmes which Toscanini eventually conducted in New York did consist entirely of Beethoven symphonies: one contained the Third and the Fifth, the other the First and the Ninth. The Fifth had already been conducted that season by Mengelberg; but while Furtwängler's schedule had originally called for the First as well as the Seventh, it is unlikely that repetition of the First could have caused any hostility. (In the end Furtwängler led the Seventh but not the First.) If there was any contention over the Ninth, clearly it was not Toscanini who initiated it. And the other statement reported by Gillis was simply false gossip about Toscanini, who had been suffering from neuritis at least since the previous October, and whose performances at La Scala had been cancelled for *real* reasons of health, just as they were in New York.

Toscanini's New York concerts all took place between 1 and 6 February 1927; one of the performances of the Ninth was broadcast on New York station WJZ and was probably Toscanini's first radio transmission. On 9 February he signed a contract to conduct 'approximately 42 concerts' with the Philharmonic the following season for a fee of $75,000 plus travel expenses and taxes. He was to be made a 'regular' rather than a 'guest' conductor; and this, according to a Philharmonic representative in a letter to Anita Colombo, had 'called forth widespread enthusiasm everywhere'.[82] Presumably Mengelberg, whose fine work was now being overshadowed, was not so enthusiastic; nor was Furtwängler, who had not even been asked to guest conduct during the following season.

By March Toscanini was working at La Scala again. Minetti, who was by then playing at the first stand of the first violins, said that the orchestra used to refer to Toscanini's trips to New York as their 'winter vacation':

'He would be away for a couple of months, and during his absence we felt as if we were on holiday! No afflictions of the spirit, no anxiety, no terror—everything ran as smoothly as oil; a little too smoothly, alas! But then, when he returned, he made us pay for our "vacation"—and with interest! He was capable of running four dress rehearsals and opening as many productions in one week (to make up for lost time, he said). . . . Gritting our teeth and grumbling in muted tones, we gave everything we had to satisfy him, and on rare occasions, we succeeded! And then, seeing him happy, we would forget the torture and the fear, the insults and the bad language, because although he maltreated us, we loved him.'[83]

Lucia returned to Toscanini's Scala repertoire for the first time in four years on 17 March, again with 'la Toti' and Pertile. He followed this with a new production of *Gioconda* a week later and a revival of *Rigoletto* on the 26th. On 7 April, two weeks after his sixtieth birthday, he led his and La Scala's first production of a masterpiece close to his heart which he had never before attempted: Beethoven's

Fidelio. As with *The Magic Flute*, *Fidelio* met with critical acclaim and public indifference. Only three performances of it were given during that Beethoven centennial season, and four more the following year.

By the end of April Toscanini had brought back *Boris*, *Nerone* and *Falstaff* and had led a new production of *Tosca* with Muzio, Pertile and Stabile. There were two other new productions in May: *Faust* and *Ariane et Barbe-bleue*. Toscanini conducted fifty performances of twelve operas during the 1926–7 season, and shared the podium with Panizza, Santini, Mascagni and Votto.

In June Arthur Judson in New York received two letters from Berta Geissmar, Furtwängler's secretary, which contained rumours that Toscanini was very ill and suffering nervous strain because of family troubles.[84] I have not been able to ascertain whether or not there was any truth to those reports; but it is interesting that Geissmar was occupying herself with this alarmist gossip. Given the fact that Furtwängler had not been invited back to New York for the 1927–8 season, one could draw some rather unpleasant conclusions from this story, especially since in the end Toscanini was healthy enough to fulfil all his commitments in both Milan and New York during that season.

Having spent part of the summer at Alpino, he conducted three concerts at La Scala on 9, 12 and 13 October. These programmes included his first performances of Haydn's Symphony No. 88, Arthur Honegger's *Pastorale d'été* and *Pacific 231*, and the 'Infernal Dance' from Stravinsky's *Firebird*, as well as works from his established repertoire.

The new season opened on 16 November with *Mefistofele*, followed by *Fidelio* on the 18th, *Manon Lescaut* on the 20th and an entirely new and eagerly-awaited production of *Otello* on the 22nd—four dress rehearsals and four openings in just over a week, as Minetti said! Verdi's masterpiece was sung by Trantoul, Stabile and Bianca Scacciata as Otello, Iago and Desdemona, respectively. In December Toscanini conducted *Cavalleria rusticana* and *Pagliacci* and he brought *Nerone* back on 1 January 1928.

He left for New York on the 9th of that month and began rehearsing very shortly after his arrival. Between 26 January and 1 April he conducted the Philharmonic in forty-three performances in Manhattan, Brooklyn, Baltimore, Washington, Philadelphia, Buffalo and Pittsburgh. His programmes included forty-two works by twenty-eight composers. He again ended his New York stay with the Beethoven Ninth.

Less than a week after his return to Milan Toscanini conducted *Falstaff*, and four days later, *Don Carlo*. The world première of Pizzetti's *Fra Gherardo* took place under his direction on 16 May, and he led *Traviata* on the 20th. This season had been shared with Panizza, Santini, Votto and Richard Strauss; and Toscanini had led forty-three performances of ten operas.

While in New York he had been told of the Philharmonic board's plan to merge the orchestra with Walter Damrosch's New York Symphony, effective the following season. This meant increasing the size and improving the quality of the orchestra; but it also meant that some of the Philharmonic's weaker players would lose their jobs to some of the Symphony's better players, and that most of the Symphony's musicians would lose their positions.

He spent part of the summer in a hotel on Isola dei Pescatori on Lago Maggiore; and it was from the town of Baveno on the opposite shore that he cabled Judson on 23 August: 'After next season I take leave definitely from theatre. You may rely upon my cooperation for carrying out [European] tour spring of 1930.'[85]

At La Scala in October Toscanini conducted four concerts, one of which was devoted entirely to Schubert for the 100th anniversary of the composer's death. His last full opera season began on 15 November with *Otello*; two nights later he presented his revival of *La forza del destino*. Twenty years had passed since he had last conducted this work, and at that time the production had closed after one very unsuccessful performance. Now the Scala public and the press were ecstatic. *Fra Gherardo* was brought back on 28 November; then, on 16 December, Toscanini realized one of his great goals when he conducted his first performance of *Parsifal*; and this too was very well received. Unfortunately, Toscanini, who never slept long or well, was then suffering from almost total insomnia resulting from the strain of overwork. He was too exhausted even to be able to assemble his Philharmonic programmes, and on 23 December Carla wired Judson that they would not be arriving in New York until 14 February—several weeks later than planned. Toscanini had also been X-rayed in November because of his shoulder and back pains; his doctor reported that the results were only slightly abnormal. Nothing was done and the pain continued.

Despite his insomnia Toscanini put *Lucia* back on the Scala stage on 23 December, and three nights later celebrated the thirtieth anniversary of his first assumption of the Scala directorship by conducting *Die Meistersinger*—the same work with which he had begun his tenure there on 26 December 1898. Journet was Sachs, Pertile Walter, and young Mafalda Favero made her Scala début as Eva. The *Corriere* reported:

'Those who were present at Toscanini's triumph can only have taken away an unforgettable memory.... To find a similar occurrence in La Scala's annals it is necessary to go back to Verdi's last appearances there. When the performance ended, at a very late hour, the demonstration began again; and it was the crowning moment of an evening truly worthy of the man who was being honoured and of the art which he represents in so unique a way.

The demonstrations in Toscanini's honour more than once echoed clamourously through the hall, which dazzled in a way rarely seen. The applause which greeted the Maestro when he first appeared on the podium went on for about ten minutes in a succession of frenetic waves, which he vainly tried to

stop several times by motioning to begin the Prelude ... and there were
numerous calls at the end of the second and third acts, in which the chorus
joined as well. Added to this applause were forms of homage and devotion
which made the evening one of the most memorable in La Scala's history. ...

At the end of the performance the public did not want to leave the hall, nor
could they be satiated with bringing Toscanini out on to the stage, calling him
with a great voice. The audience did not even seem satisfied when, to put an
end to their affectionate insistence, the lights were turned off. Toscanini was
visibly moved by the grandiose demonstration. When the theatre had emptied
about 100 of the Maestro's friends and admirers gathered in the lobby to
renew their demonstrations of approbation and their affectionate wishes.'

La Scala and the city of Milan wanted to honour Toscanini in a special way
for this event, but they knew that a monetary gift would have insulted him and
that he would not have put up with any ceremonies. They finally decided to
initiate a 'Toscanini Foundation', a fund to offer medical assistance and fresh-air
cures to any sick children of members of the Scala orchestra, chorus, or workers
and administrative staff. This idea was presented to Toscanini and he readily
accepted the 'gift'. A sum of 680,000 lire was raised immediately from admirers
all over Italy and in the United States. In 1930 Toscanini himself contributed an
additional 100,000 lire.

On 12 January 1929 he conducted the world première of Giordano's *Il re*,
which had been billed together with *Pagliacci*. He was in New York by mid-
February, where his series began on the 21st with a programme of music by
Mozart, Debussy, Wagner and Respighi; by 1 April he had led twenty-six
concerts, including tour performances in six cities. The first significant recordings
of his career were also made during this visit.

At the concert of 28 February, as Toscanini was about to begin the second
movement of the second piece on the programme—Pizzetti's *Concerto dell'estate*
—several latecomers made their way to the front of Carnegie Hall and sat down
noisily. The next day's *Herald Tribune* reported that 'the conductor turned on
his stand, crossed his arms in a Napoleonic gesture and fixed his brilliant, deep-
set eyes on them. ... "You are late!" said Mr. Toscanini sternly. The words
could be heard all over the hall. That was all, as he then turned to the orchestra,
rapped loudly and vigorously on the cello stand before him and continued the
concert.'

He was happy with the quality of the orchestra after the merger with the New
York Symphony, and Van Praag wrote to Judson on 21 February:

'During the past few days I have had several opportunities to speak to Maestro
Toscanini ... and yesterday he admitted to me that the orchestra was much
better than last season. I thereupon asked him whether he thought we should
make any changes in the personnel for next season and he replied that the

string sections were excellent. He could not understand why I insisted on making a change in the first oboe, first bassoon and the flute. He admitted that at times Mr. X was a bit dense and not quick but that he liked his tone and could see no reason for changing him for someone else.'[86]

Toscanini had by that time agreed to become the Philharmonic's principal conductor, effective the following season, and arrangements were underway for the orchestra's first European tour, which would end the season. We learn from various memoranda and letters in the Philharmonic's files that he stated emphatically and more than once that Mengelberg, whom he was succeeding, should be re-engaged as a guest conductor; that he had decided to reconsider returning to La Scala the following season, although with a greatly reduced schedule, if the Fascists would leave him alone (this never happened); that he had promised to continue leading the Philharmonic until the very end of the current season but that commitments at La Scala made him feel that he ought to leave early in April; and that the only musician in the orchestra he felt should be replaced was the second trumpet who, he said, was not bad, but also not good enough to sit next to first trumpet Harry Glantz, who was 'such a fine artist'.

After a lifetime in the Italian theatrical world Toscanini was thoroughly accustomed to a system in which individual performances or even whole productions could be re-scheduled at will if more time were needed for preparation or if an important artist were ill. So it is amusing—at a safe distance—to read of his frequent and complacent changes of mind regarding arrival and departure dates in New York, which concerts he would conduct, and so on. He had done this sort of thing for a long time and seemed blissfully unaware of the difficult scheduling exigencies which a modern concert organization like the Philharmonic faced. Mackay was 'very much disturbed' to find out that the new musical director had only the vaguest ideas, in February 1929, as to which part or parts of the following season he wished to conduct. Of course, the Philharmonic wanted and needed Toscanini much more than he wanted and needed the Philharmonic; so their attempts to pin him down were made only in the most oblique ways. All the Philharmonic correspondence with or about Toscanini presents the image of an unarmed man smilingly trying to coax a very dangerous beast to return to its cage.

Having returned to Milan, Toscanini conducted productions of *Aida*, *Germania*, *Falstaff* and one performance each of *Rigoletto*, *Lucia* and *Manon Lescaut*. His last opera of the season was to have been *Don Giovanni*, which he had conducted only once before, in Buenos Aires in 1906. But if the *Meistersinger* in this, his last Scala season, had made him think back happily—or at least without displeasure—on his very first production there, the *Don Giovanni* must have reminded him of the bitterest event of that 1898-9 season: the cancellation, at the dress rehearsal, of *Norma*. *Don Giovanni* did not quite reach the dress rehearsal, but it went all the way to the final ensemble rehearsals before Toscanini decided to withdraw it.

The cast was to have included Stabile as Don Giovanni, Vincenzo Bettoni as Leporello, Roberto D'Alessio as Ottavio, Zamboni as Elvira, Favero as Zerlina, and a Belgian soprano whose name seems to have vanished from the face of the earth as Anna; and the official reason for the cancellation was the indisposition of D'Alessio and the impossibility of replacing him at the last moment. That was definitely not the real reason; but what the real reason was is impossible to pinpoint. Favero made this statement in 1967:

'We got almost to the dress rehearsal when Toscanini said: "No, this will not be presented." We never knew the reason [although] he didn't like the soprano who was singing Donna Anna . . . At a certain point he couldn't stand it any longer; he said "Enough, I won't put it on the stage"; and we, unfortunately, were all left high and dry, because we had studied a lot. And I remember a detail, because it was the first time I had got near Mozart. I had barely been singing two years, and Maestro Fornarini was teaching me the part. . . . One day we were working on [it] when the door opened and Toscanini entered. Naturally, I felt as if I were going to die, because Toscanini was Toscanini; and he said: "I want to hear how this girl sings Mozart." I sang two *romanzas*; then Toscanini said: "Let me hear two recitatives." I did the recitatives, and he said: "Everything's all right, but I want the *acciaccature* [embellishing notes] to go from the note *below* the principal note to the principal note, and not from the one above." He had me change all the *acciaccature* in the recitatives, not in the *romanzas*. . . . Fornarini was a little—well—[he said], "Excuse me, Maestro, but I've always taught it this way!" "But no, I want it done in a different way." '[87]

It is fairly certain that other reasons for the cancellation existed beyond his dissatisfaction with one of the eight soloists. My own guess—and it is purely a guess—is that Toscanini was not convinced of his own understanding of and natural feeling for the work.

His last performance of the season took place on 14 May (*Aida*), and it was also the last time he conducted an entire opera in Italy. During his final Scala season, which was shared with Panizza, Santini, Votto and Antonio Sabino, he had led forty-five performances of thirteen operas. Now he had undertaken a special project which—although the Milanese did not yet know it—was to be his farewell to the ensemble. Five years after the idea of taking the company to Paris had fallen through, a new plan to go to Berlin materialized; and when Vienna heard about the adventure, the Italians were begged to stop in the Austrian capital as well. Just twenty-four hours after the last *Aida* performance in Milan the Scala-ites departed by train for Vienna.

The principal artists, orchestra, chorus, dancers and heads of the musical,

scenic, technical and administrative staffs all made the trip on the special train—
302 people in all. They were seen off at the station by crowds of cheering fans.
Arnaldo Fraccaroli of the *Corriere*, who was acquainted with Toscanini, accompanied the tour and sent back reports. He saw Toscanini, who was normally an
abstemious eater, devouring quantities of food on the train, and questioned him
about it. 'When I travel my appetite is always rather good,' he said in self-
justification.'[88] There were also meetings on the train to plan work schedules for
Vienna.

From 9.30 on the morning following their arrival Toscanini was at the
Staatsoper to oversee the stage installations and to test the acoustics with orchestra and chorus. 'The Maestro, who is involved with everything that makes
up the production, seems satisfied,' wrote Fraccaroli. 'The theatre is sold out at
prices which, at first, made the Viennese think there were typographical errors
on the signs.'[89] Groups of young people camped out next to the theatre beginning
at 2 a.m. the night before the first performance, in order to be sure of getting
standing-room tickets.

Falstaff was the first of the company's two Viennese offerings, and it came as
an incredible surprise to the public. Sitting in the fourth gallery and giving cues
to the head of the *claque*, who was unfamiliar with the opera, was twenty-one-
year-old Herbert von Karajan, who later said of the event:

'From the first bar, it was as if I had been struck a blow. I was completely
disconcerted by the perfection which had been achieved ... Of course, it is
known that Toscanini was for ever polishing and working at this *Falstaff* and
choosing new singers. This production was already at that time perhaps ten
or twelve years old [actually not quite eight]—not "old" in a real sense, but
mature. For the first time I grasped what "direction" meant. To be sure,
Toscanini had employed a stage director; but basically, the essential conception came from him. The agreement between the music and the stage performance was something totally inconceivable for us: instead of people
senselessly standing around, here everything had its place and its purpose. I
do not believe at all that the Viennese then understood how great a service La
Scala had performed in coming to Vienna and showing us young people, for
once, what one can make of an interpretation if everything is in its right place.'[90]

The critic for the *Neues Wiener Journal* commented:

'Now the "fabulous" Maestro Toscanini has finally come to Vienna. . . . It was
an overwhelming victory: the victory of an artist, of an art, of a nation. The
surprise began immediately with the first chords. The orchestra, under the
parlando of the first scene, bubbles like champagne. Not even a syllable of
dialogue is lost. Second scene, in the garden: Toscanini's art celebrates its first
triumph. Has one ever been able to hear a Verdi quartet sung like this in the

theatre? Or the men's quintet? And then the nine voices, with Fenton's sweet melody? . . . Those who expect only explosions of sound, passion, melodic surprises from Italian music, will have had to change their opinions after *Falstaff* conducted by Toscanini. Here there is another aspect of the Italian nature which has been made sublime: elegance, movement, gentleness.'

And the *Neues Wiener Tagblatt*:

'It is not easy to conquer the Viennese musical public, but the Italian artists succeeded; and when the Maestro attacked the first chord of *Falstaff*, no one could extract himself from the conquering force of his personality. Everything is clear, everything has its correct interpretation on the stage and in the orchestra, even if the latter does not have the abundant sonority of the Vienna Philharmonic . . .'

Julius Korngold in the *Neue Freie Presse*:

'The fusion on stage is perfect, and the marvellous vivacity of *Falstaff*, . . . has an incomparable and frankly stupefying interpreter in Maestro Toscanini . . .'

The following night the Scala company presented *Lucia* to the Viennese. Again, we have Karajan's reaction:

'*Lucia* was branded as a "stock opera" in Vienna. When we heard that Toscanini wanted to conduct this work in Vienna, I too asked myself honestly, after having played through the piano reduction, "What can there be in this?" And it is astonishing that this music which, in a normal "repertoire perform-ance" or, for instance, at the piano, sounds truly banal, was made to sound not at all banal. It was simply another type of music. . . . When one had heard it under Toscanini it had infinite significance.'[91]

Korngold wrote:

'*Lucia di Lammermoor* has been performed hundreds of times in Vienna in the past, but only now has it appeared in all its beauty. . . . The appearance of someone like Toscanini is rare in the history of art; but the orchestra, soloists and chorus of the Vienna Opera could well compete with those of La Scala if they were instructed and conducted according to the methods of the great Italian Maestro.'

Commenting retrospectively on the two performances, Paul Stefan wrote in *Die Stunde*:

'Only an ensemble like that of La Scala and a conductor like Toscanini could reach absolute perfection in the *Falstaff* performance and also disinter *Lucia* from the musical cemetery and return her to us more flourishingly alive than before. Everyone in the theatre had the sensation of being a witness to an unrepeatable artistic event.'

A great crowd gathered at the station to applaud the company as it departed Vienna on 20 May; and as the train passed through the various quarters of the city people stood on overpasses or at apartment windows to wave handkerchiefs. 'This,' said Fraccaroli, 'is the popularity which these two performances achieved in Vienna, this is the enthusiasm they aroused. Toscanini's permission to broadcast *Lucia* on the radio also contributed to this popularity. At the various stops we found people who had come to greet the singers whom they had heard the evening before . . . on the air.'[92]

Berlin heard the Scala company in one performance each of six operas, divided between the Staatsoper Unter den Linden (*Falstaff*, *Trovatore*, *Manon Lescaut* and *Aida*) and the Städtische Oper in Charlottenburg (*Rigoletto* and *Lucia*). As in Vienna, the press reports indicate a public and critical reaction of stupefied admiration. From *Vorwärts*:

'The opening, *Falstaff*, surpassed all expectations and was a very great artistic event. A product of absolute perfection is the result of the collaboration of all the musical and scenic forces under the direction of Toscanini.'

Musicologist Alfred Einstein in the *Berliner Tagblatt*:

'Let us hope that the German artists who attended this performance have learned something; in any case, the Italian opera company has given us a delightful but dangerous measuring-stick for judging German art. . . . Even if the Scala tour had nothing to offer us but a lesson in a true style for Italian opera, that would in itself be an important factor, a landmark in Berlin's musical life. . . . For the Germans, the Italian operatic style is generally considered according to traditional criteria: the singer who calmly takes his time and exaggerates high notes, orchestral crescendi violently worked up to the final dynamic explosion, savage phrasing, . . . and instead—instead, here are fortissimi which are not shouted at all, a totality not drowned in cheap melodrama, but rather passionate and without rhetoric.'

Max Marshalck of the *Vossische Zeitung* referred to the discipline imposed by Toscanini:

'It is not true that this prevents the singers from bringing out their talents: on the contrary, Toscanini sets them on the best path and makes it possible for them individually to develop their true qualities. Thus, instead of imprisoning them, he makes them freer, and this makes Toscanini's art a great thing, worthy of marvel.'

Negative remarks were aimed by several critics at Forzano's stagings: one reviewer said they were carried out in the style of the 1880s. (*Falstaff* and *Manon* were generally excepted from these criticisms.) The singers were for the most part judged to be highly competent or very good, but unexceptional. It is very hard to find any dissenting opinions on Toscanini. At the most, Oscar Bie of the *Berliner Börsen Courier* questioned his tempo modifications in *Aida*—which Alfred Einstein, however, marvelled at: '[Done in] the classical and at the same time completely personal interpretative style with which Toscanini brings the most worn-out and washed-out works back to life . . .' Einstein also said of La Scala's visit:

> 'For us, it has been much more than an extraordinary operatic event. It has been an example; it has been the discovery of an infinitely simple secret: that the exceptional can only be reached by means of the absolute will of a man possessed by music, fanatically dedicated only to music and to nothing else, and that the basis for achieving the unusual consists in working, in serving the cause, and nothing else.'

Karl Holl wrote a long article analysing La Scala's success in the *Frankfurter Zeitung* of 9 June, from which I cite excerpts:

> '. . . For six evenings, Berliners, out-of-towners and people "in the trade" thanked the Maestro and his faithful with frenetic ovations for their gift, which consisted of literally unheard-of operatic impressions. . . . Virtuosity, even in the measure in which Toscanini possesses and demands it, is and remains for him only a means towards achieving a goal. . . . Toscanini is not La Scala: one can imagine him even without it; but La Scala today is a collective Toscanini. It is his will and his work.
>
> . . . La Scala's performances moved and shook the public and sent it into ecstasy. A sea of applause interrupted and framed the performances, especially those of the most popular operas. Even granting that some part of the enthusiasm was owing to the attraction of the name and to the sensational effect of that which is foreign, it remains a success without precedent in the modern history of opera in Germany. . . . We have re-learned from La Scala to have faith in the lyric theatre, in the operatic organization and in its public. . . . The secret of this unconditional success for the ear and the heart of the vast public, above and beyond every defect or doubt, can be summarized in a few words: exceptional performance by a true ensemble.
>
> Admiration for the Italians must not, of course, take away our understanding of the special virtues of the various top-ranking German theatrical ensembles; but it must be a constant admonition to us.'

Among those present at the performances were Walter, Furtwängler, Busch, Klemperer, Kleiber, Karl Elmendorff, Paul Bekker, Siegfried Wagner, Leo Blech, Max von Schillings, Max Reinhardt and Alfred Einstein's cousin, Albert. Walter wrote that Toscanini's 'masterly performances conveyed to the German public a higher conception of the older Italian operas . . . and the very highest conception of Italian culture generally. . . . Every detail of the performances I witnessed spoke of the life-work and the imperative moral feeling of responsibility of an eminent musician.'[93] And Klemperer referred to the performances as 'wonderful and unforgettable'.[94] These were very generous statements to make, in the light of some not very delightful comparisons, implied or stated, being made in the press between Toscanini and various German and Austrian conductors. In the *Bayerischer Courier* of 29 May, for example, H. R. Gail wrote:

'This past week, all of Germany seemed like one single megaphone which echoed one single name: Toscanini. In Berlin, the excitement rose to such a fever pitch that it actually made us fear for German art, for the prestige of German musical culture. We ask ourselves whether a Blech, a Kleiber or a Klemperer would have aroused similarly delirious enthusiasm in Italy, had he gone there at the head of the Berlin Opera.—No!—Because these three conductors put together do not make one Toscanini.'

Toscanini and the entire company were welcomed joyously on their return to Italy. At every train stop from the border onwards, they were greeted by civic officials, children carrying flowers, people thanking them for the broadcasts of *Lucia* from Vienna and *Aida* from Berlin. As the train approached Milan Toscanini went down its whole length, stopping in every compartment to shake hands with and thank all the singers, players and workers. He knew—and many others had heard insistent rumours—that this was the end of his and La Scala's glorious decade together (for it was just ten years since Caldara and Albertini had begun discussing with him the formation of the *ente autonomo*). Fraccaroli reported that his voice shook with emotion, that many in the company were in tears and that the scene was an indescribable outpouring of mutual affection. As he returned down the train's corridors a great shout went up from everyone.

In Milan Toscanini received a pompous telegram from Mussolini which stated that 'La Scala's performances made known not only the great historic virtues of an artistic organization, but also the new spirit of Contemporary Italy, which unites to its will to power the necessary harmonious discipline required in every field of human activity.'[95] Toscanini understood Mussolini's implication that, like it or not, by contributing to the glory of La Scala, he was also contributing to the glory of the new Fascist society. He replied that 'today, as yesterday and as always, I am serving and shall serve my Art with humility but with intense love, certain that in so doing I am serving and honouring my Country.'[96] He must have thought, as he wrote that sentence, that he performed such a service wherever he was working, whether within or outside of Italy. On the day after his last Berlin performance the *Berliner Tagblatt* had carried news not yet made public in Italy: 'The Maestro will abandon La Scala and will give up operatic conducting.' The next time he performed with an Italian organization, Mussolini and the new Fascist society were dead.

6
To Dare To Answer 'No'

As late as June 1929 the directorate of La Scala were hoping that Toscanini would return. 'After the triumphal outcome of the tour in Austria and Germany,' wrote Scandiani to Lauri-Volpi (who had been reconciled with Toscanini at the time of the tour), 'and after the demonstrations given him on our return home, I am hoping that he will withdraw his proposal and will again dedicate part of his activity to La Scala next season.'[1] Toscanini was, in fact, considering conducting a new production of Rossini's *William Tell* for the opera's 100th anniversary, which occurred that year, with Lauri-Volpi as Arnoldo. But in July Scandiani informed the tenor: 'Maestro Toscanini has decided not to conduct at La Scala next season because of the excessive work resulting from the preparations and conducting of his American concerts.'[2]

Twenty years later Toscanini summarized his Scala years thus for B.H. Haggin:

'After [the first world] war they ask me to come back to La Scala. I do not want to go; but they say I must. I begin with five operas; next year twelve [actually eleven]; and I conduct ninety [actually about seventy-five] performances in season. Then other conductors conduct more and more, and I conduct only fifty performances. Then I feel I cannot take responsibility for season, and I resign.'[3]

Of course, Toscanini would not have returned to La Scala in 1921 had he not had *some* desire to do so; and the administration would have been overjoyed to have him lead all the performances, had he so wished.

Not many months after his departure from La Scala Toscanini had a lengthy conversation with Raffaello De Rensis, which revealed that he had for some time been considering retiring from the theatre:

'It's operatic conducting that wears me out; and I must repeat that the only reason for my departure from La Scala is the need for a less turbulent life. I had roamed the world's theatres for thirty-nine years, leaving fragments of my existence everywhere, until I decided to leave the theatre once I had brought Boito's *Nerone* to the stage. That, for me, was a debt of esteem and friendship.'[4]

At that point Toscanini showed De Rensis a Boito manuscript in his possession which he always carried with him on his travels. Its first sentence was: 'Blessed are the arts which do not require interpreters.' This led Toscanini to talk about musical interpretation.

'Conductors today generally compete to distinguish themselves from each other, so that one can refer to X's "Pastorale" and Y's "Eroica", forgetting that Beethoven is the only creator. It seems that they want to dig a little bit of everything out of the score—except what is in it. Even Verdi, in his day, complained about the arbitrariness of conductors and singers who insisted on putting themselves above the composer's creation.'

De Rensis says that Toscanini told him that he considered Furtwängler's way of conducting Wagner absolutely as valid as his own. He then went on to make a peculiar statement about contemporary operas: 'Composers today can't stand and don't love their own operas; therefore, the public can't stand or love them either.' De Rensis asked if it wasn't the scarcity of new operas which was responsible beyond all else for the operatic crisis.

' "Scarcity? No, it is rather the congestion of novelties that is disturbing the balance of our operatic seasons. The poor publishers are rich in them. But look: some operas written yesterday are already lifeless"—and here the Maestro gave me some examples; "others written today will never see a tomorrow"—more examples. "And the unfortunate part is that composers insist on blaming the publishers and conductors for the lack of vitality in their operas. Now that's really not so. At present one cannot talk about sacrificed works of art. The publishers acquire new works, the theatres put them on, we conduct them, and the public comes. Whose fault is it if the opera folds its wings and falls after a short flight? I shall go further: where is it written that all operas by modern composers must be liked? Didn't even Verdi and Rossini produce scores which have justly been laid to rest?" '

There is a final footnote to the story of Toscanini's departure from La Scala: on 13 November—that is, during the week of La Scala's reopening, when it was certain that Toscanini was not returning—news came from Rome that Mussolini's government had approved a huge new annual grant to La Scala of about $1\frac{1}{2}$ million lire.[5]

By that time Toscanini was already six weeks into his New York season. He had opened on 3 October with Schumann's *Manfred* Overture, his first performance of Strauss's *Don Quixote* and Beethoven's Seventh Symphony. The concerts continued until 24 November and also included his first performances of the Brahms Double Concerto, Berlioz's *Harold in Italy*, Mozart's Adagio and Fugue in C minor and Ravel's *Boléro*, as well as another recording session. After a long break in Italy he returned to New York to resume concerts on 27 February

1930 and to prepare the orchestra for its approaching European tour. Toscanini and Mengelberg had been listed as co-conductors for the 1929–30 season; but it is clear that Toscanini was now the *de facto* principal conductor: the orchestra and board considered him so and he led every concert on the tour. Members of the orchestra had informed Toscanini that Mengelberg had talked against him at rehearsals and Toscanini had requested the Philharmonic management to choose between Mengelberg and himself. Mengelberg did not return to New York for the 1930–1 season.

The concerts prior to the tour contained works new to Toscanini's repertoire by eleven composers. On 22 March he participated in a children's concert by leading the *Meistersinger* Prelude. This series was usually conducted by Ernest Schelling; but Toscanini had been asked to participate in the last concert of the season. He helped to hand out prize ribbons to some of the children (and received one himself from Schelling) and he actually made a short speech to them in English. His mood must have been particularly relaxed at the time, because three days later, on his sixty-third birthday, he accepted an honorary doctorate from the music department of Georgetown University in Washington. His speech of acceptance lasted approximately fifteen seconds. Honoured with him that day was Paul Claudel.

The Philharmonic's last concert took place on 20 April; three days later Toscanini and the orchestra boarded the *De Grasse*, bound for Le Havre. The European engagements had been arranged by Anita Colombo, who had acted as the Philharmonic's agent. Toscanini and family travelled with twenty-six pieces of baggage, their dog, two canaries and three elegant birdcages. Clearing customs and immigration must have been a constant headache for the orchestra's officials since the 112 musicians were natives of thirty-four different countries. (There were only about twenty American-born members at that time.) On disembarking, some of the players informed eager reporters that Toscanini had spent much time on deck, had observed the passengers' games and athletic exercises and had stayed up till the early morning hours to watch the dancing and listen to the jazz band. 'We got to know a new Toscanini,' said one musician; 'no longer the noble and stern conductor, but an affable, smiling and even joking travel companion . . .'[6] Newsmen also learned that the Philharmonic Society had spent $200,000 to underwrite the tour.

Works of nine composers then living (Elgar, Goossens, Honegger, Kodály, Pizzetti, Ravel, Respighi, Strauss and Tommasini) and fifteen others (Bach, Beethoven, Berlioz, Brahms, Debussy, Franck, Haydn, Mendelssohn, Moussorgsky, Mozart, Rossini, Schumann, Smetana, Wagner and Weber) were played in the course of the tour, which opened with two concerts at the Paris Opéra on 3 and 4 May. The reactions of the Viennese and Berlin public and critics to the previous year's Scala tour were repeated. Emile Vuillermoz, writing in *Excelsior*, set the tone for the whole month:

'Toscanini has crossed Paris like a meteor, like a shooting star. Here, truly, is a master, not only a conductor, but a master of all conductors. . . . He obtains nuances, flexibility, attacks and crescendos of a quality absolutely unique in the world. He was able to achieve a precision of execution from his orchestra which, for us, has something of the inexplicable and wondrous about it: it is absolute, unarguable and overwhelming material perfection.

There was a strange and puzzling occurrence at the second concert, which included Ravel's *Boléro*. The composer was present and, according to news reports, refused to take a bow after the playing of his piece because he felt that Toscanini's tempo had been too fast. On 6 May Ravel wrote to his friend, Hélène Kahn-Casella:

'Too bad you didn't come backstage: there was quite a little scene. People were upset that I had the audacity to tell the great virtuoso that it was twice too fast. I only went for that . . . but he is a marvellous virtuoso, all the same— as marvellous as his orchestra.'[7]

And two days later, to Ida Godebska:

'If I was seen at the Opéra it was only because I knew that Toscanini was taking a ridiculous tempo in the *Boléro* and I wanted to tell him so, which upset everyone, starting with the great virtuoso.'[8]

In September, however, Ravel wrote to Toscanini:

'My dear friend, I have recently learned that there was a Toscanini–Ravel "affair". You yourself are undoubtedly unaware of it, although I have been assured that the papers have spoken of it: it seems that I refused to stand during the applause at the Opéra in order to punish you for not having taken the correct tempo in the *Boléro*.

I have always felt that if the composer does not take part in a performance of his work, he must not receive the ovations, which must thus be directed only at the performer or the work, or both. Unfortunately, I was badly—or too well —placed to have my abstention pass unnoticed. Therefore, in order that my attitude not be misunderstood, I tried, in turning towards you, to applaud and thank you. But—wouldn't you know it—maliciousness lends itself to "sensational" news better than does the truth. . . .'[9]

And only ten days later Ravel again wrote Toscanini:

'This is only to tell you that I would very much wish to have the world première of the Concerto [in D Major for Piano (left hand) and Orchestra] which I have written for Wittgenstein given by you and the admirable orchestra which you have shaped. And I am sure that Wittgenstein will not feel differently.'[10]

One can hardly fail to notice that after all the stir over the wrong tempo, Ravel's sweet and conciliatory first letter to Toscanini—four months after the event—is followed amazingly quickly by the request for the Concerto première. I do not know whether Toscanini replied to Ravel's letters; but although he never conducted the Concerto, he continued to conduct other Ravel works during the rest of his career.

From Paris the orchestra proceeded to Zürich, Milan, Turin, Rome and Florence. The presence of the Princess of Piedmont at the Turin concert had made it necessary to have the Royal March performed; and Mussolini had made it a law that whenever the Royal March was played, *Giovinezza* must follow it. Toscanini said that he could not accept this ruling. So a compromise was reached: after the orchestra was seated and tuned a military band came out to play the hymns. In Rome the Royal family wished to attend a performance, and a similar incident—or worse—nearly took place; but the monarchs wisely backed down and announced that they were attending 'unofficially'. No hymns were played.

Ugo Ojetti attended the Florence concert and spent some time afterwards with Toscanini, his family and friends at the home of pianist Ernesto Consolo.

'. . . Toscanini eats and drinks readily. I have never seen his complexion so florid and unlined. His flesh is healthy; his lips red under his turned-up moustache; his green eyes . . . shine vividly under the ridge of shadow formed by his prominent eyebrows; and his voice, somewhere between hoarseness and vibrancy, gives his every phrase a tone of confidence drawn out by the power of sincerity. . . .

"The most important quality in a conductor? Humility, humility," he says. . . . "If something doesn't go well, it's because I haven't understood the composer. It's all my fault. Whoever thinks that Mozart, Beethoven, Wagner, Verdi are mistaken and have to be corrected is an idiot. One must study more, begin studying again, understand better. They haven't written music in order to make me look good. It is I who must make them look good by revealing them as they are, by trying to bring the orchestra and myself closer to them, as much as I can, so that nothing escapes. The conductor must not create, he must achieve. Humility, faithfulness, clarity, unity." . . . Maestro Tommasini . . . whispers in my ear, "He believes, says and does these things. But to hear about humility from——and from ——" I've forgotten the two conductors' names.

. . . From Rome to Florence he was always in the train corridor to enjoy the view. He arrived at four in the afternoon, rehearsed for an hour or two, conducted for three hours, and it is now 2 a.m. "I prefer being on my feet. You should have seen the orchestra's enthusiasm, on the train, as we went through the Roman *campagna*, then below Orvieto, then next to Lake Trasimene, then in these Tuscan hills. We should have arranged for them to travel always by day in Italy." . . .

Someone remarks: "The two faults Toscanini does not excuse are negligence and laziness." Toscanini catches the phrase. "Certainly, because they're the opposite of love, the opposite of faith. This one is lazy? That one is distracted? Then let them stay at home! Who makes them play in the orchestra? In this profession, you must give everything of yourself. Technique and mechanics aren't enough. Perfect player and perfect instrument: that's the first step, of course. But then there's the heart."

. . . "Will you make more records in America?"—"Don't talk to me about records! They're a martyrdom. You work and work; the master seems excellent. Then you get the finished record, and you want to tear your hair out. Money? What use is money? To live in peace—I mean, without doing anything? What are you talking about! My collection of paintings? Listen: In Milan, you know, I bought Telemaco Signorini's 'The Morning Toilette' at an auction. That light through the open green shutters, the woman combing her hair before the mirror, her boy friend yawning on the sofa . . . Could I deny myself such a painting? Never again. My wife (let me say it, since it's true) scolded me and made me promise in writing that I would make two more records. Is it true or isn't it? So I'm right. I have three passions: paintings—those which I like, of course—Leopardi's letters, and Mozart's letters. . . ." When he smiles, he turns affectionately towards his wife, who increases her deprecatory nods.

. . . A girl's voice repeats: "It's 4 a.m."—"You think it's late, dear? Night is so much more beautiful than day. Day is for everyone."—"But you have a reception at Palazzo Vecchio at 11."—"So? That's still seven hours away." . . .'[11]

From Florence the orchestra continued on to Munich, thence to Vienna, Budapest, Prague, Leipzig, Dresden and Berlin, arousing stupefied admiration everywhere. Thinking back on the Berlin concerts fifteen years later, Bruno Walter wrote: 'A splendid performance of Debussy's *La Mer* still sounds in my ears.'[12] Still later, German critic Heinrich Strobel recalled how Walter, Klemperer and Kleiber had been among the most enthusiastic members of the audience.

'The impartial recognition of that perfection on the part of those three great conductors is superior to any critical comment. . . . He was called a "fanatic of precision and of the artisan's faithfulness", because he completely subordinated himself and the orchestra to the work of art; and that is absolutely correct. . . . But a merely craftsman-like interpretation would never have made such a great impression had not a spirit of impassioned fire been at work in that "fanatic of conscientiousness" known as Toscanini.'[13]

Brussels received the Philharmonic for a concert at the Palais des Beaux-Arts; and the tour ended in London with two performances at the Albert Hall and two at Queen's Hall. (Orchestral life has certainly changed in the past fifty years: of the eleven non-Italian cities in which the Philharmonic played on tour, seven —including London—had never heard Toscanini before, despite the fact that he was already sixty-three years old and the most famous conductor of his time.) Response in England was very much the same as it had been elsewhere on tour: stunned and ecstatic. *The Times* commented that the orchestra's clarity was so great that 'even the Albert Hall could not obscure [it], at any rate for long at a time'. The King and Queen attended the first performance; so did a former music critic named Bernard Shaw, as well as Brahms's friend, the conductor Sir George Henschel, who wrote Toscanini a warm letter afterwards. He lauded the performance of Brahms's Second Symphony and said that Toscanini was the best of all the conductors he had ever heard. After the second concert critic W.J. Turner wrote:

'No conductor I have heard has succeeded in achieving such virtuosity and in keeping it always subservient to a purely musical intention. There is in Toscanini's conducting no trace whatever . . . of display or showmanship or self-consciousness. It is absolutely direct.'[14]

The last London concert took place at Queen's Hall on 4 June. In thirty-two days the Philharmonic had given twenty-three performances in fifteen cities and nine countries. Because Toscanini was to return to Italy when the orchestra returned to America, he sent a letter to the players before the final concert.

'My very dear friends, members of the Philharmonic Orchestra,
    I am sad at heart! The thought that this evening we shall give the last concert of our fortunate tour, and that tomorrow we must part after seven weeks spent in affectionate, family-like warmth, moves me deeply. But that is life. It is almost always made up of bitter leave-takings. When we are not saying goodbye to loved ones or close friends, we are saying goodbye to our illusions.
    This time, however, the illusion that our tour has been a magnificent artistic manifestation will not leave us. I am very sure that we shall all preserve this sweet memory for ever. But what most moves me to talk to you and to express myself to you is the great joy which I felt in witnessing, more and more each day, the enthusiasm and the faith which you put into making each concert come off better than the previous one; and you never showed the least sign of weariness! You have truly been marvellous. I thank you, and I can tell you that I am not only proud of you today, but that I love you as faithful friends.
    Now I wish you a fine crossing, and goodbye until November.'[15]

Toscanini's period of rest at home was a short one—not even three weeks. By late June he was in Bayreuth, where he was to realize one of the great goals of his career by conducting at the Wagner festival—the first non-German to do so.

He had, as we know, visited the Bayreuth festival as early as 1899. Siegfried Wagner, the composer's son, had greatly admired Toscanini since the *Tristan* production which he had seen at La Scala in 1901; and for many years he had wanted to bring Toscanini to Bayreuth, but had been opposed by conservative elements among the festival's 'great powers', to whom the idea of hiring an Italian to conduct at the German Holy of Holies was unthinkable. Karl Muck, the German conductor who had long been a bastion of the festival, was the major factor in preventing Toscanini's engagement, and he had been supported by Siegfried's sister, Eva Chamberlain, and step-sister, Daniela Thode—who later became Toscanini's most fanatical admirers. (Cosima was still alive, although past ninety, when this battle reached its climax; she was, according to Friedelind Wagner, Siegfried's daughter, still absolutely lucid, but had not taken part in decision-making since 1906. She died on 1 April 1930, and Toscanini conducted the Philharmonic in the *Götterdämmerung* Funeral Music in her memory two days later.)

In 1929 Siegfried decided to override all opposition and to extend an invitation to Toscanini. Not only would the conductor be good for Bayreuth artistically: he would also focus international attention on the festival and help to attract a fresh public. Siegfried and his young English-born wife, Winifred, went to Berlin during the Scala company's visit in the spring of 1929 and talked with Toscanini, who was interested. That autumn they went to Milan to submit a final plan to him. The fascination of conducting *Tannhäuser* and *Tristan* at Bayreuth was great; and not only did Toscanini undertake what was for him a task of enormous responsibility: he also refused to accept payment for his participation, which he considered to be like the fulfilment of a religious vow.*

* I must make reference here to a German book which was published while I was writing this book, and which in itself deserves at least a footnote in the tale of Toscanini lore and legend. It is B. W. Wessling's *Toscanini in Bayreuth*, and it is filled with new and interesting material about Toscanini and Wagner, the festival, politics and so on. Unfortunately, in attempting to follow up the many tantalizing 'leads' which the book indicated, I discovered that most of the new information was false—although I cannot say whether the fault lies with the author or with his sources. There are references to interviews which never took place, letters which were never written, untraceable verbal quotations, non-existent passages in books and many other inexplicable items. There is, for instance, a quotation from a conversation between Elgar and Toscanini which Wessling claims took place in 1928 and which he says is reported in Luisa Tetrazzini's book, *How to Sing*. Not only is such a conversation not reported (nor is there any other mention of Toscanini) in the copy of Tetrazzini's book which I saw: the book was also published in 1923, five

Bayreuth may have been a temple for Wagnerites, but it faced the same artistic problems that other opera houses faced. In some ways, in fact, its problems were more complicated, since it was not a permanent company but rather a group of performers gathered anew for several weeks each summer and then dispersed. That is fine for the solo singers, and even for the chorus, if they have enough time to prepare together—which they did at Bayreuth; but an orchestra is quite a different animal. The festival orchestra was made up of players assembled from a number of German orchestras, and there was necessarily a larger year-to-year turnover of personnel than in a permanent orchestra. Even if the members were individually of high calibre, this did not mean that a first horn from the Munich Opera and a second horn from the Berlin Philharmonic would be well-matched, or that the principal flute and principal oboe would have learned to adapt perfectly to each other after only a few weeks. Besides, the Bayreuth pit is exceptionally deep and almost entirely covered by the stage, and players therefore have the additional problem of becoming accustomed to very unusual acoustical conditions.

Before the first orchestral rehearsal Siegfried had presented Toscanini to the orchestra, and Toscanini had told the members of his deep and long-standing desire to be able to conduct at Bayreuth; but when he heard the orchestra he was dumbfounded and furious. By the time that session had ended he had decided not to conduct, and it was only when Siegfried assured him that replacements could easily be found for the weaker players that the situation was brought under control. Perhaps control is not the right word, however, because the orchestra soon found themselves subjected to Toscanini's worst sort of shock therapy. They had never experienced anything quite like it; nor were they less astonished when *der Italiener*—rehearsing from memory, as always—began to hear and correct mistakes in the parts which had gone unnoticed for decades by Bayreuth's famous conductors—as had happened at the Metropolitan.

Siegfried Wagner had prepared a new *mise-en-scène* for *Tannhäuser*, with

years before the 'conversation'! Wessling also states that Carla Toscanini's father was an early supporter of Mussolini; but in fact the poor man was dead even before his daughter met Toscanini in 1895. (Mussolini was twelve at the time.) Then there is a delightful quotation from a Toscanini letter to a certain Falconetti, a stage manager at the Metropolitan Opera; but this letter is not to be found in the Metropolitan archives, where Wessling claims to have seen it (at least neither the archivists nor I were able to find it), and there is no record of any Falconetti's ever having been employed by the Metropolitan. I found some three dozen mysteries of this sort in the book, which is only 144 pages long; and I therefore decided, for obvious reasons, not to cite any of the fascinating material which I was unable to check. I mention the whole matter only to explain why some seemingly invaluable information has not been incorporated into this book.

which Toscanini made his festival début on 22 July, with Sigismund Pilinszky as Tannhäuser, Herbert Janssen as Wolfram von Eschenbach and Maria Müller as Elisabeth. Costumes based on the medieval *Manesse-Handschrift* were created by Daniela Thode. Five performances were given in all. The night after the *Tannhäuser* opening came the first of three performances of *Tristan*, again staged by Siegfried (not a new production, however), with Lauritz Melchior and Nanny Larsén-Todsen in the title rôles, Alexander Kipnis as Marke, Rudolf Bockelmann as Kurwenal and Anny Helm as Brangäne.

Kipnis talked to Haggin about his experiences singing in *Tristan* at Bayreuth. (He also sang Hermann in one performance of *Tannhäuser*.)

> '... When King Marke says: "*MIR dies? Dies, Tristan, MIR?*"—in this quasi-*parlando* outcry I diminished the tone on *mir*, going over to a slightly breathy quality; and Toscanini looked up, but he didn't say anything. He insisted on the *rhythm* being the way he wanted it; but he never told me anything about phrasing, and he never said anything about the phrasing or accents which represented my feelings. I remember one thing he insisted on: in Bayreuth the melodic turns in *Tannhäuser* were done in the German way, as part of the rhythm of the measure; but Toscanini insisted on the more graceful Italian way, in which they were delayed and sung as a quick introduction to the next beat. ...
>
> The chief characteristics of Toscanini's *Tristan* was its lyricism, which the typical German conductor doesn't bring to this work. ... I always loved the lyrical approach to *Tristan*, which I heard many times from other conductors, but never in such a degree as from Toscanini.'[16]

Rudolf Bockelmann has also spoken of Toscanini's rehearsals at Bayreuth:

> 'He would say in German, tapping the score with his baton or his finger: "*Hier steht, hier steht*" ("It's here, it's here"). He didn't speak German, but those two words he knew. The singer who didn't remember Toscanini's observations was treated roughly. But if everything was in order, if he was happy with us, he would chat in a friendly way, he would tell us about Verdi and talk about Richard Wagner. "*C'est mon grand maître*" ("He is my great teacher"), he would say.'[17]

Conductor Hans Schmidt-Isserstedt attended the festival, and his recollections of the *Tristan* production are particularly interesting since they greatly resemble W.J. Henderson's review of Toscanini's first New York performance of the opera twenty years earlier:

> 'The prelude was very beautiful. ... The whole first act was a little disappointing to me: very slow, the rests calculated with absolute precision, and nothing that was not written in the score. Then came the second act: another world! I

have never again heard it done as beautifully as that—so fluently; one could almost hear the Italian melody. Then came the third act: grandiose, ecstatic and completely free.'[18]

Toscanini got along very well with Siegfried Wagner and held his stage directing in high regard; but he was not happy with the 'Bacchanale' in *Tannhäuser*. Friedelind Wagner says that at the moment of the scene change from the Venusberg to the Wartburg her father had made a gradual light change; but Toscanini wanted it to be sudden, as Wagner himself had indicated.[19] This request was made to Siegfried, who immediately complied.[20]

Unfortunately, Siegfried's serious heart condition worsened as the festival got under way—aggravated, according to Friedelind, by Muck's ugly behaviour over the engagement of Toscanini. On 4 August, in the middle of this very unusual season, Siegfried Wagner died at the age of sixty-one, only four months after the death of his mother. Friedelind, who was twelve at the time, had been in England when her father's condition had deteriorated, and had returned to Bayreuth shortly before he died. She wrote that immediately after her father's death, as soon as she had felt in control of herself, she had gone to be with her Aunt Eva.

'A moment later the door opened; a slight man with deep, gentle eyes and fine sensitive face took Eva in his arms, then me, the child whom he did not know. This was my first meeting with the man who thereafter came nearer than any other to taking my father's place. Toscanini!'[21]

Four days later Toscanini led the *Siegfried Idyll* during a memorial concert on the stage of the Festspielhaus. Karl Elmendorff, who was conducting the *Ring* that year, and Muck, who was leading *Parsifal*, also participated. Toscanini was as kind as he could be to Winifred and her children—Wieland, Wolfgang and Verena, in addition to Friedelind.

His last performance took place on 20 August. Winifred Wagner, who was now assuming the direction of the festival, sent him a gift in the form of a cheque for 10,000 marks: that had been a wish expressed by her husband on his deathbed. Toscanini immediately returned it, reiterating that he could accept no money for his Bayreuth labours;[22] and he told her that he would probably come back the following summer. In Italy he tried to rest, but actually spent most of his time preparing for the very demanding Philharmonic season. He visited the spa at Salsomaggiore, and on 30 October he departed for New York.

The season opened on 13 November; shortly afterwards Toscanini appeared for the first time as guest conductor of the Philadelphia Orchestra, while Philadelphia's regular conductor, Leopold Stokowski, was in New York to guest conduct the Philharmonic. Between 28 November and 8 December Toscanini conducted seven concerts (three programmes). Public reaction was excellent in both cities, but Stokowski had disciplinary problems with the Philharmonic. Just as the Scala orchestra had referred to Toscanini's absences as their 'winter vacation', so the Philharmonic tended to misbehave when released from the constant tension of his presence. Stokowski, of course, was an extraordinarily gifted conductor, too; but it may be that the orchestra resented his haughty behaviour or his sometimes grotesque tampering with the music he performed. In any case, once his visit had ended Stokowski vowed not to conduct the Philharmonic again—a vow which he maintained for quite a few years; and the Philharmonic began to develop its reputation as 'the conductors' graveyard'—a reputation which it too maintained, often justifiably, but sometimes to its own detriment.

Toscanini led a further twenty-three concerts in New York and on tour between 11 December and 18 January 1931; these included two performances of the Verdi *Requiem*. He then returned to Italy for about a month, where he rested for a few days on Isola dei Pescatori, Lago Maggiore, and worked in his study on Via Durini. Winifred Wagner visited him in Milan to finalize plans for the festival: the orchestra would be improved by the hiring of many musicians from the Berlin Staatsoper; Heinz Tietjen, who would assume the artistic directorship from 1933, would be present; Muck, who was old, ornery and ill, had been relieved of his responsibilities; and *Parsifal*, which had been Muck's property at Bayreuth for thirty years, would be given to Toscanini, along with *Tannhäuser*. (*Tristan* was given to Furtwängler, and the *Ring* to Elmendorff again.) Toscanini again refused all offers of fees or expense money—although he would, as in 1930, be lodged in one of the Wagners' homes.

His second New York series of the season began on 26 February, and by 19 April he had led thirty-two performances, including out-of-town concerts in five cities. Having come under attack for not playing American music (native composers were particularly annoyed that he had not taken a single American work on the European tour), he made his first bow to this reprimand by including Abram Chasins's *Flirtation in a Chinese Garden* and *Parade* on four of his April concerts.

A memorandum written by Van Praag on 7 March is interesting for what it reveals of Toscanini's way of dealing with hiring and firing of orchestra personnel. We learn that he had become dissatisfied with his concertmaster, Guidi, and was anxious to hear the coming audition of Mishel Piastro, then with the San Francisco Symphony. (Piastro was heard and hired.) Toscanini wanted to re-audition all the first violins before re-engaging them for the following season; he wanted two of the second violins to be fired at the end of the season because 'they did not show enough interest in their work'; a violist was to go because of chronic illness and because 'Maestro feels that he is not a viola player'. The second oboe was not to return 'as Maestro has had complaints from other conductors and he feels that Mr. X is not interested. Mr. Y, fourth oboe, is not to have the renewal of his contract as Maestro would like to engage an oboe player . . . who can play equally well English horn.' The E-flat clarinettist would not be rehired if a suitable replacement could be found. Toscanini had been upset by the personal behaviour on tour of one of the percussionists, and wanted advice on what to do; and he also wanted to talk to the two first-stand cellists before rehiring them.[23]

His attitude toward the hiring and firing of players was not entirely consistent. We shall see his indignant reaction to the Philharmonic board's proposal to release several players for economic reasons in 1935; and there were also instances of his retaining players whom he did not like (for instance, his original first clarinet in the NBC Symphony) because he felt it was not right to deprive people of their jobs. And yet, here he is ordering the release of seven players and the reconsideration of three others—not to mention the entire first violin section! (Conductors today do not have such unilateral power: they must act in conjunction with players' committees and the union.)

Also in March, Toscanini signed a contract to conduct sixty concerts in fifteen weeks during the following season, for which he would receive $110,000 plus payment of federal and state income taxes and steamship passage to and from New York. At that time, the average orchestra player's annual salary was about $3,000 for thirty weeks, before taxes. This means that on a per-service basis, Toscanini received about eighty times what an average player received.

He was again suffering from terrible shoulder and back pains, and in April he requested that the Philharmonic re-arrange his schedule for the following year so as to lengthen the period of rest between his two concert series. He also asked that Hans Lange be made full-time instead of part-time assistant conductor in order to relieve him of some of his preliminary rehearsals, and to be ready in case of emergency. The rescheduling could not be arranged; but Lange was given the position.

By the end of April Toscanini was again in Italy. At Salsomaggiore the previous summer he had been approached by the vice-mayor of Bologna, who had invited him to conduct the opening production of the city's newly restored Teatro Comunale. Toscanini declined. He was then asked whether he would like to conduct a pair of special concerts there the following May. The programmes would consist entirely of compositions by Toscanini's old friend, Martucci, who had headed Bologna's Conservatory for many years, and whose first Italian production of *Tristan* Toscanini had heard at the Comunale so long ago. He agreed, refusing—as in Bayreuth—to accept a fee.

He arrived in Bologna early in May to begin intensive rehearsals. Aldo Pais, a cellist in the orchestra, recalled:

'The Bolognese organizers had tried to form the best orchestra possible; but in spite of that, I remember that when the "sorcerer" (as he was called by the orchestra) arrived for the first time, he seemed like a furious storm, because he was never happy with anything. . . . He had a team of workers come in to raise the woodwinds, because they couldn't be heard from the podium. He broke at least ten batons that evening, with his hands and with his teeth. Then we got into shape immediately and did a fine job.'[24]

It is said that when Toscanini had heard the orchestra play for a few minutes, he called out to the manager, 'Where did you get these guys? At the morgue?'

Unfortunately, the concerts never took place. What happened instead was a nasty and brutal incident which caused international outrage and which was one of the worst embarrassments the Fascist government had faced since the Matteotti affair.

On the afternoon preceding the first performance Toscanini was asked to begin his programme with *Giovinezza*, since two Fascist ministers of state would be in attendance. He refused. When he arrived at the theatre, together with Carla and Wanda, a number of pro-Fascist hooligans surrounded the car. 'Will you play *Giovinezza*?' asked one, as Toscanini left the car. 'No.' They began to hit him in the face. (He was sixty-four at the time.) The chauffeur, who was standing next to him, pounced on him and got him quickly back into the car. At that moment, some *carabinieri* (national police), who had been standing nearby in their plumed ceremonial hats, came over to the car—when all was already done—and shouted 'Get going!' to the chauffeur, who sped the Toscaninis back to their hotel.[25]

Within a few minutes rumours of what had happened were already circulating in the packed theatre. An announcement was eventually made that the concert was being postponed because the Maestro was indisposed. Pais said that 'many shouted, "It's not true! It's not true!" . . . When we left the theatre it seemed as if the revolution had broken out in Bologna, because in the streets, everywhere, there was such commotion, such a to-do.'[26]

Respighi, who was in the audience, was informed of the occurrence. He and his wife, along with the Molinaris, left the Comunale immediately and drove quickly to Toscanini's hotel. They found him nursing cuts on the face and neck. Fortunately, he had not sustained any serious injuries; but, according to Elsa Respighi, he was 'like a caged beast'.[27] Meanwhile 200 Fascists had paraded from party headquarters to the hotel, where they gathered beneath Toscanini's windows and began shouting insults and obscenities; and there was some fear that objects might soon begin accompanying the sounds. Ghinelli, the federal party secretary, came to the hotel and asked to talk with someone in the Toscanini family. Toscanini himself was ruled out because of his quick temper, so Carla went downstairs; but she returned immediately because the Fascists did not wish to talk to a woman. Respighi then volunteered to represent Toscanini. He was told that the conductor and his family should leave the city before 6 a.m., otherwise their safety could not be guaranteed. They left at 1.20 a.m. and were in

Milan by sunrise. Their passports were taken away and their house was put under surveillance.

Arpinati—one of the government ministers—called Mussolini immediately after the incident; and Gaetano Cesari, the *Corriere della sera*'s principal music critic, who was in Bologna for the concert, bribed a telephone operator to report what had been said. According to the operator, Mussolini had responded to Arpinati's news with these words: '*Sono proprio contento. Sarà una buona lezione per questi musicisti cafoni.*' ('I am really happy. It will teach a good lesson to these boorish musicians.')[28]

Some of the details of this affair are covered in an extraordinary document written by Toscanini himself—extraordinary because he had rarely, if ever, written about himself so vividly. How the document came to be written was explained by Wally Toscanini in 1972:

'The Bologna episode upset our father. He became even angrier when he read the newspaper accounts. [Note: Within Italy, only official newspapers were allowed to carry carefully edited versions of the story. Most papers, including the *Corriere*, were forbidden for many days to mention the event at all.] . . . "I want the truth to be known," he shouted. He was very bitter. I then saw him act in an unusual way. He wrote an open letter to the papers to explain his behaviour and to defend himself from the accusations made against him. He called me to him and said: "Go to Milan and deliver this to the editor of the *Corriere*." His eyes were filled with tears. [Note: By this time Toscanini's passport had been restored and he had gone to St Moritz to relax before going to Bayreuth.]

I left immediately; but I had barely reached Milan when I learned that Papà had tried several times to get me on the telephone. I called him, and he told me: "Tear up those papers I gave you. I don't want to give anyone an account of my behaviour and ideas. Let them write and think what they will." I had read the pages during the trip. They seemed like valuable testimony to me and I didn't destroy them.'[29]

A facsimile of the letter was printed in Barblan's *Toscanini e la Scala* in 1972; this is the first time the entire document is being published in English.

'After the vile attack which I suffered in Bologna, and foreseeing either the organized silence of the press or the erroneous and biased accounts of the event, I sent the following telegram the next day (15 May) to the Head of the Government; it reflects, briefly but faithfully, the truth of what happened on the evening of the 14th.

To His Excellency *Benito Mussolini*,
Last evening, while I was going with my family to Bologna's Teatro

Comunale to fulfil a kind act of friendship and love in memory of Giuseppe Martucci (having been invited by the Mayor of that city for a religious and artistic Commemoration, not for a gala evening), I was attacked, injured and repeatedly hit in the face by an unspeakable gang. The undersecretary of the Interior was present in Bologna.—Not fully satisfied with this, the gang, now swollen in size, stood menacingly under the windows of the Hotel Brun, where I was staying, uttering every sort of insult and threat against me. Not only this, but one of their leaders enjoined me, through Maestro Respighi, to leave the city before six a.m.; otherwise, they could not guarantee my safety. I am communicating this to Your Excellency, so that despite the silence of the press or false information, Your Excellency will be able to have a precise account of the event, and so that the event will be remembered.

Regards,
Arturo Toscanini

The Head of the Government did not reply. On 16 May my passport was taken from me and my house was put under surveillance.—

Today, to deny the false statements in the press and to put an end to the repeated attempts of foreign newspapers to obtain interviews, I am breaking the silence which I had imposed upon myself and, reaffirming what I wired to the Head of the Government, I am adding some other attendant facts as a corollary and a further clarification.

The Vice-Mayor of Bologna, Professor Giuseppe Lipparini, with whom I had undertaken last August to conduct two concerts commemorating Giuseppe Martucci, announced to me only on the afternoon of the 14th, shortly before the concert, that Their Excellencies the ministers [Costanzo] Ciano and [Leandro] Arpinati would be present at the aforementioned concert, and that it would therefore be necessary to play the national hymns. This happened a few minutes after the last rehearsal, at which I had asked the members of the orchestra to take their places only two minutes before the performance, and with a maximum of concentration, conscious of the reverent and affectionate demonstration in which they were taking part—in order that no sounds other than Martucci's music should reach the public. I concluded: "Gentlemen, be democrats in life but aristocrats in art." Therefore, I could not accommodate Professor Lipparini's request—as unexpected as it was out of place—and allow the concert suddenly to take on a gala or political character, since no preliminary sign or newspaper advertisement had announced this. Instead, I very gladly accepted the conciliatory proposal later formulated by the Prefect of Bologna together with the Vice-Mayor, which they made known to me at five in the afternoon. The proposal was set forth in these terms: upon the entrance of the ministers, a band would play the national hymns in the lobby of the

Comunale. But at eight o'clock things changed. The conciliatory move did not suit the ministers; the earlier command was again brought forth, and I remained more steadfast than ever in my decision to maintain the commemorative character of the evening. At nine-thirty Mr. Brianzi of the City administration telephoned me to go to the theatre, informing me that Their Excellencies would abstain from attending the concert. And I fell right into the ambush.

But the lesson which they wanted to teach me—according to certain journalists—was to no avail, nor will it be to any avail in the future; because I would repeat tomorrow what I did yesterday, if the same conditions prevailed in Italy or in any other part of the world.

I know perfectly well the moral, political and patriotic value of a national hymn played at the proper time—and I have never refused to play that of the Nation to which I belong in any situation where its moral and patriotic meaning was unmistakable. Didn't I cross Italy and North America after the war at the head of the Scala Orchestra, in a series of concerts of national propaganda, playing my Country's national anthem everywhere? And haven't I conducted it innumerable times during my 45-year career for patriotic evenings—for example, at the Milan Arena in August 1915, or on gala evenings, or at openings of expositions, in the presence of the sovereigns? And didn't I conduct it on Monte Santo, under enemy fire? I have been accused of having played the English hymn in London on my European tour with the American orchestra. But for God's sake, that concert was given under the august patronage of the English sovereigns! And if the Queen of Italy, in Rome, very graciously considered the concert only from its artistic side, didn't the same thing happen a few days later in Brussels, before the King and Queen of Belgium? And so?

To conclude: Should I not have to judge newspapers like the *Resto del Carlino* or the *Corriere della sera* severely when, overnight, they replace the Hosannas to Toscanini with the Crucifixus? When they, like the *Popolo d'Italia* [official Fascist newspaper] even find me unsuitable for commemorating Giuseppe Martucci? And all the others which have even called me unpatriotic? How tiny and unworthy are all these poor people, hardly deserving of my compassion! "The spine curves when the soul is curved." It's true. But the conduct of my life has been, is, and will always be the echo and the reflection of my conscience, which does not know dissimulation or deviations of this type—reinforced by a proud and scornful character, yes, but as clear as crystal and just as cutting—always and everywhere ready to shout the truth loudly—that truth which, as Emerson says so well, always comes into the world in a manger but, in return, is made to live until it is completely enslaved by men.'[30]

Mussolini's delight over what had happened to this 'boorish musician' cannot have lasted long. It did not take much time for artistic and intellectual circles throughout the country to learn—at least in some degree—the facts of the case; and the international press carried detailed, if not always accurate, reports. Mussolini decided to give the Toscanini case his personal attention; government functionaries were ordered to pass whatever they learned through surveillance of the Via Durini house, wire-tapping or professional informants directly to the Duce's personal secretary. (Although Mussolini did not reply to Toscanini's telegram, he did, according to Tommasini, tell a mutual acquaintance: 'He conducts an orchestra of 100 people; I have to conduct one of forty million, and they are not all *virtuosi*.') The file which Mussolini accumulated on Toscanini from the time of the Bologna incident until 1938 still exists and provides some interesting footnotes to the history of Toscanini's relations with the Fascists.

Curiously, in the flood of intra-governmental communications on the Bologna affair, the only non-official item preserved was an anonymous letter addressed to Mussolini and dated 16 May:

'I ask whether in Year IX of the Fascist Era it be permitted to any Joe Schmoe to beat Maestro Toscanini, who is guilty of not having wanted to play *Giovinezza* on an occasion at which this hymn, despite its being so dear to Italians, would have gone like pickles with ice cream. In this period when moral values are being turned upside-down, one can expect to see Marconi, too, beaten tomorrow for not broadcasting some sleep-inducing speech by some eighteenth-ranking party hierarch. . . .

> A Fascist
> who, at the price of being called a coward, is not signing his name because he does not want to wind up in prison. (Something which happens very easily today, even if one is absolutely right) . . .

The Toscaninis learned who their friends were in those days. Since their house was being watched constantly, there were many who did not dare to call or visit; Toscanini was very hurt by this and some old acquaintances were permanently ostracized as a result. Most of his friends, however, including composers Pizzetti, Castelnuovo-Tedesco and Giordano, visited and called him repeatedly, and Mussolini's secretary was duly informed.

Five days after the incident the Minister of the Interior received a telegram from Milan's Prefect. It informed him that seven students who had shouted 'Viva Toscanini' in front of the Maestro's house had been identified and had confessed. They were being held. It continues:

'Last night, at the end of the first part of a symphony concert at La Scala, some youths in the second gallery let out shouts of "*Viva Toscanini*", which were greeted with prolonged applause by a considerable portion of the audience filling the theatre. Nine individuals were quickly arrested by guards on hand and identified as those responsible. The majority of these confessed and are being held. . . . Several hundred Fascists, meanwhile, gathered in front of the theatre; after singing *Giovinezza* they headed towards Via Durini, where they staged a hostile demonstration directed at Maestro Toscanini. Police who were there were able to stop an attempt to storm the building.'

Telegrams began arriving at Via Durini from all over the world. From Italian political exiles in France: '10,000 Italians of the Paris Assembly applaud your gesture.' From Leipzig: 'It is one year since you brought the city of Leipzig the fortune of hearing your sublime art. The Gewandhaus, always open to you, wishes to express its great affection, along with the hope of seeing you again before long.' From conductor Georg Schneevoigt in Riga: 'My unalterable affection and admiration for the great and incomparable artist.' Winifred Wagner, upset about the incident's possible effect on Toscanini's Bayreuth appearances, sent a telegram to 'Maestro Arturo Toscanini, Milano', which he did not receive; so she sent another to 'Maestro Arturo Toscanini, Italy'—and that one he did receive. Worried cables and letters reached him from friends and Philharmonic staff members in New York. Serge Koussevitzky cancelled his scheduled concerts at La Scala in protest over the affair. 'Maestro Toscanini does not belong only to Italy, but to the whole world,' he wrote to the theatre's administration. Fritz Reiner, who was preparing a concert with the Scala Orchestra, went to visit Toscanini. (But when a group of Fascists in the gallery shouted for him to play *Giovinezza* during his concert, he immediately complied.)

Pianist and conductor Ossip Gabrilowitsch heard about the Bologna affair while vacationing in Zürich. He and his wife (Mark Twain's daughter, Clara Clemens) caught the next train for Milan, where they visited Toscanini. Gabrilowitsch left an account of the meeting:

'He greeted us most cordially and seemed spontaneously inclined to describe the entire Bologna experience. He did so with undisguised indignation against the Fascist factions who had set the trap for him. In the expression of his feelings the great artist before us also divulged the great man. . . . His declaration of dislike for the present state of affairs in Italy was expressed in bold, round phrases. And this declaration he has repeatedly given outside the privacy of his home, so that no one can mistake his attitude. "Truth," he said, "truth we must have at any price, and freedom of speech, even if that price should be death. I have said to our Fascists time and again: You can kill me if you wish, but as long as I am living I shall say what I think." . . . He was in no way the broken man one might have expected to see. On the contrary, he was full of vigour and dynamic energy.'[31]

Béla Bartók—of whose music Toscanini never played a note—wrote out the following resolution and submitted it at a meeting of the UMZE (New Hungarian Music Society):

'1. The UMZE is deeply shocked and roused to indignation by the news of the grave assault that has been made on Arturo Toscanini. The Society wishes to assure him of its most wholehearted sympathy and solidarity and salutes him with the utmost admiration.

2. The UMZE views with concern the ever more numerous brutal intrusions into artistic life by factors that have nothing to do with the domain of art. These intrusions don't halt even before the worldwide authority of a Toscanini. Therefore the UMZE considers it timely to give thought to the problem of defensive action.'[32]

The Toscaninis' passports were restored to them by early June; Toscanini, Carla and Wally then went to St Moritz to relax for about ten days. A paid informer followed them there and sent back reports on the people with whom Toscanini had conversations. After this brief rest Toscanini and his wife went to Bayreuth.

'Toscanini has begun rehearsals for *Tannhäuser* and *Parsifal*,' wrote Carla to Elsa Respighi on 28 June. 'In a few rehearsals he has already read through both operas. He is very happy with the orchestra, which is much improved this year, and he has found serenity and tranquillity in his work.'[33] Carla must have returned to Italy soon afterwards, judging from Friedelind Wagner's reminiscences:

'. . . Toscanini, who was without his family this season, was a guest in the bachelor house. Every morning he took his breakfast on the little glass-enclosed balcony which got the full sun and was so hot that Wieland named it "Toscanini's Turkish bath". But the Maestro loved the sun. He was one of the most pleasant guests we ever entertained, the maids adored him because he liked his meals and gave them no trouble. He kept his own car and chauffeur and never upset the household routine with demands for service.

Toscanini was amused by my candid remarks. "You are so fonnee," he used to tell me between chuckles. On days when there were no rehearsals or performances we sometimes drove to inns up in the mountains for tea, visited the beauty spots of Franconia or just drove about in the pleasant summer afternoons.'[34]

This peaceful atmosphere was not to continue, however. In the first place, Toscanini's right shoulder began to bother him again. He had been X-rayed and had undergone some sort of treatment in Milan after the Bologna affair, but to no effect. The pain worsened as the summer progressed; at times the agony of conducting caused tears to run down his face, and he often had to resort to using only his left arm. This physical suffering did nothing to tranquillize his naturally volatile temperament.

Another problem was Toscanini's relationship with the Winifred Wagner–Furtwängler–Tietjen directorate—although the actual difficulty lay within that uneasy triangle. Toscanini, as a foreigner, neither expected nor wanted to be part of the festival's administration. He demanded the means to carry out his own work as thoroughly as possible, and that was all. Tietjen, who was a consummate politician, wished to be rid of Furtwängler in order to bring the greatest possible degree of control over Bayreuth's destinies into his own hands. This he accomplished by creating dissension between Furtwängler and Frau Wagner, by rumour-mongering and by magnifying and distorting harmless remarks. Frau Wagner who, on the one hand, was new in her position as head of the festival, and on the other, was under constant attack from her sisters-in-law and their faction, was a natural prey for this sort of tactic; and Furtwängler, who was an insecure person, was also easily manipulated.

Toscanini liked Frau Wagner personally. Her independence and energy impressed him, and he found her quite attractive. He did not, however, involve himself in Bayreuth politics, and remained friendly with the old guard as well. What he objected to in Frau Wagner was her fascination with the rising National Socialist Party and particularly with its leader, Adolf Hitler. He did not hesitate to tell her this; but she remained (and still remains, in 1978) convinced that Hitler was the right man for Germany. Instinctively, Toscanini disliked Tietjen and had as little to do with him as possible. His relations with Furtwängler were uneasy. He admired his musicianship although their views on musical interpretation were very different. (In no source have I read or heard of any uncomplimentary statement by Toscanini regarding Furtwängler, either personally or musically, until the question of the latter's involvement with the Nazis arose in 1936. Of that, more later.) But they were absolutely different personalities. Friedelind Wagner told me that 'Toscanini, as a person, was absolutely straightforward: you always knew where he stood; but Furtwängler could never be pinned down on anything. Furtwängler was very vain and, surprisingly, also very unsure of himself. It disturbed him if anyone, anywhere, began building up a career—he felt encroached upon.'[35]

On 4 August, the first anniversary of Siegfried Wagner's death, a memorial concert was scheduled in the Festspielhaus, with Toscanini, Furtwängler and Elmendorff all participating. Toscanini was to lead the *Faust* Overture. He was in excruciating pain and had asked that no one be admitted to the final rehearsal, which took place on the day of the concert; but when he arrived at the Festspielhaus, where Furtwängler's rehearsal was just ending, he found the house full: tickets had been sold to the public. He began to rehearse; but after only a few minutes he quietly put down his baton and walked out. After having told Furtwängler, who had run after him, that he would not participate in the performance, he had himself driven into the mountains, where he spent the rest of the day. While the concert was taking place without him that evening, he was placing flowers on Siegfried's grave.[36]

Despite all this, the season proceeded normally. *Tannhäuser*, which opened on 21 July, was given five performances, as was *Parsifal*, which began the next night. After having heard the *Parsifal* production, Wagner's disciple, Baron Hans Paul von Wolzogen, then eighty-three, had been moved to write an extremely laudatory letter to Toscanini, who responded on 5 August:

> 'No word of praise could be dearer and more desirable than yours. If my interpretation has been able to reawaken in you an echo of that memorable one of 1882 [Note: the première, conducted by Hermann Levi, under Wagner's supervision], it is the most I could aspire to in the fulfilment of my ideal dream—that is, to come as close as possible to expressing the composer's thoughts. You, friend of that Great Man and faithful and wise popularizer of his ideas, could not give me a greater reward.—Your praise has moved me deeply and I thank you with all my heart.'[37]

Nevertheless, by the time the last performance had ended on 19 August, Toscanini had made it clear to Frau Wagner that he was not to be expected for the 1933 festival. (There was to be no festival in 1932.) Daniela Thode later wrote that on the day following the last performance Toscanini met various members of the Wagner family—not including Winifred—over lunch and told them that he had sent back, unread, a letter from Siegfried's widow, together with a Wagner manuscript which she had offered him as a gift. He had written to thank her for her hospitality; but for the rest, he had to confess that he was deeply disillusioned with Bayreuth and would not return. He said that on coming to Bayreuth, he had thought he was entering a temple, but had found himself in an ordinary theatre.[38]

After a substantial period of rest and study in Italy, Toscanini departed for New York, where he arrived on 16 November. The Philharmonic administration was very worried lest he should have to face pro- or anti-Fascist demonstrations on the part of various Italo-American factions after the events of the past spring. Bruno Zirato, Caruso's former secretary and Toscanini's long-time friend, had been hired as the orchestra's associate manager; it was his job, above and beyond all else, to look after Toscanini, to make sure he would always have someone to whom he could express any dissatisfaction, and to report any potential problems to Judson or Mackay. Zirato was on friendly terms with both of the Italian political factions in New York, and he was successful in arranging that no demonstrations met Toscanini on his arrival at the pier. Plainclothes detectives were hired to mix with the audiences at his concerts, to stand near his dressing room and to be near him as he entered and left the hall.[39] Despite these precautions—none of which were made known to Toscanini—a few people managed to throw thousands of slips of paper from the balcony at the end of the first concert (26 November). According to Taubman, the slips said: 'Liberty is essential to Art—*Evviva* Arturo Toscanini!' (Taubman also mentions that when Italian foreign minister Dino Grandi had attended a performance at the Metropolitan several nights earlier, other slips saying 'Down with Fascism' and 'Long live Toscanini' were cast about the opera house.)[40]

To his great regret, Toscanini soon discovered that three months without conducting had not been enough to eliminate his shoulder problem. At Mackay's insistence he visited a Rockefeller Institute doctor and was given a number of diathermy treatments which did no good but for which he was charged $400. Zirato, who handled most of Toscanini's correspondence, was afraid to show him the bill, which was eventually paid either by Mackay or by the Philharmonic. The pain became so intolerable that after only a month of work—fourteen performances—Toscanini was forced to declare himself beaten. Replacements were found for the remaining programmes on his first series, and he returned to Italy after the concert of 20 December. He saw doctors in Rome and Florence, had X-rays taken, and eventually went to the village of Piazze, near Siena, where he was treated by a Dr Rinaldi. Rinaldi—original, somewhat unhinged, and confident in his cures—was one of those strange medical figures whose patients 'believe in' their healing powers. He seems to have been something of a physician and something of a witch-doctor at one and the same time. For Toscanini he prescribed twenty-four daily injections of a special serum! 'It seems a very bestial cure to everybody, but Toscanini is doing it with great enthusiasm,' wrote Signora Carla to Zirato on 23 January 1932.[41] A complete cure was predicted, but is was necessary to warn the Philharmonic that he would not be able to return in time for the first concerts of his second series.

Judson and his associates were alarmed: they feared that Toscanini's prolonged illness would have a deleterious effect on their subscription campaign for the following season, and they were having other troubles as well. Guest conductor Bruno Walter was in a state of depression because his daughter had had to undergo an operation for a stomach tumour; Sir Thomas Beecham, the next guest conductor, fell off the podium during a rehearsal, fracturing a bone in his foot; concertmaster Mishel Piastro broke two ribs in an automobile accident; and the economic depression in the United States was bringing the Philharmonic's continued existence into doubt.

In the end, Toscanini's cure at Piazze lasted three months and prevented him from fulfilling any of his New York obligations for the rest of the season. He did, however, make an extraordinary gesture of good faith and good will towards the orchestra when, in the spring, he made the long ocean voyage to America and back in order to conduct one single performance for the benefit of unemployed musicians. This concert took place on 28 April, and consisted of the Prelude and 'Good Friday Spell' from *Parsifal* and Beethoven's Ninth Symphony. While in

New York he learned that the entire orchestra and staff were accepting ten per cent salary cuts for the following season, in order to keep the Society from collapsing; so he instructed Judson to deduct $10,000 from his $110,000 salary.[42]

During his return to Europe on the *Ile-de-France*, one of Toscanini's shipboard companions was sixteen-year-old violinist Yehudi Menuhin. The boy's father, Moshe Menuhin, wrote excitedly to a friend in London about the experience.

'. . . We are having an ideal crossing. Exhilarated spiritually even more than physically. For Yehudi's life-dream has come true. Daily he and I spend hours and hours with Toscanini; making music, discussing the classics, and in a friendly, intimate atmosphere. . . . Just imagine our trunkful of scores; all of Bach's works, Mozart's, Beethoven's, Schubert's, laid out on the tables. We are the happiest people on board, and I believe (with a little immodesty) Toscanini is happy over this unlooked-for meeting.

They have decided to make music daily from 11 a.m. to 1 or 2 o'clock. Occasionally Yehudi's accompanist has been called in to assist. . . . From the beginning the boy insisted, "Please, Maestro, criticize me right and left, without hesitation. These will be my most precious lessons." . . . After Yehudi had finished Beethoven's "Kreutzer" Sonata, Toscanini burst out, "Yehudi, caro, bravo! Bravissimo! This is perfect, this is real music. How you have grown since I heard you three years ago; your heart, your mind! Oh, how little good music I hear in my life. . . . Come, my child, play, play! Go on and on!" '. . .'[43]

The few days of conducting Toscanini had done in New York had convinced him that his arm and shoulder were much improved; he returned to Piazze to continue the treatments, and an X-ray in Florence late in May confirmed that the problem had been largely cleared up. Whatever Dr Rinaldi did worked—at least temporarily. Toscanini continued to suffer from these pains from time to time, although not as severely as before. He returned to Piazze several times, and even sent other conductors with similar problems—Molinari and Artur Rodzinski, for example—until Rinaldi, as outspoken an anti-Fascist as his most famous patient, was eventually assassinated.

During this period of rest Toscanini actually responded to a questionnaire sent out to many famous musicians by the *Berliner Börsen Zeitung*.

'I love and admire all the works I conduct, symphonic or operatic, because—I conduct only those I love. My preferences in the symphonic area are for the greats: Haydn, Mozart, Beethoven. In recent years I have thoroughly studied Bruckner's monumental symphonies. I gladly leave modern works to other conductors. Among operas, I value those of Wagner and Verdi above all. It is difficult to state a preference for one of Wagner's operas. I have noticed that if I am conducting this or that Wagner opera, or playing it at the piano, which—

ever one it happens to be possesses my heart. And yet, every time I glance at
the score of *Parsifal*, I say to myself: this is the sublime one. In Verdi's operas,
I value not only the melodic richness, but also the effective and sure musical
and dramatic power. When I conduct *Falstaff* at Busseto I think about the
possibility of a Verdian Bayreuth, on the model of Wagner's Festspielhaus.
These two masters are precisely the representatives of German and Italian
national music.'[44]

Toscanini decided to go to Paris to participate in an unusual concert on
17 June which coincided with the unveiling of a monument to Debussy. The
audience at the Théâtre des Champs-Elysées first heard Gaubert conduct *Le
Martyre de Saint-Sébastien* (excerpts, presumably), then the three *Nocturnes* led
by Pierné. Next came a live broadcast into the theatre of *L'Après-midi d'un faune*
conducted in Basel by Weingartner, and then *La Mer* with Toscanini. The
evening ended with the fifth act of *Pelléas* led by D.E. Ingelbrecht, and with
Mary Garden, then fifty-five, as Mélisande, the rôle which she had sung at the
world première thirty years earlier.

During this same period, the Wagners—old guard and new—were engaged in
trying to break down Toscanini's resistance and convince him to return to
Bayreuth the following year. Eva Chamberlain-Wagner wrote him on 22 March
—three days before his sixty-fifth birthday:

'Beyond these poor words I am incapable of expressing to you the profound
feelings which move my heart towards you, dear, blessed Maestro! But I do
not doubt that you know how to read the language of the soul—and this last is
filled with an ardent prayer: "Oh kehr' zurück Du kühner Sänger!" ("O
return, Thou bold singer!").'[45]

And while Toscanini was in Paris Winifred Wagner paid him a visit. She must
have pointed out to him that the improved condition of his arm would remove
the greatest irritant from the next season; that Tietjen would not be allowed to
aggravate him; that it was unclear whether or not Furtwängler would be returning at all; that the season was to be of special significance since it would mark the
fiftieth anniversary of Wagner's death; and that in addition to *Parsifal*, Toscanini
would be given *Meistersinger* to conduct. Now, if he felt that *Parsifal* was the
most sublime of Wagner's operas, *Meistersinger* was the one he most often elected
to perform and the one which—although he would not use the word 'favourite'—
seemed to give him the greatest satisfaction. He told Frau Wagner that she could
expect him at Bayreuth in 1933.

Another question troubling Toscanini at this time concerned the possibility of
conducting again in Italy. Since reaction to the Bologna incident had calmed
down, he had nearly ceased to exist at home. The tightly controlled national press
carried very little news about him, unless there was occasion to insult him. (When

it had been thought that he would not be returning to Bayreuth, *Il popolo di Roma* had carried an article with the headline, 'The Man who Fights with Everyone: Toscanini is even dissatisfied with Beyrut [sic] and is telegraphing nasty statements about the Widow Wagner and the Hitlerites.') On 29 March—during a leave of absence he had managed to obtain from Dr Rinaldi—he had attended a concert at the Milan Conservatory. The Prefecture informed the Interior Ministry:

'As soon as his presence was noted, a part of the public directed continuous applause towards him, opposed by some whistling. After the performance, while some Conservatory students were again paying tribute to the Maestro with applause, again opposed by whistling, an individual, approaching his car, clapped his hands fervently, shouting "*Viva Maestro*" and then trying to disappear from the area. Stopped by the police, he was identified as Dr. Gino Fanoli, Socialist, and is being held pending further information.'

In August a group of orchestral musicians, obviously acting at the instigation of some person of influence in the musical world, made a request through various party functionaries to obtain an act of clemency for Toscanini '*dalla illuminata bontà del Duce*' ('from the Duce's enlightened goodness'), since the Maestro had shown himself willing to conduct a winter assistance benefit concert in Milan. Mussolini saw the request; but such a concert never took place. The following year the Prefect of Turin wired the Ministry that Toscanini would agree to conduct Beethoven's *Missa Solemnis* in that city, but had made it clear that he would not conduct the national anthems. That concert was not held either. Toscanini's tour concerts in Italy with the Philharmonic in the spring of 1930 remained his last performances in his native country for many years.

After nine months of almost complete professional inactivity, he returned to New York in September and initiated a full schedule of concerts. Between 6 October and 27 November he led thirty-three concerts in New York and on tour. Among the works new to his programmes were Schoenberg's arrangement of Bach's Prelude and Fugue in E-flat Major (the closest Toscanini ever came to Schoenberg) and Bruckner's Fourth Symphony. As usual, he spent two months in Italy between his two concert cycles, then returned to America to conduct thirty-two concerts in New York and five other cities between 1 March and 23 April. The season's last concert included the only performance he ever led of Beethoven's 'Emperor' Concerto, and the soloist was twenty-nine-year-old Vladimir Horowitz.

It was violinist Adolf Busch who had suggested Horowitz to Toscanini, whose daughter Wanda recounted in a 1972 interview:

'Horowitz was already very famous and had played throughout the world; but when he was told that Toscanini was waiting to audition him, his hands began to tremble. Besides, Busch and other friends were continually warning him, "Be careful not to arrive late; if he starts to shout, don't be frightened; if he insults you, don't reply"; and things of that sort. Horowitz, who is shy and reserved by nature, was very frightened. He arrived half an hour early at the Hotel Astor, where my father used to stay. . . . When the prearranged hour struck he introduced himself to my father. He expected a tempestuous welcome, but Papà was very gentle. He had him play a piece and then said to him: "That's very good. Now I must ask you to leave because I have a lot of work. See you at the first orchestra rehearsal." '46

At the end of January the question of Toscanini's return to Bayreuth, which appeared to have been resolved the previous June, suddenly arose again with Hitler's assumption of power in Germany. In February, on the fiftieth anniversary of Wagner's death, Toscanini (*in absentia*, of course) was made an honorary citizen of Bayreuth. He made no move, waiting to see what the Nazis would do. In March reports arrived that the Busch family had left Germany (they were not Jewish, but were strongly anti-Nazi); that Bruno Walter had been turned away from a concert with his Leipzig Gewandhaus Orchestra and had also left the country; that Klemperer was about to leave; and so on. On 14 March Toscanini allowed news to be leaked to the press that the persecution of Jewish musicians was making him think twice about returning to Bayreuth. (Obviously, he hoped that this might have some propagandistic effect in Germany.) At the end of the month he received a letter from Gabrilowitsch which ended with these words:

'Under those conditions, will you—Arturo Toscanini, the world's most illustrious artist—lend the glamour of your international fame to the Bayreuth festival? A decisive protest from you at this time would amount to a great historic fact. The world has a right to expect this noble gesture from you.'47

On 1 April a cable protesting against the boycott of Jewish musicians and the new German racist policy in general was sent to Hitler from New York. The first signature was that of Toscanini; it was followed by those of Damrosch, Koussevitzky, Bodanzky, Harold Bauer, Gabrilowitsch, Hertz, Charles Martin Loeffler, Reiner, Rubin Goldmark and Frederick Stock. The next day—a Sunday—the cable was reproduced in the morning papers; Toscanini, walking on to the stage of Carnegie Hall to begin the Philharmonic's afternoon concert, was greeted by wave after wave of applause, cheering, stamping—far exceeding the sort of reception to which even he was accustomed.

In Berlin an order was issued by the head radio commissioner on 4 April:

'According to newspaper reports, several conductors and musicians in the United States—Arturo Toscanini [*et al.*]—have lodged a complaint with the Chancellor because of the rejection of certain Jewish and Marxist fellow-musicians in Germany. Pending clarification of this matter, I direct that the compositions and records of the aforementioned gentlemen shall no longer find a place on the programmes of German broadcasters and also that no musical performance in which they in any wise have a part shall be received from concert halls or other broadcasting sources.'48

The American papers which carried this news also revealed that Winifred Wagner had dined with Hitler in Berlin that evening.

Frau Wagner had known and admired Hitler even before the Munich *putsch* of 1923. She had invited him to Wahnfried, and he had devoutly visited Wagner's grave. His love of the composer's music was only matched by his admiration for Wagner's anti-Semitic and other racial writings. When the future Führer had been jailed after the *putsch*, Winifred Wagner heard that he needed writing paper. She gladly supplied him with all he needed; and *Mein Kampf* was written on Bayreuth stationery. This natural alliance between certain aspects of the Wagnerite and Hitlerite mentalities grew stronger and stronger until, during the Third Reich's days of dubious glory, Bayreuth became Nazism's national cultural shrine and Hitler became an intimate friend of the Wagner family.

Winifred Wagner, because of her faithful support of the Nazi cause and, above all, because of the surname her husband had given her, had ready access to Hitler's ear from the moment he came to power. It is not surprising, therefore, that she was able to have dinner with him to discuss the Toscanini/Bayreuth situation; but actually, the real crisis talk had taken place by telephone two days earlier—just after Hitler had received the protest cable. Friedelind Wagner, then fifteen, was with her mother in their hotel suite in Berlin when the conversation took place:

'From the half of the conversation that I heard, I gathered that [Hitler] felt very badly treated after he had generously permitted Mother to keep her Jewish artists. On further thought he must have realized what it would mean to have such a powerful voice as that of Toscanini openly denouncing Nazi Germany, for his aides rushed back and forth from the Chancellery to the hotel all day long. Finally it was decided to send a wire in Hitler's name, urging Toscanini to reconsider. . . .

This wire was followed [3 April] by a personal letter from Hitler which he felt sure the Maestro could not resist. . . . It said among other things, "Until now it has been denied him (Hitler) to hear the great conductor but this year in his capacity as Chancellor of the Reich, he would be especially happy to greet Toscanini in Bayreuth."

When I heard this, I couldn't keep still. "It would be crazy to send such a letter," I protested. "This is the surest way to drive Toscanini away forever. If you really want him to come, don't send it, because he comes to Bayreuth for Wagner, not for Hitler. It will be sure to make him furious."

Mother glared at me and her temper flared. In an angry voice she reminded me that I was speaking like a child, and advised me to leave the operating of the festival to her. . . .'[49]

Toscanini responded to Hitler's letter on 29 April in what was for him a curiously oblique and indecisive way. The idea of giving up Bayreuth, probably forever, obviously hurt him very much, and he found it difficult to take the final, unretractable step. The reply was written in English.

'Your *Excellency*:—For your very friendly writing I want to thank you heartily, only I greatly regret that I could not answer it sooner.

You know how closely I feel attached to Bayreuth and what deep pleasure it gives me to consecrate my "something" to a genius like Wagner whom I love so boundlessly.

Therefore it would be a bitter disappointment to me if any circumstances should interfere with my purpose to take part in the coming Festival Plays, and I hope that my strength, which the last weeks have taxed severely, will hold out.

Expressing once more my thanks for your kind expressions of thought, I subscribe myself as your Excellency's sincere etc.'[50]

Shortly after having written this letter Toscanini returned to Italy. The previous year he had rented the *isolino* San Giovanni, a tiny island on Lago Maggiore, facing the town of Pallanza. For seven summers, and then again after the years of exile during the war, this was to be his favourite spot in the world. An American musical patroness, Elizabeth Sprague Coolidge, had persuaded Toscanini to agree to have the first performance of Pizzetti's String Quartet— which she had commissioned—take place on the island on 23 May 1933. The Busch Quartet came from Switzerland to play the work, and musicians and critics arrived from everywhere. German exiles like Emil Ludwig and Erich Maria Remarque were among the guests and were able to give Toscanini first-hand accounts of what was taking place in their country. Conductor Fritz Busch, brother of two of the quartet's members, was also present. In his memoirs, he wrote that Toscanini told him that he wanted to talk with him after the other guests had left.

'I felt that he was much preoccupied. When, later, we were alone in his room, he showed me a letter from Hitler, in which he declared how happy he would be "to welcome the great Maestro of the friendly Italian nation to Bayreuth before long." . . . Both he and I had come to recognize that the appearance of wounded honour means nothing compared to the true shame of serving wickedness.

What was depressing Toscanini, from his youth closely attached to the art of Richard Wagner, and its greatest interpreter, was anxiety for the future of the Bayreuth Festival. Feeling thus he asked me, "What will Bayreuth do if I refuse?" "Then they will invite me, Maestro," I said. Toscanini was speechless. "That is to say, they *have* invited me. Tietjen, who expects your refusal, has already taken steps."

I was delighted at his astonishment and added with a laugh, "Of course, I will refuse, like you." Toscanini shut his mouth, which had remained open from astonishment, and purred, in his warm, melancholy voice, "*Eh, caro amico!*" We were both silent, and a feeling of great sorrow came over us.'[51]

Toscanini telegraphed Winifred Wagner that he would not return to the Festival. In an eleventh-hour attempt, Daniela Thode was dispatched to Milan to try to make him change his mind. After a day-and-a-half of diplomatic efforts, she declared herself beaten; and Toscanini, with the advice of his lawyer and Frau Thode, wrote and sent a message to Winifred (28 May):

'The sorrowful events which have wounded my feelings as a man and as an artist have not undergone any change, contrary to my every hope. It is therefore my duty today to break the silence which I had imposed upon myself for two months and to inform you that for my tranquillity, for yours, and for everyone's, it is better not to think any longer about my coming to Bayreuth.

With unchangeable friendship for the House of Wagner,

Arturo Toscanini.'[52]

News of Toscanini's abandonment of Bayreuth reached the press on 6 June. Two days later the *New York Times* summarized reaction within Germany:

'Most Nazi organs thus far ignore Signor Toscanini's action, but the National Socialist Militant League for German Culture issued a statement saying Signor Toscanini "apparently had been unable to withstand the influence of large-scale anti-German propaganda", and added: "None of this league's authorized representatives has ever taken action against the artistic work of Toscanini. As Germans, we are convinced that artistically adequate interpreters of the works of Wagner will be found." ... The *Börsen Zeitung* said: "... We may hope he will come to Bayreuth after all, for this much is beyond doubt: the participation of Signor Toscanini was the greatest attraction of the Bayreuth festival. He guaranteed the high artistic level that the festival must have ... He also was the only guarantee for its financial success." ... The *Vossische Zeitung*: "The great musician with incorruptible ears, suspicious, pedantically insisting on the last semiquaver, has heard only the discordant tone of the great orchestra that is Germany." '

From the same article we learn that the broadcasting ban on Toscanini's recordings in Germany had been lifted—in what was obviously a last attempt to convince him to change his mind. When this attempt proved futile the ban was reinstated. Toscanini's recordings were eventually withdrawn from the market; and according to Friedelind Wagner, Hitler used to 'see red whenever the Maestro's name was mentioned'[53]—a syndrome he shared with his friend Mussolini. (Toscanini later turned down an invitation to conduct in the Soviet Union because of that country's repressive government. Stalin's reaction, if any, is not known.) The Hitler era was only four months old, and already not one of the German newspapers quoted above refers to Toscanini's real reasons for not returning to Bayreuth. Richard Strauss now informed Frau Wagner that he would gladly take over Toscanini's *Parsifal* performances at Bayreuth, just as he had taken over Bruno Walter's Gewandhaus concerts when the latter had left Germany in the spring. (Elmendorff, who was already scheduled to lead the *Ring*, directed Toscanini's *Meistersinger* as well.)

After an unexpectedly long rest period, Toscanini went to Paris to conduct three concerts at the Théâtre des Champs-Elysées with the Orchestre des Concerts Walther-Straram, on 12, 17 and 18 October. He then proceeded to Vienna, where he made his first appearances with the Vienna Philharmonic. This was the beginning of a fruitful relationship which was to last until Austria was absorbed into the German Reich.

In 1899, as we know, Toscanini had been interested in guest conducting the Vienna Philharmonic; but the orchestra's directorate had not been interested in him. In the 1920s, when he was the most sought-after conductor in the world, the Viennese had tried to convince him to conduct their orchestra. Since Toscanini did not generally want to take on extra engagements, and since he did not have a secretary or an agent, his response to Vienna's invitations was the same as it was to most of the hundreds of offers he received from around the world: silence. But in 1933 a concerted effort was made. Hugo Burghauser, the orchestra's principal bassoon and its newly elected president (the orchestra was and still is a self-governing organization), had dreamed of bringing Toscanini and the orchestra together since he had first heard him conduct at La Scala in 1923. When Toscanini's withdrawal from Bayreuth had been made known, Burghauser took the opportunity to extend a fresh invitation to Toscanini. There was no immediate response; but at the same time Toscanini was approached on the subject by the Polish violinst Bronislaw Huberman.

Huberman was a great admirer of Toscanini and, like most Jewish musicians, he was grateful for his refusal to return to Bayreuth. That summer Huberman was vacationing at Caldè on the eastern shore of Lago Maggiore, very near Toscanini's *isolino*. It occurred to him that Toscanini could make his anti-Nazi protest even more meaningful by coming to conduct in Germany's 'free' neighbour, Austria. Huberman made a quick trip back to Austria to discuss the idea with friends—notably an Austrian cabinet minister—then returned to Lago Maggiore in August to make the proposal to Toscanini, who immediately agreed to conduct the Philharmonic in the autumn.

Vienna had already heard Toscanini play German and Austrian music during his two concerts there with the New York Philharmonic in 1930; nonetheless, he wished to confront the orchestra on its own ground. Therefore, he chose Mozart's 'Haffner' Symphony, Brahms's 'Haydn' Variations, Beethoven's Seventh Symphony and the *Meistersinger* Prelude for his first concert, which took place on 24 October. (There was the traditional public dress rehearsal on the 23rd.) Toscanini had arrived in Vienna on the morning of the 20th, after a tiring trip from Paris in a sleeping-car. He asked Burghauser to postpone that day's rehearsal; but Burghauser requested that he at least rehearse for a few minutes, to forestall any rumours of trouble. This he agreed to do. After that abbreviated rehearsal and two more of normal length he was satisfied. Burghauser described Toscanini's impact on the orchestra to Haggin:

'Although I had known the orchestra more than twenty years—fifteen years as a member, and many more as a young student—I never had lived through the phenomenon of such a superhuman concentration as it showed at these rehearsals. ... The orchestra, which had been day in, day out with Strauss, Weingartner, Bruno Walter, by then also Klemperer, with this ensemble of the greatest talent of the world—the orchestra, with Toscanini, realized this was the climax of every musician's experience. Not only because he was superior to other conductors—which was taken for granted; but because he made us *superior to ourselves*—which was the phenomenon that was practically unexplainable. ... This was the essence; and also that the effect with the old Beethoven Seventh, which everyone of us knew in his sleep, and with the Brahms and the Mozart, was that they were *as newly created for us.*'[54]

Violinist Felix Galimir, who was then a student at the Conservatory, told Haggin that he had managed to sneak into one of Toscanini's rehearsals. 'And *before* the rehearsal—this was a historic event—all the violinists of the Vienna Philharmonic were actually practising their part—which had never happened since Gustav Mahler left!'[55]

Public and critical reaction was extraordinary. Critic Ernst Decsey wrote, at the end of an exultant review:

It was the great Italian artist who honoured our German masters and brought the Philharmonic musicians to a hitherto unachieved triumph. Their season began in the most auspicious way; only it will be rather hard for Toscanini's successors on the Philharmonic podium, since everyone will be measured against his vastness, everyone will be compared to what is incomparable.'

His second concert (29 October) offered Cherubini's *Anacréon* Overture, Brahms's Third Symphony, *La Mer* and *The Pines of Rome*. The reaction was the same—accompanied by astonishment, in the case of the Brahms symphony, that a Catholic from the sunny south could so thoroughly understand a Protestant from the cloudy north. (This idiotic nationalistic idea persists even today in much music criticism.) The first programme was taken to Budapest on the 30th. By the time Burghauser said goodbye to Toscanini in Vienna the next day, he had secured his promise to repeat the two concerts at Salzburg the following summer, and to conduct again in Vienna the next autumn.

After spending about three weeks at home Toscanini and Signora Carla again left Milan, this time for completely unfamiliar territory. Tullio Voghera, who had been on Toscanini's coaching staff at the Metropolitan, was now chorus master of Stockholm's Royal Theatre. His wife, Iwa, a singer, was the daughter of Tore Aulin, a well-known Swedish musician. Stockholm's *Konsertföreningens Orkester* (Concert Society Orchestra—now the Stockholm Philharmonic) had sent the Vogheras on a diplomatic mission to Italy in May, to convince Toscanini to accept an invitation to conduct the orchestra in the autumn. After inquiring about the size and quality of the orchestra Toscanini agreed to go to Stockholm. 'Your fee?' asked Voghera hesitantly . . . 'I'm incapable of making a contract,' replied Toscanini. That end of the matter was eventually handled by the orchestra and Signora Carla.[56]

His visit produced incredible excitement in Stockholm. The city's largest department store, NK, carried window displays about him, the newspapers went wild, people talked about him in trams and on the streets, and he was even mentioned in popular theatrical revues. Mrs Voghera says that the rehearsals went smoothly, and that her husband acted as interpreter when Italian musical terminology was insufficient.

'After the second rehearsal a shadow came over the Maestro's face and he hesitantly came out with a question: "Do all Swedes have such uninterested looks on their faces? I wonder if they understand me. Their faces show so little reaction." We laughed and explained . . . that that is just a part of the Nordic temperament: people don't show what they feel.'[57]

The Stockholm concerts took place on 29 November and 4 December, and Toscanini took the orchestra to Copenhagen for a concert on the 3rd. He liked the orchestra and agreed to return the following year.

A reporter for a Swedish weekly, *Vecko-Journalen*, received permission to attend a rehearsal. While present, he talked to Carla Toscanini, Mrs Voghera and —afterwards—the orchestra's principal cellist. He asked Signora Carla if her husband was shy.

' "No, not if one understands how to approach him in the right way. He lives only for his art. If he has the public with him, he feels it in the air; but he doesn't value applause very highly, still less empty flattery and false opinions—not to speak of photographers with flashbulbs. . . ."

"Yes," says Mrs. Voghera, "many people have said that he is falsely modest, but that isn't true. Toscanini is the most human and natural creature you can imagine, amiable and without airs. . . . Last evening, who but Toscanini was sitting at our place, pasting postage stamps with the children and telling fairy tales!"

"His life is only work, the eternal study of scores and texts," says Signora Toscanini. "Before each concert he goes over every score; he fixes it in his memory, driven by a perpetual anxiety that he has overlooked some dot or note. . . . My husband loves children: every Christmas he asks me to arrange parties with presents and every conceivable treat for our children, grand-children and friends' children. He enjoys children's artless happiness. . . ."

Carl Christiansen testifies: "Of course we were tense—the whole orchestra. . . . Certainly he is strict and demanding, but so human; that was the most impressive thing. . . . He is unbelievably careful; nevertheless he works to get a fresh and vital quality. . . ." '

Toscanini was to have conducted the San Francisco Symphony in December, but he asked to have the engagement postponed. (It never took place.) Instead, he was in Milan for Wanda's marriage to Vladimir Horowitz in December. She said that her father had warned her, 'You know very well that life with an artist is very difficult.' After a while he added: '*Moglie e buoi dei paesi tuoi*' ('Wife and cattle from your own village'); and he never said anything more on the subject.[58] That same month Toscanini received the Menuhin family, who had come to Milan for Yehudi's first concert there. He gave them a guided tour, spoke insultingly about the Fascists, convinced Moshe Menuhin to let him 'be Papa' during the concert—which meant acting as Yehudi's valet and moral support—and gave a party at his home in Yehudi's honour. The young violinist's playing impressed Toscanini even more than before, and he arranged immediately to have him play the Beethoven Concerto with him on a Philharmonic concert the following month.

The Menuhins re-encountered the Toscaninis aboard the *Rex* late in Decem-ber. Fellow shipmates also included the newly wed Horowitzes, Nathan Milstein, Gregor Piatigorsky and Molinari. It may well have been on this trip that Piati-gorsky tried to get Toscanini to play the cello for him. He wrote in his memoirs:

'I finally succeeded in luring him to my cabin. My cello, with the pin out, waited for him. He sat on a chair but when I handed him the cello he said, "No—no pin—it's a modern invention." He pushed the pin back inside. I gave him the bow and he began tuning. "The A is too high; the G is too low," he grumbled. Fifteen minutes passed and he was still tuning. I hoped he would start playing. "*O bestia, stupido*, now the D is too high!" He continued tuning until it was time to go to lunch. I never heard him play the cello.'[59]

On 11 January 1934, one week after his arrival, Toscanini opened his Philhar-monic series with the first concert in a Beethoven cycle which was scattered over the next two months. In addition to all the symphonies and various other works, it included his first performance of the *Missa Solemnis*, with soloists Rethberg, Onegin, Althouse and Pinza.

Menuhin's performances with the Philharmonic took place on 18 and 19 January. Some days earlier the boy had gone to the Hotel Astor to go over the concerto with Toscanini. At the most serene moment in the second movement, the phone rang—although Toscanini had left orders at the hotel desk that calls were not to be sent through. They continued playing; but after the third ring Toscanini got up from the piano bench, strode to the telephone with murder in his eye, and ripped it out of the wall, plaster and all. Then, as if nothing had happened, he returned to the piano, and they calmly began where they had left off.[60]

In an interview several years ago Menuhin told me:

'I remember that he was always so respectful of the score. There are several markings in the first and second movements. In the slow movement, it's on the G-string, and the bowing is marked over two bars together, tied. We discussed it at great length when we rehearsed together, and I said, "Well, I'll try taking it in one bow on the G-string". And the next day, the very afternoon of the concert, I got a message from him, handwritten, saying, "After all, I think you'd better take it in two bows on the D-string." He was very conscientious, very meticulous about every detail.'[61]

The Philharmonic's Sunday afternoon concerts were now being broadcast in many American cities, and the orchestra, pressed by its financial difficulties, invited its radio audience, as well as its subscribers and benefactors, to send any contribution they could afford. Toscanini understood the situation and co-operated, even to the extent of allowing a fund to be initiated in his name on his sixty-seventh birthday; but he was disgusted by the way in which the arts had to go begging in a country as rich as the United States. He later told New York's mayor, Fiorello La Guardia, that entertainment and radio taxes should be instituted in America, as had been done in many European countries, in order to subsidize artistic organizations. This idea was, however, anathema in the States.

The Philharmonic campaign aimed at raising $500,000; and while it was reasonably successful, the press did not refrain from remarking on Toscanini's reputedly (and in fact) enormous salary, or that this went to a man 'who does little to help American music'. This last phrase meant that Toscanini had played very little music by American composers, which was true. These composers' more recent products were generally written in idioms which were foreign to him; and works by past generations of native musicians did not interest him. But he did begin to make an attempt, and by the time his career had ended he had performed works by about twenty American composers, including Barber, Copland and

Gershwin; however, he did not feel at home in this repertoire, and the results were often unsatisfactory—as so commonly happens when performers play music out of a sense of obligation or under pressure. Furthermore, it seems rather unfair to accuse a man who was giving America one magnificent musical experience after another of doing little to help American music—or music in America, at any rate. He certainly engendered more enthusiasm for music in America than did most American composers.

The General Motors Company sponsored a Philharmonic broadcast on 11 February, in which Toscanini's soloist was Lotte Lehmann, who sang arias from *Tannhäuser* and *Fidelio*. The great German soprano had been invited to sing Eva in *Meistersinger*—in Italian—at La Scala a decade earlier; but she had heard that Toscanini was a difficult person to work with, and had declined. 'My refusal was one of the great blunders in life that can never be made good,' she said later.[62] Toscanini had heard her in the Viennese première of Strauss's *Arabella* in October 1933 and had invited her to appear with him in New York. She related that at the piano rehearsal for the concert

> 'I trembled so much that I could scarcely sing my programme. . . . But the object of my terror seemed so mild and friendly that my fears vanished and I sang with my usual freedom. Later I had the privilege of singing under his baton on various occasions. I was subjugated to his fanatical will like everybody else who came under the spell of that marvellous personality. I saw how he suffered when something was not done exactly as he wanted to have it—not from caprice, but from a relentless pursuit of the very highest perfection. He demanded absolute precision and at the same time the most complete spiritual surrender to the music. . . . And so it is always a fearful pleasure to sing under him.'[63]

Several writers have suggested that Lehmann and Toscanini became lovers. When, after the soprano's death, I wrote to her friend Frances Holden to see whether there was any correspondence between the two of them, I was told that Lehmann had destroyed the letters she had received from Toscanini, and that he was said to have done the same with her letters to him.

Having led forty-six concerts in fourteen weeks (with only one out-of-town performance) Toscanini sailed for Europe on the *Ile-de-France* on 5 May. Much of the late spring and summer was spent on the *isolino*; but he was in Paris to conduct the Orchestre Walther–Straram in a French programme on 25 and 27 May and a mixed programme on 3 and 6 June.

In July 1934 Austrian Chancellor Engelbert Dollfuss was assassinated by a pro-Nazi group who tried unsuccessfully to assume power. The country was in a period of grave instability. Burghauser says that no one believed Toscanini would fulfil his promise to conduct at Salzburg that summer. But early in August he received a telegram from Toscanini stating simply that he would arrive in ten days for rehearsals; and on 23 August he led his first performance at the Fest-spielhaus—a repetition of his first Viennese concert of the previous autumn. Three days later he conducted an all-Wagner concert with Lehmann as soloist; and a final concert on the 30th consisted of the Brahms Third Symphony and various other works.

After another stay in Italy Toscanini went to Vienna in October for more concerts with the Vienna Philharmonic. On the 10th he led a Wagner programme in which Lehmann sang the *Liebestod* from *Tristan*. She was nervous about finding her first note correctly after the Prelude, and Toscanini said he would hum it for her softly. She recalled that it was hard to get the right note from his croaking voice, but she managed somehow. 'To the end of his days he was happy that he had helped me to sing right.'[64] There was another concert on the 14th, and parts of these two programmes were combined for a performance in Prague on the 15th. Kodály's *Psalmus Hungaricus* and Beethoven's Ninth Symphony were presented in Vienna on the 21st and in Budapest the next night; and the Verdi *Requiem* was performed in memory of Dollfuss on 1 November. Working for the first time as Toscanini's rehearsal assistant in the *Psalmus* and the Ninth was twenty-two-year-old Erich Leinsdorf.

'Toscanini has taken leave of Vienna after a glorious sojourn of several weeks,' wrote Paul Stefan in a correspondence which appeared in *Musical America* on 25 November. He continued:

'... There were many who said (your correspondent among them) that they had never heard the finale of the Ninth Symphony in such marvellous clarity. The first three movements provided a great series of climaxes. Excellent, also, the impression made by the Psalmus Hungaricus in which the Budapest Chorus earned its laurels. It sang in place of the Vienna Opera Chorus because the latter declined to appear under Toscanini in order—so the accepted story runs—not to "hurt the feelings" of the opera director, Clemens Krauss. There have been those who have asserted openly that the opera director did not exactly relish the explosive successes of Toscanini in Vienna.

All sorts of little difficulties arose before Toscanini's last concert ... despite the fact that this concert was a memorial tribute of all federal theatres for Chancellor Dollfuss, a memorial event ordered by the government, itself, and one for which Toscanini accepted the conductorship without any compensation. Finally, after delays and postponements of three days, the concert took place on November 1 (a holiday in this country) before noon. ... It was the crowning moment of his Viennese activities, all the members of the government were present. ...'

The 'little difficulties', according to what Burghauser told Haggin, began with Toscanini's being denied entrance to the Opera for the first rehearsal ('No stranger may enter here!' said the doorman), and continued with the failure of

the Opera's directorate to send a rehearsal pianist to Toscanini's first rehearsal
with the solo soprano.

'Toscanini himself had to sit down at the piano, put his pince-nez on his nose,
and begin to play for the soprano. . . . Soon after they began, Toscanini
stopped and asked her to sing a phrase in one breath, instead of breaking it to
take breath; and she answered that she was accustomed to doing it her way, and
showed him her score in which Bruno Walter had marked it to be sung that
way. Toscanini, still quiet, told her she would have to sing it as he asked. There
were a few more exchanges, increasing the danger of a storm; and then an
abrupt movement of Toscanini's head caused his pince-nez to fall off his nose
to the floor. Before Burghauser could get there, Toscanini was on the floor
groping nearsightedly for the pince-nez, which he found; and sitting down
again he put it back on his nose, only to discover that he could see nothing
because the lenses had fallen out. In exasperation and fury he jumped up and
stamped his feet; and at the terrible sound of the lenses being crushed, the
soprano burst into tears and fled from the room.'[65]

It was this incident which caused the three-day delay, because a new soprano had
to be found. The replacement, Anna Bathy, was also singing the *Requiem* in
Budapest at the time and had to fly back and forth to accommodate rehearsals and
performances in both cities—in that blessed day when 'winged' singers were a
very rare phenomenon.

Toscanini's conducting the Verdi *Requiem* in memory of Dollfuss was a
strange act on the part of a convinced democrat. Since becoming Chancellor in
1932 Dollfuss, who belonged to the Christian Socialist Movement, had abolished
parliament, abrogated the constitution, governed by emergency decree, allied
Austria with Italy (Dollfuss and Mussolini were trying to use each other as
'buffers' against Hitler), savagely put down a rebellion by Social Democrats and
workers in February 1934, and declared that party illegal. In short, he governed
like any other dictator. It could be said in Dollfuss's favour that he did not adopt
an anti-Semitic policy, and the attempted Nazi *coup* which resulted in Dollfuss's
death was deplorable. Clearly, for Toscanini Dollfuss symbolized opposition to
Hitler's Germany; but to honour the dead Chancellor with a performance of the
Verdi *Requiem* seems, today, an incredibly naive and ill-advised action—and one
imagines that it must have disappointed a considerable segment of the Austrian
population.

In thanks for the performance, the new Austrian Chancellor, Kurt von
Schuschnigg, gave Toscanini a copy of the first edition piano-vocal score of
Fidelio, which contained Beethoven's inscription to his landlord, Baron
Pasqualati, and some corrections in the composer's hand.

He returned to Milan for a few days—long enough to complain that La Scala
was wasting tax money by commissioning Respighi to do a worthless adaptation

of Monteverdi's *Orfeo*—then left for Paris to conduct concerts on 15, 16, 22 and 23 November which included three performances of the Beethoven Ninth as well as Brahms's Fourth Symphony and works by four other composers. The Orchestre Walther-Straram also performed at Brussels' Palais des Beaux-Arts under his direction on 19 and 20 November.

From Paris he proceeded directly to Stockholm, where he conducted music of Mozart, Brahms, Mendelssohn, Sibelius and Rossini on the 28th and, four nights later, the 'Eroica' and Wagner excerpts. People queued all night in order to obtain tickets to the concerts; and as in 1933 parts of the second concert were broadcast.

Toscanini and his wife returned to Milan for the holidays, made especially pleasant by the presence of Sonia Horowitz, their granddaughter born in October. They then left for New York on the *Conte di Savoia*, arriving on 17 January.

During Toscanini's absence a proposal had been made to merge the Philharmonic and the Metropolitan Opera. This was a cost-cutting project resulting from the economic strain of the Depression. The Metropolitan orchestra would be replaced by the Philharmonic, which would play both a reduced opera season and a reduced concert season at the opera house, under the artistic direction of Toscanini. Naturally, the chorus, *corps de ballet* and above all the orchestra at the Metropolitan were incensed at the news, which would mean reduced employment for some and dismissal for others. Zirato had been dispatched to Milan in December to present the idea to Toscanini, and had cabled Judson:

'Had several talks with the Maestro. . . . He believes the merger would not help either organization artistically. Giving concerts at the Metropolitan, the Philharmonic would lower its standards achieved so far. He believes it impossible that only forty performances of ten operas would satisfy the public. Anyway, he never could recommend giving concerts at the Metropolitan on account of the acoustic conditions there, despite proposed stage improvements. The Maestro, however, wishes you to tell the members of the board that this honest opinion should not carry any weight in their minds, or arrest any negotiations if they still consider advantageous a merger with the Metropolitan.'[66]

The board could not have failed to realize that were they to accept the proposed amalgamation, they would lose Toscanini; and although they lost him not long afterwards anyway, it is obvious that, put into practice, the plan would have had a disastrously limiting effect on New York's musical life.

His 1935 Philharmonic series opened on 24 January—Bruckner, and a Respighi Bach arrangement. The second programme included Castelnuovo-Tedesco's cello concerto with Piatigorsky as soloist. The cellist says that he had just arrived in New York after a terrible crossing—cold, fever and seasickness—

when he received a telephone call from Toscanini to come and read through the score with him immediately. As Piatigorsky was taking his cello out of its case, Toscanini

'. . . moved towards me, closer and closer, until his face almost touched mine. He stared at me scrutinizingly with his near-blind eyes, as if I were a terrible misprint in a score. He twisted his moustache, shook his head, and said, "Bad, very bad. Hemorrhoids again? Didn't you try the medicine I gave you in Milano? It helped Puccini. Your face is green," he concluded gravely.
. . . Maestro banged on the piano in a true Kapellmeister manner. He spoke and he sang, and his spontaneity and vigour carried me away. By the end of our long and exhilarating session I had miraculously regained my strength, and I returned to the hotel in an exuberant frame of mind.'[67]

Toscanini directed thirty-seven Philharmonic concerts, including perform-ances in Hartford and Providence. The highlight of the series was a six-part Brahms cycle which contained all the symphonies, the First Piano Concerto with Horowitz, the Double Concerto with Piastro and principal cellist Alfred Wallenstein, the Violin Concerto with Heifetz, the *German Requiem* with Elisabeth Rethberg and Friedrich Schorr, and most of the other orchestral compositions. (The Second Piano Concerto was scheduled with Gabilowitsch; but Toscanini had heard him play the work with the National Orchestral Association some weeks earlier and had decided that their views of it were so different that the performance should be cancelled.) Toscanini ended the Philharmonic season with three performances of the *Missa Solemnis*.

He and his wife left New York on 2 May and returned to Italy. Soon after-wards, however, they found themselves travelling again: he had agreed to participate in the BBC Symphony's Summer Music Festival—his first appear-ance with a British orchestra. Sir Adrian Boult, who was then the BBC's musical director, has confessed how nervous he was about this new guest conductor. He accompanied Toscanini to the podium at the first rehearsal:

'I introduced the orchestra to him, and said something about our achieving the desire of every one of us, using the word "greatest". At this the Maestro gave me a hearty thump on the shoulders: "No, no, no, no, no. Not that at all: just an honest musician." So we all laughed and I left them to it . . . The two middle movements of the Brahms E minor went through without interruption. "Bene, bene, bene," he said, "just three things." He then found three passages, put them right, and went straight on. Toscanini never believed in "ploughing through" after a thing was once right. . . .
Needless to say, the orchestra worshipped the Maestro from the first rehearsal. . . . Alas, one person was not amused: Koussevitzky. The over-whelming reaction of the London public to Toscanini in 1935 had, of course,

faded out the memory of his own fine contribution to that Festival. It was obviously not practical politics to invite them both again, and I wonder whether I was ever forgiven.'[68]

In addition to the Brahms Fourth Symphony, Toscanini's first BBC programme (3 June) included works by Cherubini and Wagner, and Elgar's 'Enigma' Variations. This last piece was the only one which received adverse criticism in the press: Toscanini's performance was considered 'un-English'. Sir Landon Ronald, well-known conductor and friend of Elgar, dismissed this opinion in a letter which appeared in *The Times* on 6 June:

'This great conductor rendered the work exactly as Elgar intended, and the composer's idiom has obviously no secret for Toscanini. Some of the best performances I have ever heard were from the composer himself, but Toscanini excelled because he has a genius for conducting and Elgar had not.'

Conductor John Barbirolli, whose father and uncle had played in the Scala pit with Toscanini at the world première of *Otello*, wrote to his future wife, oboist Evelyn Rothwell:

'The Toscanini concert was grand. I was at rehearsal too and was much moved by his attitude to music, which is one of the greatest sincerity, humility and ideal of service. It is extraordinary how a man of such individual power can yet create the illusion that there is nothing coming between you and the music. A lovely tone quality he gets, and such endless lines of phrase, and all with such impeccable taste and dignity. The orchestra played well for him, strings especially, but the intonation was frankly *bad*. I really cannot understand it.'[69]

And in a subsequent letter:

'Had rather a wonderful day yesterday. The two hours spent with Toscanini were lovely. He talked much of Father and their times together, also I was able to ask him many things about the licence permissible in Verdi operas, and very relieved to find I was perfectly right in the stand I had taken in this matter. On telling him of some of the things I had heard at Covent Garden under so-called distinguished Italian conductors he proceeded to describe them as men who are not only ignorant, but traitors to music. . . . But the most moving thing of all was the man's great simplicity and burning sincerity in his love of music. . . . He was so sweet to me, and to hear him call me "Caro Maestro" tickled me to death. I got him on to the subject of Glyndebourne to tell him about you, and apparently he had never heard of a female oboe player for he called it a "cosa buffa" (comic thing). . . . The orchestra played better last night . . . The Brahms and Wagner were unforgettable. Such nobility of music-making becomes a great inspiration . . .'[70]

While in London, Toscanini received a diplomatic emissary from the New York Philharmonic—his assistant conductor Hans Lange. At that time the musicians' union in New York was making demands of the board which were causing the Philharmonic's administrators to consider reducing the size of the ensemble from 110 to 95. Lange had been instructed to place the matter before Toscanini, and to try to convince him that the reduction would not be artistically harmful; but Toscanini immediately decided that the idea was a bad one. Lange wrote Zirato on 7 June:

> 'It is his opinion that if the Board of Directors cannot raise the money to comply with the demands of the Union they should rather disband the whole orchestra than reduce it. Maestro considers the proposal . . . a very inartistic one. Especially the letting out of the fourth wind instruments . . . Besides all this, Maestro is of the opinion that letting out of so many is a very *inhuman* and unjust action, to which he never will agree. Since it is not the fault of the members of the orchestra, but the fault of the Union that this situation has come about, he does not want the poor musicians to suffer for it. Especially not in times like these, where there is no hope for them to get other engagements.
>
> His decision is : If the Board . . . finds ways and means to keep the orchestra at its full strength, he will come and conduct next season. If that is not possible and a reduction should take place, he would prefer to stay in Europe and will *not* come to America.'[71]

This letter was read and approved by Toscanini. In a separate, private letter, Lange told Zirato:

> 'You made my life miserable. . . . Instead of enjoying my vacation I have to fight with Maestro. Hell!!! He has trouble with his arm again since yesterday and you know how irritable he is when that happens. Now I have written all to you and I am begging you to try your best to comply with his wishes. I am very much afraid that we are going to lose him otherwise. He seems to like now guest conducting and hates a steady position. He is tired and he wants a change.
>
> The concerts have been an unbelievable success. The audience is just crazy. London tries hard to get him for a longer time, he likes the orchestra and they pay him more than New York (at least the papers say so). It is a dangerous situation, Bruno. For heaven's sake, do your best in New York and I do my best here to persuade him not to leave us flat. . . .'[72]

On 11 June Toscanini cabled the Philharmonic:

> 'I cannot understand why Philharmonic Board has not the courage to fight to the limit in order to have its sacred rights recognized instead of yielding and

therefore sacrificing so many musicians who will increase unemployment. If you insist in reducing orchestra I will have to resign!'[73]

Despite the added annoyances of this problem and his painful arm, he was able to conduct all four of his London concerts, and with great success, as Lange's letter indicates. According to Boult, Toscanini agreed to return to London for eight concerts in 1936, and a fee was set:

'As the correspondence went on it seemed that seven concerts would form a better pattern and this was agreed. Soon after this the contract was sent to the Maestro, and an unimaginative accountant, loyal to the BBC, filled it in for seven-eighths of the originally agreed fee . . . Toscanini's mind did not work like that. Was it likely that a great artist's would? Correspondence abruptly ceased. We could not understand why, but when we found out the reason for his sudden silence it was too late.'[74]

He was able to spend a little time on the *isolino* following the London excursion, and was surrounded there by his entire family: his wife; his son Walter with *his* wife, ballerina Cia Fornaroli, and their six-year-old son Walfredo; his daughter Wally, by then Countess Castelbarco, with her husband and daughter Emanuela; and of course the Horowitzes with their little Sonia. Conductor Artur Rodzinski and his wife, Halina, visited them at this time, and Toscanini told them that he was planning to leave the Philharmonic before long. '*Sono stufo e sono stanco!*' ('I'm fed up and I'm tired!') he said.[75]

Stufo and *stanco* were adjectives he may have applied to himself; but those are the last words anyone who saw him .at work then or who has heard his recordings from that period would have used to describe him. Tape transfers exist of the *Missa Solemnis* he had led in New York the previous April, of the Brahms's Fourth with the BBC, and so on. The intellect which shapes them and the energy which propels them are surpassed by no other conductor I know— not even by Toscanini himself later in his life. These performances are of breathtaking depth and majesty; they are relaxed and flexible, yet precise and fluent. And further revelations were about to take place at Salzburg.

At the time of his Salzburg concerts in 1934 the festival's administration had approached him about conducting an opera there the following year; and the work proposed had been *Fidelio*. Toscanini assented—but on condition that he also be permitted to lead a production of *Falstaff*. Clemens Krauss, who had created difficulties with the Verdi *Requiem*, decided to do the same with the *Falstaff* plan by scheduling a *Falstaff* production of his own for Vienna (in German). This, in accordance with custom, would be transferred to Salzburg, conductor and all. It was obvious that Krauss was engaging in a test of strength: were the administrators more interested in having Krauss as musical director of the Staatsoper, or in having Toscanini as guest conductor in Salzburg? Toscanini was asked whether he would be willing to replace *Falstaff* with another opera; but he replied, 'No *Falstaff*, no Toscanini.' It was Chancellor Schuschnigg who decided that *Falstaff* would be conducted in Salzburg by Toscanini; and when, in December 1934, Furtwängler resigned as director of the Berlin Staatsoper in protest over action taken by the Nazis against Hindemith, Krauss, who felt that the golden future lay with Hitler, abandoned Vienna (and Salzburg with it) for Berlin.

Most of the singers Toscanini engaged for the Salzburg *Falstaff* were members of his old Scala cast: Nessi as Bardolph, Autori as Pistol, Vasari as Meg and, above all, Stabile as Falstaff. Badà was Cajus, a rôle he had sung with Toscanini at Busseto in 1913; and all but three of the remaining singers had worked with him at La Scala. Guido Salvini received the title of stage director, although Burghauser says that Toscanini did most of the directing himself; Margarete Wallmann, who was then Burghauser's wife, was responsible for the choreography in the last act; and the sets were the ones Robert Kautsky had designed for Krauss's Viennese production. One of these nearly caused a disaster. In Vienna the previous autumn, Toscanini, on his way to a choral rehearsal for the Verdi *Requiem* in the Staatsoper, had passed through the auditorium, where a stage rehearsal of the first scene of Act III of *Falstaff* was under way; and he had been outraged to see Falstaff not drying himself in the sun in front of the Garter Inn, as Verdi prescribes, but in bed, under a pile of blankets. He informed Burghauser that if this set were to appear in Salzburg he would walk out. Burghauser informed the proper authorities; but the set did appear in Salzburg, causing Toscanini to walk out; and only a frantic effort that produced an acceptable set within twenty-four hours brought him back to the theatre.

Despite this and other difficulties, the production was an extraordinary one. Haggin reports Burghauser's saying that Weingartner, then seventy-two, 'leapt' into the pit after the first act and exclaimed to the orchestra: 'Children, such perfection I have never experienced or dreamed of.'[76] Leinsdorf says that although the opening (29 July) was a 'performance of unmatchable perfection', Toscanini asked him to get the cast together for a piano rehearsal one day before the second performance (3 August). He relates that after Toscanini and the singers had sat around telling stories for an hour, the Maestro had cheerfully dismissed everyone. When the young man questioned him about this afterwards, Toscanini told him that it was important to remind the cast—even without saying a word about it—that a performance was about to take place, to bring them into the right state of mind. ' "Since all went well at the première, there was nothing for us to rehearse." '[77]

French critic Emile Vuillermoz wrote:

'Toscanini with *Falstaff* is a medium bringing Verdi back from the hereafter. Barely a few weeks ago I heard this score at the Opéra, interpreted by an

Italian company and a famous maestro. Well! At Salzburg I had the dumb-
founding impression of being present at the first performance of an unpublished work. Truly, I did not know *Falstaff* . . .'[78]

The *Fidelio* cast included Andreas von Rösler as Florestan and Lehmann as
Leonore. She wrote of the new experience of working with Toscanini in the
theatre:

'. . . The fanatical frenzy of this extraordinary personality compels all who
work under him to give their utmost. He won't stand any slackness or "routine
work". Every rehearsal is like the actual performance to him, and every performance is a "festival performance". . . . It amazed me to find how a pure
musician like him works from the dramatic text. A vividly acted performance
is as important to him as a complete realization of the music. . . . Nothing
escapes that keen, relentless eye. . . .

His *Fidelio*—impregnated with intense tragedy—was a tremendous and
sensational success. . . . Rehearsals with him were a perpetual "shaking and
quaking in anguish and pain. . . ." But what a compensation that *Fidelio*
was!'[79]

Lehmann was already forty-seven at that time, and she had some problems
with the high notes in Leonore's great first act aria. Leinsdorf has described the
situation:

'Toscanini . . . wanted to spare her anxiety and attempted to provide relief.
First he proposed to transpose the entire piece, and I was assigned to read
through it with the orchestra in a special rehearsal on the day of the second
repeat performance. . . . After performing the aria transposed, Maestro felt, as
we all did, that the recitative had suffered in the lower key, particularly
Leonore's phrase "*Da leuchtet mir ein Farbenbogen*", which came off poorly in
B major. . . . To remedy this and still help Lotte, Toscanini then devised a
clever transitory harmony that left the entire recitative in the original key and
yet transposed the aria into E flat. There were plenty of raised eyebrows
over such interference with Beethoven . . . While the whole enterprise was
open to legitimate criticism, I found it a document for Toscanini's approach
to a complex masterwork. . . . He was a pragmatist and not a stickler for the
printed dot on the i. And it showed that he went to great lengths to
accommodate an artist whom he admired and appreciated.'[80]

The last *Fidelio* performance of the summer (31 August) was broadcast, and
the first part of it (through Leonore's aria) was received via shortwave in America.
An extremely poor quality recording exists of this whole segment—unfortunately
unavailable commercially; yet even on the basis of this horrible recording it is
obvious that this was an outstanding *Fidelio*. It is quite unlike the concert version

which Toscanini conducted with the NBC Symphony in 1944 and which is available on commercial records. The pacing is generally much broader in the Salzburg version, the singing is better and the playing does not have the occasional tenseness which the NBC betrays; but above all, there is a sustained and monumental dramatic power (no doubt helped by the fact that it comes directly from the theatre) which one experiences with astonishment. Some highlights: the shock of the two groups of Allegro bars and the contrast of the incredibly slow and increasingly tense sextuplet bars in the introduction of the Overture; the full, rich and sustained quality of the lower strings in the opening bars of the Quartet (No. 3), and the perfection of detail in the phrasing of both singers and orchestra; the electric tension of Pizarro's aria (No. 7), which transforms the prison governor from a vaudeville villain into a monster; and of course Leonore's aria, which is breathtaking in every respect, excepting the offensive harmonic change mentioned above. It begins with barely a moment's wait after the Pizarro–Rocco duet; the remarkable expressiveness of the recitative is followed by a *'Komm, Hoffnung'* of equally remarkable breadth and warmth; Lehmann's singing is gripping and the orchestra's playing excellent; and the *'Ich folg' dem innern Triebe'* reaches a level of intensity which is almost unbearable. One hopes that someday, somewhere, a complete and somewhat better recording of this production will be discovered. (Fred Gaisberg, the British recording pioneer, tried to convince Toscanini to make commercial recordings of the Salzburg operas, as well as to do further symphonic recordings in England, but Toscanini was not interested. Furthermore, Gaisberg's biographer, J.N. Moore, reports that Toscanini told Gaisberg that the New York Philharmonic paid him an annual $20,000 retainer so that he would not make recordings elsewhere[81]— but surely it must have been RCA Victor, if anyone, and not the Philharmonic, who paid this fee. We read elsewhere that Toscanini's wife and daughters tried to convince him to make more recordings during this period; and they seem to have won at least a partial victory by 1936, from which point he began to record more frequently.)

In addition to the four performances of *Falstaff* and four of *Fidelio*, Toscanini also conducted the Vienna Philharmonic in three concerts at Salzburg in August. The repertoire ranged from Handel to Debussy. In September the Toscaninis returned to Italy.

Some time earlier, when Barbirolli had told him that he looked very well, Toscanini's immediate comeback had been: 'My boy, five years *without* opera.'[82] Toscanini must have been tired after the Salzburg exertions, despite the fact that he had rented a pleasant villa at nearby Liefering and that he was able to spend time in the company of Bruno Walter, Stefan Zweig, Thomas Mann and quite a few Italian and American friends who had come to Salzburg in order to hear him and be with him. This tiredness and his recurring shoulder problem certainly had not put him in a positive frame of mind, when he was routinely informed by the New York Philharmonic that Beecham had been engaged as one of the guest conductors for the coming season. He cabled Zirato protesting against the engagement, which had been made without his approval. (He was, after all, the musical director.) And he added, 'Please inform the Board of Directors not to count on me for season after next.'[83]

It has been suggested that Toscanini was jealous of Beecham. This is an absurdity. Conductors who were at least of Beecham's stature—Walter, Klemperer, Kleiber, *et al.*—had been engaged repeatedly during Toscanini's directorship. Beecham had guest conducted during the 1931–2 season; and whether because of Van Praag's less than enthusiastic reports about him ('I am not quite in favour of Sir Beecham's [sic] idea of rehearsing') or because on his return he had felt that the orchestra's playing was not as disciplined as he had left it and had blamed this, rightly or wrongly, on Beecham, the fact remains that Toscanini did not wish to have him engaged. In December there had been the proposed Metropolitan merger, and in June the proposed reduction of the Philharmonic's personnel—both of which Toscanini had regarded as preposterous. Although these matters had been resolved to his satisfaction, he was not one to forget about such sins; and he considered the Beecham engagement the final offence.

Meanwhile, his stays in Italy were becoming less and less pleasant because of the political situation, and it was becoming ever clearer that sooner or later he would have to leave permanently. Here is a transcript of part of a phone conversation between Toscanini and a lady friend, identified only as Signora Ada, on 19 October 1935—shortly after the government had put a ban on all foreign newspapers:

'Toscanini: It's a really dirty piece of work to put a country in this situation! It's unheard of that a person can't read the paper he wants to and has to believe everything that they print! It's something from another planet! And it isn't even clever, because they will generate still more doubts. To force a people in this way—with a slip-knot at its throat! . . . You have to read and know only what they want—there must be only one head! This is no longer living!

Ada: It's frightful! Worse than Russia! In the past few days the newsstands already had orders not to display foreign papers. . . . You can see that they're plotting something.

T: No, it's only this: the people must be kept in complete ignorance . . .

A: It gives you a sense of suffocation.

T: I can't wait to leave, because I can't stand it any longer! These things shock me . . . To see people enslaved in this way! Talk about black slavery . . . We are white slaves.

A: Don't say that you want to leave. If you weren't here to keep me from it, I too would leave tomorrow. . . .

T: . . . You have to think the way *that* head thinks... And I'll never think the way he thinks... I never have thought that way! I was weak only for a moment, and now I'm ashamed of myself! You can only read their newspaper—because you can say that in Italy there exists only one newspaper. . . . And yet there are people who don't feel anything, who live like this... For me, though, it's a suffering that annihilates me.'

There is a notation on this government transcript: 'This proves what we already knew—that Toscanini is unchangeable.'[84]

He was in Paris in November to conduct two concerts (19th and 26th) at the Opéra which were broadcast all over Europe. From there he proceeded to Vienna for a series of performances (1, 7, 8, 15 December; 3 December in Budapest) which included the 'Eroica', Brahms's *German Requiem* and Schubert's 'Great C Major' Symphony. Burghauser spoke at length to Haggin about Toscanini's untraditional approach to the Schubert Symphony; I talked with both Burghauser and Otto Strasser, who played principal second violin in the orchestra, and they said that the orchestra members were completely convinced by this performance, whereas they were not so convinced by some of Toscanini's Mozart performances.

By the end of December Toscanini was in Monaco, where he conducted the Monte Carlo Orchestra on 1 January 1936 in works of Beethoven, Debussy, Wagner and Verdi. Critic Ernest Newman, who had written one of the best-known Wagner biographies, was also present and met Toscanini, whom he greatly admired. After their first conversation, Newman reported to his wife: 'What a brain! What a fascinating man! I wish I had known him years ago. *There* is someone I can listen to and talk to with pleasure.' The Newmans attended some of Toscanini's rehearsals.[85]

Between 23 January and 29 April Toscanini led thirty-eight Philharmonic concerts in New York and two out-of-town performances. He also 'underwent' his first recording sessions since 1929: three Wagner pieces, the Beethoven Seventh, Brahms's 'Haydn' Variations and two Rossini overtures. All rank among the great classic Toscanini recordings, and document the most extraordinary of all the realizations of the distinctive, unique 'Toscanini sound' Klemperer spoke of—Toscanini's realization of it with the New York Philharmonic. The season's soloists included Casadesus in the Brahms Second Piano Concerto, Serkin making his American début in the Beethoven Fourth and Mozart B-flat (K. 595), and Milstein in the Mendelssohn Violin Concerto.

On his arrival in America Toscanini had reconsidered his resignation from the Philharmonic, and had discussed with Zirato the possibility of leading a reduced series—four to six weeks—during the 1936–7 season. By early February, however, the Philharmonic's gruelling schedule had already tired him; so he made up his mind to resign after all, and informed the management. As much pressure as possible was exerted upon him by all concerned, but Toscanini remained adamant. Mackay made the announcement to the board on 12 February, and a letter of regret was delivered to Toscanini that same evening.[86]

A search began at once to find a successor. His own first recommendation was to make Furtwängler principal conductor and to have Rodzinski share the season with him. Furtwängler was offered the job and willingly accepted; but a scandal broke out immediately over his political affiliations in Germany. Furtwängler was never a member of the Nazi party and he helped in saving many German Jewish musicians and their families, often at great personal risk. In 1933, however, he had delivered what Alban Berg called 'a Nazi-inspired speech which made me depressed all day' at a Brahms festival, and had conducted the *Egmont* Overture at the opening of the *Reichskulturkammer* on 15 November, at which Goebbels made a speech. In 1934 he had toured Italy with the Berlin Philharmonic, and had been received by Mussolini and given a decoration; in 1935 he had conducted a *Winterhilfe* concert at which he was photographed shaking hands with Hitler,[87] and in 1936 he had agreed to return to the Bayreuth festival for the first time in five years. Because of these things, his appointment created an uproar in New York, especially since a great percentage of both the orchestra and the audience was Jewish. Toscanini must have been aware of Furtwängler's activities in Germany, and he must also have known that the reaction in New York would not be positive. Personally, I believe that he recommended Furtwängler as his successor not only because he held him in high esteem as an artist, but also because he wished to give him a clear alternative to remaining in Germany. Furtwängler, however, could not face giving up his country (his widow, Elisabeth Furtwängler, told me that Goebbels had warned her husband that if he conducted in countries other than those okayed by the German government, he would not be allowed to return to Germany); and so, when the critical moment arrived, he felt compelled to withdraw from the Philharmonic post.

Toscanini's next suggestion for principal conductor was Fritz Busch, a musician whom he respected very much and who was above suspicion on the Nazi question. Busch felt honoured; but he was happy conducting in Copenhagen and did not want the responsibilities and pressures of the Philharmonic position. He turned it down with thanks. A final decision on the succession was postponed because the Philharmonic had problems which were even more pressing: economic survival, union–management disputes, falling subscriptions—only Toscanini's concerts drew the public in consistently large numbers—and possible player resignations in the wake of Toscanini's departure. (Mass resignations did not take place, because the employment situation was very difficult at the time.)

A special farewell concert was arranged for 29 April, and Toscanini requested that all proceeds be divided among the musicians, staff, Carnegie Hall personnel and the Musicians' Emergency Fund. The programme consisted of Beethoven's

Leonore Overture No. 1 and Violin Concerto (with Heifetz), and four Wagner pieces. The concert was announced in the morning papers on 16 March, and by one in the afternoon the tickets had all been sold. Nearly $25,000 was raised. On the day of the concert people began lining up at 7 a.m. for the 140 standing-room tickets which would go on sale more than thirteen hours later. By the time the doors opened at 8.06, there were 5,000 people in line, and pandemonium broke out as the crowd swept two mounted policemen back against the wall and struggled with fifty other officers. A few of the fortunate 140 opened a fire-escape door and let in an additional 150 people before police were able to stop the leak.

Toscanini received frenzied applause before and after each piece; but after the very last work—the 'Ride of the Valkyries'—a reporter rushed to the stage and snapped a picture of him. The flash directly in front of his weak eyes nearly blinded him, if only temporarily, and he rushed from the stage, not to return.

When he recovered he was presented, backstage, with gifts from the board, including a Beethoven letter dated 1814. Then he returned to the Astor, where he gave a party for the orchestra members and their wives. The next day he received a telegram of regret and appreciation from President Roosevelt, to which he replied gratefully. On 2 May he departed aboard the S.S. *Champlain*, after having issued a rare press statement in which he thanked the Philharmonic, its board and its public, and bade goodbye to America.[88]

In Paris, Toscanini conducted a special concert of French music at the Salle Pleyel on 22 May, to raise money for a monument to Saint-Saëns. After staying at least two more weeks in Paris he returned to Italy where, on 30 June, he passed the fiftieth anniversary of his conducting début.

His next engagement was at Salzburg in July and August. Something had upset him about the festival in the spring, because we find Bruno Walter writing him on 1 June—when they were both in Paris:

'I am deeply moved and agitated by what I have heard. I can no longer imagine Salzburg without you. Salzburg needs you, we all need you. I am sure that your reasons are very strong—but I am also sure that the fault of Kerber [the festival director] or others is nothing other than that Austrian "laisser aller" which is certainly unacceptable but which—at the same time—is far from being a bad intention and very far from being a lack of comprehension or of respect for you.

I beg you with all my heart to let me know what must be done to satisfy you; and I shall take it upon myself to see to it that everything is done. Tomorrow, Tuesday, I shall be terribly busy. But Wednesday afternoon I shall be able to free myself to visit you and to learn what your conditions are.

You know better than I—and it will be remembered from last summer—that Salzburg is perhaps the last non-political place where art still has a roof over its head. Do not leave this place—I repeat that we need you. . . .'[89]

The situation appears not to have been settled very easily: Walter had to interrupt his holiday at Sils Maria to go to Milan to intercede with Toscanini on
behalf of the Austrian Minister of Education. In the end, Toscanini did agree to
return.

Besides *Fidelio* and *Falstaff*, he conducted *Meistersinger* in 1936. He was to
have led Wagner's comedy at Bayreuth in 1933; now, any German who wanted
to hear his production of it had to go to Austria.

A grave problem arose during the rehearsals when Toscanini became dissatisfied with Friedrich Schorr, the bass-baritone whom he had engaged for the rôle
of Hans Sachs. Schorr had sung in Brahms's *German Requiem* with him in New
York a year earlier; nevertheless, as preparations went on, Toscanini was
increasingly convinced that the part of Sachs was absolutely wrong for him. They
did not agree on anything and Schorr would not accept his suggestions and
demands. Eventually Toscanini sent the singer a letter asking him to withdraw,
and word was given out that Schorr was indisposed. He was replaced by Hans
Hermann Nissen.

Eva was sung by Lehmann and Walther by Charles Kullmann. Taubman says
that at one ensemble rehearsal, Toscanini shouted at Kullmann from the pit:
' "Stand up straight. You're playing a nobleman." Kullmann squared his
shoulders and drew himself up, murmuring, "I thought he was nearsighted." '[90]
Burghauser talked to Haggin about this production:

'His *Meistersinger* lasted fully five hours; but it *seemed* fast because it was so
lively in expression. For example, at the beginning of Act 3, in the scene of
David and Sachs, he made us play with a much lighter tone than we were
accustomed to produce. He said: *"Come una commedia, non tragedia."* ... The
first and third acts, you could say, were of course the highest standard, but
well-known standard, no surprises—convincing, and yet what we were well
acquainted with—except for the scene ... which I mentioned.... *But—the
second act*—was the literally unheard-of! The poetry of what went on with
Sachs and Eva! ... And again those subtle modifications of tempo! In the
dialogue of Sachs and Eva the subtlety, the tender polyphony in the orchestra!
By then I had heard *Die Meistersinger* for 25 years; but this second act was an
entirely new experience for me. In sound and dynamics, in clarity, in expression—this was the ultimate. And afterwards, when we ran up to Toscanini's
dressing room, I never saw him as he was then. He said: *"Com'un sogno*. Like a
dream.'[91]

It was an interesting experience—although it had happened to him before—to
conduct Verdi's and Wagner's comic masterpieces alternately during the same
period. A few months later he commented on this juxtaposition to composer
Adriano Lualdi during a chance encounter on a train:

'*Meistersinger* is a magnificent opera, but *Falstaff* is really something different. There is no opera more beautiful, more complete, newer and more Latin
than *Falstaff*. *The Marriage of Figaro* is very beautiful: many years ago I heard
a performance of it conducted by Richard Strauss and I was exalted by it. But
I thought—and I said so to the person I was with—there's something that I
don't understand, that I'm not able to find, and that I miss. *The Barber of
Seville* is a magnificent opera, but it has its arguable moments—pages which
are unnecessary and not all beautiful, which must be cut; however, in comparison with *The Marriage of Figaro*, how much sun, how much variety and how
much real cheerfulness there is in that music!

I think that there is the same basic difference between *Falstaff*, which is the
absolute masterpiece, and *Meistersinger*, which is an outstanding Wagnerian
opera. Just think for a moment how many musical means—beautiful ones,
certainly—Wagner must make use of to describe the Nuremberg night. And
look at how Verdi gets a similarly startling effect at a similar moment *with three
notes*.'[92]

Toscanini also conducted two concerts at Salzburg: the Brahms programme
which he had led in Vienna in December and a programme centred around the
Schubert 'Great C Major' Symphony—which, according to Otto Strasser, he did
not rehearse, although eight months had passed since they had performed it in
Vienna. He had also been instrumental in obtaining a guest engagement for
Rodzinski, and had attended the younger man's rehearsals and performance with
enthusiasm. Other conductors saw him at their rehearsals and performances, too.
Margarete Wallmann recalls, in her memoirs, sitting with him at one of Walter's
Tristan rehearsals. Towards the end of the long love scene in the second act,
Toscanini turned to her and said: 'If they were Italians, they would already have
seven children; but they are Germans, so they're still talking.'[93]

One evening after a performance of *Don Giovanni* led by Walter, Toscanini
went to a café with Mario Labroca, a well-known Italian musician who was then
general director of Florence's Maggio Musicale festival. Labroca had been asked
by the governing board of the festival to sound Toscanini out on the possibility of
his returning to conduct in Italy—and specifically, of course, at the festival.

'At one point I asked him point-blank: "Would you like to conduct again in
Italy?" I expected one of his violent reactions; instead, he answered with
naturalness: "Of course I would!" "So why don't you come back?" I persisted, moved. He remained silent, and he, too, was moved. He said: "Thanks,
Labroca," and didn't add another word. I persisted; I assured him of the
welcome he would have, of the certainty that no untoward incident would take
place. He listened as if the invitation interested him, but didn't speak again.'[94]

In September he conducted two extra performances of the Salzburg *Fidelio* at the Vienna Staatsoper as a gesture to Bruno Walter, who had succeeded Wein-gartner as its chief conductor. He then returned to Italy, but was back with the Vienna Philharmonic two months later for an important series of concerts—four performances in Vienna (plus the customary open dress rehearsals) and two in Budapest. The last concert, 29 November, was devoted to the *Missa Solemnis*. A German basso had originally been engaged as one of the soloists, but the Nazis had denied him permission to leave on the day before the first scheduled rehearsal. Fortunately, Kipnis was available to substitute. He felt that the *Missa* was one of Toscanini's greatest achievements. 'The real feeling of [it] came to me only when I sang it with Toscanini,' he told Haggin.[95]

From Vienna Toscanini flew to Paris on 1 December and began preparing for his concerts at the Théâtre des Champs-Elysées on the 8th, 10th and 13th, which turned out to be his last in France.

French conductor D.E. Ingelbrecht wrote perceptively about Toscanini in a book called *The Conductor's World*, which appeared during the period when Toscanini was a frequent guest in Paris. The book is out of print, so it is worth citing a few passages.

'. . . While I was listening one day in wonderment to Toscanini rehearsing *La Mer*, I heard behind me two conductors, and not at all of a lowly rank, remark with a smile: "Fancy telling the orchestra that he always wants to hear the melody—how typically Italian!" They were quite wrong. What Toscanini asked for was a specific *musical* issue. What he called melody was actually the line, that thread of Ariadne which the performer must never allow the listener to lose.

. . . It took a long time before it was acknowledged what influence his genius could bring to bear also upon all non-Italian music. For example, I had always heard it said that Wagner was a closed secret to him. Therefore, passing through Milan, I did not miss the chance of hearing him conduct *The Master-singers*. Is it necessary to describe the unforgettable memory of this per-formance...? "That may be," other critics had told me, "but never listen to him conducting Debussy...!" At that time, the colossal revelation of *La Mer*, one evening at the Opéra, was still a thing of the future for me.

. . . Hardly has he left the orchestra, dripping even more with perspiration after a rehearsal than after a concert, his voice husky from continual comment and explanation, he will still talk of music as he moves away. If anything could be more striking than his unequalled mastery of conducting and his prodigious memory, it would be this constant fervour of his. . . . He knows, of course, that an orchestra will not go all out at rehearsals, giving its best only when in front of the public, like the majority of conductors. So he harasses them. *He* would *never* do that—spare himself! "You always do things *one-half*...! Don't play *as if it were a habit*...!" . . . He threw his score down with a burst of anger which caused a grumbling in the orchestra. But this did not make him feel put out. Far from it. He did not leave the instrumentalists with any illusion concerning his own attitude in the future, but roared: "And I'll always behave like this!" Another time after long attempts at getting what he wanted by persuasion, and not having been very successful, he calmly closed his score and said: "It isn't what I wanted, I did not enjoy it, but my conscience is easy." . . .

. . . You have only to hear him rehearse the Funeral March from *The Twilight of the Gods* to become aware that, whatever you may have thought yourself, it is mostly he who is right. . . . So long as he does not achieve the same tone-value for the two harsh chords at the beginning, he will persevere. He will explain that they had been wrong in *always* playing the second chord of the first beat and the chord preceding the third beat less strong. Then he will proceed to the fourth beat of the *same* bar, dwelling on the chromatic triplet-figure of the basses, which he will take neatly to pieces, because it is being hurried, and this always and everywhere, in the attempt of somehow patching it up. "I have given this triplet lesson in vain all over the world," he says. . . .'[96]

If Vienna and Paris were by now familiar territory for Toscanini, the site of his next engagement was not. The story of this unusual adventure begins in New York the previous February, when he received a letter from Huberman—who was also in the city—requesting a meeting to discuss 'a constructive idea in the artistic field' with which the violinist was 'obsessed'.[97] Toscanini readily agreed to see him, and Huberman was able to relate the details of his project to organize a first-rate orchestra in Palestine, to be made up entirely of Jewish musicians— largely those who were fleeing actual and potential persecution in central Europe. He had also been able to find some financial support, particularly among American Jews, for the project. Now he was asking Toscanini to go to Palestine and conduct the orchestra's inaugural concerts. Not only would this be a great show of solidarity with the innocent victims of an abhorrent political system and a means of attracting attention to and finding further economic aid for the orchestra: it would also be the best possible musical start for this new ensemble. Toscanini immediately declared himself willing and enthusiastic, and he refused to hear about accepting a fee or reimbursement for his travel expenses.

The news was quickly made public; and among the first to show their gratitude was Albert Einstein, who wrote Toscanini from Princeton on 1 March:

'Honoured Master!
    I feel the necessity of telling you for once how much I admire and honour you. You are not only the unmatchable interpreter of the world's musical literature, whose forms deserve the highest admiration. In the fight against the Fascist criminals, too, you have shown yourself to be a man of greatest

dignity. I also feel most deeply thankful because you have given the soon-to-be-founded Palestine Orchestra a push forward of inestimable significance.

The fact that such a contemporary exists cancels many of the delusions one must continually experience from the *species minorum gentium!*

With love and greatest respect, cordial greetings from your
                                                    Albert Einstein.'[98]

By 23 March Huberman was able to inform Toscanini that most of the money needed for the first three years of the orchestra's existence had been raised and that Einstein had accepted the honorary presidency of the orchestra's American committee. The opening was originally scheduled for October but political problems caused a postponement until December. Less than a week after his last Paris concert, Toscanini was again leaving Milan accompanied by Signora Carla. They travelled by train to Brindisi, and by plane to Athens, Alexandria and Tel-Aviv, arriving there on 20 December. 'Huberman was desperate because he had no news of us,' wrote Signora Carla to Wanda; 'but Papà was calm and happy to have taken this long and relaxing journey.'[99]

There was incredible excitement throughout Palestine over Toscanini's visit, and great nervousness in the orchestra. Huberman was particularly concerned lest Toscanini should find the orchestra unsatisfactory. The string players were all of very high calibre: most of them had been principal players in leading European orchestras; the wind section was not quite as strong. Hans Wilhelm Steinberg—later known simply as William Steinberg—himself a refugee from German persecution, had set the orchestra up and had given it some preliminary training. One journalist persuaded an orchestra member to tell him about Toscanini's first rehearsals.

'You can well believe that we were all in an extraordinary state. . . . Toscanini arrived, dressed in the jacket he wears at rehearsals, stepped on to the podium and simply said: "The Brahms Symphony". Everything went excellently and the Maestro declared that he was satisfied. At the second rehearsal we felt that we had not worked as well as the first time. Toscanini said nothing. We were very unhappy, thinking he didn't take us seriously. At the following rehearsal, he bawled us out terribly; we were delighted.

. . . We didn't understand Italian, so he made an effort to speak German. It was time wasted. Huberman suggested a mixture of gestures and words. . . . We were quite able to understand each other, in every respect.

. . . You lose all nervousness, because his baton is so sure. With him, you can never miss your entrance. . . . He demands that every musician hear the whole work, and not just his own part. . . . He says that the orchestra is so good because many of its members were chamber music players. . . ."[100]

Signora Carla wrote to Wanda:

'On the day of our arrival Papà had his first rehearsal and is satisfied with the orchestra. There are two rehearsals a day, but they are short and not tiring. . . . They put us in a lovely little villa on the outskirts of town. As far as beauty and comfort go, it is everything one can desire, and we have at our disposal a car, a valet and cook-maid. We are treated as if we were royalty. But at night we are isolated, and the villa, being modern, has enormous windows on the ground floor; and for the first time in my life I am uneasy. I'm afraid—afraid of everything. Papà laughs at me, but I gave up my beautiful big room, and we are sleeping in a smaller one together. Until now, I still have the same amount of money with me as the day I arrived here. Although Papà protests, I let them pay.'[101]

The first programme was a large and demanding one: Brahms's Second Symphony, Rossini's *La scala di seta* Overture, Schubert's 'Unfinished' Symphony, the Nocturne and Scherzo from Mendelssohn's *Midsummer Night's Dream* and Weber's *Oberon* Overture! Free tickets were distributed to artists and workers for the final rehearsal, which took place on Christmas day in the Great Hall of Tel-Aviv's Exhibition Grounds, and the public's response was one of overwhelming emotion. The president of the Hebrew University broke into uncontrollable tears. At the end, Toscanini insisted that Huberman appear to share the ovations with him.

At the official first concert the following night, the British High Commissioner was in attendance, as were Dr Chaim Weizmann and David Ben-Gurion. The hall was packed, and people without tickets surrounded the area and even climbed on to the roof in the hopes of hearing something. A burst of applause lasting several minutes greeted Toscanini as he made his way to the stage. As at his last New York concert in April, the excitement of the evening ended badly with the explosion of a flash bulb before his eyes.

The concert was given again in Tel-Aviv and repeated in Jerusalem and Haifa, and a second programme—all Beethoven—was also given in all three cities. Everywhere and always, the ecstasy and gratitude were the same. The first Haifa concert (31 December) was, however, marred by an unfortunate musical accident, recounted to Haggin by Felix Galimir, one of the orchestra's violinists:

'It had happened that at one rehearsal of the Brahms, in the third movement, the first trumpet overlooked the marking 'third movement *tacet*", and began to play the fourth movement in the third movement. Toscanini gave him a look; but it was only a rehearsal, and it was a little mistake that could happen. But we repeated the same program many times . . . It starts to become a little routine for the player; he doesn't pay attention, and so in Haifa the trumpeter made the same mistake at the concert. You remember the fourth movement starts very *piano*, with the trumpet playing just one note: ta. And the trumpeter played that one note at the beginning of the *third* movement.

Toscanini got furious: while he conducted he cursed, he threw dagger-glances
at the poor trumpeter, who was dying with fear; he continued to curse all the
time while we played the rest of the symphony; he got faster and faster; he
didn't hold the *fermata*; he ended in a fury, *prestissimo* and *fortissimo*. The
audience, which of course didn't know what was going on, never heard such
fire and such sounds; and there was tremendous applause. But Toscanini
rushed out, kicking over the music stands ... and didn't come back on the
stage again. The intermission lasted an hour and a half ...'[102]

Toscanini was very anxious to see Palestine—its Biblical and other historic
sites, its potash plants and agricultural settlements, and the daily life of its
people. He was highly impressed by a performance of *The Merchant of Venice* at
the Habimah Theatre; he toured the Hebrew University and was greeted with
thunderous applause when he entered a hall to attend a lecture on Hebrew
literature, which was translated into English for him; he attended several
receptions—despite his normal hatred of such events; and he was driven all
around the country, to *kibbutzim* and experimental farms. Toscanini and
Huberman were out for a drive one day when a storm overtook them. Their
chauffeur pulled into the nearby agricultural village of Ramoth Hashavim, and
they entered the main building, to the surprise of the settlement's inhabitants.
One of its administrators recalled years later:

'Nearly all of these farmers were professors, doctors, lawyers, who had
decided ... to become agriculturalists in Palestine after the destruction of their
existences in Germany. All these people had been raised in the world of
German culture; they were all music lovers and, like the whole country, were
full of love and gratitude for Toscanini and Huberman, who had brought such
unexpected musical events to their new country. They had a lively conversation
that afternoon, and Toscanini was so impressed by these people that he said
he would come back soon. A few days later, he returned ... with his wife, and
they passed several hours of animated conversation at the house of one of the
directors. The farmers were overjoyed to be able to present Mrs. Toscanini
with a basket of eggs from their henhouses. There were more visits. As a token
of gratitude for Toscanini's action toward the Jewish people ... the village
dedicated a piece of land to him.'[103]

The Toscaninis and Huberman planted trees on this piece of land at a special
ceremony, and school children sang folk songs and children's songs for them.
Toscanini said it was difficult for him to speak because of the power of the
impressions he had received, and Signora Carla wept openly. She wrote to Wanda
of this 'magnificent farm of fifty houses'.

'The young people have adapted themselves, but for those who are fifty and
over, it is very sad. There was one who spoke beautiful French, and it was so

sad that we were in anguish. But he did not utter one word of rebellion. One sensed only an infinite sadness, and when we left we were both crying. If you stop to think what they have achieved through sheer labour, it is nothing short of miraculous.'[104]

One of the Jerusalem concerts was broadcast; and traffic in the country came nearly to a halt as people listened to the programme in their own homes or in cafés. Toscanini was so moved by the musical appetite of the populace that he opened another general rehearsal to the public, in order to accommodate some of those who had been unable to obtain concert tickets. As he was driven up to the hall, half an hour early, he saw no one entering and thought that perhaps interest was not so great, after all. Once inside, however, he discovered that the entire audience had arrived much earlier and that every seat was taken.

One afternoon, Toscanini's young chauffeur arrived two minutes late to drive him to rehearsal. He found that the angry Toscanini, who was a bear for punctuality, had already left and was walking towards the hall. The car soon caught up with him, but Toscanini refused to get in; so the poor chauffeur simply drove along behind him at walking pace. When they reached the hall Toscanini turned, smiled at the driver, said '*Shalom*', and that was that. The same driver told Toscanini one day how sad he was that his wife could not attend the concert, because she was expecting a baby very shortly. So Toscanini and his wife visited the young couple for tea one day.

The orchestra and Toscanini repeated each of their concerts in Cairo and Alexandria between 7 and 12 January 1937; but before leaving Palestine Toscanini told Huberman: 'I am so sad to be leaving this country, this people, its public, its orchestra. I must come back—and I shall come back!'[105]

In Egypt, violinist Lorand Fenyves was part of a group of musicians who visited the pyramids and other archaeological sites with Toscanini.

'He was excited about everything that had to do with beauty. He was interested in archaeological finds. . . . Whatever he saw, he wanted to know everything about, he wanted to get to the core of the thing. He would listen very carefully, and questioned until he understood the significance of a place or thing. He sought a real knowledge and understanding of things that interested him.'[106]

In fact, he was so fascinated by Egypt that he accepted an invitation to travel up the Nile. From Luxor, Signora Carla wrote to Huberman:

'It is a month since we left Italy, a month which we have passed happily and which we shall always remember with real emotion and sweetness. Toscanini thinks nostalgically about the days in Tel-Aviv. I think that those were the most moving days for him.

I think they will have written you that after a long discussion with our friend Dr. Simon, we arranged with Colonel Kisch to accept a trip to Upper Egypt!

So here we are, still your guests!! And here, too, we have spent nine delightful
and restful days. Thanks, thanks, thanks! We shall return to Cairo on the 24th
and will leave again on the 27th for Bengasi and Rome directly in an Italian
plane. On the evening of the 25th we'll attend Busch's concert in Cairo. . . .
Thanks again, from Toscanini as well, and our most friendly greetings to
you.'[107]

Before Toscanini had left New York the previous April, he had told Zirato that
he might eventually consider returning for a tour with the Philharmonic. The
orchestra's management immediately began investigating possibilities. Finally, in
December, they reached an agreement with David Sarnoff, head of the Radio
Corporation of America, the organization which produced Toscanini's Victor
records and which ran the National Broadcasting Company: Toscanini would be
invited to conduct a five-week, twenty-five-concert American tour with the
Philharmonic, beginning 19 April 1937. He would be paid $50,000, taxes and
steamship passage. Zirato said that someone should be sent to Europe to present
the plan to him, but Sarnoff vetoed the idea. Instead, a cable was sent to Toscanini
who was then in Paris; he did not answer. Another cable was sent, and this time
he replied (14 December): 'For this year impossible. Only possibility April
recordings, benefit concerts. . . .' New plans were formulated in New York, and
at the end of December Toscanini received a cable in Tel-Aviv saying that if he
wished to make recordings, he would be paid either his full concert fee (approximately $2,000) for each recording session, or a five per cent royalty on the
records, as he pleased. On 15 January Mrs Toscanini replied from Aswan:
'Toscanini will absolutely not make records. Sorry. Thanks.' A letter followed in
which she explained that a cable had come from HMV in London—RCA's
European affiliate—at the same time as RCA's cable; but the British company
was offering a twelve and a half per cent royalty. Toscanini, she said, would
accept neither proposal, in fairness to the Philharmonic.[108]

Within a very short time, however, this indebted feeling to the Philharmonic
was to disappear. An announcement had been made in December that young
John Barbirolli had been given a three-year contract with the orchestra. When
Toscanini heard about it he was incensed—in the first place because he had
recommended Rodzinski over Barbirolli, and in the second place because the
Philharmonic had not consulted him over their choice. It is unlikely that he had
any personal grudge against Barbirolli; but it was his opinion that Rodzinski
could better have kept the Philharmonic's quality at a high level. Shortly afterwards Zirato received a letter from Signora Carla, the contents of which he
restated to Judson:

'Maestro did not think it was right to announce the engagement of Barbirolli
after only a brief period with the orchestra and before the other conductors
started their terms. As far as he remembers this is a new procedure in the

annals of the Society, to announce the conductor for the next season as early as December. In this way, he adds, the conductors whose terms follow Mr. Barbirolli's, meet the public under unfavourable conditions because in engaging Mr. Barbirolli the Society has already made the decision of his superiority against others who have not even been heard. Secondly, Mr. Toscanini himself would have liked an official communication of the engagement of Mr. Barbirolli just as a matter of courtesy. He heard of this engagement through private letters from Mr. Walter Price and myself. He was quite offended by this lack of respect and courtesy.'[109]

Toscanini had every right to express his professional opinions of Barbirolli and the Philharmonic situation; but later on, when he was back in New York, he was fed and helped to spread unkind gossip about his successor. He eventually apologized for this to both Barbirolli and his wife, and told them that he had 'behaved like a pig'.

The next part of this tale becomes even more Byzantine in its intricacy; and its central figure is David Sarnoff. Sarnoff had immigrated to the United States from Russia in 1900, at the age of nine, and by 1929 he had become president of RCA. He did not know much about music, but he knew that Toscanini represented high quality and was an enormous audience attraction. It may well have been at the time of RCA's negotiations with the Philharmonic over the proposed but never realized Toscanini tour that the idea of forming a special radio orchestra of superb quality—as the BBC had done in London—had occurred to him. Of course, the situation was and is quite different in the two countries: the BBC is public and RCA is private; and while there were public service rulings which governed some aspects of broadcasting in the States, the major networks were so powerful that they were largely able to decide among themselves what the interpretation of those rulings should be. Sarnoff must also have been quite aware that RCA's giant subsidiary, NBC, would soon be negotiating with the very strong American Federation of Musicians regarding an increase of network spending for 'live' music. (In the summer of 1937 NBC was, in fact, forced to agree to raise its number of New York staff musicians for 1938 from 74 to 115 and to increase its annual expenditure on live music by an additional $500,000.)

In December Sarnoff had opposed sending a personal emissary to Europe to discuss the proposed Philharmonic tour with Toscanini; in January, however, he sent his own hand-picked emissary to Milan to discuss his new proposal. This representative was Samuel Chotzinoff, who had once been an accompanist for several well-known singers and instrumentalists—including Heifetz, whose sister he married. Later he was music critic for New York's *The World* and *The Post*. He worshipped Toscanini and had been part of what several people I have spoken with have called the 'clique of sycophants' who had surrounded him—whenever possible—during his Philharmonic years.

I assume that the account of Chotzinoff's mission in the article in *Fortune* magazine of January 1938—which was written by Chotzinoff's friends, Russell and Marcia Davenport—is what he told them when he returned, and therefore probably true (whereas his totally different account in *Toscanini, An Intimate Portrait* is what he invented for his purposes eighteen years later). According to the account in *Fortune* Chotzinoff had cabled Toscanini, then in Cairo, 'that he had an "important proposition" to present to him in person and that "this commits neither you nor me". And Toscanini's reply had designated Milan.' Chotzinoff and his wife arrived in Milan on 31 January—not more than two or three days after the Toscaninis' return from Egypt; and it was only at his second meeting with the Maestro that he summoned up the courage to present the proposal for the new broadcast orchestra. Toscanini examined the various contract possibilities that were offered him and chose the shortest one: ten broadcasts in a ten-week period, to begin the following December, at a fee of $4,000 per broadcast, with his taxes paid by NBC. The orchestra would also have to be of the highest possible quality, and he wanted Rodzinski to choose and begin to train it.

Chotzinoff immediately phoned New York from the Toscanini home. Within a day or two he and Sarnoff had prepared a precise contract which Toscanini then signed. Since the Fascists tapped Toscanini's phone and read incoming and outgoing telegraph messages, the *Corriere della sera* and then the whole world quickly knew the entire story. (Interestingly, Leinsdorf says that he met Toscanini in Rome when the latter was returning from the Middle East, and that Toscanini already knew, at that time, exactly what Chotzinoff was coming to discuss with him.)[110]

Rodzinski's wife received a letter from Walter Toscanini's wife to the effect that the whole Toscanini family were outraged by the brush-off they felt Rodzinski had been given by the Philharmonic, and that Toscanini had agreed to take the NBC job partly in order to teach a lesson to his former associates.[111] And the Philharmonic board and directorate certainly were upset! Zirato cabled Signora Carla on 8 February:

> 'Very surprised acceptance radio proposal. Want to know if Maestro considered bad effects this contract would make our season in case he permits public attendance broadcasts, gratis or with payment, and further, if these broadcasts will be transmitted Thursday evenings or Sunday afternoons [when Philharmonic subscription concerts were given].'

Toscanini himself answered this cable in no uncertain terms:

> 'Was surprised at your surprise. I will ask nothing of Sarnoff, who will arrange things to suit his own interests just as the Philharmonic has done and will always do.'

Zirato rebutted:

'My surprise was due to the fact that after your Farewell Concert I never could imagine that you would agree to conduct in America again and especially to broadcast, which you always hated. I consider the radio not the altar for the god of the musical world. Inasmuch as you say you will ask nothing of Mr. Sarnoff, I have nothing to add, but cannot help telling you that evidently you are wrongly advised and falsely informed.'

And Toscanini:

'For the priest who preaches the truth it does not matter if the altar is located in St. Peter's in Rome or in a little church in the most obscure village of Italy. My information is based on evidence of facts. Greetings.'[112]

A month after returning from Palestine Toscanini departed for the Netherlands to conduct two special concerts of the Residentie Orkest which was based in the Hague. These were his first appearances with a Dutch ensemble, and the engagement had been arranged by Jaap Stotijn, the orchestra's principal oboist who, in December, had rushed to Palestine at the last moment to replace a player whom Toscanini had found completely unsatisfactory. During the intermission of the Cairo concert Stotijn had told Toscanini that the Residentie Orkest was a very good orchestra, 'but I am not the best player in it'. Toscanini was very impressed with Stotijn's playing and accepted his invitation, on behalf of his orchestra's board, to come to the Hague.[113]

He seemed content with the orchestra at the first rehearsal; and one of the players reported that the musicians, gathered for coffee during the break at that rehearsal, couldn't stop talking about 'this unique event. You hear the words "magnificent", "unique", "unbelievable" in every corner of the room. It is best to be silent and to be grateful that we are permitted to witness this event.'[114] But the next day Toscanini became very upset over the poor quality of some of the brass players, threw a tantrum of cataclysmic proportions and walked out. He said that there was 'no discipline' in the orchestra and, according to one of the musicians, he was right—because there was at that time no permanent conductor, only series of guests. George Szell, who became the regular conductor the following season, reported that the orchestra's president begged Toscanini not to leave, told him that it would destroy the orchestra, and offered him as much rehearsal time as he wished. He consented; two players were replaced and the performances took place in Rotterdam on 6 March and in the Hague two nights later. In the end he was quite happy with the orchestra's work and even agreed to return the following year.[115]

While in Cairo Carla Toscanini had written to the Vogheras that her husband was willing to return to Stockholm in March; so the Concert Society Orchestra turned its schedule upside-down to accommodate him for two concerts. The

Toscaninis flew to Stockholm from Holland, and he started rehearsing for his first concert. He began having terrible shoulder pains again and had himself examined and X-rayed by a Swedish doctor (the doctor framed the X-ray and mounted it on his office wall); but to no avail. Rehearsals were tense, and Mrs Voghera saw him pacing back and forth in his room complaining, 'My arm no longer speaks.' On top of all this, a mysterious telegram arrived from Italy which put him even more out of sorts. (The Vogheras never discovered its contents.) After the first concert (16 March) he wrote to Mrs Voghera, asking her to make his letter public:

'I am sorry to have to give you an unpleasant task, but I cannot avoid doing so, considering the short time available and the urgent work to be done before the second concert. *I feel tired*, really tired, and I haven't the nerve or the strength to begin again tomorrow morning with the rehearsals which, considering the very few days until the concert, would have to be rushed ... I would need a few days of rest. I have trusted too much in my physical strength and am now punished for it. If I had time at my disposal, I would say, let's postpone the concert to next week; but as you well know, I must be in Milan next Monday. Therefore, I am obliged to be indebted to the Concert Society for this cancelled concert. I shall pay it off in the near future, when I have more time.'

He never did return to Stockholm.

He had to be back in Milan because he had agreed to let his family give him a seventieth birthday party which would include friends from many countries. Signora Carla reported on the event in a letter to Iwa Voghera:

'The 25th of March was a day of great emotion! At 8 in the morning the Busch Quartet came to serenade Toscanini in the courtyard... then the mayor of Salzburg arrived to present the plans for the [new]* theatre; then the Minister of Fine Arts spoke on the radio, then presents, telegrams, flowers ... In the evening there were more than 120 friends in our house where, besides the Busch Quartet, Horowitz also played ...'

'I am now an old man,' Toscanini told Burghauser at the party. 'And who knows: every new day is a gift of heaven, which I cannot even expect and hope for. I am not sick, but after seventy where are you? Should I even go out and conduct?'[116]

In April Toscanini flew to Vienna to hear a performance of *The Magic Flute*, which he was to direct that summer in Salzburg. What he heard did not please him at all. His visit, however, turned into a special event in Vienna, as reported by Herbert F. Peyser in a dispatch to the *New York Times*:

* Probably blueprints of the new Festspielhaus. See p. 261.

'... After the "Magic Flute" Toscanini was guest of honour at a reception in company with the chairman of the Philharmonic, Prof. Hugo Burghauser. Taking advantage of the circumstance that the master seemed in great good humour, Prof. Burghauser ventured to suggest a concert for the following Saturday and Sunday. Instantly, and enthusiastically, Toscanini agreed. The rest was easy. Front-page stories in the next day's papers sent half the town scurrying to the Philharmonic box office, the more so as ticket prices were not raised. The program ... contained the "Italian Girl in Algiers" overture of Rossini, the "Pastoral", Haydn's B-flat London Symphony and Strauss's "Death and Transfiguration".

There was particular satisfaction that Toscanini would at last give Vienna a chance to hear his "Pastoral" ... It surpassed all expectations. Can any conductor ever have encompassed quite this incorruptible rectitude of tempo, this exquisite simplicity, ... this translucence of sonorities?

The Haydn symphony which Toscanini, contrary to prevailing German and Austrian usage, played with a reduced orchestra was another of those experiences which stand out like milestones in a musical lifetime. If the master had never done anything more than the introductory Adagio he would still be one of the supreme conductors of all time. In some ways one regretted that Strauss's tone poem had to follow Haydn and Beethoven. Magnificent as was every detail of Toscanini's reading the piece sounded by comparison banal and theatrical. Tremendous ovations greeted the conductor at every opportunity. And the Philharmonic never sounds quite that way under anyone else.

... Toscanini went to the Staatsoper almost every night for a week ... I would give a great deal to know what was in Toscanini's thoughts as he listened to "Carmen", one of the most heathenish of the Staatsoper's offenses and generally recognized as such in Vienna. "Tristan", at all events, had Bruno Walter in the conductor's chair and Kipnis's King Mark on the stage. In "Figaro" it was Josef Krips who had the doubtful satisfaction of brandishing the baton while both Walter and Toscanini looked and listened. ...'

After returning to Milan for a few weeks, Toscanini went to London, where he conducted six completely different concerts (for a total fee of £3,000) with the BBC Symphony between 26 May and 16 June. Oxford had offered him an honorary degree; but apparently after the aberration of the Georgetown degree a few years earlier he had decided not to accept any further academic awards. To show that he appreciated the thought, however, he took the orchestra to Oxford on 8 June for a special concert in aid of the university's appeal fund. It was a mammoth programme, consisting of a Rossini overture and three symphonies —the 'Pastoral', Brahms's First and Haydn's No. 92 ('Oxford'). The Toscaninis renewed their acquaintance with Ernest and Vera Newman and had an enjoyable visit with them at their Tadworth home; and Toscanini attended performances of *Pelléas* and *Tosca* at Covent Garden, conducted by Albert Wolff and Barbirolli, respectively.

After another two- or three-week stay in Italy, he was in Salzburg for most of July and all of August. In addition to conducting the new *Magic Flute* production, he revived his three previous Salzburg operas. *Fidelio* now had Kipnis singing the part of Rocco. He told Haggin:

'Toscanini was completely absorbed in the music of *Fidelio*: I think he was not *there*, actually. He was like a high priest of this work: in what he did, it was as if he felt Beethoven was present; and we had a beautiful performance. At the first rehearsal with piano we started from the very beginning; and after each number we stopped and waited for corrections from Toscanini. He was brief and to the point . . . After Florestan's aria at the beginning of the second act there is the famous digging duet; and when the Fidelio [Lehmann] and I finished it, we waited for corrections. Toscanini sat with his head bent down deep in his hands, and didn't say a word. After a few minutes he looked up at us and said, "What music!" '[117]

The Magic Flute, which was staged by Herbert Graf, and which included Kipnis, Helge Roswaenge, Jarmila Novotna and Willi Domgraf-Fassbaender in its cast (and Georg Solti at the glockenspiel in the pit), aroused great controversy —even among those who participated in it. Many of Toscanini's tempi were unconventional—both on the fast side and on the slow side. I do not generally admire his Mozart performances; but I find this particular performance (judging from a 'pirate' recording which I have heard) original, fascinating and, for the most part, very beautiful. Toscanini, incidentally, insisted on having the dialogue done almost uncut; and Kipnis—who was one of the singers who remained unconvinced by Toscanini's way with the opera—also mentioned to Haggin that

'Toscanini asked us to modulate the dialogue into the key of the aria which followed it. He asked me, for instance, to modulate into F major for the aria "*O Isis und Osiris*", and into E major for "*In diesen heiligen Hallen*".'[118]

All four of the operas conducted by Toscanini that summer were recorded by the Austrian Broadcasting Corporation on a machine called the Selenophone, which cut a vertical recording into 8 mm acetate film. According to Robert Hupka, whose detailed research into the history of Toscanini's recordings is of great importance (and whose photographs of Toscanini at work in Antek's book, *This Was Toscanini*, are the most beautiful of their kind), John N. Royal, an NBC executive, wrote to Austria requesting copies of these recordings; but through a secretarial error *Fidelio* was not included in the request. NBC received and filed away the other three operas, and the omission was not even noticed for several years. During the war the original films in Vienna were either destroyed or stolen; and so the fragment of the 1935 *Fidelio* shortwave broadcast mentioned earlier is the only part of Toscanini's Salzburg *Fidelio* known to exist today.

It is unfortunate that the other three recordings are not yet available to the public. The sound quality of the originals is poor, but good engineering could at least remedy some of the pitch problems. Dietrich Fischer-Dieskau has called the *Meistersinger* 'wonderful', and the *Falstaff* and *Magic Flute* are no less worth hearing.*

It was at Salzburg during that summer of 1937 that Toscanini broke with Furtwängler, who had come to conduct a performance of the Beethoven Ninth. According to Burghauser, Furtwängler insisted on talking with Toscanini about the possibility of the former's conducting *Der Freischütz* at Salzburg the following summer. Toscanini's reply had been that he could do as he pleased, 'but I will not be here'.[119] But Elisabeth Furtwängler says that her husband told her that Toscanini had simply said, 'You must choose between Bayreuth and Salzburg.' Obviously, Toscanini felt that Furtwängler was trying to have the best of both worlds without taking a firm stand; and Furtwängler probably realized when it was too late how much better it would have been for him to have taken such a stand.

Toscanini's 1937 Salzburg appearances also included a performance of the Verdi *Te Deum* and *Requiem* and two other concerts. As he conducted the last performance of the season on 31 August, work crews gathered to prepare for the demolition of the stage and backstage areas; and they began that very night. Toscanini had been very aware of the shortcomings of the old Festspielhaus; and he had met, the previous year, with Schuschnigg and the governor of Salzburg province—with Burghauser as translator—to formulate a plan for a new theatre. He personally contributed his royalties from the American broadcast of his festival performances and volunteered to conduct benefit concerts to aid the project.

For the following summer he planned to add *Tannhäuser* (with Lehmann, Kipnis, *et al.*) to his other four Salzburg operas; and he was already thinking about *Boris Godunov*, *The Barber of Seville* and Gluck's *Iphigenia in Aulis* for future seasons.

In October he was back in Vienna to find out how work was proceeding at Salzburg, and he even made a stop in Salzburg to check on the progress. He conducted the Philharmonic in two concerts in Vienna and one in Budapest, and immediately after his last Vienna concert on 17 October he departed for London. Austria never saw him again.

---

* *The Magic Flute* was released in 1978 by Fonit-Cetra in Italy. However, the pitch varies (it is often a semitone sharp, which also makes the tempi faster), the beautifully-done dialogue has been cut entirely, and sections often run together without a moment's pause. In short, some of the poor pirate versions in circulation are actually superior to this commercial release.

This time his BBC work began with three days of recording sessions, which yielded Beethoven's First and Sixth Symphonies and Brahms's 'Tragic' Overture. On 30 October he conducted a Brahms programme and on 3 November a Beethoven concert.

He was to have returned to Palestine after his London visit; but it was decided to postpone the trip until the spring. 'A great anxiety has been lifted from me,' wrote Daniela Thode to Enrico Polo. 'For me, it was an intolerable idea that the Maestro should again be in that land and among those people who crucified Our Lord.'[120] It is not hard to imagine what Toscanini's reaction would have been, had Polo shown him this letter from one of his most fervent admirers in the House of Wagner.

Before returning to Italy from London he found himself embroiled in unexpected problems having to do with the formation of the new NBC Symphony. The following is part of the text of a press release issued by the American Radio Telegraphists Association on 8 November:

'Kendall E. Davis, Vice-President of the Broadcast Division of the ARTA, a CIO affiliate, today sent the following radiogram to Maestro Arturo Toscanini in London:

... NBC DISCHARGING NUMEROUS EMPLOYEES CITING COST OF YOUR ENGAGE-MENT NECESSITATES BUDGET SLASH STOP THIS ORGANIZATION CONFIDENT THAT YOU AS AN ARTIST AND A LIBERAL WILL NOT TOLERATE THIS MISUSE OF YOUR NAME AND URGES THAT YOU TAKE IMMEDIATE STEPS TO FORCE NBC TO ADMIT THESE DISCHARGES PART OF VICIOUS OPEN SHOP POLICY AND STOP ATTEMPTING TO CONCEAL ANTI-LABOUR ACTIVITIES UNDER THE CLOAK OF THE EXPENSES DUE YOUR ENGAGEMENT. THANKS AND GREETINGS. AMERICAN RADIO TELEGRAPHISTS ASSOCIATION'[121]

Toscanini, outraged, cabled that he was withdrawing from the NBC engagement, causing Chotzinoff and others to suffer collective heart failure. They knew that Toscanini had not been told everything about the formation of the new orchestra, and were afraid of what he might find out. Chotzinoff had told Toscanini in Milan that NBC was going to 'build him a great orchestra', which he, like everyone else, took to mean it was going to engage a new orchestra for the exclusive use of himself and selected guest conductors. What he had not told him was that the 92 players of the NBC Symphony would be part of NBC's staff orchestra, increased from 74 in 1937 to 115 in 1938, and would be dividing their weekly thirty hours of work equally between Toscanini's rehearsals and broadcast and NBC's other programmes; and that the 92 NBC Symphony players comprised 31 men retained from the 1937 staff orchestra and 61 newly engaged (1) as higher-calibre replacements of members of the 1937 staff orchestra, most of whom *had*, then, presumably lost their jobs, and (2) as additions for the 1938 staff orchestra.

Chotzinoff's cabled reply to Toscanini—that, far from costing even one musician his job, his engagement had caused NBC 'to take on a full symphony orchestra' and other personnel—was, therefore, untrue. But since Chotzinoff was a personal friend, Toscanini believed him, and decided to continue with the project.

There were other difficulties in the formation of the orchestra: Rodzinski, who was paranoiac to begin with, was extremely worried that his selection of players would not satisfy Toscanini. He had second thoughts about some of the men he had chosen—especially some of the younger ones—when it was too late to do anything about them; and he gave those players a hard time at rehearsals. There was nervousness and apprehension within the orchestra and its administration, and in the end Pierre Monteux was asked to conduct its first concerts instead of Rodzinski. Monteux led two concerts and Rodzinski then led three. The last of these took place in mid-December and was attended by Toscanini, who had just arrived in New York; and the next day he began rehearsing for his first concert. Violinist Samuel Antek wrote about that first rehearsal:

'. . . From a door on the right side of the stage, a small, solidly built man emerged. Immediately discernible were the crowning white hair and the impassive, square, high-cheekboned, bemoustached face. He was dressed in a severely cut black alpaca jacket, with a high clerical collar, formal striped trousers, and pointed, slipperlike shoes. . . .

As he stepped up to the podium, by prearranged signal we all rose . . . He looked around, apparently bewildered by our unexpected action, and gestured a faint greeting with both arms, a mechanical smile lighting his pale face for an instant. Somewhat embarrassed, we sat down again. Then, in a rough, hoarse voice, he called out, "Brahms!" He looked at us piercingly for the briefest moment, then raised his arms. In one smashing stroke, the baton came down. . . .

With each heart-pounding timpani stroke in the opening bars of the Brahms First Symphony his baton beat became more powerfully insistent, his shoulders strained and hunched as though buffeting a giant wind. His outstretched left arm spasmodically flailed the air, the cupped fingers pleading . . . His face reddened, muscles tightened, eyes and eyebrows constantly moving.

As we in the violin section tore with our bows against our strings, I felt I was being sucked into a roaring maelstrom of sound—every bit of strength and skill called upon and strained into being. . . . I sensed, more than I heard, with near disbelief, the new sounds around me. Was this the same music we had been practising so assiduously for days? . . . With what a new fierce joy we played!'[122]

The first concert took place on Christmas night, 1937, from NBC's Studio 8H —its largest broadcasting hall, which had a seating capacity of 1,200. The studio was acoustically very dry and prevented Toscanini's unique sound quality from being heard, except when the orchestra gave benefit performances at Carnegie Hall or played occasional tour concerts. It was also partly responsible for some of the more atrocious-sounding recordings which represent Toscanini to today's listeners. Admittance to the NBC concerts was free, and tickets were always very hard to get. Besides the Brahms symphony, the first programme consisted of Vivaldi's Concerto Grosso in D minor, Op. 3 No. 11, and Mozart's Symphony No. 40 in G minor. It was heard by millions.

Toscanini conducted the ten broadcasts he had agreed to do, as well as two benefit concerts at Carnegie Hall: Beethoven's First and Ninth Symphonies on 6 February 1938 and the Verdi *Requiem* on 4 March. Recording sessions were held on 7 and 8 March. The new orchestra so satisfied him that he agreed to sign a contract for the next three years, with sixteen broadcasts per season.

Sarnoff was also satisfied: in a speech during the last broadcast of the season he said that 'the National Broadcasting Company is a business. It has employees; it has stockholders; and it serves them best by serving the public best'. In other words, there was a profit potential in this venture into 'high culture'.

The proceeds from the two special concerts were to have gone to the new Salzburg Festspielhaus; but by the time the first one took place, Austria's situation *vis-à-vis* Germany was so hopeless that Toscanini directed that the money go to other beneficiaries. He also cabled that he himself would not return to Salzburg that summer. The government asked both Bruno Walter and Huberman to intercede with him, but he remained firm. A few weeks later Austria was swallowed up by the German Reich; and just as Strauss had filled Toscanini's place at Bayreuth five years earlier, so Furtwängler now agreed to conduct what had been Toscanini's *Meistersinger* production. All productions made use of the new facilities which Toscanini had helped to build. Once again Daniela Thode poured out her dismay to Polo:

'In the midst of all these new and agitating events, I have in mind only our beloved, great, heroic brother—but a mistaken brother. . . . He, the enemy— but why!—of Fascist Italy and Fascist Germany, cannot conduct in a Fascist Austria; it is a consequence of his principled stand. But why take this stand? Why not render unto Caesar what is Caesar's, with Christian wisdom, and withdraw into the realm where he is the sovereign, absolute king, completely independent and incomparable?'[123]

Why not? His reason was made clear in his phone conversation with 'Signora Ada' in 1935: 'There are people who don't feel anything, who live like this... For me, though, it's a suffering that annihilates me.'

Toscanini must have departed for Europe almost immediately after his last NBC recording session (8 March): between the 21st and 25th he again led

Holland's Residentie Orkest, this time in four concerts—three in the Hague and one in Rotterdam.

In April—the month in which the Italian government pleased Hitler by proclaiming its shameful anti-Semitic 'racial manifesto'—Toscanini returned to Palestine. There were serious Arab–Jewish disturbances at the time and Weizmann had told Huberman to ask Toscanini to cancel his trip, since his safety could not be guaranteed. Huberman wired Toscanini and later met with him in the Hague, but found it impossible to dissuade him. He and his wife arrived by plane on 8 April. On the 13th he conducted a concert for workers in Haifa; the next night he repeated the programme for regular subscribers. The same pattern was followed in Tel-Aviv on the 16th and 17th, and a combined concert was given in Jerusalem on the 20th. He led a second concert in Tel-Aviv and Jerusalem on the 24th and 26th; and this programme contained, among other pieces, what must have been the only music of Wagner ever done by the orchestra, either before or after the creation of the state of Israel: the Preludes to Acts I and III of *Lohengrin*.

While there, the Toscaninis again toured the country, spent a day with Weizmann at Rehovoth, and returned to Ramoth Hashavim, where they wept on being given the first oranges from 'their' plot of land. They left by plane from Haifa Bay at the end of the month, promising to return as soon as possible. International events were to render that promise unfulfillable.

From mid-May to mid-June Toscanini was in London, where he led six concerts and three recording sessions with the BBC Symphony at Queen's Hall. Cellist Emmanuel Feuermann was soloist in Strauss's *Don Quixote* at one of these performances; another featured the Verdi *Requiem*. At about this time, a book called *The Orchestra Speaks*, written by the BBC's principal violist, Bernard Shore, appeared in Britain. It is a perceptive work in every respect, and the chapter on Toscanini is very fine.

'. . . Under Toscanini orchestral playing becomes a different art. He stimulates his men, refreshes their minds; and music that has become stale is revived in all its pristine beauty. Rehearsals are looked forward to. There is never a moment of dullness—everything is far too concentrated and vital— nor is there any vain repetition. The time-factor disappears. Sheer physical fatigue takes the place of the clock . . .

. . . With Toscanini there is no wasting a moment. Rehearsals finish as soon as he feels there is no more to be done. He is never satisfied, but he seems to have an exact picture of the utmost any orchestra can achieve. His continual striving for perfection is felt to apply to himself rather than to spring from dissatisfaction with the orchestra. If he cannot please himself he does not allow the players to feel they are to blame.

. . . Without any cut-and-dried scheme, Toscanini covers all the ground at preliminary rehearsals, and the final rehearsal—with so many conductors a violent race against time—he directs with calm and smooth organization, though electrical in vitality. . . . His modest, deprecatory gesture after the concert, sharing the honours with the orchestra, is utterly natural. Whatever the ovation, having appeared once or twice in an increasing tumult, he whispers to the principal first violin to lead the orchestra from the platform—and that's the end.

. . . This concentration of his, which must be very near the root of his greatness, enables him to live and think the music he is recreating so deeply and intensely that all who are working with him feel drawn to the composer's very heart. It is a state of mind which blots out everything save the subject desired; he enters into another world, taking the orchestra with him. It is frequently noticeable at rehearsal that when he is deeply engaged upon a line of thought and anything unexpectedly happens to snap it, he reacts violently, though at the performance proper nothing seems to upset him.

Once he has started, a slight mistake brings no calamitous look to his face. Yet at rehearsal, if he is building up a climax and a heavy instrument just fails to rise to the occasion by not giving its utmost power, Toscanini will become violent. Score and stick will fly and inferno is let loose for a moment or two. . . . All technical difficulties and passage work seem to become more playable with Toscanini. He feels the tempo at which a piece will sound most effective. . . . It is a very subtle matter, and perhaps not perceived at all by the audience, but the orchestra is supremely aware of it. Only a hair's breadth lies between ease and great difficulty in a technical matter, and Toscanini succeeds invariably in finding ease.'[124]

He returned to Italy after his London concerts and spent most of the summer relaxing and preparing for his second NBC season. He did, however, accept a short engagement in August.

Not long after the Austrian *Anschluss*, the mayor of Lucerne and some of the Swiss city's other important citizens decided to attempt to set up a small music festival which would draw upon some of the musicians who were now unable or unwilling to play at Salzburg. Toscanini was invited to come and he quickly agreed to conduct one concert. Before long a series of eight concerts had been organized, and the participants included Cortot, Ansermet, Feuermann, Serkin, Fritz and Adolph Busch, Walter and Mengelberg. A 'Swiss Festival Orchestra' was formed, with members of the Busch Quartet as string section leaders and with five of Switzerland's other leading quartets in the ranks. Polo came up from Milan to join in the ensemble as well.

All of the concerts except Toscanini's were held either in the *Kursaal* or at the *Kunsthaus*; his was held in the park next to the villa of Triebschen, on Lake Lucerne, where Wagner had lived and worked from 1866 to '72. A special wooden shell was erected for the event, which took place on 25 August. Toscanini contributed his services gratis; but ticket prices for his performance were four times those of the other concerts. The programme, in addition to the *Siegfried Idyll*, which had been written and first performed in the villa, included works of Mozart, Beethoven, Rossini and more Wagner. Since the demand for tickets had been so great, he agreed to conduct a second concert two days later in the *Kunsthaus*—this time Cherubini, Brahms, Mendelssohn and Wagner. He was very happy with the atmosphere of the new festival and promised to come back the following summer.

On his return to Italy his passport was taken away, and efforts to get it back were futile at first. His existence was a terrible irritant to Mussolini, and the previous spring the Fascist press had begun a smear campaign against him. One slanderous article in Cremona's *Il regime fascista* was entitled 'The Honorary Jew'. After making gratuitous calumnies against Toscanini, it lists the licence plate numbers of some Italian cars noticed by informants in Lucerne, and incites 'comrades' in the various cities of provenance to take appropriate action.[125]

Toscanini realized that it was becoming foolishly dangerous for his family and himself to continue to return to Italy, even as visitors. While awaiting his passport, he spent some time at an old farmhouse-villa he owned at Ripalta Guerrina, near Crema, and on the *isolino*; and he paid a visit to Parma to see his only surviving sister, Ada, and to look nostalgically and tearfully around the Conservatory and some other places dear to him.

In Venice, Wally saw Fulvio De Suvich, Italy's ambassador to the United States, about the restitution of her father's passport. The ambassador spoke with Count Galeazzo Ciano, the foreign minister, who warned him not to involve himself in the affair: 'The Duce flies into a rage if you talk to him about Toscanini.' So Wally herself went to speak with Ciano, who wrote in his dairy on 7 September:

> 'I received Countess Castelbarco Toscanini who cried over the withdrawal of her father's passport and worried over reaction in America, where he has to conduct concerts soon. The Duce is annoyed because many Italians, and above all the Princess of Piedmont, went to Lucerne for the Wagnerian concert. But the withdrawal of the passport is related to a wiretap, from which it seems that Toscanini attacked the Duce for his anti-Semitic policy, terming it "medieval stuff".'

Suvich met Mussolini in Trieste and broached the subject despite Ciano's warning, mentioning that a worldwide outcry could ensue. Mussolini agreed to give back the passport, but Toscanini would have to request it himself. Toscanini refused. A plan was formulated to have him escape in a hydroplane which would take him from the Italian to the Swiss part of Lago Maggiore. This appealed to his sense of adventure, but he feared reprisals against his family and friends.

Finally, Walter Toscanini encouraged a Swiss journalist friend to begin an uproar in the world press. The Duce gave in and Toscanini left for America. He was seventy-one then and the Fascists were firmly entrenched. There was a good chance that he would never see his country again.

He reached New York aboard the *Normandie* on 10 October and began rehearsals the next day. The orchestra now had ninety-four permanent players, and twenty of these were replacing people who had left after the first season. (I do not know whether any of those departures were involuntary.) Steinberg had been engaged as his assistant conductor and had worked with the orchestra for ten days before Toscanini's arrival. At Toscanini's first rehearsal, the orchestra— aware of the problems he had faced in Italy—gave him a great ovation as he walked on to the stage. He motioned his thanks, but his gesture to stop the applause and cheering did not work. This time, his 'boys' really wanted him to know how they felt. Several minutes passed before he could begin the session.

The broadcasts were resumed on 15 October. The second concert featured Feuermann in *Don Quixote*; the third included Toscanini's first performance in over forty years of Tchaikovsky's 'Pathétique' Symphony; on the fourth he led Samuel Barber's Adagio for Strings and *Essay* for orchestra; William Primrose played the solo part in *Harold in Italy* on 21 January 1939; and in February there were all-Brahms, all-Sibelius and all-Wagner programmes. Toscanini also took the orchestra to Newark, Baltimore, Boston, Chicago, Pittsburgh, Providence and Washington for concerts which were not broadcast, and he led several recording sessions in February, March and April. He broke with Rodzinski that winter: according to Rodzinski's wife it was because of a lie told Toscanini by H. Leopold Spitalny, the orchestra's personnel manager, which is quite possible since he was fed numerous lies by NBC officials. But one friend close to the Toscanini family told me that in this case the lie had been Rodzinski's: he had told Toscanini that NBC had not paid for one of his engagements; and when Toscanini questioned NBC officials, they showed him the cancelled cheque, endorsed by Rodzinski. I do not know which—if either—of these stories is correct.

He returned to the BBC Symphony for a seven-concert Beethoven cycle which was spread through nearly the whole month of May, and which included all the symphonies, two performances of the *Missa Solemnis*, and shorter works. (His total fee was £3,675.) Only a fraction of the 75,000 people who had applied for tickets were accommodated. There was also a recording session on 1 June.

He attended a performance of Sir Arthur Bliss's ballet, *Checkmate*, which he liked. Bliss, on his part, attended Toscanini's rehearsals and was deeply impressed by 'this man, so obviously dedicated to music'. The Toscaninis invited him to their hotel for a visit.

'I shall not forget his first words to me, as they were an example of how courteously to put a humbler musician at his ease. Leading me by the arm to a sofa, and settling me down by him, he said "Tell me, Mr. Bliss—do *you*, as an English musician, think that I, as an Italian, take the slow movements of Beethoven rather fast?" At once I found myself talking eagerly and naturally, while Madame Toscanini bustled around, supervising our tea. I have at times in my life suffered from the arrogant manner assumed by some famous conductors, so I like to recall this hour with Toscanini as a signal proof of my contention that a great man is usually also a modest one.'[126]

Toscanini also attended a performance of Verdi's *Macbeth* conducted by Busch at Glyndebourne. Later, Busch invited Toscanini—through Alberto Erede—to conduct *Falstaff* there. He replied that he liked Glyndebourne but simply did not have the time. And he added: '*Macbeth* is wonderful. Busch can do *Falstaff* very well—I couldn't do it better.'[127]

He was in Lucerne for much of the summer. The festival had been expanded and its participants—in addition to those of the previous year—included Rachmaninoff, Horowitz, Casals, Boult and Huberman. This year Toscanini conducted seven times—four concerts in the *Kunsthaus*, two performances of the Verdi *Requiem* in the Jesuit church, and a special performance, for a few invited guests—including Friedelind Wagner and her two old aunts—at which a small group of musicians played the *Siegfried Idyll* inside the Triebschen villa where it had first been performed in 1870.

His mood was grim during the festival. Like everyone else, he knew that Europe was about to face another catastrophe. A few friends were in tears while listening to his last rehearsal for his last concert of the summer. There were two beautiful actresses, Luisa Rainer and Madeleine Carrol; an old granddaughter of Mathilde Wesendonck; Italian journalist Camilla Cederna; and Renato Levi, who had a record shop on Via Verdi, near La Scala, and who was to die in a German concentration camp five years later. That concert took place on 29 August and included Brahms's Second Piano Concerto with Horowitz. Three days later Germany invaded Poland. It was to be a long time before Toscanini again conducted in Europe.

The Phenomenon

Toscanini was now an exile. On his return to New York in that terrible autumn of 1939 he joined the Mazzini Society—a group of liberal and socialist Italian expatriates who favoured the establishment of an Italian republic following the downfall of Fascism, which they all ardently hoped for. Their leaders included the historian Gaetano Salvemini, art critic Lionello Venturi, church historian Giorgio La Piana, literary historian Giuseppe Antonio Borgese, Colonel Randolfo Pacciardi, Alberto Tarchiani (later Italy's ambassador to the United States) and Count Carlo Sforza, who was a minister of state both before and after the Fascist period. These men asked Toscanini to accept the presidency of the society; he refused, but told them they could count on him for support at any time.

The Toscaninis moved from the Hotel Astor to a large home which they had rented in suburban Riverdale. The house, called Villa Pauline, had a dark-panelled central hall, a large parlour, a library, a glass-enclosed sun room and an external balcony on the ground floor. From the balcony, and also from Toscanini's study on the next floor—which was reached by a grand staircase—one could look out over the five-acre estate, down to the Hudson River and across it to the New Jersey Palisades. The environment was a peaceful one, and Toscanini was able to study, receive visitors and relax there. In the autumn of 1942 they moved to a different house in the same area. It was called Wave Hill, and had once been Mark Twain's residence; but they bought and returned to the Villa Pauline a few years later.

Signora Carla supervised the household and managed her husband's finances, about which he knew—and wished to know—nothing. She was a naturally friendly, helpful and generous person, and her main concern during the pre-war and war years was helping to secure American entry visas, jobs and homes for refugee European friends and musicians less fortunate than her husband. One of her favourite pastimes was shopping, and she was an intrepid bargain-hunter. Nearly everyone who knew her recalls her as an intelligent and pleasant person. Although she had no formal musical training, she was the only person in the world who would freely and regularly criticize Toscanini's performances to his face; and he always took her opinion seriously.

Now in his seventies, he made few concessions to age in his daily life. He generally went to bed in the early hours of the morning and awoke by 6.30, and he often took pills to help him sleep four or five hours. A cup of thick Italian coffee would be served to him in bed, and he would read or study until 8.00, when he and his wife would have another coffee and rolls. More study occupied most of his morning, although he would often take walks and look at the flowers in his greenhouse. Lunch was served at 1.30. He loved *minestrone* and other thick soups, but he might also eat a *risotto* or *polenta* as a first course. The second course was often veal, followed by cheese and coffee and perhaps fruit. No dessert. Wine was, of course, served with the meal. Supper was lighter than lunch.

He dressed very formally, as always, and was extremely fastidious in his personal habits. His wife cut his hair, he always shaved himself without looking in the mirror, and he used an old-fashioned fire-heated moustache iron to keep his moustache bristly. He was still an incredible philanderer, too, thanks to his vivacity, fame, good health, good looks and—above all—undiminished appetite. One of his loves at that time was Eleonora von Mendelssohn, a great-grandniece of the composer. Her father, Robert, was an eccentric Berlin financier who had married Giulietta Gordigiani, a friend of the actress Eleonora Duse; and the younger Eleonora was the older one's namesake and goddaughter. She herself was an actress of moderate ability who had led a wild life from her youth. According to one person who knew her, she had two great loves in her life: Max Reinhardt and Toscanini. She emigrated to America with the advent of Hitler, and worked tirelessly with Signora Carla—with whom she got on well—to help other refugees. Her devotion to Toscanini, who was more than twice her age when they met, was fanatical for a number of years; but their relationship eventually ended and she died some years later under mysterious circumstances.

He was often surrounded by young, beautiful and admiring women, and by all indications he continued to take full advantage of the situation until he had far surpassed the average human life expectancy. Considerably less amusing and enviable than this aspect of his life, however, is the story of his relationship with his circle of 'friends' in New York.

Someone who knew Toscanini quite well said that his most serious problem in his day-to-day relations with other people was his love of gossip, and that this flaw, inconsequential in a person armoured with an average amount of cynicism, was dangerous in Toscanini's case because he was basically rather guileless, and because people would upset him and whip him into a frenzy by reporting things about mutual friends or colleagues which others would have taken with a grain of salt, but which he tended to swallow whole. (Sacchi makes a similar observation in the second Italian edition of his Toscanini biography; and he also knew Toscanini personally.)

A woman named Margherita De Vecchi, the daughter of an Italo-American banker, whom the Toscanini's had known since the Philharmonic years, who acted as self-appointed factotum to the Toscanini household, is said to have been a very friendly person but a fantastic gossip. Like Toscanini, she was a night owl; they would phone each other at 2 or 3 a.m. and exchange news about various people. He also enjoyed calling other friends to *chiacchierare*—an Italian verb meaning 'to chat' but also containing a trace of 'to gossip'. Unfortunately, by indulging in this seemingly harmless pastime, he often made himself the victim of skilled *intrigants* and favour-seekers, and kept at a distance people with whom he could have had more fruitful and enjoyable relationships. This, however, is vain moralizing on the part of this author. It seems reasonable to say that the involvement with the entourage which Toscanini acquired in his later years resulted from the fact that he was not as busy as he had been earlier in his life, that he had time to fill. That Toscanini was aware of the fact that people 'used' him is clear from an account given by Haggin of a visit to Riverdale in 1948 during which he and Toscanini had listened to a recording of the previous year's broadcast of Berlioz's *Romeo and Juliet*:

> 'Later, as he was putting away the score, he looked at me with a smile and said: "Now, Haggin, what would you like?"
>
> "Anything you would like to hear," I answered.
>
> "No"—still smiling—"what would you like—what would you like to have?" And as I stared at him uncomprehendingly he added: "You come only to see me?"
>
> "Yes, of course," I managed to answer, so shocked that I didn't until later apprehend what he was telling me in this way . . .'[1]

Two of the Toscaninis' children were now living in America. Walter, who, together with his brother-in-law Count Castelbarco, had run a fine antiquarian bookshop in Milan (and who had been extremely kind in giving employment and other help to Socialists and other 'untouchables' who had lost their positions during the régime) had moved with his wife and son to Camden, New Jersey, where his father had arranged a job for him with RCA. They later moved to New York and eventually occupied the third floor of the Villa Pauline. Walter then acted more or less as his father's manager. The Horowitzes lived in Manhattan; but little Sonia, whose grandfather absolutely adored her, very often stayed with her grandparents while her parents were on tour. Only Wally remained in Italy with her husband and daughter.

Toscanini's third NBC season began with two mixed programmes in October and continued with six all-Beethoven concerts—his first Beethoven cycle in America in over six years. He then took a long mid-season break, which was interrupted by his participation in a special benefit programme for the Chatham Square Music School on New York's Lower East Side. For his part in the performance, he dressed in an old-fashioned schoolmaster's frock coat and conducted a small orchestra whose players included Heifetz, Milstein, Busch,

19 Toscanini with his wife, Carla, at their summer home on the *isolino* San Giovanni, Lago Maggiore, between 1947 and 1949

20 Toscanini rehearsing for his last concert with the Scala orchestra, La Scala, Milan, September 1952 (© *E. Piccagliani, La Scala*)

21 Toscanini leaving the stage after his last concert at La Scala, 19 September 1952 (© *E. Piccagliani, La Scala*)

22 Toscanini in his dressing room at La Scala with Iris and Guido Cantelli, 19 September 1952 (© *E. Piccagliani, La Scala*)

23 Title page of one of Toscanini's published pieces

24 Toscanini on the *isolino*, talking with Antonio Ghiringhelli, Summer 1954

25 Toscanini attends a rehearsal of Spontini's *La Vestale*, La Scala, December 1954. With him: Victor De Sabata, Antonino Votto (back to camera) and Maria Callas (© *E. Piccagliani, La Scala*)

26 First page of a song written by Toscanini during his student years

27 Another song from Toscanini's student days, written out from memory in his old age. (Note his English translation of the words written beneath the original Italian.)

28 Toscanini consults the score during a rehearsal of Schubert's 'Great C Major' Symphony, 25 February 1947 (© *Robert Hupka*)

29 and 30
At a recording
session for Debussy's
La Mer,
4 March 1947
(© *Robert Hupka*)

31 The funeral procession gets underway, Milan, Piazza della Scala, 18 February 1957

Primrose and Feuermann in Mozart's *A Musical Joke* and Gillet's *Loin du Bal*. The players, all dressed in short pants, were billed as 'Toscanini's Children's Orchestra'.

In February he led a tour performance in Newark and in March recorded the Beethoven Violin Concerto with Heifetz; he then conducted the last eight concerts of the NBC season. There was another recording session in May (Brahms's Second Piano Concerto with Horowitz), followed by a special broadcast concert in Washington, given at the invitation of the US government for the American Scientific Congress. At the end of the month, he and the orchestra departed aboard the *Brazil* for a major tour of South America.

For years, South American musical organizations had tried to get Toscanini to return to their continent; but he had always refused. In 1939, however, a prominent financier and music-lover named Bogdan had written Chotzinoff from Buenos Aires to suggest that Toscanini bring the NBC Symphony to South America. 'We are willing to go to any lengths to meet your and Toscanini's conditions,' he said. When Toscanini was told that the tour would be a grand gesture of international friendship, he accepted. He and the musicians all agreed to cuts in their fees, and financial backing came from NBC and from committees in the four cities in which the orchestra was to play.

The voyage to Rio de Janeiro took nearly two weeks. Toscanini and his wife were often out on deck, talking and joking with the men in the orchestra. On 10 June, one of the last days at sea, news arrived by radio that Italy had attacked France, which so upset Toscanini that he locked himself in his room and raged like a wild beast.

An enormous crowd greeted the orchestra on its arrival at Rio, where two concerts were given. These were Toscanini's first appearances in the city since his début season fifty-four years earlier. The orchestra then proceeded to São Paulo for one performance, followed by eight in Buenos Aires—where Toscanini had last been seen in 1912 and where enthusiasm was particularly great—and two in Montevideo. Pro-Nazi demonstrations were anticipated in the Uruguayan capital but did not take place. Another concert was given in São Paulo on 8 July and two more in Rio on the next two nights.

The orchestra returned home on the *Uruguay*, reaching New York on 22 July. Only on the last day of the voyage was Toscanini informed that one of his violists, Jacques Tuschinsky, had been killed in a traffic accident on the day of the last concert in Rio. On hearing the news he burst into tears and refused to emerge from his suite or to eat. He contributed $1,000 to a fund which the orchestra had set up for the musician's family.

Later in the summer Toscanini and his wife made a trip to the west to visit the Grand Canyon. His fourth NBC season began with a benefit performance of Verdi's *Te Deum* and *Requiem* at Carnegie Hall on 23 November. The soloists were Zinka Milanov, Bruna Castagna, Jussi Bjoerling and Nicola Moscona. (I

have heard recordings of about half a dozen performances of the *Requiem* led by
Toscanini between 1938 and 1951; but this one, to me, is the greatest of all.) His
fifth programme of the season, another benefit at Carnegie Hall, offered the
Missa Solemnis, with the same soloists as for the *Requiem*, except for Kipnis in
place of Moscona. An incident at a rehearsal for this performance resulted in a
serious rift between Toscanini and NBC.

The orchestra Toscanini had begun to conduct in 1937 included a large number of young string virtuosos who had given up concert careers and positions in
string quartets to play with him, and who delighted him with their exceptional
talent, their youthful energy and their warm responsiveness. Gradually, however,
he found himself baffled and frustrated by the fact that on some days they played
like 'tired old men'. 'It took him some time to discover that the orchestra NBC
said it created for him played in other programmes under other conductors,'
cellist Alan Shulman told Haggin; 'and it made him angry because it affected our
work with him.' Shulman went on to relate the following story:

'On a Friday in December 1940 we were scheduled to rehearse from 5 to 7:30
in Carnegie Hall for a performance of the *Missa Solemnis* the next night. There
was a concert of the Chicago Symphony in Carnegie Hall that afternoon, after
which the platform had to be set up on the stage for the chorus in the *Missa*;
so the rehearsal didn't start until 5:30, which meant it would go on to 8. But
35 men of the orchestra had to play with Frank Black in the Cities Service
program in Studio 8H at 8; and they had to leave at 7:30 if they were to . . .
be ready for the broadcast at 8. And since this was the first time we were doing
the *Missa* with Maestro he was really out to work. So 7:30 came, and he kept
right on working; then it was 7:32, and 7:33; and at that point the personnel
manager stood behind Maestro and signaled to the men one by one to sneak
out. I saw Carlton Cooley, right under the Maestro's nose, get down on his
hands and knees and crawl out; and it was only after a number of men had
done this that the Old Man's eye caught the movement of the bassoon that
one of the men was holding as he crawled out, and he discovered what had
been going on. He was so infuriated that he threw down his stand and walked
out. He conducted the performance the next night and finished the season; but
a couple of months later when the conductors for 1941–42 were announced he
was not among them, and we learned that Stokowski was going to conduct us
instead.'[2]

After the *Missa* incident rumours began circulating within the orchestra that
Toscanini was about to resign. One of the principal players told me recently that
he had had lunch with Steinberg one day, and that Steinberg had encouraged
him to write a letter to Toscanini urging him to stay, 'because he'll listen to
orchestra members'. This musician wrote the letter and brought it to the next
rehearsal, with the intention of inviting any of his colleagues who so wished to

co-sign it with him; and before the rehearsal began he announced that he had something he wanted to discuss afterwards.

It was a very rough rehearsal: Toscanini stormed and screamed about everything. (The rehearsals were gruesome at that time because Toscanini was so outraged over what was happening.) Afterwards the musician did not want to raise the matter, feeling it was the wrong moment. The orchestra insisted, however. So he said that they had all heard rumours to the effect that Toscanini was going to leave, and that he had written a letter to Toscanini expressing his wish that he stay. He said he hoped that other members of the orchestra would be willing to add their signatures. Everyone said Yes, and he was about to read the letter to the orchestra when Spitalny, the personnel manager, jumped up and said: 'You have no right to read that letter here!' 'Why not?' Spitalny, before he had thought about what he was saying, blurted out: 'How do you know we *want* him back?' He then realized what he had said and closed his mouth. The orchestra men said that it was of no matter whether the letter were read aloud or not: they would sign it. But its writer had changed his mind, feeling it would be more useful if each one were to write his own.

A few days later Toscanini called him and invited him to his home for lunch. At one point during the meal, Toscanini said to him: 'I cannot understand something. When my son-in-law give concert in a city, if they don't want him back the next year, they don't ask him to write letter of resignation.' 'Why do you mention that, Maestro?' 'Because NBC want me to write letter of resignation.' 'You mean they don't want you back?' 'That is right.'

When contracts came up for renewal in the spring, this player's was 'overlooked' by the management; and it was not until Stokowski insisted on retaining him that he was given a new contract.

At about the same time as the *Missa Solemnis* incident Toscanini was angered when he learned that Burghauser, who had come to America at the time of the Austrian *Anschluss*, had been refused a place in the NBC Symphony—a job for which Toscanini had recommended him when the position became available. Spitalny and Chotzinoff told Burghauser in no uncertain terms that while Toscanini had the right to veto players who had been accepted by them, only *they* had the right actually to hire people. But despite these upsets, Toscanini led thirteen broadcasts and several recording sessions during that difficult 1940–1 season. In April he guest conducted the Chicago Symphony for the first and only time, and he accepted an invitation to return to Buenos Aires in June and July to conduct four performances of the Beethoven Ninth (plus shorter pieces) and three of the Verdi *Requiem* with the Teatro Colón Orchestra and Chorus. (He took six wind players from the US along with him to strengthen the ranks.) These were his last appearances in South America.

The Toscaninis re-encountered Friedelind Wagner in Buenos Aires. She had been with them in Lucerne when the war had broken out, and since she—unlike her mother—was a convinced anti-Nazi, Toscanini had arranged with the mayor of Lucerne that she could stay in Switzerland. She eventually made her way to England, only to find herself interned on the Isle of Man. Toscanini pestered the British authorities for months on her behalf and she was finally allowed to go to Argentina in March 1941. The Toscaninis obtained a US entry visa for her and told her that she could return to New York with them. She recalled that their flight back to New York was delayed because of bad weather, and she was amused to find that news of Toscanini's delay had already appeared in a Buenos Aires paper while they were still awaiting the flight. She showed the article to him. 'Put it away,' he told her; 'it is bad taste to read about oneself.'[3] (He actually did read about himself—reviews and other items, too—which he sometimes referred to in conversation; but he regularly told people that he did not do so.)

It is obvious that Toscanini was unsure how to proceed in regard to the NBC affair. During the previous half-century he had developed a very effective way of dealing with orchestra boards and opera impresarios: he made what he considered to be reasonable demands, and if those demands were not met, he left. At La Scala, at the Metropolitan, at the Philharmonic and at countless other places he had always been the central figure, the person whose presence had been the best guarantee of excellence and whose departure had almost always given rise to general mourning. But the NBC Symphony did not have a board of directors to be tyrannized over: it was one tiny accessory of a huge business corporation; and although RCA considered Toscanini an asset—that is, although his name brought prestige to the corporation, attracted radio listeners and sold RCA records—no one in the organization was mad enough to believe that RCA's future depended upon Toscanini's continued presence. On the contrary, many executives felt that the NBC Symphony cost more than it was worth and that it ought to be dropped altogether. So Toscanini learned that while fawning concern was shown him by the people directly involved with the section of the corporation in which he was employed, the whole fate of the orchestra (let alone its artistic standards and achievements) was of little importance to the people who were actually in control.

During the time when he was most angry with NBC he went so far as to talk with William Paley, head of the rival CBS, but nothing came of their meeting; and he accepted invitations from the Philadelphia Orchestra and the New York Philharmonic to guest conduct during the 1941–2 season. But he was not satisfied. He wanted to do more, yet he no longer wanted the permanent conductorship of a regular orchestra, with the numerous repetitions of concerts, tours, administrative decisions and fund-raising and subscription campaigns which went along with such a position. This problem plagued him for months; and the very mild and friendly letter of resignation which he sent Sarnoff in April 1941 indicated that he did not wish to break off all relations with NBC.

The desire to conduct opera took hold of him occasionally, as was natural in a man who had spent so much of his life in the theatre; and he discussed this more than once with stage director Herbert Graf, one of his Salzburg collaborators, who was now living in the States. Graf recalled:

'During my stay in New York he tried twice to present complete operas: at the New York World's Fair in 1939 and later for the Red Cross. He wanted to do *Falstaff* and *La traviata*; but since the financial guarantees necessary for a perfect realization were not forthcoming, he had to satisfy himself with conducting them on the radio . . .'[4]

What a loss for American opera!

In November 1941 Toscanini returned to the Philadelphia Orchestra for the first time in eleven years, and he came back again in January and February; three programmes were given twice each in Philadelphia and there were two tour performances—one in Washington and one in New York. Quite a few of the works played on this series were recorded during eight sessions at Philadelphia's Academy of Music. The recordings comprised Schubert's Ninth Symphony, Mendelssohn's Incidental Music to *A Midsummer Night's Dream*, Berlioz's 'Queen Mab' Scherzo, Debussy's *La Mer* and *Ibéria*, Strauss's *Death and Transfiguration*, Tchaikovsky's Sixth Symphony and Respighi's *Feste romane*. The story of these magnificent recordings is given in detail in B.H. Haggin's *The Toscanini Musicians Knew* and must be summarized here. Toscanini listened to the test pressings in the autumn of 1942, approving some of the sides but rejecting others. In the normal course of events, the rejected sides would have been re-made at a time mutually convenient to Toscanini and the orchestra; but the American Federation of Musicians had meanwhile forbidden its members to record, pending a new agreement with the recording companies. This ban was in effect for two years, and by the time it ended the Philadelphia Orchestra was under contract to Columbia instead of RCA. Haggin reports:

'The orchestra would have been available for the correction and completion of its Victor recordings with Toscanini; but Walter Toscanini told me at that time that Victor wanted the Philadelphia Orchestra recordings abandoned and new ones made by Toscanini with the NBC Symphony, and that "we are trying to get Father to forget the Philadelphia recordings". He didn't say why Victor wanted this; and one could only conjecture that it didn't want Toscanini's name to promote a Columbia orchestra, and rather than have this happen preferred to sacrifice recordings which documented the collaboration of this great conductor and great orchestra in some of the greatest performances Toscanini ever put on records; and that for Victor's purpose one Toscanini performance was as good as another . . . The argument that the Philadelphia was now a Columbia orchestra wouldn't have counted for much with Toscanini; and Victor could hardly argue that the performances were poor; but it could, and did successfully, argue that the Philadelphia Orchestra recordings were mechanically defective beyond hope of remedy.

Quite possibly, Victor, in persuading Toscanini, also persuaded itself that the recordings were atrocious—in particular that the musical sound couldn't be heard because of the noise—and that therefore they couldn't be issued. But it wasn't true: the surface noise was stronger than the usual surface noise from 78-rpm records; but it didn't prevent one from hearing the musical sound: one's ear separated it from the musical sound, which was clearly audible and marvellously beautiful. . . .'⁵★

In 1963 the Toscanini–Philadelphia recording of Schubert's Ninth Symphony was released by RCA, after engineer John Corbett had spent 800 hours in reducing the level of surface noise and eliminating the clicks from the deteriorated metal masters. And in the autumn of 1976, thirty-five years after they were recorded, the remaining performances were released, giving evidence of less remedial effort applied to the increased deterioration.

Toscanini's return to the New York Philharmonic occurred in April and May 1942, as the ending of the orchestra's 100th anniversary season. He had been invited a year and a half earlier by the Philharmonic board and had vacillated for months on whether or not to accept. In fact, he did not finally make up his mind until the season in question had already begun and until Walter Price, one of the board members, had told him to his face that he was behaving very badly towards an organization which had always done everything to satisfy him. A heated argument had ensued; but in the end Toscanini had decided that Price was right, and he made up his mind to give them more than they had hoped for: with incredible energy and stamina for a man who had just passed his seventy-fifth birthday, he rehearsed and performed all nine Beethoven symphonies, the *Missa Solemnis*, the Triple Concerto and four overtures in a six-concert series—all within a period of two weeks! The rehearsals went very well. Haggin, who was present, said that the orchestra responded to Toscanini at the first rehearsal as if 'not six years but one day' had passed since he had last stood before it; that he was 'radiant' after the second rehearsal (' "My dear Haggin—today I can hope." '); and that in the few remaining minutes of one rehearsal, 'turning to the finale of the First Symphony, he led the orchestra through it without interruption and produced the performance of six . . . years earlier in all its beautiful detail.'⁶

Toscanini did conduct the NBC Symphony in five war bond benefit concert-broadcasts during the 1941–2 season—two in December and one each in January, March and April—and he led recording sessions in December and March. NBC was finding Stokowski as hard to handle as Toscanini had been, and

---

★ Several years later Haggin was told by one of RCA's chief producers that it had been Walter Toscanini who had compelled the company to abandon the recordings on the grounds of their technical defects.

the orchestra and public wanted Toscanini back; so Walter was asked to try to induce his father to return. It probably did not take much effort to persuade him: he did not want to stop conducting, the major American orchestras already had conductors under contract, Europe was destroying itself, the NBC season was tailored to his requirements and the salary was unmatchable. He agreed to take up his position again, with the proviso—according to one orchestra member —that Spitalny and Chotzinoff should not show their faces in the studio during his rehearsals; and Walter received a letter from NBC thanking him for his work on behalf of the 'RCA family'.[7] Toscanini shared the following two seasons with Stokowski (who presumably had been given a three-year contract), then with other conductors whom he selected.

On 19 July Toscanini conducted the American première of Shostakovich's Seventh Symphony, which had been written the previous year as a tribute to Russian resistance during the German siege of Leningrad. The score had been microfilmed in Kuybyshev, flown and driven to Teheran, and from there to Cairo and New York. Stokowski had persuaded NBC the previous December to buy the rights to the American première; but NBC now wanted Toscanini to conduct it. He insisted on seeing the score before deciding. It was handed to him on 14 June; he read through it and decided to conduct it. Stokowski immediately wrote to ask him to relinquish the première to him. Toscanini answered:

'I do not want nor will I attempt in any way to refute the arguments you display in your letter in order to prove and claim your right to give the first radio performance of Shostakovich Seventh Symphony. During my long career, I never urged the honour to conduct first performance of any composer! [Note: There was an incident concerning *Salome*, however . . .]

I admire Shostakovich music but I don't feel such a frenzied love for it like you. I had promised a time ago to receive the new score as it arrives from Russia. In effect, two men of the Am-Russ Music Corporation brought to me the film and some days later the first copy of the score....

As you can imagine, I eagerly looked into it for a few days.... At once I was deeply taken by its beauty and its anti-Fascist meanings, and I have to confess to you, by the greatest desire to perform it.

Don't you think, my dear Stokowski, it would be very interesting for everybody, and yourself, too, to hear the old Italian conductor (one of the first artists who strenuously fought against Fascism) to play this work of a young Russian anti-Nazi composer. I haven't a drop of Slavonic blood into my veins—I am only a true and genuine Latin.... Maybe I am not an intense interpreter of this kind of music, but I am sure I can conduct it very simply with love and honesty....

Beside that this performance will have for me *today* a special meaning.

Think it over, my dear Stokowski, only a few minutes and you will convince yourself not to give much importance to the arguments you displayed in your last letter....'[8]

Stokowski interpreted this in his own way and wrote, 'I am glad you are willing for me to make the first radio broadcast.' Toscanini replied:

'Your letter of Wednesday troubled me very much because I saw in it the complete result of some misunderstanding—maybe my poor English language has certainly been the cause, and I am sorry for it....

I don't know if you are aware that in the season 1938–1939 at the NBC, I renounced to be the first interpreter of the Shostakovich Fifth Symphony because of my scanty interest in it—and I want to repeat again that this time after a careful reading of the Seventh, I felt the strongest sympathy and emotion for this special work, so I urged the NBC to have it performed by me. Try to understand me, my dear Stokowski, only because of the special meaning of this Symphony. Happily, you are much younger than me, and Shostakovich will not stop writing new symphonies. You will certainly have all the opportunities you like to perform them. Be sure you will never find me again in your way....'[9]

He conducted the Philharmonic again in October and November. One of the programmes offered his first performance of Berlioz's complete Dramatic Symphony, *Romeo and Juliet*; and the last was an all-Wagner programme for the benefit of the Red Cross. He wanted to be sure that the beneficiary would realize at least $20,000 from the event, so he sent a signed blank cheque to the orchestra management in case the goal were not reached. In the end, his contribution was about $1,000.

His 1942–3 NBC season began on 1 November with a programme consisting entirely of American music (works by Loeffler, Creston, Gould and Gershwin), and there was a similar concert (Gilbert, Kennan, Griffes and Grofé) in the spring.* He led thirteen broadcasts in all, including a six-concert Brahms cycle, and also guest conducted both the Cincinnati and Philadelphia orchestras in February. On 25 April he conducted a special Tchaikovsky concert at Carnegie Hall with Horowitz as soloist. Seats were obtained only by the purchase of war bonds, and the total sales amounted to well over $10 million. The manuscript of Toscanini's orchestration of 'The Star-Spangled Banner' was sold at auction for $1 million in bonds during the interval. He conducted four more concerts for the war bonds drive in June, July and September. The broadcast of 25 July was a

---

* Other American composers whose music Toscanini led during his NBC years were Copland, Gillis, Rieti (naturalized American), Siegmeister, Sousa and Strong. He had conducted works by Chasins, Hanson, Harris and Schelling with the Philharmonic; so his list of American composers eventually numbered eighteen. (See Appendix II—B for names of pieces.)

programme of Verdi excerpts, and Toscanini and soprano Gertrude Ribla had just left the stage after the aria '*Pace, pace mio Dio*' from *La forza del destino* when an announcement was broadcast into the hall and over the air: Benito Mussolini had been deposed. Toscanini, beside himself, rushed back on to the stage, clasped his hands and gazed heavenwards, in a sign of thanksgiving, while the audience, equally beside itself, applauded, cheered, screamed, and all but tore the studio to pieces. Toscanini did not know that on that same day, printed posters were pasted all over La Scala's sign-boards. They said only: '*Evviva Toscanini, Ritorni Toscanini.*'

Earlier that year, in publishing their short work *What to Do with Italy*—which anticipated the post-Mussolinian political struggle—Salvemini and La Piana had written the following dedication (I translate from the Italian edition, which is the only one I have seen):

'To Maestro Arturo Toscanini who, in the darkest days of Fascist crimes, of Italy's dishonour, of the world's madness, remained intransigently faithful to the ideals of Mazzini and Garibaldi and, with tenacious faith, anticipated the dawn of the second Italian *Risorgimento*.'[10]

Now the crucial moment had come; these men of good will wished to see to it that none of the people who had compromised with the Fascists in any way would be allowed to participate in the new Italy. They attempted, mostly in vain, to make their voices heard in the US State Department, and they tried to influence American public opinion. They asked Toscanini if he would make a public statement, in print; and for the first time in his life he accepted. The editors of *Life* gave him the editorial page of their issue of 13 September 1943. He wrote directly in English and with great care. (I understand that he made a critical reference to the Church's position on Fascism which was removed before publication.)

In the statement ('To the People of America'), Toscanini said that he felt he could act as interpreter of the wishes of the Italian people who had been 'choked for more than twenty years'. He asserted—and this was his main point—that the King and Badoglio (Mussolini's successor) 'cannot be dissociated in any way from the fascist and militarist clique. They cannot be the representatives of the Italian people: they cannot in any way conclude peace with the Allies in the name of Italy, so betrayed by them.' He predicted that there would be a revolution in Italy, and that for this to 'result in an orderly democratic government, as we hope, it will be necessary for the Allies to support all democratic elements currently arrayed against the King and Badoglio'. These 'elements' of course included the long-suppressed Socialists and Communists, and the idea of supporting them, instead of dealing with the King and Badoglio, was unlikely to be greeted with enthusiasm by the Western Allies.

Toscanini went on to suggest that Italy's frontiers, as established before

Mussolini's accession, should be respected; that economic assistance should be given the new government; and that 'the Allies permit our volunteers to fight against the hated Nazis under the Italian flag with conditions substantially similar to those of the Free French' in order to facilitate an unconditional surrender of the Italian armed forces. Citing *Henry VI* he said:

'Do not forget that we Italians have been the first to endure the oppression of a tyrannical gang of criminals, supported by that "fainthearted and degenerate King" of Italy—but that we have never willingly submitted to them. Countless thousands of men and women in Italy shed blood, met imprisonment and death, striving fiercely against that horde of criminals, enduring also the apathy and indifference of the world then full of admiration for Mussolini.'

When, however, the Allies did conclude a surrender with the King and Badoglio, the Mazzini Society split: Sforza, Tarchiani and their faction accepted the compromise; but Toscanini, Salvemini and others remained adamant and left the Society. Sforza wrote Toscanini to explain his position. Toscanini replied unequivocally on 10 October:

'From this moment on you can consider me a *traitor to my Country*! Not even to save Italy could I come to terms with those who have shamefully betrayed her for more than twenty years! I could not even speak to or look at those two wretches. I am sorry for you..... Our tastes are very different... Your politics may be intelligent and shrewd, but I condemn them and despise them—and I declare myself against you and the Allied government which has fully demonstrated its complete ignorance and ineptitude in understanding the honest and simple Italian soul. Their policy regarding Italy has been a shameful fiasco— and, as Dorothy Thompson says, a complete failure. Their *"unconditional surrender"* is ridiculous..... And today they want to put the anti-Fascist forces into the hands of those who have betrayed them for long and, alas! sorrowful years!'[11]

The same day Toscanini answered a letter from an Italo-American named Gian Luca Cicogna, who had written him:

'Your article . . . thoroughly disgusted me. Why don't you continue to occupy yourself only with music and leave politics alone, since you don't understand anything about them? Who authorized you to express the feelings of Italians regarding His Majesty the King? I respond to your ignorant statements with a: Long live the King, Long live the House of Savoy!'[12]

Toscanini's reply:

'No—I have never had the bad taste to express to the American people the feelings of those shameless Italians who, like you, admire and respect that degenerate coward, the King of Italy, who has betrayed *everything* and *everyone*.

A constitutional monarch betrayed the Constitution and signed the Statute which made a free people into the slaves of a gang of criminals! For more than twenty years he has sanctioned with his signature all the iniquities which his *worthy* cousin Mussolini, the mad criminal, set before him. In the end, to save himself, he even betrayed Mussolini and the ignominious alliance with Germany. Where can you find a more vile being???? Where??

—No—Noble Gian Luca Cicogna—my letter to the American people interpreted the feelings of the other Italians . . . the good ones—the pure ones—those who sincerely love Italy and liberty... You have nothing to do with it —and neither do those Fascists who de-Fascisticized themselves at the last minute out of convenience and cowardice!... You misunderstood my letter.'[13]

On 9 September Toscanini conducted the NBC Symphony in a special broadcast which he called 'Victory Symphony, Part I', to mark the fall of Italian Fascism. Among other pieces, it included the first movement of Beethoven's Fifth Symphony. He planned to conduct the entire symphony when Germany fell.

During the same period he agreed to participate in a film. In Paris in 1936 he had almost accepted director Max Ophüls's offer of 1 million lire to conduct in a sound film—after having seen and enjoyed Ophüls's film version of Smetana's *The Bartered Bride*; then he had had second thoughts and had withdrawn. Since then he had turned down major American film company offers of up to $250,000 to appear on the screen. Now the US Office of War Information asked him to contribute his services gratis to the making of a propaganda film which could be sent to the liberated portions of Europe. He said Yes. The film shows him conducting the Overture to *La forza del destino* as well as a deservedly less-known Verdi work called the *Hymn of the Nations*—a potboiler written for London's International Exposition of 1862, which makes use of the themes of *God Save the Queen*, the *Marseillaise* and the *Garibaldi Hymn*. Toscanini changed the text of this last from '*Italia, patria mia*' ('Italy, my country') to '*Italia, patria mia tradita*' ('Italy, my betrayed country'); and he wrote a bridge passage at the end and added the Socialist 'Internationale' and 'The Star-Spangled Banner' in tribute to the other two major allies.

One of the people who occasionally enjoyed Toscanini's company during the years of exile—and especially during this final phase of the war—was the Italian anarchist Armando Borghi, who wrote very charmingly of their acquaintanceship in an article which appeared in *Il mondo* not long after Toscanini's death. Borghi mentions that until the war, the anti-Fascists were a very small minority among influential Italo-Americans.

'. . . As far as the roughnecks of the colony were concerned, Toscanini had betrayed Italy and the Duce . . . Let's reflect on the fact that Toscanini was the

only [Italian] world celebrity who never went to visit the Pope, never surrounded himself with priests and friars and nuns, never conducted music in
the churches [Note: he actually did do so on three or four occasions, but never
for religious functions], who never gave benefit concerts for religious organizations—either in Italy or in America.

. . . Toscanini, it should be repeated, was not the sort of man who restyles
himself with the passing of time, even (one ought to say *above all*) when in
foreign lands. Even when surrounded by adorers of high rank he remained
the son of an artisan-tailor from Parma's *Oltretorrente*. A famous journalist
wanted to know who was the musician Toscanini loved most. The Maestro
responded, "Verdi." "And why?" "Because he remained a peasant." Of
course, Toscanini said these things to people who didn't understand a thing.
What Toscanini meant was that Verdi was not a *runaway* from his world, from
his origins.

Once he asked me: "How are you able to speak while facing the public?"
I answered that without looking at the public I wouldn't know how to open my
mouth. He said to me: "If I didn't show my tail to my public, I couldn't
conduct."

. . . He was a thousand times stronger than we others, who acted with
"political" preparation and premeditation. He was *defenceless* at the time of
Fascism's rise; he was not furnished with that armour of diffidence which we
had and which resulted from our political convictions. Toscanini was . . . absorbed by the majesty of his art; but his internal world predestined him to be
what he was. . . . Had it not been for the "now you see me, now you don't"
concerning the rescue, not of poor devils, but of big guns like Farinacci and
Starace . . . the dissensions among the anti-Fascist leaders [in New York]
would have remained in the background. This necessity *not to soften*, in what
was by then the conclusive hour of the war, showed everyone and everything
in its correct light. In that hour Toscanini openly ranked himself against
compromise and against the compromise-brokers. As a result he broke with the
Mazzini Society, at the moment in which it was about to . . . act as a Noah's
Ark for saving the black-shirt big guns of the entire colony. . . .

We were often in touch at that time. We discussed politics and post-Fascist
society. We also discussed anarchy, which he found a "reasonable" ideal. He
laughed at those who called him a future Paderewski. In fact, he had never
accepted, nor did he later accept, honours or decorations which he could have
had for the asking in Italy, in America, in the whole world. . . .'[14]

On 12 June 1944 *Life* magazine carried a lengthy article entitled 'An Italian
Manifesto', co-signed by Salvemini, Toscanini and four other leading Italian
émigrés. Once again, they urged the British and Americans to stop standing
behind the King and Badoglio, and also went further in their condemnation of

Allied policy. It was a desperate, heartfelt and impassioned plea; and it was disregarded.

Along with the public anxiety there was of course personal anxiety. Toscanini was very preoccupied about Wally, who had remained in Italy. Occasionally they managed to exchange letters through clandestine channels. He had written her on 17 May 1943, when she was staying on the estate near Crema with her family and a group of Milanese friends who feared remaining in the city during the aerial bombardments:

> 'I finished my concerts some weeks ago and am resting in this delightful Riverdale, which reminds me so much of our dear Isolino—if in subdued tones. I'll conduct a few concerts from time to time ... but only benefit performances—then the real musical season begins on 31 October.
>
> As you see my activity hasn't diminished despite my 76 years—it's a sign that the good Lord (or someone in his place) is protecting me, keeping me in good health and with the ever more fervent hope that we'll see each other much sooner than we had thought. Dear Wally, how many times my thoughts —or rather our thoughts (because Mamma, Walter and Wanda don't love you any less than I do) are with you, longing to know how your life, how the lives of all of you, are going. You can well imagine it from the worry which you feel for us. But, again, I hope that we'll be together much sooner than we thought....
>
> And our dear Emanuela? How we all would like to see her! Sonia and Walfredo are adorable. Still beautiful, lively and good. I'm so happy about the Colony you've created. Good for you! You're a marvel of goodness and prudence. And I'm happy not only for you but for our relatives and friends. I embrace and kiss you with infinite tenderness ...'[15]

On 27 September 1944 he wrote to her again. By this time her marriage had ended and she and Emanuela had escaped to Switzerland.

> 'The mere thought that in a few days you will receive these few lines which I'm setting down on this page with nervous hand and suffering heart makes me breathe a little more easily. But I can't stand it anymore. It seems like a thousand years since I saw you. The complete absence of news about you makes me "irrational". I can understand that you can't write us. There are reasons of *force majeure*—but that none of our friends can do so for you seems unlikely to me. But I don't want to sadden you with my complaints. God willing, it seems to me that the beginning of the end of this monstrous tragedy has already started—let's hope for a quick resolution and that you can soon return home.—Our health is fine. I'll begin my concerts again in a few weeks. I'll conduct sixteen this year—four more than last year. So you see that your old father is still going strong and holding up quite well.'[16]

And on 9 November:

'Your long letter was like a divine "sunbeam". How I needed it—after long months of sorrowful waiting. My dear daughter, it was a serious mistake not to have left with Emanuela when we were in Switzerland!

I'll just tell you today that I began working three weeks ago. Yes, it serves to take my mind off things, but not to remove the heaviness and anguish from my heart. I think of my poor, dear Italy, mishandled and torn asunder by enemies and friends alike, and I don't know why I'm not there to do something better than what I can do here. I assure you that I feel remorse because of it. . . .'[17]

Despite the agitation of those days, Toscanini continued to carry out his duties at NBC with his usual energy, love and intransigence. He led thirteen broadcasts during the 1943-4 season.* A Wagner–Verdi concert was given at Madison Square Garden on 25 May for the benefit of the Red Cross—which realized $100,000. This event made use of the combined NBC Symphony and New York Philharmonic and the All-City High School Chorus and Glee Clubs. The remarkable recording of the last act of *Rigoletto*, with Milanov, Merriman, Peerce, Warren and Moscona, which is still in the record catalogues in 1978, was made at this concert. His only guest performance that season took place in February with the Philadelphia Orchestra—an all-Beethoven programme for the orchestra's pension fund, and his last appearance with that ensemble. The NBC Symphony gave four summer broadcasts under his direction, again on behalf of the war bond drive.

The first nine broadcasts of the 1944-5 season were devoted to Beethoven. This particular cycle ended with a concert performance of *Fidelio* (Act I on 10 December, Act II a week later), which was the first of seven operas he directed for the radio during his NBC years. In October and February he conducted special concerts which were not broadcast—the first in the New York City Centre, the second at Carnegie Hall, with Horowitz as soloist; on 13 January he conducted the New York Philharmonic for the last time, in a pension fund concert which repeated the programme of his very first concert with that orchestra (14 January 1926); and on 8 May, for 'Victory in Europe Day', he led,

---

* The orchestra was now being sponsored by General Motors; so NBC had officially turned public service into private profit. When General Motors later dropped the broadcasts and no other sponsor could be found, NBC sold the prime Sunday afternoon hour then occupied by the concerts to Ford and moved Toscanini to Saturday at 6.30, when vast numbers of Americans were eating supper and/or preparing to go out. Toscanini, however, was told by NBC that more people would be able to listen to the broadcasts at that hour; and people close to him, who knew better, allowed him to believe this.

as promised, a complete performance of Beethoven's Fifth Symphony at NBC. Since the union's ban had now been lifted, he began making many records.

He also visited the west coast for the first time to conduct a pension fund concert of the Los Angeles Philharmonic on 19 April. One of the last pieces on the programme was Weber's *Invitation to the Dance*, during which a young woman ran on to the stage, barefoot, and began dancing. Toscanini stopped the orchestra; the woman eventually danced into the arms of backstage policemen and was taken to a psychiatric hospital for examination. The concert then proceeded normally.

As soon as the war had ended Toscanini received invitations to come back to Italy. Rumours of his imminent return began circulating—and not only in Italy. Milanese artist Aldo Carpi, waiting to be transported home from Mauthausen concentration camp, wrote in his diary on 2 June: 'Is it true that Toscanini is in Milan and has spoken at La Scala?' It was not true; but Toscanini's re-entry was looked forward to as a sign that the nightmare had really ended.[18]

La Scala had been heavily damaged by Allied bombs in August 1943. Toscanini authorized Wally—who had rejoined her family in America—to contribute 1 million lire in his name towards the reconstruction; the rest was done by the Allied government and other donations. However, Toscanini refused to return to Italy until the monarchy had been eliminated—or at least until the people were given a chance to vote on the issue. He responded thus to an invitation from the Scala Orchestra:

'. . . I have been near you with all my spirit throughout these sorrowful years of struggle, of mourning and of despair. I never doubted, not even during the blackest and saddest hours, the generous contribution that Italian patriots were making in the struggle for world liberation, at the moment of redemption from Nazi-Fascist tyranny.

But the tens of thousands of Italian patriots who fell heroically alongside the Allied soldiers in this war, the decisiveness and discipline demonstrated by you Milanese in the hour of revolt, the inexorable and rapid execution of the major Fascist criminals, make me certain that the republican ideals of Cattaneo, Garibaldi and Mazzini will all be fully actuated by you and by the Italian people. Every vestige of the ignominious past and of betrayal must disappear.

Justice also requires that he who gave the Fascist tyranny full moral and material support, arms and legal powers to silence, subjugate and oppress the Italian people for twenty sorrowful years, be called upon to account for his own complicity in the crimes perpetrated by the Fascists in his name, and for all those violations of the Statute which made the Italian people the first victims of Nazi-Fascist terror. You Milanese who, in 1848, began the revolt against German tyranny, well deserved to conclude this battle of our *Risorgimento*. I

am proud to return among you as a citizen of a free Italy and not as a subject of
the kings and princes of the House of Savoy."[19]

I cannot refrain from imagining the bitter tears shed by Claudio Toscanini's
unflinching, seventy-eight-year-old son as he signed this letter, which indefinitely
postponed his return home.

On 1 September Toscanini conducted a broadcast of the 'Eroica' Symphony to
mark the end of the war in the Pacific. During the same month he led two more
broadcasts, a recording session and a Beethoven concert (including the Ninth
Symphony) at Carnegie Hall, with ticket sales to benefit various Italian welfare
societies and the War Orphans Committees. After this performance Mayor La
Guardia and Ambassador Tarchiani tried to visit him in his dressing room, but he
would not receive them: Tarchiani was one of those who had compromised with
the 'demo-Fascists'.

That performance of the Ninth was the first occasion on which young Robert
Shaw had prepared the chorus for Toscanini; and Toscanini came to consider
Shaw the finest choral director with whom he had ever collaborated. Shaw talked
to Haggin about their first meeting:

'I went up to check the tempo changes with him and to ask him about certain
technical things. Because we were a little short of men's voices during the war
years we'd been in the habit of using some altos occasionally in high tenor
parts; and in the Ninth I thought it would be wise occasionally to use some
tenors in low alto parts too. I asked Toscanini if this would be all right with
him. He said: "Will it make the score sound?" I said: "Maestro, I think this is
the only way it *can* be made to sound." And he said: "Anything which makes
the score sound is right." Then he said: "You know, I have never had a good
performance of this work. Sometimes the chorus is bad; sometimes the
orchestra is bad; many times the soloists are bad. And many times *I* am
terrible." '[20]

Toscanini's regular NBC broadcasts began on 28 October and he conducted
sixteen programmes that season, as well as recording sessions in March and
April. On 3 and 10 February 1946 he led a two-part concert performance of *La
Bohème*, for the fiftieth anniversary of the première which he had directed at
Turin's Teatro Regio. In mid-April it was announced that a referendum on the
abolition of the monarchy would be held in Italy in June. Fritz Busch's son, Hans
who was with the Allied forces in Milan, phoned Toscanini in New York and
invited him to return to conduct La Scala's re-opening. He could wait no longer
and departed for Italy.

The Toscaninis made what was then a long flight to Europe, landing in Geneva
on 22 April. The next day they proceeded by train to Chiasso at the Swiss–Italian
border, where they were met by Wally and Emanuela (who had since returned
home), a group of close friends, Toti Dal Monte, and La Scala's special

commissioner—later general director—Antonio Ghiringhelli. The homes in Milan and on the *isolino* were not yet ready to be occupied, so they went directly to Ripalta Guerrina.

He and Ghiringhelli began that same evening to discusss the Scala re-opening, and their conversation continued the next day. The restoration work in the theatre was not yet complete, the orchestra had to be reconstituted (Toscanini insisted that people who had been forced out for political or religious reasons be reinstated), programmes and other conductors had to be decided upon.

It was on one of the last days of April that Toscanini re-entered La Scala to see how the work was proceeding. Sixty years earlier, less a few months, he had accompanied the Figners in an audition on that stage; fifty years ago that very week he had conducted there for the first time; twenty-five years earlier he had begun rehearsals for the first season of the *ente autonomo*; and sixteen years had already passed since he had last appeared there—with the New York Philharmonic. As he walked from the stage entrance into the auditorium, one of the staff people offered to hang up his hat for him. 'Thank you,' he replied, 'but I'm not the *prima donna*—and I'm not even the baritone.' He had not changed

He pronounced the restoration excellent and called the first rehearsal for 3 May; but he wished to get together with his old orchestra before the rehearsal, since he knew that their first meeting would be an emotional one and he didn't want anything to disturb the working atmosphere of the rehearsals. They met in La Scala's *Sala gialla* (Yellow Room), where he and the 'old-timers' embraced and wept openly, and where he shook hands with the younger members.

Minetti, at that time (and for quite a while thereafter) still occupying the concertmaster's chair, has written of how the older musicians had prepared the younger ones for what would happen at the rehearsals:

'. . . We had described . . . the reality of those far-off years passed with him, his artistic intransigence, inflexible will, faithful and pure dedication to music and (why not) his outbursts, his nerves, the scenes and—our fear!

We began the rehearsals in an atmosphere of absolute cordiality (on his part, of course!). He even smiled a few times. A real idyll! The young men, in ecstasy, looked at us almost with sympathy. Was this the Toscanini we had described? Was this Bluebeard? the terror of orchestras? But it was a matter of time: little by little the Maestro's observations became rather more authoritative, more incisive, less kindly; the invitations to "make an effort", the exhortations to "sweat" were peremptory, accompanied by the well-known gesture of the accusatory index finger; and his glances began to delve again into our eyes and into our hearts. We again saw a few scores fly into the new and beautiful auditorium and (nothing new under the sun) more than one handkerchief was pitilessly torn up and many batons were broken and thrown to the winds!

The youngsters had stopped looking at us and appeared rather stricken. It was our turn to smile then. . . . At last we had found "our" Maestro again, just as we remembered him from distant times, just as we had known, admired, feared and loved him. . . .'[21]

The concert took place on 11 May. La Scala, which still smelled of fresh paint, was filled beyond normal capacity: ten and twelve people were jammed into loges which normally held four or six and standees were massed in unusual numbers in the galleries. Tens of thousands had gathered in Piazza del Duomo—the cathedral square—to hear the performance on loudspeakers set up for the event, and the concert was broadcast throughout the country and via shortwave. As Toscanini came on to the stage at precisely 9 p.m., the audience jumped to its feet, shouting, applauding, cheering the man who, to the Milanese public, was no longer *a* conductor, as he had been half a century earlier, nor even *the* conductor, as a quarter-century earlier, but who had become a living symbol of musical excellence, of personal integrity, and of that mixture of healthiness, severity and humanity which had given their country a Dante, a Michelangelo, a Verdi.

The programme was all Italian music—Rossini, Verdi, Puccini and Boito; and the soloists included some of Toscanini's old companions—Stabile, Pasero, Nessi, Favero—and young Renata Tebaldi, whom he had auditioned shortly after his arrival. La Scala's old choral director, Vittore Veneziani, who had been distanced from the theatre by the racial laws, was also back at his post, by Toscanini's edict. Each piece was followed by unrestrained outbursts of enthusiasm and Toscanini was radiant, almost ecstatic. He stopped to talk with some of his wind players and pat them on the back as he walked off stage after his bows. No one, not even Toscanini himself, could quite believe this was really happening. Afterwards the orchestra gave him a gold medallion with the inscription: 'To the Maestro who was never absent—his Orchestra.'

He was to conduct three other programmes as well in May and June, and was scheduled to take the orchestra to Paris and London for special performances. The second programme was a tough one for a newly reconstituted orchestra: it included *La Mer* and Brahms's Fourth Symphony. One person who was present at the rehearsals wrote down some of Toscanini's not always patient remarks:

'Make the bow jump a bit—separate those two bloody notes.

The whole crescendo, all of it, ALL of it! Put something into your work!

We're going before other countries and travel is tiring... Wake up! Let's go! Come on! I've had to conduct for sixty years to hear playing like this! It's shameful! What an awful day.

It's sixty years since I started out, and I never feel as though I've made it. I'm still the simple student of those days. Maybe you've played well, but you can still play badly—it's much easier.

Fool that I am, I thought you'd understood for the next time as well, but you don't have it in your heads yet.

Horn... I know you, X, with that hand of yours. Play open, *open*, OPEN—and if you don't know how to play, change professions!—He wants to play the way *he* likes, but he drives me crazy.

Don't ever think you've succeeded. Always try to do better—otherwise, drop dead.

[Fourth movement of the Brahms] It says *Allegro energico e passionato*. *Energico*—you don't play with energy! *Passionato*—you don't play with passion!! It's written in Italian, but here are Italians who don't understand it.'[22]

His programmes also included music by Shostakovich, Kabalevsky and Gershwin—composers whose works had been banned in Italy during the war—and a performance of the Beethoven Ninth. On 2 June he voted in the referendum which abolished the monarchy. Then, at the end of the month, as he prepared to depart for Paris with the orchestra, news came that the Allied government had decided to cede a tiny piece of Italy (Briga and Tenda) to France. All arrangements had been made and the train was ready to depart that afternoon, but Toscanini decided to cancel the trip. Ghiringhelli and music critic Franco Abbiati rushed to Via Durini to try to change his mind—as impossible a task as ever. Finally, they composed a statement to the press:

'The Directorate of La Scala wish to inform the public that Maestro Toscanini, who learned this morning of the decisions concerning Italy made by the four-power Conference, has decided to cancel the concert which was to have taken place in Paris on Sunday evening [30 June]. . . . This decision was made in complete agreement with the City Council and the entire Scala Directorate. The cancellation of the concert—the receipts from which were to have gone entirely to the French Red Cross—was not caused by injured nationalism; it merely confirms the Italians' state of mourning for these new humiliations.'[23]

The London concert, which was to have taken place at Covent Garden on 3 July, was also cancelled. The Soviet news agency, Tass, labelled Toscanini a reactionary for this act of protest. Interestingly, Toscanini had felt that the Soviet government had acted as reactionaries when they had officially condoned Victor Emanuel's post-Mussolinian government in 1944.

Organizers of the Lucerne festival quickly took advantage of the situation and invited the Scala ensemble to participate. Toscanini agreed and the group made the short trip on 4 July. The concerts took place on the 5th and 7th and were a great success.

There were those who believed that Toscanini would assume the position of artistic director of La Scala; but he wanted nothing of the sort. He did, however,

agree to return for the opening production of the first post-war opera season—
Otello, with Ramón Vinay in the lead rôle. It seems, though, that he later argued
with Ghiringhelli; and what would have been an historic event never took place.
Scenographer Nicola Benois recalled the conversations he had had with Tosca-
nini concerning the production (which was conducted, in the end, by De
Sabata):

> '. . . He gave me very valuable suggestions which I put into practice. One
> of the most interesting was that of dividing the third act of *Otello* into two
> scenes, in order to give the first part, which contains the handkerchief episode,
> a more intimate and dramatic setting. Toscanini suggested that I make the
> scene dark and small-scale, and advised me to use four large columns, which
> would serve to make the action, the play among the four characters, more
> interesting.
>
> Actually, Toscanini did not conceive the sets only in an aesthetic sense, but
> above all in relation to the action. Again according to the Maestro's suggestion,
> this scene was then to be transformed into an enormous reception hall for the
> arrival of the ambassadors; the change was to take place [in complete darkness]
> during the off-stage trumpet fanfares . . .'[24]

On 20 August Toscanini returned to New York and began preparations for
the NBC season, which opened on 28 October. There was a performance of
Tchaikovsky's 'Manfred' Symphony in November; and it may have been at one
of these rehearsals that he interrupted the orchestra near the very beginning:

> '*E passione, dolore*—sorrow, passion, ENTUSIASMO—*ma* no SLEEP when you
> play! Put *entusiasmo*, like me! I don't enjoy to conduct—no, no, I 'ate to
> conduct, I 'ATE!! Because I suffer too much—TROPPO! [Then, disarmingly:]
> What—you look at me? Why? You are astoni-ed? You think that I am crazy?
> No, no. [Pause to find the right English word.] Sensitive, yes! Don't look at
> me in this way.'

In December he led a two-part concert performance of *La traviata*. Robert
Merrill, who sang the rôle of Giorgio Germont, recalled that during a rehearsal
of the second act duet with Violetta (Licia Albanese) he had trouble with the
syncopations in the phrase '*Siate, siate l'angiol consolator*'. Toscanini cured him
of the problem by tapping the beats on Merrill's head.[25] Stravinsky's friend
Nicholas Nabokov reports that he spent an entire evening with the composer
listening to records of this performance which NBC had made at Stravinsky's
request. It was later issued on commercial records.

He again performed Berlioz's entire *Romeo and Juliet* in February, together
with a scene from *The Damnation of Faust*. His eightieth birthday occurred on
25 March, and he marked it only by sending 2 million lire to the Verdi home for

aged musicians in Milan. Ugo Stille, a reporter for the *Corriere della sera* who visited Riverdale during that period wrote that Toscanini spent a great deal of time listening to radio broadcasts by various American orchestras, and that he did quite a bit of reading, trying especially to follow contemporary Italian literature.

After his sixteen broadcasts and several recording sessions Toscanini flew back to Italy and went almost immediately to the *isolino*. There, on 21 June, he and his wife celebrated their fiftieth anniversary with Walter, Wally, the Polos and a few intimate friends. Natale Gallini, a musician and collector of rare manuscripts, who was on the Scala board at the time, recalls that Toscanini came down to meet these guests at the boat landing:

'... As we walked up towards the villa, the youngest of the ladies, passing near an ancient tree, jumped up and grabbed a branch, trying to pull herself up ... She did not succeed, however. Then the Maestro, eighty years old, grabbed the branch nonchalantly and pulled himself up four or five times, without the least effort. "To will is enough," he said, smiling. ... I brought forward the albums of Verdi manuscript letters which I had brought with me ... and presented them to Toscanini. So as not to embarrass him, I said: "Your Wally wants you to choose the nicest of these letters, the most interesting one to you."

He took off his glasses and stared at me for a few seconds with a rather severe look; then, calming down, he looked at his daughter and, with a smile, picked up the two volumes. After having meditated over numerous letters ... he invited me into the garden with Signora Carla. We sat down on the little wall overlooking the lake; and resuming his reading of some of the letters sent by Verdi to Francesco Maria Piave he exclaimed: "What a man! What precise ideas! Wagner wrote his own libretti while Verdi had to depend upon librettists; but he crucified them, he insisted on his ideas. Look at this letter: he himself transforms the personality of his characters and resolves the most important stage situations." ... Toscanini was for an updated re-publication of the correspondence, while I favoured using the complete correspondence as the outline of a great biography of Verdi, his life and works. The idea of proposing Franco Abbiati to write the great work on Giuseppe Verdi was born at that moment.

Before going back inside Toscanini chose the letter which most interested him. It wasn't the most important one ... but it was the most remote in time and referred to an opera which Verdi intended to compose especially for Parma's Teatro Ducale, before *Oberto*—an opera which he never wrote.

... Our conversation fell on composer Giovanni Bottesini from Crema, the double bass virtuoso who later directed the Parma Conservatory ... Commenting on the opera which Bottesini had composed to Boito's libretto *Ero e*

Leandro, I was imprudent enough to refer to the verses of the opera's pro-
logue: "*Canto pei cuori innamorati, canto | per gli occhi vaghi e per le guance
smorte ...*" The Maestro, with a decisive gesture, stopped me and began
to declaim: "*Canto la storia di Leandro e d'Ero | su cui con tanti secoli passati ...*"
—that is, he began to recite the verses of the prologue right from the beginning,
which left me astonished since a bit earlier he had said that he knew Bottesini's
opera from having read it once as a student at Parma's Conservatory, more
than sixty years earlier. . . .'[26]

Toscanini was back in New York by the end of August. On 6 September he
led a benefit concert with a group of players from the NBC Symphony at the
Ridgefield, Connecticut, high school. He directed a summer series broadcast on
21 September, then resumed the regular broadcasts on 25 October. There was a
Mendelssohn programme on 1 November, for the centenary of the composer's
death, and on 6 and 13 December there were the historic broadcasts of *Otello*,
fortunately preserved and still available on records. On 20 March, five days
before his eighty-first birthday, his NBC concert (all-Wagner) was televised for
the first time, and two weeks later there was another telecast—this time of the
Ninth Symphony. (A *New York Times* reporter watched the first programme in a
Greenwich Street tavern, and wrote the next day that one customer, 'who
obviously had not seen Mr. Toscanini before, remarked: "He knows his onions,
dat old boid. See the signals he got?" ') In fact, ten Toscanini–NBC concerts
were televised between 1948 and 1952. All of these were preserved on film, but
not one of them has been shown again in its entirety. This is a misfortune,
because these are among the most extraordinary documents of one of the most
extraordinary performing musicians in history. (Eight of the telecasts and the
Hymn of the Nations film can now be viewed by members of the Museum of
Broadcasting in New York.)

Again, there were sixteen broadcasts that season, plus numerous recording
sessions and a benefit concert (Verdi *Te Deum* and *Requiem*) for the New York
Infirmary fund at Carnegie Hall on 26 April. He had received and accepted an
invitation to conduct a programme at La Scala in June commemorating the
thirtieth anniversary of Boito's death. Leaving New York aboard the *Saturnia*
on 3 May, he arrived in Naples a week later and thence returned to Milan.

The programme took place on 10 June and consisted of excerpts from *Mefistofele* and *Nerone*, done in complete operatic form. Toscanini found himself
rehearsing singers on stage, demonstrating gestures and placement, for the first
time in eleven years—and for the last time in his life. During a break in one of the
rehearsals he stood in the aisle on the ground floor and, while talking to some
friends about Boito, he said: 'I remember how he sat there—it was right in that
seat—during a rehearsal for my first *Meistersinger*. I can see him as clearly as if it
had been yesterday.' It was, in fact, exactly fifty years that month since Boito had

convinced La Scala's governing council to accept Toscanini as musical director; and the *Meistersinger* production had taken place later that year.

He spent most of the summer relaxing, then returned to La Scala for a concert on 19 September which included Schubert's Ninth Symphony. During one of the rehearsals, he couldn't get the orchestra to begin the third movement with the quickness and lightness he wanted. After several attempts he said: 'You must stop thinking of Schubert as a sad man, feeble, reduced by illness to groping his way desperately through the streets of Vienna. Schubert was young, loved cheerful company, songs, wine, women.... Anyway, if he didn't like them, so much the worse for him.' Laughter in the orchestra, and the passage went more freely.[27]

In May Toscanini had attended the rehearsals of twenty-eight-year-old Guido Cantelli, who was preparing to conduct his first Scala concert. He was very impressed with the young man's musicianship, seriousness and intensity, and he began to take an interest in his career. He arranged for Cantelli to guest conduct four concerts during the next NBC season; these performances were very well received, and afterwards Toscanini wrote to Cantelli's wife, Iris:

'I am happy and moved to inform you of Guido's great success and that I introduced him to my orchestra, which loves him as I do. This is the first time in my long life that I have met a young man so gifted. He will go far, very far. Love him well, because Guido is also good, simple and modest. His departure will leave a great gap here.'[28]

Having returned to New York on 10 October, he readied himself for his sixteen-concert NBC series which opened with a six-part Brahms cycle. The season ended with a two-part concert performance of *Aida*, which was also televised (as had been two concerts earlier in the season), and later issued on records. Toscanini had planned to leave for Italy a week after his benefit concert for the City College of New York at Carnegie Hall on 20 April 1949; but he slipped in the bathtub, bruising a rib, and had to postpone his departure by a month.

Most of the summer was spent on the *isolino*; but on 3 September he inaugurated Venice's twelfth contemporary music festival, conducting the Scala Orchestra in a programme whose most contemporary work was Strauss's *Don Juan*, written more than sixty years earlier. He attended a rehearsal of Berg's *Lulu* at the Teatro La Fenice, and someone told the young stage director Giorgio Strehler that he should meet Toscanini. He was led to the proper loge; but on opening the door he heard Toscanini cursing the music and its composer. Strehler turned tail and fled. Later, Toscanini gave some friends who had come to visit him in his hotel room a demonstration of what he thought *Lulu* sounded like: he opened the piano lid and sat down on the keyboard. He also talked about *Wozzeck* with Minetti:

'I don't know—I think I have an excellent memory, and in fact I don't experience any difficulty in studying a score; but with *Wozzeck*, which isn't part of my spirit, I give up after a couple of pages. And I can't understand how Mitropoulos is able to knock all that stuff into his head.'[29]

Toscanini also conducted two concerts at La Scala (8 and 10 September), then returned to New York. On 7 October he led another benefit performance in Ridgefield, Connecticut, then resumed his regular broadcasts on the 29th.

He had an upset in December when Luigi Einaudi, then President of Italy, cabled to inform him that he had been nominated Senator for life. Two years earlier he had been told that something similar was being prepared and he had categorically refused; this time it had come without warning. He was shaken by the news, but finally replied thus:

'It is an old Italian artist, greatly disturbed by your unexpected telegram, who addresses himself to you and begs you to understand how this announced nomination ... profoundly contrasts with his sensibilities, and how he is forced, with great regret, to refuse this honour.

Averse to accepting any honours, academic degrees or decorations; desiring to end my existence in the same simple state in which I have lived it; grateful and happy for the recognition shown towards me on behalf of my Country; ready to serve her again in any eventuality—I beg you not to interpret my wish as a discourteous or arrogant act, but rather in the spirit of simplicity and humility which inspires it. Please accept my deferential greetings and respectful homage.'[30]

Toscanini conducted sixteen broadcasts in all during the 1949–50 season, and he again concluded with a magnificent performance of a Verdi opera— *Falstaff*. Nan Merriman, who sang the rôle of Meg Page, later wrote that the piano rehearsals averaged six hours a day for six weeks. NBC had engaged a fine coach to accompany the sessions, but Toscanini did most of the playing himself. In that way, he could indicate all the dynamics and tempo inflections he wanted without having to resort to verbal explanations. 'His powers of evocation were enormous,' said Merriman.[31]

In 1910 Toscanini had taken the Metropolitan Opera to Paris, in 1920 the Scala Orchestra to North America, in 1930 the New York Philharmonic to Europe, in 1940 the NBC Symphony to South America. Now, in 1950, at the age of eighty-three, he was to lead the NBC on a six-week tour that would take them all the way across the United States and back.

Orchestra musicians generally hate tours: they are constantly playing, travelling or checking into and out of hotels. They get to see very little of the places they visit, they play worse and worse as the tour progresses, and they return home exhausted. This tour, however, was different. An entire twelve-car train was chartered for the trip; the men had pleasant sleeping and dining accommodation right on the train; and concerts were given only once every two or three nights, so there was time for sightseeing. Furthermore, an orchestra which was accustomed to playing together only a few hours each week under good conductors, and generally in an unpleasant-sounding broadcast studio, now spent six weeks playing numerous rehearsals and twenty-one concerts together, under relaxed circumstances, in more-or-less decent halls—all with Toscanini. And since he didn't want his players to become bored, he took along twenty-eight works by Beethoven, Brahms, Debussy, Dukas, Dvořàk, Glinka, Kabalevsky, Mendelssohn, Ravel, Rossini, Saint-Saëns, Schubert, Smetana, Strauss, Tchaikovsky and Wagner—more than five completely different (and lengthy) programmes.

The last car on the train was reserved for him and it was a completely equipped suite of rooms. Signora Carla was unwell—she was recovering from two strokes which she had suffered during the winter—so Walter went along to look after his father. Walter and Alfred Walker, who had been Toscanini's errand boy and 'bodyguard' since 1938, had their hands full trying to satisfy all his needs—finding celluloid tie clasps, snap-together cuff links and a new hat in Atlanta; having his glasses repaired (he was constantly sitting on them accidentally); taking his soiled shirts to the airport to be flown to Forziati's New Shirt Laundry in New York; and seeing to dozens of other details. But their main problem was simply keeping up with him. 'He will kill us all yet with his energy,' said Walter one night, as the train was about to leave Richmond after a concert.

'He wears me out, really. The moment we reached his car after the concert tonight, he insisted on walking through the train; said he wanted to see the musicians. "Father," I said, "the musicians have not yet arrived at the train." But no, he goes through every car, first one way, then the other. Then he had some soup and red wine, and *then* he said, "Walter, I will show you a trick," and he stood in front of a divan and jumped up on it backwards.'[32]

Walter's son Walfredo, who was then studying architecture at Yale, told me: 'I flew down to go along on part of the tour, and after a few days I was sick and exhausted. And all *I* did was listen to the concerts and go sightseeing. Grandfather did the sightseeing *plus* conducting rehearsals and concerts.'[33]

Violinist Samuel Antek recalled a free day which most of the orchestra spent at Sun Valley:

'At ten in the morning I came upon Toscanini, stretched out full length on the lawn, drinking a toast in champagne to the beautiful mountains! Later that day, while up on the 10,000-foot Mt. Baldy, we were amazed to see him coming up the ski tow, and broke into a cheer as his chair swung into view. The jaunty beret on his head and his waving arms gave him the appearance of a happy boy playing hooky. . . . "Maestro," I said to him, "you are a brave man. Some of the boys were afraid to come up." He looked at me very earnestly and said, "I've never been afraid of anything in my life. I like to try everything." All through the day he was "one of the boys", joining us in a marvellous outdoor barbecue and applauding the buffoonery of the "Sad Symphony", performed with pots, pans, and kazoos by the men, who were burlesquing the numbers we had been playing on the tour. We cheered wildly as he rather dazedly accepted an invitation to lead us in the "Stars and Stripes Forever". That night, a more exhausted, happier lobster-red group of musicians could not have been found.'34

It need hardly be mentioned that the concerts were completely sold out and totally successful in all the twenty cities where the orchestra played. And Antek said, 'The performances all along were undoubtedly the finest I ever heard our orchestra give. No wonder Toscanini was delighted and pleased as I had never seen him before.'35 Having opened in New York on 14 April, the tour ended 8,600 miles later in Philadelphia on 27 May. On the 29th Toscanini gave an enormous party at his home for the orchestra, its staff and their wives, greeting all 300 guests personally and remaining on his feet for four hours; then, on the evenings of 1 and 2 June he led recording sessions which lasted nearly three hours each, and which produced his excellent records of *La Mer* and *Ibéria*.

He was back in Milan on 17 June and, inexhaustible, immediately began rehearsing for a performance of Verdi's *Te Deum* and *Requiem* at La Scala on the 24th. The concert did not satisfy him, and he later wrote to a friend:

'At La Scala, after my performance of Verdi's *Requiem Mass*, which left a bad taste in my mouth, I heard Beethoven's *Missa Solemnis* and Bach's *Mass in B minor* with the Vienna chorus and orchestra [with Karajan] . . . The public was cold towards the Beethoven and warmed up for the Bach. I was bored by both. Not even the divine "Kyrie" moved me as it did in a performance many years ago by a Berlin chorus [with Georg Schumann at La Scala in 1928]. Then I wept and wept. Maybe my advanced age has hardened my heart. After those two performances I came to the Isolino, where I am now. I'm living the contemplative life. I've thought back over a bit of my life, from the day I first came here in 1932. 18 years ago. I look forward 18 years and see myself at 101. The idea of being able to reach that age makes me smile. What do you think, my dear friend? Oh well, I wouldn't want to live that long.'36

And to another friend he wrote:

'What a delight! What beauty! This is truly an enchanting site! It seems to have rained down from the sky for the joy of man... I brought my piano, and I bang on it every once in awhile.'37

In Rome to visit Dr Cesare Frugoni about pains he was experiencing in a knee, Toscanini also saw Elsa Respighi and other old friends. Architect Marcello Piacentini took him to see the huge new Auditorium Pio at the Vatican; he was very favourably impressed with the acoustics and said that he would like to conduct the inaugural concert—which he never did.

At home in Milan he spent many hours each day listening to the radio. Among other things he heard Furtwängler's broadcast of *The Damnation of Faust* from the Lucerne festival, and let him know through a mutual friend that he had found it excellent. (It has been stated that Toscanini was involved in the campaign to keep Furtwängler out of America after the war; but I seriously doubt that theory—in the first place, because I have never seen any documentation, even of the questionable sort, to support it, and secondly, because he did not attempt to keep Furtwängler from returning to La Scala, which was still 'his' territory.)

Meanwhile, Chotzinoff—who was again *persona grata*—had informed Toscanini that 8H was being converted into a television studio and would no longer be available to the orchestra. Would he prefer Carnegie Hall or the Manhattan Centre? Toscanini loathed the Centre and, naturally, chose Carnegie Hall. He then received a cable saying that Carnegie Hall was no longer available because of scheduling problems, and the broadcasts would take place at the Centre.

He returned to New York furious, and also suffering increasingly because of his knee. As a result of both these situations, he cancelled his autumn broadcasts. A clinic in Philadelphia received him frequently for treatments, and at the same time the Carnegie Hall problem was resolved. Finally, he felt well enough to return to his orchestra for a recording session on 10 January and for a benefit performance of Verdi's *Te Deum* and *Requiem* on 27 January, the fiftieth anniversary of the composer's death, with the proceeds for the Casa Verdi in Milan. Three more broadcasts followed, the last of which (17 February) contained music by Debussy, Respighi and Elgar. His energy was astonishing. Finding the orchestra's playing too phlegmatic in the finale of the 'Enigma' Variations, he said to them: '*Quando sarò morto, avrò più vita di voialtri tutti!* Yes, when I will be dead, I am alive—OOOOHHH! more than EVERYBODY!' But his knee was not bearing up well under the strain; and since he refused to contemplate sitting down at rehearsals or concerts he began to be convinced that that concert would be his last. He requested that there be no applause.

1951 had worse in store for him. At his doctor's suggestion he had had a stationary bicycle set up at home for the purpose of exercising his knee; but he was so impatient that he pedalled too furiously. During an exercise session on 1 March he suddenly felt terribly ill; however, he managed to keep himself from falling and even dragged himself upstairs, where he sat down in the bathroom doorway. His unbelievable pride kept him from calling out, and members of his family found him there sometime later. He had suffered a minor stroke; and although he recovered quickly and well, it seemed clear to him that the end was near.

It had been his dream to conduct *Falstaff* again, and possibly also *Macbeth*, at Busseto in this 'Verdi year', and he had promised the organizers of the Verdi celebrations that he would do so. (He had also auditioned and accepted Maria Callas for the rôle of Lady Macbeth.) Now he had to cancel that project as well as a scheduled return to London for the opening of the Royal Festival Hall. NBC, however, optimistically announced that he would be back in the autumn.

Then, early in April, he received a call from Milan: his wife, whose health had not permitted her to accompany him to New York that season, had suffered a serious heart attack and was not expected to survive. He caught a plane for Italy in order to be with her. Fortunately, she recovered, albeit temporarily. Wally said that 'Papà was very affectionate, full of tenderness'; but Carla no longer believed him. ' "He's always been a liar," Mamma sighed.'[38] His knee had improved somewhat and he began taking solitary walks through the city late at night. A cellist from Parma once saw him walking in the rain without an umbrella. When Toscanini stopped to read an election poster at Piazza San Babila, the cellist summoned up his courage and approached him. 'Maestro, you're getting wet,' he said. 'And you aren't?' Toscanini replied. But he let his fellow-townsman accompany him to his door. Lauri-Volpi visited him one day and told him that he hoped Toscanini would live to be 100. 'And what if I do? Sixteen years pass quickly. And then?' He also met Carlo Maria Giulini at this time: after having heard him on the radio he invited him to visit. 'I always tried to seek out his ideas, his conversation, his experience of music, and not to ask him favours,' said Giulini years later. 'He was not only unbelievably gentle, but also very kind. Of course he could be incredibly rude as well and he often terrified his orchestras, but he was also kind, which is often forgotten by people who talk about him now.'[39]

In mid-June Carla Toscanini suffered another attack. She remained in a coma for several days, and her husband stayed near her bedside. Thus they passed their fifty-fourth wedding anniversary on 21 June. Surrounded by her family, she died two days later, not long before her seventy-fourth birthday, and was laid to rest in the tomb built for little Giorgio Toscanini so many years earlier.

Toscanini's grief, insomnia, abstinence from food, and general mental state caused serious worry in his family for several weeks. Then he made a decision: he had long ago promised to make some recordings with the Scala Orchestra, the sale of which would benefit the Casa Verdi. Now he felt that this would be an opportunity—away from the public eye—to see whether he could go on.

So he returned to La Scala early in August for three lengthy sessions which produced recordings of the Overture to *I vespri siciliani* and the two *Traviata* Preludes. He later rejected the *Vespri* Overture, and the *Traviata* Preludes were released only in Brazil. Nevertheless, there could be no doubt, as those who saw him at work testified: he had overcome all the shocks of the first half of the year and was ready and able to work again. NBC was informed that he would be back.

Following the Scala sessions he made a trip to Ischia; and from there he wrote to Maria Cecchini—Emanuela's tutor and a friend of the Toscanini family—on 26 August:

'What beauty—what luminosity in these parts! It seems as though sun—air—stars are more luminous than at home! Dream country. Man could live with a handful of grass if he had eyes for seeing and a heart for feeling.'

He returned to the *isolino*, then flew back to New York in mid-September to begin a series of recording sessions on the 28th. On 3 October he wrote to Wally:

'I can't forgive myself for having departed without first having made a visit to the cemetery! Then the departure, so hurried, without my having been able to be with all of you calmly for an instant, poisoned the trip for me. It seemed eternal and sad to me, and I felt at every moment as if I were suffocating—to the point where I swore that I wouldn't go by plane again.

The arrival in Riverdale wasn't happy either! Cia [his daughter-in-law] was in bed for some days with those blessed heart palpitations. She still doesn't have permission to go down to Mamma's rooms. She is always good and patient.

I am as always—well, according to others—not well, according to me. I'm homesick for my old house on Via Durini. But what can be done? I want to work. I can't in Italy. This alone is my working environment. And work I must, otherwise life is unbearable! I made two records. About an hour-and-a half was enough. Howe [his physician, who also made his batons, as a hobby] took my blood pressure afterwards—122 over 80. I didn't feel tired. Next Friday I have another rehearsal. Beethoven Second Symphony and *Don Pasquale* Overture. So you see that your old father has put himself to work with enthusiasm. . . .'[40]

The first broadcast of the new season (3 November) was also televised. It consisted of Weber's *Euryanthe* Overture and Brahms's First Symphony; and there were three further telecasts that season. Altogether, Toscanini conducted twelve broadcasts and twenty-one recording sessions and ended by performing the Ninth Symphony for the last time—four days after his eighty-fifth birthday—and then recording it. Tapes made at rehearsals during this period, not to mention the performances themselves, show him at the height of his powers—an almost frightening phenomenon.

Early in May he broke his hastily made vow not to fly again and returned to Milan by plane. At the end of the month violinist Michelangelo Abbado brought his chamber orchestra to Via Durini to play for him. Abbado's nineteen-year-old son, Claudio, played the piano in Bach's Concerto in D minor and Toscanini told him that his playing 'fit like a glove'.[41] One afternoon, a painter, Renato Vernizzi, came to do Toscanini's portrait, accompanied by Parmesan writer Ubaldo Bertoli. Toscanini chatted about various things during the sitting. He recalled his childhood in Parma:

'There was a little church, Santa Teresa, where my mother used to go to Mass; and there was a fat priest with a violet-coloured nose. He was always agitated. In those days it was a peaceful street. A cart would pass by "every time a bishop died", as we used to say.

I went to Parma recently. I got out in Piazza del Duomo to go and see again Antelami's "Deposition", the most beautiful sculpture in the world, a stupendous symphony of sorrow and serenity. On the steps, a little man came up to ask if I needed a guide. I told him that I knew the Duomo very well, but I said it in dialect. It was a big mistake! He stared at me and shouted: "*Ma lu l'è al mestor Toscanen.*" ["But you're Maestro Toscanini."] I begged him not to tell anyone, then I got back into the car quickly.

[He talked about Stefan Zweig, who had committed suicide during the war.] It's not for man to kill himself. Dignity and courage must be involved, even if these have become difficult words. He was a friend and I loved him; but I've never been able to forgive him his suicide.'[42]

Toscanini decided to visit Frugoni in Rome again about his knee. He had hoped to sleep in the car on the way down, but instead enjoyed the trip immensely, waking Wally occasionally to point out sights of interest. At the home of a Roman friend, Mimì Finzi, he saw an old journalist acquaintance, Raffaele Calzini, who wrote about their meeting:

'. . . He looked at me: "You've put on weight! Even you have put on weight! Everybody's getting fat, by God! Look at me! Look! . . . No stomach. You have to have fire inside not to get fat. You people don't have fire inside!" He was very cheerful, smiling, happy. I thought he would talk to me about Rome, or maybe some museum, or some lady admirer, or his future plans. No: he talked to me about music.

"I'm enthusiastic: I'm just coming back from the RAI [Italian Radio] on Via Asiago where I heard twelve fine, excellent kids, a perfect chamber orchestra —twelve young people, you know, eighteen or twenty years old—Barbara Giuranna's orchestra. They play without a conductor. I told those kids—I applauded them and thanked them. No, music won't die. They study more these days. In my day there were many *dilettanti* and Bohemians and drunkards. There are orchestral ensembles in Italy which do honour to the country, to our traditions—like the Roman *Collegium* that went to America and was very well received. Right, Wally? Right? Where'd she run off to? She's like her mother, like poor Carla: can't stand still for a minute! Wally, Wally, where'd you run off to?" Wally came suddenly; he caressed her black hair, as if she were eighteen years old. "Tell him how they played, tell him, tell him!" But it was a formality: he had already started talking about music again. . . . "Giuranna's son, whom I heard a moment ago with this group, which is called *I musici*, played the viola d'amore as few can play it; and it's hard to play the viola d'amore, it's tiring. You see, Wally?"

He doesn't address me, he addresses Wally; but Wally had run to the telephone. "You see?" he said to me, satisfying himself with my presence. And, lifting his left arm as if he were holding a viola d'amore, he showed me how the fingers must be placed on the strings. "Like this, you know." He knew that I didn't know, and he smilingly changed the subject. "Smell that perfume? It's the perfume of Rome. I had never noticed it; I discovered it during my sleepless hours. Here I don't have music on the radio to keep me company at night, so I've analysed the odours: jasmine, pittosporum, magnolia and, above all, pine—pine resin."

". . . It did me good to get to know those young people, those fine young people. But I've also fished up certain old wrecks like myself during my visit! Pintorno, who taught singing at the Milan Conservatory, came to see me. He's ninety. Gurcha, a singer who's 96, I only talked to by phone. . . . I want to get back to Milan as soon as possible. I must, I must. My son Walter sent me the test pressing of the Ninth from America; I want to hear and check how it came out, and possibly to correct it. These long-playing records often make me happy. . . . You've got to work, always work." . . .'[43]

And work he did! On 8 July he flew back to New York to lead two broadcasts and two recording sessions of light classics—among which two pieces by Catalani, whom he had never forgotten. Then, by the end of August, he was again in Milan. There, on 19 September, he conducted at La Scala for what turned out to be the last time—an all-Wagner programme. The orchestra found him in even better shape than the previous year. 'I'm embarrassed to have to make these remarks,' he said, after correcting some basic rhythmic problems at one of the first rehearsals; and during Isolde's *Liebestod* he shouted: '*Crescendo, voce, voce!* For God's sake—what do you have where your hearts should be?'[44] Mario Labroca was backstage after the concert and reported:

'As we escorted Toscanini [to his dressing room] (he needed to rest) we saw before our eyes a very famous foreign conductor who was a guest in the theatre that evening. Approaching the Maestro, he said in French: "What a marvellous concert, marvellous, marvellous!" Toscanini, who had had to stop before the unforeseen obstacle, looked at him for a second and exclaimed—in Italian, of course: "Ass!" We were all taken aback; but our fears turned into wonder when we saw a brilliant smile appear on the conductor's face, as he said happily: "Oh, how kind, how kind!" Fortunately, he didn't understand a word of Italian.'[45]

Five days later Toscanini arrived in London to begin preparing two all-Brahms concerts with the Philharmonia Orchestra—his first performances in England in thirteen years, and his farewell to the country (although not announced as such). Tickets ranging in price from five shillings to £5 had disappeared within hours of going on sale, and standees queued up to forty-eight hours for the 300 available places. Toscanini's fee was £1,800 per concert, according to the papers—the largest sum ever paid to a musician up to that time in Britain. Both concerts were broadcast by the BBC and were heard by an estimated 15 million listeners; and since they were recorded, the beauty and transparency of those performances *could* still be heard today by the public.

Charlie Chaplin, his wife Oona, Sir Laurence Olivier and his wife Vivian Leigh greeted Toscanini backstage after the first concert and had supper with him at his room at the Savoy. After the second performance a laurel wreath wound around an Italian flag was presented to him on behalf of the standees, who had each contributed a few pence for the gift. He was genuinely moved and asked them to visit him backstage afterwards.

Once again he returned to New York and prepared for another NBC series. This year there were fourteen broadcasts and eleven recording sessions. On 22 November he led a concert performance of the second act of Gluck's *Orfeo*, with Nan Merriman in the principal rôle, which she had already sung with him in 1945. She later wrote that rehearsals for the 1952 performance were spread over an eight-month period, and that Toscanini had had her study directly from the orchestral score. Thus he made her aware of every detail of colouring in the work, and explained his reasons for everything he required her to do.[46]

The season ended on 28 March 1953 with his last performance of the *Missa Solemnis*, and he recorded the work during the following few days. Before the performance, he had written to a friend about Beethoven:

'If, with my enthusiasm and adoration for that saint, I could achieve something worthy, it would be the greatest reward for my long, too long, artistic life.'[47]

Afterwards he wrote to Maria Cecchini to thank her for having sent him newspaper clippings about a group of young singers trained at La Scala:

'I should have written this letter long ago, as soon as I had received the reviews of the Scala cadets; but I was so busy and worried over Beethoven's *Missa Solemnis* that I was no longer living a normal life. . . . You can't imagine my joy in reading about those dear young artists. When I return to Italy you must take me to hear their rehearsals. I love the young more than the old and famous. . . . Excuse me for writing badly, but I am very nervous and my hand is slipping on the paper. I am old, very old. I can't stand it any longer.

Remember me to your family, and please ask your mother to excuse me for the visit I didn't make. Tell her that I am old, very old, and in very bad humour.'[48]

He wrote her again on 16 May, beginning with the same phrases about his poor writing and his age. Then he went on:

'I am not well, and no one believes me, the asses, but I'm not the same as I was. My eyes have worsened so much that I can no longer find glasses which can help me. My legs and my memory fail me. I sleep little and badly, tormented by tragic, commonplace or fearful dreams. All in all, a poor unhappy man—and they have had the bad taste to force me to accept another year of concerts. And I, imbecile that I am, and tired of hearing myself bothered, have given in. The American public will again have to have the patience to put up with having an old man of 86 before its eyes.'[49]

Of course no one had—or could have—forced him to accept again. In recent months he had begun to show signs of decline; and no one was more aware of these signs than he himself was. He had always severely criticized other musicians whom he felt had gone on too long; but now, for the first time in his life, he found himself unable to face an important decision. 'And work I must, otherwise life is unbearable,' he had written to Wally not many months earlier. It was too horrible to contemplate stopping.

Back in Italy for the summer, he again went to Rome for a medical examination, then returned to Milan. On 3 August he wrote to Maria Cecchini:

'I spent four days in Rome to see Frugoni... Everything was better than two or three years ago. I discovered that Frugoni, a brilliant and good-looking man, cares about his beauty.—He weighs himself every day... I marvelled that a scholar like him finds the time to worry about that. I have returned to Milan and am about to go to the Isolino, where I've spent two Sundays; but now I'll stay there because Walter and Cicogna [an engineer] are preparing for me the means for listening to the records, which I must study without the help of people more intelligent than myself—*just like you*!' [Note: He was notoriously incompetent at handling mechanical equipment, including gramophones.][50]

Journalist Enzo Biagi found him strolling with Emanuela one day in Milan and stopped to talk with him. Toscanini told him that the coming season would be his last. 'I hope for God's help, because I would like successfully to complete this trip as well,' he said, and added: 'Verdi passed away at my age, but you must remember that he ate a lot more.'

He returned to New York in September to plan his season. Eventually, he conducted eleven broadcasts; but Arthur Fierro, who was Walter Toscanini's assistant during the 1960s, told me that the original schedule had been more elaborate. Toscanini had wanted, for example, to do the second 'Brandenburg'

Concerto, which he had not performed in fifteen years; but his first trumpet, Harry Glantz, who had been with him since the Philharmonic days, told him that he felt he was no longer young enough to play the difficult solo part. Toscanini had also wanted to perform Kodály's *Psalmus Hungaricus* again, and had wished to end the season with Brahms's *German Requiem*; but his health did not permit this. In fact, he was not well enough to conduct the first two concerts of the season, which were taken over by Monteux, who was only seventy-eight years old. Toscanini's first concert took place on 22 November and included Brahms's 'Tragic' Overture and Strauss's *Don Quixote*. The broadcasts were now sponsored by the Socony-Vacuum Oil Company, who transmitted a commercial over the air and into Carnegie Hall after the overture, while Toscanini remained on the podium, chatting with one of his players.

He was beginning to have memory difficulties, and his painful awareness of the situation is hinted at in a letter to Maria Cecchini's mother, written on 25 November:

'Your dear letter, which arrived on the 15th, I read only after many days had passed... I was in such a depressed state that I didn't have the courage to get any news or to confront any work... A real wretch... I am having trouble writing. I conducted a concert on the 22nd as well as possible. Your beautiful letter is too moving for me, I was not worthy of it. Signora Elena, believe me always your true, simple friend—I am so tired of being M... Arturo Toscanini that it bores me even to read my own name. . . .'[51]

(Verdi had written a similar phrase to Boito many years earlier.)

His big project of the season was a two-part concert performance of Verdi's *Un ballo in maschera* on 17 and 24 January 1954. According to Della Corte, when the second broadcast had ended Toscanini said: 'This was my last opera performance. I began by hearing a performance of *Un ballo in maschera* at the age of four, up in the gallery; and I've finished by conducting it at eighty-seven. From now on I'll do what I can: short symphonic concerts and, as far as operas are concerned, overtures at most.'

The performance of Verdi's *Te Deum* on 14 March—later released on record—was a magnificent one; but Haggin reports that the Tchaikovsky 'Pathétique' Symphony the following week lacked the 'continuity of impetus and tension' which one normally heard in Toscanini's music-making. An NBC musician told him: 'He was all there in the rehearsal, but not in the performance.'[52]

Also in March, various sources reported that Toscanini would lead a European tour with the NBC Symphony at the end of the season; but the real story was considerably different. It is still impossible, nearly a quarter-century after the event, to determine the truth about Toscanini's departure from NBC. The best one can do is to present the bits of information available.

At least as early as 1951 there were persistent rumours that when Toscanini eventually retired the orchestra would be disbanded. (This was perfectly in keeping with NBC's then-current policy that 'every programme must pay for itself'. Symphony orchestras can never pay for themselves in monetary terms; so it was obvious that whenever Toscanini decided to stop, NBC would use the event as an excuse to rid itself of a cultural burden in whose importance it did not believe.) Several musicians left at about that time, feeling that the job market would be flooded if and when this happened. We know that in the spring of 1953 Toscanini had signed a contract for the following season and had then regretted having done so, and that he had stated explicitly during the summer that the coming season would be his last. It may be that Walter Toscanini wished to avoid the possibility that his father would change his mind, sign yet another contract and subject himself to the strain of yet another season. This would corroborate the story Sarnoff told Wallenstein in the autumn of 1953—that when he and Chotzinoff had gone to Riverdale with Toscanini's contract for the 1954–5 season, they had been intercepted by Walter, who had asked them not to present it to his father.

According to what Cantelli told a friend—who, in turn, told Haggin—what Walter reported to his father was that Chotzinoff had informed him that NBC would be ending its broadcasts in the spring of 1954 and that his father might wish to resign for appearances' sake. This, said Cantelli, produced violent scenes at Riverdale.

A letter of resignation was eventually prepared for Toscanini. One member of his family told me that the letter was written by the family; but I don't dismiss the possibility that NBC officials may have made some substantial suggestions in its formulation. 'And now the sad time has come when I must lay aside my baton and say goodbye to my orchestra,' it said. Several weeks passed before he put an unsteady signature on it on 25 March, his eighty-seventh birthday. Sarnoff replied, accepting the resignation, on the 29th.

Some normally reliable sources have told me that Toscanini had long known that NBC would disband the orchestra when he resigned, and that one of his main reasons for continuing as long as he did was to postpone that event. Others said that neither Toscanini nor the orchestra knew until shortly before the last concert in 1954 that the orchestra was definitely finished. Both of these versions conflict, at least in part, with the statements of Cantelli and with Sarnoff's report to Wallenstein. It seems highly unlikely that the full story will ever be known. When I asked Wally Toscanini about her father's resignation, she said simply: 'He realized that he was very old and thought it was time to stop.'

The final concert—an all-Wagner programme—was scheduled for Sunday, 4 April. At the first rehearsal on Thursday afternoon he told the orchestra that he would beat *alla breve* (two-to-the-bar) in the *Lohengrin* Prelude, but had trouble maintaining this and sometimes lapsed into four, following and confusing the orchestra; and Haggin says that in the *Meistersinger* Prelude which followed he

was surprised 'that Toscanini did nothing about the nerveless, poor playing'.
He continued:

> 'Then *Dawn and Rhine Journey* from *Die Götterdämmerung*, in which there
> were several stops for corrections that I don't remember, and one stop for
> something that was to have great importance two days later. The place was the
> entrance of the kettle-drum in the passage immediately after the off-stage horn
> calls; and Toscanini contended that the timpanist had come in too soon. "It's
> the same part I always play," said the timpanist. "Maybe," said Toscanini.
> "All right, I'm always——" I didn't catch the timpanist's last word but
> presumed it was "wrong". Eventually the passage was played the way
> Toscanini considered correct, and the piece was completed.'

The following morning's rehearsal went well and Haggin noted, 'power all
there'. Then came the final rehearsal on Saturday afternoon.

> 'Power was all there again in the performances of the *Lohengrin* Prelude, the
> *Forest Murmurs* from *Siegfried*, and the *Götterdämmerung* piece as far as
> Toscanini got in it. My notes record his stopping at one point in the *Dawn*
> portion and shouting: "Staccato! Staccato! *Ignoranti, tutti!*" And they record
> his stopping in a fury at the point where the trouble with the kettle-drum had
> occurred two days before. While Toscanini raged I heard Frank Miller call
> out to the timpanist: "Make it thirteen measures rest instead of twelve."
> Twelve was right, and the timpanist had waited that number of measures;
> but Toscanini mistakenly thought it should be one more; and Miller was telling
> the timpanist to do what would seem right to Toscanini. "*E' vergogna!
> Vergogna!* ["It's shameful!"] he shouted. And when the passage was repeated,
> as he thought, correctly, he stopped again and exclaimed: "*Finalmente!*"
> Then, in bitter anger: "*L'ultima prova!*" ["The last rehearsal!"].[53]

With that, Toscanini walked out without completing the rehearsal.

The next day's performance began with the *Lohengrin* Prelude; then came the
Siegfried piece, in which Toscanini forgot to indicate some changes of time
signature. The orchestra, however, did not go wrong. The *Götterdämmerung*
excerpts proceeded normally and were followed by the *Tannhäuser* Overture and
'Bacchanale'. After the climax in the 'Bacchanale', Toscanini suddenly stopped
conducting and put his left hand over his eyes; the strain on his mind and the
emotion of the moment were too much for him. The orchestra began to make
wrong entrances and Cantelli, who was in the radio control booth, insisted that
the concert be taken off the air. Technical difficulties were announced and Toscanini's recording of the Brahms First Symphony was broadcast. In the meantime,
Miller had begun giving cues and Toscanini finally regained a measure of self-
control. He began to beat time again, and the programme was put back on the
air. At the end of the 'Bacchanale' he stepped down from the podium and

prepared to leave the stage; but Miller stopped him and reminded him that he still had to conduct the *Meistersinger* Prelude. Toscanini nodded, returned to the podium and beat numbly through the last piece. As the orchestra hammered out those final, affirmative bars of C Major, as the strings tumbled downwards towards the final resolution, the numbness must have given way to a feeling of suffocation, to a need for release and escape stronger even than his ironclad sense of duty towards the music and towards the orchestra; for while the last chords were still being played, he dropped his baton, stepped slowly from the podium and made his way to the exit. An enormously long life, full of love and work, a life that had been whole and healthy and that, above all, had been lived completely without cynicism and without calculation, had, in effect, ended.

8
Last Years

Toscanini's retirement began with that slow walk from the podium to his dressing room, where he tearfully closed himself in. Later that evening, at dinner, no mention was made of what had happened; but as he rose to go to his bedroom, he said: 'I conducted as if it had been a dream. It almost seemed to me that I wasn't there.'[1]

As had happened in many earlier years, a post-season party was arranged in Riverdale for the orchestra. In fact, three parties were organized this time, with part of the orchestra invited to each. Bassist David Walter, who was present at the first one, told Haggin that Toscanini was not present to greet the orchestra, as he had always been before.

> 'Eventually Ghignatti [English horn] and Cooley went upstairs to see him. They reported that he was in tears, exclaiming "My poor orchestra! My poor orchestra!"—feeling that he was responsible for the disbanding of the orchestra, and that he couldn't face us. And the other two parties were cancelled.'[2]

At some point Sarnoff also went to Riverdale to visit him, but Toscanini was so upset that he wouldn't see him. He stayed in his room, sitting on his bed and crying.[3]

But when, on 3 and 5 June, he returned to Carnegie Hall to conduct two long sessions for the purpose of re-recording some unacceptable passages in the broadcast performances of *Ballo* and *Aida*, 'He came in,' said Alan Shulman, 'like a house afire . . . We said, "My God, he's a rejuvenated man!" ' And the power and beauty of the remade passages prove to us, as they must have proved to him, that he was *not* finished, as it had seemed at the last broadcast, but was still in possession of his powers. He got Herva Nelli to sing the long climactic phrase of Aida's aria '*O cieli azzurri*' ('*no, mai più! non ti vedrò, non ti vedrò mai più!*'), with its high C, in one breath, as Verdi indicates; and when Toscanini stepped off the podium, she put her arms around him and he gave her an affectionate whack on the behind. Friedelind Wagner, who was present, recalls that during one of the sessions Toscanini became infuriated over something that had gone wrong, picked up the heavy full score of one of the operas, and threw it with such force that it landed in the tenth row of the auditorium.

Two days later he was back in Milan, surrounded by family, old friends, and the relics of his past. It cannot have been a happy time for him. Critic Beniamino Dal Fabbro saw him at a rehearsal of Beethoven's Fourth Piano Concerto with Rubinstein and Cantelli at La Scala, and wrote in his diary (24 June):

> 'Rubinstein came off the stage . . . and Toscanini stood up. Rubinstein kissed his hand, and kissed it again before taking his leave. Everyone kisses his hand nowadays, men and women, as if he were a pope . . . Faded, distracted, . . . he is venerated as a sort of living mummy of that which was the great Toscanini.'[4]

One evening, Michelangelo Abbado brought his chamber orchestra to Via Durini to play for Toscanini, as he had done two years earlier. Abbado recalled that after playing five or six short pieces by well-known Baroque composers, they began the D Major Violin Concerto of Francesco Bonporti, a student of Corelli. Abbado himself was playing the solo part and giving conducting indications. At a certain point Toscanini stood up, walked to within two feet of where Abbado was standing, faced him, and remained in that position until the piece had ended. 'I can't say that I felt very comfortable,' said Abbado. 'In fact, those were the most agonizing moments I can remember ever having experienced. Finally the ordeal ended. There were several seconds of dead silence; then Toscanini, who had never heard the work before, suddenly said: '*Per la madonna!—Questa è la perfezione!*' I can't tell you what a sigh of relief went up from all of us.'[5]

During those same weeks, Toscanini was afflicted with a superstitious fixation that he was going to die at exactly the same age as Verdi, eighty-seven years, three months and seventeen days, which would have occurred on 12 July. (Several years earlier, he had got it into his head that he would not survive beyond the age at which his mother had died, eighty-four.) The previous evening, Guido and Iris Cantelli came to visit him, along with engineer Sandro Cicogna; after much begging, they convinced him to accompany them to the nearby town of Vigevano, to see the illuminated main piazza.

'Oh God, I've got my slippers on!' he said as he walked out on to the landing with Anita Colombo. Turning to go back inside, he tripped, rolled down a few steps, and banged his head against the wall. Surprised to find himself unhurt, he decided to go anyway. At Vigevano he walked all around the piazza and looked in shop windows; but he was all the more preoccupied about the next day. In the morning he called Wally, who was in Venice for a theatre opening, and asked her to come back to Milan, which she could not do. The day passed uneventfully, and at midnight he drank a glass of chilled champagne. When friends laughed at this story he snapped, 'You tell *me* what kind of risk it is for someone my age to bang his head like that!' Then he laughed at himself and muttered, 'My God, how old I am!'

He still shaved, as he always had, without looking in the mirror, and he could still recite poems by Arnaldo Fusinato which he had been taught at the tailor shop in Parma when he was four. He wanted very much, despite everything, to work again. 'You were born well!' his doctor, Augusto Murri, told him when he went for a check-up. 'But this shoulder is bothering me,' Toscanini complained. 'So you'll conduct with the other arm,' Murri replied. Conduct? It was really unthinkable. And yet . . .

Late in July RCA engineer Richard Gardner arrived in Milan to go over the tapes of the 1951 broadcast of the Verdi *Requiem*; with Cicogna, they began their long and painstaking labour. Toscanini was finally convinced that the recording should be released only when Gardner played him parts of other conductors' versions. It is an excellent performance; but those who are familiar with one or another of the various privately circulated editions of his 1940 broadcast might wish that the earlier version, with its greater elasticity, its staggering perfection of detail, and its exceptional singing, had been offered to the public as well. Gardner returned to America, but Toscanini continued to go over his recordings with Cicogna. He had not wanted to listen to the tape of his 1944 performance of the last act of *Rigoletto*; Cicogna, however, eventually wore down his resistance. 'I'm warning you: it will make me angry,' Toscanini said before they began. 'By the end of the performance Toscanini was in tears,' reports Cicogna. 'He said: "I don't know whether I would be able to conduct that as well today." It was the closest I ever heard him come to praising himself or anything he had done.'[6]

In August Walter's wife, Cia, died after having suffered from heart disease for years. Toscanini had been very fond of her, and these unhappy months must have been made more difficult for him by this event.

A telegram reached him from those members of the NBC Symphony who had regrouped as the Symphony of the Air, inviting him to return to New York to conduct them whenever he wished. He cabled his thanks, but stated that he could not really contemplate such a project, and the new organization played its first concert in October under unusual circumstances:

> 'Because none of us feels that another conductor should take your place on this, our first public concert, we have decided to play our concert with the podium empty with only the inspirational memory of your guiding hands before us, dedicating our future to the high ideals and years of tradition that you, as our beloved Maestro, have given the world. Please accept our love and very best wishes . . .—Your Orchestra.'

But it is clear that Toscanini was, in fact, contemplating various projects. Yehudi Menuhin visited him at the *isolino* that summer, and Toscanini confided in him that he felt he still had something to offer. He wanted to return to London to conduct again, but the idea was never realized.[7] This wish, however, was nothing compared to his great desire to conduct the opening of the Piccola Scala, the small theatre then under construction next to La Scala itself. Even before Toscanini's recent return to Italy, Emilio Radius had reported in Bologna's *Il resto del carlino* (23 May) that Toscanini was thinking about conducting Puccini's *La rondine*—an opera he had never performed before—for the thirtieth anniversary of the composer's death (29 November), if the new theatre were completed in time. When it became clear that it would not be ready, he made up his mind to do *Falstaff* there the following spring.

Early in August he wrote to Maria Cecchini: 'I haven't decided to go to the Isolino yet. I stay riveted here between my bedroom and my study. I work with my mind because I can't with my wretched eyes . . .'[8] He did go to the *isolino* shortly afterwards, and wrote: 'After a sleepless night, in the early morning hours I dreamed of Gubbio. That magnificent, delightful little city was under a magical lunar light. It seemed like a magic painting by my painter friend, Marius Pictor.'[9]

In the autumn he was with Wally at Sirmione on Lago di Garda for mud cures for his arm. Natale Gallini was also at the resort with his wife. They all met one afternoon at the villa which Toscanini had rented. At one point, while Gallini and Toscanini happened to be seated together across the veranda from Signora Gallini and Wally, Toscanini told Gallini of his desire to conduct *Falstaff*. Gallini replied with enthusiasm, but said that he did not know whether the theatre would be ready by the spring. Toscanini insisted on the Piccola Scala because he wanted to do the work in intimate surroundings, as he had done at Busseto in 1913 and '26. Meanwhile, Gallini noticed Wally signalling him, unseen by her father, with gestures obviously indicating that Gallini should not encourage him. He tried to be as non-committal as possible, and he later found out that Wally felt the strain of conducting a staged opera would have been too great for her father.[10]

She was right. Obstinately, he proceeded with his plans, because life without such plans, without the prospect of making music, was no life at all. Having overcome a bout of pneumonia later that autumn, he started thinking about a cast and held discussions about staging with Luchino Visconti, grandson of Duke Guido Visconti di Modrone, who had been president of the board of La Scala when Toscanini was chosen as conductor in 1898. When Visconti was a child, Toscanini used to scold him for riding his bicycle too fast with his books and Wanda on the handlebars; and Wanda had been Visconti's leading actress in the first theatrical events he had staged at home. 'Why don't you young people try to think up something different and propose it to me?' Toscanini asked him. 'I can only imagine the old scenes—the usual tavern, the usual garden. Suggest something fresh, something nice.'[11]

'He wanted the real *Falstaff*,' said Visconti, 'in which the characters would truly recite the comedy even more than singing it.'[12]

Falstaff was announced for La Scala's 1954-5 season, and Toscanini became increasingly upset because the work on the Piccola Scala was proceeding so slowly. 'Yes, I'm fine,' he would tell people. 'But it's not surprising that I'm in a hurry. Only the young can be patient; at my age, one can't be any more. I can't wait too long. Now I'm all right, but in a few months—who knows?' Journalist Camilla Cederna sat next to him at table at a gathering in Via Durini in November. There was a fad about Chinese mushrooms at the time, and she talked about their salutary effect. Toscanini's eyes lit up. 'Do you have any?' When she said that she did, he begged her to send him some immediately. 'I can't wait too long; I've got to do everything to stay well.' Then he told her that if he had managed to keep his good health, it was because he had never had indigestion (which was absolutely untrue), had never been drunk, had never smoked. 'My mouth is always fresh; I don't stink like an old man.' He had also given up coffee for the previous two years—a great sacrifice—in an attempt to teach Walter to stop smoking. He slept poorly, but occasionally had a 'restful' dream in which he saw himself closed in a coffin and felt fine there.[13]

While everyone else thought he was deluding himself, he had already come to terms with the fact that he probably would not be able to bring his *Falstaff* plan to fruition. He attended one of Visconti's rehearsals of Spontini's *La vestale*, which was to open the Scala season in December. Victor De Sabata, then artistic director (with whom Toscanini had not been on good terms for many years), Antonino Votto, who was conducting the production, and Maria Callas, the protagonist, all came off the stage to greet him. De Sabata later recalled that 'Toscanini whispered to me: "You know, it's useless to think about choosing the other singers [for *Falstaff*] since I won't be able to conduct it. I look fine, but actually . . ." I almost felt my heart stop from the anguish.'[14]

Visconti said that 'later, Maestro called me to him, saying, "I like very much what you do, but you must understand that my eyesight is poor. I find this Callas woman very good, a beautiful voice and an interesting artist, but her diction is unintelligible . . . Opera is theatre, and the words are more important than the music." I was stupefied—surely Toscanini could not mean this—and I explained that Maria was a Greek-American and did not speak perfect Italian. But Toscanini held to his point. "No! No! You *must* hear every word, otherwise it is a concert." '[15]

Toscanini sat in Ghiringhelli's loge directly over the stage at the opening night of *La vestale*, and the audience went wild when Callas, while taking a bow, walked over to the loge and graciously handed him a bouquet of flowers which had been thrown to her. Docilely, he accepted. Afterwards, Toscanini, Wally, Giulini, Visconti and a few others went to a restaurant. Smiling at Visconti from across the table, the old man proposed a toast: '*Al nostro Falstaff* '![16]

One evening Ghiringhelli came to decide on the *Falstaff* cast with Toscanini, who was still determined to see how far he could go. 'That evening was one of Papà's happiest,' wrote Wally to a friend, some two years later. 'He saw his dream becoming a reality. During the night, perhaps because of the sense of responsibility and the fear of having taken on too heavy a task for his age, he worked himself into such a state that in the end it provoked a heart attack. When it had passed, Papà understood immediately that he was condemned to giving up . . .'[17] Walter, in New York, wrote to Cicogna:

'I'm very happy that the *Falstaff* idea has finally been laid to rest. It was a nightmare for me . . . Then, too, it seemed to me cruel to let him delude himself in preparing for a task which he can no longer bring off, given the fact that the soloists, starting with Valdengo [Falstaff], are in worse shape than they were four years ago [at the time of the NBC broadcast] . . .'[18]

The attack was a mild one and was kept secret from the public. Toscanini recovered well, but his intimates were warned to prevent him from having any emotional upsets. Previously, friends had often come to visit him, to talk about the past or to listen to test pressings of recordings with him (at an unbelievable volume, according to Votto). Now, even these visits became oppressive to him because they reminded him of his impotence. But his pride was still unshaken. He was determined to work as long as possible at the editing of his recordings, and he was even more determined not to have those old friends who remained see him slip into senility and physical decay; and so he renounced the right to die in his beloved native country. Wally wrote later that her father was ashamed of his age and felt the need 'to hide himself, to finish in exile, forgotten by all'. A few friends visited him the evening before his departure for New York. Gallini tried to convince him to stay, to head an institute for Verdi studies. 'Maestro,' he said, 'bring me that plane ticket so I can tear it up!' But his mind was made up, and on 28 February he was back in Riverdale. (A few hours before Toscanini was to leave, Votto telephoned to say goodbye. 'He didn't speak at all about not feeling well. He asked me about my plans. I told him that La Scala had proposed that I conduct Donizetti's *Poliuto*, with Callas, Corelli and Bastianini. He was enthusiastic, said that it was a great opera, and right there on the phone began to sing parts of it. His memory was still formidable, incredible.')[19]

For nearly two years Toscanini, Walter and the RCA engineers worked as much as the old man was able at the business of tape editing. Other than that, he lived amid his family, with the devoted Anita Colombo always present. A few friends were occasionally invited to visit, and some ex-NBC musicians once came to play quartets for him. Mario Delli Ponti, a very young Italian pianist, visited Toscanini in America several times during concert tours in 1955 and '56. The first time (October 1955) Toscanini greeted him warmly, asked about his tour, and inquired solicitously about his honorarium. Delli Ponti recalled:

'It was below the minimum; by saving, I could pay my expenses. The Maestro was very worried. "How will you do it?" Then he said, "I'll teach you a secret. Excuse me a moment." So I waited. I couldn't understand what he was doing;

I saw him walk back and forth, imprecating. Finally, he came into the room and handed me a coin, saying, "You see this? This is a ten-cent piece. It's called a 'dime'. Now I'm going to give you my private telephone number and you must write it down. You'll certainly run out of money, but don't worry: call me at this number—and since you won't even have enough money for the call, just say 'collect call'. This is America, you know, and you're a young man. If you go out with a woman it'll cost you a fortune. First of all, in the afternoon you have to send her a corsage"—which must have been a custom in Woodrow Wilson's day; "then there's the restaurant... You'll go broke." He said all this without laughing, almost sombrely, shaking his head.'[20]

Toscanini's eyes became almost useless, but he kept up his contacts with the few old friends in Italy who were still alive. In August 1956 Wally wrote a letter for him to his ex-schoolmate Guido Zavadini, English hornist and music historian. She wrote:

'I have been with Papà for some months, and we often speak of you. Papà talks about past times and his distant friend. I re-read your interesting biography of Donizetti to him, and he wants me to send you ... his words: "Dear Zavadini, I have been thinking so much about you in recent days, and I would like to have some news of you. I am well, but my legs have become a bit weak and my eyes do not allow me to write you myself. I want, though, to send you an affectionate embrace ... Your very old friend, Arturo Toscanini." '[21]

He received Delli Ponti again in October and December of 1956 and talked at length about music and musicians.

'He spoke well of Tullio Serafin: "He is serious." But he spoke badly of Antonio Guarnieri and De Sabata. He reproached De Sabata for having withdrawn from active life, from work: "The last time I saw him, he already smelled like a corpse." To him, people were divided into those who worked and those who didn't work, and he would speak of the relationship between work and the good aroma of the *minestra*, the lunch soup. Of Puccini he spoke with great affection. I also heard, apropos of Catalani, a sort of discourse on the artist and hunger—hunger as a stimulus for the imagination.

I asked him about Moussorgsky's *Pictures at an Exhibition*, which I was then studying. He told me that he didn't like Horowitz's arrangement of it, and he also mentioned that he felt the composer himself had originally intended to orchestrate it, just as *Night on Bald Mountain* had first been written in a piano version. He admired Ravel's orchestration of the piece enormously, and said that the two great treatises on instrumentation were the one written by Berlioz and Ravel's orchestration of *Pictures*.

We talked about Schumann, about *Kreisleriana* and the *Humoreske*—he knew and remembered the entire repertoire in great detail and had ideas about everything. His admiration for Schumann the composer was boundless, but he considered Schumann's critical writings worthless.

One day we were listening to a tape of his performance of the "Dance of the Seven Veils" from *Salome*. Shortly after it began, Toscanini, who was sitting in one of the big, straight-backed chairs in the living room, began gently beating time with his right hand; then, as the music became more heated, he really began "conducting" with full gestures. But on the long trill, just before the end, he stopped, as if embarrassed, and I would swear that he nodded his head and pretended to be asleep. He told me that he wished he could have destroyed all his recordings; but he also gave me two of them. One was the Mozart G minor Symphony, and as he gave it to me he told me that Bruno Walter's recording was better than his own.

I told him about my experiences playing in Alaska. He was surprised to learn that I had played chamber music with good amateur quartets, and that there were educated music lovers there. Toscanini told me that those were the people we professional musicians play for; without them there would be no point in continuing to play music. I also mentioned that a friend of mine, a collector of musical manuscripts and letters in California, had asked me to get his opinion as to whether certain little-known Verdi letters to a woman, which showed Verdi in a somewhat less holy light than usual, ought to be published. He had seen the letters I was referring to and said emphatically: "I *forbid* that they be published!" '22

The unfailing friendship of Guido Cantelli, who visited, telephoned and sent detailed letters about his activities, was a great consolation to Toscanini in his last years. 'Lucky Guido,' he would say, 'who is conducting and who has a whole life ahead of him. But he is capable and good, he deserves all the best luck.'23 Then came the terrible plane crash in Paris, 23 November 1956, in which Cantelli was killed. Toscanini was never told.

That Christmas, Hugo Burghauser and conductor Jonel Perlea visited him in Riverdale. Burghauser told Haggin:

'He reminisced about Salzburg and *Falstaff* and talked about the short-comings of Walter and Furtwängler and this and that—how it's never *all* good and therefore it's really *never* good ... But there was one who was good: Nikisch. And Ernst von Schuch in Dresden ... And what did he talk about at the end? He said: "Preparation for my ninetieth birthday on March 25—exactly three months from now. They tell me they prepare something nice; and I am going to enjoy it." ...'24

The next day, Delli Ponti came to play for him.

'I said I would play a piano version of a piece by Michelangelo Rossi, an obscure 17th-century composer who had been Frescobaldi's pupil. When I named the piece Toscanini said immediately, "There are two editions of it, but both of them have a mistake in the fourth bar"; and he told me what the mistake was. I was stupefied. I mean, even granted the fact that he memorized with extreme facility, when had he ever had the *time* to go into the furthest reaches of the musical repertoire—and not just to look at these works perfunctorily, but to develop ideas about them, about how they should be played?* In any case, I played the piece, and afterwards I played a toccata by Frescobaldi himself, which delighted Toscanini. He talked at length about Frescobaldi— how it was unnecessary to go to *Parsifal* to hear extraordinary harmonies: one could hear them in Frescobaldi. And he talked about Frescobaldi's having been a popular composer, which was very important to Toscanini—that a composer write music for people to listen to. Then I played some Bach and then the Schubert B-flat Sonata, which was particularly dear to him. I believe that that was the last time anyone played for him.—Afterwards, I told him that I had been renting a piano studio by the hour in the apartment of an old Russian woman, not far from my hotel in New York. One day, the woman had to leave and asked me to let in any of the other studio lessees. The bell rang many times, and each time I opened the door, there would be a man with a young girl standing there, and I would show them to a studio. After a while, I began to see the same girls coming back with different men, and I realized that I was the gatekeeper in a brothel. When the old woman came back, I said nothing; but when I attempted to pay her for my hours of piano rental, she said, "No, no, I really couldn't accept money from you today; you've been a great help to me." I never saw Toscanini laugh so heartily as he did at this story; and he laughed even more when I mentioned that the old woman had an autographed photo of Caruso on her grand piano, with an inscription which said something like, "The face of Caruso, who is not so old after all, thanks to you." Toscanini talked about Caruso's amatory abilities which, despite everything, even he was able to envy.'[25]

31 December 1956—a New Year's Eve party in Riverdale. Toscanini was feeling well, lively, talkative; and he was ecstatic that his granddaughter Emanuela, who had married Filippo D'Acquarone, was soon to present him with his first great-grandchild. All his children and grandchildren were present, as were Anita, Martinelli, Wallenstein and several other friends, including tenor Virginio Assandri, a fellow-Parmesan who had managed to get an enormous

---

* This interest in pre-Baroque and early Baroque music—very uncommon in musicians of Toscanini's generation—was not something he developed in old age. The *Corriere della sera* of 18 July 1920 reports that at Toscanini's suggestion, a fund had been set up under the auspices of the Milan Conservatory library to cover preliminary research expenses for a projected Ricordi edition of ancient Italian music; and he himself contributed 500 lire.

culatello (a special Parmesan sausage) for the Maestro. There was plenty of good food and drink, toasts and excited conversation. At midnight Toscanini embraced each guest, as well as the cook, the chauffeur and the maid.

According to an article which appeared in Milan's *Il giorno* in 1967, and which was based on information related by Wally and Anita, at about 1 a.m. Wanda said: 'Papà, you must be tired. Do you want to go to bed?' 'I wouldn't dream of it! I'm just fine.' After 2 a.m., he accompanied his guests to the door and went up to his room. The article continued:

'For some time, he hadn't been sleeping alone. He liked to have someone near him. So Wally and Anita Colombo kept him company each night. They took turns sleeping in the bed and he slept on a reclining chair, because the bed was too high and it was difficult for him to climb on to it. He usually slept in short spells, often agitated, full of dreams and nightmares which he would then relate meticulously on awakening: there was a train which never came out of a long tunnel, or he and a friend were stowaways on a ship . . .

That morning he awoke at 7:00, put on his bathrobe and went to the bathroom. When he reappeared in the doorway, he was very pale and tottering. He leaned against the doorpost and put his hand to his forehead. Anita ran to him, held him up, accompanied him with difficulty to the bed . . . Walter was called from his room, and the doctor arrived soon afterwards. It was a cerebral thrombosis.'[26]

He regained consciousness, and when Sonia Horowitz came to be with him that afternoon, he whispered to her, '*Cara, cara*, you've come in time, because your grandfather is dying.' He recovered to the point of trying to walk. 'That iron will of his helped him to conquer the pain,' said Wally; 'but it was no longer he. For me, Papà died that New Year's morning.' Other strokes followed. Returning to the article in *Il giorno*:

'. . . The news was kept in the family for fifteen days . . . His fibre was tough and resistant. One morning, Wally saw him move his hands . . . Toscanini opened his eyes and saw a male nurse whom they had hired on the doctor's advice. Toscanini had never been able to stand nurses. "Who is that man?" he asked. They made the nurse hide . . .

"Once in a while," said Anita Colombo, "one had the impression that he heard voices. He would nod his head and say 'Yes' or 'Sì' or a word in Parmesan dialect. On one of the last days . . . he murmured, '*No, non così, più morbido, prego, più morbido. Ripetiamo. Più morbido. Ecco, bravi, così va bene.*' ('No, not like that, more smoothly, please, more smoothly. Let's repeat. More smoothly. That's it, good, now it's right.')" . . .'[27]

While still in Italy, Wally had tried to persuade Don Carlo Gnocchi, a family friend who was the only priest Toscanini could tolerate, to come to America to confess her father, who had not confessed since his Conservatory days, well over seventy years earlier! Padre Gnocchi, probably guessing what sort of reception would have met his attempt, replied: 'It isn't necessary that I go to America. Your father has done so much good in his life that he doesn't need my absolution.'[28] Now, when it had become clear that the old man could not last much longer, a priest was called to administer extreme unction. Toscanini's eyes were closed; he opened them for an instant only when, during the recitation of the liturgical formula, he heard his name pronounced.

He died the next morning, 16 January 1957, at 8.40, two months and nine days before his ninetieth birthday, surrounded by his children, his grandchildren and Anita Colombo. It was Wally's birthday.

Thousands of people filed past his open coffin at the Frank Campbell chapel in Manhattan, and a funeral was held at St Patrick's cathedral. A month later the body was flown to Italy. Between 7.30 and 9.30 on the morning of 18 February an estimated 40,000 people passed before the coffin in the foyer of La Scala. After the benediction, the inside doors of the theatre were opened, and the Scala Orchestra, conducted by De Sabata, could be heard playing the Funeral March from the 'Eroica', which was also broadcast into the jammed Piazza della Scala. The enormous crowd followed the hearse past Piazza San Babila to Via Durini, where there was a brief pause in front of Toscanini's house, then on to the cathedral, where the archbishop, Cardinal Montini (later Pope Paul VI), read the mass, and De Sabata led the Scala company in the *Libera me* from Verdi's *Requiem*, with Leyla Gencer as soloist. From there, the procession moved on to the Cimitero Monumentale, where the coffin was to be placed in the family tomb. At the cemetery entrance, the combined choruses of La Scala, the Radio italiana and the Conservatory sang 'Va, pensiero' from *Nabucco*, the same piece which Toscanini had conducted in the same place fifty-six years earlier, in tribute to its composer.

Some Observations

A well-known American music critic who had at one time even played under Toscanini in the New York Philharmonic published a review some years ago of a Karajan performance of Tchaikovsky's Fifth Symphony. He used the interesting method of making a rather detailed comparison between Karajan's approach to the work and Toscanini's. Toscanini, however, had never conducted Tchaikovsky's Fifth Symphony—and one of the critic's readers quickly wrote to point that out to him. It was one of those first-rate critical blunders which fill the hearts of performing musicians with wicked and perfectly justifiable joy. But the critic in question did not declare himself beaten: he apologized for his 'mistake', but went on to say, in effect, that he was so familiar with Toscanini's style of music-making that he felt he knew how his performance of that work would have sounded had it ever existed!

This is an extreme case of the kind of presumptuous stupidity which characterizes much music criticism in general and Toscanini criticism in particular. Nearly everything one reads and hears today on the subject of Toscanini's performances (excepting remarks by some older observers) is as foolish and futile as the above remarks on the phantasmal Tchaikovsky Fifth.

During the 1920s and '30s, when he was at the height of his powers and of his fame, Toscanini was considered by overwhelming numbers of musicians and listeners as someone whose stature was greater than that of anyone else in his field. This did not mean that he was above criticism, that everything he did was great or even good: it meant, rather, that his capabilities were so striking and his results so convincing that musicians as diverse as Kreisler, Paderewski and Monteux—to name but a few—thought of him as a phenomenon, as someone 'apart' from his colleagues, as *le plus grand de tous* (Monteux's words). The situation has changed drastically, however, in recent years. It seems that there are now two main groups of people involved in the 'Toscanini Question': fan-clubbers who would rather listen to a 'pirate' tape of Toscanini conducting Bolzoni's *Medieval Castle Serenade* than to anyone else doing a Beethoven symphony; and detractors who will tell you that they 'know the Toscanini recordings' and that he took everything too fast.

It is obvious that the whole problem of Toscanini criticism at this date—nearly a quarter-century after the conductor's retirement—and certainly in the future, is and will continue to be indissolubly bound up with his recordings. Unfortunately, those recordings do not and cannot represent him adequately. When he made his first records with the Scala orchestra in America in 1920–1, he was fifty-three years old and had been conducting for thirty-four years. His career was exactly at its half-way point. Those sessions produced about fifty minutes of nearly worthless commercial material which, in any case, is not on the market today. Between that point and his seventieth birthday he made less than three and a half hours of commercial recordings, and only a fraction of that modest quantity is available to record-buyers in the late 1970s. Toscanini did not begin to record regularly until he was past seventy; and nearly all of the currently available recordings of his core repertoire were made when he was in his eighties —all of the Beethoven and Brahms symphonies, three Schubert symphonies, *La Mer* and *Ibéria*, his four Strauss tone poem recordings, his five complete Verdi opera recordings (although *Traviata* was actually recorded a few months before his eightieth birthday), and nearly all of his Wagner excerpts.

I am not suggesting that these very late Toscanini recordings are not to be taken seriously, or that they have no value in themselves. On the contrary: they all testify to the unceasing investigative and analytical passion of an extraordinary musician, and in most cases their inherent musical value and beauty is very great. The point is that they do not give us any real perspective on his work. For example: an air-check recording exists of Toscanini's April 1935 performance of the *Missa Solemnis* with the New York Philharmonic. Most of his tempi are the slowest I have ever heard in any performance of this work, either live or on record. There is exceptional flexibility in the handling of every section, and the total effect is uniquely gripping and moving, despite the very poor quality of the recording itself and the unsuitability of Martinelli's voice in combination with the other soloists. Pirate copies also exist of Toscanini's December 1940 performance of the work with the NBC Symphony. Although its duration is only a minute less than that of the 1935 version, the general conception of the work has become less massive, more dramatic. Finally, we come to the March 1953 recording—the only one available to the public. The timing of this performance totals 1 hour, 14 minutes and 52 seconds, as opposed to 1 hour, 23 minutes and 45 seconds in 1940—a very considerable difference. Not only have the tempi become faster, but the modifications *within* those tempi have been reduced to the barest minimum: everything is done with greatest simplicity. All of these performances took place in Carnegie Hall, so the question of different tempi in different acoustical situations does not come into play here. Nor can we say that arteriosclerosis caused an increase in the speed and rigidity of Toscanini's tempi, as some have implied: while it is true that his tempi often became faster and less subject to inflection as he grew older, one can point to many contrary examples—a 1953 'Tragic' Overture much slower and weightier than that of 1937, a 'Pastoral' Symphony more lyrical in 1952 than fifteen years earlier, a Brahms Second Symphony in which an eighty-five-year-old Toscanini takes the tempo of the second theme in the last movement considerably slower than that of the first theme, and so on.

My own preference among the three *Missas* is for the earliest; but I find it fascinating and instructive to follow the evolution of Toscanini's thinking on this work over an eighteen-year period. Choose as one will—choose all or none of them, for that matter—the fact remains that Toscanini was not a musician whose work can be intelligently judged primarily on the basis of what he did *circa* 1950. Anyone who has heard his startlingly divergent recordings of the Schubert 'Great C Major' Symphony (1941, '47 and '53; all commercially available at one time or another) ought to restrain himself from making sweeping generalizations about Toscanini's 'way' of conducting. One wonders, futilely, what his performance of that work was like when he first led it in 1896 and in all the intervening years . . . 'They say that I have always been the same,' the octogenarian Toscanini told Gianandrea Gavazzeni one day. 'Nothing more foolish has ever been uttered about me. I've never been the same—not even from one day to the next. I knew it even if others didn't.'[1] His way of performing given pieces of music changed radically over the years, because he was a highly reflective and self-critical artist who was very rarely convinced that he had done his job decently, let alone well.

Another problem (actually a non-problem converted into a problem) which falls within the category of Toscanini criticism is that of 'objectivity versus subjectivity' in music-making. This contrasting of Toscanini's so-called 'literal' approach with the more 'personal' approach of, let's say, Furtwängler, has almost become a sport in certain circles; and we poor devils who try to write biographies of performing musicians frequently find ourselves attempting to digest lengthy and extremely unpalatable discussions of *die neue Sachlichkeit* and *le divin imprévu*.

Let it be stated categorically that the whole notion of 'literal' and 'objective' performances is a fallacious one! A piece of printed music will be interpreted in a different way by every performer, and even its composer will not interpret it exactly the same way every time he studies or plays it. All performers interpret all the music they perform within the limits imposed upon them by their technical and intellectual capacities, instincts, convictions, psychological make-up, and so on. This is inescapable. Finding 'the right way' to play a piece is an ideal sought by many conscientious musicians who, nonetheless, are fully aware of the fact that such a goal is unreachable. Toscanini, like other great musicians, tried as hard as possible to get to the heart of the works he performed. It is true that in, for instance, the third movement of Beethoven's Fifth Symphony, he tried to play the *poco ritardando* written over the seventh and eighth bars as Beethoven indicated, and not as a *molto ritardando* beginning two bars earlier, as many conductors before and after him have felt it should be done. It is true as well that the word 'Allegretto' written at the beginning of the second movement of the

Seventh Symphony suggested to Toscanini that Beethoven did not want that movement to have a dirge-like quality. And it is also true that Toscanini was convinced that when Verdi wrote the aria 'Caro nome' in *Rigoletto*, he put into it all the ornamentation that he considered desirable. If these are examples of pettifogging pedantry, then Toscanini—and a number of other excellent musicians—can be called pedants, literalists, and anything of the sort.*

One of the incorrect legends about Toscanini which books like Chotzinoff's helped to foster is that of a completely one-sided genius who demonstrated phenomenal spiritual profundity in his work, knew very little about anything else, and spent much of his time behaving like a petulant three-year-old. That Toscanini was capable of behaving petulantly is quite obvious; but I hope it has been made clear that he was also capable of personal generosity and nobility. Furthermore, he was anything but an idiot in many areas outside his immediate field. His knowledge of classical and romantic literature was very substantial. He had learned most of Dante and a good deal of Shakespeare (in English) by heart. Nineteenth-century Italian writers, particularly Leopardi and Carducci (the prose works), were his constant companions; and in his seventies, when he lived in Riverdale, he became fascinated by early American literature, notably Washington Irving, whose tales of the Hudson appealed to him. His reading included the French and Russian novelists, Emerson, the Greek dramatists and theories of world government—and given his extraordinary powers of concentration and memorization, to read was to absorb completely. In his own field his reading encompassed everything he could put his hands on—histories of music, biographies and correspondence of composers, analytical works—and he was eternally pursuing every bit of information which could conceivably contribute something to his work. Erich Leinsdorf called Toscanini 'an extremely intelligent and highly aware person who certainly knew everything there was to know about his profession'.[2]

His knowledge of the visual arts was also very impressive. 'I don't know,' he once told Sacchi, 'whether I like music or painting better.'[3] Although he was, of course, familiar with Renaissance art, his great passion was for his contemporary turn-of-the-century Italian artists, many of whom became his closest friends—the pointillist painter Vittore Grubicy and sculptor Leonardo Bistolfi, for example. He would spend hours at a time in Grubicy's studio, and he used to accompany another painter friend, Arturo Tosi, on his sketching forays into the countryside. Eventually he developed a fine collection of works by these artists as well as by Signorini, Sernesi, Lega, and even Tiepolo and Fontanesi. His daughter Wanda said that it relaxed her father to re-hang the canvases:

* It must be mentioned that Toscanini, like many of his colleagues, often made changes—generally minor but occasionally major—in the orchestration of works he conducted; and these re-touchings were sometimes in questionable taste.

'He always had a hammer and nails, and liked to change the position of the paintings. Often he did this in the middle of the night when he couldn't sleep. He really adored paintings. When he would buy a new one he would take it to his bedroom, sit in bed and look at it. Mother said that one night she woke up and found Father asleep with a painting in his hands. She was glad that she had awakened, or the painting would have fallen on his face.'[4]

All this is not to demonstrate that Toscanini was an intellectual. He was not—and woe to the artist who thinks he is; but neither was he the totally one-sided creature that some have made him out to be. It must also be mentioned that he enjoyed watching television when it was introduced in America after the Second World War, and he especially liked children's shows, slapstick comedians, prize fights and wrestling matches. He became interested enough in boxing to read about it, and he eventually got to know personally Primo Carnera, Antonino Rocca and other Italo-American fighters. (I once heard a funny interview with Rocca, in which he put forward the theory that since Toscanini's health was so good and his physique so strong, 'if he had been training hard, he could have been a champ'.)

Performing musicians—great ones, decent ones and poor ones—come and go; even the best of them leave a mark which quickly fades. Recordings have proved that nothing can stop this from happening: the percentage of today's record-buyers who will choose a performance of a Beethoven symphony by Furtwängler or Toscanini over a more modern version is very small indeed. Walter and Beecham, who lived long enough to make stereophonic recordings, have already been transferred to the so-called 'budget' labels, and the same fate awaits Klemperer and others. Of course there are fine and beautiful modern recordings of much of the repertoire, and there is no reason why they should not be enjoyed. But the fact is that people have short memories, even for what they once loved; and new generations arise who, except in special cases, do not feel a need to listen to performances that took place in their grandparents' day. Those who like to hear how Nikisch, Mengelberg, Weingartner or Strauss did certain pieces are either professionals or exceptionally impassioned amateurs.

What *is* the point in caring? Admitting that European civilization is but one segment of a vast fabric, admitting that 'professionally-composed' polyphonic music is but one strand in that segment, it seems absurd that a highly gifted human being like Toscanini should have lavished his vital energies on trying to realize this or that melodic figure in one way instead of another. The most amazing thing about Toscanini, however, was that his struggle to achieve a beautiful performance was absolutely a matter of life and death—the struggle itself even more than the achievement. His objective in driving himself and everyone else so ferociously was certainly not to please an audience made up largely of casual listeners. The beauty simply had to be re-created, and to him the world was no good without it. This passion, fanaticism, madness—call it what you will—possessed him so entirely that his work *became* communication at a level undreamed of by most performers.

Personally, I find his performances—or what remains of them today—to be valuable and often uniquely beautiful. This book, however, has not been written in praise of Arturo Toscanini's achievements (which in any case do not require my praise), but rather in tribute to his concentratedness, his terrible honesty, his unfailing sense of direction and his relentless self-dissatisfaction.

Notes

FOREWORD (pp. 1–4)

1 Walter Toscanini, letter to the author, 10 August 1964.
2 Peter Heyworth, interview with Otto Klemperer, broadcast by the Canadian Broadcasting Corporation, 1969.
3 Fedele D'Amico *et al.*, *La lezione di Toscanini*, p. 226.

CHAPTER 1 (pp. 5–21)

1 Gaspare Nello Vetro, *Toscanini alla Regia Scuola del Carmine*, pp. 20–2.
2 Filippo Sacchi, *Toscanini*, p. 28.
3 Luciana Frassati, *Il Maestro*, pp. 270–1.
4 Vetro, op. cit., p. 15.
5 Camilla Cederna, *La voce dei padroni*, pp. 13–14.
6 Vetro, op. cit., pp. 128–9.
7 ibid., p. 138.
8 ibid., p. 101.
9 Alfredo Segre, 'Toscanini—The First Forty Years', p. 162.
10 Vetro, op. cit., pp. 171–2.
11 Walter Toscanini, letter to Mario Medici, 6 June 1964.
12 Ayres de Andrede, 'Um episódio brasileiro na carreira de Toscanini'.
13 This and subsequent direct quotations of Toscanini's words in this chapter are taken from a tape made (without Toscanini's knowledge) of a conversation he had on 1 September 1955 at his home in New York with his son, Walter, his daughter, Wally, and his friends Anita Colombo and Wilfrid Pelletier.
14 Eugene Weintraub, 'A Visit to Toscanini', *Musical America*, 10 February 1943.
15 Igor Stravinsky, *Stravinsky*, p. 204.

CHAPTER 2 (pp. 22–59)

1 See note 13 to preceding chapter.
2 D'Amico *et al.*, op. cit., pp. 176–7.
3 Carlo Gatti, *Catalani*, pp. 140–1.
4 Andrea Della Corte, *Toscanini visto da un critico*, p. 25.
5 Sacchi, op. cit., pp. 89–90.
6 *L'Elettore*, Casale Monferrato, 10 June 1887.

7 Guglielmo Barblan, *Toscanini e la Scala*, p. 28.
8 Howard Taubman, *The Maestro*, p. 40.
9 George R. Marek, *Toscanini*, p. 112.
10 D'Amico *et al.*, op. cit., p. 181.
11 Ambrogio Brocca, *Il Politeama Genovese*, p. 171.
12 Giulio Gatti-Casazza, *Memories of the Opera*, p. 52.
13 Much of the information on the Voghera season was found in the article by Giuseppe Mazza, 'Teatro Sociale: Stagione lirica 1889', *Ultrapadum*, Voghera, September 1957.
14 Segre, op. cit., p. 157.
15 Barblan, op. cit., p. 37.
16 Segre, op. cit., p. 157.
17 G. B. Vallebona, *Il Teatro Carlo Felice*, p. 194.
18 ibid.
19 ibid.
20 Segre, op. cit., p. 158.
21 Catalani letter to Giulio Ricordi, 19 February 1892, Museo Teatrale alla Scala, Milano.
22 Segre, op. cit., p. 158.
23 Vallebona, op. cit., p. 195.
24 Museo Teatrale alla Scala.
25 ibid.
26 Barblan, op. cit., p. 315.
27 John W. Klein, 'Toscanini and Catalani—A Unique Friendship', p. 221.
28 Barblan, op. cit., p. 316.
29 Della Corte, op. cit., p. 37.
30 ibid., p. 38.
31 ibid.
32 Segre, op. cit., p. 160.
33 Frassati, op. cit., p. 20.
34 Gatti, op. cit., p. 142.
35 Klein, op. cit., p. 213.
36 Mario Morini, '*Pagliacci*, Leoncavallo e Toscanini', p. 93.
37 Gatti-Casazza, op. cit., p. 51.
38 Franco Abbiati, *Giuseppe Verdi*, vol. IV, p. 565.
39 ibid., p. 566.
40 Segre, op. cit., p. 163.
41 *La Gazzetta di Venezia*, 21 April 1895.
42 *Il Pianoforte*, June 1924, pp. 174–5.
43 D'Amico *et al.*, op. cit., p. 176.
44 Stanley Jackson, *Monsieur Butterfly*, p. 70.
45 Giacomo Puccini, *Carteggi Pucciniani*, p. 137.
46 ibid., p. 139.
47 Frassati, op. cit., p. 73.
48 B. H. Haggin, *Conversations with Toscanini*, p. 79.
49 Della Corte, op. cit., p. 54.
50 Barblan, op. cit., p. 37.
51 Barblan, op. cit., p. 316.
52 ibid., pp. 317–18.
53 Renzo Allegri, 'Nostro Padre Arturo Toscanini', 1 April 1972.

54 Giuseppe Valdengo, *Ho cantato con Toscanini*.
55 Haggin, op. cit., p. 68.
56 Istituto di Studi Verdiani, Parma.
57 Raffaelle De Rensis, *Lettere di Arrigo Boito*, p. 243.
58 ibid., pp. 243-4.

CHAPTER 3 (pp. 60-102)

1 Carlo Arner, 'Storia della questione della Scala', *Annuario dell'Arte Lirica e Coreografica*, Milano 1899.
2 *Parma a Toscanini*, 1958, pp. 61-2.
3 Barblan, op. cit., pp. 319-20.
4 ibid., p. 320.
5 Della Corte, op. cit., pp. 73-4.
6 ibid., p. 75.
7 Gatti-Casazza, op. cit., p. 74.
8 *Il Pianoforte*, June 1924, p. 175.
9 Museo Teatrale alla Scala, Milano.
10 Paul Stefan, *Arturo Toscanini*.
11 Barblan, op. cit., p. 323.
12 ibid., pp. 322-3.
13 Abbiati, op. cit., p. 637.
14 ibid., pp. 637-8.
15 Giuseppe Verdi, *I Copialettere*, p. 256.
16 ibid.
17 *La Gazzetta musicale di Milano*, 16 March 1899.
18 Abbiati, op. cit., p. 638.
19 ibid.
20 Istituto di Studi Verdiani, Parma.
21 Abbiati, op. cit., p. 640.
22 Vienna Philharmonic Orchestra, archives.
23 Barblan, op. cit., p. 61.
24 Segre, op. cit., p. 170.
25 Barblan, op. cit., p. 65.
26 Puccini, op. cit., p. 195.
27 ibid., pp. 195-6.
28 Allegri, op. cit., 1 April 1972, p. 60.
29 Puccini, op. cit., p. 204.
30 Interview with Friedelind Wagner by the author, 1977.
31 Barblan, op. cit., p. 324.
32 ibid., p. 86.
33 Gatti-Casazza, op. cit., p. 110.
34 Haggin, op. cit., p. 61.
35 Feodor Chaliapin and Maxim Gorky, *Chaliapin*, pp. 146-7.
36 Haggin, op. cit., p. 78.
37 Romeo Carugati, in *Lombardia*, 3 April 1902.
38 Sacchi, op. cit., p. 177.
39 Museo Teatrale alla Scala, Milano.
40 Jackson, op. cit., p. 117.

41 *Il Pianoforte*, June 1924, p. 171.
42 Barblan, op. cit., p. 330.
43 Enrico di San Martino, *Ricordi*, p. 100.
44 Toscanini Memorial Archives, Library of the Performing Arts, Lincoln Center, New York.
45 Sacchi, op. cit., facing p. 176; and Barblan, op. cit., p. 119.
46 Della Corte, op. cit., p. 101.
47 Barblan, op. cit., p. 121.
48 Guglielmo Barblan, 'Toscanini Alpinista', p. 60.
49 *Il Pianoforte*, June 1924, p. 182.
50 Enzo Biagi in *La Stampa*, 27 April 1972.
51 Barblan, *Toscanini e la Scala*, pp. 329–30.
52 ibid., pp. 330–1.
53 ibid., pp. 331–2.
54 ibid., p. 332.
55 ibid., p. 334.
56 Richard Strauss, *Die Welt um Strauss in Briefen*, p. 175.
57 Frances Alda, *Men, Women and Tenors*, pp. 83–4.
58 Gatti-Casazza, op. cit., p. 148.
59 Metropolitan Opera Archives.
60 Mario Morini, 'Toscanini visto dai cantati', in *Fenarete letture d'Italia*, 1967, p. 35.
61 Barblan, op. cit., p. 343.
62 ibid., p. 146.
63 ibid., p. 146.

CHAPTER 4 (pp. 103–41)

1 Emma Eames, *Some Memories and Reflections*, p. 294.
2 Gustav Mahler, *Briefe*, p. 430.
3 Alma Mahler, *Gustav Mahler* (Italian edition).
4 Alma Mahler, *Gustav Mahler* (American edition), p. 145.
5 ibid., p. 146.
6 Bruno Walter, *Theme and Variations*, p. 278.
7 Taubman, op. cit., p. 119.
8 Haggin, op. cit., p. 77.
9 Museo Teatrale alla Scala, Milano.
10 Interview with Erich Leinsdorf by the author, 1972.
11 Eames, op. cit., p. 298.
12 Interview with Carlo Maria Giulini by the author, 1977.
13 Anne Homer, *Louise Homer*, pp. 276–7.
14 Frieda Hempel, *Mein Leben dem Gesang*, p. 184.
15 Barblan, op. cit., p. 174.
16 Puccini, op. cit., p. 376.
17 Score in the archives of the Ricordi Company, Milano.
18 Puccini, op. cit., p. 377.
19 ibid., p. 379.
20 ibid., p. 383.
21 ibid., p. 384.
22 Ferruccio Busoni, *Letters to His Wife*, p. 184.

23 Edward J. Dent, *Ferruccio Busoni*, p. 209.
24 Allegri, op. cit., 8 April 1972, p. 60.
25 Barblan, op. cit., pp. 339–40.
26 Frassati, op. cit., p. 53.
27 Labroca and Boccardi, op. cit., pp. 62–3.
28 Della Corte, op. cit., pp. 127–8.
29 ibid., pp. 128–9.
30 Frassati, op. cit., p. 102.
31 De Rensis, op. cit., p. 245.
32 Haggin, op. cit., p. 78.
33 Max Smith, 'Toscanini at the Baton', in *The Century*.
34 Haggin, op. cit., p. 68.
35 Interview with Giulio Riccardi by the author, 1977.
36 Verdi, op. cit., pp. 255–7.
37 ibid., pp. 264–5.
38 Barblan, op. cit., p. 183.
39 Haggin, op. cit., p. 79.
40 Allegri, op. cit., 1 April 1972, p. 60.
41 Morini, op. cit., p. 96.
42 Della Corte, op. cit., p. 239.
43 Interview with Giovanni Martinelli by Edward Downes, Metropolitan Opera broadcast, March 1967.
44 Giovanni Martinelli, 'Singing Verdi', *Musical America*, March 1963.
45 Barblan, op. cit., pp. 337–8.
46 Taubman, op. cit., pp. 119–20.
47 Metropolitan Opera archives.
48 ibid.
49 Irving Kolodin, *The Metropolitan Opera*, p. 215.
50 Barblan, op. cit., pp. 338–9.
51 Labroca and Boccardi, op. cit., p. 69.
52 Puccini, op. cit., p. 450.
53 Allegri, op. cit., 1 April 1972, p. 60.
54 Dora Setti, *Eleonora Duse ad Antonietta Pisa*.
55 Vincent Seligman, *Puccini among Friends*, pp. 292–3.
56 Taubman, op. cit., p. 141.
57 Della Corte, op. cit., pp. 150–1.
58 Metropolitan Opera archives.

CHAPTER 5 (pp. 142–95)

1 Della Corte, op. cit., p. 160.
2 Metropolitan Opera archives.
3 Nuccio Fiorda, *Arte, beghe e bizze di Toscanini*, p. 49.
4 Enrico Minetti, *Ricordi scaligeri*, p. 75.
5 *Il Pianoforte*, June 1924, p. 177.
6 ibid., p. 170.
7 Della Corte, op. cit., p. 168.
8 Ignace J. Paderewski and Mary Lawton, *The Paderewski Memoirs*, p. 124.
9 *Parma a Toscanini*, 1958, p. 52.

10 Interview with Giuseppe Marchioro by the author, 1976.
11 Interview with Antonino Votto by the author, 1977.
12 *Il Pianoforte*, June 1924, pp. 167–8.
13 D'Amico *et al.*, op. cit., pp. 214–18.
14 Toti Dal Monte, *Una voce nel mondo*, p. 107.
15 ibid., p. 108.
16 Giacomo Lauri-Volpi, *Voci parallele*, p. 21.
17 D'Amico *et al.*, op. cit., p. 226.
18 Domenico Silvestrini, *Aureliano Pertile*, p. 34.
19 Ezio Pinza and Robert Magidoff, *Ezio Pinza*, p. 100.
20 Renato Simoni, *Ritratti*, pp. 20–1.
21 Maria Labia, *Guardare indietro: che fatica!* p. 117.
22 Carlo Paladini, *Giacomo Puccini*, p. 154.
23 Puccini, op. cit., pp. 509–10.
24 Barblan, op. cit., p. 204.
25 Puccini, op. cit., p. 512.
26 ibid., p. 521.
27 Barblan, op. cit., p. 205.
28 Puccini, op. cit., p. 534.
29 Barblan, op. cit., pp. 345–7.
30 Frassati, op. cit., p. 161.
31 Dal Monte, op. cit., pp. 118–19.
32 D'Amico *et al.*, op. cit., p. 222.
33 Silvestrini, op. cit., pp. 30–2.
34 Barblan, op. cit., p. 206.
35 ibid., p. 207.
36 Berta Geissmar, *The Baton and the Jackboot*, p. 35.
37 Labroca and Boccardi, op. cit., pp. 99–100.
38 Facsimile of Toscanini's message in *L'illustrazione italiana*, Milano, 13 June 1948.
39 Sacchi, op. cit., pp. 298–9.
40 D'Amico *et al.*, op. cit., p. 189.
41 Labroca and Boccardi, op. cit., p. 159.
42 Dal Monte, op. cit., p. 125.
43 ibid., pp. 126–7.
44 Minetti, op. cit., pp. 76–8.
45 Della Corte, op. cit., p. 234.
46 Piero Nardi, *Vita di Arrigo Boito*, p. 722.
47 Barblan, op. cit., p. 207.
48 Puccini, op. cit., pp. 553–4.
49 Barblan, op. cit., p. 208.
50 Puccini, op. cit., p. 555.
51 Allegri, op. cit., 8 April 1972, p. 56.
52 Enzo Biagi, in *La Stampa*, 27 April 1972.
53 ibid.
54 Giuseppe Adami, *Puccini*, p. 218.
55 Ugo Ojetti, *I Taccuini*, pp. 156–7.
56 Labroca and Boccardi, op. cit., p. 106.
57 Fritz Busch, *Pages from a Musician's Life*, p. 183.
58 Interview with Gianandrea Gavazzeni by the author, 1972.

59 Sacchi, op. cit., pp. 263-4.
60 New York Philharmonic archives.
61 ibid.
62 ibid.
63 ibid.
64 Louise Varèse, *Varèse: A Looking-Glass Diary*, p. 249.
65 ibid.
66 Barblan, op. cit., facing p. 113.
67 Interview with Antonino Votto by author, 1977.
68 Frassati, op. cit., p. 182.
69 D'Amico *et al.*, op. cit., p. 210.
70 ibid.
71 ibid., p. 211.
72 Minetti, op. cit., p. 79.
73 Igor Stravinsky, *Stravinsky*, pp. 203-5.
74 ibid., p. 206.
75 Eric Walter White, *Stravinsky*, p. 518.
76 New York Philharmonic archives.
77 ibid.
78 Walter, op. cit., p. 278.
79 Conversation between Louis Fourestier and the author, 1971.
80 Daniel Gillis, *Furtwängler in America*, pp. 18-19.
81 New York Philharmonic archives.
82 ibid.
83 Minetti, op. cit., p. 73.
84 New York Philharmonic archives.
85 ibid.
86 ibid.
87 D'Amico *et al.*, op. cit., pp. 201-2.
88 Arnaldo Fraccaroli, *La Scala a Vienna e a Berlino, Maggio 1929*.
89 ibid.
90 Ernst Haeussermann, *Herbert von Karajan*, p. 112.
91 ibid.
92 Fraccaroli, op. cit.
93 Walter, op. cit., p. 286.
94 Peter Heyworth, *Conversations with Klemperer*, p. 91.
95 *Ente Autonomo Teatro alla Scala:* 'Cronistoria della stagione 1928-29', p. 142.
96 ibid.

CHAPTER 6 (pp. 196-269)

1 Museo Teatrale alla Scala, Milano.
2 ibid.
3 Haggin, op. cit., pp. 79-80.
4 Raffaelle De Rensis, *Musica vista*, p. 117.
5 *Emporium*, Bergamo, December 1930.
6 Della Corte, op. cit., p. 250.
7 René Chalupt, *Ravel au miroir de ses lettres*, p. 244.
8 ibid., pp. 244-5.

9 Barblan, op. cit., p. 362.
10 ibid., p. 363.
11 *Arturo Toscanini: Parma nel centenario della nascita*, pp. 85–7.
12 Walter, op. cit., p. 290.
13 Labroca and Boccardi, op. cit., pp. 130–1.
14 B. H. Haggin, 'Toscanini and his Critics'.
15 Barblan, op. cit., p. 361.
16 B. H. Haggin, *The Toscanini Musicians Knew*, pp. 63–4.
17 Labroca and Boccardi, op. cit., pp. 133–4.
18 ibid., p. 133.
19 Interview with Friedelind Wagner by the author, 1977.
20 Interview with Wanda Toscanini Horowitz by Edward Downes, Metropolitan Opera broadcast, March 1967.
21 Friedelind Wagner and Page Cooper, *Heritage of Fire*, p. 54.
22 Daniela Thode, 'Bayreuth seit 1930', typed manuscript, Richard Wagner Gedenkstätte, Bayreuth.
23 New York Philharmonic archives.
24 Labroca and Boccardi, op. cit., p. 136.
25 See note 20.
26 Labroca and Boccardi, op. cit., p. 137.
27 Interview with Elsa Respighi, RAI broadcast, August 1977.
28 Interview with Natale Gallini by the author, 1977.
29 Allegri, op. cit., 15 April 1972, pp. 48, 51.
30 Barblan, op. cit., facing p. 360 *et seq*.
31 Clara Clemens, *My Husband Gabrilowitsch*, p. 206.
32 Josef Szigeti, *With Strings Attached*, pp. 347–8.
33 Frassati, op. cit., p. 206.
34 Wagner and Cooper, op. cit., p. 62.
35 Interview with Friedelind Wagner by the author, 1977.
36 Thode, op. cit.
37 Barblan, op. cit., p. 364.
38 Thode, op. cit.
39 New York Philharmonic archives.
40 Taubman, op. cit., p. 195.
41 New York Philharmonic archives.
42 ibid.
43 *New York Times*, May 1932.
44 Della Corte, op. cit., pp. 281–2.
45 Barblan, op. cit., pp. 364–5.
46 Allegri, op. cit., 8 April 1972, p. 56.
47 Clemens, op. cit., p. 211.
48 ibid., p. 212.
49 Wagner and Cooper, op. cit., pp. 88–9.
50 Richard Wagner Gedenkstätte, Bayreuth.
51 Busch, op. cit., p. 217.
52 Frassati, op. cit., p. 249.
53 Wagner and Cooper, op. cit., p. 89.
54 Haggin, op. cit., pp. 154–5.
55 ibid., p. 192.
56 Unpublished reminiscences of Iwa Aulin Voghera.

57 ibid.
58 Allegri, op. cit., 8 April 1972, p. 56.
59 Gregor Piatigorsky, *Cellist*, p. 242.
60 Robert Magidoff, *Yehudi Menuhin*, p. 157.
61 Interview with Yehudi Menuhin by the author, 1971.
62 Lotte Lehmann, *Midway in My Song*, p. 157.
63 ibid., pp. 225–6.
64 Lotte Lehmann, taped reminiscences of Toscanini, Metropolitan Opera broadcast, March 1967.
65 Haggin, op. cit., pp. 229–30.
66 New York Philharmonic archives.
67 Piatigorsky, op. cit., pp. 225–6.
68 Sir Adrian Boult, *My Own Trumpet*, pp. 101–2.
69 Michael Kennedy, *Barbirolli*, p. 96.
70 ibid.
71 New York Philharmonic archives.
72 ibid.
73 ibid.
74 Boult, op. cit., p. 102.
75 Halina Rodzinski, *Our Two Lives*, p. 129.
76 B. H. Haggin, 'Vienna's Great Conductors', p. 34.
77 Erich Leinsdorf, *Cadenza—A Musical Career*, pp. 41–2.
78 Adriano Lualdi, *L'arte di dirigere l'orchestra*, p. 230.
79 Lotte Lehmann, op. cit., pp. 231–2.
80 Leinsdorf, op. cit., pp. 40–1.
81 J.N. Moore, *A Voice in Time*.
82 Kennedy, op. cit., p. 95.
83 New York Philharmonic archives.
84 Fascist government file on Toscanini, St Antony's College, Oxford.
85 Vera Newman, *Ernest Newman*, p. 150.
86 New York Philharmonic archives.
87 Haggin, op. cit., p. 40.
88 New York Philharmonic archives.
89 Barblan, op. cit., p. 366.
90 Taubman, op. cit., p. 215.
91 Haggin, *The Toscanini Musicians Knew*, pp. 169–70.
92 Lualdi, op. cit., pp. 228–30.
93 Margarete Wallmann, *Les Balcons du ciel*.
94 Labroca and Boccardi, op. cit., pp. 142–3.
95 Haggin, op. cit., p. 70.
96 D. E. Ingelbrecht, *The Conductor's World*, pp. 19–29.
97 Bronislaw Huberman Archive, Central Library for Music and Dance, Tel-Aviv.
98 Casa natale di Toscanini, Parma.
99 *Arturo Toscanini*, America–Israel Cultural Foundation.
100 *La Bourse Egyptienne*, 7 January 1937.
101 See note 99.
102 Haggin, op. cit., pp. 193–4.
103 See note 97.
104 See note 99.

105 See note 97.
106 Interview with Lorand Fenyves by the author, 1971.
107 See note 97.
108 New York Philharmonic archives.
109 ibid.
110 Leinsdorf, op. cit., pp. 47–8.
111 Rodzinski, op. cit., p. 159.
112 New York Philharmonic archives.
113 Jaap Stotijn, *Even uitblazen*, p. 32.
114 *Het Vaderland*, The Hague, 2 March 1937.
115 Interview with George Szell by the author, 1965.
116 Haggin, op. cit., p. 174.
117 ibid., p. 68.
118 ibid., p. 67.
119 Haggin, 'Vienna's Great Conductors', pp. 38–9.
120 Barblan, op. cit., p. 308.
121 New York Philharmonic archives.
122 Samuel Antek, *This Was Toscanini*, pp. 15–16.
123 Barblan, op. cit., p. 308.
124 Bernard Shore, *The Orchestra Speaks*, pp. 161–82.
125 Della Corte, op. cit., p. 321.
126 Sir Arthur Bliss, *As I Remember*, p. 116.
127 Grete Busch, *Fritz Busch*, p. 156.

CHAPTER 7 (pp. 270–309)

1 Haggin, *Conversations with Toscanini*, p. 66.
2 Haggin, *The Toscanini Musicians Knew*, pp. 35–6.
3 Interview with Friedelind Wagner by the author, 1977.
4 Labroca and Boccardi, op. cit., pp. 156–7.
5 Haggin, op. cit., pp. 221–2.
6 Haggin, *Conversations with Toscanini*, pp. 20–2.
7 Conversation between Arthur Fierro and the author, 1977.
8 Booklet accompanying RCA's 'A Toscanini Treasury of Historic Recordings', LM 6711.
9 ibid.
10 Gaetano Salvemini, *L'Italia vista dall'America*, vols. I and II, p. 165.
11 Salvemini archives, Rome.
12 ibid.
13 ibid.
14 Armando Borghi, 'Esilio americano', *Il mondo*, 14 May 1957.
15 Barblan, op. cit., p. 368.
16 ibid., p. 369.
17 ibid., p. 370.
18 Aldo Carpi, *Diario di Gusen*, p. 174.
19 Della Corte, op. cit., pp. 337–8.
20 Haggin, *The Toscanini Musicians Knew*, pp. 80–1.
21 Minetti, op. cit., pp. 67–8.
22 Notes made by Lily Seppilli.

23 Frassati, op. cit., p. 267.
24 Labroca and Boccardi, op. cit., p. 226.
25 Interview with Robert Merrill by Edward Downes, Metropolitan Opera broadcast, March 1967.
26 *Il giorno*, Milano, 25 March 1967.
27 Labroca and Boccardi, op. cit., p. 201.
28 Della Corte, op. cit., p. 370.
29 Minetti, op. cit., p. 20.
30 Della Corte, op. cit., p. 382.
31 Nan Merriman, 'A Singer's View of Toscanini', *Saturday Review*, 25 March 1967.
32 Philip Hamburger, 'Toscanini Train', *New Yorker*, 20 May 1950.
33 Interview with Walfredo Toscanini by the author, 1977.
34 Antek, op. cit., pp. 99–100.
35 ibid., p. 101.
36 Allegri, op. cit., 22 April 1972, p. 50.
37 Courtesy Maria Cecchini Montarsolo.
38 Enzo Biagi, in *La Stampa*, 27 April 1972.
39 Richard Osborne, 'All in Good Time', *Records and Recordings*, February 1973.
40 Barblan, op. cit., p. 371.
41 Interview with Michelangelo Abbado by the author, 1977.
42 *Il giorno*, 25 March 1967.
43 Della Corte, op. cit., pp. 394–8.
44 Cederna, op. cit., pp. 9–10.
45 Labroca and Boccardi, op. cit., p. 274.
46 See note 31.
47 Allegri, op. cit., 22 April 1972, p. 53.
48 ibid.
49 Courtesy Maria Cecchini Montarsolo.
50 ibid.
51 ibid.
52 Haggin, *Conversations with Toscanini*, p. 103.
53 ibid., pp. 103–5.

CHAPTER 8 (pp. 310–20)

1 Della Corte, op. cit., p. 426.
2 Haggin, *The Toscanini Musicians Knew*, p. 15.
3 Conversation between Arthur Fierro and the author, 1977.
4 Beniamino Dal Fabbro, *Musica e verità*, p. 173.
5 Interview with Michelangelo Abbado by the author, 1977.
6 Conversation between Sandro Cicogna and the author, 1977.
7 Interview with Yehudi Menuhin by the author, 1971.
8 Courtesy Maria Cecchini Montarsolo.
9 ibid.
10 Interview with Natale Gallini by the author, 1976.
11 D'Amico *et al.*, op. cit., pp. 179–80.
12 Luchino Visconti, 'Il vero *Falstaff*', *Il contemporaneo*, Rome, 26 January 1957.
13 Cederna, op. cit., pp. 10–12.

14 *Oggi*, 31 January 1957.
15 John Ardoin and Gerald Fitzgerald, *Callas*, p. 89.
16 See note 12.
17 *Arturo Toscanini: Parma nel centenario della nascita*, p. 136.
18 Courtesy Sandro Cicogna.
19 Gualtiero Trambali, 'Sono vecchissimo, non ne posso più', *Epoca*, 26 January 1977.
20 Conversation between Mario Delli Ponti and the author, 1977.
21 *La Gazzetta di Parma*, 20 January 1957.
22 See note 20.
23 Giuseppe Tarozzi, *Non muore la musica*, p. 284.
24 Haggin, *The Toscanini Musicians Knew*, pp. 173–4.
25 See note 20.
26 *Il giorno*, Milano, 25 March 1967.
27 ibid.
28 Allegri, op. cit., 22 April 1972, p. 56.

SOME OBSERVATIONS (pp. 321–6)

1 Interview with Gianandrea Gavazzeni by the author, 1972.
2 Interview with Erich Leinsdorf by the author, 1972.
3 Sacchi, op. cit., p. 244.
4 Interview with Wanda Toscanini Horowitz by Edward Downes, Metropolitan Opera broadcast, March 1967.

Appendix I

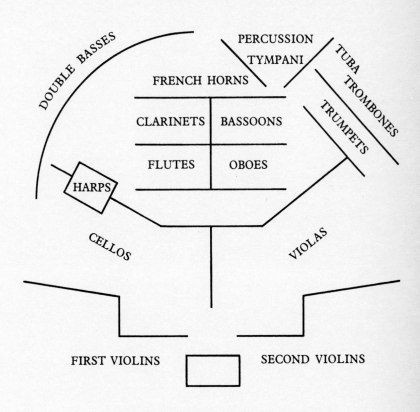

TOSCANINI'S NORMAL ORCHESTRAL SEATING

Appendix II

If and when the archive assembled by Walter Toscanini is ever made available for scholarly investigation, it should be possible for a comprehensive Toscanini repertoire list to be published. As it is, the information uncovered by previous researchers and myself would fill a fair-sized volume. What follows is the barest skeleton of a catalogue. In the 'Theatre' section, I have listed names of composers and operas, as well as the cities in which Toscanini conducted each opera; in the 'Concert Hall' section, not even that much detail could be given: only names of the composers and their works are furnished. In sections C and D I have attempted to fill in some of the biggest gaps.

The statistics, as they now stand, are impressive and even overwhelming. In the theatre, Toscanini led 117 operas (plus Debussy's *Le Martyre de Saint-Sébastien*) by 53 composers; in the concert hall, 175 composers (38 of them overlapping the opera composers) were represented by over 480 works—*not* including operas or excerpts from operas which he had conducted in stage performances. In total, there are approximately 600 works, great and small, by 190 composers—and everything rehearsed and performed from memory. No doubt the family archive would increase these figures, although probably not by very much.

I have used the following abbreviations: arr—arranged; BA—Buenos Aires; Balt—Baltimore; Ber—Berlin; Bo—Bologna; Bos—Boston; Brkln—Brooklyn; Byrth—Bayreuth; Chi—Chicago; Gen—Genoa; Mi—Milan; Mont—Montevideo; mvt—movement; NY—New York; orch—orchestrated; Par—Paris; Phila—Philadelphia; Pitts—Pittsburgh; recit—recitative; Rio—Rio de Janeiro; Ro—Rome; Sg—Salzburg; Tur—Turin; Ven—Venice; Vn—Vienna.

A   IN THE THEATRE

Beethoven, Ludwig van. *Fidelio* (Mi, Sg).
Bellini, Vincenzo. *Capuleti e Montecchi* (Barcelona); *I puritani* (Brescia); *Norma* (Palermo, Tur).
Berlioz, Hector. *The Damnation of Faust* (Mi, BA, Mont, Tur).
Bizet, Georges. *Carmen* (Verona, Tur, Gen, Ro, Mi, NY, Phila, Brkln).
Boito, Arrigo. *Mefistofele* (Tur, Mi, BA, Mont); *Nerone* (Mi, Bo, Tur).
Buzzi-Peccia, Arturo. *La forza d'amore* (Tur).
Cagnoni, Antonio. *Francesca da Rimini* (Mi, Gen).
Canti, Natale. *Savitri* (Bo, Gen).

Catalani, Alfredo. *Edmea* (Tur); *Loreley* (Gen, Palermo, Treviso, Tur, BA, Mont); *La Wally* (Lucca, BA, Mont, Mi, NY).

Charpentier, Gustave. *Louise* (Mi).

Cilea, Francesco. *Adriana Lecouvreur* (BA, Mont); *Gloria* (Mi).

Debussy, Claude. *Le Martyre de Saint-Sébastien* (Mi); *Pelléas et Mélisande* (Mi).

De Lara, Isidore. *Messalina* (Mi).

De Leva, Enrico. *La Camargo* (Tur).

Donizetti, Gaetano. *Don Pasquale* (BA, Mont, NY); *L'elisir d'amore* (Mi, BA, Mont); *La favorita* (Rio, Voghera, Bergamo); *Linda di Chamounix* (Mi, BA, Mont); *Lucia di Lammermoor* (Mi, Vn, Ber); *Lucrezia Borgia* (Verona).

Dukas, Paul. *Ariane et Barbe-bleue* (NY, BA, Mi).

Franchetti, Alberto. *Asrael* (BA, Mi); *Cristoforo Colombo* (Gen, Treviso, Bo, Pisa, Ven, Trento, BA, Mi); *La figlia di Iorio* (BA); *Germania* (Mi, BA, NY, Phila, Chi).

Galeotti, Cesare. *Anton* (Mi).

Giordano, Umberto. *Andrea Chénier* (Tur); *La cena delle beffe* (Mi); *Madame Sans-Gêne* (NY, Phila, Brkln, Mi); *Il re* (Mi); *Siberia* (BA, Tur).

Gluck, Christoph Willibald. *Armide* (NY); *Orfeo ed Euridice* (Mi, NY, Brkln).

Gnaga, Andrea. *Gualtiero Swarten* (Ro).

Gnecchi, Vittorio. *Cassandra* (Bo).

Goldmark, Karoly. *The Queen of Sheba* (Mi, BA).

Gomes, Carlos. *Salvator Rosa* (Rio).

Gounod, Charles. *Faust* (Rio, Tur, BA, Mont, Paris [final scene only], Mi).

Humperdinck, Engelbert. *Hänsel und Gretel* (Mi, BA, Bo); *Königskinder* (BA).

Leoncavallo, Ruggero. *I pagliacci* (Mi, Palermo, Ro); *Zazà* (Mi).

Lozzi, Antonio. *Emma Liona* (Ven, Tur).

Machado, Augusto. *Laurianna* (Rio).

Mancinelli, Luigi. *Ero e Leandro* (Tur).

Mascagni, Pietro. *L'amico Fritz* (Gen); *Cavalleria rusticana* (Senigallia, Tur, Palermo, Gen, Mi, NY, Phila); *Iris* (Mi, BA, Mont, NY); *Le maschere* (Mi).

Masetti, Umberto. *Vindice* (Gen).

Massenet, Jules. *Griselda* (BA, Mont); *Manon* (Brescia, BA, Mont, NY, Atlanta); *Le Roi de Lahore* (Ravenna, Mi).

Meyerbeer, Giacomo. *L'Africaine* (Casale Monferrato); *Dinorah* (Bo); *Les Huguenots* (Rio, Novara, Mi); *Le Prophète* (Gen).

Montemezzi, Italo. *L'amore dei tre re* (NY, Phila, Mi).

Moussorgsky, Modeste Petrovich. *Boris Godunov* (NY, Mi).

Mozart, Wolfgang Amadeus. *Don Giovanni* (BA); *The Magic Flute* (Mi, Sg).

Paer, Ferdinando. *Le Maître de chapelle* (Tur).

Panizza, Ettore. *Medio Evo latino* (BA).

Pizzetti, Ildebrando. *Dèbora e Jaéle* (Mi); *Fra Gherardo* (Mi).

Ponchielli, Amilcare. *La gioconda* (Rio, Casale Monferrato, Brescia, Palermo, BA, Mi, NY, Phila, Balt, Brkln, Chi, Atlanta); *I lituani* (Mi); *Marion Delorme* (Rio); *I promessi sposi* (Mi).

Puccini, Giacomo. *La bohème* (Tur, Brescia, Ven, Mi, BA, Paris [Act III only], NY); *La fanciulla del West* (NY, Phila, Brkln, Ro); *Madama Butterfly* (BA, Mont, Bo, Tur, NY, Brkln, Phila, Balt, Chi, Pitts, Albany, Atlanta, Ro [Act II only], Mi); *Manon Lescaut* (Pisa, Mi, BA, Mont, Paris, Ber); *Tosca* (Mi, BA, Mont, NY, Phila, Brkln, Atlanta); *Turandot* (Mi); *Le Villi* (Brescia, Ven, Bo, NY, Phila).

Rossini, Gioacchino. *The Barber of Seville* (Palermo, BA, Mont); *William Tell* (Mi).

Saint-Saëns, Charles-Camille. *Samson and Delilah* (Tur, BA).

Smareglia, Antonio. *Oceana* (Mi).

Strauss, Richard. *Salome* (Mi).

Tchaikovsky, Piotr Ilich. *Eugene Onegin* (Mi).

Thomas, Ambroise. *Hamlet* (Rio, Mi); *Mignon* (Verona, Gen, Tur).

Verdi, Giuseppe. *Aida* (Rio, Macerata, Novara, Voghera, BA, Lugo, Mont, Mi, NY, Phila, Brkln, Chi, Pitts, Bos, Par, Montreal, Cleveland, Ber); *Un ballo in maschera* (Trento, Mi, NY, Atlanta); *Don Carlo* (Mi); *Falstaff* (Treviso, Bo, Gen, Pisa, Ven, Tur, Mi, BA, NY, Phila, Par, Ro, Busseto, Vn, Ber, Sg); *La forza del destino* (Mi, Novara, Ro, Gen, Ven); *I lombardi* (Casale Monferrato); *Luisa Miller* (Tur, Mi); *Otello* (Pisa, Mi, BA, NY, Phila, Brkln, Chi, Par, Cleveland, Cincinnati, Atlanta); *Rigoletto* (Rio, Palermo, BA, Mont, Brkln, Mi, Ber); *Simon Boccanegra* (Gen); *La traviata* (Rio, Brescia, BA, Mont, Busseto, Mi); *Il trovatore* (Rio, Mi, NY, Ber).

Wagner, Richard. *The Flying Dutchman* (Palermo); *Die Götterdämmerung* (Tur, Mi, NY, BA); *Lohengrin* (Mi, BA, Mont); *Die Meistersinger* (Mi, BA, Mont, Bo, NY, Bos, Chi, Sg); *Parsifal* (Mi, Byrth); *Siegfried* (Mi, Bo, Tur); *Tannhäuser* (Gen, Treviso, BA, Byrth); *Tristan und Isolde* (Tur, Mi, BA, Mont, NY, Phila, Bos, Par [Act II only], Byrth); *Die Walküre* (Tur, Mi, BA).

Weber, Carl Maria von. *Euryanthe* (Mi, NY, Brkln); *Der Freischütz* (BA).

Wolf-Ferrari, Ermanno. *L'amore medico* (NY); *Le donne curiose* (NY); *Il segreto di Susanna* (Mi).

Zandonai, Riccardo. *I cavalieri di Ekebù* (Mi).

B IN THE CONCERT HALL

Aguirre, Julian. Two Dances.

Alaleona, Domenico. Two Italian Songs ('*La mama lontana*,' '*Canzone a ballo*'); Mirra: Intermezzo.

Atterberg, Kurt. Symphony No. 6.

Bach, Johann Christian. Sinfonia in E-flat, Op. 18 No. 1; Sinfonia in D, Op. 18 No. 3.

Bach, Johann Sebastian. 'Brandenburg' Concerto No. 2; 'Brandenburg' Concerto No. 6; Cantata No. 46; Cantata No. 209; 'Christmas' Oratorio: Pastoral Prelude to Part II; Concerto for 4 Harpsichords (played on pianos); Concerto for Violin in A minor; Concerto for Two Violins in D minor; Mass in B minor: Kyrie; *St Matthew Passion:* Final Chorus; Suite No. 3 in D.

Bach, J.S., arr. Abert. Prelude, Chorale and Fugue.

Bach, J.S., arr. Mahler. Suite No. 2 in B minor.

Bach, J.S., arr. Respighi. Three Chorale Preludes; Passacaglia and Fugue in C minor; Prelude and Fugue in D.

Bach, J.S., arr. Schoenberg. Prelude and Fugue in E-flat.

Bach, J.S., arr. Wood. Toccata and Fugue in D minor.

Barber, Samuel. Adagio for Strings; Essay for Orchestra.

Bazzini, Antonio. Allegro drammatico for Violin and Orchestra; *Saul:* Overture.

Beethoven, Ludwig van. Concerti for Piano, Nos. 1, 3, 4, 5; Concerto for Violin; Concerto for Violin, Cello and Piano; 'Consecration of the House' Overture; *Coriolan:* Overture; *Egmont:* Overture; Fantasia for Piano, Chorus and Orchestra; *Fidelio:* complete (concert form), Overture, Recit. and aria *Abscheulicher! wo eilst du hin?* . . . *Komm, Hoffnung;* 'King Stephen' Overture; *Leonore:* Overtures Nos. 1, 2, 3; *Missa Solemnis; Prometheus:* Overture, Adagio, Andante, Allegretto; Septet (with reinforced string parts); String Quartets Op. 59 No. 3 (Andante con moto from first mvt, Coda to third mvt and Allegro molto), Op. 130 (Cavatina), Op. 135 (Lento and Vivace); Symphonies Nos. 1–9.

Bellini, Vincenzo. *Norma:* Act 1—Introduction and Druids' Chorus.

Berlioz, Hector. *Benvenuto Cellini:* Overture; *The Damnation of Faust:* 'Rákóczy' March, Dance of the Sylphs, Scene 7; *'Les Francs-Juges'* Overture; *Harold in Italy;* 'Roman Carnival' Overture; *Romeo and Juliet:* complete, Love Scene, *Roméo seul, Grande fête chez Capulet,* 'Queen Mab' Scherzo; *Symphonie Fantastique:* mvts 4 and 5 only.

Bizet, Georges. *L'Arlésienne:* Suites Nos. 1 and 2; *Carmen:* Suite No. 1; *La Jolie fille de Perth:* Suite; *La Patrie* Overture.

Bloch, Ernest. *Three Hebrew Poems.*

Boccherini, Luigi. Concerto for Cello in B-flat; Quartet in D; Quintet in E: Minuet.

Boito, Arrigo. *Mefistofele:* Prologue.

Bolzoni, Giovanni. *Capriccio sinfonico;* Dramatic Suite; 'Medieval Castle' Serenade; Minuet in B; *Il ruscello; Tempesta in un bicchier d'acqua;* Theme and Variations for Strings.

Borodin, Alexander. *In the Steppes of Central Asia; Prince Igor:* 'Polovtzian' Dances; Symphony No. 2.

Bossi, Marco Enrico. *Intermezzi goldoniani;* Suite in D.

Brahms, Johannes. 'Academic Festival' Overture; Concerti for Piano Nos. 1 and 2; Concerto for Violin; Concerto for Violin and Cello; *Ein deutsches Requiem; Gesang der Parzen; Gesänge für Frauenchor* (3); *Liebeslieder* Waltzes; Serenades Nos. 1 and 2; Symphonies Nos. 1–4; 'Tragic' Overture; Variations on a Theme of Haydn.

Brahms, orch. Dvořák. Hungarian Dances Nos. 1, 5, 6, 17, 20, 21.

Brahms, orch. Rubbra. Variations on a Theme of Handel.

Bruch, Max. Concerto for Violin in G minor; 'Scottish' Fantasy.

Bruckner, Anton. Symphonies Nos. 4 and 7.

Busch, Adolf. Variations on a Theme of Mozart.

Busi, Alessandro. *Elegia funebre.*

Busoni, Ferruccio. *Berceuse élégiaque; Rondò arlecchinesco.*

Buzzi-Peccia, Arturo. *Re Harfagar.*

Castelnuovo-Tedesco, Mario. Concerto for Cello; Concerto No. 2 for Violin; Overture to a Fairy Tale; *Taming of the Shrew* Overture; Violin Variations.

Catalani, Alfredo. *A sera; Dejanice:* Prelude to Act IV; *Loreley:* 'Dance of the Water Nymphs'; *La Wally:* Preludes to Acts II and IV.

Celega, Nicola (?). *The Enchantment;* Gavotte for Strings; *The Heart of Fingal.*

Chabrier, Emmanuel. *Gwendoline:* Overture.

Chasins, Abram. *Flirtation in a Chinese Garden; Parade.*

Cherubini, Luigi. *Ali Baba:* Overture; *Anacréon:* Overture; *Faniska:* Overture; *Medea:* Overture; *Requiem;* String Quartet in E-flat: Scherzo; Symphony in D.

Cimarosa, Domenico. *Il matrimonio per raggiro:* Overture; *Il matrimonio segreto:* Overture.

Copland, Aaron. *El Salón México.*

Corelli, Arcangelo. Andante and Gigue for Strings; Concerto grosso No. 8.

Corelli-Geminiani. Concerto grosso No. 12 ('La follia').

Cowen, Frederick. 'Scandinavian' Symphony: 'An Evening on the Fjord'.

Creston, Paul. 'Choric Dance' No. 2; *Frontiers.*

Da Venezia, Franco. *Allegro di Concerto.*

Debussy, Claude. *La Cour des lys*; *La Demoiselle élue*; *Ibéria*; *Marche écossaise*; *Le Martyre de Saint-Sébastien*; *La Mer*; *Nocturnes:* 'Nuages' and 'Fêtes'; *Prélude à l'après-midi d'un faune.*

Debussy, orch. Ravel. *Danse.*

De Falla, Manuel. *El amor brujo.*

De Sabata, Victor. *Gethsemane; Juventus.*

D'Indy, Vincent. *The Enchanted Forest;* 'Istar' Variations.

Donizetti, Gaetano. *Don Pasquale:* Overture; *Maria di Rohan:* Overture; Miscellaneous operatic excerpts.

Dukas, Paul. *Ariane et Barbe-bleue:* excerpts; *The Sorcerer's Apprentice.*

Dvořák, Antonín. 'Carnival' Overture; Concerto for Cello; 'Othello' Overture; Scherzo Capriccioso; Slavonic Dance No. 6; Symphony No. 9 ('New World'); Symphonic Variations.

Elgar, Edward. 'Enigma' Variations; Introduction and Allegro for Strings.

Enesco, Georges. Rumanian Rhapsody No. 1.

Ernst, Heinrich Wilhelm. Fantasia on Rossini's *Otello* for Violin and Orchestra.

Faccio, Franco. *Amleto:* Funeral March.

Ferraria, L.E. (?). Adagio and Allegretto for Strings.

Foroni, Jacopo. Overture in C minor; Overture in A.

Franchetti, Alberto. *Cristoforo Colombo:* Nocturne; *Nella foresta nera*; Symphony in E-flat: first mvt.

Franck, César. *Les Eolides*; *Psyché:* 'Psyche's Slumber' and 'Psyche and Eros'; *Rédemption:* Symphonic Interlude; Symphony.

Franck, orch. Pierné. Prelude, Chorale and Fugue.

Fuchs, Robert. *Des Meeres und des Liebes Wellen:* Overture.

Geminiani, Francesco. Concerti grossi Op. 2 No. 2 and Op. 3 No. 2.

Gershwin, George. *An American in Paris*; Concerto for Piano in F; *Rhapsody in Blue.*

Gilbert, Henry F.B. Comedy-Overture on Negro Themes.

Gillet. *Loin du bal.*

Gillis, Don. Symphony No. 5½.

Giordano, Umberto. *Il re:* Moor's Dance; *Siberia:* Prelude to Act II.

Girard, Narcisse. Sarabande for Strings.

Glazunov, Alexander. Symphony No. 6.

Glinka, Mikhail. *Jota aragonesa*; *Kamarinskaya.*

Gluck, Christoph Willibald. *Armide:* Dances; *Iphigenia in Aulis:* Overture; *Orfeo:* Act II.

Goldmark, Karoly. *Prometheus Bound:* Overture; *Queen of Sheba:* Prelude to Act II; 'Rustic Wedding' Symphony: mvts 2, 3, 4; *Sappho:* Overture.

Golinelli, Stefano, orch. Mugellini. Sonata: Scherzo.

Gomes, Carlos. *Fosca:* Duet; *Il Guarany:* Overture.

Goossens, Eugene. Sinfonietta.

Gould, Morton. *A Lincoln Legend.*

Gounod, Charles. *Colombe:* Intermezzo.

Graener, Paul. *The Flute of Sans-Souci.*

Grieg, Edvard. *First Meeting* for Strings; 'Holberg' Suite; Lento and Presto al saltarello for Strings; *Peer Gynt:* Suite No. 2 and other excerpts.

Griffes, Charles T. *The White Peacock.*

Grofé, Ferde. 'Grand Canyon' suite.

Handel, George Frederick. Concerto grosso No. 5 (?); Concerto grosso Op. 6 No. 12; Largo for Oboe and Strings; Minuet for Strings; *Susanna:* Overture.

Hanson, Howard. Symphony No. 2.

Harris, Roy. Symphony No. 3.

Haydn, Franz Josef. Quartet Op. 3 No. 5: Serenade; Quartet Op. 76 (No. 37): Adagio con variazioni; Sinfonia concertante in B-flat; Symphonies Nos. 31, 88, 92, 94, 98, 99, 101, 104.

Hérold, Ferdinand. *Zampa:* Overture.

Honegger, Arthur. *Pastorale d'été; Pacific 231.*

Humperdinck, Engelbert. *Hänsel und Gretel:* Overture; *Königskinder:* Prelude to Act III.

Kabalevsky, Dmitri. *Colas Breugnon:* Overture; Symphony No. 2.

Kalinnikov, Vassily S. Symphony No. 1.

Kennan, Kent. *Night Soliloquy.*

Kodály, Zoltán. 'Dances of Marosszék'; *Háry János:* Suite; *Psalmus Hungaricus; Summer Evening.*

Kozeluch, Leopold Antonín. Quartet No. 2: Andante and Allegro.

Lalo, Edouard. Norwegian Rhapsody.

Lassen, Eduard. *Festouvertüre.*

Liadov, Anatol. *Kikimora.*

Liszt, Franz. *From the Cradle to the Grave;* Hungarian Rhapsody No. 2; *Danse macabre;* 'Mephisto' Waltz; *Orpheus; Les Préludes.*

Loeffler, Charles M. *Memories of My Childhood.*

Lorenzo Fernandez, Oscar. *'Batuque'* from *Reisado do pastoredo.*

Lualdi, Adraiano. *Figlia del re:* Interlude.

Lully, Jean-Baptiste. Minuet for Strings.

Malipiero, Gian Francesco. *Pause del silenzio.*

Mancinelli, Luigi. *Cleopatra:* Barcarolle; Inaugural Cantata, Turin Exposition 1898; *Scene veneziane:* Excerpts.

Manfredini, Vincenzo. 'Christmas' Concerto.

Marcello, Benedetto. Psalm No. 47.

Martucci, Giuseppe. *Canzone dei ricordi;* Concerto for Piano in B-flat minor; *Danza (Tarantella); Notturno; Novelletta; Piccola Suite;* Symphonies Nos. 1 and 2.

Massenet, Jules. *Le dernier sommeil de la vierge; Les Erinnys; Scènes alsaciennes; Scènes napolitaines; Sous les tilleuls.*

Mendelssohn, Felix. Concerto for Violin; 'Hebrides' Overture; *Meeresstille und glückliche Fahrt* Overture; *A Midsummer Night's Dream:* Overture, Intermezzo, Nocturne, Song with Chorus, Wedding March, Scherzo, Chorus and Finale; Octet (arr.); Quartet in E-flat: Canzonetta; Quintet: Adagio and Lento; 'Ruy Blas' Overture; Symphonies Nos. 3,4, 5; 'The Tale of Lovely Melusine' Overture.

Meyerbeer, Giacomo. *Dinorah:* Overture.

Mignone, Francisco. *Congada; Fantasia brasileira;* 'Symphonic Impressions of Four Old Brazilian Churches'.

Montemezzi, Italo. *Cantico dei cantici.*

Monteverdi, Claudio, arr. Molinari. Sonata sopra 'Sancta Maria'.

Morlacchi, Francesco. *Francesca da Rimini:* Overture.

Mossolov, Alexander. *Iron Foundry.*

Moussorgsky, Modeste Petrovich. *Boris Godunov:* Introduction and Polonaise from Act III; *Khovantchina:* Prelude; *Night on Bald Mountain.*

Moussorgsky, orch. Ravel. *Pictures at an Exhibition.*

Mozart, Leopold. 'Toy' Symphony.

Mozart, Wolfgang Amadeus. Adagio and Fugue in C minor; Concerto for Bassoon K. 191; Concerti for Piano K. 466, 467, 595; Concerto for Violin No. 6; Divertimento K. 287; *Don Giovanni:* Overture, *Là ci darem la mano* (?); *The Magic Flute:* Overture; *The Marriage of Figaro:* Overture; *A Musical Joke;* Overture in the Italian Style, K. 318; Sinfonia concertante K. 364; Symphonies Nos. 1, 28, 29, 35, 38, 39, 40, 41.

Nicolai, Carl Otto. *The Merry Wives of Windsor:* Overture.

Orefice, Giacomo. 'Forest' Symphony: Suite; *Quattro anacreontiche.*

Paer, Ferdinando. *Ero e Leandro:* Overture; *Il sargino:* Overture.

Paganini, Niccolò. *Moto perpetuo.*

Paisiello, Giovanni. *Nina, pazza per amore:* Overture.

Pedrollo, Arrigo. Symphony.

Perosi, Lorenzo. *Mosé; La risurrezione di Lazzaro.*

Pick-Mangiagalli, Riccardo. *Notturno e Rondò fantastico; Sortilegi.*

Pizzetti, Ildebrando. *Concerto dell'estate; Introduction to the Agamemnon of Aeschylus; Ouverture per una farsa tragica; La Pisanelle:* Suite; *Rondò veneziano;* Three songs for Voice and String Quartet.

Ponchielli, Amilcare. *La gioconda:* Dance of the Hours; *I lituani:* Overture; *Marion Delorme:* Funeral March, Intermezzo Act IV.

Prokofiev, Sergei. Symphony No. 1 ('Classical').

Puccini, Giacomo. *La bohème* (complete, concert form); *Edgar:* Prelude and Funeral Elegy; *Manon Lescaut:* Act III (complete, concert form), Act III Intermezzo; *Requiem; Le Villi:* Act II Prelude.

Rabaud, Henri. *Nocturnal Procession.*

Rachmaninoff, Sergei. *The Island of the Dead.*

Raff, Josef Joachim. 'Dance of the Dryads'; Quartet, *Die schöne Müllerin:* excerpts; Symphonies in E and F.

Ravel, Maurice. *Boléro; Daphnis et Chloé:* Suite No. 2; *Rhapsodie espagnole; La Valse.*

Reinecke, Carl H.C. Concerto for Harp: first mvt.

Respighi, Ottorino. Ancient Airs and Dances; *Ballata delle gnomidi; The Fountains of Rome; The Pines of Rome; Roman Festivals.*

Rieti, Vittorio. *Sinfonia tripartita.*

Rimsky-Korsakov, Nicolai. *Antar; Sheherazade:* Part II; 'Russian Easter' Overture; *Snow Maiden:* Suite.

Rocchi, Guido. Gavotte.

Roger-Ducasse, Jean-Jules. Sarabande.

Rossini, Gioacchino. Overtures to *The Barber of Seville, La Cenerentola, La gazza ladra, L'italiana in Algeri, Semiramide, The Siege of Corinth, La scala di seta, Il Signor Bruschino, William Tell;* Sonata No. 3 for Strings; *William Tell:* Act I *Passo a sei,* Act III Soldiers' Dance, Wedding Chorus; Various operatic excerpts.

Roussel, Albert. *The Spider's Feast;* Symphony No. 4.

Rubinstein, Anton, orch. Mueller-Berghaus. *Valse Caprice.*

Saint-Saëns, Charles-Camille. Concerto for Cello; Concerto No. 4 for Piano; *Danse macabre; Suite algérienne:* 'Un soir à Blidah'; Symphony No. 3.

Sammartini, Giovanni Battista. Symphony No. 3.

Scarlatti, Domenico, orch. Tommasini. *The Good-Humoured Ladies.*

Schelling, Ernst. *Impressions from an Artist's Life.*

Schubert, Franz. *Der Teufel als Hydraulicus* Overture; Serenade for Contralto, Women's Chorus and Orchestra; Symphonies Nos. 2, 5, 8, 9.

Schubert, orch. Brahms. Ellen's Second Song.

Schubert, orch. Joachim. 'Gastein' Symphony.

Schubert, orch. Liszt. Hungarian Dances; Hungarian March; 'Wanderer' Fantasy (paraphrase).

Schubert, orch. Mottl. *Tecla.*

Schumann, Robert. Concerto for Cello; *Hermann und Dorothea:* Overture; *Konzertstück* for Piano and Orchestra; 'Manfred' Overture; Symphonies Nos. 2, 3, 4.

Schumann, orch. Berlioz. *Abendlied.*

Sgambati, Giovanni. Concerto for Piano in G minor; Symphony in D: Excerpts.

Shostakovich, Dmitri. Symphonies Nos. 1 and 7.

Sibelius, Jean. *En Saga; Finlandia; Pohjola's Daughter; Lemminkäinen's Home-coming; The Swan of Tuonela;* Symphonies Nos. 2 and 4.

Siegmeister, Elie. 'Western' Suite.

Sinigaglia, Leone. *Le baruffe chiozzotte;* 'Piedmont' Suite; *Hora mistica;* Scherzo for Strings; Concerto for Violin; *Danze piemontesi nuove.*

Smareglia, Antonio. *Oceana:* Overture.

Smetana, Bedřich. *The Bartered Bride:* Overture; *The Moldau.*

Sonzogno, Giulio. *Il negro;* Tango.

Sousa, John Philip. Marches: 'El Capitan', 'Semper Fidelis', 'The Stars and Stripes Forever'.

Stanford, Charles Villiers. 'Irish' Symphony.

Strauss, Johann jun. Waltzes: 'The Blue Danube', 'Voices of Spring'; 'Tritsch-Tratsch' Polka.

Strauss, Richard. *Death and Transfiguration; Don Juan; Don Quixote; Ein Heldenleben; Salome:* Dance of the Seven Veils; *Till Eulenspiegel.*

Stravinsky, Igor. *Fireworks; Firebird:* 'Infernal Dance'; *Petrouchka:* first and fourth scenes.

Strong, George T. *Die Nacht.*

Suppé, Franz von. 'Poet and Peasant' Overture.

Svendsen, Johan S. *Carnival of Paris;* Symphony No. 4.

Tansman, Alexander. Four Polish Dances.

Taubert, Karl. Pizzicato for Strings.

Tchaikovsky, Piotr Ilich. Concerto for Piano No. 1; *Eugene Onegin:* Waltzes; 'Manfred' Symphony; *The Nutcracker:* Suite No. 1; 'Romeo and Juliet' Overture-Fantasia; String Quartet Op. 11: Andante cantabile; Symphony No. 6; 'The Tempest' Overture-Fantasia; 'The Voyevoda' Overture.

Thomas, Ambroise. *Mignon:* Overture.

Tommasini, Vincenzo. *The Carnival of Venice; Chiari di luna;* Prelude, Fanfare and Fugue; *Tuscan Landscapes.*

Toscanini, Arturo. Andante and Scherzo.

Trucco, Edoardo. Little Suite in B-flat.

Vaughan Williams, Ralph. Fantasia on a Theme of Thomas Tallis.

Verdi, Giuseppe. *Aida* (complete, concert form), Overture (unpublished), *O cieli azzurri; Attila: Allor che i forti corrono; Un ballo in maschera* (complete, concert form), *Teco io sto, Eri tu; La battaglia di Legnano: Inno e giuramento; Don Carlo: O don fatale; Falstaff* (complete, concert form); *La forza del destino:* Overture, Act II Finale, *Rataplan, Col sangue sol cancellasi, Pace, pace mio dio; Four Sacred*

Pieces (excepting *Ave Maria*); *Hymn of the Nations; I lombardi: O signore, dal tetto natio, Qui posa il fianco; Luisa Miller:* Overture, *Quando le sere; Nabucco:* Overture, *Va pensiero sull'ali dorate; Oberto:* Prelude; *Otello* (complete, concert form), Ballet music, *Ave Maria; Requiem; Rigoletto:* last act (complete, concert form), *Bella figlia dell'amore;* String Quartet in E minor; *La traviata* (complete, concert form), Preludes to Acts I and III; *I vespri siciliani:* Overture; Various operatic excerpts.

Vieuxtemps, Henri. Ballade and Polonaise.

Viotti, Giovanni Battista. Concerto for Violin in A minor, No. 22.

Vivaldi, Antonio. Concerto in A (?); Concerto in D minor, Op. 3 No. 11; Concerto for Violin in A minor; Concerto for Violin in B-flat; *The Seasons:* 'Spring', 'Winter'.

Wagenaar, Bernhard. Symphony No. 2.

Wagner, Richard. 'A Faust Overture'; *Flying Dutchman:* Overture; *Götterdämmerung:* 'Dawn and Siegfried's Rhine Journey', 'Siegfried's Death and Funeral Music', 'Immolation' Scene and Finale; *Lohengrin:* Preludes to Acts I and III; *Meistersinger:* Preludes to Acts I and III; *Parsifal:* Preludes to Acts I and III, 'Good Friday Spell', 'Klingsor's Magic Garden', unspecified excerpts from Act III; *Rheingold:* 'Entrance of the gods into Valhalla'; *Rienzi:* Overture; *Siegfried:* 'Forest Murmurs'; *Siegfried Idyll; Tannhäuser:* Overture (Dresden version), Overture and Bacchanale (Paris version), Prelude to Act III (original version), *Dich, teure Halle; Tristan und Isolde:* Prelude, excerpts from Act II, *Liebestod; Die Walküre:* Act I Scene 3, 'Ride of the Valkyries', 'Magic Fire Music', 'Wotan's Farewell'; *Wesendonck' Lieder* (3).

Waldteufel, Emil. 'Skaters' Waltz'.

Weber, Carl Maria von. *Euryanthe:* Overture; *Freischütz:* Overture; 'Jubel' Overture; *Oberon:* Overture; 'Ruler of the Spirits' Overture; Various operatic excerpts.

Weprik, Alexander. Dances and Songs of the Ghetto.

Wetzler, Hermann. Symphonic Dance: 'The Basque Venus'.

Williams, Alberto. Symphony No. 7.

Wolf-Ferrari, Ermanno. *Le donne curiose:* Overture; *Il segreto di Susanna:* Overture.

Zandonai, Riccardo. Suite: *Patria lontana.*

C SOME IMPORTANT TOSCANINI OPERATIC PRODUCTIONS

s—soprano, ms—mezzo-soprano, t—tenor, bar—baritone, b—bass

Dates given are the opening dates of each production.

30.6.86 —Rio, Teatro Imperial—Verdi: *Aida* (Boulicioff, s; Mei, ms; Figner, t; Lhérie, bar) Toscanini's professional début

4.11.86 —Tur, Teatro Carignano—Catalani: *Edmea* (Ferni-Germano, s; Figner, t) Toscanini's Italian début

21.5.92 —Mi, Teatro Dal Verme—Leoncavallo: *Pagliacci* (Stehle, s; Giraud, t; Maurel, bar) World première

22.12.95—Tur, Teatro Regio—Wagner: *Die Götterdämmerung* (Ehrenstein, s; Grani, t) First production by an Italian company and Toscanini's first production as head of the Regio

1.2.96 —Tur, Regio—Puccini: *La bohème* (Ferrani, s; Gorga, t; Wilmant, bar) World première

14.2.97 —Tur, Regio—Wagner: *Tristan und Isolde* (Prossnitz, s; Dupeyron, t) Toscanini's first *Tristan* production

26.12.98—Mi, La Scala—Wagner: *Die Meistersinger* (Pandolfini, s; De Marchi, t; Scotti, bar) Toscanini's first production as head of La Scala

26.12.99—Mi, Scala—Wagner: *Siegfried* (Bianchini-Cappelli, s; Borgatti, t) First performance by an Italian company

7.4.00 —Mi, Scala—Tchaikovsky: *Eugene Onegin* (Carelli, s; Zeni, t; Giraldoni, bar) Italian première

29.12.00—Mi, Scala—Wagner: *Tristan* (Pinto, s; Borgatti, t)

9.2.02 —Mi, Scala—Verdi: *Il trovatore* (Calligaris, s; Bruno, ms; Biel, t; Magini-Coletti, bar)

2.4.02 —Mi, Scala—Weber: *Euryanthe* (Storchio, s; Cossira, t) Italian première

22.12.02—Mi, Scala—Berlioz: *The Damnation of Faust* (Petri, s; Zenatello, t; Renaud, bar)

11.3.03 —Mi, Scala—Verdi: *Un ballo in maschera* (Micucci-Betti, s; Parsi-Pettinella, ms; Zenatello, t; Magini-Coletti, bar)

6.8.04 —BA, Teatro de la Ópera—Weber: *Freischütz* (Pandolfini, s; Borgatti, t; Didur, b) Toscanini's only production of this work

29.7.06 —BA, T. de la O.—Mozart: *Don Giovanni* (Tolexis—Anna; Storchio—Zerlina; Clarenti—Elvira; Anselmi—Ottavio; De Luca—Don Giovanni; Didur—Leporello) Toscanini's only production of this work

26.12.06—Mi, Scala—Strauss: *Salome* (Krusceniski, s; Borgatti, t)

2.4.08 —Mi, Scala—Debussy: *Pelléas et Mélisande* (Ferrani, s; Giraud, t; Amato, bar) Italian première

16.11.08—NY, Metropolitan Opera House—Verdi: *Aida* (Destinn, s; Homer, ms; Caruso, t; Scotti, bar; Didur, b) Toscanini's North American début

10.12.08 NY, Met—Wagner: *Die Götterdämmerung* (Fremstad, s; Schmedes, t)

20.3.09 —NY, Met—Verdi: *Falstaff* (Destinn—Alice; Scotti—Falstaff; Campanari—Ford)

17.11.09—NY, Met—Verdi: *Otello* (Alda, s; Slezak, t; Scotti, bar)

27.11.09—NY, Met—Wagner: *Tristan* (Gadski, s; Burrian, t)

23.12.09—NY, Met—Gluck: *Orfeo ed Euridice* (Gadski, s; Homer, ms)

26.3.10 —NY, Met—Wagner: *Die Meistersinger* (Gadski, s; Slezak, t; Soomer, bar)

14.11.10—NY, Met—Gluck: *Armide* (Fremstad, s; Homer, ms; Caruso, t; Amato, bar)

10.12.10—NY, Met—Puccini: *La fanciulla del West* (Destinn, s; Caruso, t; Amato, bar) World première

29.3.11 —NY, Met—Dukas: *Ariane et Barbe-bleue* (Farrar, s; Rothier, b) American première

19.3.13 —NY, Met—Moussorgsky: *Boris Godunov* (Homer, ms; Althouse, t; Didur, b) American première

20.9.13 —Busseto, Teatro Verdi—Verdi: *La traviata* (Bori, s; Garbin, t; Amato, bar) Verdi centenary

28.9.13 —Busseto—Verdi: *Falstaff* (Bori—Alice; Amato—Falstaff; Giardini—Ford) Verdi centenary

22.11.13—NY, Met—Verdi: *Ballo* (Destinn, s; Matzenauer, ms; Caruso, t; Amato, bar)

2.1.14 —NY, Met—Montemezzi: *L'amore dei tre re* (Bori, s; Amato, bar; Didur, b) American première

19.11.14—NY, Met—Bizet: *Carmen* (Farrar, s; Caruso, t; Amato, bar)

19.12.14—NY, Met—Weber: *Euryanthe* (Hempel, s; Sembach, t)

25.1.15 —NY, Met—Giordano: *Madame Sans-Gêne* (Farrar, s; Martinelli, t) World première

20.2.15 —NY, Met—Verdi: *Il trovatore* (Destinn, s; Ober, ms; Martinelli, t; Amato, bar)

26.12.21—Mi, Scala—Verdi: *Falstaff* (Cannetti—Alice; Stabile—Falstaff; Badini —Ford) First production of the reorganized Ente Autonomo Teatro alla Scala

14.1.22 —Mi, Scala—Verdi: *Rigoletto* (Dal Monte, s; Lauri-Volpi, t; Galeffi, bar)

16.2.22 —Mi, Scala—Moussorgsky: *Boris Godunov* (Casazza, ms; Zalewski, b)

23.4.22 —Mi, Scala—Wagner: *Die Meistersinger* (Caracciolo, s; Merli, t; Journet, bar)

26.12.22—Mi, Scala—Puccini: *Manon Lescaut* (Caracciolo, s; Pertile, t)

22.3.23 —Mi, Scala—Donizetti: *Lucia di Lammermoor* (Dal Monte, s; Pertile, t; Stracciari, bar)

12.5.23 —Mi, Scala—Mozart: *The Magic Flute* (Sari—Queen; Alfani-Tellini— Pamina; Ciniselli—Tamino; Badini—Papageno; Melnik—Sarastro) Toscanini's first production of this work

28.11.23—Mi, Scala—Verdi: *Traviata* (Dalla Rizza, s; Pertile, t; Montesanto, bar)

20.12.23—Mi, Scala—Wagner: *Tristan* (Larsén-Todsen, s; Bielina, t)

1.5.24 —Mi, Scala—Boito: *Nerone* (Raisa, s; Pertile, t; Galeffi, bar; Journet, b) World première

30.4.25 —Mi, Scala—Verdi: *Trovatore* (Raisa, s; Anitùa, ms; Pertile, t; Franci, bar)

17.5.25 —Mi, Scala—Debussy: *Pelléas* (Heldy, s; Legrand, t; Journet, bar)

14.11.25—Mi, Scala—Verdi: *Ballo* (Carena, s; Anitùa, ms; Pertile, t; Galeffi, bar)

25.4.26 —Mi, Scala—Puccini: *Turandot* (Raisa—Turandot; Zamboni—Liù; Fleta—Calaf) World première

14.11.26—Mi, Scala—Verdi: *Don Carlo* (Scacciati, s; Cobelli, ms; Trantoul, t; Galeffi, bar; Pasero—Philip IV; Marone—Inquisitor) Toscanini's only production of this work

7.4.27 —Mi, Scala—Beethoven: *Fidelio* (Pasetti—Leonora; Ferraris—Marzelline; Merli—Florestan; Franci—Pizarro; Bettoni—Rocco) Toscanini's first production of this work

22.11.27—Mi, Scala—Verdi: *Otello* (Scacciati, s; Trantoul, t; Stabile, bar)

17.11.28—Mi, Scala—Verdi: *La forza del destino* (Scacciati, s; Merli, t; Franci, bar)

16.12.28—Mi, Scala—Wagner: *Parsifal* (Pasetti, s; Fagoaga, t; Rossi-Morelli, bar; Pasero, b) Toscanini's first full production of this work

22.7.30 —Bayreuth Festival—Wagner: *Tannhäuser* (Müller—Elisabeth; Jost-Arden—Venus; Pilinszky—Tannhäuser; Janssen—Wolfram) Toscanini's Bayreuth début

23.7.30 —Bayreuth—Wagner: *Tristan* (Larsén-Todsen, s; Melchior, t)

22.7.31 —Bayreuth—Wagner: *Parsifal* (Ohms, s; Wolff, t; Janssen, bar; Andrésen, b)

29.7.35 —Salzburg Festival—Verdi: *Falstaff* (Caniglia—Alice; Stabile—Falstaff; Biasini—Ford)

7.8.35 —Salzburg—Beethoven: *Fidelio* (Lehmann—Leonore; Helletsgruber—

Marzelline; von Rösler—Florestan; Jerger—Pizarro; Baumann—Rocco)

8.8.36 —Salzburg—Wagner: *Die Meistersinger* (Lehmann, s; Kullmann, t; Nissen, bar)

30.8.37 —Salzburg—Mozart: *The Magic Flute* (Osvath—Queen; Novotna— Pamina; Roswaenge—Tamino; Domgraf-Fassbaender—Papageno; Kipnis—Sarastro)

Complete operas in concert form with the NBC Symphony Orchestra (always done in two parts):

10, 17 Dec 44 —Beethoven: *Fidelio* (Bampton—Leonore; Steber—Marzelline; Peerce—Florestan; Janssen—Pizarro; Belarsky—Rocco)

3, 10 Feb 46 —Puccini: *Bohème* (Albanese, s; Peerce, t; Valentino, bar) 50th anniversary of the world première

1, 8 Dec 46 —Verdi: *Traviata* (Albanese, s; Peerce, t; Merrill, bar)

6, 13 Dec 47 —Verdi: *Otello* (Nelli, s; Vinay, t; Valdengo, bar)

26 Mar, 2 Apr 49—Verdi: *Aida* (Nelli, s; Gustavson, ms; Tucker, t; Valdengo, bar; Scott, b)

1, 8 Apr 50 —Verdi: *Falstaff* (Nelli—Alice; Valdengo—Falstaff; Guarrera— Ford)

17, 24 Jan 54 —Verdi: *Ballo* (Nelli, s; Turner, ms; Peerce, t; Merrill, bar)

D TOSCANINI'S VOCAL SOLOISTS IN FOUR MAJOR CHORAL-ORCHESTRAL WORKS

Beethoven—*Missa Solemnis*, Op. 123:
NY 8, 9, 11 Mar 34: Rethberg, Onegin, Althouse, Pinza. NY 25, 26, 28 Apr 35: Rethberg, Telva, Martinelli, Pinza. Vn 28, 29 Nov 36: Vincent, Thorborg, von Pataky, Kipnis. London 26, 28 May 39: Milanov, Thorborg, von Pataky, Moscona. NY 28 Dec 40: Milanov, Castagna, Bjoerling, Kipnis. NY 22 Apr 42: Kirk, Castagna, Johnson, Kipnis. NY 28 Mar 53: Marshall, Merriman, Conley, Hines.

Beethoven—*Symphony No. 9 in D minor*, Op. 125:
Mi 20, 25, 27 Apr 02: Silvestri, Cernuschi, Borgatti, Nicoletti. NY 13, 18 Apr 13: Hempel, Homer, Jörn, Griswold. Tur 7, 8, 10 Jun 19: Dal Monte, Bergamasco, Di Giovanni, Ludikar. Mi 14, 15, 16, 18 Jun 19: (same soloists as preced.). Mi 25, 29 Jun, 2, 12 Jul 22: Dal Monte, Bertana, Alabiso, Pinza. Mi 12, 17 (Tur), 20 Oct 26: Ferraris, Stignani, Menescaldi, Righetti. NY 5, 6 Feb 27: Rethberg, Homer, Crooks, Gange. NY 29, 30 Mar, 1 Apr 28: Morgana, Braslau, Crooks, Pinza. NY 28 Apr 32: Rethberg, Matzenauer, Martinelli, Pinza. NY 15, 16, 18 Feb 34: Tentoni, Onegin, Althouse, Pinza. Vn 20, 21, 22 (Budapest) Oct 34: Schumann, Szanto, von Rösler, Mayr. Paris 16, 22, 23 Nov 34: Mahé, Cernay, Cathelat, Cabanel. NY 5, 6, 8 Mar 36: Tentoni, Bampton, Kullman, Pinza. London 3 Nov 37: Baillie, Jarred, Jones, Williams. NY 6 Feb 38: Bovy, Thorborg, Peerce, Pinza. London 22 May 39: Baillie, Balfour, Jones, Williams. NY 2 Dec 39: Novotna, Thorborg, Peerce, Moscona. BA 20, 25, 29 Jun, 24 Jul 41: Hellwig, Kindermann, Maison, Kipnis. NY 3 May 42: Kirk, Eustis, Johnson, Kipnis. NY 25 Sep 45: Andreotti, Merriman, Peerce, Alvary. Mi 24, 26 Jun 46: Gatti,

Barbieri, Prandelli, Pasero. NY 3 Apr 48: McKnight, Hobson, Horne, Scott.
NY 29 Mar 52: Farrell, Merriman, Peerce, Scott.

Brahms—*A German Requiem*:
NY 7, 8, 10 Mar 35: Rethberg, Schorr. Vn 7, 8, Dec 35: Bathy, Sved. Sg 12 Aug 36:
Bathy, Sved. London 30 Oct 37: Baillie, Sved. NY 24 Jan 43: Della Chiesa,
Janssen.

Verdi—*Requiem Mass*:
Mi 27 Jan 02: Bruno, Karola, Cossira, Nicolay. NY 21, 28 Feb, 28 Mar, 9 Apr 09:
Destinn, Homer, Martin, Hinckley (first two)/Witherspoon (last two). NY 6 Feb,
13 Mar 10: Destinn, Homer, Martin, Witherspoon. Ro 4, 6, 8 Jul 11: Gagliardi,
Guerrini, Martinelli, Mardones. Mi 12, 14, 18 Oct 13: Gagliardi, Guerrini,
Giorgini, De Angelis. Mi 22 May 23: Besanzoni, Rinolfi, Merli, Pinza. NY 15,
16 Jan 31: Rethberg, Matzenauer, Chamlee, Pinza. Vn 1 Nov 34: Bathy, Rünger,
Kullmann, Manowarda. Sg 14 Aug 37: Kunz, Thorborg, Roswaenge, Kipnis.
NY 4 Mar 38: Milanov, Castagna, Kullmann, Moscona. London 27 May 38:
Milanov, Thorborg, Roswaenge, Moscona. Lucerne 16, 17 Aug 39: Milanov,
Thorborg, Bjoerling, Moscona. NY 23 Nov 40: Milanov, Castagna, Bjoerling,
Moscona. BA 15, 19, 22 Jul 41: Milanov, Castagna, Maison, Kipnis. NY 26 Apr 48:
Nelli, Merriman, McGrath, Scott. Mi 24 Jun 50: Tebaldi, Elmo, Prandelli, Siepi.
NY 27 Jan 51: Nelli, Barbieri, Di Stefano, Siepi.

Bibliography

BOOKS

Abbiati, Franco. *Giuseppe Verdi*. Milano: Ricordi 1959.
Adami, Giuseppe. *Edoardo Marchioro*. Milano: Emilio Bestetti 1945.
———. *Puccini*. Milano: Fratelli Treves 1935.
Alda, Frances. *Men, Women and Tenors*. Boston: Houghton, Mifflin 1937.
Antek, Samuel, and Hupka, Robert. *This Was Toscanini*. New York: Vanguard 1963.
Ardoin, John, and Fitzgerald, Gerald. *Callas*. New York: Holt, Rinehart & Winston 1974.
Ashbrook, William. *The Operas of Puccini*. London: Cassell 1969.
Barblan, Guglielmo. *Toscanini e la Scala*. Milano: Edizioni della Scala 1972.
Beetz, Wilhelm. *Das Wiener Opernhaus, 1869 bis 1945*. Zürich: The Central European Times Verlag 1949.
Blaukopf, Kurt. *Gustav Mahler*, trans. I. Goodwin. London: Allen Lane 1973.
Bliss, Sir Arthur. *As I Remember*. London: Faber & Faber 1970.
Bonardi, Dino. *Toscanini*. Milano: Libreria Editrice Milanese 1929.
Borghi, Armando. *Mezzo secolo di anarchia*. Napoli: Edizioni scientifiche italiane 1954.
Boult, Sir Adrian. *My Own Trumpet*. London: Hamish Hamilton 1973.
Briggs, John. *Leonard Bernstein*. Cleveland: World Publishing Co. 1961.
Brocca, Ambrogio. *Il Politeama Genovese*. Genova: Antonio Montorfano 1895.
Busch, Fritz. *Pages from a Musician's Life*, trans. M. Strachey. Westport, Connecticut: Greenwood Press 1953.
Busch, Grete. *Fritz Busch*. Frankfurt: S. Fischer Verlag 1970.
Busoni, Ferruccio. *Letters to his Wife*, trans. R. Ley. New York: Da Capo Press 1975.
Carelli, Augusto. *Emma Carelli, Trent'anni di vita del teatro lirico*. Roma: Edizioni Maglione 1932.
Carner, Mosco. *Puccini*. London: Duckworth 1974.
Carpi, Aldo. *Diario di Gusen*. Milano: Garzanti 1971.
Casella, Alfredo. *Music in My Time*, trans. S. Norton. Norman, Oklahoma: University of Oklahoma Press 1955.
Cederna, Camilla. *La voce dei padroni*. Milano: Longanesi 1962.
Cernicchiaro, Vincenzo. *Storia della musica nel Brasile*. Milano: Fratelli Rusconi 1926.
Chailly, Luciano. *Cronache di vita musicale*. Roma: Edizioni De Santis 1973.
Chaliapin, Feodor, and Gorky, Maxim. *Chaliapin*. London: Macdonald 1968.

Chalupt, René. *Ravel au miroir de ses lettres*. Paris: Robert Laffont 1956.

Cherubini, Renato. *Come ho visto Toscanini*. Reggio Emilia: 1961.

Chotzinoff, Samuel. *Toscanini—An Intimate Portrait*. New York: Alfred A. Knopf 1956.

Ciampelli, Giulio Mario. *Toscanini*. Milano: La Modernissima 1923.

Ciano, Galeazzo. *Diario, 1937–1938*. Bologna: Cappelli 1948.

Clemens, Clara. *My Husband Gabrilowitsch*. New York: Harper and Brothers 1938.

Cortopassi, Rinaldo. *Il dramma di Alfredo Catalani*. Firenze: La Voce 1954.

Cozzani, Ettore. *Arturo Toscanini*. Milano: Eroica 1927.

Cushing, Mary W. *The Rainbow Bridge*. New York: G.P. Putnam's Sons 1954.

Dal Fabbro, Beniamino. *Musica e verità*. Milano: Feltrinelli 1967.

Dal Monte, Toti. *Una voce nel mondo*. Milano: Longanesi 1962.

D'Aroma, Nino. *Mussolini segreto*. Bologna: Cappelli 1958.

De Filippis, F., and Arnese, R. *Cronache del Teatro San Carlo*. Napoli: Edizioni Politica Popolare 1963.

Della Corte, Andrea. *Toscanini visto da un critico*. Torino: ILTE 1958.

Dent, Edward J. *Ferruccio Busoni*. London: Oxford University Press 1933.

De Rensis, Raffaelle. *Lettere di Arrigo Boito*. Roma: Novissima 1932.

——. *Musica vista*. Milano: Ricordi 1961.

Eames, Emma. *Some Memories and Reflections*. New York: D. Appleton 1927.

Eaton, Quaintance. *Opera Caravan*. New York: Farrar, Straus and Cudahy 1957.

Erskine, John. *The Philharmonic-Symphony Society of New York: Its First Hundred Years*. New York: MacMillan 1943.

Ewen, David. *The Man with the Baton*. New York: Thomas Y. Crowell Co. 1936.

Ferrari, Vittorio, and Albertini, Cesare. *Il Teatro della Scala*. Milano: Tamburini 1921.

Ferrarini, Mario. *Parma teatrale ottocentesca*. Parma: Casanova 1946.

Fiorda, Nuccio. *Arte, beghe e bizze di Toscanini*. Roma: 1969.

Forzano, Giovacchino. *Come li ho conosciuti*. Torino: ERI 1957.

Fraccaroli, Arnaldo. *La Scala a Vienna e a Berlino*. Milano: *Corriere della Sera* 1929.

Frassati, Luciana. *Il Maestro*. Torino: Bottega d'Erasmo 1967.

Furlong, William B. *Season with Solti*. New York: MacMillan 1974.

Gara, Eugenio. *Caruso*. Milano: Cisalpino-Golliardica 1947.

Gatti, Carlo. *Catalani*. Milano: Garzanti 1953.

——. *Il Teatro alla Scala rinnovato*. Milano: Fratelli Treves 1926.

Gatti-Casazza, Giulio. *Memories of the Opera*. New York: Vienna House 1973.

Gavazzeni, Gianandrea. *Non eseguire Beethoven*. Milano: Il Saggiatore 1974.

Geissmar, Berta. *The Baton and the Jackboot*. London: Hamish Hamilton 1944.

Giazzotto, Remo. *Quattro secoli di storia dell'Accademia Nazionale di Santa Cecilia*. Roma: Accademia Nazionale de Santa Cecilia 1970.

Gillis, Daniel. *Furtwängler and America*. New York: Maryland Books 1970.

Gilman, Lawrence. *Toscanini and Great Music*. New York: Farrar 1938.

Guerrieri, G. *Eleonora Duse nel suo tempo*. Milano: Quaderni del Piccolo Teatro 1962.

Haeussermann, Ernst. *Herbert von Karajan*. Gütersloh: C. Bertelsmann Verlag 1968.

Haggin, B.H. *Conversations with Toscanini*. Garden City, N.Y.: Doubleday 1959.

——. *A Decade of Music*. New York: Horizon Press 1973.

——. *Music in the Nation*. Freeport, N.Y.: Books for Libraries Press 1971.

Haggin, B.H. *The Toscanini Musicians Knew*. New York: Horizon Press 1967.

Hempel, Frieda. *Mein Leben dem Gesang*. Berlin: Argon Verlag 1955.

Herzfeld, Friedrich. *Wilhelm Furtwängler*. Leipzig: Wilhelm Goldmann Verlag 1941.

Heyworth, Peter. *Conversations with Klemperer*. London: Victor Gollancz 1973.

Hoeller, Susanne Winternitz. *Arturo Toscanini, a Photobiography*. New York: Island Press 1943.

Homer, Anne. *Louise Homer*. New York: William Morrow 1974.

Hughes, Spike. *The Toscanini Legacy*. London: Putnam 1959.

Incagliati, M. *Il Teatro Costanzi*. Roma: Tipografia editrice 1907.

Ingelbrecht, D.E. *Le chef d'orchestre parle au public*. Paris: René Julliard 1957.

——. *The Conductor's World*, trans. G. Prerauer and S. Kirk, London: Peter Nevill 1953.

Jackson, Stanley. *Monsieur Butterfly*. London: W.H. Allen 1974.

Jellinek, George. *Callas*. New York: Ziff-Davis 1960.

Kennedy, Michael. *Barbirolli*. London: McGibbon & Kee 1971.

——. *Portrait of Elgar*. New York: Oxford University Press 1968.

Kolodin, Irving. *The Metropolitan Opera*. New York: Oxford University Press 1940.

Kralik, Heinrich von. *Die Wiener Philharmoniker*. Wien: Verlag Wilhelm Frick 1938.

Kupferberg, Herbert. *The Mendelssohns*. New York: Charles Scribner's Sons 1972.

Labia, Maria. *Guardare indietro: che fatica!* Verona: Bettinelli 1950.

Labroca, Mario, and Boccardi, Virgilio. *Arte di Toscanini*. Torino: ERI 1966.

Lauri-Volpi, Giacomo. *Voci parallele*. Milano: Garzanti 1955.

Lehmann, Lotte. *Midway in My Song*. New York: Bobbs-Merrill 1938.

——. *My Many Lives*, trans. Frances Holden. Westport, Connecticut: Greenwood Press 1974.

Leibowitz, René. *Le Compositeur et son double*. Paris: Gallimard 1971.

Leinsdorf, Erich. *Cadenza—A Musical Career*. Boston: Houghton, Mifflin 1976.

Lenotti, Tullio. *I Teatri di Verona*. Verona: Edizioni di Vita Veronese.

Levy, Alan. *Bluebird of Happiness (The Memoirs of Jan Peerce)*. New York: Harper & Row 1976.

Lezuo-Pandolfi, Amina. *Toscanini: Ein Leben für die Musik*. Zürich: Apollo Verlag 1957.

Lockspeiser, Edward. *Debussy, His Life and Mind*. London: Cassell 1962 and 1965.

Lualdi, Adriano. *L'arte di dirigere l'orchestra*. Milano: Hoepli 1940.

Mack Smith, Dennis. *Italy: A Modern History*. Ann Arbor: University of Michigan Press 1959.

Magidoff, Robert, and Raynor, Henry. *Yehudi Menuhin*. London: Robert Hale & Co. 1973.

Mahler, Alma. *Gustav Mahler*, ed. D. Mitchell. London: John Murray 1973.

——. *Gustav Mahler*, ed. L. Rognoni, trans. Laura Dallapiccola. Milano: Il Saggiatore 1960.

Mahler, Gustav. *Briefe, 1879–1911*, ed. A. Mahler. Berlin: Paul Zsolnay 1924.

Malipiero, Gian Francesco. *Il filo d'Arianna*. Torino: Einaudi 1966.

Mandelli, Alfredo. *Toscanini: Appunti per un bilancio critico*. Milano: Nuove Edizioni 1972.

Marchetti, Arnaldo. *Puccini com'era*. Milano: Edizioni Curci 1973.

Marek, George R. *Toscanini*. New York: Atheneum 1975.

Marsh, Robert C. *Toscanini and the Art of Orchestral Performance*. London: George Allen & Unwin 1956.

Martin, George. *Verdi*. New York: Dodd, Mead & Co. 1963.

Matthews, Denis. *In Pursuit of Music*. London: Victor Gollancz 1966.

Melba, Nellie. *Melodies and Reflections*. London: Butterworth 1925.

Minetti, Enrico. *Ricordi scaligeri*. Milano: Edizioni Curci 1974.

Monleone, Giovanni. *I cent'anni del Teatro Carlo Felice*. Genova: Teatro Carlo Felice 1928.

Monteux, Doris. *It's All in the Music*. London: William Kimber 1956.

Moore, J.N. *A Voice in Time*. London: Hamish Hamilton 1976.

Morini, Mario. *Pietro Mascagni*. Milano: Sonzogno 1964.

Mucci, E. *Bernardino Molinari*. Lanciano: Carabba 1941.

Myers, Rollo. *Ravel*. London: Duckworth 1960.

Nabokov, Nicholas. *Old Friends and New Music*. Boston: Little, Brown & Co. 1951.

Nardi, Piero. *Vita di Arrigo Boito*. Verona: Mondadori 1944.

Newman, Vera. *Ernest Newman*. London: Putnam 1963.

Nicotra, Tobia. *Arturo Toscanini*. New York: Alfred A. Knopf 1929.

O'Connell, Charles. *The Other Side of the Record*. Westport, Connecticut: Greenwood Press 1970.

Ojetti, Ugo. *I Taccuini*. Firenze: Sansoni 1954.

Paderewski, I.J., and Lawton, Mary. *The Paderewski Memoirs*. New York: Charles Scribner's Sons 1938.

Paladini, Carlo. *Giacomo Puccini*. Firenze: Vallecchi 1961.

Paumgartner, Bernhard. *Erinnerungen*. Salzburg: Residenz Verlag 1969.

Pelletier, Wilfrid. *Une Symphonie inachevée*. Ottawa: Editions Leméac 1972.

Piatigorsky, Gregor. *Cellist*. Garden City, N.Y.: Doubleday 1965.

Pinza, Ezio, and Magidoff, Robert. *Ezio Pinza*. New York: Rinehart & Co. 1958.

Prawy, Marcel. *The Vienna Opera*. London: Weidenfeld & Nicolson 1970.

Prezzolini, Giuseppe. *Prezzolini alla finestra*. Milano: P.A.N. 1977.

Puccini, Giacomo. *Carteggi Pucciniani*, ed. E. Gara. Milano: Ricordi 1958.

Reid, Charles. *John Barbirolli*. London: Hamish Hamilton 1971.

———. *Malcolm Sargent*. London: Hamish Hamilton 1968.

Respighi, Elsa. *Ottorino Respighi*. Milano: Ricordi 1954.

Rinaldi, Mario. *Musica e musicisti a controluce*. Roma: Edizioni De Santis 1972.

Rizzi, F.G. *Gilda Dalla Rizza*. Venezia: Tipografia Commerciale 1964.

Rodzinski, Halina. *Our Two Lives*. New York: Charles Scribner's Sons 1976.

Rossi, Cesare. *Personaggi di ieri e di oggi*. Milano: Casa editrice Ceschina 1960.

Rossi, Michele. *Cento anni di storia del teatro di Lugo*. Lugo: Ferretti 1916.

Russell, John. *Erich Kleiber*. London: André Deutsch 1957.

Sacchi, Filippo. *Toscanini*. Milano: Arnoldo Mondadori 1951.

———. *Toscanini, un secolo di musica*. Milano: Longanesi 1960.

Saerchinger, César. *Artur Schnabel*. New York: Dodd, Mead & Co. 1957.

Salvemini, Gaetano. *L'Italia vista dall'America*, ed. E. Tagliacozzo. Milano: Feltrinelli 1969.

San Martino, Enrico di. *Ricordi*. Roma: Danesi 1943.

Schonberg, Harold. *The Great Conductors*. New York: Simon & Schuster 1967.

Seligman, Vincent. *Puccini Among Friends*. London: Macmillan 1938.

Seltsam, William. *Metropolitan Opera Annals*. New York: Wilson 1947.

Seroff, Victor. *Renata Tebaldi*. Freeport, N.Y.: Books for Libraries Press 1970.

Setti, Dora. *Eleonora Duse ad Antonietta Pisa*. Milano: Ceschina 1972.

Shanet, Howard. *Philharmonic*. Garden City, N.Y.: Doubleday 1975.

Shore, Bernard. *The Orchestra Speaks*. London: Longmans, Green & Co. 1938.

Silvestrini, Domenico. *Aureliano Pertile*. Bologna: Aldina 1932.

Simoni, Renato. *Ritratti*. Alpes 1923.

Stefan, Paul. *Arturo Toscanini*, trans. L. Emery. Milano: Fratelli Bocca 1937.

Stotijn, Jaap. *Even uitblazen*. Nieuwkoop: Uitgeverij Heuff 1975.

Strauss, Richard, and Zweig, Stefan. *Briefwechsel*. Frankfurt: S. Fischer Verlag 1957.

——. *Die Welt um Strauss in Briefen*. Tutzing: Hans Schneider 1967.

Stravinsky, Igor. *Stravinsky*. New York: Simon & Schuster 1936.

——, and Craft, Robert. *Memories and Commentaries*. Garden City, N.Y.: Doubleday 1960.

Szigeti, Josef. *With Strings Attached*. New York: Alfred A. Knopf 1967.

Tarozzi, Giuseppe. *Non muore la musica*. Milano: SugarCo Edizioni 1977.

Taubman, Howard. *The Maestro*. New York: Simon & Schuster 1951.

Thomson, Virgil. *Virgil Thomson*. London: Weidenfeld & Nicolson 1967.

Thompson, Oscar. *Debussy, Man and Artist*. New York: Tudor 1940.

Toobin, Jerome. *Agitato*. New York: Viking Press 1975.

Valdengo, Giuseppe. *Ho cantato con Toscanini*. Como: Pietro Cairoli 1962.

Vallebona, G.B. *Il Teatro Carlo Felice*. Genova: Cooperativa fascista poligrafici 1928.

Varèse, Louise. *Varèse: A Looking-Glass Diary*. New York: W.W. Norton 1972.

Verdi, Giuseppe. *I copialettere*. Milano: 1913.

Vergani, Orio. *Toscanini nella pittura di Caselli*. Bergamo: Instituto italiano d'arti grafiche 1953.

Vetro, Gaspare Nello. *Arturo Toscanini alla Regia Scuola del Carmine in Parma*. Parma: Tipolito la Ducale 1974.

Wagner, Friedelind, and Cooper, Page. *Heritage of Fire*. New York: Harper & Bros. 1945.

Wallmann, Margarete. *Les Balcons du ciel*. Paris: Robert Laffont 1976.

Walter, Bruno. *Briefe*. Frankfurt: S. Fischer Verlag 1969.

——. *Theme and Variations*, trans. J.A. Galston. New York: Alfred A. Knopf 1947.

Wessling, Berndt. *Gustav Mahler*. Hamburg: Hoffmann und Campe 1974.

——. *Lotte Lehmann*. Salzburg: Residenz Verlag 1969.

——. *Toscanini in Bayreuth*. München: Verlag Kurt Desch 1976.

White, Eric Walter. *Stravinsky*. Berkeley: University of California Press 1969.

Wooldridge, David. *Conductor's World*. London: Barrie & Rockliff 1970.

Miscellaneous Books and Pamphlets

Arrigo Boito: scritti e documenti, a cura del comitato per le onoranze. Milano 1948.

Arturo Toscanini. America-Israel Cultural Foundation 1967.

Arturo Toscanini: A Complete Discography. RCA 1965.

Arturo Toscanini: Parma nel centenario della nascita, a cura di Carlo Allodi. Parma 1967.

Due secoli di vita musicale: Storia del Teatro Comunale di Bologna, a cura di Lamberto Trezzini. Bologna: Edizioni ALFA 1966.

Ente Autonomo del Teatro alla Scalla: 'Cronistoria della stagione 1928–1929'.

Esposizione Generale in Torino, 1898: Programmi illustrati dei Concerti Orchestrali A. Toscanini.

La lezione di Toscanini, a cura di F. D'Amico e R. Paumgartner. Firenze: Vallecchi 1970.

Milano/Scala, a cura di Giuseppe Morazzoni. Milano: Ente Provinciale per il Turismo 1976.

Nerone: numero unico ufficiale, Stagione lirica, Teatro Comunale. Bologna: IBIS 1924.

Parma a Toscanini, a cura di Mario Medici. 1958.

La Scala nel 1830 e nel 1930. Milano: Libreria editrice milanese 1930.

Un secolo di scenografia alla Scala. Milano: Edizioni d'Arte 1945.

Théâtres des Champs-Elysées, 1913–1963. Paris: Olivier Perrin éditeur 1963.

Il Teatro Regio di Torino, a cura di V. Mazzonis *et al.* Torino: Editrice AEDA 1970.

Leyden, Norman. Doctoral thesis: *A Study and Analysis of the Conducting Patterns of Arturo Toscanini.* Columbia University, New York, 1968.

MAJOR ARTICLES

Abbado, Michelangelo. 'Nel centenario della nascita di Enrico Polo', *Annuario del Conservatorio G. Verdi*, Milano (1967).

Adorno, Theodor W. 'La maestria del Maestro', *Questioni*, Torino (January to April 1959).

Allegri, Renzo. 'Nostro Padre Arturo Toscanini', *Gente*, XVI, 12–16 (1972).

Andrede, Ayres de. 'Um episódio brasileiro na carreira de Toscanini', *O Jornal*, Rio de Janeiro, 27 January to 2 February 1957.

Barblan, Guglielmo. 'Toscanini al Conservatorio', *Annuario del Conservatorio G. Verdi*, Milano (1967).

——. 'Toscanini Alpinista', *Le vie d'Italia*, Milano (1965).

Davenport, John and Marcia. 'Toscanini on the Air', *Fortune* (January 1938).

De Angelis, A. 'Le direzioni di Toscanini a Roma', *Santa Cecilia* No. 2 (1957).

Haggin, B.H. 'Genius Betrayed—Toscanini and Chotzinoff', *Tri-Quarterly*.

——. 'Toscanini and His Critics', *Encounter* (January 1973).

——. 'Vienna's Great Conductors', *Encounter* (July 1977).

Klein, John W. 'Toscanini and Catalani—A Unique Friendship', *Music and Letters* XLVIII, No. 3.

Mazza, Giuseppe. 'Teatro Sociale: Stagione Lirica 1889', *Ultrapadum* (September 1957).

Morini, Mario. '*Pagliacci*, Leoncavallo e Toscanini', *Associazione Amici della Scala: Conferenze 1968–70*.

Il Pianoforte (issue largely devoted to Toscanini) V, No. 6 (June 1924).

Segre, Alfredo. 'Arturo Toscanini—The First Forty Years', *Musical Quarterly* No. 2 (1947).

Smith, Max. 'Toscanini at the Baton', *The Century* (March 1913).

Editor's Note

Since this book was first published in 1978, Harvey Sachs has written several major articles in English and Italian based on new discoveries and developments in the Toscanini story. Interested readers are referred to the following items:

'Arturo Toscanini: Some New Discoveries', in *Ovation*, New York (January 1982).
   Newly discovered documents regarding Toscanini's work in Turin (1895–98) and Bayreuth (1930–31), and various other matters.

'Guardando Toscanini dirigere', in *Atti e memorie della Accademia Petrarca di lettere, arti e scienze*, Anno 1982 (pub. Arezzo, 1984).
   Describes Toscanini's conducting technique as observed in tapes of parts of his ten televised NBC Symphony concerts.

'Toscanini, Hitler, and Salzburg', in *Grand Street*, New York (Autumn 1986). Reprinted (under various titles) in: *La Stampa*, Turin (October 30–31, 1986 [abridged]); *Le Monde de la Musique*, Paris (May 1987); *Neue Zeitschrift für Musik*, Mainz (June–July 1987 [abridged]); *Nuova Rivista Musicale Italiana*, 1987, No. 2.
   Makes use of a cache of previously unknown papers, belonging to New York Public Library, to document Toscanini's break with the nazified Salzburg Festival in 1938. Includes correspondence of Toscanini, Bruno Walter, Max Reinhardt, Gaetano Salvemini, and Lotte Lehmann.

'Historic Anniversary at La Scala', in *Opera Canada*, Toronto (Fall 1986).
   On the occasion of the concert conducted by Carlo Maria Giulini at La Scala in 1986 to celebrate the fortieth anniversary of the theater's re-opening, under Toscanini's direction, this article describes the 1946 event in detail.

'Un guardiano del bel canto', in *Antologia Vieusseux*, Florence (1986).
   In the context of a review of Rodolfo Celletti's book, *Memorie d'un ascoltatore*, Sachs discusses revisionist notions of Toscanini's position in the history of Italian operatic performance.

'Toscanini e il fascismo: appunti e scoperte', in *Piano Time*, Rome (January 1987).
   Makes use of recently discovered papers in the Central State Archives in Rome to document Toscanini's turbulent relations with Mussolini's government during the 1930's.

'L'oro di Toscanini', in *La Stampa*, Turin (April 1, 1987).
   Outlines the vicissitudes, describes the contents, and assesses the importance of the Toscanini archives, recently acquired by the New York Public Library.

'The Maestro Maligned', in *The New Republic*, Washington (June 1, 1987); reprinted in a slightly different version in *La Stampa* ("Tuttolibri"), Turin (June 20, 1987).
   Substantial review of Joseph Horowitz's book, *Understanding Toscanini*.

'Toscanini mio padre', in *La Stampa*, Turin (August 14, 1987).
   Interview with Wally Toscanini, the conductor's elder daughter.

Arturo Toscanini from 1915 to 1946: Art in the Shadow of Politics, EDT, Turin (1987); also available in Italian.
   Catalogue of the exhibition held at the Teatro Farnese, Parma, August–October 1987;

at the Library and Museum of the Performing Arts, New York, November 1987–January 1988; and in other major cities throughout the world in 1988. Contains introductory essay by Sachs, a full description of the 200 items on display (with ample quotations from documents), and transcripts of Sachs's interviews with Gianandrea Gavazzeni, Erich Leinsdorf, James Levine, Yehudi Menuhin, Randolfo Pacciardi, George Szell, Walfredo Toscanini, and seven orchestral musicians who worked with Toscanini.

'The Toscanini Case', final chapter in the book *Music in Fascist Italy* by Harvey Sachs, W. W. Norton, New York (1987).
A 34-page resume of Toscanini's relations with fascism, based on all the information currently available.

Harvey Sachs is also responsible for the script (1985) of the television documentary "Toscanini, the Maestro" (Host: James Levine; Producer: Peter Rosen; Adviser: Walfredo Toscanini), available on videocassette through Video Arts International, Inc., New York.

Index

Abbado, Claudio, 302
Abbado, Michelangelo, 301, 311
Abbiati, Franco, 291, 293
Abert, 176
Adami, Giuseppe, 170
Adriana Lecouvreur (Cilea), 85
Africaine, L' (Meyerbeer), 27–8
Agrigento, 87
Aida (Verdi), Berlin, 193, 194, 195; Buenos Aires, 79, 85, 116; Lugo, 83; Macerata, 30; Milan, 26, 97, 161, 189, 190; NBC broadcast, 295, 310; New York, 105–9, 112, 116, 123, 126; Novara, 31; Paris, 110–11; Rio de Janeiro, 16, 17–18; Turin, 13; Voghera, 32–3
Alaska, 317
Albanese, Licia, 292
Alberti, Luciano, 164
Albertini, Cesare, 92, 121, 142, 148–9
Albertini, Luigi, 141, 142, 166, 174, 195
Alceste (Gluck), 97, 109
Alda, Frances, 98, 107, 110
Aldrich, Richard, 106, 110, 112, 120
Alexandria, 250, 253
Alfano, Franco, 177–9
Allodi, Eurialo, 121
Alpino, 172, 186
Althouse, Paul, 118, 230
Am-Russ Music Corporation, 279
Amato, Pasquale, 122; in Buenos Aires, 86; in *Forza del destino*, 100; in *Pelléas et Mélisande*, 101; in *Rigoletto*, 107; in New York, 109, 112–13; in Paris, 110; Verdi centenary, 121, 123; in *Madame Sans-Gêne*, 126; in *Il trovatore*, 127
American Federation of Musicians, 255, 277
American Radio Telegraphists Association, 262
American Scientific Congress, 273
Amico del popolo, L', 43
Amico Fritz, L' (Mascagni), 38–9, 45, 90
Amore dei tre re, L' (Montemezzi), 123, 126, 177

Amore medico, L' (Wolf-Ferrari), 123
Andante and Scherzo for Orchestra (Toscanini), 14
Andrea Chénier (Giordano), 53
Andreae, Volkmar, 172
Anitùa, Fanny, 166, 171
Anselmi, Giuseppe, 91, 116–17
Ansermet, Ernest, 181, 266
Antek, Samuel, 263, 297–8
Antelami, Benedetto, 302
Anton (Galeotti), 73
Appia, Adolphe, 163–4, 166
Arabella (Strauss), 231
Arena, L', 29–30
Argentina, 78–9, 85–6, 276
Ariane et Barbe-bleue (Dukas), 113, 116, 186
Armide (Gluck), 112, 113, 116
Arpinati, Leandro, 210, 211
Aspromonte affair, 5, 6, 8
Asrael (Franchetti), 79, 83
Assandri, Virginio, 318–19
Associazione unitaria democratica, 7
Asti, 25
Athens, 250
Aulin, Tore, 228
Austria, 6, 7, 60, 132, 136, 226–8, 231, 233, 264
Austrian Broadcasting Corporation, 260
Auteri-Manzocchi, Salvatore, 13
Autori, Fernando, 239
Autunno (Toscanini), 29
Avanti, 117
Avemaria (Leoncavallo), 125

Bach, J.S., 55, 83, 176, 198, 234, 318; 'Brandenburg' Concertos, 305–6; Concerto in D minor, 302; *Mass in B minor*, 298; Prelude and Fugue in E-flat Major, 221
Badà, Angelo, 239
Badoglio, Pietro, 281–2, 284
Bagnolesi, Garibaldo, 46–7
Bakst, Léon, 177